Extending SAP S/4HANA®

SAP PRESS

SAP PRESS is a joint initiative of SAP and Rheinwerk Publishing. The know-how offered by SAP specialists combined with the expertise of Rheinwerk Publishing offers the reader expert books in the field. SAP PRESS features first-hand information and expert advice, and provides useful skills for professional decision-making.

SAP PRESS offers a variety of books on technical and business-related topics for the SAP user. For further information, please visit our website: *www.sap-press.com*.

Philipp Herzig, Henning Heitkötter, Sander Wozniak,
Akhil Agarwal, Johannes Wust

Extending SAP S/4HANA®

Side-by-Side Extensions with the SAP S/4HANA Cloud SDK

Rheinwerk
Publishing

Editor Hareem Shafi
Copyeditor Yvette Chin
Cover Design Graham Geary
Photo Credit iStockphoto.com/174833886/© malerapaso
Layout Design Vera Brauner
Production Hannah Lane
Typesetting III-Satz, Husby (Germany)
Printed and bound in the United States of America, on paper from sustainable sources

ISBN 978-1-4932-1715-1

1st edition 2018

Library of Congress Cataloging-in-Publication Data
Names: Herzig, Phillipp, author.
Title: Extending SAP S/4HANA : side-by-side extensions with the SAP/S/4HANA cloud SDK / Phillipp Herzig, Henning Heitkotter, Sander Wozniak, Akhil Agarwal, Johannes Wust.
Description: 1st edition. | Bonn ; Boston : Rheinwerk Publishing, 2018. | Includes index.
Identifiers: LCCN 2018011450 (print) | LCCN 2018012676 (ebook) | ISBN 9781493217168 (ebook) | ISBN 9781493217151 (alk. paper)
Subjects: LCSH: SAP HANA (Electronic resource) | Database management. | Management information systems. | Business enterprises--Data processing. | Cloud computing.
Classification: LCC QA76.9.D3 (ebook) | LCC QA76.9.D3 H487 2018 (print) | DDC 004.67/82--dc23
LC record available at https://lccn.loc.gov/2018011450

Contents at a Glance

Dear Reader,

One size doesn't fit all.

From our phones to our computers to our cars, the ability to customize the things we use to our lifestyles and personal tastes has proven to be a big draw. For businesses, tailoring enterprise software to their specific needs is also a way to stand out from the crowd—the crowd of competitors. Optimized business processes, faster innovation, and increased flexibility can give companies the competitive edge they're looking for.

When it comes to customizing SAP S/4HANA, SAP Cloud Platform and the SAP S/4HANA Cloud SDK are invaluable tools. In *Extending SAP S/4HANA: Side-by-Side Extensions with the SAP S/4HANA Cloud SDK*, our expert author team will help you understand how to extend the functional scope and individual reach of your SAP S/4HANA system. Philipp Herzig, Henning Heitkötter, Sander Wozniak, Akhil Agarwal, Johannes Wust, and 21 other contributors have worked tirelessly over the past few months to compile their extensive knowledge and bring you a resource that explains the end-to-end development of extension applications. It has been a pleasure working with them, and I am sure you'll find their book as impressive as I do.

What did you think about *Extending SAP S/4HANA: Side-by-Side Extensions with the SAP S/4HANA Cloud SDK*? Your comments and suggestions are the most useful tools to help us make our books the best they can be. Please feel free to contact me and share any praise or criticism you may have.

Thank you for purchasing a book from SAP PRESS!

Hareem Shafi
Editor, SAP PRESS

hareems@rheinwerk-publishing.com
www.sap-press.com
Rheinwerk Publishing · Boston, MA

Contents

PART IV Advanced Concepts

14 Building a Custom SAP Fiori User Interface 403

15 Integrating with Java Frameworks 425

PART V In-App Extensibility

Foreword

Thank you for taking the time to read this book about extending SAP S/4HANA with the SAP S/4HANA Cloud SDK. When I was first given the outline for this book, I was amazed by the scope of topics covered. This book goes well beyond presenting the capabilities of the SDK, providing multiple perspectives on how to build cloud-native, future-proof extensions to SAP S/4HANA using the SAP Cloud Platform. From my own perspective, I'm struck by how all the pieces need to be in place to deliver truly cutting-edge business software. This book touches on these individual elements. From architecture and frameworks, to integration, methodologies, DevOps, and much more.

SAP has a history of delivering tools that enable developers to build applications quickly. We had built reusable functions into the core of ABAP, but reusability does not compare with the cloud-native approach we have today. The SAP S/4HANA Cloud SDK provides out of the box capabilities to enable developers to develop modern cloud applications with ease by breaking down the barriers to innovation. Developers can quickly test new functionality with rapid testing, bringing the functionality closer to the end user. In these ways, the SAP S/4HANA Cloud SDK is a core element of our overall cloud strategy.

Over the past few years, the digital transformation has been a heavily discussed topic, and SAP has led the way in this space. I have spoken on stage at various events, talking to our customers and partners about the challenges of running IT at two speeds. We have brought these two speeds of IT together with our cloud technology, and the SDK is an essential part of that. However, the SDK is also part of a much more important change that will bring us to a new era of intelligent computing, and ERP is going through a major transformation to prepare itself.

First, an ERP needs to be truly cloud-native. Sometimes I am asked the question, "Will the future of ERP be a big monolithic system or will it be a lean core with line of business cloud applications surrounding it?" But, this question assumes that a compromise is required to move from one pattern to the other. In a monolithic system, easy integration is a benefit by default but suffers from limited flexibility. On the other hand, the best-of-breed does not always easily integrate. I do not see the need for a compromise. With the technology available to us today, you can define modularity using a microservice architecture, while providing standard integration services to connect functional modules. This book takes us through the concepts that make this reality.

Second, core components of ERP are evolving to prepare themselves for the intelligent era. Systems of record are becoming systems of intelligence through machine learning. Business intelligence systems now include predictive analytics and natural language processing, where insights from analytics are delivered in spoken form, delivering a new user experience that augments human capabilities with context relevant information and decision support. A similar transformation is going to be required of many business applications and processes, where hyperautomation will drive productivity.

It is important to remember that intelligence evolves through interaction. We handle millions of these interactions: in our core processes, across our edge applications in the cloud, between customers, suppliers, devices, employees, our whole ecosystem. These interactions all contribute to, and mutually benefit from, being connected to an intelligent system. From these interactions, we gain intelligence that can then be used to drive automation and differentiation. The SAP S/4HANA Cloud SDK opens up these channels of interaction. I believe that the SDK will have a knock-on network effect that will help us to deliver something much greater. Only the cloud can deliver intelligence at scale. Only the cloud will enable companies to get access to the data they need for their systems to become intelligent, and only a unified process landscape wins in the intelligent economy.

In the near future, artificial intelligence will be by far the biggest disrupter to businesses and the global economy alike. The opportunities to apply this technology within SAP and beyond are boundless and, I believe, far outweigh any perceived downside. A combined effort is needed, but as long as we ensure the right standards are in place, we will see the development of new intelligences that will help us all change the world and improve people's lives. Today, SAP is in the best position to deliver the vision of the intelligent enterprise—one that connects humans and machines together to directly impact business outcomes, and not just answer questions or automate a function point.

Before I finish, I would like to remind you of the vital role that the SAP Cloud Platform plays. The SAP S/4HANA Cloud SDK resides on the SAP Cloud Platform, which provides a layer of consistency in how we extend our applications, manage business and technical services, and deploy applications. The ecosystem is building around it. Our customers and our partners bring their knowledge and expertise to deliver amazing extension solutions, so I am sure they will appreciate this new SDK at their disposal.

I would like to finish by thanking the authors who worked tirelessly to deliver such a comprehensive introduction to our cloud technologies and ecosystem. They have made these topics accessible while being in-depth and communicating with clarity and definition. The online community discussing the SAP S/4HANA Cloud SDK has been growing, and we are seeing real traction within the development community. I will use this book as a reminder of what we can do and how we can help our customers achieve their goals. So again, I would like to offer a big thanks to everyone who contributed to this insightful read. Enjoy!

Bernd Leukert
Member of the Executive Board of SAP SE
Products & Innovation

Preface

SAP S/4HANA is the all-new, standard product for enterprise resource planning (ERP), on-premise as well as in the cloud. Based on SAP HANA and a dramatically simplified data model, SAP S/4HANA has already enabled thousands of customers to run their systems with less total cost of ownership (TCO), to get unparalleled real-time insights from their business data, and to make informed decisions without information loss. These benefits are possible thanks to the flexibility offered by working on the finest level of data granularity (line item data) at all times. Furthermore, SAP has introduced SAP Fiori to provide a radically new, modern, and lean user experience. Based on the speed and data granularity offered by SAP HANA, SAP S/4HANA is now able to leapfrog business applications into the space of artificial intelligence and machine learning, enabling intelligent enterprises. In this context, we'll see completely new business processes and applications that were not imaginable before and, at the same time, we'll see incredible productivity gains with the existing application suite.

To make this high-paced innovation cycle possible, updates to SAP S/4HANA Cloud are released every quarter without compromise. At the same time, customers want to extend or customize SAP S/4HANA to tailor the system to reflect company-specific business models and processes. Partners of SAP want to extend SAP S/4HANA to provide their key expertise from the cloud and fill out industry-specific verticals. A perennial question for SAP has been how to deliver fast-paced business innovations while not interfering with the extensions built by customers and partners. These extensions shouldn't break when SAP S/4HANA is updated, nor should SAP's updates be delayed because of extensions in the ecosystem.

The answer to this important question lies in two main forms of extensibility: in-app and side-by-side extensibility. This book will describe these methods in great detail and provide you with all the background information you'll need to understand how to transform your business, on our common journey, to the cloud.

Purpose

With SAP S/4HANA, SAP has introduced a next-generation ERP system for the digital age. With this change, not only the core applications but also the extension mechanisms have been adapted to the fast-paced digital business world and cloud delivery models. This book describes what it takes to extend SAP S/4HANA, from simple extensions for an individual business to fully-fledged, cloud-native applications. We'll describe the concepts as they apply to SAP S/4HANA Cloud, but most of the information also holds true for SAP S/4HANA on-premise installations unless mentioned otherwise.

The primary purpose of this book, therefore, is to educate decision-makers, developers, architects, engineers, and other professionals in the SAP ecosystem on what to expect when extending their SAP S/4HANA systems and, at the same time, what they can no longer can expect. This guidance will help you decide on the best implementation strategy by balancing the required effort with the promised benefits. This book will provide in-depth guidance on the vision and the goals of the SAP S/4HANA architecture and present the various options for extending the system using both side-by-side extensibility and in-app extensibility.

This book's second purpose is to provide clear guidance and hands-on examples for software engineers to learn to extend SAP S/4HANA. We'll cover the entire development cycle and give developers all the necessary resources they need to build applications effectively and efficiently, with a focus on side-by-side extensions in the cloud. Cloud-based applications require a different approach compared to traditional enterprise IT approaches, especially with respect to application development, lifecycle management, delivery, and release strategies as well as application operations. This book introduces all the required underlying concepts as well as best practices and tools to help developers deliver on the promises of cloud-native applications for SAP customers and partners alike.

Who Should Read This Book

The target audience for this book is twofold. We'll address decision-makers on the customer's side, namely, chief information officers (CIOs) and managers who are in charge of deciding their enterprise's landscapes and would like to evaluate the available options in terms of costs, efficiency, or time-to-availability. The same applies to decision-makers in the SAP partner ecosystem who would like to understand the options and limits on how they can extend the scope of SAP S/4HANA seamlessly for their customers.

We'll also address software and solution architects as well as software developers of existing SAP ecosystems who would like to understand the benefits they can derive from SAP S/4HANA in conjunction with SAP Cloud Platform. Moreover, software engineers and architects may find the examples and in-depth material in the book relevant to evaluate the various technologies involved and thus advising decision-makers on the available options.

Additionally, this book invites every software engineer or decision-maker already familiar with cloud-native application development but new to SAP S/4HANA to study the opportunities offered by SAP Cloud Platform and evaluate the technologies provided for future projects that may have to integrate with SAP S/4HANA.

Structure and Content of the Book

This book comprises six major parts that explain all the required concepts for extending SAP S/4HANA. In Part I, we'll outline the vision, rationales, design principles, and implications of the SAP S/4HANA architecture and outline its extensibility strategy to give a comprehensive picture of options for chief information officers (CIOs), chief technology officers (CTOs), partners, and architects. Based on this general consideration, we'll dive deeply into the concepts and implementation details of how to build side-by-side extensions to SAP S/4HANA using SAP Cloud Platform as the extension platform, including important technologies such as the SAP S/4HANA Cloud SDK and the SAP Cloud Platform SDK for service development in Part II. After we successfully build our first example application, the Business Partner Address Manager application, we'll move on to Part III, where we'll describe how this application can be delivered and operated on SAP Cloud Platform using cloud-native principles like continuous delivery and DevOps. In Part IV, we'll extend the application from Part II by introducing advanced engineering and architectural topics discussing various trade-offs of advanced frameworks, as well as the integration to SAP's machine learning and blockchain offerings. Then, Part V switches back to SAP S/4HANA and explains how in-app extensibility can be leveraged to customize SAP S/4HANA, and then explores touchpoints between in-app extensibility and side-by-side extensibility. Finally, the book wraps up with a concrete use case description of how an SAP partner, msg, has successfully utilized the concepts presented in the previous parts to implement a fully-fledged, microservice-based architecture for reinsurance use cases.

Let's look at the structure of the book in more detail.

Nomenclature Used in This Book

"SAP S/4HANA" will always refer to both SAP S/4HANA on-premise and SAP S/4HANA Cloud when no substantial difference exists in the concepts and methods we're describing, unless noted otherwise. When there is a difference, the cloud version will explicitly be called "SAP S/4HANA Cloud," while the on-premise version will be called "SAP S/4HANA on-premise" or "on-premise" will be referred to explicitly in context.

"SAP Cloud Platform" will implicitly refer to the Cloud Foundry environment on the SAP Cloud Platform, unless noted otherwise.

"Example application" will refer to the Business Partner Address Manager application that we'll develop throughout the book.

"Cloud application or app" will refer to any nonspecific cloud application.

Part I—The Intelligent ERP, provides a general introduction into the new architecture of SAP S/4HANA, its design imperatives, and rationales. Based on the design principles we'll discuss, the supported extension patterns will be explained covering side-by-side as well as in-app extensibility.

- *Chapter 1* introduces the vision and design principles of SAP S/4HANA as the intelligent ERP. Overall, we'll introduce eleven important design principles, and we'll explain how SAP S/4HANA is ready for the fast-paced digital age and how extensions fit into the overall picture.
- *Chapter 2* provides a general overview on the various options, patterns, and use cases that can be realized with both in-app and side-by-side extensibility.

Part II—Building Side-by-Side Extensions with SAP Cloud Platform, dives directly into the characteristics of side-by-side extensions and explains the various concepts you'll need to understand when developing extensions on SAP Cloud Platform. Throughout these chapters, a concrete use case and our example application will be used to give foundation to the lessons and provide a rough idea of the effort and engineering requirements necessary for implementing cloud-native extensions.

- *Chapter 3* introduces the rationales and design principles of building cloud-native applications that are future-proof, scalable, and resilient. Moreover, this chapter explains why SAP Cloud Platform is the preferred choice for building side-by-side extension applications for SAP S/4HANA. Therefore, we'll introduce the theoretical characteristics of microservices, continuous delivery, containerization, and DevOps as well as the twelve-factor principles to guide architects and developers on implementing cloud-native applications the right way. Based on these characteristics, this chapter introduces SAP Cloud Platform in more detail, outlining the Cloud Foundry and Neo environments and their benefits. Furthermore, this chapter introduces the SAP S/4HANA Cloud SDK as well as the SAP Cloud Platform SDK for service development as two of the cornerstones of successful, efficient, and future-proof application development. Finally, this chapter introduces the architecture of example Business Partner Address Manager application that we'll develop throughout the book.

- *Chapter 4* is the first hands-on chapter, showing how to implement a cloud-native application from the start, including setting up the environment and developing a "Hello World!" service, until the first running deployment of our Business Partner Address Manager application to the Cloud Foundry environment of SAP Cloud Platform. While implementing the application, we'll introduce important programming concepts of the SAP S/4HANA Cloud SDK, such as the virtual data model (VDM) for OData, resilience patterns, and caching.
- *Chapter 5* presents all concepts required to secure SAP Cloud Platform applications with authentication and authorization. We'll introduce components such as the application router (AppRouter) and Extended Services for User Authentication and Authorization (XSUAA) as well as important security flows, such as OAuth2, which are used in the SAP Cloud Platform today. Based on these theoretical considerations, we'll also show you how to secure microservices on an implementation level and how user roles and authorizations are managed at runtime.
- *Chapter 6* presents integration options with SAP S/4HANA on-premise and SAP S/4HANA Cloud that are handled by the SAP S/4HANA Cloud SDK. We'll introduce the various components and concepts that connect to both versions of SAP S/4HANA in a transparent way. We'll also present detailed instructions on how to set up and configure these components in a customer landscape and discuss design trade-offs for productive use.
- *Chapter 7* introduces the concepts of multitenancy for cloud-native application development. This chapter starts with a conceptual introduction by outlining important terminology, design trade-offs for realizing multitenancy, and the involved components during design-time and at runtime. Based on the theoretical considerations, the knowledge is applied by enhancing our example Business Partner Address Manager application with a local, multitenant persistence scenario, where new business partner addresses can be proposed and locally stored in SAP Cloud Platform before being approved by a different user and promoted into SAP S/4HANA.
- *Chapter 8* discusses the importance of RESTful APIs by comparing them to traditional approaches, such as SOAP, and talks about why to use an API-first strategy

for cloud services and applications. We'll also introduce OData as a concrete realization of the RESTful approach and its benefits. Based on this theory, this chapter leverages the SAP Cloud Platform SDK for service development to expose comprehensive OData services by enhancing the example application.

- *Chapter 9* presents a deep-dive into the various forms and methods of automated testing for cloud applications that are continuously delivered. With our example application, we'll demonstrate how the SAP S/4HANA Cloud SDK facilitates the testing of applications developed for SAP Cloud Platform and integrated with SAP S/4HANA.

Part III—Delivering and Operating Side-by-Side Extensions, builds further on the concepts discussed in Part II and continues to develop our example application. On top of the existing application, we'll show you how to deliver, release, and operate extensions in a cloud-native manner. Besides practical and technological guidance, this part also explains the paradigm shifts and benefits associated with continuous integration, continuous delivery, and DevOps, and how they impact organizational and cultural changes in the organization compared to the traditional approaches that are still often found in enterprise IT scenarios today. These paradigm shifts are important to understand before using the corresponding technologies. This chapter, therefore, presents many references to related work in this emerging field.

- *Chapter 10* introduces the methods and the mindset of continuous delivery and DevOps, respectively. We'll start with a comprehensive discussion on why these fields have emerged during the last ten years and how organizations can benefit from them to react more quickly to changing market demands, interact more closely with end users, streamline their organization, and deliver on the promises of a lean culture.
- *Chapter 11* introduces the continuous delivery pipeline artifacts that are shipped and closely integrated with the SAP S/4HANA Cloud SDK. After a conceptual overview of concepts and design-time considerations, this chapter provides a detailed step-by-step guide to setting up the first continuous delivery pipeline for our example application introduced in Part II and to delivering the application with zero downtime in the cloud instead of via manual deployment.
- *Chapter 12* is an in-depth consideration of enterprise and cloud-native qualities built into the continuous delivery pipeline artifacts of the SAP S/4HANA Cloud SDK. We'll introduce comprehensive design-time and runtime checks that are automatically executed by the pipeline to help developers adhere to functional

correctness and discuss several qualities such as clean code, resilience, logging and tracing.

- *Chapter 13* wraps up Part III by introducing important operational topics for gathering and using telemetry data from a running cloud application. We'll introduce a logging service based on Kibana for comprehensive log analysis as well as Dynatrace for application monitoring and alerting. In addition, we'll discuss several best practices on monitoring the health of the application and explore concepts related to the general principles of DevOps.

Part IV—Advanced Concepts, introduces several advanced concepts relevant to building side-by-side extensions that make application development more powerful and efficient and extend the breadth and depth of the application's capabilities.

- *Chapter 14* discusses frontend options and trade-offs of our application more thoroughly. While Part II only assumed that some frontend code exists, written in SAPUI5, this chapter introduces how the frontend of the application has been built and which deployment options exist, including their advantages and disadvantages. This discussion will help architects decide where to put frontend code and its implications in terms of operability, costs, and efficiency.
- *Chapter 15* introduces two popular Java frameworks: Java Platform, Enterprise Edition (Java EE) and Spring Boot. These are typically used to make application development more efficient and scalable across multiple teams due to its certain standardization of certain concepts. Besides presenting how these frameworks can be utilized, this chapter shows you how the SAP S/4HANA Cloud SDK is highly interoperable with these frameworks.
- *Chapter 16* introduces the topic of events and event-driven architecture from SAP S/4HANA to SAP Cloud Platform leveraging typical patterns such as message queues or publish-subscribe patterns. Previous chapters have relied primarily on an API-based integration approach, that is, the extension always needs to actively call the S/4HANA system. Leveraging event capabilities, architects and developers can realize patterns such as event notifications, event-carried state transfers, or event sourcing.
- *Chapter 17* enhances our example application with a use case for machine learning and blockchain, leveraging additional services and capabilities from SAP Leonardo, such as SAP Leonardo Machine Learning Foundation or SAP Leonardo Blockchain, which are available on SAP Cloud Platform. Thus, this chapter demonstrates

how application developers can benefit from the rich cloud ecosystem of services to provide application capabilities that had not been possible before.

Part V—In-App Extensibility, switches the perspective from SAP Cloud Platform back to what is possible within SAP S/4HANA with regards to extensibility. Customers seeking to customize their SAP S/4HANA systems natively without using SAP Cloud Platform should find this part useful. At the same time, partners can see which mechanisms to rely on and how to leverage in-app extensions from their side-by-side extensions on SAP Cloud Platform.

- *Chapter 18* provides an overview on the concepts, ideas, and capabilities of in-app extensibility in general and how they have been realized in SAP S/4HANA Cloud.
- *Chapter 19* provides a detailed, step-by-step guide on realizing the concepts introduced in Chapter 18. This chapter enhances the data model of SAP S/4HANA so we can prepare our Business Partner Address Manager application for consumption as a side-by-side extension on SAP Cloud Platform.
- *Chapter 20* builds on Chapter 19 and shows how the provided in-app extensions can be easily consumed from an SAP Cloud Platform extension. Our Business Partner Address Manager application will be enhanced so that it can consume the extended SAP S/4HANA data model and interact with it.

Part VI—Partner Case Study and Outlook, concludes the book by presenting an exemplary use case that leverages most of the methods and approaches discussed throughout the book.

- *Chapter 21* introduces a reinsurance scenario that msg, an SAP partner, has implemented on SAP Cloud Platform. We'll briefly introduce the motivation for moving a highly specialized industry application into the cloud by examining the architecture of a reinsurance scenario that msg implemented. We'll discuss certain design decisions and show you how the architecture was realized using the technologies introduced throughout this book. We'll also present how SAP Cloud Platform helped msg implement their use case more quickly and with higher quality than ever before.
- *Chapter 22* summarizes the lessons learned throughout this book and describes the benefits, from a partner's perspective, of using the SAP Cloud Platform, the SAP S/4HANA Cloud SDK, and SAP S/4HANA. We'll also provide recommendations for your ecosystem.

How to Read This Book

Now that we've outlined the book's structure and content, you may find some chapters more interesting than others depending on your organizational role. This book has been organized in such a way that chapters related to business, organizational, and cultural aspects can be read independently from the technical chapters that target software architects, engineers, and developers with the goal of realizing concrete outcomes. Therefore, we'll provide an overview of all chapters and their focus topics in Table 1 to guide the reader in pursuit of their specific priorities and professional preferences.

Chapters		Business	Technical
	Foreword by Bernd Leukert	X	X
Part I: The Intelligent ERP			
1	SAP S/4 HANA: The Intelligent ERP	X	X
2	SAP S/4HANA Extensibility	X	X
Part II: Side-by-Side Extensibility			
3	Side-by-Side Extensibility	X	X
4	Building the Application		X
5	Application Security		X
6	Integrating with SAP S/4HANA		X
7	Multitenancy		X
8	REST APIs		X
9	Automated Testing		X
Part III: Delivering and Operating Side-by-Side Extensions			
10	DevOps and Continuous Delivery	X	X
11	Implementing Continuous Delivery		X
12	Quality Assurance		X
13	Cloud Operations		X

Table 1 Focus of the Book's Chapters

Chapters		Business	Technical
Part IV: Advanced Topics			
14	Building a Custom SAP Fiori User Interface		X
15	Integrating with Java Frameworks		X
16	Event-Based Integration		X
17	Extending SAP S/4HANA with Machine Learning and Blockchain Technologies	X	X
Part V: In-App Extensibility			
18	In-App Extensibility in SAP S/4HANA	X	X
19	Forms of In-App Extensibility	X	X
20	Consuming In-App Extensions in a Side-by Side Extension		X
Part VI: Partner Case Study and Outlook			
21	Partner Application Development Using the SAP S/4HANA Cloud SDK (Case Study)	X	
22	Outlook	X	X

Table 1 Focus of the Book's Chapters (Cont.)

How to Use the Code Examples

This book contains plenty of code examples to put concepts and theories into action. For the majority of the examples, you'll only need a computer and a working Internet connection. Additionally, we'll assume that you have installed the latest Java Development Kit (JDK) and the latest version of Maven. Furthermore, you may use your favorite integrated development environment (IDE) such as SAP Web IDE, Eclipse, Netbeans, or IntelliJ IDEA. More detailed installation instructions can be found in Chapter 4.

While reading and using the examples in this book, please take the following into consideration:

- Some examples and command line instructions may, for formatting reasons, contain line breaks that are not meant to be typed. A small arrow symbol (↩) indicates that the line should be continued without a break.

- To save space, all examples are shown without import statements for packages. We assume that you are either using an IDE that can help resolve imports automatically, or you can use the publically available version of the code examples in this book's GitHub repository at *https://sap.github.io/cloud-s4-sdk-book/*. More details about this repository are provided in the next section.

In addition, we assume in some chapters that you have a working SAP Cloud Platform account or an SAP S/4HANA system on hand.

For SAP Cloud Platform, SAP offers a free and open 90-day trial version for the Cloud Foundry environment. At the time of this writing, the trial version includes the following resources:

- 1 GB of memory for applications
- 2 GB of instance memory
- 20 routes
- 20 services
- Two configured on-premise systems with the Cloud Connector
- Usage of HDI containers in a shared SAP HANA database

The trial version of the Cloud Foundry environment can be used for 90 days and will be deleted after the expiry date.

For the Neo environment of SAP Cloud Platform, SAP offers a free, unlimited-time trial with the following capabilities:

- 1 GB of memory for applications
- 1 GB of database storage
- 1 GB of document storage
- One SAP HANA MDC tenant database
- 100 MB of memory for all Git repositories
- Two configured on-premise systems with the Cloud Connector

You can get access to both trial environments at *https://cloudplatform.sap.com*. After registering for a free public user (P-user), you'll be able to access the trial tier of SAP Cloud Platform and use all available services while working through this book. Please note, as the offerings described in this book may change in the future, you should consult the SAP Help Page at *http://tiny.cc/scpaccounts* for the most up-to-date information about trials.

Some of the programming examples we use require access to APIs provided by SAP S/4HANA. If you have either an SAP S/4HANA Cloud instance or a corresponding SAP S/4HANA on-premise installation available, we recommend using these systems as we describe throughout the book. All examples have been developed with an SAP S/4HANA Cloud 1805 system. If you do not have an SAP S/4HANA system available, we provide the set of APIs necessary for running the examples from the book on a small mock server in the book's GitHub repository at *https://sap.github.io/cloud-s4-sdk-book/*.

In some rare cases, this book requires you to download additional development artifacts from the SAP Service Marketplace (for example, the security libraries in Chapter 5). Thus, you'll need a so-called support user (S-user), which you can get by following these steps:

1. Go to *https://launchpad.support.sap.com/*.
2. Click on the **User Management** tile.
3. Click **Request User** on the lower right.
4. Enter your user details.
5. Click **Submit**.

Please note that an S-user may take up to 24 hours to create.

Note on Alpha and Beta Features

In some places in this book, we'll be using beta and sometimes even alpha services, but we'll let you know when we do. Please note that such early-access services are not meant for productive use, may be changed by SAP at any time, or may never become generally available. We nevertheless want to point you to those services to give you a glimpse of potential future innovations and to showcase how to integrate them in general.

Additional Resources and Feedback Channels

Besides being a book of business, architectural, and other high-level concepts for long-term use, this book is full of in-depth examples and how-to guides intended to help developers get started as easily as possible and to put concepts immediately into practice. Nonetheless, we're fully aware that these examples might be rather short-lived and do not provide any formal contract about future enhancements, improvements, and design decisions that SAP may undertake. In addition, despite our best efforts to provide a thorough didactic approach, we acknowledge that you might get stuck with the examples as we cannot provide a completely executable codebase but instead only show the important parts for illustration purposes.

Therefore, we'll provide the latest running version of the Business Partner Address Manager application, which we develop throughout this book, as an open source reference implementation at the GitHub repository for this book: *https://sap.github.io/cloud-s4-sdk-book/*. This will also be available as a download on this book's web page at *www.sap-press.com/4655*.

The source code for our example application is available under an Apache License version 2.0 (*www.apache.org/licenses/LICENSE-2.0*). You may use the GitHub issue mechanism let us know if you encounter any problems.

Furthermore, various teams at SAP provide community support and additional content on SAP S/4HANA, the SAP Cloud Platform, the SAP S/4HANA Cloud SDK, or the SAP Cloud Platform SDK for service development and its related artifacts, that go beyond the scope of this book. To find more information, you should visit the SAP Community, GitHub, and StackOverflow.

SAP Community

The SAP Community is the primary places for additional content; SAP shares blogs from its own developers, answers general questions, and maintains a vital community of other developers in an open manner.

For example, the main entry for the community blog space for SAP S/4HANA Cloud SDK can be found at *http://tiny.cc/s4sdk-blogs*. At the time of this writing, this space contains over twenty additional tutorial blogs, in-depth guides, and frequently asked questions.

You can use the following tags in SAP communities to find more learning content.

- On side-by-side extensibility with SAP Cloud Platform:
  - *https://blogs.sap.com/tag/sap-s4hana-cloud-sdk/*
  - *https://blogs.sap.com/tag/sap-cloud-platform/*
  - *https://blogs.sap.com/tag/extensibility/*
- On in-app extensibility with SAP S/4HANA:
  - *https://blogs.sap.com/tag/in-app-extensibility/*
  - *https://blogs.sap.com/tag/s4hana-cloud-extensibility/*
  - *https://blogs.sap.com/tags/73554900100800000266/*

StackOverflow

The SAP S/4HANA Cloud SDK team can be contacted at StackOverflow for any in-depth programming-related issues that you might encounter while working with the examples or the artifacts presented in this book. All questions with the "s4sdk" tag are actively monitored:

https://stackoverflow.com/questions/tagged/s4sdk

GitHub

Besides using the examples for this book provided in the public GitHub repository, you may want to use the specific open source artifacts introduced throughout the book. You can also learn more about the code itself, raise issues, or contribute actively using pull requests as with any open source project.

Additional example applications can be found at *https://github.com/SAP/cloud-s4-sdk-examples*. The open source artifacts for continuous integration and delivery, as introduced in Part III of this book, can either be found in the vanilla pipeline project at *https://github.com/SAP/cloud-s4-sdk-pipeline* or the corresponding library at *https://github.com/SAP/cloud-s4-sdk-pipeline-lib*. Furthermore, you can check out SAP's Jenkins library GitHub repository for additional library steps and implementations at *https://github.com/SAP/jenkins-library*.

Acknowledgements

We would like to thank all those who have contributed to this book significantly with their time, dedication, and passion.

First and foremost, we would like to thank all our coauthors without whom this book would not have been possible: Dr. Richard Birenheide, Pablo Caceres, Marco Dahms, Alexander Dümont, Michael Emerson, Dr. Frank Essenberger, Jürgen Göbl, Benjamin Heilbrunn, Ramachandra Kamath, Ekaterina Kruse, Helmut Königseder, Georg Köster, Daniel Kurzynski, Dr. Christian Lechner, Arun Bhaskaran Nair, Tatjana Pfeifer, Jan Rumig, Mathias Rup, Junjie Tang, Felix Wente, Florian Wilhelm, and Carsten Ziegler.

Furthermore, we would like to thank Sabrina Merx and Colin Wernicke for managing and editing the illustrations of the book.

Besides the coauthors, editors, and designers, we are extraordinarily thankful for all the great minds who either acted as reviewers or gave invaluable input to the contents of the individual chapters. In particular, we would like to thank Thomas Bieser, Dr. Martijn De Boer, Peter Eberlein, Manuel Heibel, Artem Korsun, Oleg Koutyrine, Andreas Krompholz, Dennis Kuhnert, Florian Kunzke, Marika Marszalkowski, Thomas Meigen, Florian Richter, Joel Rosenberger, Dr. Andreas Roth, Dr. Arne Scherrer, Katrin Schneider, Dr. Thomas Schneider, Christoph Schubert, Dr. Volker Schulz, Tobias Stein, Nikolai Tankov, Dr. Sebastian Wieczorek, and Torsten Zube.

We would like to thank Dr. Wieland Schreiner, Executive Vice President for SAP S/4HANA, for his great support on the book project as well as his relentless push of making the intelligent enterprise based on SAP S/4HANA a reality for the business world.

Moreover, we would like to thank Bernd Leukert, member of the Executive Board, Products and Innovation, for his vision and strategy that inspired and shaped many of the developments and software artifacts that you'll find throughout the book. We are also very grateful to him for writing the foreword outlining SAP's vision and commitment to the intelligent enterprise, putting the book into perspective.

In addition, we would like to thank the publisher, SAP PRESS, for accepting the book proposal in the first place and delivering a high-quality book in the very ambitious time frame we set on short notice. We are particularly grateful for all the work of the book's editor, Hareem Shafi, who worked relentlessly to give us input and help. Her final editing gave the book the quality you deserve as the reader.

Finally, a book on extending SAP S/4HANA would not exist without all its involved products. Therefore, we would like to thank everyone who has contributed to the development of SAP S/4HANA and SAP Cloud Platform for their continued hard work to expand SAP's Cloud solutions every day and to regularly incorporate important feedback from the ecosystem. Special thanks go to the teams behind the SAP S/4HANA Cloud SDK as well as the SAP Cloud Platform SDK for service development for their continued commitment and hard work. Furthermore, we would like to thank all SAP application development teams, for example SAP RealSpend, SAP Financial Statement Insights, and SAP S/4HANA Cloud for credit integration as well as all SAP partners who acted as early adopters for the latest technologies. Their validation, input, and feedback have been extraordinarily important to the quality of many artifacts described in this book.

Legal Disclaimer

Any statements contained in this document that are not historical facts are forward-looking statements as defined in the U.S. Private Securities Litigation Reform Act of 1995. Words such as "anticipate," "believe," "estimate," "expect," "forecast," "intend," "may," "plan," "project," "predict," "should" and "will" and similar expressions as they relate to SAP are intended to identify such forward-looking statements. SAP undertakes no obligation to publicly update or revise any forward-looking statements. All forward-looking statements are subject to various risks and uncertainties that could cause actual results to differ materially from expectations.

PART I

The Intelligent ERP

Chapter 1
SAP S/4HANA: The Intelligent ERP

SAP is committed to supporting its customers' digital transformation with SAP S/4HANA. While customers ask for the ability to quickly set up new digital processes, they also often need a stable upgrade path from older business suite solutions to SAP S/4HANA. This chapter explains the evolution of SAP S/4HANA and its major design principles such as simplification, compatibility, and its public model as well as decoupled extensions.

This book is about building cloud-native applications that extend or otherwise integrate SAP S/4HANA. To maintain the primary focus of the book, we won't dive deeply into the individual features of SAP S/4HANA. However, a basic understanding of some fundamentals of SAP S/4HANA will be helpful when you build extensions of SAP S/4HANA on the SAP Cloud Platform.

In the following sections, we'll introduce the history of SAP S/4HANA and the design principles that have shaped the new architecture. Understanding these principles and SAP S/4HANA in general will help you when you extend SAP S/4HANA with applications on the SAP Cloud Platform. You'll learn how SAP S/4HANA's architecture impacts the way extensions can be built and learn about the benefits of flexible innovation via extensions that help you and your customers through digital transformation.

1.1 Digital Transformation

Digital transformation describes the change introduced in human society by digital technologies. Starting with the invention of computers, technology has pushed the limits of previously paper-based processes to new scales at a significantly higher speed with lower costs. This transformation penetrates all aspects of the society by disrupting or converting traditional business models. In the last decade, Apple has revolutionized the mobile phone market by merging the capabilities of phones and personal computers into one device, the smartphone. Car or accommodation sharing was not available. Neither was video streaming. Within ten years Uber, Airbnb, and Netflix have emerged as global players on new markets. Spikes in technical advancements can lead to the collapse of traditional business models at an unprecedented speed in economic history. While media streaming has already replaced the traditional rental model, other business models have not yet proven they can adapt.

Common to many digital products is that the delivery of a service is separate from the physical world, such as music, books, articles, connectivity with friends in a social network, training courses, and so on. Consumption may happen instantly at any time. Digital products do not require the repetitive production of physical goods and shipments to consumers. Production rather refers to digital copies (data) that is transmitted to consumers.

Digital transformation won't end soon but rather will continue until almost all aspects of life are transformed. In 2018, technologies such as 3D printing and machine learning have led to new waves of disruption with completely new business models. Companies that embrace a mindset of change and IT infrastructures will likely grow more quickly than their competitors. SAP is committed to accompanying customers on their way through the digital transformation, a key design principle of SAP S/4HANA.

1.2 SAP S/4HANA Evolution

From its beginning, SAP has continuously transformed the IT industry and helped its customers embrace best practices. The evolution of SAP S/4HANA exemplifies SAP's constant push towards innovation and its dedication to redefining the way companies do business:

- 1973: SAP R/1
- 1979: SAP R/2
- 1992: SAP R/3
- 2004: SAP ERP/SAP Business Suite
- 2010: SAP HANA
- 2013: SAP Business Suite on SAP HANA
- 2015: SAP S/4HANA

In 1979, SAP introduced its mainframe-based SAP R/2 solution to the market. For the first time, standard software allowed enterprises to integrate business processes such as inventory management, purchasing, or invoice verification in real time. Following the success of SAP R/2 in 1992, SAP released SAP R/3. With SAP R/3, the mainframe architecture was replaced by a client-server model, allowing interaction with the system in real time from a desktop by using a graphical user interface (GUI). In 2010, SAP released its revolutionary in-memory database SAP HANA, and then moved the SAP Business Suite, the successor to SAP R/3, to SAP HANA in 2013. Ultimately, SAP S/4HANA emerged as the next generation of intelligent enterprise software in 2015 (Figure 1.1). SAP S/4HANA builds on the foundations of SAP Business Suite and its deep integration with SAP HANA. The cloud version of SAP S/4HANA was released in 2016. Today, SAP S/4HANA provides the most comprehensive suite of business applications tailored for small, medium, and large enterprises on-premise as well as in a cloud deployment model.

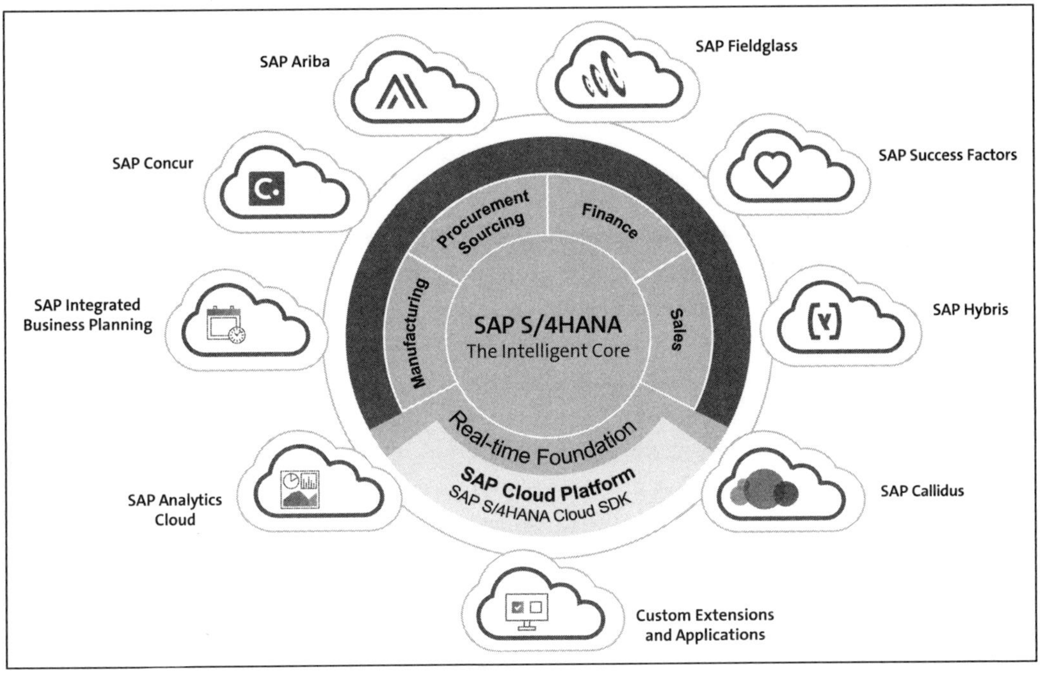

Figure 1.1 SAP S/4HANA and the Modular Suite

1.3 SAP S/4HANA Design Principles

To support its customers' digital transformation roadmaps, SAP has applied a set of key design principles in the development of SAP S/4HANA. These principles are the natural and logical result of SAP's cloud strategy for the future and thus can be considered a frame for past, present, and future development activities around SAP S/4HANA. The principles are:

- Simplification
- SAP HANA
- Compatibility
- Single codeline
- Cloud-first
- SAP Fiori
- Flexible deployment
- Integration
- Public model
- Intelligence
- Decoupled extensions

While the focus of the book is decoupled extensions, the other principles are important for an understanding of extension options. Let's look at each of these guiding principles in more detail in the next sections.

1.3.1 Simplification

The simplification principle manifests itself in several ways. Compared to SAP Business Suite, SAP S/4HANA eliminates many redundancies in terms of frameworks, data models, user interfaces, and business solutions. For example, SAP S/4HANA uses one global business partner model, one global field for the material number, one simplified data model for financials, logistics, and other areas. Best practice configuration is provided in combination with a wizard to help you scope and fine-tune SAP S/4HANA reducing initial setup times and ongoing postproduction support needs. The necessity of programming to optimize the system to your needs is significantly reduced with adaptation tools to help adjust user interfaces to specific end-user needs. Without any data dictionaries or programming experience, you may extend data structures from a database layer, over OData APIs, to a user interface. A clearer separation between internal and external API simplifies creating extensions.

1.3.2 SAP HANA

With SAP Business Suite on SAP HANA, SAP has relinquished multidatabase support in favor of concrete optimizations for SAP HANA. SAP HANA allows you to combine transactional and analytical processes in one database instance so that persisted aggregates and index tables could be eliminated. Consequently, the data model for many processes was simplified and optimized so that totally new processes could be developed, such as real-time Inventory Management in SAP Materials Management that implemented an insert-only and lock-free data model, thus drastically increasing throughput.

1.3.3 Compatibility

SAP S/4HANA's functionality is based on the huge feature scope of the SAP Business Suite. Although a majority of the codebase has been rewritten and the data models have been significantly simplified, SAP has ensured that external interfaces are mostly compatible. Therefore, you can continue running many of the processes from SAP ERP or SAP Business Suite on SAP HANA also in SAP S/4HANA. From the beginning, SAP wanted to facilitate migration from other SAP products to SAP S/4HANA. SAP S/4HANA has been kept semantically compatible with SAP ERP and SAP Business Suite on SAP HANA. In addition to the data model, integration interfaces like BAPIs and IDocs are largely compatible (exceptions are called "deprecations"), and their use is the result of intentional simplification and additional functionality.

1.3.4 Single Codeline

SAP S/4HANA Cloud and SAP S/4HANA on-premise share the same development codeline. Based on this, extensions can target both versions. However, the two products are not identical. SAP S/4HANA Cloud does not provide some previously available functionality. In particular, this is true for deprecated features such as simplification, and compatibility scope. The term *compatibility scope* describes functionality provided to support migration to SAP S/4HANA on-premise. These functionalities are not provided in SAP S/4HANA Cloud because today other cloud solutions cover its scope, for example, SAP SuccessFactors instead of the classic SAP

Human Capital Management module from SAP ERP. The remaining scope differences are gradually reduced with SAP S/4HANA Cloud's quarterly updates. Major additions to SAP S/4HANA Cloud are the cloud enablement qualities, such as the SAP Fiori web-based UI, OData APIs, or optimizations for cloud operations. These qualities are also available for SAP S/4HANA on-premise based on yearly shipments from the single code line that underlies both products. Figure 1.2 shows schematically the differences between both options of SAP S/4HANA as well as SAP ERP based on scope, targeted qualities, and shipment model.

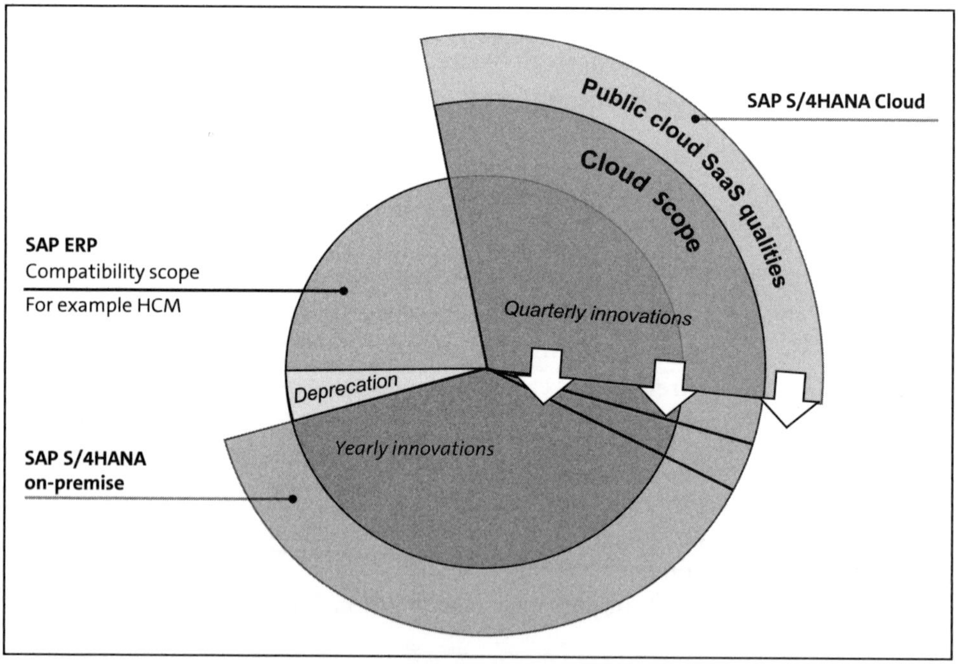

Figure 1.2 Cloud Enablement Strategy for SAP S/4HANA

1.3.5 Cloud-First

SAP S/4HANA Cloud is offered as a true software-as-a-service (SaaS) solution. You can almost instantly explore and configure the system. SAP is responsible for the operations aspects to ensure highest availability, scalability, security, and other cloud qualities. In this regard, the principle *cloud-first* has many shapes. SAP releases innovations to SAP S/4HANA Cloud on a quarterly basis to respond quickly to market trends and customer needs. Only one version of SAP S/4HANA for all cloud customers, which is automatically updated, exists at any given time. Based on SAP S/4HANA Cloud's quarterly updates, updates to SAP S/4HANA on-premise are delivered on a yearly schedule. Therefore, cloud innovations are also made available in the traditional delivery model. The cloud-first approach also expresses itself in the public model (Section 1.3.9) and the simplified customer experience (Section 1.3.6).

1.3.6 SAP Fiori

SAP S/4HANA provides a modern, web-based user interface based on SAP Fiori. SAP Fiori provides a consistent design and a responsive user experience for various form factors, such as mobile devices and workstations. The SAP Fiori launchpad provides a role-based way to organize applications and enables various personalization capabilities to tailor the experience to the end users' needs. SAP Fiori also features SAP CoPilot, a digital assistant that supports natural language processing. SAP Fiori communicates with the backend through RESTful OData APIs so that backend and frontend are well separated and decoupled.

1.3.7 Flexible Deployment

For many companies, replacing a working on-premise system completely with a cloud-based SaaS platform all at once is hard to justify. Furthermore, business units such as subsidiaries, divisions, and acquired companies may want to configure and extend their own systems as needed. Consequently, the deployment model needs to reduce complexity and total cost of ownership (TCO) by providing the agility to support new business models alongside traditional operations. Because SAP S/4HANA shares one development code line, the same data model, and the same user experience, integration between the cloud and on-premise versions is easier than in any other setup.

As a result, smaller units can innovate more quickly without learning a new system and isolating themselves from the parent company's processes. Consolidation and closing activities are facilitated by operational consistency across subsidiaries. Moreover, SAP S/4HANA on-premise can act as an intermediate step for transitioning from any older ERP releases to SAP S/4HANA Cloud. This step might be helpful to drive the necessary changes and adaptions in your existing systems, such as migrating custom extensions to the public model or to SAP Cloud Platform, before moving into a pure SaaS-based solution. Refer to Chapter 7 for more detailed information.

1.3.8 Integration

SAP S/4HANA provides plug-and-play integration with SAP's other cloud solutions such as SAP Fieldglass, SAP Concur, SAP Ariba, or SAP Leonardo. Several processes are supported with predefined integration content, such as invoice and discount management with sell-side SAP Ariba, supply chain finance with SAP Ariba Financial Supply Chain, cost centers with SAP SuccessFactors, and payment advices with SAP Fieldglass, to name just a few. For SAP S/4HANA Cloud, integration points can be managed and operated by SAP. In addition, integration might be managed centrally with SAP Cloud Platform Integration for structural mappings or based on direct calls to the public APIs offered mostly as OData or SOAP services in the SAP API Business Hub (*http://api.sap.com*).

In general, three main integration approaches exist. First, so-called SAP-managed integration involves completely predefined integration scenarios that are operated by SAP; that is, no additional customer input is necessary to set up the integration. Second, in template-based integration scenarios, SAP provides verified content to serve main integration activities such as APIs and field mappings, adaptations, and customer operations. Third, partner- or customer-driven integration scenarios based on released APIs from SAP can be set up, developed, and operated solely by the partner or customer. This third approach is a core topic of this book.

To enable flexible integration options between on-premise and cloud solutions, SAP provides the Cloud Connector. For example, the Cloud Connector might be used to establish a secure tunnel between SAP S/4HANA on-premise and the SAP Cloud Platform and its services. The Cloud Connector supports various protocols such as HTTP, SQL, RFC, and IDocs.

1.3.9 Public Model

Stable APIs for integration and extensibility are a key factor for the success of SAP S/4HANA. The SAP API Business Hub provides access to public APIs in the form of catalogues grouped around business domains. APIs consist of OData services based on SAP S/4HANA's public data model, also referred to as the virtual data model (VDM), which uses core data services (CDS) as the underlying implementation technology. Also the basis for transactional apps and analytics, the VDM is comprehensive, semantically rich, understandable, stable, and meant for reuse.

Next to the APIs, in the form of OData services, SOAP APIs or traditional RFC-based APIs, such as BAPIs or IDocs, are available. In contrast to SAP Business Suite or SAP

ERP, SAP S/4HANA clearly separates between public and private APIs. In SAP S/4HANA Cloud, only public APIs can be used, while private APIs are not even visible. The on-premise version of SAP S/4HANA has more degrees of freedom. To facilitate migration, SAP S/4HANA still allows access to private APIs and deprecated code, thus, these features can be used temporarily during the transition to the public model. In this context, SAP classifies development objects into three categories to clearly define the risks associated with using each objects with respect to future compatibility and migration efforts.

First, *whitelisted* objects are part of the public model and are recommended for use by developers as they provide a stable contract. Second, *graylisted* objects are not part of the public model. Those objects might become incompatible in the future or even be completely removed. The risk for future migration efforts is significantly increased when relying on such objects. Thirdly, *blacklisted* objects are not part of the public model and, if not already removed, are likely to be removed in a future version. SAP does not recommend using them at all.

Customers and partners should adapt their extensions to make use of the public model only, even in the on-premise version, to guarantee hassle-free upgrades to newer versions of SAP S/4HANA. For the reasons we've just mentioned, SAP S/4HANA Cloud only provides the public model and related tools for in-app and side-by-side extensions, as outlined throughout this book. In the on-premise version of SAP S/4HANA, ABAP extensions can be ported by using many of the traditional capabilities for ABAP add-on development such as the traditional graphical user interfaces or the development of function groups. Nonetheless, customers and partners alike should take migration and forward-compatibility considerations regarding graylisted and blacklisted functionality into account.

Additional Information on Migrating Custom Code

SAP S/4HANA System Conversion: *http://tiny.cc/s4h-conversion*

SAP S/4HANA Custom Code Migration Worklist: *http://tiny.cc/s4h-worklist*

ABAP Custom Code Adaptation for SAP HANA: *http://tiny.cc/s4h-abap*

1.3.10 Intelligence

With the rise of computational power and novel algorithms, artificial intelligence and machine learning continue to penetrate business processes. Artificial intelligence services such as speech and image recognition have already surpassed human capabilities. An intelligent ERP contextualizes information on all levels of interaction with the system. The evolution towards an intelligent enterprise starting from the classical transactional world is shown in Figure 1.3. In a traditional transactional enterprise, many simple and repetitive tasks are being executed manually, leaving little time for high-value tasks such as customer interactions, product innovation, or collaboration. Moving from a transactional enterprise over a digital enterprise into an intelligent enterprise, an ever-increasing number of repetitive tasks can be replaced by artificial intelligence.

As a result of this process, employees of an enterprise can spend more time on more complex high-value activities that eventually lead to more effective outcomes and higher productivity.

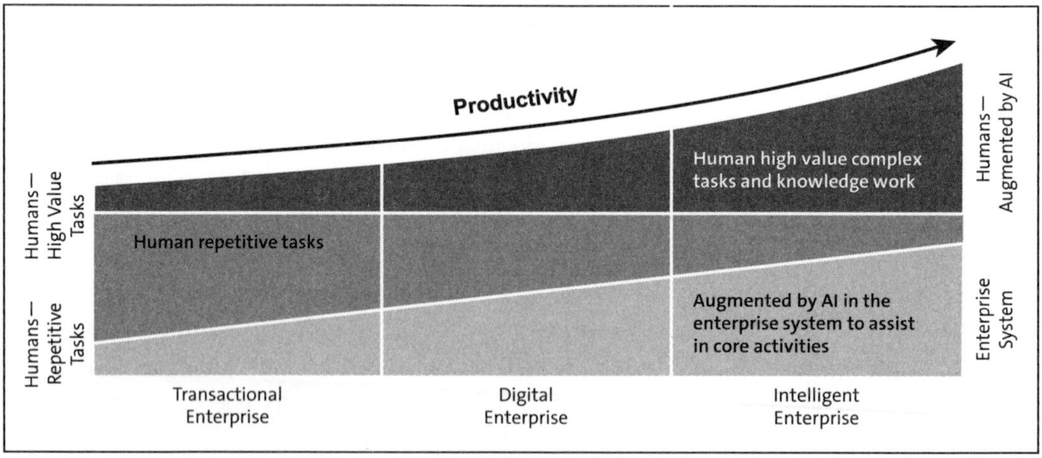

Figure 1.3 The Intelligent Enterprise: Augmentation of Human Capabilities and Automation of Repetitive Tasks

SAP S/4HANA includes artificial intelligence on several levels such as the user interface and the database across various business processes. As an example, SAP S/4HANA provides intelligent payment clearing capabilities that include image recognition based on neural networks to allow automated matching and payment of incoming invoices. Other example scenarios include the reliable prediction of contract expirations or goods consumptions allowing for more effective and proactive supplier negotiations and relationships. Furthermore, SAP S/4HANA's situations concept proactively displays issues requiring attention and automatically provides related information and actions. As such, machine learning enables intelligent businesses beyond traditional insight-to-action scenarios.

With SAP Leonardo, artificial intelligence services are also available for customer and partner extensions of SAP S/4HANA, again, using the SAP Cloud Platform. Chapter 17 provides guidance and how-to examples on how to leverage these services in any partner or customer extension.

1.3.11 Decoupled Extensions

While SAP S/4HANA provides end-to-end functionality across a broad array of businesses, individual organizations will often require additional functionality that is unique to their business. For many years, the SAP NetWeaver Application Server (AS) was not only used by SAP for its products but also was used by many customers to extend the SAP standard in many ways. Extensions can range from simple ABAP reports extracting data from business module database tables to developing huge add-ons to implement completely new processes. The ability to debug and analyze the source code of SAP's modules has helped customers learn a lot about the internal structure of those modules. Often, customer and partner extensions benefitted from existing code and data structures by calling into the business modules' classes and function modules or by selecting from the business modules' database tables. Development costs were kept at a moderate level, and operations costs were low as no additional servers were needed. As a consequence of this tight coupling of customer code and SAP modules, SAP could not easily refactor and improve its code in the past. Any change would have vast effects on custom extensions so companies found it difficult to upgrade their systems or benefit from SAP's best practices and improvements.

Therefore, SAP S/4HANA provides two modes for extensions: First, in-app extensibility provides expert or key user tools to create extensions inside SAP S/4HANA itself. Second, side-by-side extensions are based on the SAP Cloud Platform to create extensions in conjunction with SAP S/4HANA.

In both cases, the public model provides a stable contract that you can rely on when upgrading to future versions of SAP S/4HANA without the need to update the custom code built on top. Although semantically deeply integrated, side-by-side extensions are technically decoupled from SAP S/4HANA so that extensions can be developed independently from the SAP NetWeaver AS. For example, you can use other languages than ABAP, apply different lifecycle concepts, consider independent release timelines, and scale extensions independently of SAP S/4HANA. Moreover, the SAP Cloud Platform includes additional technical and business services to facilitate the effective and efficient creation of side-by-side extensions. Several of these services are explained in this book.

1.4 Summary

In the next chapter, we'll explain both extension options in greater detail by presenting archetypes, patterns, and use cases that can be realized with these novel extension concepts.

Chapter 2
SAP S/4HANA Extensibility

This chapter explains the various forms and modes through which SAP S/4HANA can be extended. This chapter, in particular, includes in-app extensibility (i.e., all extensions made with key user tools inside of the SAP S/4HANA core) as well as side-by-side extensibility (i.e., all extensions on SAP Cloud Platform). We'll provide an overview of extension capabilities and their corresponding integration points and outline patterns for extensibility and their characteristics. Although the book touches on in-app extensibility, our primary focus is on side-by-side extensibility.

After introducing the general design principles and rationales of the SAP S/4HANA architecture, this chapter explains SAP S/4HANA's extensibility options and their business implications in more detail.

The majority of customers using one of SAP's ERP solutions have significantly adjusted and extended the standard software provided by SAP to implement business processes that are specific to their organizations. Extensions range from simple reports or modifications of a few lines to SAP's ABAP source code to newly developed applications for an industry-specific adaptation of a standard process. Furthermore, many partners have provided significant industry-specific or line of business (LOB)-specific enhancements, usually in the form of large ABAP add-ons.

This chapter explains SAP S/4HANA's new extensibility strategy and how it differs from the traditional approaches. While the following chapters of this book dive into specific details of extensibility, the goal of this chapter is to provide an overview of extensibility options and capabilities.

The extensibility strategy is based on two pillars: in-app extensibility and side-by-side extensibility. As the name implies, in-app extensions are implemented using key user tools directly inside the SAP S/4HANA system, while side-by-side extensions leverage the SAP Cloud Platform as extension platform. For both approaches, we'll give examples as well as typical use cases that use both options in combination.

2.1 Separation of Concerns

In this section, we'll introduce how the new extensibility strategy differs from the well-known traditional approaches that were possible in the traditional architecture of the past. Faster innovation cycles demand a different approach that gives appropriate freedom both to SAP and to extension developers.

2.1.1 "The Good Old Days"

For decades, the SAP NetWeaver Application Server (AS) for SAP ERP was used to develop and run extensions, from simple enhancements like adding some validation logic on a business object to huge add-ons. Several circumstances led to the perception that developing extensions was simple. Let's explore these in the next sections.

Integration

SAP's ERP modules were deeply integrated because they ran on the same application servers and shared the same database instance. Custom applications and extensions could use this tight integration in the same way as SAP did, which made upgrades more difficult.

Access to Source Code

The ABAP source code and the data dictionary (that is, the metadata) of the database was fully available to customers and accessible for extension development. Many customer extensions copied major parts from existing SAP modules or reused code from the modules so that customers could easily replace parts in their own implementations, which again made lifecycle management more difficult.

Infrastructure

Customers often deployed extensions into the existing infrastructure so that the extension code ran on the same infrastructure as the SAP modules. By doing so, purchasing hardware, installing servers, and managing users as well as other administrative tasks were avoided.

Change Management

SAP's change and transport management was for many years an unmatched advantage of the SAP NetWeaver AS. SAP has shaped many industry best practices with its way of handling multiple software versions and the infrastructure of transporting changes from development to quality and production systems.

ABAP

ABAP is SAP's programming language, which was designed exclusively for business application development and features all the capabilities generally expected from a fourth-generation language. SAP has added many frameworks, libraries, and tools, such as the internal table concept or business partner APIs so that application and extension development was efficient. Consequently, SAP also made ABAP available to customers and partners for extension development.

Reliability

The SAP NetWeaver AS introduced the client-server approach to enterprise software, which is stable and reliable. By simply adding more application servers, SAP NetWeaver AS can scale from the smallest installations to the demands of the largest enterprises in the world.

2.1.2 Principle of Least Knowledge

In SAP S/4HANA on-premise, all capabilities mentioned in the previous section are still available and valid, although SAP imposes a more strict separation of internal and external APIs (public model) as explained in Chapter 1. Customers are strongly advised to build on the public model only and to avoid using or removing any other software artifact so that future upgrades can be executed smoothly.

In contrast, SAP S/4HANA Cloud exposes the public model only. The basic approach taken by SAP can be expressed with the *principle of least knowledge*, also known as the *law of Demeter*, introduced by Ian Holland in 1987. This principle postulates that any consuming component may not know the internal details of another provider component, but only uses its exposed functionality. Based on this principle, SAP can regularly update SAP S/4HANA Cloud without any adaptation needed on the part of customers and partners, enabling a faster innovation cycle. Consequently, long and error-prone upgrade procedures are significantly reduced, which increases customers' ability to benefit from new innovations faster. Furthermore, even for SAP, the violation of this principle reduced the ability to optimize the internals of the modules. Thus, code and objects created by SAP, by customers, and by partners code must be clearly and logically separated. That is, customers can no longer modify objects delivered by SAP in SAP S/4HANA Cloud.

While all traditional modification techniques are still possible in the on-premise version of SAP S/4HANA, to support the migration to SAP S/4HANA, we strongly recommend that customers *not* use these capabilities anymore. Technically, the separation of concerns by using decoupled extensions is one of the most important aspects of SAP S/4HANA and one of its major differences with SAP ERP and SAP Business Suite.

However, we'll need to determine the technologies, tools, and methods to use in conjunction with SAP S/4HANA if the traditional approaches are either no longer supported or are at least discouraged. In general, SAP S/4HANA provides two main types of extensions, which implement the separation of concerns:

- In-app extensions
- Side-by-side extensions

In-app and side-by-side extensions can be used individually but also in a seamlessly integrated way. As discussed earlier, in SAP S/4HANA Cloud, these options are the only ones available today. In contrast, in SAP S/4HANA on-premise, customers may also use traditional extension approaches, for example, using ABAP development tools such as ABAP in Eclipse and the ABAP Workbench (Transaction SE80). However, the traditional approach is no longer recommended for new developments and, therefore, is not covered in this book at all.

2.2 In-App Extensions

All in-app extensions are technically implemented inside the core of SAP S/4HANA, that is, on the same servers as SAP S/4HANA. As a result, no remote communication between the extension and the extended app is required. Many processes in SAP S/4HANA support extensions with key user tools integrated into the SAP Fiori user interface for SAP S/4HANA. As such, in-app extensions enable business experts without deep technical knowledge, typically referred to as *key users*, to implement key types of customer extensions, such as creating custom business objects and adding custom fields to business objects.

Note that the in-app extension concept is essential for SAP S/4HANA Cloud. However, this concept is also invaluable for traditional, on-premise deployments in order to align with the separation of concerns philosophy. With the inevitable move to the cloud, we recommend thinking of extensions from a cloud-first perspective even when applications are still running on-premise. In other words, in-app extensibility features should also be considered in SAP S/4HANA on-premise.

Definition: Key User

A key user in SAP S/4HANA is a member of a functional team that adopts the software to the needs of his or her business department—being either a direct employee or an external person, such as a consultant. As this person typically has some level of technical knowledge but no in-depth knowledge like a developer, all extension steps need to be covered by tools that hide complexity and technical detail. The old, strict separation of requestors stating requirements and developers implementing those requirements is no longer the preferred model for many SAP customers. Especially in software-as-a-service (SaaS) applications, for simple cases, customers expect to create custom forms, reports, fields, and even small pieces of business logic with appropriate tools that hide the technical complexity involved in connectivity, deployment, or lifecycle management.

This set of tools applies consistently across all applications in SAP S/4HANA; in other words, there is exactly one way to add custom logic to a business object or to extend a business object's data model with a field. This unification was achieved through SAP S/4HANA's overall streamlined architecture. The layers of a modern SAP Fiori application in SAP S/4HANA are shown in Figure 2.1.

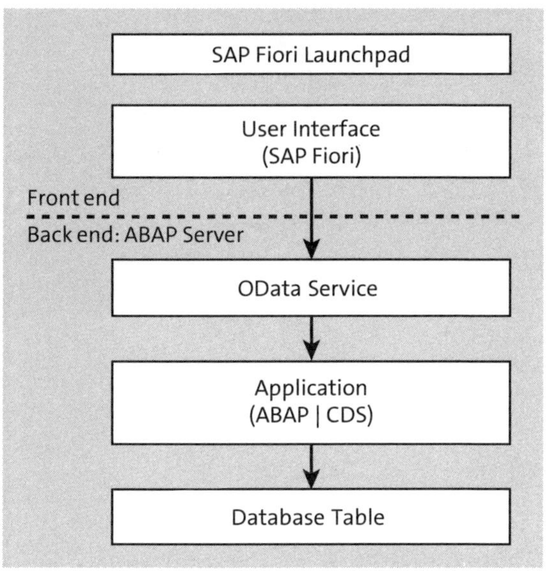

Figure 2.1 Anatomy of an SAP Fiori Application

An application consists of five layers. At the bottom, the database model contains database tables, which are used by an application layer. In the application layer, the core data service (CDS) model contains views for efficient consumption and analytical requests. In addition, this layer may contain ABAP source code, organized in business objects, for example, to implement validation logic. On the third layer from the bottom, the functionality of the business objects is exposed in the form of RESTful Open Data Protocol (OData) services, which can be considered the communication layer. At the top are the responsive SAP Fiori user interface and the SAP Fiori launchpad.

Open Data Protocol

OData was originally developed by Microsoft but today falls under the leadership of the OASIS organization. OData is an open protocol that standardizes the creation and use of RESTful HTTP communication APIs. OData client and server libraries are available for all major programming languages.

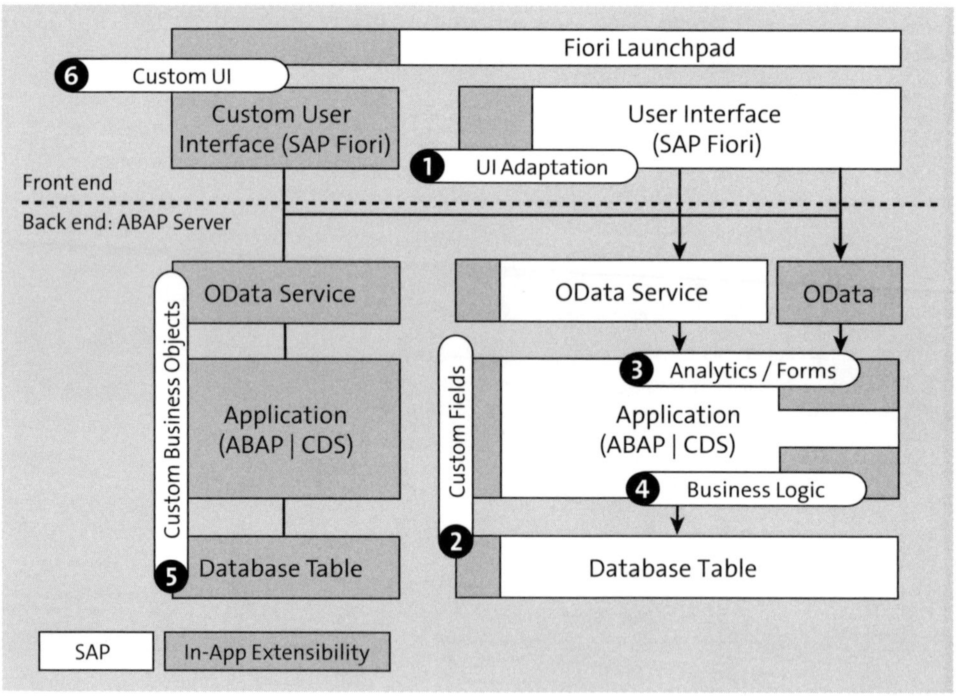

Figure 2.2 In-App Extensibility Points

On any layer, customers may apply in-app extensions. The diagram shown in Figure 2.2 provides an overview of the most important in-app extension points. We'll go through each extension point following the outlined numbering schema. Note that all the concepts we'll mention next will be described in more detail in Chapter 18 of this book.

- ❶ **User Interface Adaptation**
  Key users may change the layout of tables and forms directly in the running user interface. A special graphical user interface adaptation mode provides the mechanisms to hide fields in existing forms, tables, or filters; to rename labels; to add fields to the user interface from the field repository; and to move fields or entire blocks to other sections of the screen.
- ❷ **Custom Fields**
  In the Custom Fields and Logic SAP Fiori application, you can add and edit custom fields to extend SAP database tables, CDS views, and OData APIs. Moreover, this extension application helps to define how custom fields are used in user interfaces, reports, or forms. Furthermore, you can use custom fields along with predefined business scenarios so that all involved business objects are extended and values are passed along automatically.
- ❸ **Custom CDS Views, Analytics, Forms**
  The SAP S/4HANA data model, with its public views based on CDS, might not always provide the best technical option to fetch data. When related data needs to be pulled out of various views, pushing the join and aggregation operators into the SAP HANA database by creating a custom view might be more convenient or efficient.

  The Custom CDS View application provides an overview of all CDS views in the public model as well as custom CDS views. This app enables customers to create new views based on an existing view model supporting features like associations, joins, transformations, field relabeling, selections, etc. With OData APIs on top of these views, customers may, in addition, expose the data for consumption outside the SAP S/4HANA core. Furthermore, the custom views might be used as data sources to define analytical queries. Those queries are used in embedded analytic user interfaces integrated into SAP S/4HANA applications. Another use case for custom views is to build forms with the Forms Designer application. Forms can consume data from custom OData services and use the data, for example, in custom email templates.

❹ Business Logic

Many SAP S/4HANA applications have enhancement spots (also called Business Add-Ins [BAdIs]). With the ABAP web editor (Figure 2.3), customers may create custom logic for the BAdIs. Typically, customers implement additional checks, set default values, or create mappings in combination with custom fields. The available features of the ABAP language in the web editor are limited compared to the capabilities in the SAP NetWeaver AS to ensure no negative impact on the robustness of the system as well as to comply with high security and data consistency standards. For example, you cannot perform database updates or generate source code dynamically from the web editor.

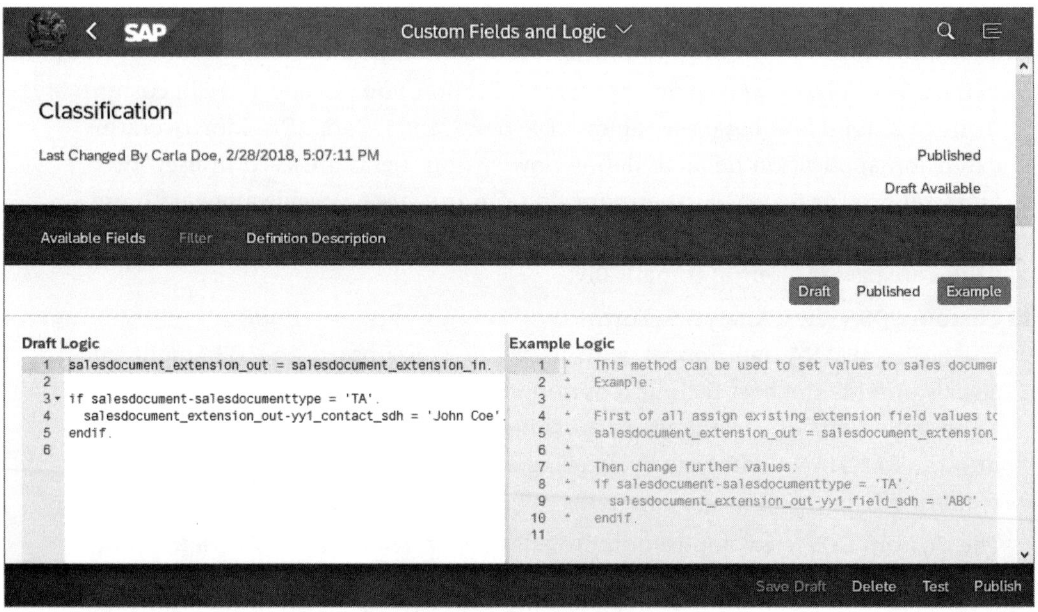

Figure 2.3 Custom Fields and Logic SAP Fiori Application

❺ Custom Business Objects

Besides custom views, you can create completely new business objects using the Custom Business Objects application. This application helps define the business object structure in the form of business object nodes, which automatically create the required database tables (Figure 2.4). A built-in web editor supports with writing the corresponding code. Again, for writing customer business objects, you can only use whitelisted APIs.

Changing existing SAP business objects is not supported. However, the creation of custom business objects can be supported by reusing custom CDS views, OData APIs, and custom user interfaces so that a fully-fledged, self-contained extension to SAP S/4HANA can be created.

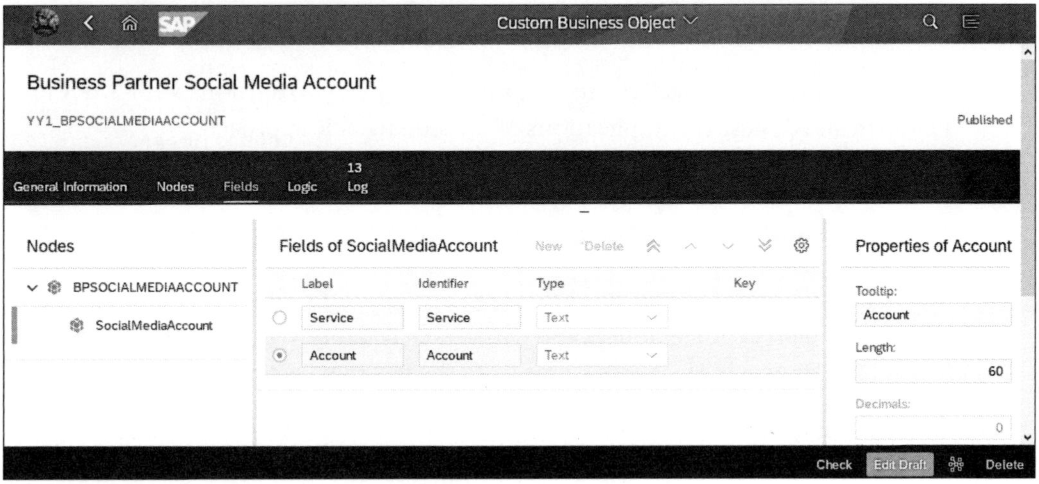

Figure 2.4 Creation of a Node in a Custom Business Object

❻ **Custom User Interfaces**

You can use the SAP Web IDE to create your own SAP Fiori user interfaces either from scratch or based on templates. The SAP Fiori user interfaces consume SAP S/4HANA's RESTful OData interfaces. After creation and successful testing, you can deploy these user interfaces into SAP S/4HANA's user interface repository and integrate them into the customer's SAP Fiori launchpad as new tiles using the Custom Tiles and Custom Catalog Extensions application.

In SAP S/4HANA Cloud, the transport of adaptations from the test system to the production system is also performed by the key user with another SAP Fiori application. These tools can be used without interaction with the service provider and outside the service provider's maintenance window. The extensibility transport tools are available as part of the Manage Software Collection application.

Thus concludes our overview of in-app extensibility as one major form of SAP S/4HANA extensibility. More details on in-app extensibility and its intersection with side-by-side extensibility can be found in Chapter 20 of this book. Furthermore, we can recommend some additional literature on this topic in the box below.

Further Information on In-App Extensions

Online Help on Extensibility: *http://tiny.cc/sap-help-in-app*

SAP S/4HANA Extensibility Tutorial: *http://tiny.cc/in-app-tutorial*

SAP S/4HANA Extensibility: Use Case Overview: *http://tiny.cc/in-app-overview*

Now, we'll switch perspectives to building side-by-side extensions with SAP Cloud Platform and discuss the implications of the side-by-side approach.

2.3 Side-by-Side Extensions

Scenarios exist where in-app extensions are not sufficient, which we'll explain in Section 2.4. In such cases, customers and partners may use side-by-side extensions as an alternative approach. The name stems from the fact that, in contrast to in-app extensions, side-by-side extensions are only implemented using the SAP Cloud Platform.

2.3.1 Overview of the SAP Cloud Platform

The SAP Cloud Platform is a platform-as-a-service (PaaS) offering for creating applications or extensions in a secure cloud-based computing environment managed by SAP. It is the default choice for building side-by-side extensions to SAP S/4HANA Cloud or on-premise. The platform also serves extension cases for other SAP products, be it other on-premise applications or the modern LOB-specific SaaS solutions such as SAP SuccessFactors (Figure 2.5). With SAP Cloud Platform, SAP offers a product as well as a methodology to develop technically decoupled extensions and cloud applications to meet challenging requirements in terms of cloud qualities such as availability and scalability, which we'll explain in Chapter 3.

SAP Cloud Platform provides a broad range of managed services as well as open source technologies that can be used to build new solutions. Business services include a currency service, a translation hub, and business logging. Furthermore, SAP Cloud Platform contains a broad range of technical services such as SAP Cloud Platform Integration, SAP Leonardo Internet of Things (IoT), or SAP Leonardo Machine Learning to name just a few. Finally, SAP Cloud Platform also provides storage services such as SAP HANA and open-source technologies like Redis or PostgreSQL. The entire list is continuously extended with new services on all levels of the platform.

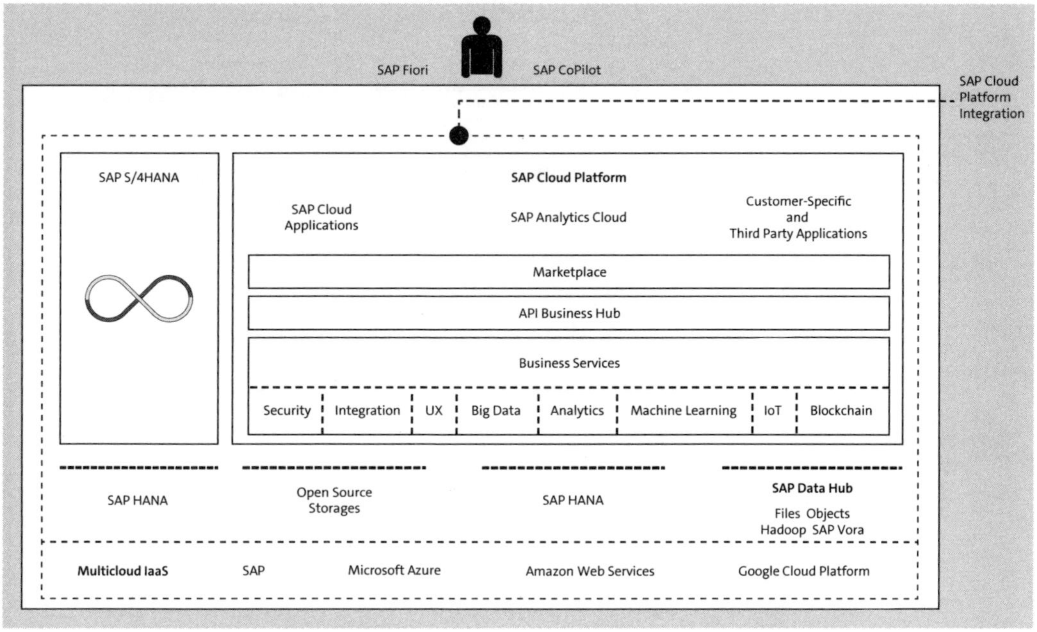

Figure 2.5 High-Level Overview of SAP Cloud Platform as the Extension Platform

In addition, SAP provides several programming environments and runtimes. First, the SAP Cloud Platform Neo environment is an SAP-proprietary environment for Java and HTML5 applications. Second, various runtimes are available as part of the Cloud Foundry environment on the SAP Cloud Platform, such as Java, Node.js, Python, and basically any other runtime supported by Cloud Foundry. Cloud Foundry is an open source industry standard to provide a PaaS standard that can run on multiple clouds. Cloud Foundry helps automate, scale, and manage cloud applications throughout the application lifecycle. SAP supports the Cloud Foundry Foundation as a Platinum member with code contributions and helps advance the evolution of open cloud computing technologies along with other companies such as Cisco, Dell, IBM, Pivotal, Suse, Google, and Microsoft. Complementing the existing capabilities of Cloud Foundry, SAP offers tools for developing applications such as the SAP Web IDE, the SAP API Business Hub, and an operations cockpit as well as several services for application management and monitoring. Figure 2.6 presents a high-level overview of the capabilities that are part of the SAP Cloud Platform. You may check out the overview of capabilities on the SAP Cloud Platform web page (*http://tiny.cc/scp-services*) for a more recent picture since the portfolio continuously expands.

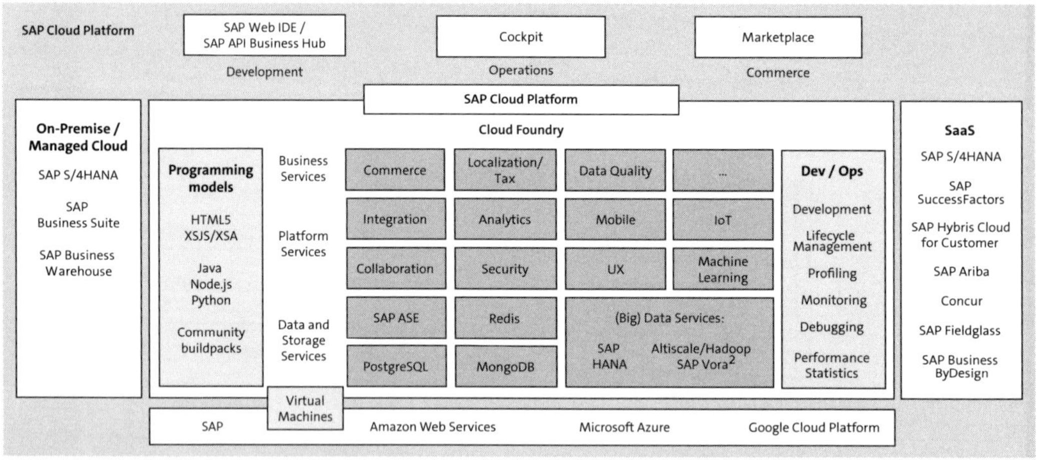

Figure 2.6 High-Level Overview of SAP Cloud Platform Capabilities

Thanks to SAP's multicloud strategy, you can use SAP Cloud Platform on multiple infrastructures, such as SAP's own data centers, Amazon Web Services, Microsoft Azure, and Google Cloud Platform. Customers can use SAP Cloud Platform in combination with other cloud services or co-located to existing cloud infrastructure and services.

2.3.2 Connectivity between SAP Cloud Platform and SAP S/4HANA

Connectivity between SAP Cloud Platform and SAP S/4HANA Cloud uses HTTPS communication, mostly via OData APIs. SAP S/4HANA Cloud exposes public APIs that can be directly called from applications on SAP Cloud Platform, and vice versa. Connectivity between SAP Cloud Platform and SAP S/4HANA on-premise is often more complex because you may not want to expose your internal networks for direct internet access. For this purpose, SAP offers the Cloud Connector to establish a secure tunnel for the communication. The tunnel can support ODBC, RFC, and HTTPS communication protocols so that you can, for example, invoke classic BAPIs, perform data replication from the database, or call OData APIs. The Cloud Connector is a small server installed inside the customer's landscape and acts as a reverse proxy to establish a connection with the connectivity service on SAP Cloud Platform. Once the connection is established, the Cloud Connector accepts calls from SAP Cloud Platform and routes them through to the correct endpoint of one of the on-premise systems, as shown in Figure 2.7.

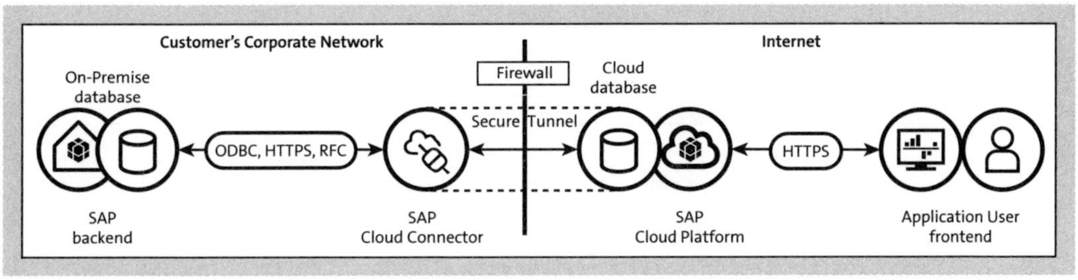

Figure 2.7 The Cloud Connector in a Hybrid Scenario

We'll go into more detail on how to set up the connection between SAP S/4HANA and the SAP Cloud Platform in Chapter 6. We'll also include detailed instructions on the differences between SAP S/4HANA Cloud and SAP S/4HANA on-premise as well as discuss some security concerns with delegating business users between the two stacks.

2.3.3 Side-by-Side Extension Scenarios

Side-by-side extensions are by design technically decoupled from the SAP S/4HANA standard. Consequently, an extension on the SAP Cloud Platform can be scaled and delivered independently from SAP S/4HANA. The extension may even provide its business function in case SAP S/4HANA or the connection to it has limited availability or other technical issues. Highly agile teams may use side-by-side extensions to update and improve parts of the system without close alignment with SAP S/4HANA teams and release plans. The following patterns cover the most important extension points next to the ones already introduced for in-app extensions. The patterns themselves consider typical, disjointed usage scenarios and, thus, do not reflect every possible combination that might be possible across patterns. Thus, you'll have to pick and combine various patterns depending on your use case and requirements.

Custom User Interfaces

The SAP Web IDE provides the tools for customers to create web-based user interfaces. The SAP Web IDE puts special focus on SAP Fiori and SAPUI5 with many templates for commonly used patterns such as the master-detail page layout. The user interfaces can then be deployed to an SAP Cloud Platform account for testing purposes or for productive use. The user interfaces may use existing whitelisted OData services from SAP S/4HANA (Figure 2.8). This functionality might be especially helpful for you to copy existing SAP standard user interfaces as a starting point.

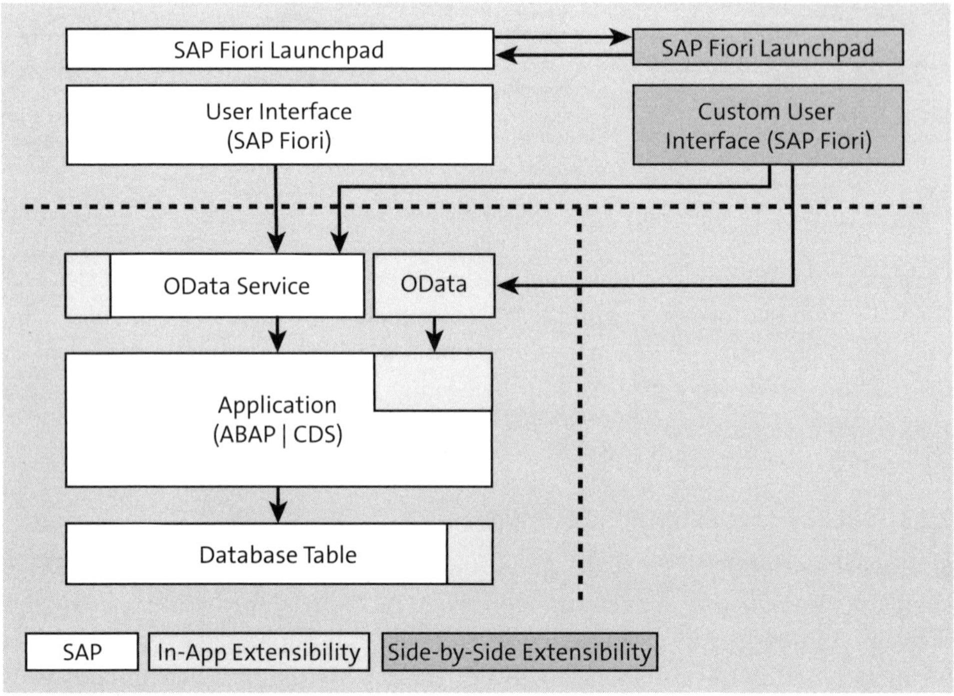

Figure 2.8 SAP Fiori User Interface as a Side-by-Side Extension

However, you can combine in-app extensions with side-by-side extensions by creating new OData services inside the core of SAP S/4HANA that can be consumed from SAP Cloud Platform. As explained earlier, such OData APIs may either serve additional data, for example, from a custom business object, or can combine data from several existing views so that roundtrips between the user interface and the backend are reduced (Section 2.2).

Custom Applications

As shown in Figure 2.9, you can also create completely new applications spanning across user interfaces, application logic, and the storage layer. For partner applications, this structure is expected to be the dominant extension pattern. On all layers, the SAP Cloud Platform provides numerous technologies and tools so that customers or partners may choose the best ones to fulfill their requirements. Although the

Cloud Foundry environment on the SAP Cloud Platform allows you to write applications in almost any programming language, SAP is primarily investing in Java, JavaScript, and ABAP. For example, SAP provides libraries to create OData services or to use the SAP S/4HANA public data model inside Java and JavaScript backend services. A good part of these libraries and options, such as the SAP S/4HANA Cloud SDK, are covered in this book.

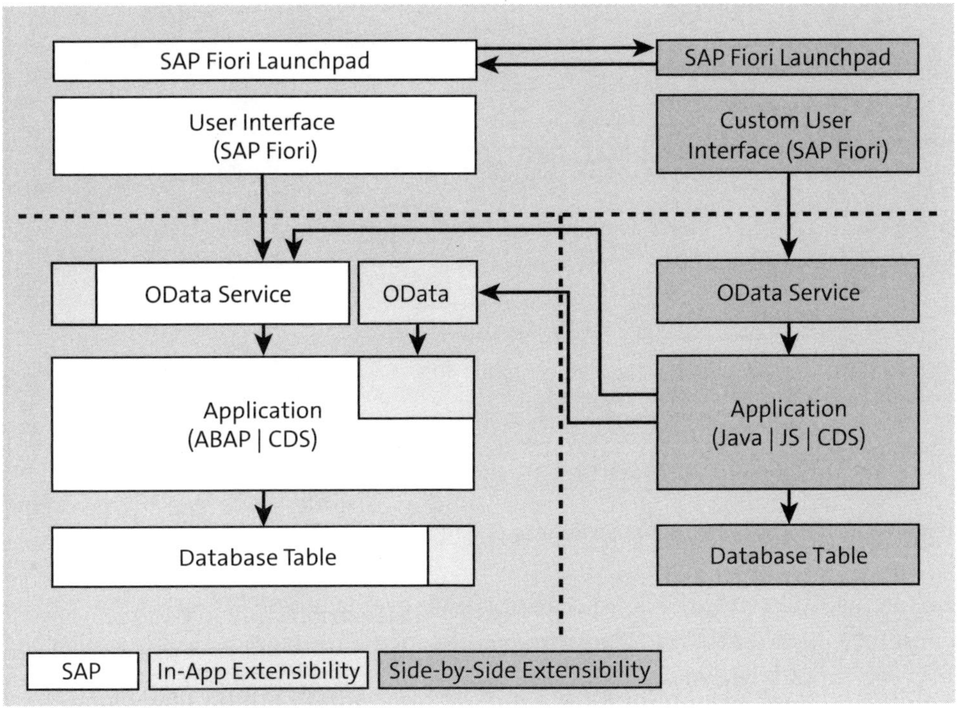

Figure 2.9 Side-by-Side Extension App on SAP Cloud Platform

Again, the extension application may integrate with SAP S/4HANA Cloud through existing public APIs or by additional APIs created with in-app extensions. In addition, SAP S/4HANA on-premise exposes APIs in the form of BAPIs using the RFC protocol or the HTTP-based SOAP protocol.

Side-by-Side Service and Events

Sometimes, an in-app extension, in the form of a code extension or a custom business object, may require capabilities not provided by SAP S/4HANA. For this purpose, customers may implement a service on the SAP Cloud Platform and invoke the service by a RESTful call from the in-app extension to the SAP Cloud Platform service, as shown in Figure 2.10.

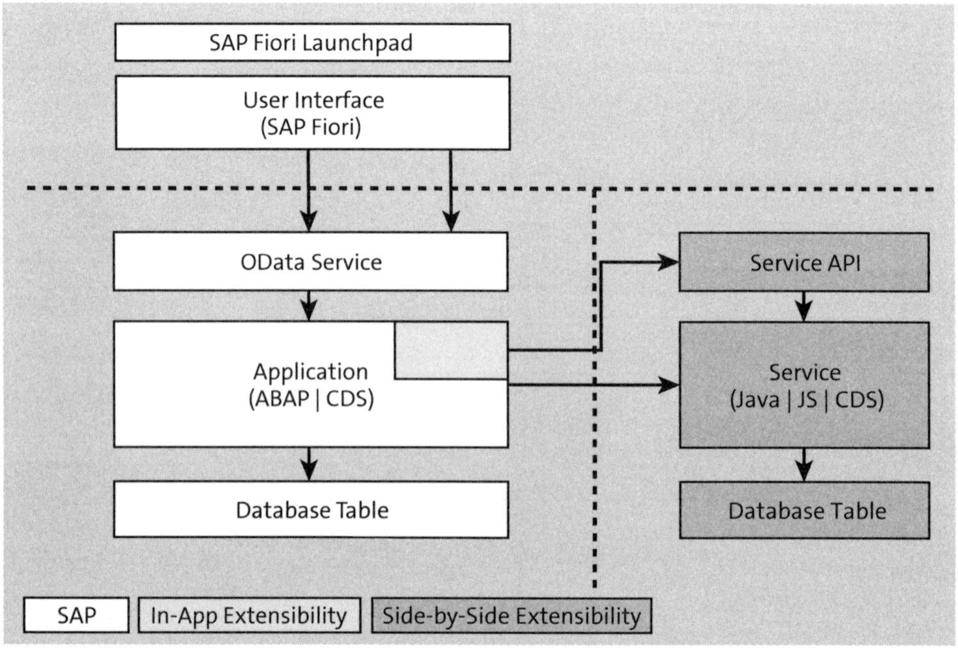

Figure 2.10 Side-by-Side Extension Service on SAP Cloud Platform

Besides RESTful service calls, you can also emit events in SAP S/4HANA that can be consumed on the SAP Cloud Platform. Events contain messages with data similar like in a service call. The main difference, however, is the asynchronous nature of an event. The process continues after emitting the event without waiting for a response. The eventing capabilities between SAP S/4HANA and the SAP Cloud Platform will be explained more detail in Chapter 16.

Data Mart Extension

Analytical applications implementing data mart-like scenarios, may need to bring data together in one database so that the response to an analytical query is fast (Figure 2.11). With SAP HANA being the database on both sides, you can replicate data from the SAP S/4HANA system into the database of the analytical application on the SAP Cloud Platform. The basis for the replication is the public model so that, after replication, the same views can be used in selects and joins. To use the replication mechanisms with SAP S/4HANA Cloud, a fully managed SAP service exists. At the time of this writing, the service is in restricted mode, accessible only to pilot customers.

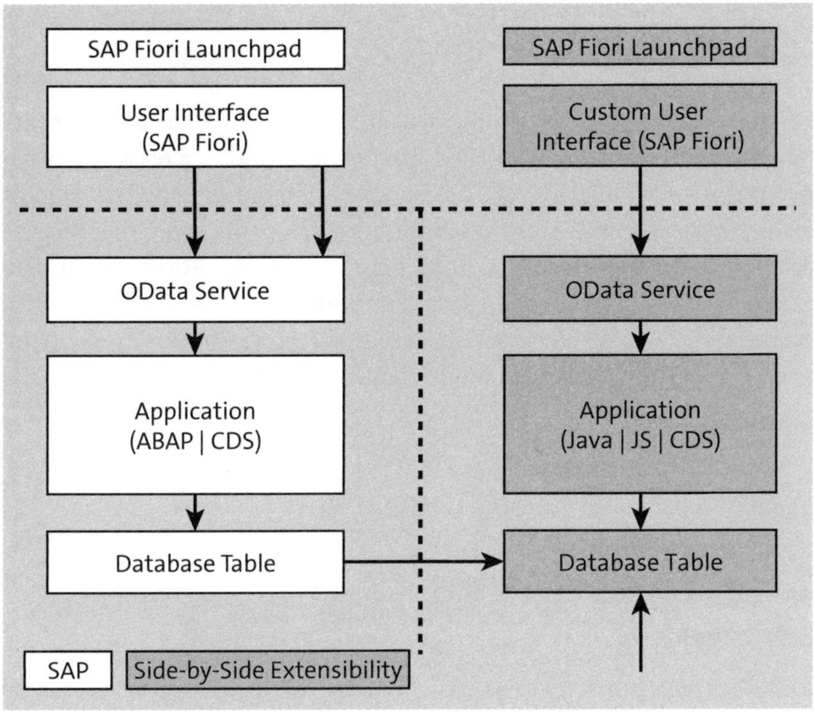

Figure 2.11 Data Mart on SAP Cloud Platform as a Side-by-Side Extension

For SAP S/4HANA on-premise and other SAP solutions, customers can perform the replication with help of the Cloud Connector and, optionally, also SAP Landscape Transformation Replication Server. Further, you can copy data from various other sources into the analytical application using RESTful services so that customers can join data across business applications and processes as part of the analytical application.

Further Information on Data Replication to SAP Cloud Platform

Replicate ABAP CDS Views from SAP S/4HANA Cloud to SAP Cloud Platform: *http://tiny.cc/data-replication*

Replicating Back-End Data to the Cloud: *https://sap.github.io/cloud-s4ext/week-4/unit-3/*

This concludes our review of the general patterns possible using the side-by-side extension approach. In the next section, we'll discuss typical extension use cases based on the presented patterns and principles.

2.4 Extension Use Cases

With the side-by-side and in-app extensibility features explained in the previous sections, you can build additions to SAP S/4HANA that significantly increase the reach and the scope of the system. SAP S/4HANA can be connected in processes that engage internet users, such as in an online store, on mobile devices, or via experimental user interface technologies. Furthermore, you may extend existing processes but also invent completely new processes while easily combining SAP S/4HANA data with data from other systems. As a result, we've observed several typical extension archetypes that our customers or partners are implementing, as follows:

- Proxy applications
- Convenience applications
- Substitute applications
- Preprocessing applications
- Postprocessing applications
- Analytical applications

Note that this list does not claim to be exhaustive and you can combine several of these archetypes within one process or even within one application. The presented archetypes are typically driven from a side-by-side extension perspective. However, in most real-life scenarios, they are complemented and supported by in-app extensions.

Let's discuss these archetypes individually next.

2.4.1 Proxy Applications

Proxy applications are highly connected applications that shield the SAP S/4HANA system from internet traffic. In other words, these applications "buffer" data and communicate with the SAP S/4HANA in batch mode for more efficient data exchange. These applications often work with identities only known in the proxy application but not in SAP S/4HANA, for example, the end consumers of a retail enterprise who may not require an SAP S/4HANA backend user. Typical proxy applications include online stores, registration web sites, or any other publicly available web sites. A proxy application on a mobile phone could also be used by customers to learn about promotions and products. These applications typically have high requirements with respect to availability and scalability to cater for traffic bursts at peak times.

2.4.2 Convenience Applications

Convenience applications aim at simplifying the user experience and, thus, often do not add many new features but instead make using existing features significantly easier. You can, for example, build a convenience application for a mobile device to support field engineers. In a convenience application, fields can be defaulted to the most commonly used values or can be hidden altogether because reasonable values can be provided automatically.

2.4.3 Substitute Applications

Substitute applications replace a specific process or process step in SAP S/4HANA. The reasons to use a substitute application might be to provide a functionality missing in SAP S/4HANA or existing processes that shouldn't be changed when deploying SAP S/4HANA. Substitute applications typically execute service calls on SAP S/4HANA in the background while end users can work in a completely different user interface with capabilities that are not part of SAP S/4HANA's scope.

For example, let's consider time recording in the service industry. Typically, external tools are used for project management and scheduling, such as Atlassian Jira. Jira ticket numbers and other fields can be added to the SAP S/4HANA data model using an in-app field extension for simplified end-to-end reporting of SAP S/4HANA. Then, the substitute application on SAP Cloud Platform may join the information from SAP S/4HANA (i.e., costs from a cost center) with information from Atlassian Jira (i.e., project times, statuses, and schedules).

2.4.4 Preprocessing Applications

Preprocessing applications are often used to collect data before a process is started in SAP S/4HANA. In preprocessing applications, data is collected until a certain status or state is achieved. Then, a process in SAP S/4HANA is started using the collected data. An example might be an app to create and maintain new products as a side-by-side extension of SAP S/4HANA. Once details about the new product have been approved, the product is promoted to and stored in SAP S/4HANA. Subsequently, SAP S/4HANA processes are triggered such as pricing or production-related activities.

2.4.5 Postprocessing Applications

Postprocessing applications receive events from SAP S/4HANA when certain processes or process steps are completed. Based on these events, additional activities are performed in a side-by-side extension of SAP S/4HANA. An example could be an application that updates a customer record. If the customer relationship ends, data may have to be deleted from corresponding applications or data stores hosted on the SAP Cloud Platform.

2.4.6 Analytical Applications

Analytical applications connect data from multiple sources into one analytical database so that analytical queries can be answered quickly and interactively. Ad hoc reporting is also available. For this purpose, data from SAP S/4HANA and other systems might be replicated into a SAP HANA database on SAP Cloud Platform. Then, analytical applications can leverage all the capabilities provided by SAP HANA, such as columnar storage, in-memory execution, and rich view building as well as the analytical user interface controls of SAPUI5.

2.5 Nonfunctional Requirements of Extension Applications

So far, we've presented extension archetypes and described common use cases for extensions from a functional perspective. Functional requirements specify the behavior of the system, that is, what it is supposed to do. However, other, nonfunctional requirements also exist that relate to the underlying qualities of the system such as performance, costs, availability, or resilience.

By definition, in-app extensions inherit their nonfunctional properties from SAP S/4HANA. In contrast, for side-by-side extensions, customers and partners are mainly responsible for ensuring certain qualities such as scalability and availability. To achieve these qualities, customers are supported by appropriate SAP Cloud Platform services, software development kits (SDKs), and best practices, many of which we'll explain in this book. However, not all qualities are equally important for all extensions. Some business cases may also not justify the efforts to build highly scalable and available extensions. Therefore, you'll need to understand the design trade-offs, when to invest, and how to achieve a high degree of quality.

Generally, we recommend identifying extensions that are mission critical; any failure in this extension would have a severe impact on business operations. For example, customers often consider employee self-service applications less critical than applications involved in core business processes. In certain situations, such as a leave request, an employee may accept poor user interface performance and simply retry at a later point in time. On the other hand, an application intended to be used by the customers of the business such as an online shop or a customer-facing mobile application can have severe impact on the business success when customers cannot place orders (revenue loss) and instead select competitive products. This distinction between mission-critical and non-mission critical capabilities can help you find the right trade-offs.

Mission critical applications are business processes that involve customers, partners, suppliers, etc., for example, an internal application the sales force needs for daily operations. Mission critical applications may also target different users or interact with systems that are not under the control of the organization. Often, non-mission critical applications accept a much lower level of certain nonfunctional requirements for the sake of lower development or operations costs. In mission critical applications, certain nonfunctional requirements such as availability cannot be sacrificed, and higher development and operational costs might be acceptable.

Typical properties of internal applications include the following:

- Known user (e.g. SAP S/4HANA user), single-sign on
- Predictable scalability (e.g. based on number of users)
- SAP Fiori UI with moderate usability requirements
- Downtimes and times of limited availability are considered acceptable

Typical properties of external applications include the following:

- Known user and internet user (not a user in one of the organization's systems)
- Unknown scalability needs or high peaks (e.g. due to seasonal events), load impact on internal systems unclear
- SAP Fiori and freestyle UIs (e.g. created by an agency)
- Downtimes unacceptable (24/7) with continuously high performance

Based on these considerations and to best serve business needs, we recommend building external applications as side-by-side extensions to cope with the additional nonfunctional challenges introduced by cloud software. For internal applications, a careful trade-off analysis should be conducted to identify whether the functionality might be provided by either a pure in-app extension or by a side-by-side extension.

The criteria above may guide you in finding the appropriate trade-offs for your application scenario.

We'll further explore the qualities of cloud-native application development, the predominant development style for side-by-side extensions, in the next chapter.

2.6 Summary

In this chapter you learned about the various options you have for extending SAP S/4HANA. In the next chapter we'll dive into the specifics of side-by-side extensibility and cloud-native application development. You'll learn how the principles of cloud-native development, such as DevOps, microservices, continuous delivery, and containerization, can help you craft highly scalable, resilient, and consistently available applications on the SAP Cloud Platform.

PART II
Building Side-by-Side Extensions

Chapter 3
Side-by-Side Extensibility

This chapter discusses the concepts at the heart of cloud-native side-by-side extensions. You'll also learn about the key capabilities of the Cloud Foundry and Neo environments on the SAP Cloud Platform, and the architecture and key functionalities of the SAP S/4HANA Cloud SDK.

In this chapter, we'll introduce methods relevant to building SAP S/4HANA side-by-side extensions based on cloud-native development principles and the commonly referenced twelve-factor application. We'll then present an outline of the SAP Cloud Platform, including its terminology, components, and services, as well as the available platform environments, Cloud Foundry and Neo. Finally, we'll describe our example side-by-side extension on SAP Cloud Platform, the Business Partner Address Manager application, which allows you to manage business partner addresses in an SAP S/4HANA system. This application will be gradually built up over the course of this book, serving as our primary example to highlight fundamental concepts and technologies for developing and operating a side-by-side extension from end to end.

3.1 Cloud-Native Development

Before outlining the features of SAP Cloud Platform in more detail, let's cover the fundamental principles and rationale that govern the development and delivery of *cloud-native applications*. These development principles serve as essential guidelines for building side-by-side extensions.

3.1.1 Motivation

According to Pivotal, the developers of Cloud Foundry, *cloud-native* refers to an "approach for building and running applications that fully exploits the advantages of the cloud computing delivery model" (*https://pivotal.io/cloud-native*). This statement reflects the idea that developing, building, and running applications should be independent of the underlying cloud infrastructure. The primary goal of cloud-native development is to enable fast innovation and swift delivery of ideas to the market. This focus, in turn, can give a business a competitive advantage by allowing the business to enter a market sooner and adapt to changes more flexibly.

3.1.2 Benefits of Cloud-Native Applications

In comparison to traditional enterprise applications, cloud-native applications offer several advantages, as outlined by Pivotal at *https://pivotal.io/cloud-native* (see also M. Stine, *Migrating to Cloud-Native Application Architectures*). The following sections describe the most relevant benefits of cloud-native applications.

Speed and Agility

The speed of developing software, and thus providing value to end consumers, can define a strong competitive advantage in the market against traditional development models. Because traditional models are often limited to publishing releases over several weeks and months, experimenting and trying out new and more innovative approaches becomes harder and more risky. Innovative approaches, however, define the key differentiators of an enterprise. The ability to deploy hundreds of times each day effectively translates into the capability of almost instantly correcting and recovering from mistakes without any impact on the availability of the application. This capability provides the freedom to experiment and to quickly adjust to changes.

However, speed not only relates to the frequency of software delivery. It also refers to the notion of agility in relation to the development and delivery process. For instance, fostering closer collaboration between development and operations teams, as well as offering self-service options instead of manual ticket-based procedures, can contribute to the company's speed and competitive advantage.

Safety and Reliability

While speed is the motor of innovation and differentiation, it means nothing without safety and reliability. Eventually, customers will be frustrated and abandon an application if the "latest breaking changes" interrupt workflows several times per day. As a result, ensuring high quality in code and engineering for stability, reliability, and fault tolerance are key to fast development cycles. The following aspects enhance safety and reliability (M. Stine, *Migrating to Cloud-Native Application Architectures*):

- **Visibility**
  Within an application, failures must be detected as quickly as possible. This feature requires detailed monitoring of the application state to judge what represents exceptional conditions, in contrast to normal, expected states.
- **Fault isolation**
  An additional measure for reliability is the isolation of the failures of individual components, controlling how they affect the overall application, which represents a distributed system. This separation may be achieved, for example, by isolating calls to remote systems into dedicated thread pools to avoid requests stalling the overall thread pool in an application, an approach commonly called the *bulkhead pattern* (M. T. Nygard, *Release It! Design and Deploy Production-Ready Software*). Inspired by bulkheads, that is, water-tight, metal compartments that keep ships from sinking in the event of a hull breach, this pattern describes the isolation of operations to remote services into separate partitions like isolated thread pools. Another approach that can contribute to such an isolation of failures is the use of separate service instances, which naturally leads to isolating logic into separate processes.
- **Fault tolerance**
  Cloud applications usually represent distributed systems where services are invoked over a well-defined API. Fault tolerance requires not only limiting failures to a single service, but also stopping failures from propagating. This situation may be achieved by failing fast via timeouts if remote services are not responding to avoid stalling dependent services. In addition, if services are not reachable, that is, if multiple timeouts are triggered within a certain amount of time, subsequent calls to the service should be avoided. This approach is called as the *circuit-breaker pattern* and can be compared to an electrical safety switch that opens in case of danger (M. T. Nygard, *Release It! Design and Deploy Production-Ready Software*). In terms of fault tolerance, this pattern refers to the idea of not calling the remote system at all for a certain amount of time if a certain number of failures are detected over some time frame (for example, if a certain number of timeouts occur during a defined time interval). This pattern further improves the stability of a service with respect to unresponsive downstream services.
- **Automated recovery**
  While detecting and protecting against failures are essential, recovering from failure should not necessarily require manual intervention and should include mechanisms to automatically restart or redeploy failed services.

Scalability and Elasticity

To benefit from an economy of scale, cloud applications must be designed in such a way that scaling and adjusting to cost-efficient, right-sized capacities are easy.

Traditionally, scaling an application is achieved by using servers with increasingly powerful hardware (commonly referred to as *vertical scaling*, also known as *scale-up*). However, ordering and delivering physical hardware tends to be too rigid and slow for quickly adjusting to the varying loads that usually appear during business and rush-hour peaks. These effects of "burstiness" must always be accounted for in an application since internet traffic is a statistical process with self-similar characteristics and tends to follow a heavy-tailed distribution (W. E. Leland et al., *On the Self-Similar Nature of Ethernet Traffic*). Even when assuming that requests from a client to a server follow the benign *Poisson process* (which is too optimistic in reality), *Little's law* (J. D. Little, *A Proof for the Queuing Formula:* $L = \lambda W$) suggests to only aim for not more than 50% or 60% utilization of theoretically possible capacity on a queueing-based system like the internet, to keep the delay in response times acceptable. Thus, with vertical scaling, the only remaining option is strong overprovisioning, which requires even more expensive hardware and is not cost-efficient since the average load should never reach full utilization anyway to keep the application responsive.

An approach to addressing the challenge of overprovisioning with expensive, specialized hardware is to rely on *horizontal scaling* (also known as *scale-out*) instead of vertical scaling. Instead of using larger machines, the idea with horizontal scaling is to rely on a large number of small, cheap, and easily acquirable machines with commodity hardware and scale via parallelization and distribution of computing tasks.

Furthermore, to better utilize the available hardware during idle times, mechanisms for abstracting from the actual hardware—such as virtualization and containerization—have been introduced by cloud infrastructure providers like Amazon. Now, the task of provisioning computing power can be delegated to such infrastructure-as-a-service (IaaS) providers, accordingly, relieving developers of the burden of expensive, upfront investments based on capacity planning efforts that may rest on incorrect or incomplete assumptions. The IaaS can quickly adjust to varying load conditions at a reasonable, traffic-based price.

Nevertheless, this approach requires designing and building applications differently from the traditional, state-oriented model. The use of horizontal scaling demands that applications become stateless units of work that can be spawned and disposed without ideally any effort. Therefore, to keep applications stateless, managing and interacting with the necessary state of an application, like persistence, require considering mechanisms for externalizing the state to separate services that rely on their own, specialized techniques for handling scalability.

An example for achieving such scalability can be the relaxation of certain aspects of the strict ACID (atomicity, consistency, isolation, durability) properties, which are typically found in traditional relational databases. By offering software engineers certain trade-offs between ACID and BASE (basically available, soft state, eventual consistency) properties, applications gain more flexibility for choosing or adjusting such a state-managing persistence service around their individual requirements. In this context, the CAP theorem (Fox and Brewer, *Harvest Yield and Scalable Tolerant Systems*) suggests a model that describes the implications and restrictions of the possible trade-offs between consistency, availability, and partition tolerance.

3.1.3 Enabling Cloud-Native Applications

To develop and operate cloud-native applications, four fundamental pillars should be considered (*https://pivotal.io/cloud-native*):

- DevOps
- Continuous delivery
- Microservices
- Containers

The following sections provide a detailed overview of these aspects.

DevOps

The basic idea of DevOps originates from lean software and agile development principles. Put simply, DevOps aims to avoid the traditional separation of teams into development and operations units, which tends to lead to information silos, unnecessary hand-off friction due to misaligned assumptions, and—ultimately—delayed delivery of software. In contrast, instead of handing over tasks between different development and operations teams, DevOps strengthens joint, collaborative end-to-end responsibility, starting from early development to finally operating the software within the production environment. This notion of joint responsibility fosters a culture of reproducibility, high automation, continuous improvement, and mutual understanding that reduces bottlenecks and friction in the process of delivering software. DevOps is therefore generally considered as a key enabler for shipping high-quality, value-adding software as fast and as often as possible.

Continuous Delivery

While traditional software development based on the so-called "waterfall model" tends to follow rigid, long-term plans with release cycles of several months or years, agile development principles embrace a culture of change and delivering value to customers in short release cycles of only a few days, ideally allowing for changes to be delivered up to several times per day. In this case, agile methodologies offer a wide variety of benefits over the traditional "waterfall" approach. First of all, they provide an increased level of transparency and awareness of the work that is ongoing and still pending which strengthens effective collaboration among cross-functional teams. Given short iterations of work in well-prioritized batches of usually only one to two weeks, defects can be removed quickly, eventually allowing features to be delivered in a more predictable, business- and value-oriented way. In particular, within agile methodologies, the definition of value is strongly driven and continuously evaluated by the direct feedback of real users early in the development process.

For a detailed overview of the principles and practice of DevOps and continuous delivery with the SAP S/4HANA Cloud SDK, refer to Chapter 10 and Chapter 11.

Microservices

The term *microservices* refers to small, autonomous, independently deployable services (*http://tiny.cc/microservices*). They are often referenced in the context of the *microservice architecture*, which describes an approach in software engineering where applications are developed as a distributed system of microservices designed around certain characteristics such as business domains, organizational team structures, or components that must scale independently of each other. In simple terms, this architectural style refers to an approach where an application is developed as a set of small services that run in their own processes and communicate with more or less lightweight mechanisms such as HTTP-based APIs. Microservices have emerged from the challenges that have been observed in traditional development and the architecture of three-tiered enterprise applications—consisting of a client-side user interface, a server-side application, and a relational database system—that run as a single, monolithic unit on the application server. In this architecture, even small changes in the backend require adjustments of the monolithic application.

When building cloud applications, delivering functionality can become cumbersome since all changes are strongly tied together. In addition, in order to scale, all parts of an application must be replicated, making it impossible to flexibly scale individual components based on their loads in a more fine-grained manner. These issues have led developers to split up their monolithic cloud applications into smaller components focused around the *single responsibility principle*: doing one specific thing very well.

As indicated earlier, splitting up a large monolithic application into individual services increases the complexity of the distributed system. Therefore, the question arises how to best define service boundaries and granularities. One common answer—aside from individual experience and knowledge about the application and its domain—is to follow the approach of *domain-driven design* and organize logic around *bounded contexts* that correspond to specific business capabilities (*http://tiny.cc/microservices*). To determine these boundaries, following a "monolith-first" approach can lead to necessary experience and knowledge about the application domain (*http://tiny.cc/monolith-first*). Once the application is understood well enough, you can gradually split it into microservices according to the discovered boundaries. In this way, you'll avoid the initial complexity and risk of premature decomposition into a distributed system along suboptimal dimensions, which can result in an application that is hard to refactor and test across the boundaries of its microservices.

Nevertheless, the "monolith-first" approach also has some risks. Therefore, some experts, such as Stefan Tilkov, recommend directly starting with microservices instead of persuing a "monolith-first" approach since a monolith can increase the risk of introducing strong dependencies that are difficult to resolve and split up later (*http://tiny.cc/dont-start-monolith*). In particular, monolithic applications, naturally, tend to favor tight coupling. An example of such tight coupling is a shared persistence model that is usually extremly difficult to seperate later on as separation would require migrating code and data.

In addition to the individual microservices and their boundaries, microservice architectures also come in different flavors depending on the type of communication being used. On one hand, you can rely on *orchestration*, that is, using certain microservices synchronously to trigger communication with other microservices following a request/response pattern. A potential disadvantage of this scenario is that the microservice that triggers a process can become a central governing entity that can be harder to refactor later on. On the other hand, instead of synchronuous communication, microservices may rely on asynchronous communication to notify other microservices about certain events via a message broker like RabbitMQ (*https://www.rabbitmq.com*). With such a *choreography* of events, a distributed system of microservices can be more adaptable to change. Nevertheless, such an *event-driven architecture* runs the risk that, once events start to become too fine-grained and only address a single consuming microservice, the system of microservices will again twist towards an orchestrated approach as a single governing entity (*http://tiny.cc/event-driven*). For more details on event-driven architectures and how to integrate eventing in an SAP S/4HANA side-by-side extension, please refer to Chapter 16.

The key benefits and trade-offs of using a microservice architecture can be summarized as follows:

- **Technology heterogeneity**
  One of the primary advantages of using a microservice architecture is the ability to build an application by leveraging a rather heterogeneous set of technologies. Instead of using a one-size-fits-all approach, microservices can use the technologies and frameworks best suited for a task, thus enabling your business to quickly leverage, evaluate, and embrace new technologies and foster experimentation with only limited risk. If a microservice that is built on a certain technology turns out to be unfit for the job, replacing such a small service with a new implementation becomes less risky for an organization. In contrast, a monolithic application enforces the use of certain technologies that can lead to conflicts with new technologies or dependencies. While, in the past, existing technologies may have been introduced based on well-defined assumptions, their underlying rationale may no longer be relevant. Accordingly, in a monolithic application, changing certain initial decisions later on can be difficult or even impossible.
- **Organizational alignment**
  In traditional software development, the use of heterogeneous technologies is rather unpopular because of the effort of handing off software between different departments such as development and operations. While this burden may seem contradictory to embracing various technologies within a single application, it actually confirms the benefits of using a microservice architecture to align an organization according to the principles of DevOps. Since, as described by *Conway's law* (*http://tiny.cc/conways-law*), any organization that designs a system will produce a design that reflects an organization's communication structure, microservices tend to be shaped, not around domains like the frontend or the backend, but rather around the actual business capabilities of an application. This scenario encourages organizations to rely on cross-functional teams with end-to-end responsibility for developing and operating their microservices, thereby reducing hand-offs and alignment meetings, which are inefficient for larger teams working across different locations.
- **Scaling**
  In large monolithic applications, scaling small parts can become difficult since only the full application may be replicated and scaled. In contrast, microservices

can be scaled independently of each other, giving more fine-grained control over the necessary computational resources and thus costs for running an application.

In addition to these key benefits, a variety of other qualities justify using microservices. Nevertheless, these come with more significant trade-offs that should be carefully taken into account:

- **Resilience**
  Following the bulkhead pattern as described in Section 3.1.2 on the benefits of cloud-native applications with respect to safety and reliability, microservices offer the advantage of isolating components into separate processes. Nevertheless, given the resulting distributed system of microservices that may eventually fail, the overall resilience of an application must still be carefully considered and engineered into its design. Furthermore, depending on the underlying technology, even monolithic applications can provide a certain degree of failure isolation by, for example, employing separate, dedicated thread pools to realize bulkheads.
- **Ease of deployment**
  With a large monolithic application with millions of lines of code, the effort for only changing a single line of code can become extremely high due to the resulting efforts and underlying risks. As a result, delivering updates for an application becomes increasingly difficult, preventing the frequent, continuous delivery of functionality. Even worse, as the changes that need to be delivered build up over time, the fear of publishing a release can rise, again increasing the delay in delivering functionality and value to end consumers. A microservice architecture, in contrast, allows you to reduce effort greatly and thereby lower the risk of delivering changes to the overall application since each microservice can be deployed independently. Despite these clear benefits, note that not all deployments challenges will vanish with a microservice architecture. For example, for changes that affect multiple services, versioning strategies must be introduced—at least for some time span—so that breaking changes are delegated to different API versions. Consequently, migrations from different API versions must be aligned between the teams that maintain the relevant microservices. Furthermore, while microservice boundaries are ideally well defined and therefore stable, over time, legacy microservices might need to be deprecated to introduce new microservices, which can to some degree again increase complexity of deployments.
- **Optimizing for replaceability**
  With microservices representing dedicated components around certain business capabilities, we expect long-lived applications to be maintained more easily and

evolve better over time. This belief is based on the assumption that, while certain components are likely to end up as legacy parts of an application, migrating such components can become easier if an application has been designed around certain bounded contexts and business functionalities that facilitate their replacement. However, these benefits should be considered carefully. While an individual microservice may be easier to maintain and replace, the overall application may consist of a rather complex choreography of services. Accordingly, maintaining, evolving, and testing an application across various microservices may not be easy, for example, if the microservices turn out to focus around business functionalities with suboptimal boundaries.

- **Composability**
  A beneficial side effect of building an application based on microservices is the ability to reuse the functionality that is encapsulated into microservices in different contexts. While this flexibility is similar to more traditional mechanisms for componentization, like modules or libraries, microservices can provide additional flexibility when composing business-oriented services based on different programming languages and technologies. Nevertheless, this advantage requires appropriately designed microservices and comes at the price of an increasingly complex distributed system. Therefore, the use of libraries and modules usually represents the first logical choice in terms of composability, modularization, and well-defined API contracts. In particular, modularization represents a principle in software engineering that you should consider regardless of whether a monolithic or microservice-based architecture is employed. Modularization includes best practices like avoiding breaking changes and migrating between software versions using deprecation schemes where old and new APIs are offered in parallel for some time. Finally, you should consider that certain functionalities may not lend themselves well to being shaped around a specific business domain. Generic functionality (like parsing a configuration format that is shared across microservices) can typically be reused more effectively by providing a library. This is also the case for functionality that requires high throughput, where method invocations are cheaper compared to calling a REST API.

In summary, based on these relative advantages and disadvantages, as well as considering various observations about and experiences with a "monolith-first" approach, you should carefully consider which approach to take based on their specific requirements, existing knowledge, and assumptions about the individual application and its business domain.

Containers

Containers are a concept that originates from the Linux operating system. In contrast to virtual machines that run a full guest operating system on a host operating system, containers represent a more lightweight approach for running multiple processes in an isolated and restricted way on a single host operating system or virtual machine (M. Stine, *Migrating to Cloud-Native Application Architectures*). To realize these restrictions with respect to resource allocation and process isolation, containers rely on Linux concepts such as *control groups (cgroups)* and *namespaces*. A control group is an approach for organizing processes in a hierarchical structure that allows you to control and configure the distribution of resources, while namespaces isolate and virtualize global resources such as hostnames or user identifiers. Put simply, a control group defines what processes can do whereas a namespace defines what processes can see. These mechanisms enable you to realize the degree of isolation that is otherwise achieved with virtual machines but with less overhead. In addition, processes have read-only access to most of the file system while read-write access is limited to only a small part. Furthermore, file systems relate to the concept of *images*, which represent a set of serialized file systems with configuration and metadata. When deploying an image to a container, the file systems of the image are mounted as a file system to the namespace of the container process.

Overall, containers enable a reliable, flexible, and easy way to move software between different computing environments, from developers' laptops to the physical machines located in various data centers around the world running the software in production.

For more details on how containers are used in the SAP S/4HANA Cloud SDK, please refer to Chapter 11.

3.1.4 Cloud-Native Architecture: The Twelve-Factor Application

Based on the motivation and possible benefits of cloud-native applications, the so-called *twelve-factor application* (*https://12factor.net*) is often cited as a best practice that specifies a set of principles in order to provide guidelines and to facilitate the development of cloud-native applications (J. Long and K. Bastani, *Cloud Native Java*). The following paragraphs describe each of the twelve factors in more detail.

Codebase

"One codebase tracked in revision control, many deploys."

The idea behind this factor is that the source code of an application should only reside within a single source code repository such as Git. In particular, specifics of different deployment and runtime environments—such as development, staging, or production—should not be part of the application code itself.

Dependencies

"Explicitly declare and isolate dependencies."

According to this factor, the dependencies of an application should be declared in a *manifest*, which makes such dependencies explicit. An example in the Java space is using Apache Maven with its explicit declaration of dependencies in a POM file. Additionally, this factor demands that the existence of implicitly available dependencies via, for example, system- or container-provided dependencies is never relied upon.

Config

"Store config in the environment."

This factor requires you to cleanly separate application code from configuration. The motivation behind this aspect of only providing configuration via the respective environment (for example via environment variables) is to avoid the need to redeploy an application in case configuration has to be adjusted.

Backing Services

"Treat backing services as attached resources."

Backing services are required for the operation of the application and usually consist of, for example, databases, message brokers, or external RESTful APIs. Considering such backing services as resources that only need to be attached to the application at runtime provides greater flexibility and reduces the complexity of the application, for example, to enable the use of an embedded database for local testing and an externally hosted database in production. Thus, this aspect avoids the need to adapt application code for consuming such resources under different circumstances and makes scaling and deploying in different environments and data centers easier.

Build, Release, Run

"Strictly separate build and run stages."

Twelve-factor applications clearly distinguish between build, release, and run stages. In this context, the build stage refers to the process of retrieving the source code and compiling or bundling it into a package that represents the *build*. A *release* refers to the combination of a build with its separately stored configuration and corresponds to the unit that can be subsequently executed and operated in a certain environment, which then reflects the *run* stage. Each release is expected to provide a unique version identifier (for instance, by using *semantic versioning* or generating a timestamp). This separation is used so that changes to the application code are only possible by adjusting the source code in its repository and triggering the build stage, which fosters traceability of changes as well as reproducibility of builds.

Semantic Versioning

Semantic versioning (*https://semver.org/*) refers to a scheme that suggests the use of a version number "MAJOR.MINOR.PATCH," where MAJOR indicates incompatible API changes, MINOR new functionality with backwards compatibility, and PATCH backwards-compatible bug fixes.

Processes

"Execute the app as one or more stateless processes."

Motivated by the advantages of shared-nothing architectures (such as the ability to run in parallel on cheaper commodity hardware, see also [M. Stonebraker, *The Case for Shared Nothing*]), twelve-factor applications aim to be stateless and only rely on the necessary state-like persistence via backing services (attached resources) that offer storage in relational databases or document stores. In particular, states are not stored within the runtime environment, which allows applications to be easily destroyed and re-created and provides a foundation for load balancing and scaling the application.

Port Binding

"Export services via port binding."

This factor refers to the concept of providing fully self-contained applications that don't rely on a web server. Accordingly, an application should expose itself via an HTTP port. For example, in terms of Java, newer versions of Spring Boot offer the option to provide a self-contained JAR file, which includes an embedded application server like Apache Tomcat instead of a more traditional WAR file that must be deployed to an existing application server.

Concurrency

"Scale out via the process model."

As suggested by its name, this factor describes the requirement that applications should leverage concurrent processing models that allow running an application in parallel and distributed processes, as well as using in-process parallelization via threads. This factor provides the foundation to scale applications horizontally and balance their load appropriately.

Disposability

"Maximize robustness with fast startup and graceful shutdown."

Based on their statelessness, twelve-factor applications should be disposable, meaning that processes can be stopped at any time during their execution and applications will gracefully handle the destruction of processes. Accordingly, the startup times of processes should be minimal so that disposed processes can be resolved almost instantly (ensuring high availability of the application), both for quickly recovering as well as for swiftly scaling processes based on the current application load.

Dev/Prod Parity

"Keep development, staging, and production as similar as possible."

To prevent development and production environments from diverging, eventually increasing the complexity of development and operations, twelve-factor applications should avoid the following gaps. First of all, no *time gap* should exist between a development change and its deployment to production to avoid the introduction of differences across environments which, in the moment, seem to be useful workarounds for delays. . Furthermore, no *personnel gap* should exist, that is, software engineers should be responsible end to end for bringing a change from development into production in order to avoid time-consuming hand-offs. Finally, no *tool gap* should exist, which means that all tools, technologies, and frameworks should be consistently mirrored across environments, including the local development environment.

Logs

"Treat logs as event streams."

Twelve-factor applications are expected to only write logs to the standard output *stdout*) without managing the storage of these logs. Instead, the execution environment is expected to handle log output, including tasks related to managing storage and archiving of log files.

Admin Processes

"Run admin/management tasks as one-off processes."

One-time administrative tasks in twelve-factor applications are expected to be based on scripts that are checked into the application's source code repository. An example for such an one-time task is a database migration, which usually requires elevated privileges due to the sensitivity of the data. To remain consistent across environments, administrative tasks should be run in the execution environment of the application while being based on the scripts maintained in the source code repository.

3.1.5 Conclusion

Cloud-native development practices and the twelve-factor application offer several principles and guidelines that have proven to be useful for successfully delivering cloud applications. The following sections now provide an overview and highlight the relationship of these concepts to the SAP Cloud Platform, the SAP Cloud Platform SDK for service development, and the SAP S/4HANA Cloud SDK for building SAP S/4HANA side-by-side extensions.

3.2 SAP Cloud Platform

SAP Cloud Platform is SAP's enterprise platform-as-a-service (PaaS) offering and provides comprehensive application development services and capabilities that allow you to build, extend, and integrate business applications in the cloud while supporting multiple cloud infrastructure providers such as Amazon Web Services (AWS), Google Cloud Platform, or Microsoft Azure. In particular, SAP Cloud Platform provides the tools and infrastructure to achieve the following goals:

- **Extend on-premise and cloud applications**
  Personalize and extend existing applications, independent of whether they run on-premise or in the cloud, in order to achieve agility and quicker time-to-market.
- **Integrate on-premise and cloud applications**
  Bring together disparate systems and IT landscapes to streamline processes and increase the efficiency of your business.

- **Build new cloud applications**
  Develop new cloud applications with a small investment of capital in software and hardware.

3.2.1 Development Environments

SAP Cloud Platform offers two development environments—Cloud Foundry and Neo—along with a broad choice of programming languages that are supported to fulfill the requirements of applications. Environments represent the actual SAP Cloud Platform PaaS offering, which allows you to develop and operate business applications. Cloud Foundry is open source, whereas Neo is based on open standards. The availability of different environments offers choices for technologies, runtimes, and services, thereby providing great flexibility in the development process. Note that, in addition to the Cloud Foundry and Neo environments, environments like Kubernetes or ABAP are planned. In this book, however, we'll only consider Cloud Foundry and Neo.

The Cloud Foundry Environment

The Cloud Foundry environment contains the Cloud Foundry application runtime, which is based on the open source application platform managed by the Cloud Foundry Foundation. Cloud Foundry focuses less on being a typical infrastructure-as-a-service (IaaS) but instead aims to provide an offering designed around the development of applications and services (J. Long and K. Bastani, *Cloud Native Java*). SAP is offering the Cloud Foundry environment in different data center locations so that applications can be deployed in different regions. The Cloud Foundry environment offers a multitude of buildpacks that largely abstract away details about containers, including both community- and SAP-specific buildpack variants. This runtime platform provides the ability to develop and deploy web applications, supporting multiple runtimes, programming languages, libraries, and services.

Application developers can use the Cloud Foundry environment to extend SAP products and to integrate business applications, as well as to develop entirely new enterprise applications. The Cloud Foundry environment allows you to use multiple programming languages, such as Java or Node.js, and community/bring-your-own language options. SAP recommends using the Cloud Foundry environment for twelve-factor and/or microservices-based applications, for the Internet of Things (IoT) and machine learning scenarios, as well as for developing applications using SAP HANA extended application services, advanced model (SAP HANA XSA).

Within this book, we'll primarily focus on the Cloud Foundry environment on the SAP Cloud Platform, which is the go-to environment for twelve-factor applications, providing great flexibility for choosing technologies and programming languages based on the requirements for your application.

The Neo Environment

The Neo environment is a feature-rich and easy-to-use development environment that allows you to develop, deploy, and run applications built with HTML5, Java, and SAP HANA extended application services (SAP HANA XS). We recommend using the Neo environment for developing HTML5 and complex Java applications as well as for complex integration and extension scenarios.

Applications can be deployed and managed by using a command line interface or the SAP Cloud Platform cockpit, which also provides the ability to monitor applications. The Neo environment provides virtual machines to deploy and run applications. A virtual machine is the virtualized hardware resource (CPU, RAM, disk space, installed OS) that blurs the line between PaaS and IaaS.

3.2.2 Overview of Terminology, Concepts, and Services

Every customer of the SAP Cloud Platform is represented by a *global account*. This account contains all entitlements for purchased services and resources. Customers can assign dedicated administrators to their global account. Finally, a global account encompasses all regions; that is, even if a customer is active in both Europe and US East regions of AWS, still one single global account is sufficient.

A *subaccount* is used to structure global accounts. In contrast to global accounts, subaccounts are specific to a certain region. One subaccount can host applications from supported environments such as Cloud Foundry and Neo. You can assign quotas and define dedicated administrators for each subaccount. For user management, a subaccount comes with a standard Identity Provider (IdP) for maintaining users and roles. In addition, a custom IdP can be configured. All environments, services, and subscriptions to software-as-a-service (SaaS) applications are accessed from a subaccount. Furthermore, subaccounts rely on *subdomains* that correspond to the respective subdomain of applications running within a certain subaccount.

Technically, a subaccount represents a tenant at runtime for multitenant applications in both SaaS and PaaS scenarios (see Chapter 7). In SaaS scenarios, subaccounts subscribe to applications in order to consume them. In PaaS scenarios, subaccounts consume services in order to enable the development of applications that are based on these services within the relevant subaccounts. For the latter, subaccounts can be further structured depending on the environment in which applications are developed. For instance, in Cloud Foundry, a subaccount maps to an *organization* that can be further subdivided into *spaces* that offer separate areas for developing and running applications based on different teams and permissions.

Figure 3.1 shows the relationship of the concepts we've outlined, including the various environments, global accounts, and subaccounts as well as services and subscriptions for multitenant applications on the SAP Cloud Platform.

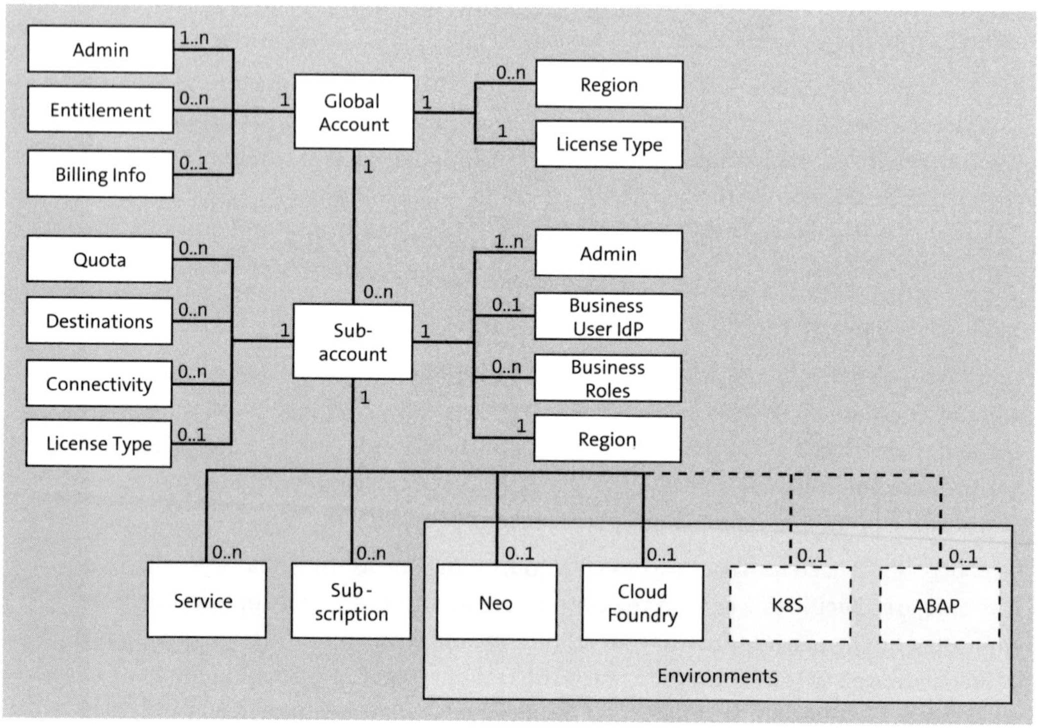

Figure 3.1 Conceptual Overview of Terminology and Relationship of SAP Cloud Platform Components and Services

In addition to these concepts, SAP Cloud Platform offers several platform-specific services. Some services presented throughout of this book are highlighted as follows:

- **Authorization and trust service**
  The authorization and trust service—also referred to as the *XSUAA* service—provides functionality for authenticating and authorizing users on the SAP Cloud

Platform. A detailed overview on the consumption of this service including the underlying security concepts is presented in Chapter 5.

- **Destination service**
  The destination service provides subaccount-specific access to the configuration for consuming other services or microservices. A *destination* is described by an identifier or name that is unique within the subaccount in which it is maintained. Furthermore, the destination service contains essential configuration like the URL to a service, as well as security-relevant information (certificates or authentication headers) necessary for applications to access and consume the APIs of the relevant services. Details on how to configure destinations in order to access, for example, an SAP S/4HANA system is outlined in Chapter 6.
- **Connectivity service**
  As described earlier, destinations provide the required configuration for accessing other services. However, this configuration is not necessarily sufficient if a service or system such as SAP S/4HANA is located in an on-premise network. In this case, an application depends on the availability of a secured tunnel that enables access to the on-premise network of a customer. Therefore, the connectivity service offers customers the ability to easily set up and configure a secured tunnel via the *Cloud Connector*, which operates as a reverse proxy that is installed in the on-premise environment. Once installed and configured, the Cloud Connector opens a tunnel to the SAP Cloud Platform and allows administrators to expose certain systems and service URLs to the cloud in a well-defined manner. Chapter 6 describes this procedure and the configuration steps for the connectivity service in detail.

Based on this overview of SAP Cloud Platform, the following section now describes the SAP S/4HANA Cloud SDK and the SAP Cloud Platform SDK for service development. These products offer essential tools and functionality for building SAP S/4HANA side-by-side extensions.

3.3 The SAP Cloud Platform SDK for Service Development and the SAP S/4HANA Cloud SDK

To simplify the development of cloud-native applications on SAP Cloud Platform, SAP provides two complementary Java-based software development kits (SDKs), which offer a variety of modules that focus on specific development purposes.

The *SAP Cloud Platform SDK for service development* provides generic development libraries and tools (for example, OData consumption, OData provisioning, business events) to enable application developers to easily create generic extensions on SAP Cloud Platform.

The *SAP S/4HANA Cloud SDK* is based on the SAP Cloud Platform SDK for service development and provides SAP S/4HANA-specific end-to-end capabilities (such as convenient consumption of data models from SAP S/4HANA), tools, and codified processes (for example, for ensuring quality and interoperability) to enable application developers to easily create SAP S/4HANA side-by-side extensions. The SDK represents the generalized knowledge and experience from building several productively running SAP S/4HANA side-by-side extensions on SAP Cloud Platform. Amongst others, these extensions include partner-built applications as described in Chapter 21 of this book, as well as SAP RealSpend (*https://www.sap.com/realspend*), which represents the first side-by-side extension for SAP S/4HANA developed following the cloud-native application principles outlined earlier in this chapter.

Figure 3.2 highlights the relationship of both SDKs with the SAP Cloud Platform and SAP S/4HANA. As outlined earlier, the SAP Cloud Platform SDK for service development builds upon SAP Cloud Platform whereas the SAP S/4HANA Cloud SDK builds on top of the SAP Cloud Platform to further simplify the development of side-by-side extensions.

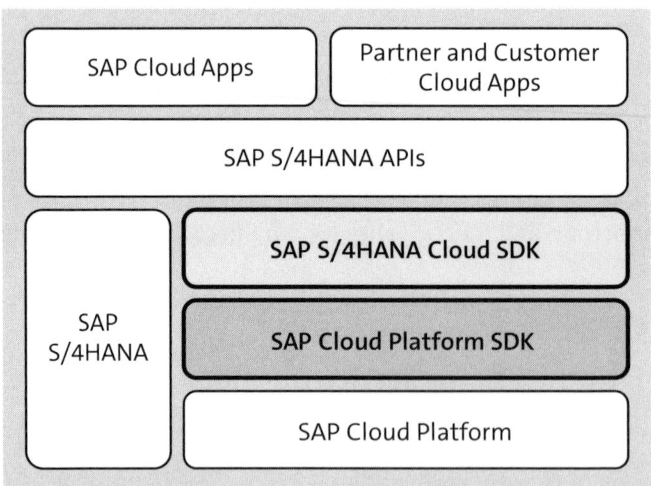

Figure 3.2 Overview of SAP S/4HANA Cloud SDK and SAP Cloud Platform SDK for Service Development

Java-based side-by-side extensions on SAP Cloud Platform tend to follow a certain structure, as shown in Figure 3.3, which depicts the essential components in the stack of side-by-side extensions according to the traditional layers of a three-tiered application.

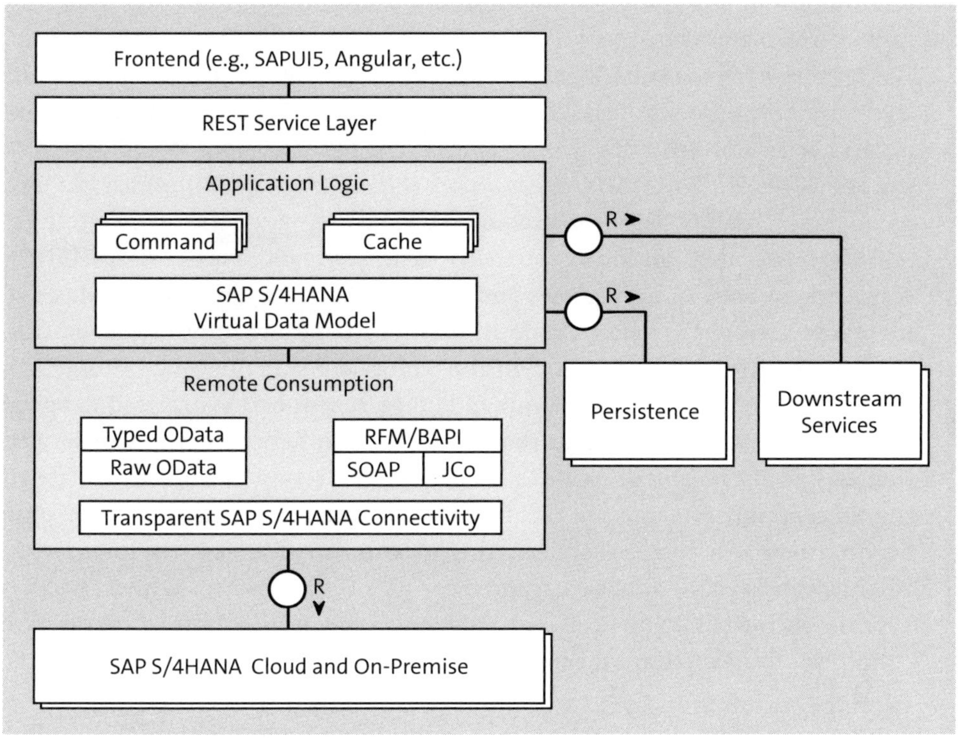

Figure 3.3 Typical Structure of Java-Based Side-by-Side Extension on SAP Cloud Platform Showing Various Application Layers

These essential components are:

- **Frontend layer**
  The consumer-facing part of a side-by-side extension is usually the frontend of the application. This layer is usually built in JavaScript or TypeScript using frontend technologies such as SAP Fiori, SAPUI5, Angular, and more (see also Chapter 14).
- **REST service layer**
  Below the frontend layer, the REST service layer exposes the functionality of a side-by-side extension using RESTful APIs. This layer may consist of simple JSON-based

APIs or more sophisticated APIs built on the OData standard. The service layer can be exposed with Java-based frameworks such as Java Platform, Enterprise Edition (Java EE), Spring, or plain web servlets. In addition, the SAP Cloud Platform SDK for service development offers functionality for exposing OData services in an easy and convenient way (see Chapter 8).

- **Application logic layer**
  The Java-based application logic is at the heart of a side-by-side extension. This layer primarily consists of classes that realize the functionality of the application (such as persistence). For this layer, to efficiently build extensions for SAP S/4HANA, the SAP S/4HANA Cloud SDK offers a *virtual data model* (*VDM*), which is a Java-based representation of the logic required to consume services that are offered by SAP S/4HANA. The VDM allows you to invoke the relevant APIs of SAP S/4HANA—consisting of both OData services and specific BAPIs—in a type-safe and convenient way from within the Java code. In addition, to retrieve information via other systems or microservices in a resilient and fault-tolerant manner, the SAP S/4HANA Cloud SDK offers *commands*. Commands represent function-oriented wrappers around specific parts of the code that interact with other components or services that may be unavailable or prone to latency issues (Section 3.1.2). Closely related to the concept of commands are caches that can store results that were previously been retrieved via remote services. This functionality allows us to improve the responsiveness of the application and reduce the load on downstream services or systems such as SAP S/4HANA. For a detailed overview on how integrate these concepts into an application, refer to Chapter 4.

- **Remote consumption layer**
  Finally, the remote consumption layer represents the foundation for integration capabilities such as the SAP S/4HANA VDM by realizing a transparent connectivity layer to SAP S/4HANA systems. This layer includes abstractions that allow the consumption of both OData services and BAPIs via different underlying protocols—SOAP and the RFC protocol, which is implemented based on the *SAP Java Connector* (JCo). In particular, these abstractions facilitate the development of cost-efficient multitenant applications where customers (or their administrators) can configure connections to their relevant SAP S/4HANA systems. For developers of a side-by-side extension, whether data is retrieved from an SAP S/4HANA system in the cloud or from a system that resides in an on-premise environment remains fully transparent, and the data is exposed to a side-by-side extension with the Cloud Connector. Chapter 6 describes configuring to different SAP S/4HANA systems in detail.

In addition to the application layer-specific functionality offered by the SAP Cloud Platform SDK for service development and the SAP S/4HANA Cloud SDK, a wide variety of tools and components are available to address additional aspects across the layers we've just described. These tools also refer to capabilities focusing on both the development and the operation of a side-by-side extension. Figure 3.4 shows an overview of these components.

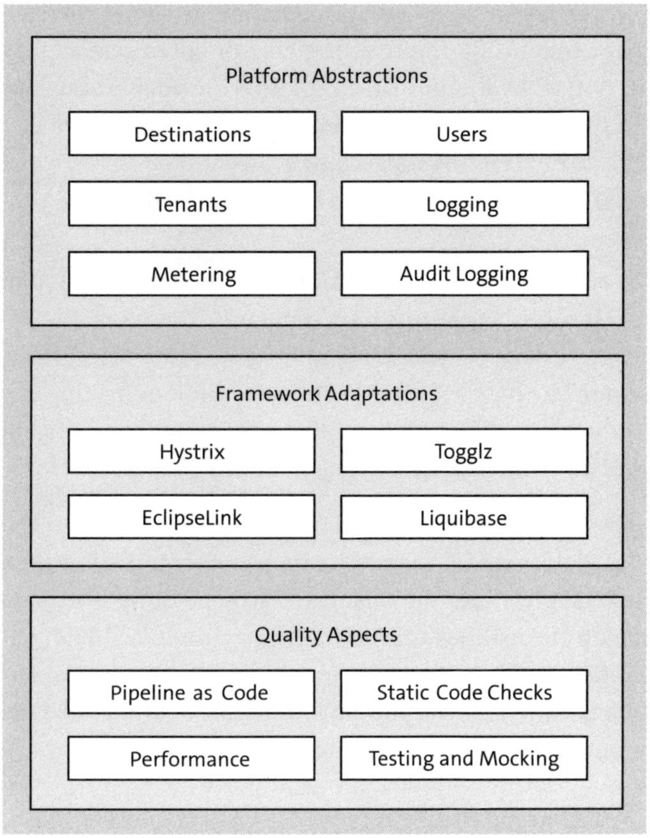

Figure 3.4 An Overview of Functionality and Tools Provided by the SDKs Across Application Layers for Both Development and Operations

Let's explore these components in more detail:

- **Platform abstractions**
  The SAP S/4HANA Cloud SDK supports both SAP Cloud Platform environments: Cloud Foundry and Neo. Therefore, it abstracts from the specific implementations

of each underlying environments. It offers generic interfaces for environment-specific tasks such as accessing destinations, as well as tenant and user data. This facilitates testing across SAP Cloud Platform environments and offers increased flexibility for running the same code on Cloud Foundry and Neo.

- **Framework adaptations**
  Open source libraries offer powerful capabilities for developing SAP S/4HANA side-by-side extensions. Nevertheless, open source components sometimes rely on assumptions that do not fully fulfill the requirements of enterprise applications. Therefore, the SAP S/4HANA Cloud SDK offers specific adaptations and extensions to certain open source frameworks to consider these requirements. An example of an adaptation is the extension Togglz (*https://www.togglz.org*), which supports feature toggling on both the user level and the tenant level.
- **Quality aspects**
  Delivering a cloud-native side-by-side extension not only requires developing code efficiently but also continuously ensuring high standards. Therefore, the SAP S/4HANA Cloud SDK offers a variety of tools for testing as well as a ready-made, codified, and fully containerized pipeline that enables continuous testing and delivery of side-by-side extensions. For details on the underlying concepts and how to use these quality-related functionalities, please refer to Chapter 12.

Given this high-level overview of the capabilities and purpose of the SAP S/4HANA Cloud SDK and the SAP Cloud Platform SDK for service development, the following section describes our example application, the Business Partner Address Manager application, which we'll develop throughout this book. This example will highlight how to best leverage both SDKs to effectively develop side-by-side extensions. Furthermore, our example application will show you how to embrace and realize the cloud-native qualities we've outlined so far.

3.4 Business Partner Address Manager Application

In this book, we'll gradually build up a complete side-by-side extension that allows you to read business partner information and manage business partner addresses in an SAP S/4HANA system. Such information can be maintained directly in SAP

S/4HANA, but doing so generally requires users with elevated privileges. To enable users with lower privileges to manage business partner information, our application, the Business Partner Address Manager application, uses a new approval workflow for creating, updating, and deleting business partner addresses. On one hand, casual business users are empowered by allowing them to maintain this information by themselves. On the other hand, the workload on data administrators for maintaining all the information is reduced because now they only need to review the suggested changes before accepting them into SAP S/4HANA.

Following the terminology of extension use cases from Chapter 2, Section 2.4, our application is both a proxy and a convenience application. Thus, the Business Partner Address Manager application must be able to read and write the following data to and from an SAP S/4HANA system:

- **Reading a list of business partners**
  To maintain business partner addresses, the application should be able to retrieve a list of business partners with a minimal set of information per business partner (business partner ID, first name, and last name).
- **Reading a specific business partner**
  To list business partners, the application should be able to retrieve business partner details, including the business partner's addresses, for a single selected business partner. Business partner details are fields, such as the creation date of a business partner entry.
- **Writing business partner addresses**
  Finally, the application should be able to maintain (create, update, and delete) the address information of a specific business partner, for example, its country, city name, postal code, street name, and house number for addresses.

In the following chapters, we'll first focus on a simple side-by-side extension that directly reads and writes business partner entries and addresses to and from the SAP S/4HANA system. Figure 3.5 shows a simplified workflow of how addresses are directly maintained in SAP S/4HANA.

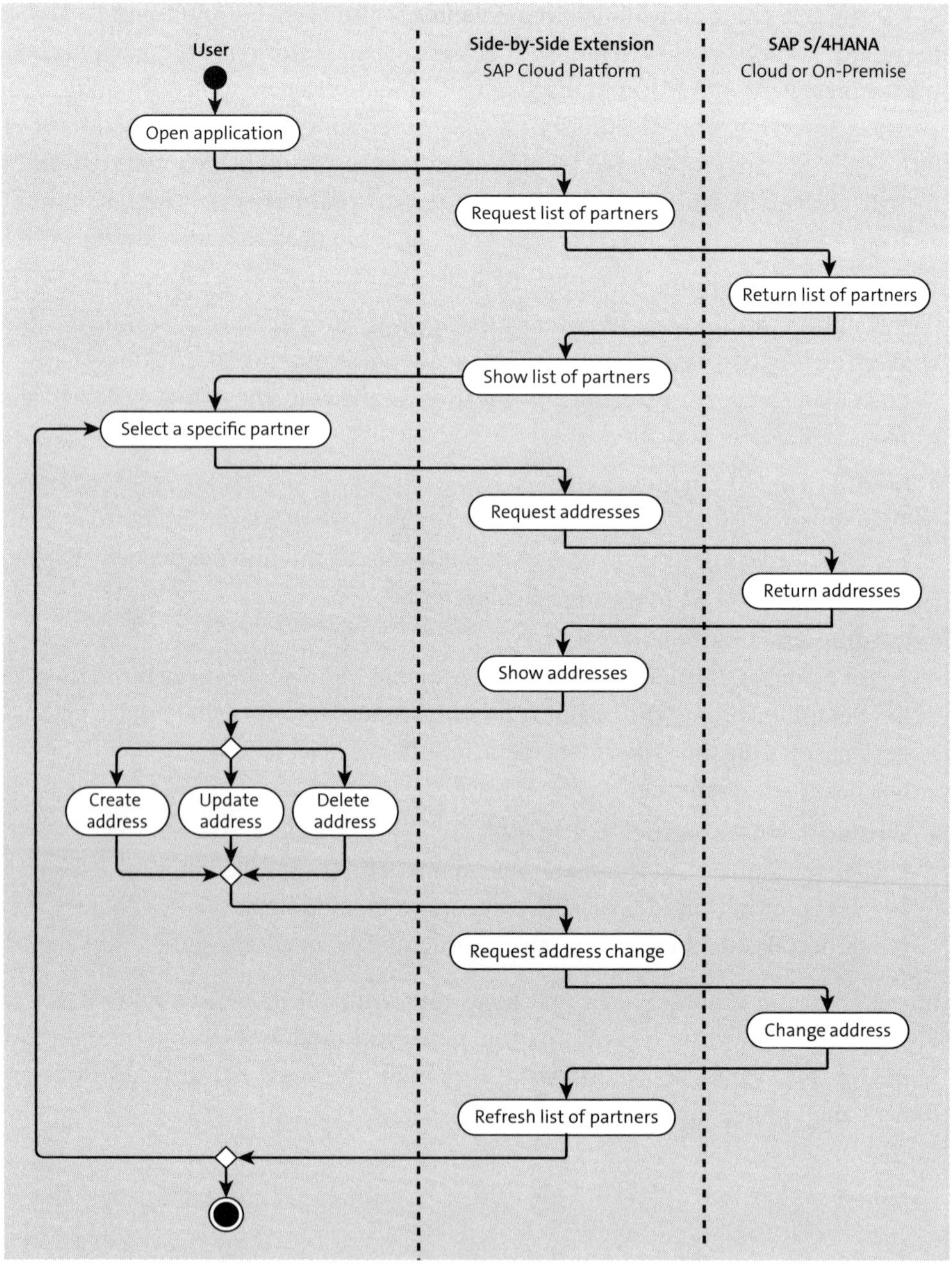

Figure 3.5 Overview of Simple Workflow of the Example Side-by-Side Extension for Managing Business Partner Addresses

To support the full approval workflow, Chapter 7 introduces the basics of persistency on SAP Cloud Platform, allowing us to first maintain business partner addresses within a local database on the SAP Cloud Platform instead of directly writing the changes back to SAP S/4HANA. By first only persisting changes within our application, we can follow an approval workflow where suggested changes in the local database are written to the actual SAP S/4HANA system, in line with the preprocessing extension use case. Thus, the action of maintaining address entries within the local database on SAP Cloud Platform is separated from the action of writing a suggested change to SAP S/4HANA in two separate business user roles. Figure 3.6 shows the final approval workflow for creating a new address. Finally, the approval for a new address that has been suggested is shown in Figure 3.7

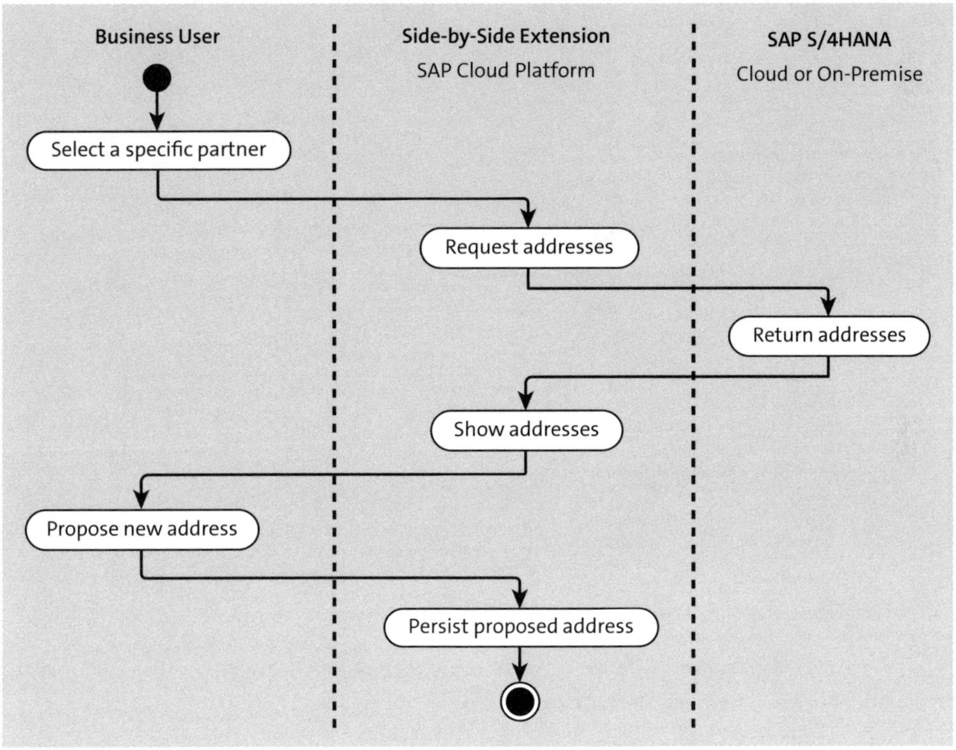

Figure 3.6 Workflow of a Casual Business User Creating an Address

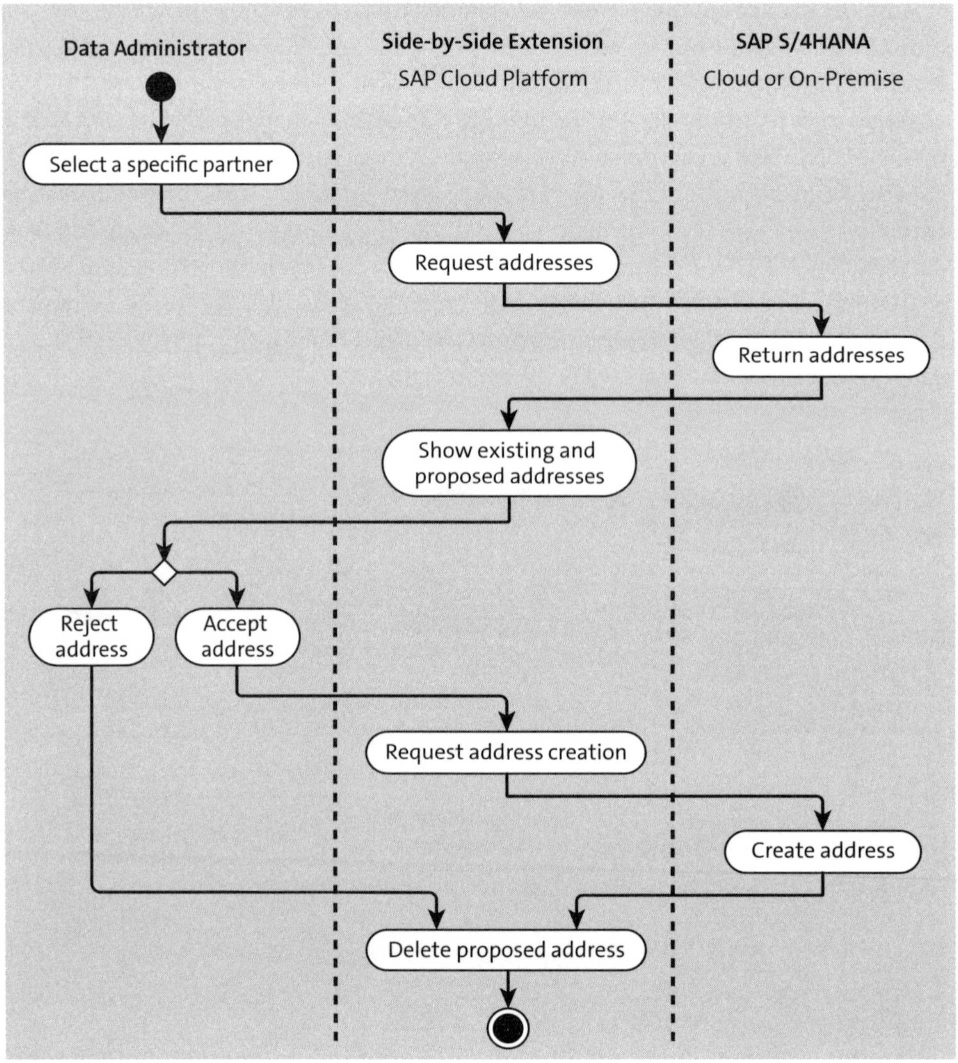

Figure 3.7 Approval Workflow with Data Administrator Rejecting or Accepting a Suggested New Address for a Business Partner

3.5 Summary

This chapter highlighted the reasons behind, the benefits of, and the enablers of cloud-native application development concepts. In addition, we outlined the principles suggested by the so-called twelve-factor application. Furthermore, we presented an overview of SAP Cloud Platform, its basic terminology, components, and services, as well as the SAP S/4HANA Cloud SDK and the SAP Cloud Platform SDK for service development. Finally, we described our example side-by-side extension that we'll gradually build up over the course of this book.

In the next chapter, we'll start building the Business Partner Address Manager application with the SAP S/4HANA Cloud SDK.

Chapter 4
Building the Application

This chapter describes how to build our example application using the SAP S/4HANA Cloud SDK. We'll implement the basics of our Business Partner Address Manager application as we outlined in Chapter 3. We'll integrate an SAP S/4HANA API and include a predefined front-end. The basic app we build in this chapter will be expanded in the following chapters with additional features and technologies.

In previous chapters, we explained the motivation for side-by-side extensions of SAP S/4HANA. In particular, Chapter 3 sketched out our sample application, a web-based application to manage business partner addresses. In this chapter, we'll implement an early version of that application that will contain the basic functionality of displaying and managing business partner addresses. Our focus will be on using the SAP S/4HANA Cloud SDK to implement the integration to SAP S/4HANA according to cloud qualities. At the same time, you'll also learn how to apply general principles for cloud-native applications during implementation.

To start building our app, in Section 4.1, we'll use the project templates provided by the SAP S/4HANA Cloud SDK and explain how to quickly create a working skeleton for our application that incorporates some best practices for cloud-native application development. Then, in Section 4.2, we'll implement the first part of our backend including integration with SAP S/4HANA for reading business partner data. In Section 4.3, we'll integrate a prebuilt user interface, and in Section 4.4, we'll deploy the application to the Cloud Foundry environment of SAP Cloud Platform. At this point, we'll have a fully running application, but it will still be missing the transactional capabilities of modifying address information in SAP S/4HANA—the topic of Section 4.5. With this final part, the basic functionality of the application will be complete, and we'll have a solid foundation for the remainder of the book. The last section looks at the cloud qualities expected of a cloud-native application from a theoretical as well as hands-on perspective and discusses how to leverage the SAP S/4HANA Cloud SDK to make our application more resilient.

4.1 A First "Hello World!" Microservice

You can use the SAP S/4HANA Cloud SDK in any Java project, whether an existing Java Platform, Enterprise Edition (Java EE)-based project or a newly created Spring Boot application. To start a new project, the SDK offers project templates to quickly create an initial project structure, already set up for continuous delivery, as we'll discuss in Chapters 10 and 11. We recommend using these so-called *archetypes*, which are based on established best practices, when you create new side-by-side extension projects. Chapter 15 walks through the steps for integrating the SAP S/4HANA Cloud SDK into any Java project, without using archetypes.

To get started quickly with our example application without assuming too much prior knowledge, we'll use the SDK's archetype for the Cloud Foundry environment of the SAP Cloud Platform on a simple Apache TomEE application server. An archetype is also available based on Spring Boot. When implementing the application on top of the generated project, we'll avoid introducing too many frameworks such as Java EE at first. Instead, we'll aim for a straightforward implementation, which we'll adapt and expand continuously, not only with additional functionality but also with more advanced technology. Chapter 15 explains how you can quickly begin using the SDK together with other enterprise application frameworks such as Java EE or Spring Boot.

4.1.1 Prerequisites

To build applications using the SAP S/4HANA Cloud SDK, you'll need a minimal set of prerequisites installed on your developer machine. The GitHub repository for this book provides instructions on how to install these prerequisites on all popular operating systems. Install the following before proceeding with the next subsection:

- **Java Development Kit (JDK), version 8 (1.8.0+) or above**
  The JDK is necessary for compiling Java applications and allows you to run Java applications locally.
- **Apache Maven, version 3.5.0 or above**
  Maven is a build automation tool for Java projects (and other programming environments). Maven manages project structures and dependencies to other libraries, as well as the build lifecycle. Maven also generates projects via the archetypes provided by the SAP S/4HANA Cloud SDK.
- **(Optional) Integrated Development Environment (IDE)**
  While using an IDE instead of a simple text editor to write code is entirely optional,

an IDE can greatly simplify the development lifecycle, especially in later chapters. In general, you can do everything described in this book with a plain text editor and command line tools. The SAP S/4HANA Cloud SDK does not make any assumptions on your IDE; so, you're free to choose any IDE you like, for example, Eclipse or IntelliJ IDEA.

A few additional tools are used as soon as we go beyond the local development and testing stages, as follows:

- **Cloud Foundry command line interface (CLI)**
  The Cloud Foundry CLI allows you to interact with Cloud Foundry from the command line. You can deploy, start and stop applications, consume services, and do much more, via simple commands on your local command line. In principle, you can perform many of the tasks also with the SAP Cloud Platform cockpit. However, we'll mostly describe the approach using the command line.
- **Git**
  The distributed version control system (VCS) Git is important when talking about continuous delivery and DevOps in Chapters 10 and 11. A VCS such as Git enables collaboration in development teams. Version control also forms the basis for any continuous delivery pipeline. Until we get to this topic in Chapter 10 and Chapter 11, you're free and encouraged to store your code in a Git repository but are not required to. We won't explain how to use Git in detail. Especially if you haven't worked with Git before, you may first want to skip using a VCS entirely.

Most of these prerequisites are part of a standard development setup, so you likely already have some or all of these tools on your machine. In any case, these tools will help you in any development project, at least if based on Java, whether you're using the SAP S/4HANA Cloud SDK or not. Once you've installed Java and Maven, you're ready to proceed to the next subsection and generate the initial project structure for our application.

4.1.2 Generating the Project

The first step is to launch the project creation using a simple command. Open a command line interface (CLI) on your computer, for example, the Command Prompt or Windows PowerShell on Windows, the Terminal on Mac OS, or any shell on Linux. Navigate to the folder where you want to create your project folder. Type the command in Listing 4.1 *as a single line* (as indicated by the symbol ↩, but don't type that symbol) and press `Enter`. The double quotes "..." around the arguments may not be necessary or should be replaced by single quotes '...', depending on your command line interface.

```
mvn archetype:generate ↩
    "-DarchetypeGroupId=com.sap.cloud.s4hana.archetypes" ↩
    "-DarchetypeArtifactId=scp-cf-tomee" ↩
    "-DarchetypeVersion=RELEASE"
```

Listing 4.1 Generate Project Using Archetype

This command instructs Maven to launch the project based on the archetype `scp-cf-tomee` of the SAP S/4HANA Cloud SDK, as specified by the arguments. With this command, Maven downloads the archetype from its repository, Maven Central; the actual version used will depend on the latest available release of the SAP S/4HANA Cloud SDK. At the time of this writing, that release is 2.0.0. During execution, the generator will ask for several parameters of the project to be generated, outlined in Table 4.1 along with the values used in our example. We recommend using those values as they are referenced throughout our app project.

Parameter	Explanation	Value in Example
groupId	Identifier of the group or company creating the project	`com.sap.cloud.s4hana.examples`
artifactId	Identifier of the application	`address-manager`
version	Initial version of the application	`1.0-SNAPSHOT` (press `Enter` to accept the default)
package	Top-level package of the Java artifacts in the project	`com.sap.cloud.s4hana.examples.addressmgr`

Table 4.1 Parameters of the Project Generation

Afterwards, Maven will display the chosen values and ask for a final confirmation, which you can confirm by pressing `Enter`. Then, Maven will create a folder with a name like *artifactId* and generate the initial project structure.

The generated project contains a multimodule Maven project with three Java modules in separate subfolders:

- The *application* folder for the source code and configuration of the backend application

- The *unit-tests* folder for the unit tests of the backend application
- The *integration-tests* folder for the integration tests

The file pom.xml in the top-level folder of the project describes the overall multi-module Maven project with the group and artifact identifiers, as well as the general properties and configuration for the Java build. Furthermore, this file specifies the version of the SAP S/4HANA Cloud SDK used in the project, as shown in Listing 4.2. If you later want to update the version of the SAP S/4HANA Cloud SDK used in your project once a new release is available, you only need to change the version identifier in this file; all submodules will immediately reference this version.


```
<dependencyManagement>
    <dependencies>
        <dependency>
            <groupId>com.sap.cloud.s4hana</groupId>
            <artifactId>sdk-bom</artifactId>
            <version>2.0.0</version>
            <type>pom</type>
            <scope>import</scope>
        </dependency>
    </dependencies>
</dependencyManagement>
```

Listing 4.2 SAP S/4HANA Cloud SDK Dependency in Maven

The generated content also includes a folder named *cx-server*, as well as files named *Jenkinsfile*, the manifest.yml file, and the pipeline_config.yml file. These are relevant for the continuous delivery pipeline described in more detail in Chapters 10 and 11. Chapter 9 explains the testing setup in more detail, so we'll focus on the structure of the *application* folder in the following sections. The generator has created a simple "Hello World!" application, which we'll explore in the remainder of this section.

We'll take a closer look at the generated source code and configuration files in Section 4.1.4. But first, let's build and run our project locally, to see the initial "Hello World!" application in action.

4.1.3 Building and Running the Project Locally

The generated source code can be compiled without any modification to create a simple service that returns "Hello World!" when called. You can then start a local server and run the service locally. The steps described in this subsection apply whenever you want to build the project or run it locally.

To compile the Java source code and package it in a Java web archive, execute the following command in the top-level folder of your project:

```
mvn clean package
```

Executing Commands

Unless noted otherwise, all commands that are executed on a command line interface should be executed in the top-level folder of the project. Use the `cd` command to switch to that folder:

```
cd path/to/address-manager
```

With this command, Maven removes any files from previous builds (`clean`) and assembles the project (`package`). Ahead of assembling the archive, Maven compiles the Java code and runs the tests defined in the corresponding modules. When the command has finished successfully, as indicated by the "BUILD SUCCESS" message, you'll find a file called address-manager-application.war in the folder *application/target*. This Web Application Archive (.war) file can be deployed on a suitable, Java EE-compatible application server.

The SAP S/4HANA Cloud SDK archetype already includes a plugin into the generated Maven project, so we can start an Apache TomEE server and deploy our application on this server in a single command in a few seconds:

```
mvn tomee:run -pl application
```

This command instructs Maven to execute the TomEE plugin and run a server within the application module. Once the server has started, you'll see a line in the log output similar to "INFO: Server startup in 9544 ms."

By default, the server is accessible at the URL *http://localhost:8080/* on your local machine. If you enter this URL in your browser, you'll see a standard static welcome page provided by the SAP S/4HANA Cloud SDK, as shown in Figure 4.1.

Open the URL *http://localhost:8080/hello* to see the simple "Hello World!" service that has been automatically generated as a sample. The service simply returns the text "Hello World!" as shown in Figure 4.2.

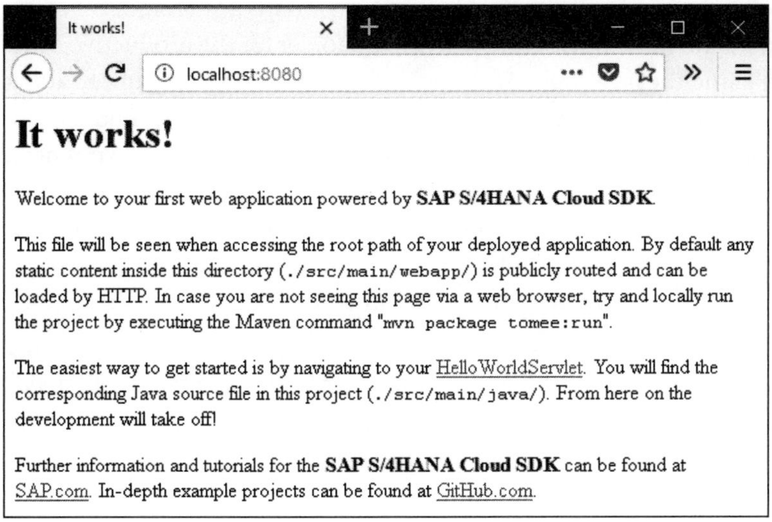

Figure 4.1 Welcome Page of the SAP S/4HANA Cloud SDK

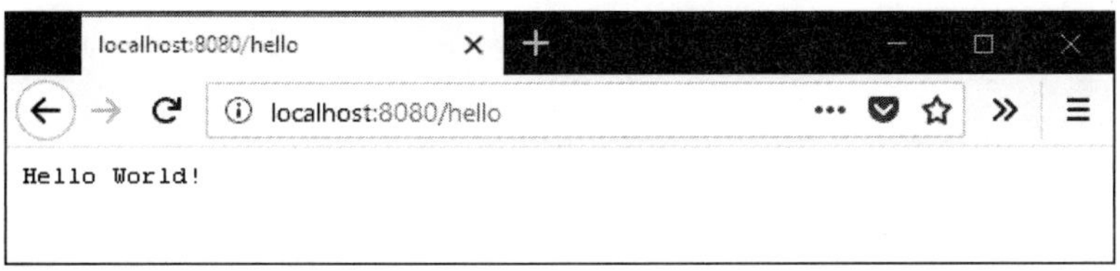

Figure 4.2 "Hello World!" Service

In the next section, we'll briefly explore the structure of this generated application.

4.1.4 Structure of the Application Code

In the application folder of the generated project, you'll again find the pom.xml file, which defines the Maven module of the application itself, that is, its dependencies and build instructions. If you study the file, you'll see that it defines the identifiers of the module, references the top-level multimodule project as a parent, lists the required dependencies, and contains build instructions including the TomEE plugin used earlier. The list of dependencies already includes the central modules of the SAP S/4HANA Cloud SDK, so that we can immediately use the modules in our code in the next section.

In addition to the pom.xml file, the application folder contains a subfolder called *src* that follows the standard Maven structure with a *main* folder for the productive code. In this folder, you'll find the Java code of the application under *java/*, organized along the Java package structure, where we'll put most of our source code in folders. The folder *resources* contains additional configuration and resource files that do not need to be compiled by Java. The folder *webapp* contains static resources for the welcome page and the web application deployment descriptor file at *WEB-INF/web.xml*. We'll put our frontend application into this folder. You can ignore the Maven-standard *src/test* folder, because we have separate modules for unit and integration tests.

Of special interest for our purpose is the HelloWorldServlet.java file automatically created by the archetype, usually under *application/src/main/java/com/sap/cloud/s4hana/examples/addressmgr* if you used the example package name. The file contains a class `HelloWorldServlet`, as shown in Listing 4.3.

```
@WebServlet("/hello")
public class HelloWorldServlet extends HttpServlet
{
  private static final long serialVersionUID = 1L;
  private static final Logger logger =
      CloudLoggerFactory.getLogger(
          HelloWorldServlet.class);

  @Override
  protected void doGet( final HttpServletRequest request,
      final HttpServletResponse response )
      throws ServletException, IOException
  {
    logger.info("I am running!");
    response.getWriter().write("Hello World!");
  }
}
```

Listing 4.3 HelloWorldServlet Generated by Archetype

The class uses the simple Java Servlet API 3.1 to define a *servlet*, which will run on a server and respond to requests at a certain endpoint. In this case, we have a servlet for the HTTP protocol to responds to specific HTTP methods such as `GET` requests. The class inherits from `HttpServlet`, which already provides the necessary functionality and only requires that the subclass overrides and implements the methods that it intends to support. In the case of `HelloWorldServlet`, the servlet shall respond to `GET` requests, and thus, the class overrides the `doGet` method. The `@WebServlet` annotation in the first line specifies the path of the URL where the servlet can be called. All `GET` requests to the */hello* path of the web application, relative from its root path, will be served by an `HelloWorldServlet` object. The application server will prepare the request as a Java object and call the `doGet` method.

The method has access to the request via the corresponding parameter, including the query string and the headers. The `response` parameter can be used to send a response with content to the caller. The sample code above does not consider the incoming request parameter and always writes "Hello World!" into the response. Before that, the code also sends an info log statement. These capabilities are everything we need from the application server to implement the first features of our Business Partner Address Manager application in the next section. For this reason, at first, we won't use more complex and powerful frameworks, but instead stick to the simple Java Servlet standard.

4.2 Reading Business Partners

The generated project gives us a good basis for implementing our Business Partner Address Manager application. In this section, we'll focus on retrieving business partners from an SAP S/4HANA system and exposing them to the frontend as JSON objects. Two different requirements need to be supported by the API to read business partners: (1) retrieving all relevant business partners with their basic information for the list and (2) retrieving more specific information about a specific business partner, including his or her addresses, for the detailed view.

We'll implement both with the same servlet because of the similar nature of the request. In Section 4.2.1, we'll implement the list of business partners and then, in Section 4.2.2, show you how to run this locally including creating a connection to an SAP S/4HANA API. We'll explain the concept behind and benefits of using the Java virtual data model (VDM) for the SAP S/4HANA OData services used to implement the feature in Section 4.2.3. Finally, in Section 4.2.4, we'll expand the servlet to cover the case of retrieving a single business partner.

For the first iteration in this section, we'll focus on a straightforward implementation. To get to the main point quickly, we won't digress into important topics such as error handling. We recommend you consider this topic as part of extending the example on your own because error handling concepts are generic and require standard Java coding.

4.2.1 Retrieving the List of Business Partners

The HelloWorldServlet from the generated project already hints at how we can implement a servlet for retrieving business partners. We'll call the servlet BusinessPartnerServlet and serve it from the path */api/business-partners*. Thus, we've defined the basic structure of the file BusinessPartnerServlet.java, as shown in Listing 4.4, which we'll place in the same package as the HelloWorldServlet:

```
@WebServlet("/api/business-partners")
public class BusinessPartnerServlet extends HttpServlet {
  private static final Logger logger = CloudLoggerFactory
      .getLogger(BusinessPartnerServlet.class);
  // implementation of doGet goes here
}
```

Listing 4.4 Outline of BusinessPartnerServlet

According to the requirements of the application, each call to this endpoint shall retrieve all business partners from SAP S/4HANA that are natural persons with first and last names. Additionally, we'll retrieve the unique identifier for each business partner to reference the person in subsequent calls to SAP S/4HANA, for example, when retrieving the details for a specific business partner. Finally, we want results to be ordered by last name.

With the SAP S/4HANA Cloud SDK and its VDM for OData services, these requirements translate into a simple implementation, as shown in Listing 4.5.

```
new DefaultBusinessPartnerService()
    .getAllBusinessPartner()
    .select(BusinessPartner.BUSINESS_PARTNER,
        BusinessPartner.LAST_NAME,
        BusinessPartner.FIRST_NAME)
    .filter(BusinessPartner.BUSINESS_PARTNER_CATEGORY
        .eq("1"))
    .orderBy(BusinessPartner.LAST_NAME, Order.ASC)
    .execute();
```

Listing 4.5 Using the VDM to Select Business Partners

The DefaultBusinessPartnerService of the VDM represents the business partner API of SAP S/4HANA and gives access to various operations available in this API, such as the operation to query all business partners, exposed by the VDM by the method getAllBusinessPartner. When we call this method, we'll get a helper object that exposes a fluent API. This approach conforms the notion of a fluent interface (M. Fowler, *FluentInterface*) and allows us to construct the query step-by-step in a type-safe manner before the query is finally executed. The following actions occur from line 3 and beyond in Listing 4.5:

- First, we'll specify which of the many fields of a business partner we want to retrieve for each entity returned by the query. We'll supply the fields to the select method of the fluent query helper. The BusinessPartner class of the VDM allows easy access to all available fields as static fields in Java, for example, BusinessPartner.**LAST_NAME**.
- Then, in line 6, we'll define the filter to be applied by the OData service in the SAP S/4HANA system. The fluent query helper exposes the filter query option of OData via the filter method, which expects a filter expression as a parameter. To define such an expression, we'll use the VDM again. Natural persons in SAP S/4HANA are identified by the category *1*, which is what we've specified in a fluent manner, using the representation of the business partner field BUSINESS_PARTNER_CATEGORY and comparing it to the String "1" (or a constant CATEGORY_PERSON of that value, as in Listing 4.6).
- Last, we'll finish defining the query by specifying a sort query operation in line 7. To this end, we'll supply, to the orderBy method, the field to sort by and the sort order Order.ASC to specify an ascending sort.

Having defined the query in this manner leveraging the VDM of the SAP S/4HANA Cloud SDK, we'll call the execute method to send the query to the SAP S/4HANA system connected to our application. A lot happens in the background when calling execute, as the SAP S/4HANA Cloud SDK takes over a lot of the burden from the developer. We don't need to specify in our code where to find the SAP S/4HANA system of the current tenant, nor establish connectivity to the system ourselves, which may reside on-premise in the customer's network. Nor do we need to deal with authentication and authorization. On top of all this, the VDM also handles the actual call to the OData service at its defined path, by constructing the query as expected by SAP S/4HANA and handling the response.

The response of SAP S/4HANA is converted into a set of Java objects, in this case, a list of business partners. The business partner type is defined by the VDM as well and gives easy and type-safe access to the returned entities and their properties. In our case, however, we only want to convert the result list retrieved from SAP S/4HANA to a JSON response object and return it as a response to the caller. The code to achieve this operation can be seen in Listing 4.6. We'll store the return value of the call to the OData service in a variable `result`, convert it to JSON using the GSON library, and write the JSON into the response. As the call to the OData service may fail for several reasons, we'll need to wrap it in a try-catch block. However, we'll deal with proper error handling only later, so for now, we'll just log the error and wrap the exception in a `ServletException` to throw this wrapped exception again.

```
@Override
protected void doGet(final HttpServletRequest request,
           final HttpServletResponse response)
    throws ServletException, IOException {
  final List<BusinessPartner> result;
  try {
    result = new DefaultBusinessPartnerService()
        .getAllBusinessPartner()
        .select(BusinessPartner.BUSINESS_PARTNER,
            BusinessPartner.LAST_NAME,
            BusinessPartner.FIRST_NAME)
        .filter(BusinessPartner.BUSINESS_PARTNER_CATEGORY
            .eq(CATEGORY_PERSON))
        .orderBy(BusinessPartner.LAST_NAME, Order.ASC)
        .execute();
  } catch (ODataException e) {
    logger.error("Error retrieving business partners", e);
    throw new ServletException(e);
  }

  response.setContentType("application/json");
  response.getWriter().write(new Gson().toJson(result));
}
```

Listing 4.6 Implementation of the doGet Method for Retrieving All Business Partners

In the same manner, the VDM provides simple, type-safe, and fluent access to each operation of every OData service available in an SAP S/4HANA Cloud system. Before we look into the Java VDM in more detail, let's start up the local server to see our new API in action.

4.2.2 Running Locally

To run our service, we'll need to connect it to an OData service. On SAP Cloud Platform, corresponding services are available that deal with connecting to SAP S/4HANA or other downstream systems. The SAP S/4HANA Cloud SDK integrates with those services as well. However, we do not have an SAP Cloud Platform instance running on our local machine. And you may not have an SAP S/4HANA system readily available and accessible while reading this book. Thus, we'll need to define the destination to connect to in a different way.

The SAP S/4HANA Cloud SDK offers an easy solution to the first problem by using an environment variable, as we'll explain briefly. For the second problem, we offer a dummy OData service, available in the GitHub repository for this book.

For the following steps, you'll need to know the URL of the SAP S/4HANA system or of your instance of the dummy service, as well as the credentials for a user authorized to call the business partner API. We'll explain how to set this up for an SAP S/4HANA system in Chapter 6. For now, we assume that you'll use the dummy service with dummy credentials or that you already have access to SAP S/4HANA.

Before you start the local server, you'll need to specify the destination to connect to in an environment variable called `destinations`. The SAP S/4HANA Cloud SDK will look for this environment variable and use it to determine how to connect to SAP S/4HANA. If this variable is not available, only then will other destinations, such as the destination service on the Cloud Foundry environment of the SAP Cloud Platform be used. For our purposes, a local deployment without SAP Cloud Platform, the `destinations` variable is exactly what we want. For a general introduction to the concept of destinations, either see the short overview in Chapter 3 or the detailed discussion in Chapter 6.

The environment variable needs a JSON representation as its value that conforms to the format displayed in Listing 4.7. The value is a JSON array with one or many objects, where each object represents one destination configuration. Each object has a property `name` that can be used to identify the destination. By default, the SAP S/4HANA Cloud SDK looks for a destination named "ErpQueryEndpoint" to connect to SAP S/4HANA. As we haven't specified anything else in our code above, we'll need to use this name here as well. Furthermore, the destination JSON object needs to have a property `url` whose value is the URL to the SAP S/4HANA system or dummy service. Finally, a user name and password are required.

```
[
    {
        name: "ErpQueryEndpoint",
        url: "https://URL",
        username: "USER",
```

```
        password: "PASSWORD"
    }
]
```

Listing 4.7 Format of Destinations Environment Variable

To store this configuration in the environment variable `destinations`, run the corresponding command from your command line interface, for example, on the Windows command prompt:

```
set destinations=[{name: "ErpQueryEndpoint", url: ↩
"https://URL", username: "USER", password: "PASSWORD"}]
```

On Mac OS or Linux, the command will be `export`. After we've defined this environment variable, we can execute the usual commands to build the application and run the local server in the top-level folder of our project:

```
mvn clean package
mvn tomee:run -pl application
```

That's all! Now, if you access the URL *http://localhost:8080/api/business-partners*, you should see a list of business partners formatted as JSON objects with exactly the fields we selected in our code, as shown in Figure 4.3.

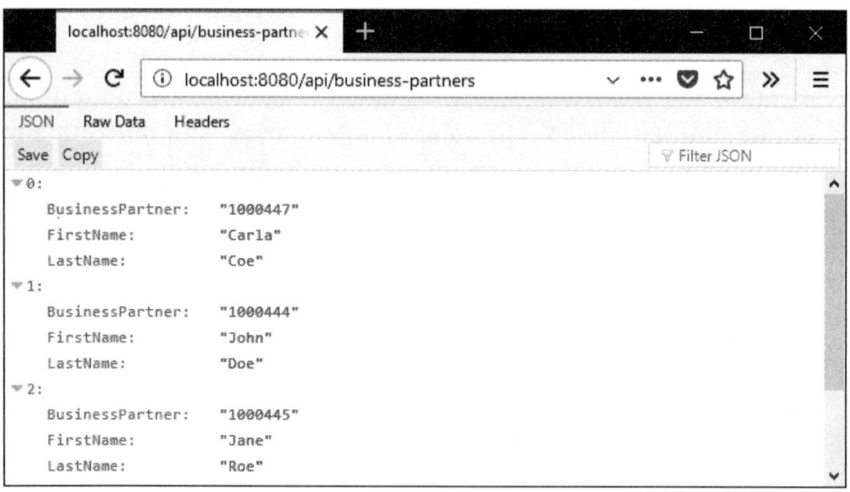

Figure 4.3 JSON Result of the First Service

4.2.3 The SAP S/4HANA Virtual Data Model in Java

In Section 4.2.1, we used the SAP S/4HANA VDM in Java, which is part of the SAP S/4HANA Cloud SDK, to connect to the OData service of the business partner API. As mentioned earlier, the business partner service is only one of many APIs available in SAP S/4HANA Cloud. The VDM is available for all APIs of SAP S/4HANA Cloud that are exposed as OData services. As such, the VDM of the SDK is a Java representation of the public subset of the ABAP virtual data model that underlies SAP S/4HANA. You can find an overview of the APIs also in the SAP API Business Hub in the SAP S/4HANA Cloud section at *http://tiny.cc/s4-api-hub*.

The VDM is regularly updated for new releases of SAP S/4HANA Cloud as part of new versions of the SAP S/4HANA Cloud SDK, so that you can call any OData service of SAP S/4HANA Cloud. If the same service is available in your on-premise SAP S/4HANA system, you can likewise use the VDM to connect to it as well.

To understand the full breadth of benefits of the VDM, we recommend comparing our implementation so far with a call to SAP S/4HANA that does *not* use the SAP S/4HANA Cloud SDK. With a framework such as the SAP Cloud Platform SDK for service development introduced in Chapter 3, calling an OData service is already significantly easier than building the HTTP request by hand and implementing the response handling from scratch. Nevertheless, as the SAP Cloud Platform SDK for service development does not provide specific features for SAP S/4HANA, we would have to write generic code, such as Listing 4.8, to achieve the same as in Section 4.2.1.

```
final List<MyBusinessPartnerType> businessPartners =
    ODataQueryBuilder
        .withEntity("/sap/opu/odata/sap/API_BUSINESS_PARTNER",
                "A_BusinessPartner")
        .select("BusinessPartner",
                "LastName",
                "FirstName",
                "IsMale",
                "IsFemale",
                "CreationDate")
        .build()
        .execute()
        .asList(MyBusinessPartnerType.class);
```

Listing 4.8 Calling an SAP S/4HANA Service without the VDM (Slightly Simplified)

The generic `ODataQueryBuilder` requires you know the exact OData endpoint path and the entity name `A_BusinessPartner`, which are specified as plain String parameters of the `withEntity` method. Then, each field to select is specified as a plain String as well, which needs to match the actual property names of the OData entity type, without any possibility of checking their accuracy at compile time. The same applies for other query options such as *filter* or *orderby*. Finally, you'll need to create your own Java class `MyBusinessPartnerType` (which is not shown here) that models the return value (or the input to a modifying operation).

Compare this process with the benefits achieved when using the VDM of the SAP S/4HANA Cloud SDK, which specifically targets SAP S/4HANA services and already embodies the following knowledge about their definitions:

- The VDM uses typed Java representations of properties for select, filter, and other query options, instead of hardcoded strings, thus eliminating the possibility of spelling errors and incompatible types, which might otherwise remain unnoticed at compile time.
- The Java types for entities of OData services are provided out of the box instead of requiring you to create Java representations on your own. The Java representation is used to return values of service calls as well as input parameters to create, update, or delete requests and model the full structure of the OData entity type, which often contain up to a hundred properties. The VDM also handles the required type conversions automatically.
- Thanks to the fluent API of the VDM, you can discover the available services, operations, options, and properties more easily directly from the IDE, instead of studying separate documentation and translating the gained insights manually to Java.

All in all, the VDM improves not only development efficiency, but also quality, by embodying best practices and making errors much less likely.

How are these benefits achieved? Conceptually, the VDM is a Java representation of the APIs that already embodies the knowledge you would have to put in by hand when using a generic approach to call the OData service of SAP S/4HANA. The VDM consists of services, fluent helpers, property representations, and entity types. Internally, it uses the SAP Cloud Platform SDK for service development but makes the SAP S/4HANA APIs available and accessible with less effort. When working with the VDM, the individual components of the VDM are easily accessible and almost unnoticeable. Nevertheless, understanding the structure of the VDM will help you harness its full potential.

The VDM represents each API with a service interface and a default implementation that provides the entire functionality. Both the service interface and the implementation class for each API reside in the package `com.sap.cloud.sdk.s4hana.datamodel.odata.services` available from the Maven module `odata-api` (group `com.sap.cloud.s4hana.datamodel`). Each VDM service representation in Java contains one method per operation that is available from the underlying OData service. Each method returns an object of a specific fluent helper class. The fluent helper provides fluent and type-safe access to the options of the operation. For type-safe access, the VDM models each available property of entity types used in the service with a corresponding Java representation that you can use to define queries.

The entity types for the return values of queries and for the parameters of writing operations are modeled as Java types of the VDM, available as a separate package for each API under the root package `com.sap.cloud.sdk.s4hana.datamodel.odata.namespaces`. Such a Java type, representing an entity type of the OData service, models the structure of the entity including associated entities in Java. Each property of the entity type is transferred to a Java property with an appropriate Java type.

4.2.4 Retrieving a Specific Business Partner

So far, we've implemented the first part of our API for retrieving business partners, the list of all business partners with the most important properties. In our Business Partner Address Manager application, we'll also want to display detailed information about a specific business partner, including the addresses, when a user clicks on a business partner in the list. To reduce the amount of data transferred between frontend, backend, and SAP S/4HANA, we'll only retrieve the specific information when the user selects a single business partner. Thus, we'll need to extend our existing API with an option to retrieve a single business partner with more fields than just the name, in particular, addresses. Again, this information will come from SAP S/4HANA. While a call to */api/business-partners* without any parameters can retrieve all business partners as before, a call like */api/business-partners?id=12* that includes the query parameter `id` will retrieve the information for the business partner with the specified identifier.

To prepare, we'll rewrite the `doGet` method, as shown in Listing 4.9. First, we'll access the query parameter `id` from the request. If the caller did not provide the query parameter, the return value will be `null` according to the servlet specification. Within the try-catch block, we'll use this information to either ❶ call the SAP S/4HANA service (as before in Listing 4.6) if `id` is `null` or ❷ to call the service for a single business partner. We'll implement the latter in a moment, but first, note that we introduced a variable jsonResult to hold the JSON-formatted body of the eventual response, which will now either represent a list of business partners or a single business partner.

```
@Override
protected void doGet(final HttpServletRequest request,
                     final HttpServletResponse response)
    throws ServletException, IOException {
  final String id = request.getParameter("id");

  final String jsonResult;
  try {
    if (id == null) {
      final List<BusinessPartner> result =
          new DefaultBusinessPartnerService()
              .getAllBusinessPartner()
              // ❶
      jsonResult = new  Gson().toJson(result);
    } else {
      final BusinessPartner result = // ❷
      jsonResult = new  Gson().toJson(result);
    }
  } catch (ODataException e) {
    logger.error("Error retrieving business partners", e);
    throw new ServletException(e);
  }

  response.setContentType("application/json");
  response.getWriter().write(jsonResult);
}
```

Listing 4.9 Skeleton for doGet for Retrieving All Business Partners or a Single Business Partner

Listing 4.10 shows how to use the VDM to fulfill the requirement for retrieving a single business partner we outlined earlier. This code goes to the else branch in Listing 4.9 ❷. Again, we'll use the business partner service representation of the VDM, but this time, we'll call the method representing the operation to retrieve a business partner by its key. This method expects the key of the business partner as the identifier and returns a specific fluent helper for the *get-business-partner-by-key* operation of the OData service. We'll pass the ID retrieved from the query parameter as its identifier. We won't apply any validation right now, for the sake of simplicity. Validating user inputs such as a query parameter is, however, a must before using a query in such a manner anywhere, to avoid the security threat of injection. You can implement the validation on your own using standard Java code.


```
BusinessPartner result = new DefaultBusinessPartnerService()
    .getBusinessPartnerByKey(id)
    .select(BusinessPartner.BUSINESS_PARTNER,
        BusinessPartner.LAST_NAME,
        BusinessPartner.FIRST_NAME,
        BusinessPartner.IS_MALE,
        BusinessPartner.IS_FEMALE,
        BusinessPartner.CREATION_DATE,
        BusinessPartner.TO_BUSINESS_PARTNER_ADDRESS.select(
            BusinessPartnerAddress.BUSINESS_PARTNER,
            BusinessPartnerAddress.ADDRESS_ID,
            BusinessPartnerAddress.COUNTRY,
            BusinessPartnerAddress.POSTAL_CODE,
            BusinessPartnerAddress.CITY_NAME,
            BusinessPartnerAddress.STREET_NAME,
            BusinessPartnerAddress.HOUSE_NUMBER
        ))
    .execute();
```

Listing 4.10 Call to VDM to Retrieve a Single Business Partner Including Addresses

The fluent query helper returned by the VDM again exposes the `select` query option, but not a `filter` or `orderBy` option, which are not supported and not needed for retrieval by key in OData. This time, the parameters to the `select` method are more sophisticated, compared to Section 4.2.1, since we not only want to retrieve more parameters, but also associated addresses.

OData allows us to model associations via *navigation properties*, which are special properties of an entity type that represent the associated entities. To retrieve associated entities via navigation properties, OData has the notion of an `expand` query option. The VDM supports this expand query option and incorporates it into the `select` method to allow you to define all the properties to be retrieved in a single place, independent of whether they are defined on the main entity, the navigation properties, or the properties of entities reached via navigation properties. Similar to other properties, we'll use the Java representation of the navigation property for business partner addresses, to specify that it shall be retrieved as part of the query, which implicitly means that `expand` will be used by the query. If we don't specify anything further, all the properties of the associated address entities would be retrieved. The Java representation of a navigation property, such as the addresses of a business partner, provides a nested `select` method, to which we can then supply the properties of the associated entities, if we want to retrieve only a subset of properties. In this case, we'll retrieve the most relevant properties of the addresses that we need, including the identifiers of the business partner as well as the address, which together form the composite key necessary for later operations on the entity.

With these steps, we've defined our API to retrieve business partners. Now, rebuild the application and run it locally, as described in Section 4.2.2. When you launch the URL *http://localhost:8080/api/business-partners*, you'll still see the list of all business partners. Note down the identifier (property `BusinessPartner`) from any business partner and open *http://localhost:8080/api/business-partners?id=<identifier>* in your browser, replacing *<identifier>* with the corresponding value. You should see a result similar to Figure 4.4. If your chosen business partner does not have an address, the corresponding property has an empty array as its value.

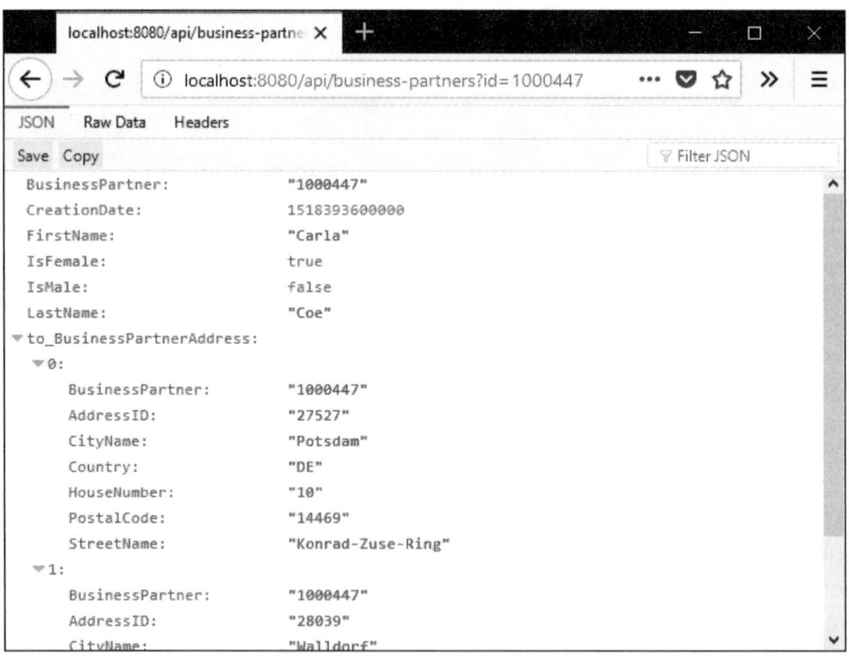

Figure 4.4 Result when Retrieving a Single Business Partner

With the API to retrieve a list of all business partners and to retrieve details on a specific business partner completed, we have everything in place for our first version of the frontend, which we'll integrate next.

4.3 Integrating the Frontend

Based on the API we've implemented so far, our first version of the frontend should display the list of business partners, allow the user to select one, and display detailed information about that business partner. Support for editing addresses will be available once we implement the corresponding API in Section 4.5.

Since this book is about implementing side-by-side extensions that integrate with SAP S/4HANA in a Java backend, developing a user interface is not our primary focus, so we won't build the UI ourselves in the following section but instead use an implementation which we'll provide in the GitHub repository for this book. Chapter 14 provides a brief introduction on building custom SAP Fiori UIs for side-by-side extensions and will explain how the provided UI is built up.

To integrate the user interface for our Business Partner Address Manager application, download the frontend from the GitHub repository for this book. The frontend application is provided as an archive that contains the full application based on SAPUI5.

In our first iteration, we'll host the HTML-based user interface as part of the Java web application. Other options are explored in Chapter 14. As explained earlier in Section 4.1.4, any content in the *webapp* folder within *application/src/main* will be hosted by the application server as static content. Thus, to integrate the downloaded frontend application, extract its archive and place its files into a folder called *address-manager* within the *webapp* folder.

If you now rebuild the application and run the local server, the frontend can be found at *http://localhost:8080/address-manager*. Launch the URL in your browser to see the application, as shown in Figure 4.5. If you study the source code or observe the network traffic using your browser's developer tools, you'll see the calls to our previously implemented API, still available at */api/business-partners* as before.

You can see the list of business partners, search for a specific person, change the sort criterion, select a specific person, and view his or her details. Actions to modify the data will not work yet.

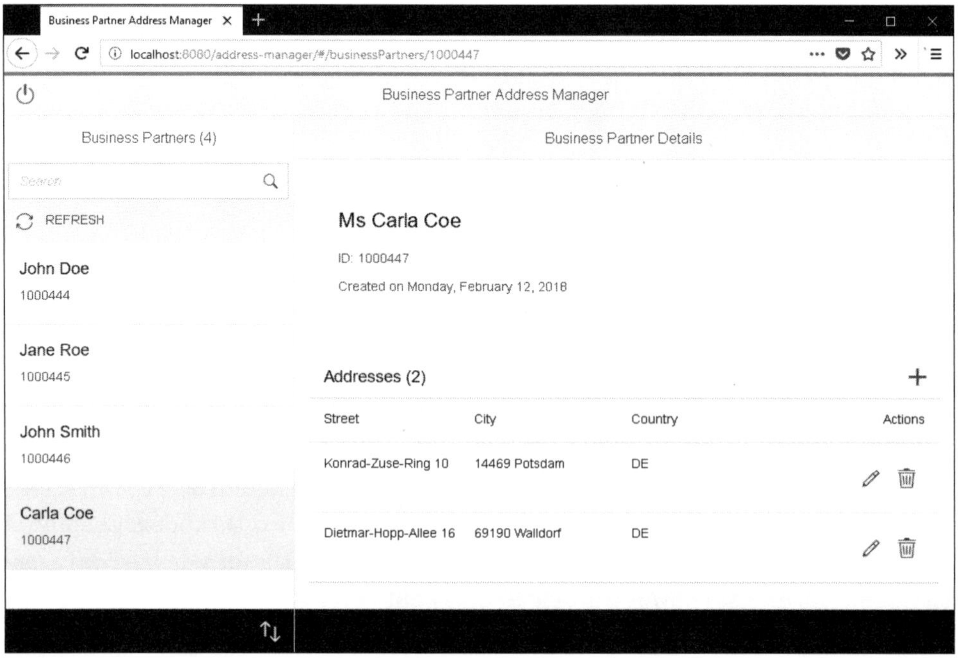

Figure 4.5 Business Partner Address Manager

4.4 Deploying the Application to Cloud Foundry

So far, we've only run the application locally. Of course, our goal is to build a side-by-side extension on SAP Cloud Platform that also uses the rich set of services offered by SAP Cloud Platform. Now that we have the first SAP S/4HANA integration implemented and a partly working frontend, let's deploy our application to the Cloud Foundry environment of the SAP Cloud Platform. You need to fulfill two prerequisites before proceeding:

- You'll need at least a trial account in the Cloud Foundry environment of SAP Cloud Platform. Refer to the Preface on how to get a trial account.
- You'll need to have installed the Cloud Foundry command line interface, as described in Section 4.1.1.

Once you've fulfilled both prerequisites, proceed to deploy the application as implemented so far. If you prefer to continue with the local server first, you can also skip this section and return later to deploy your application to Cloud Foundry.

To deploy your application, you'll need to log in to your Cloud Foundry account at SAP Cloud Platform. Open a command line interface and execute the following commands:

```
cf api https://api.cf.eu10.hana.ondemand.com
cf login
```

Replace the URL in the first line with the API endpoint of your SAP Cloud Platform Cloud Foundry account, visible on the subaccount page in the SAP Cloud Platform cockpit, if it's different from the one in the example. The second command will ask you for the credentials of your SAP Cloud Platform account and possibly prompt you to select an organization and a space to connect to in the Cloud Foundry environment. For more details on subaccounts, orgs, and spaces, refer to Chapter 3.

All the following commands with the Cloud Foundry CLI will target this space. To finally deploy the application, we'll need to upload our packaged Java web application to Cloud Foundry. To do this, we'll navigate to the top-level folder of our project, make sure that the latest state has been build, and push it to the connected Cloud Foundry space, using the following commands:

```
cd path/to/address-manager
mvn clean package
cf push
```

The last command looks for a manifest.yml deployment descriptor in the current folder and creates an application in the connected Cloud Foundry space according to the configuration of the deployment descriptor. We'll examine the descriptor later in this section, but first let's open our app running on Cloud Foundry. Once the `cf push` command has finished, it will—as part of its longer output—print the URL where the application can be reached, similar to the output line beginning with `urls:` shown in Figure 4.6. As we're using a random route for now, the URL will be different for everyone, but should look similar to *address-manager-unsparse-subutopian.cfapps.eu10.hana.ondemand.com*. Type this URL into your browser. You should see the welcome page for the SAP S/4HANA Cloud SDK.

The business partner API will not work yet, because we have not yet defined the destination where the SAP S/4HANA system can be reached. We can use the same approach with the `destinations` environment variable as we did locally (Chapter 6). In this case, we'll need to set the variable for the application running on Cloud Foundry. The CLI provides a corresponding command. Use the same value for the environment variable as you did locally. We assume that your SAP S/4HANA system or the dummy

OData service used so far is publicly accessible. Run the following two commands in sequence:

```
cf set-env address-manager destinations '[{name: ↩
"ErpQueryEndpoint", url: "https://URL", username: "USER", ↩
password: "PASSWORD"}]'

cf restart address-manager
```

The second command restarts the application to ensure that it has access to the newly defined environment variable. Whenever you change the variable, you'll need to restart the application.

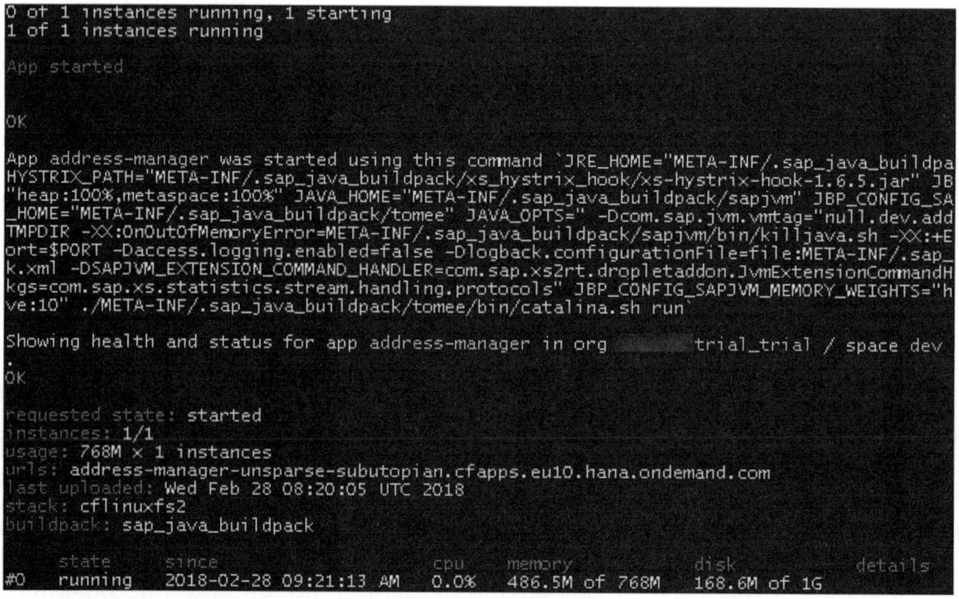

Figure 4.6 Output of the Deployment to Cloud Foundry

Now, you can access our Business Partner Address Manager application at the URL of our Cloud Foundry application by appending the path */address-manager* to the random URL.

How does Cloud Foundry know how to run the application, based on the simple `cf push` command? The CLI inspects the file manifest.yml that was created by the archetype when we generated the project. Listing 4.11 shows the content of this so-called *Cloud Foundry deployment descriptor*, written in the YAML markup language. (You can find more information about the YAML syntax at *yaml.org*.) Most importantly, the deployment descriptor specifies the type of the application by defining the Cloud Foundry buildpack to use for deploying the application, in our case, the Java buildpack provided by SAP. The `path` property contains the path to the Web Application Archive (.war file) to use, which has been created by Maven during `mvn clean package`. A few additional properties of the descriptor define the name of the application, determine how much memory to allocate, and specify that the app will be hosted at a random route.


```
---
applications:

- name: address-manager
  memory: 768M
  random-route: true
  path: application/target/address-manager-application.war
  buildpack: sap_java_buildpack
  env:
    TARGET_RUNTIME: tomee
    JBP_CONFIG_SAPJVM_MEMORY_SIZES: 'metaspace:96m..'
```

Listing 4.11 Content of manifest.yml Deployment Descriptor

We'll explore and use the different options of the Cloud Foundry manifest file throughout this book. For now, let's turn to implementing the remaining features in our backend.

4.5 Writing Business Partner Addresses to SAP S/4HANA

In this section, we'll implement the modifying operations, that is, the ability to create, update, and delete business partner address information in the SAP S/4HANA system. Thus, we'll implement the missing endpoints accessed by the frontend for the address management options. All three operations will be developed in a separate `AddressServlet` and will be reachable at the base path */api/addresses*.

Thus, the skeleton of the servlet should look like Listing 4.12, which we'll expand over the course of the following sections on create, update, and delete capabilities.

```
@WebServlet("/api/addresses")
public class AddressServlet extends HttpServlet {
  private static final Logger logger = CloudLoggerFactory
```

```
      .getLogger(AddressServlet.class);
  // implementation of operations goes here
}
```

Listing 4.12 Skeleton of AddressServlet

As before, we want to focus on implementing the actual functionality of integrating with SAP S/4HANA, this time for modifying operations using the VDM. Thus, we'll defer advanced cloud qualities, such as resilience, to Section 4.6 and fully-fledged error handling to your own study. You can also refer to the GitHub repository for this book, which contains the full source code of our example application, including error handling features. Other important concepts are described in separate chapters such as Chapter 9 on testing or Chapter 8 on designing a REST API.

4.5.1 Creating Addresses

In a RESTful API, creating an entity happens via an HTTP POST request to the endpoint representing the collection to which the entity shall be added. In our case, that endpoint is the list of addresses. Thus, we expect consumers of our API, for example, the frontend, to send a POST request to */api/addresses* with the address to create, in JSON format, in the body of the request. Our implementation shall transfer the body into the address to be created, call the SAP S/4HANA system to create the address there, and respond with a success code. The response shall also contain the just created address in the body, including the identifier and any other fields assigned by SAP S/4HANA when creating the entity.

The actual call to SAP S/4HANA will again be made using the VDM of the SAP S/4HANA Cloud SDK. As already mentioned, this Java representation of the SAP S/4HANA API includes methods for modifying operations in addition to the read operations we used in Section 4.2. As earlier, we'll need an implementation of the service that offers a method to create an address of a business partner. We'll need to supply the address to create as an object of the VDM entity type BusinessPartnerAddress. Assuming this object is stored in the variable addressToCreate, the complete code necessary to execute the call to SAP S/4HANA looks like Listing 4.13.

```
addressCreated = new DefaultBusinessPartnerService()
  .createBusinessPartnerAddress(addressToCreate)
  .execute();
```

Listing 4.13 Using the VDM to Create a Business Partner

As with reading operations, the VDM takes care of all infrastructure code and lets us focus on the business logic at hand: creating an address. The call to execute connects to the SAP S/4HANA API to create the new address and to associate it with the business partner mentioned in the address. The call returns the created entity parsed from the response of SAP S/4HANA, including the new address identifier.

The only major thing missing is constructing the object that represents the address to create from the JSON-formatted body of the request. The SAP S/4HANA Cloud SDK enables different approaches to constructing the entity that will eventually be sent to SAP S/4HANA. We could use the builder for addresses and construct the entity in a fluent manner, after extracting the property values for the address from the request body. For example, if the identifier of the business partner of the new address is stored in a String variable `businessPartner` and the country in a String variable `country`, the call in Listing 4.14 creates an address entity that we could supply to the `create` method shown in Listing 4.13.

```
final BusinessPartnerAddress addressToCreate =
    BusinessPartnerAddress.builder()
        .businessPartner(businessPartner)
        .country(country)
        // further properties
        .build();
```

Listing 4.14 Creating a Business Partner Address Entity using the Builder Pattern in the VDM

A second approach, which we'll use here, leverages the fact that VDM entity types can, out of the box, be serialized to and deserialized from their JSON representation. That is, an object of type `BusinessPartnerAddress` can be transformed into JSON, as we have seen before when reading business partners, and can also be created out of a similar JSON representation, as shown in Listing 4.15.

```
{
    "BusinessPartner": "1000000",
    "Country": "DE",
    ...
}
```

Listing 4.15 JSON Representation of a Business Partner Address as Used by the VDM

In our simple case, we can follow this approach because we don't need to transform the object sent by our API consumer yet. We simply need the frontend to supply the address to be created in the expected format. We'll define a method that gets the address VDM entity from the request body. This method will first transform the input stream of the request that contains the request body into a String, which we'll then supply to a JSON deserializer to create a Java object of the expected type. To this end, we'll specify the BusinessPartnerAddress entity type as the target class. Listing 4.16 display the entire method to be part of the AddressServlet, which should be expanded with input validation checks as appropriate.

```
private BusinessPartnerAddress getAddressFromBody(
    final HttpServletRequest req)
    throws IOException {
  final String body = CharStreams.toString(
      new InputStreamReader(req.getInputStream(),
          Charsets.UTF_8));
  return new Gson().fromJson(body,
      BusinessPartnerAddress.class);
}
```

Listing 4.16 Method for Deserializing Request Body to VDM Entity

Now, we have everything in place to implement the doPost method of the servlet, which is similar to the doGet method we discussed in Section 4.2, but handles request done with the HTTP method POST. Listing 4.17 contains the complete source code that implements the creation of addresses.

```
@Override
protected void doPost(final HttpServletRequest request,
                      final HttpServletResponse response)
    throws ServletException, IOException {
  final BusinessPartnerAddress addressToCreate =
      getAddressFromBody(request);

  final BusinessPartnerAddress addressCreated;
  try {
    addressCreated = new DefaultBusinessPartnerService()
        .createBusinessPartnerAddress(addressToCreate)
        .execute();
  } catch (ODataException e) {
    logger.error("Error creating address", e);
```

```
      throw new ServletException(e);
    }

    response.setStatus(HttpServletResponse.SC_CREATED);
    response.setContentType("application/json");
    response.getWriter().write(
        new Gson().toJson(addressCreated));
}
```

Listing 4.17 Complete Implementation of Creating Addresses

You may now rebuild and redeploy the application locally or on Cloud Foundry as described earlier to test the create functionality. In the frontend, click the **+** icon next to the table of addresses, which will open the popup window shown in Figure 4.7, into which you'll enter the details of the address. When you click **Submit**, the frontend will issue a call to our just implemented backend, supplying the address in the body.

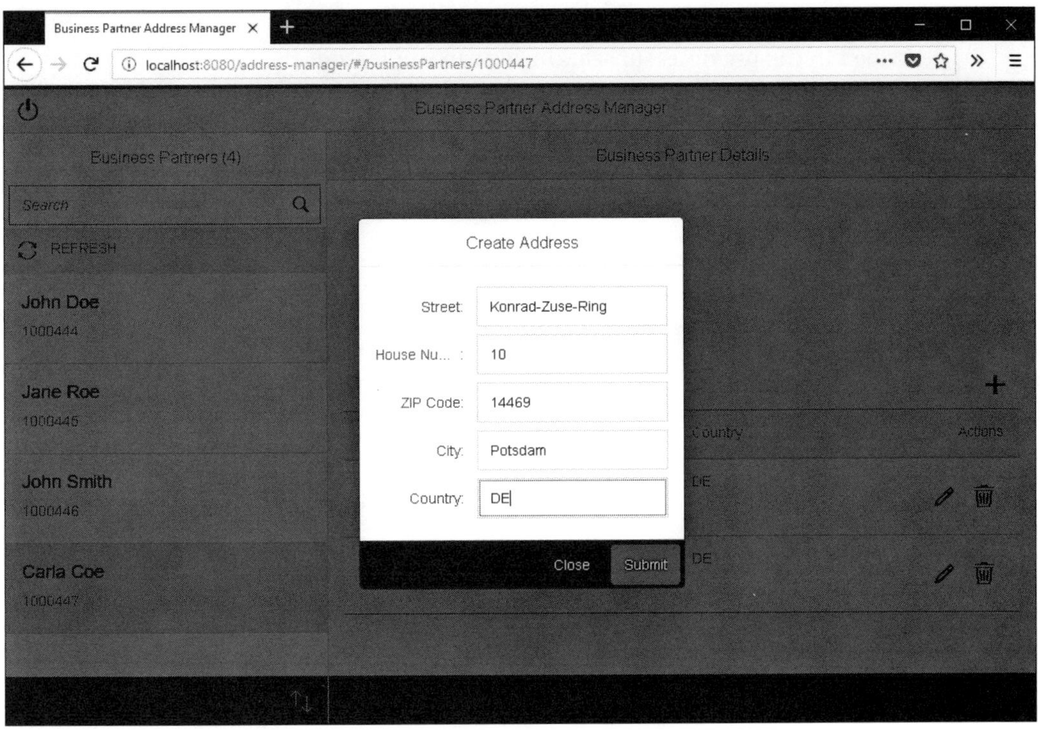

Figure 4.7 Create Dialog

4.5.2 Deleting Addresses

The next operation on our list to implement is the deletion of addresses, for which the appropriate HTTP method is delete. For this operation, the backend needs to know the composite key of the address to delete, which is made up of the business partner and the address identifier. Following a RESTful style, we expect those details to be part of the URL, for simplicity, as query parameters. Thus, a delete request to */api/addresses?businessPartnerId=10&addressId=1* will delete the address with ID 1 of business partner 10. We can retrieve the values of those query parameters from the request object using the getParameter method, for example:

```
final String businessPartnerId =
    request.getParameter("businessPartnerId");
```

The business partner service of the VDM provides a method for deleting addresses, which like all delete methods expects an object representing the entity to delete. The object needs to be of the VDM entity type to be deleted. Only the key fields of that entity need to be filled. With this knowledge and by making use of the builder described in the previous subsection, we can implement the deletion of the address in SAP S/4HANA as described in Listing 4.18. First, we'll create the address to delete as a Java object of the BusinessPartnerAddress entity type. Then, we'll supply this object to the delete method and execute the call. In this case, the return value is not relevant.

```
final BusinessPartnerAddress addressToDelete =
    BusinessPartnerAddress.builder()
        .businessPartner(businessPartnerId)
        .addressID(addressId)
        .build();

new DefaultBusinessPartnerService()
    .deleteBusinessPartnerAddress(addressToDelete)
    .execute();
```

Listing 4.18 Source Code to Delete Address in SAP S/4HANA

Based on the previous sections, you should be able to complete the implementation of the method for deleting addresses: retrieve the identifiers from the query string, use the VDM as described earlier to delete the entity, introduce the usual try-catch block, and finally return an empty response with status code "NO_CONTENT". To get started quickly, use the skeleton provided in Listing 4.19.

```
@Override
protected void doDelete(final HttpServletRequest request,
                        final HttpServletResponse response)
    throws ServletException, IOException {

  // your implementation goes here

  response.setStatus(HttpServletResponse.SC_NO_CONTENT);
}
```

Listing 4.19 Skeleton for Implementing the Delete Operation

With the delete operation in place, you can now use the frontend to delete addresses, after rebuilding and redeploying the application. The final missing basic feature is the editing of addresses.

4.5.3 Updating Addresses

Updating an existing entity in a RESTful API can occur in two slightly different ways:

- You can use the standard PUT method of HTTP. The semantics of this method require you send the complete entity with all properties as part of the request. The entity of the request then overwrites the existing entity.
- At times, sending the complete entity is not appropriate or is too cumbersome. Instead, you only want to send a subset of the properties of the entity, or, more specifically, only the changed properties. An extension of the HTTP standard introduces the PATCH method for partial modifications (*https://tools.ietf.org/html/rfc5789*).

For our purposes, the PATCH method is more appropriate because we're always dealing with a subset of address properties anyway. The selected fields of the address represent only an excerpt of all properties available in SAP S/4HANA. The body of the PATCH request will again contain a JSON representation of the entity. Only the fields available to the frontend will be supplied. For the sake of simplicity and because the entity is small, the frontend sends both updated and unmodified fields. According to REST conventions, the path of the request shall specify the identifier of the entity to be updated, similar to the delete operation created in the previous section.

In our backend entity, we'll need to transform the JSON request body to a VDM entity. Then we'll create a second VDM entity for the address that we'll use to maintain the changed property values, so that we are only sending those to SAP S/4HANA. You will create a new address object using the builder and supply the corresponding identifiers from the query parameters. Afterwards, you can set the values of the changed properties. Then you'll provide this entity to the VDM method for updating business partner addresses.

We've seen how to retrieve a VDM entity from a JSON body when we created an address in Section 4.5.1, and in Section 4.5.2, we explained how to retrieve identifiers from query parameters using the example of deleting addresses. With this combined prior work, you should be able to implement the update operation yourself. To set the property values on an existing entity, use the set methods available for all properties of entity types.

Put your implementation into a method called `doPatch` with the usual signature with request and response parameters. Because the `PATCH` method is a later addition to the HTTP standard, this method is not yet included in the Java servlet specification. As a result, the standard HTTP servlet does not handle `PATCH` requests and does not contain a `doPatch` method for us to override. However, a simple remedy is to put the extended `HttpServlet` class, which we provide in the GitHub repository for the book, into the package `com.sap.cloud.s4hana.examples.addressmgr.util` and have the `AddressServlet` extend that `HttpServlet` instead of the `HttpServlet` from package `javax.servlet.http`. This custom extended `HttpServlet` supports the `PATCH` method.

After you've implemented the update operation, the basic functionality of our backend is complete. For reference, you can always compare your implementation with the source code in the GitHub repository for this book. All features of the web application should now work after you rebuild and redeploy the application. Nevertheless, we can still improve several nonfunctional aspects of our application and make the source code more robust, which we'll discuss in the remaining section of this chapter.

4.6 Engineering with Cloud Qualities

In the previous sections of this chapter, we implemented the basic functional requirements of our Business Partner Address Manager application. We focused on functional integration with SAP S/4HANA using the VDM and experienced how the SAP S/4HANA Cloud SDK makes the integration easy. Another important topic for any cloud-native application is engineering for cloud qualities that positively impact the stability of the system. In this section, we'll take a closer look at selected cloud qualities to increase the stability of our application beyond the straightforward paths we've considered so far. More qualities of cloud-native applications will be considered throughout this book, for example, multitenancy in Chapter 7 or continuous delivery in Chapters 10 and 11.

We'll use the SAP S/4HANA Cloud SDK to integrate cloud qualities into our application. Let's take an in-depth look at the concepts of designing stable systems next (see also Chapter 3).

4.6.1 Designing for Stability

Implementing an application that conforms to the essential functional requirements is easy, especially when using frameworks such as the SAP S/4HANA Cloud SDK to do a lot of the heavy lifting for you. This statement may sound provocative and is certainly oversimplifying. However, writing source code that, in a controlled environment, fulfills the specification described in a test suite for straightforward functional requirements (such as creating an address in SAP S/4HANA) is easy compared to the task of making the application stable in a production environment with adverse conditions everywhere. Significant additional effort is required to design applications that keep running and also allow users to efficiently fulfill their tasks regardless of real-world setbacks. For example, a productively running distributed system needs to be resilient in the face of failing network calls, unavailable remote systems, traffic spikes, slow responses, and much more.

For a cloud application, stability is measured as the availability of the system. While different definitions of availability exist, often for the contractual purposes of service level agreements (SLAs), all definitions boil down to the ratio a system is available to serve its purpose. Availability also requires acceptable response times. Whole books deal with the topic of building stable systems. We can only provide a glimpse of the reasons for the following improvements and otherwise refer you to the literature for more details, in particular M. T. Nygard's *Release It!*. In particular, we'll consider the case of stability in distributed, multitenant productive systems.

What's different in production than during development or even in testing environments? One difference is the time that an application is up and running. Usually, a test environment will only stay on for a limited period of testing and be discarded afterwards. Each new commit will require a new deployment and test to be run. In contrast, productive applications will keep running between at least two deployments. While with continuous deployment the time span may be small, this duration is still longer than a usual test cycle and handles more requests. Thus, in production, certain kinds of issues can create more and unique problems, compared to a test environment, also called *longevity bugs* (M. T. Nygard, *Release It!*, p. 26):

- **Long-running requests**
  Tests are designed to run quickly to give immediate feedback. Many tests will only simulate downstream dependencies with mocking. In contrast, productive calls will always hit the actual downstream system and thus be exposed to much higher variability in response times.
- **Memory leaks**
  If not carefully designed, certain requests may lead to a long-lasting or even permanent increase in memory consumption, for example, when unsuccessful request are not cleaned up properly.
- **Thread exhaustion**
  Asynchronous calls to downstream systems or resources will most often be executed in separate Java threads, and each HTTP request will also need a thread for execution. Thread pools are limited, and if threads keep running for a long time, no threads may be left to serve new requests. This bottleneck can occur if requests are made without a timeout setting and take a long amount of time.
- **Failures of dependencies**
  In production, applications interact with real, productive downstream services, systems, or resources. The distributed systems we deal with in this book will have a large network of dependencies. Outside the controlled test environment, those downstream dependencies out of our control may be unavailable, unreachable, or unstable themselves at times.

All of these scenarios, especially the network of dependencies, are multiplied when looking at multitenant applications: Each customer (tenant) of our app will bring his own set of downstream SAP S/4HANA systems to connect to, which may be residing in different networks, for example, on-premise at customers. The SAP S/4HANA Cloud SDK explicitly considers these cases and helps us write code to deal with such issues, as we'll discuss in the following subsections.

You can, and we recommend you to, expand the test suite to also cover such situations, but you'll have to consider the cost-benefit trade-off. In any case, the application needs to be designed to handle such threats to stability gracefully, which requires a mindset that accepts failures will happen when calling dependencies and accepts that effort is required to handle them, even if a significant portion of an application's code deals with handling failures. When building an application, on each step, you must actively consider what happens when something goes wrong, whether an error caused by the user or his configuration, for example, results in a bad request to create an address for a nonexistent business partner or the user lacks the authorization to modify addresses. You might encounter a system failure such as network outages in a customer's on-premise network that hosts the SAP S/4HANA system connected to your application, system downtimes of another customer's system, or performance issues because of high loads on a third customer's database.

Handling such situations means keeping the overall system running; that is, not allowing the original trigger cause issues in other layers of your application. Your front-end application should keep running if you temporarily lose connection to a database; the application should work for other customers if one customer's SAP S/4HANA system is not reachable; a user should be able to complete his work if his colleague keeps making erroneous requests at high volumes. In addition to dealing with stability in our code, as discussed earlier in this section, we also need to actively monitor our application as part of our operations, described in more detail in Chapter 13.

What forces can make our or similar applications unstable? These forces are sometimes called *anti-patterns* (M. T. Nygard, *Release It!*, Chapter 4) and are threats to stability, which we can summarize as follows:

- **Integration points**
  Any sophisticated application will integrate with other dependencies, and failures are inevitable when dealing with integration points such as SAP S/4HANA. Even if up and running, your system could still be unreachable because of a network issue. Thus, we need to prepare for those failures, which may come in many different forms, such as network issues or bad requests. The root causes of problems at integration points may also be hidden under several layers of abstractions.
- **Cascading failures**
  Integration often spans several layers, particularly in a microservice architecture. Without proper countermeasures, a failure in one layer may propagate up the chain. As integration points are bound to fail eventually, we must ensure that our application keeps running even during failures and degrades gracefully so that the failure does not cascade to applications that depend on others.
- **Users**
  Users are the necessary evil of any application: Serving users is the purpose of the application, but the application would be more stable if no user ever accessed it. But an unused application is certainly not what we want, so we need to prepare for many users appearing all at once, for users doing adverse actions at exactly the worst possible moments, and for irresponsible or outright malicious users.

- **Blocked threads**
  In modern managed programming languages such as Java, a crash of the whole application is seldom the cause of failures. Instead, more commonly, threads still run but are blocked, in other words, not doing any actual work. If you don't carefully manage resources and apply timeouts, a chain reaction can occur where, for example, all threads that could do meaningful work are instead waiting for something that will never happen because an integration point failed.
- **Slow response**
  The response of integrated systems may be slow for a number of reasons, perhaps insufficient hardware, a sudden increase in resource consumption, or network issues. Slow response may eventually trigger cascading failures if timeouts are exceeded. Waiting forever is definitely not an option, either; often, failing fast is preferable to a slow response because failing fast frees up resources.
- **SLA inversions**
  When committing to a certain SLA, such as a 99.99% uptime, you'll need to consider the SLAs of your dependencies. If you depend on a system that guarantees only 99.5% uptime, you cannot promise a higher SLA yourself, unless you apply measures for your application to continue working without the dependency. As you'll have multiple dependencies, the probability of failure is the combined probability of failure of all systems you depend on.
- **Unbounded result sets**
  Test systems will usually have a small dataset to ensure fast response. In production, the results of external calls may be orders of magnitude larger. Forgetting to apply limits to queries is all too easy when developing against small datasets (in fact, we have not used the top and skip options of OData ourselves so far when querying SAP S/4HANA, so now may be a good time to learn about these options on your own: *http://tiny.cc/odatatopskipcount*).

This list demonstrates why we need to implement resilience measures against threats to the stability of our application. In the next subsection, we'll look at certain patterns to help deal with these threats and discuss how the SAP S/4HANA Cloud SDK supports applying these patterns in our applications, using our ongoing example application.

4.6.2 Implementing Resilience

Several design patterns can be used to build stable systems in the face of unreliable dependencies. These patterns include the following stability patterns (M. T. Nygard,

Release It!, Chapter 5) that we'll employ, along with their corresponding features in the SAP S/4HANA Cloud SDK:

- **Timeouts**
  Each request to a resource should have a timeout that causes the request to fail once the specified time has passed without response. Otherwise, requests may wait forever for any number of (unexpected) reasons. Consistently applying timeouts helps deal with the threats to stability at integration points, such as blocked threads and slow response. By explicitly expecting a timeout to occur, we also avoid some potential causes for cascading failures, if timeouts are handled properly. The underlying rationale for timeouts is that they free up resources and signal to callers that something is wrong, instead of silently ignoring the problem, which will cause the problem to spread throughout the system.
- **Bulkheads**
  The term *bulkhead* comes from shipbuilding, where spaces seal separate watertight compartments to prevent a leak from spreading across compartments and sinking the whole ship. In software engineering, a bulkhead refers to a way of partitioning resources to ensure that parts of the functionality of the system stay available if some other part goes down. Separate integration points should use separate resources, such as thread pools, so that one failing integration point does not drain the available resources for other integration points. In multitenant applications, each customer's SAP S/4HANA system can be seen as a separate integration point: We don't want our application to stop working for all our customers just because our application cannot connect to the SAP S/4HANA system of one specific customer, who for example may be having problems with his on-premise network.
- **Circuit breakers**
  After, say, five successive attempts to reach a resource such as a specific customer's SAP S/4HANA have failed, common sense dictates we should give the integration point time to recover instead of flooding the network or system with further requests likely doomed to fail. The circuit-breaker pattern, an analogy drawn from electrical wiring, helps achieve such a behavior. By default, a circuit breaker is closed, allowing requests to the integration point to execute normally. In this state, the circuit breaker monitors, via different possible metrics, whether the integration operates normally, for example, by measuring the number of successive failures or the ratio of failures in a certain time slot. If some threshold is reached, the circuit breaker *trips* open. In the open state, the circuit breaker will

not pass a request through, but instead the request fails directly. After a specified time has passed, allowing the integration point to recover, the circuit breaker will become half-open and allow the next request to pass through to test if the integration point is working properly again. If the request succeeds, the circuit breaker becomes closed and operates normally, until the next issue. If the request fails, the circuit breaker will trip open, reset the timeout, and continue to reject requests. A circuit breaker protects against cascading failures and saves capacity at the calling system, while avoiding an overload of the called system under trouble by not sending more and more requests.

These patterns represent a subset of ways to increase stability or, put differently, to increase the resilience of a system against failures. These patterns are most effective when combined and used consistently. Implementing these patterns from scratch can be a daunting task that not only requires significant effort, but also the highest quality, as these patterns will run at the core of our system. Luckily, there are well-tested open-source libraries available for these tasks.

For example, Netflix created the Hystrix library to run its distributed microservice-based video streaming service (*http://tiny.cc/hystrix*). Hystrix implements several of the patterns we suggested for building resilient, stable systems. The SAP S/4HANA Cloud SDK provides an integration of Hystrix into SAP Cloud Platform with its multitenancy and user concept and also provides easy-to-use ways for implementing resilient calls to SAP S/4HANA, with the optional added benefit of caching.

In Section 4.2 and Section 4.5, we called the SAP S/4HANA system directly, without any consideration to resilience. The call to SAP S/4HANA will use any arbitrary timeout defined by the underlying library, and a single customer network that cannot be reached may bring down the application for all users. So, let's now adapt our application to make those calls resilient by specifying explicit timeouts, isolating the different types of requests, and leveraging tenant-aware circuit breakers.

The SAP S/4HANA Cloud SDK provides the abstract class `ErpCommand` that we can use to wrap our calls to SAP S/4HANA or any other potentially risky operation. We'll create one command per operation that interacts with SAP S/4HANA. In other words, we'll create two commands for reading business partners and three for writing addresses. The basic structure of such a command looks like Listing 4.20, using as example the command to retrieve the list of business partners.

```
public class GetAllBusinessPartnersCommand
    extends ErpCommand<List<BusinessPartner>> {
  public GetAllBusinessPartnersCommand() {
```

```
    super(GetAllBusinessPartnersCommand.class);
  }

  @Override
  protected List<BusinessPartner> run()
      throws Exception {
    return new DefaultBusinessPartnerService()
        .getAllBusinessPartner()
        // select, filter, etc as before
        .execute();
  }
}
```

Listing 4.20 Basic Structure of a Hystrix Command with the SAP S/4HANA Cloud SDK

The command extends the `ErpCommand` and specifies the type of its return value as a generic parameter, in this case, a list of business partners. A default constructor calls the constructor of the superclass with this class as the command type used to isolate different commands according to the bulkhead pattern. The command class needs to implement the `run` method, which returns an object of the specified type. We already know the logic to retrieve the business partners from Section 4.2.1. Now, we'll simply move the VDM call into the `run` method of our command and exchange the call to the VDM in the `BusinessPartnerServlet` with creating a new instance of our command and calling `execute` on this instance as follows: `new GetAllBusinessPartnersCommand().execute()`.

This code will execute the logic defined in the `run` method in a resilient manner using a Hystrix command. The command will, by default, use a circuit breaker per user or tenant, a sensible default value for timeouts, and isolated thread pools for different commands. These recommended default parameters for the specific use cases of multitenant applications on SAP Cloud Platform are automatically applied whenever you use any of the command classes provided by the SAP S/4HANA Cloud SDK, such as `Command`, `ErpCommand`, or `CachingCommand`. You can modify or augment the default commands by supplying them explicitly to the superclass constructor during the initialization of your command. For example, you can specify your own value of 10 seconds for timeouts through the code in Listing 4.21.

```
public GetAllBusinessPartnersCommand() {
  super(HystrixUtil
      .getDefaultErpCommandSetter(
          GetAllBusinessPartnersCommand.class,
```

```
            HystrixUtil.getDefaultErpCommandProperties()
                .withExecutionTimeoutInMilliseconds(10000)));
}
```

Listing 4.21 Supplying a Specific Timeout Value to Commands

With the potentially failing call to SAP S/4HANA wrapped in a command, we've improved the resilience of our application. The productive application will not be bogged down by individual, unreachable SAP S/4HANA systems after we have wrapped the remaining operations in commands as well. If the same call fails repeatedly, a circuit breaker will trip open. Hystrix ensures that, during a cooling off period, no additional attempts are made that may overload the dependency further, in favor of failing fast. This circuit breaker helps with several of the forces threatening stability, most importantly, slow responses and blocked threads. Of course, our application will still show an error if anything goes wrong during the call to SAP S/4HANA or if the circuit breaker is open. In some cases, nothing can be done about that—after all, the integration to SAP S/4HANA is one of the major features of our application. Nevertheless, we can do more, for example, caching previous responses (Section 4.6.4) or setting up fallbacks in case of errors.

These fallbacks, once designed, can be implemented into the commands quite easily. Fallbacks can potentially be quite elaborate; for example, we could store addresses to be created in a queue while SAP S/4HANA is not available and retry them later. For the sake of demonstration, we'll implement a simple fallback for our command that retrieves the list of business partners: If anything goes wrong while calling SAP S/4HANA, we'll simply return an empty list that is then displayed on the frontend. All we need to do is implement the method `getFallback` in our command class, as shown in Listing 4.22.

```
@Override
protected List<BusinessPartner> getFallback() {
  logger.warn("Fallback called because of exception:",
      getExecutionException());
  return Collections.emptyList();
}
```

Listing 4.22 Fallback Method for GetAllBusinessPartnersCommand

The method has the same signature as the `run` method, but simply returns an empty list, without making any potentially failing external calls. Hystrix will attempt to execute the actual command logic and resort to the fallback if the actual call fails or the circuit breaker is open. A good practice is to log the original exception (create a logger, as discussed in Section 4.2), which will help you investigate the causes of errors, in addition to the metrics that Hystrix collects automatically.

With this information, you can implement your first resilient command with a fallback and call it from the servlet, replacing the previous direct call to SAP S/4HANA. Before you redeploy the application locally or on Cloud Foundry, you be sure to set the environment variable `ALLOW_MOCKED_AUTH_HEADER` to `true`, using commands such as in Listing 4.23 for local and Cloud Foundry deployment, respectively.


```
set ALLOW_MOCKED_AUTH_HEADER=true
cf set-env address-manager ALLOW_MOCKED_AUTH_HEADER true
```

Listing 4.23 Setting the Environment Variable ALLOW_MOCKED_AUTH_HEADER Locally and on Cloud Foundry

ALLOW_MOCKED_AUTH_HEADER Explained

As mentioned earlier, the SAP S/4HANA Cloud SDK integrates the fault tolerance offered by the Hystrix library with SAP Cloud Platform, in particular, the tenant and user information, among other things. As we don't have a complete multitenant setup including security yet (we will set one up in Chapter 5), we'll need to mock the setup using this environment variable inspected by the SDK.

This variable is only a temporary workaround until we secure our application in Chapter 6. This setting is inherently unsecure and must not be used in production. Remove the environment variable from your Cloud Foundry application when you have the full setup in place with the code:

```
cf unset-env firstapp ALLOW_MOCKED_AUTH_HEADER
```

When you launch the application afterwards, you shouldn't notice any differences at first glance. Under the hood, however, our application just got more fault-tolerant. However, we still have four other operations that directly call SAP S/4HANA. We'll deal with those in the next section.

Asynchronous Execution of Commands

Another nice side effect of using commands is the ability to run any command asynchronously. Simply call the `queue` method of the command instead of `execute`, as shown in Listing 4.24. The `queue` method will return a so-called Future and schedule the execution of the command in an asynchronous task. Your code can run other tasks, if any, and later use this object to retrieve the results of the task. Similarly, Hystrix supports reactive programming via observe (see Chapter 16 for more details on reactive programming and Chapter 17 for the integration via Hystrix).

```
Future<List<BusinessPartner>> async =
    new GetAllBusinessPartnersCommand(service).queue();
// do other work
result = async.get(10, TimeUnit.SECONDS);
```

Listing 4.24 Using a Hystrix Command Asynchronously

4.6.3 Advanced Commands

Implementing the remaining operations in a resilient manner requires, in principle, the same steps we performed with the GetAllBusinessPartnersCommand:

1. Create a command that inherits from ErpCommand.
2. Move the previously implemented logic to the run method of the command.
3. Replace the direct call in the servlet with the command.

Now, we only have to pay attention to the fact that all of the other commands require additional parameters to run, such as the identifier of the business partner to retrieve in the GetSingleBusinessPartnerByIdCommand.

To make the identifier (or other parameters such as the entity to create) available to the command, simply add them as fields of the command class, which can, for example, be set via the constructor, as shown in Listing 4.25.

```
public class GetSingleBusinessPartnerByIdCommand
    extends ErpCommand<BusinessPartner> {
  private final String id;

  public GetSingleBusinessPartnerByIdCommand(final String id){
    super(GetSingleBusinessPartnerByIdCommand.class);
    this.id = id;
  }

  // run method uses field "id"
}
```

Listing 4.25 Command with a Parameter

The modifying create, update, and delete operations should be put into a command as well. Most likely, these operations do not have a proper fallback, but otherwise follow the same pattern as earlier.

With our command implementation so far, any exception raised while executing the `run` method will be considered a failure that triggers the fallback, if available, and will be counted into a metric that decides when to trip the circuit breaker. While this fallback is desired for all connectivity-related exceptions, a few exceptional cases may be the result of erroneous user input instead of connection issues to SAP S/4HANA. For example, the consumer of our API may have supplied a nonexistent identifier for the business partner, which would result in an `ODataException` with a status code representing "not found." In most cases, such illegal arguments should not trigger a circuit breaker, as the connection is in fact working. To signal to Hystrix that a certain exception thrown by the logic of the command should not be considered as a failure, we'll have to wrap this exception in a `HystrixBadRequestException`. An exception of this kind thrown by a run will simply be propagated by Hystrix and not trigger any fallback or be considered for circuit-breaker logic. You need to be careful though, to only wrap those exceptions that will only be triggered by illegal arguments and never by system-level failures. For example, a remote server may return a response with HTTP status code 404, "Not Found," not only if the requested cannot be found, but also if the service handling the requested path is currently not running and the path of the request is thus not mapped.

4.6.4 Caching

In the previous section, we improved the stability of our application by integrating fault tolerances and circuit breakers into all external calls. As we've seen, slow response is another threat to stability. Any operation that requires network traffic will be significantly slower than a local operation. Furthermore, certain information will not change frequently or does not need to be up-to-date all the time. In these cases, caching the results for a limited amount of time is acceptable and can reduce overall network traffic, reduce load on downstream systems, and improve response times, all at the expense of additional memory consumption of the application.

Let's assume that, in our use case, the list of business partners can, by default, be as old as five minutes, because rarely will a just created business partner immediately need to be assigned a new address. Similarly, managing the addresses of recently deleted business partners is rare as well. Thus, we'll implement caching for the list of business partners based on our existing command with a few small modifications, thanks to the commands available from the SAP S/4HANA Cloud SDK. All we have to do to implement caching for our `GetAllBusinessPartnersCommand` is the following:

1. Extend `CachingErpCommand` instead of `ErpCommand`.
2. Rename the `run` method to `runCacheable`.
3. Create a cache object.
4. Create a `getCache` method that returns the cache object.

Let's take a closer look at the last two steps. The corresponding source code is shown in Listing 4.26.

```
private static final Cache<CacheKey, List<BusinessPartner>>
    cache = CacheBuilder.newBuilder()
        .maximumSize(50)
        .expireAfterWrite(5, TimeUnit.MINUTES)
        .build();

@Override
protected Cache<CacheKey, List<BusinessPartner>> getCache() {
  return cache;
}
```

Listing 4.26 Providing a Cache for a Caching Command

For caching, the SAP S/4HANA Cloud SDK leverages Google's Guava libraries (*http://tiny.cc/guava*). We'll create a Guava cache as a static field using the `CacheBuilder` provided by Guava. We can configure the builder with specific properties. To manage memory consumption, we'll set an explicit maximum size. To fulfill the requirement to not display stale data, we'll specify that cache entries will expire five minutes after they've been written into the cache. The `getCache` method returns a static field. The cache must be static or in some other way shared across command instances; otherwise, each command execution would use its own cache.

The cache is parameterized with a cache key and the type of the values stored in the cache, which in our case are lists of business partners. The cache key instances will be used to differentiate the cached values. The SAP S/4HANA Cloud SDK already makes the cache key consider the current tenant and user to ensure that cached values are properly isolated. Moreover, you can configure the cache key for each command execution yourself by overwriting the `getCommandCacheKey` method. For example, parameterized commands need to add their parameters to the cache key: `super.getCommandCacheKey().append(parameters)`.

Invalidating the Cache

Sometimes, we want to retrieve the newest results instead of the cached values. Guava allows you to invalidate cache entries to force a new execution of the logic retrieving the result by using these commands:

```
cache.invalidateAll();
cache.invalidate(key);
```

In our case, applying caching to the other commands does not make much sense because we always want the latest address information to be shown when retrieving a single business partner. Write operations can't be cached anyway.

4.7 Summary

With this chapter, we have the first version of our backend application available, including necessary cloud qualities. Some topics we skipped for reasons of space, for example, validating user input and error handling. You should implement these and other nonfunctional requirements on your own based on the examples provided in this book's GitHub repository. In the following chapters, we'll gradually expand our sample application with additional functionalities and capabilities, starting with security measures in the next chapter.

Chapter 5
Application Security

This chapter outlines how to secure our example application, which consists of several microservices in a multitenant fashion. This chapter involves an overview of the architecture and the interaction among the corresponding components such as the application router (AppRouter) and the Identity Provider (IdP), as well as other relevant microservices. In addition to how to configure authentication and authorization between services and users, we'll cover essential security fundamentals and web security topics such as cross-site request forgery (CSRF) and clickjacking.

In this chapter, we'll introduce you to all concepts that you need to understand to secure your application in the Cloud Foundry environment on the SAP Cloud Platform. Before we dive more deeply into implementation details, in this chapter, we'll provide a comprehensive overview of the architectural components (e.g., the AppRouter, Extended Services for User Account and Authentication [XSUAA]) and patterns (e.g., OAuth) you'll need to understand for the full conceptual picture. Based on this overview, we walk through step-by-step how to protect our Business Partner Address Manager application so that only authenticated and authorized users can use the application. Additionally, we'll introduce some common web application threats, such as cross-site request forgery and clickjacking, and discuss how SAP technologies can help you to reduce your application's vulnerability to these threats.

5.1 Security on SAP Cloud Platform

Figure 5.1 presents the general architectural setup of security configuration in the Cloud Foundry environment on the SAP Cloud Platform. So far in this book, we learned about the single Java-based microservice that comprised our application, which consists of a few backend APIs and the UI (a micromonolith if you will). However, instead of accessing this service directly, we'll now use the AppRouter, which serves three main purposes.

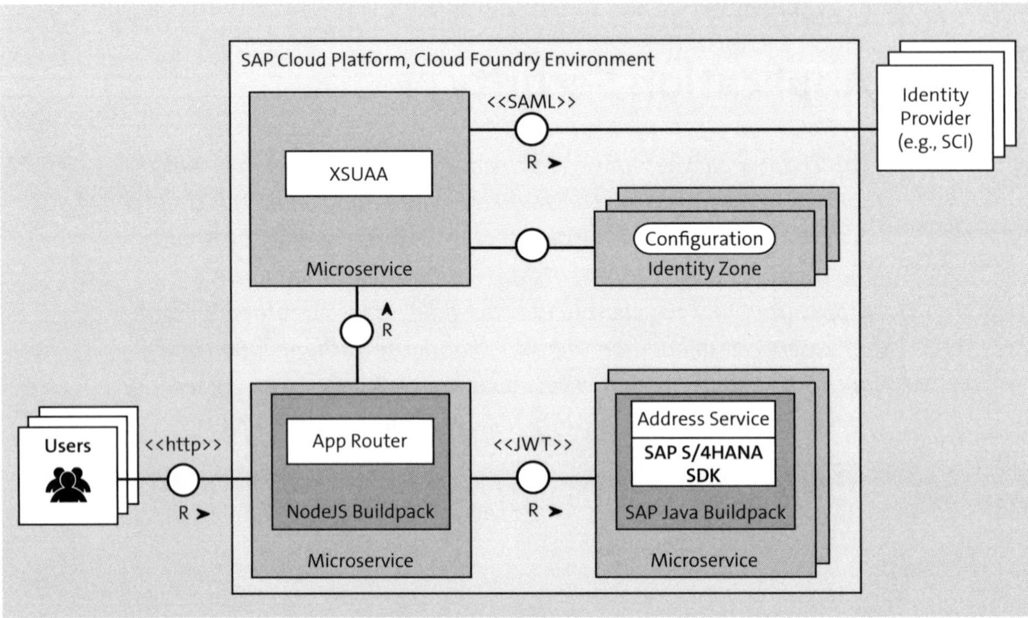

Figure 5.1 High-Level Authentication Setup with AppRouter and Extended Services for User Account and Authentication (XSUAA)

First, the AppRouter is the central entry point for our application into the world of real microservices. We can dissect our application into multiple microservices while hiding the resulting complexity from our end users. As such, the AppRouter dispatches requests to our backend microservices, thus acting as a reverse proxy, in particular, since the backend microservices should not be directly accessible by the client.

Second, the AppRouter can serve static content such as web pages, SAPUI5, or any other client-side code. We'll postpone discussion about static content until Chapter 14.

Third, the AppRouter is an important component for managing the authentication flows for our entire application and is, in addition, capable of strengthening our application against common web application threats. We'll focus on these features throughout this chapter.

For the purposes of authentication (who the user is) and authorization (what the user is allowed to do), the AppRouter takes all incoming, unauthenticated request and initiates an OAuth2 flow (authorization code grant) with the *Extended Services for User Account and Authentication (XSUAA)* service of the SAP Cloud Platform in the Cloud

Foundry environment. The XSUAA is a specific service provided by SAP to deal with authentication and authorization for business applications instead of using the standard user account and authentication service available in the Cloud Foundry environment. By default, the XSUAA uses the SAP ID service as user provider managing all users of the SAP Cloud ecosystem such as public users (P-users) or support user (S-users). Customers may replace the default configuration with any other Security Assertion Markup Language (SAML) 2.0-compliant Identity Provider (IdP) like the SAP Cloud Platform Identity Authentication service.

The full runtime flow of all involved components for authentication is shown in Figure 5.2. If you're not comfortable with OAuth yet, we recommend studying the RFC at *https://tools.ietf.org/html/rfc6749*.

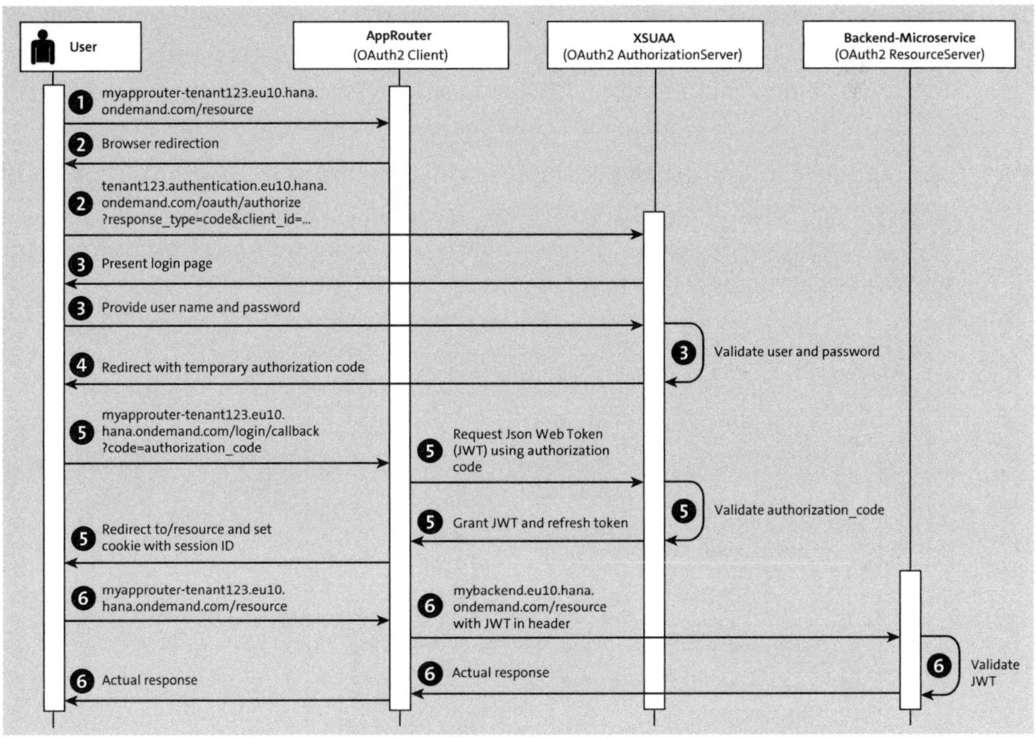

Figure 5.2 Runtime Flow for Authentication in SAP Cloud Platform

In the first step of the runtime flow ❶, a nonauthenticated user may request a certain backend resource from one of our microservices using the AppRouter as the single entry point. Since the user is not authenticated, in the second step ❷, the AppRouter, acting as an OAuth client, will respond with a URL redirect to the XSUAA service, which serves as the OAuth authorization server. In Step ❸, the XSUAA now responds with a login page asking the user for a valid user name and password. If the login information is correct, the XSUAA responds with a redirect back to the AppRouter including a temporary authorization code in Step ❹. In the fifth step ❺, the AppRouter exchanges the authorization code against an access token, represented as a JSON Web Token (JWT). The JWT contains all the information about the user: the formal user name, the tenant the user belongs to, any granted authorizations as OAuth scopes, etc. The JWT is also digitally signed so that every involved party can check its validity and integrity. The AppRouter stores the received JWT in the user's session for future use. For more information on the JWT standard, refer to the official RFC at *https://tools.ietf.org/html/rfc7519*. In the sixth and final step ❻, the AppRouter will forward the original request with the granted JWT to our backend resource which, after also validating the validity of the JWT, will return the correct response payload to the user. Note that this entire flow needs to be repeated only when the session of the user inside the AppRouter expires or the user has issued an explicit logout.

As mentioned earlier, the JWT contains a signature that must be verifiable by every microservice constituting our application. Therefore, every service must maintain a service binding to the XSUAA service, which provides this information at runtime for verification purposes and to fulfill the OAuth flow (Figure 5.3).

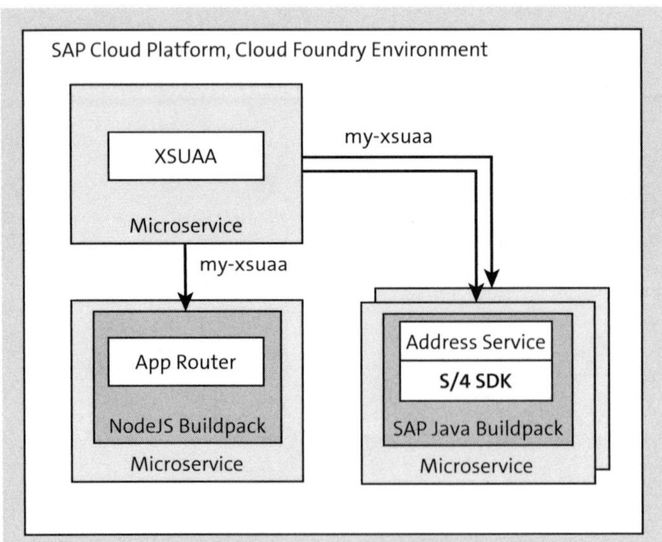

Figure 5.3 Runtime Binding between Microservices and XSUAA

Technically, every microservice needs aa binding to the specific XSUAA instance that writes this information into the VCAP_SERVICES environment variable, which the microservices can use to check the JWT's validity. With these basics in mind, let's create the setup shown in Figure 5.1 in the following sections.

5.2 Configuring Authentication

In the following section, we'll show you how to secure our Business Partner Address Manager application so that only authenticated users can access it.

5.2.1 Setting Up the Application Router

As a first step, we'll need to get and set up the AppRouter as explained in the previous section. The AppRouter is a Node.js component distributed via the publically available SAP NPM registry.

To download and install the AppRouter, follow these steps:

1. Go to your favorite *<destLocation>*, which represents your preferred development directory.

```
cd <destLocation>
mkdir approuter
cd approuter
```

2. Place the package.json shown in Listing 5.1 in the newly created *approuter* directory. Please note that we're using version 4.0.1, which is the most recent version at the time of this writing. You may update the AppRouter's version in this file to the latest version.

```
{
  "name": "approuter",
  "dependencies": {
    "@sap/approuter": "4.0.1"
  },
  "scripts": {
    "start": "node node_modules/@sap/approuter/approuter.js"
  }
}
```

Listing 5.1 The package.json for the Application Router

3. Install AppRouter dependencies using the following commands:

```
npm config set @sap:registry https://npm.sap.com
npm install
```

4. If successful, you should find a *node_modules* folder in the same location as the package.json.

Install via Service Marketplace

Alternatively, you may download the AppRouter from the SAP Service Marketplace at *http://tiny.cc/xsjavascript* and pick the latest XS JavaScript package, which includes the AppRouter among other dependencies. However, at the time of this writing, only an older version was available. We don't recommend this option.

Now, we need to provide some design-time configuration to the AppRouter. The main configuration file is called xs-app.json (Listing 5.2), which we create and place under *<destLocation>/approuter*.

```
{
  "welcomeFile": "index.html",
  "routes": [{
  "source": "^/api/(.*)",
    "target": "/api/$1",
    "destination": "app-destination"
  },{
  "source": "^/address-manager/(.*)",
  "target": "/address-manager/$1",
  "destination": "app-destination"
  }]
}
```

Listing 5.2 The AppRouter's Design Time Descriptor xs-app.json

So far, this file contains two routes to our backend microservice: one for our backend APIs and a second for static frontend content. During runtime, a route is identified through a matching pattern provided under the `source` path matched against the relative URL requested by the client. Then, the relative URL for the backend service is calculated based on the expression under `target` and combined with the base URL read from the `destination` variable, which is provided as an environment variable. In this way, we can flexibly change destinations later at runtime when our deployment model changes but leave all design-time parameters constant.

The Application Router's Design-Time Descriptor: xs-app.json

The xs-app.json file can be used to configure many more aspects at design-time of the AppRouter like authentication types, cache control, compression threshold for outgoing traffic (by default, 1 KB), client-initiated logout, custom settings for CSRF protection, and much more. We'll use some of these settings throughout this book. However, we recommend studying the up-to-date specifications and more detailed settings at *http://tiny.cc/approuterconfig*.

To correctly deploy our AppRouter, we'll create an additional manifest.yml file inside *<destLocation>* as the next step with the example content shown in Listing 5.3.

```
---
applications:
- name: approuter
  routes:
    - route: approuter- ↩
        <subdomain>.cfapps.eu10.hana.ondemand.com
  path: approuter
  memory: 128M
  env:
    TENANT_HOST_PATTERN: 'approuter- ↩
          (.*).cfapps.eu10.hana.ondemand.com'
    destinations: '[{"name":"app-destination", "url": ↩
          "https://address-manager-unsparse-subutopian ↩
          .cfapps.eu10.hana.ondemand.com", ↩
          "forwardAuthToken": true}]'
  services:
    - my-xsuaa
```

Listing 5.3 Providing a Deployment Descriptor for the AppRouter

Note

Replace the `route` parameter with your subaccount's subdomain as well as the URL parameter of the `destinations` variable with the correct base URL of our previously deployed Business Partner Address Manager microservice. For example, if you created a trial account on SAP Cloud Platform previously with a P-user, the route of the AppRouter will look like `approuter-p1942765239trial`, and the URL to the microservice might be `address-manager-unsparse-subutopian` based on the random route generated in Chapter 4.

As we discussed in Chapter 4, we'll use the standard Cloud Foundry manifest.yml file to instruct the AppRouter to describe basic metadata for deployment as we did already for the Java-based backend microservice. Additionally, we'll utilize two important user-provided environment variables, which are understood by the AppRouter.

First, the `destinations` variable will declare the base URL of our `app-destination` destination that we referenced earlier in the xs-app.json. You must provide an absolute URI including the protocol (*https://*), without any relative information as that information will be used to identify routes as specified in *xs-app.json*. We'll also specify that any JWT from the AppRouter shall be forwarded to this destination.

Second, the `TENANT_HOST_PATTERN` variable will define how tenants should be identified in our application's URL. Upon request, the AppRouter will match the incoming base URL against the provided regular expression and will consider the first matching group of the expression as the tenant. Then the AppRouter will use the matched string to identify the corresponding XSUAA tenant. If you need a different URL scheme for your tenants, you'll need to change this pattern accordingly. As we assume to build multitenant applications throughout this book, this parameter is required but can be omitted if implementing a single-tenant application only.

The AppRouter's Runtime Configuration

Besides destinations and tenant host patterns, the AppRouter understands many different parameters that can be changed during runtime, without redeploying the entire AppRouter, which is consistent with the twelve-factor application principles outlined in Chapter 3. Recognized parameters include cross-origin policies, session timeouts, compression thresholds, JWT refresh times, etc. You can find a full list of these parameters at *http://tiny.cc/approuterparams*. Besides declaring these variables in manifest.yml, please note that you can always use `cf set-env <appName> <variableName> <variableValue>` to set them.

Finally, in manifest.yml, we introduced a binding to a service instance, called `my-xsuaa` in our example. Our XSUAA service instance will be bound to the AppRouter so that JWTs issued by the XSUAA can be verified and, therefore, trusted by the AppRouter. Technically, this binding will issue a VCAP_SERVICES entry for the AppRouter, which holds all required information such as the client secret or the public key, to verify all security-related artifacts, as shown in Listing 5.4.


```
{
 "VCAP_SERVICES": {
  "xsuaa": [{
    "binding_name": null,
    "credentials": {
     "clientid": "<clientid>",
     "clientsecret": "<clientsecret>",
     "identityzone": "<subdomain>",
     "identityzoneid": "<subaccountId>",
     ...
     "verificationkey": "-----BEGIN PUBLIC KEY----- ...",
     "xsappname": "<xsappname>"
     ...
```

Listing 5.4 XSUAA Binding Information

However, before we can deploy the AppRouter, we'll need to instantiate our my-xsuaa service instance as described in the next section.

5.2.2 Extended Services for User Account Authentication (XSUAA)

With the AppRouter, we've already set up the largest part required for authentication. Besides acting as an OAuth client, the AppRouter is required for many other aspects in SAP Cloud Platform and, thus, is an important prerequisite. Eventually, authentication and authorization will be performed by the XSUAA. Therefore, we'll need a service instance to the XSUAA service, which is then bound to our AppRouter.

To create a service instance, we'll require the xs-security.json descriptor file, which we'll put into our initially chosen *<destLocation>* for the AppRouter:

```
{
  "xsappname": "address-manager-<subdomain>",
  "tenant-mode": "shared"
}
```

Like with the AppRouter, this file provides important design-time information such as roles, authorizations, etc., to the service instance we are about to create. For authentication purposes, the file looks simple as we are basically telling the XSUAA to create an instance with a unique identifier. As a best practice, we'll again use the application's name and subaccount's domain, but you can use any other arbitrary identifier not yet taken. Furthermore, we'll use the XSUAA in multitenant mode (`tenant-mode: shared`). We'll enhance this file in Section 5.3, when we introduce authorization concepts.

The Application Security Descriptor: xs-security.json

The xs-security.json descriptor is an important design-time artifact to provide authorization scopes, role templates, and other attributes of the application itself as well as foreign applications. For full specifications, refer to *http://tiny.cc/securitydescriptor.*

We'll then create a service instance called `my-xsuaa` of the XSUAA service by issuing the following command and using the xs-security.json file as a configuration input:

```
cf create-service xsuaa application my-xsuaa -c xs-security.json
```

By creating this instance, we are now explicitly declaring our XSUAA tenant as a platform-as-a-service (PaaS) tenant, that is, as a tenant whose security configuration can be shared with software-as-a-service (SaaS) tenants of consumers subscribing to our application later (see also Chapter 3 and Chapter 7). Thus, the consumers of our multitenant application can see, configure, and assign scopes and roles to their tenant-specific users (Section 5.3.2).

5.2.3 A First Test

If you successfully went through the previous two sections, you should have in your file or version control system a structure that looks like the following:

```
.
├── approuter
│   ├── node_modules
│   ├── package.json
│   └── xs-app.json
├── manifest.yml
└── xs-security.json
```

Note that you may have different content in the *approuter* folder depending on your individual setup. Ensure that xs-app.json, package.json, manifest.yml, and the *node_modules* directory with correct contents are present at least. If your structure is sufficient, you're ready for the first test. Deploy the AppRouter using the following commands:

```
cd <destLocation>
cf api https://api.cf.eu10.hana.ondemand.com
cf login
cf push
```

Now, you should be able to locate the AppRouter from within your browser using the host name of your deployment as well as the subaccount's subdomain following the pattern as specified earlier. For example, using our example user P1942765239, the final URL would be *https://approuter-p1942765239trial.cfapps.eu10.hana.ondemand.com/address-manager/*. This address should present a page similar to Figure 5.4 where you'll use your email address and password to log in.

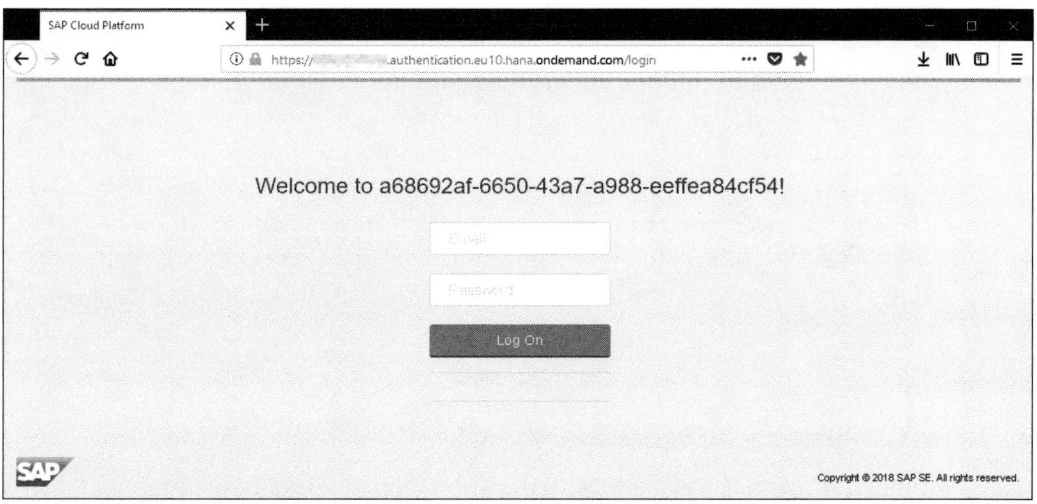

Figure 5.4 Login Screen of Our Application Based on Application Router and XSUAA

After logging in, you should also see our Business Partner Address Manager application, as shown in Figure 5.5, now being served via the AppRouter as you can see from the URL.

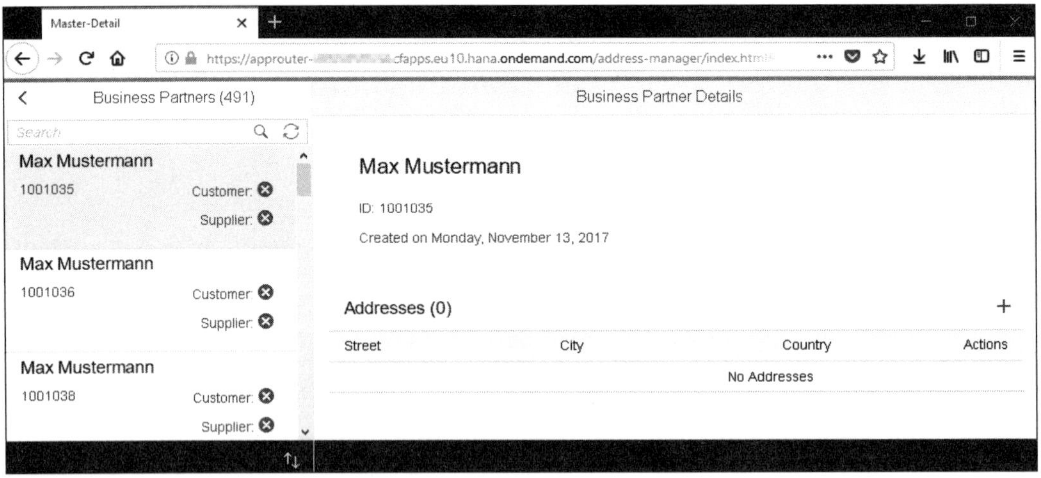

Figure 5.5 Business Partner Address Manager Application Delivered over Application Router after Authentication

> **Did You Know? Running the Application Router Locally**
>
> Sometimes it might be helpful to run the AppRouter locally for testing or debugging purposes, in particular, when you want to experiment with different settings and do not want to deploy the AppRouter to SAP Cloud Platform all the time. To run the AppRouter locally, place two required files called default-env.json (which contains the required environment variables) and default-services.json (which contains the XSUAA service binding information) next to xs-app.json. Check out the GitHub repository for this book for a concrete example. You may run the AppRouter locally using `npm start`.

5.2.4 Protecting Our Backend Microservice

Although authentication works with the AppRouter, our Java-based backend microservice is still fully visible in the web and not protected. We'll therefore need to protect our backend microservice as well so that it only accepts requests with valid and trusted JWTs. Two simple steps are all that's required.

First, we'll need to modify our Java backend's web.xml and introduce the lines of code shown in Listing 5.5.

```
<login-config>
    <auth-method>XSUAA</auth-method>
</login-config>
<security-constraint>
  <web-resource-collection>
    <web-resource-name>Read business partners ↩
        </web-resource-name>
    <url-pattern>/api/business-partners</url-pattern>
  </web-resource-collection>
    <auth-constraint>
        <role-name>ViewAddresses</role-name>
    </auth-constraint>
</security-constraint>
<security-role>
    <role-name>ViewAddresses</role-name>
</security-role>
```

Listing 5.5 Declarative Security Configuration for Backend Microservices

This code essentially leverages the SAP Java buildpack to validate incoming requests and only accept requests with a valid JWT for users who possess the `ViewAddresses` role (which we'll introduce in the next section).

Second, we'll also need to bind our Java backend service to our previously created XSUAA instance `my-xsuaa`. Therefore, we'll slightly modify the manifest.yml definition of our Java backend and introduce the `my-xsuaa` service instance to the services section:

```
services:
- my-xsuaa
```

Now, we're ready to rebuild and redeploy our backend microservice with the commands:

```
mvn clean install
cf push
```

As a result of this change, accessing the backend service directly will reject any requests and show a 401 HTTP status (Unauthorized) because we are not providing any valid JWT (Figure 5.6).

Figure 5.6 Java Microservice Rejecting Unauthenticated Traffic

When using the AppRouter as the entry point, the backend service will now respond with a 403 HTTP status (Forbidden) as authentication has worked, but now, the user lacks the `ViewAddresses` authorization required to protect the endpoints accordingly (Figure 5.7). Giving the user access to the roles will be the topic of the next section.

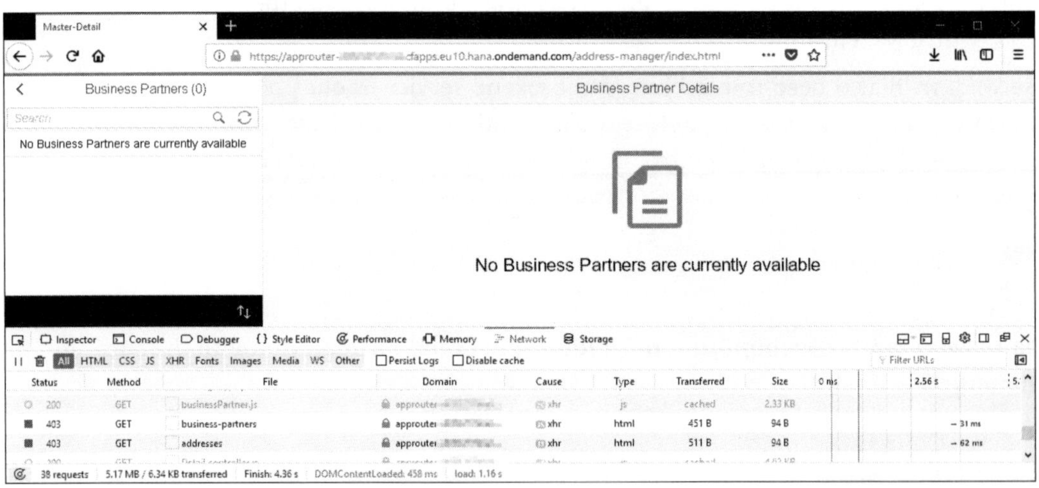

Figure 5.7 Backend Requests Authenticated over the AppRouter but Forbidden Due to Missing Authorizations

Did You Know? Providing Logout Functionality

While experimenting with different authentication and authorization options, you may require logging out every now and then to explicitly invalidate established session information on the server- and client-sides. This forced logout can be an important capability for your productive application later on.

Fortunately, the AppRouter also provides a mechanism for client-initiated logout that provides a central logout facility in our distributed system. By adding the snippet in Listing 5.6 to xs-app.json, we can tell the AppRouter under which relative URL we want to expose the logout (for example, */logout*):

```
"routes": [{<route_definitions>}],
"logout" : {
  "logoutEndpoint": "/logout",
  "logoutPage": "/logout.html"
}
```

Listing 5.6 Adding Logout Functionality to AppRouter

Troubleshooting JSON Web Tokens

In some cases, you might need to investigate the content of the JWT to identify any potential issues. The JWT is passed using an HTTP header with key `Authentication`, and the value always starts with `Bearer:` followed by a Base64-encoded string. You can, for example, create an arbitrary servlet for debugging purposes and log the header to the console. Afterwards, you may use a page like *https://jwt.io* to decode the token. However, *never* do this with any productive tokens and use local solutions instead, such as the publically available *jwt-cli* tool.

5.3 Configuring Authorization Using OAuth2

Now that we've secured our application against unauthenticated traffic, let's now turn to how to check concrete business authorizations as part of the application semantics.

5.3.1 Overview

In the previous section, we provided the setup required to authenticate our users end-to-end using the AppRouter and our previously built Business Partner Address

Manager application. However, we haven't yet considered any business authorizations, the more fine-grained controls over our exposed business capabilities. For example, let's say we only want to allow certain users *read* rights on business partner addresses while other users might be allowed to also *write* new addresses. For this distinction, we'll require authorization definitions at design-time and corresponding runtime checks, which we'll introduce in this section. Figure 5.8 provides a high-level overview on how authorization concepts are modelled and handled in the Cloud Foundry environment on SAP Cloud Platform.

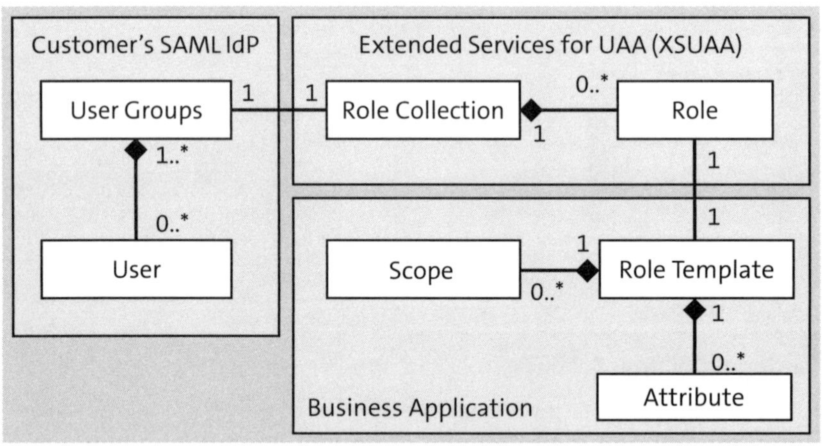

Figure 5.8 Relationships of Authorization Concepts on SAP Cloud Platform

We, as the developers or architects of our business application, can define *role templates*, which may contain multiple (OAuth) scopes. OAuth scopes refer to specific authorizations such as DISPLAY or WRITE permissions, which are checked by the microservice. We'll provide our scope and role template design using the xs-security.json descriptor (Section 5.2.2) when creating the XSUAA service instance.

The consumer of our application (for example, an administrator in a client company) can then instantiate the provided role templates into concrete roles in his subscriber accounts (for example, giving them customer-specific names) and may aggregate multiple roles (for example, from different providers) into role collections that can finally be assigned to individual users or groups of users. In this way, we can achieve, on one hand, fine, granular authorization control for microservices and, on the other hand, compose authorization in a flexible way with more coarse role collections. The idea behind this process is that, for example, a "Business Partner Manager" role collection may span multiple applications while its underlying microservices all have individual scopes. The role collections can resolve all associated roles and return a union of all associated scopes as part of the JWT issued by the XSUAA.

5.3.2 Defining Scopes and Role Templates

For our Business Partner Address Manager application, let's say we want to define two role templates: the `BusinessPartnerViewer`, which is only allowed to view existing addresses (scope: `ViewAddresses`), and a `BusinessPartnerManager` template, which is also allowed to write new addresses to the system (scope: `ViewAddresses` and `WriteAddresses`). To define these role templates, we'll enhance our existing xs-security.json descriptor as shown in Listing 5.7.

```
{
  "xsappname": "address-manager-<uniqueId>",
  "tenant-mode": "shared",
  "scopes": [{
    "name": "$XSAPPNAME.ViewAddresses",
    "description": "Scope to view business addresses"
  },{
    "name": "$XSAPPNAME.WriteAddresses",
    "description": "Scope to write business addresses"
  }],
  "role-templates": [{
    "name": "BusinessPartnerViewer",
    "description": "Role to view business addresses",
      "scope-references" : [
        "$XSAPPNAME.ViewAddresses"
      ]
    },{
      "name": "BusinessPartnerManager",
      "description": "Role to manage all business addresses",
      "scope-references" : [
        "$XSAPPNAME.ViewAddresses",
        "$XSAPPNAME.WriteAddresses"
      ]
    }
  ]
}
```

Listing 5.7 Enhancing the Application Security Descriptor with Scopes and Role Templates

Note that all scopes must be prefixed with "$XSAPPNAME," which will be replaced during runtime with the actual name of the application.

Finally, we'll need to update our existing XSUAA service instance `my-xsuaa` and make it aware of our design changes using the following command:

```
cf update-service my-xsuaa -c xs-security.json
```

5.3.3 Protecting Our Application

Now that we've introduced scopes and role templates to the XSUAA service instance, we'll need to protect our application accordingly. Basically, two places exist where you can check authorizations: inside the AppRouter and in the backend microservices.

Checking Scopes inside the AppRouter

First, let's check OAuth scopes inside the AppRouter and protect certain routes with scopes. For example, we could check on our */api* route that we only allow users with the `ViewAddresses` scope to pass; otherwise, the AppRouter should reject the request. However, we won't pursue this option in our example further because these checks are declarative in nature on routes only and might be used as a second line of defense. Therefore, we'll omit this option in the remaining chapter for the sake of simplicity.

```
"routes": [{
  "source": "^/api/(.*)",
  "scopes": ["$XSAPPNAME.ViewAddresses"]
}
```

Checking Scopes Declaratively in Backend Microservices

Checks can also be performed in the backend microservices where the actual business logic resides. We always recommended introducing authorization checks in your backend microservices so that the check is closely related to your business logic and semantics. In some cases, you might even need to check authorizations programmatically inside the business logic, which can be only done inside the microservice itself. To check scopes in our Java-based microservice, we can either use the declarative or programmatic approach.

The declarative approach works either by using the web.xml as before or by using annotations directly in the servlet (Servlet specification 3.0 or later). For servlets, we can rely on the SAP-provided buildpack for Java and let it work out of the box.

With the web.xml approach inside the */application/webapp/WEB-INF/* folder, you can protect resources declaratively outside your code. For example, in the last section, we showed you how to protect the URL pattern under */api/business-partners* with the `ViewAddresses` role, which corresponds exactly to the scope we just defined. In this process, you can add different URL patterns with different authorization constraints to protect your endpoints accordingly, as shown in Listing 5.8. (Please refer to the official Servlet 3.0+ specification for more details.)


```
<security-constraint>
  <web-resource-collection>
    <web-resource-name>Read business partners ↩
        </web-resource-name>
    <url-pattern>/api/business-partners</url-pattern>
  </web-resource-collection>
  <auth-constraint>
      <role-name>ViewAddresses</role-name>
  </auth-constraint>
</security-constraint>

<security-role>
  <role-name>ViewAddresses</role-name>
</security-role>
```

Listing 5.8 Protecting Java Microservices Declaratively

Alternatively, with the annotation-based approach, you can directly annotate the relevant servlet using the `@ServletSecurity` annotation, for example, inside the `BusinessPartnerServlet` class:

```
@WebServlet("/api/business-partners")
@ServletSecurity(@HttpConstraint(rolesAllowed = ↩
    {"ViewAddresses"}))
public class BusinessPartnerServlet extends HttpServlet
```

However, this code is just a different syntactical way of expressing the same semantics. If you prefer annotations, you can safely remove the protection from web.xml.

No matter which approach you use, you'll need to rebuild and push the application using the command:

```
mvn clean install
cf push
```

Checking Scopes Programmatically in Our Backend Microservices

Authorizations can be also checked programmatically in your backend microservices by leveraging the XS2 security libraries, which are currently distributed by SAP through the SAP Service Marketplace.

> **Note**
>
> At the time of this writing, a Maven Central delivery is not available. Please check if the artifacts are available when you read this chapter; if so, you can skip the instructions in the next paragraph.

To get the latest version of the XS2 security libraries, you'll need to download them from *http://tiny.cc/xs2seclibs* and pick the latest version. At the time of this writing, the latest version is XS_JAVA_1-70001362 (19.03.2018). Please note that you'll require a support user to access the SAP Service Marketplace (see the preface for information on getting one). Once you've downloaded the library, unzip the downloaded package to a temporary directory *<tempDir>*. Afterwards, install the libraries to your local Maven repository as follows:

```
cd <tempDir>
mvn clean install
```

After you've installed the XS2 security libraries, you'll need to reference them as dependencies from *<projectDir>/application/pom.xml*, as shown in Listing 5.9. Note that the depicted dependency versions may be outdated in the code and should be replaced with the latest available versions.

```
<!-- replace with latest available versions -->
<dependency>
    <groupId>com.sap.xs2.security</groupId>
    <artifactId>security-commons</artifactId>
    <version>0.27.2</version>
</dependency>
<dependency>
    <groupId>com.sap.xs2.security</groupId>
    <artifactId>java-container-security</artifactId>
    <version>0.27.2</version>
</dependency>
<dependency>
    <groupId>com.sap.xs2.security</groupId>
    <artifactId>java-container-security-api</artifactId>
```

```
    <version>0.27.2</version>
</dependency>
<dependency>
    <groupId>org.springframework</groupId>
    <artifactId>spring-core</artifactId>
    <version>4.3.0.RELEASE</version>
</dependency>
<dependency>
    <groupId>org.springframework.security</groupId>
    <artifactId>spring-security-jwt</artifactId>
    <version>1.0.9.RELEASE</version>
</dependency>
<dependency>
    <groupId>org.springframework.security.oauth</groupId>
    <artifactId>spring-security-oauth2</artifactId>
    <version>2.3.2.RELEASE</version>
</dependency>
<dependency>
    <groupId>com.sap.security.nw.sso.linuxx86_64.opt</groupId>
    <artifactId>sapjwt.linuxx86_64</artifactId>
    <version>1.0.19</version>
</dependency>
```

Listing 5.9 Additional Dependencies for Programmatic Security Checks

Next, the scopes can be checked programmatically using the SAP S/4HANA Cloud SDK shown in Listing 5.10. Thanks to the abstractions of the SDK, the same code can be reused in both the Cloud Foundry and the Neo environment.

```
try {
  final Scope scope = new Scope("ViewAddresses");
  if(!UserAccessor.getCurrentUser().hasAuthorization(scope)) {
    response.setStatus(HttpStatus.SC_FORBIDDEN);
    response.getWriter().write("Forbidden");
    return;
  }
} catch(UserNotAuthenticatedException | UserAccessException e) {
  e.printStackTrace();
}
```

Listing 5.10 Checking Authorizations Programmatically

Finally, we'll need to rebuild and push our application to SAP Cloud Platform using the command:

```
mvn clean install
cf push
```

Did You Know? XS2 Libraries Enable the Spring Security Framework

The downloaded security libraries aren't just helpful for programmatic authorization checks, they also enable you to secure your microservices with *Spring security* as an alternative to the standard servlet security approach we've presented so far. Moreover, the XS2 libraries allow you to use any buildpack from the community instead of the SAP buildpack for Java. To enable Spring security, the archetype generated with the SAP S/4HANA Cloud SDK contains a spring-security.xml file in the *WEB-INF/* folder of your application, which you can enable by adding the `ContextLoaderListener` and `DelegatingFilterProxy` to your web.xml. The entire approach is described in more detail in a blog post at *http://tiny.cc/sapsecurityblog*.

Securing Applications in the Neo Environment on SAP Cloud Platform

All methods for protecting applications with the declarative servlet security approach as well as the programmatic approach can be equally used in the Neo environment of SAP Cloud Platform. The only difference is that, for Neo applications, the login configuration must be changed from `XSUAA` to `FORM`:

```
<login-config>
    <auth-method>FORM</auth-method>
</login-config>
```

Furthermore, you won't need to add any additional XS2 security libraries to your project.

5.3.4 Assigning Users to Application Roles

Now that we have a new XSUAA configuration in place and have protected our backend microservices, we'll need to assign the corresponding roles to our users. We can assign roles using the SAP Cloud Platform cockpit, for example, using *https://account.hanatrial.ondemand.com/cockpit*.

In the first step, open the **Role Collections** tab under the **Security** ribbon of your Cloud Foundry subaccount as shown in Figure 5.9.

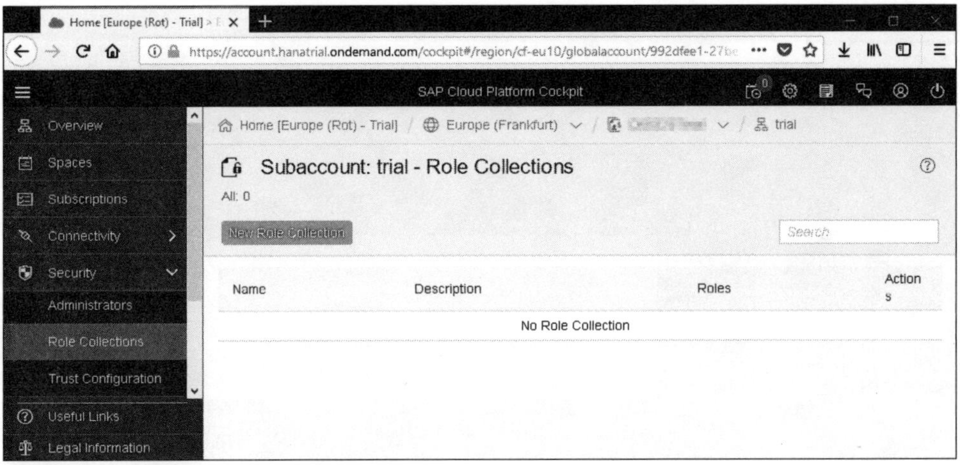

Figure 5.9 The Empty Role Collections Menu to Define A New Collection

Then, we'll create a new role collection to which you can give an arbitrary name. In our example, we call our role collection "Business Partner Manager" and click **Save**, as shown in Figure 5.10.

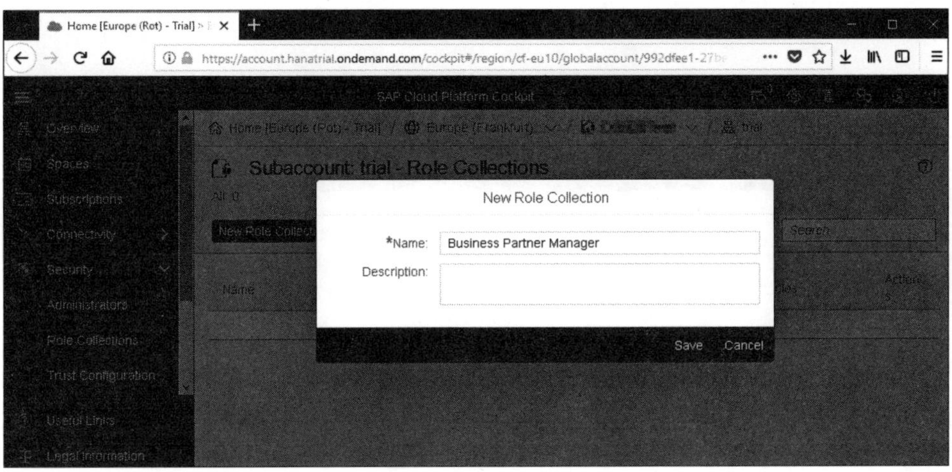

Figure 5.10 Defining the Business Partner Manager Role Collection

Third, select the newly created **Business Partner Manager** role collection and select **Add Role**. From the menu, select your application presented as the application identifier `xsappname` from your xs-security.json and the corresponding role template we defined earlier (Figure 5.11).

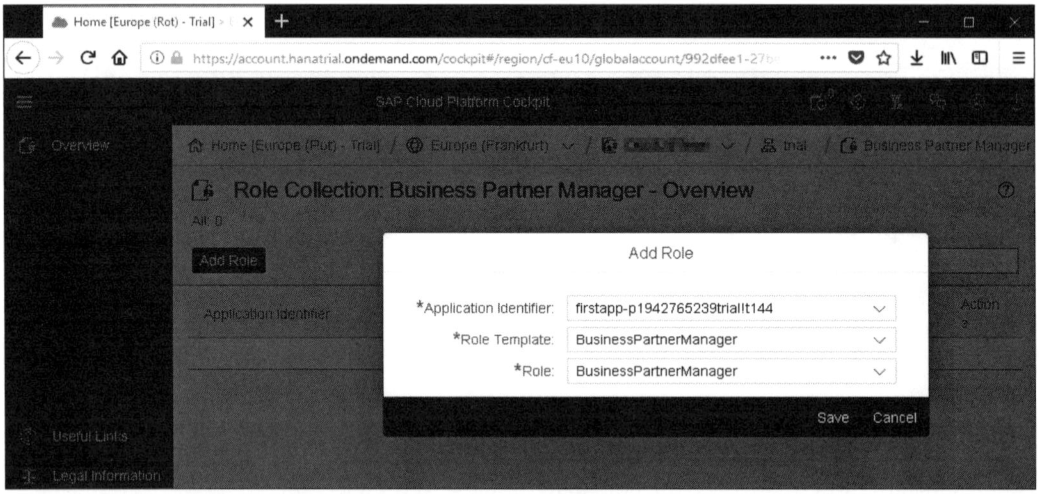

Figure 5.11 Add Role Template to Role Collection

In the next step, we'll need to assign our user to the newly created **Business Partner Manager** role collection to grant the `ViewAddresses` and `WriteAddresses` scopes. Therefore, we'll select the **Trust Configuration** from the **Security** menu and select the **SAP ID Service** from the list as shown in Figure 5.12.

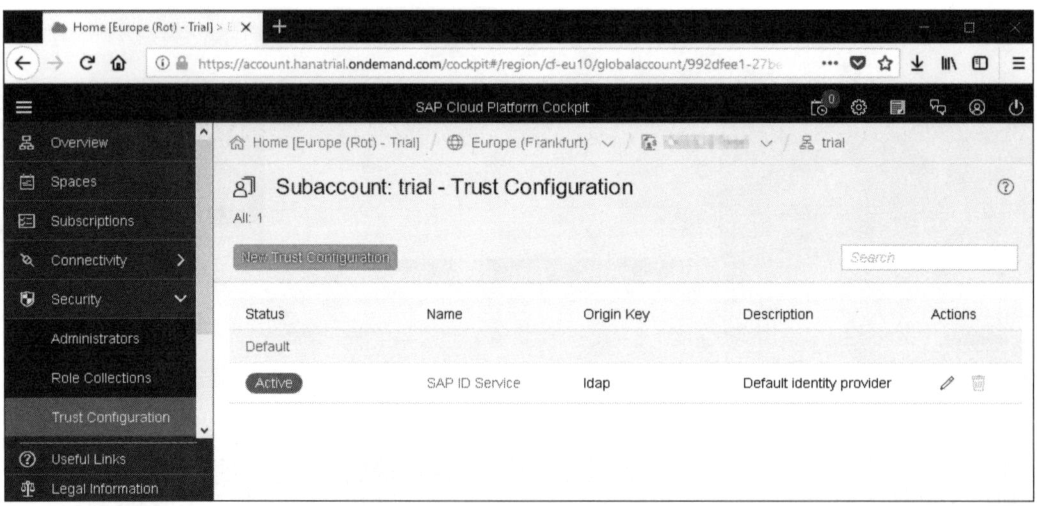

Figure 5.12 Trust Configuration in SAP Cloud Platform with the SAP ID Service as Default Identity Provider

In the opening dialog, enter your email into the user field and click **Show Assignments** (Figure 5.13).

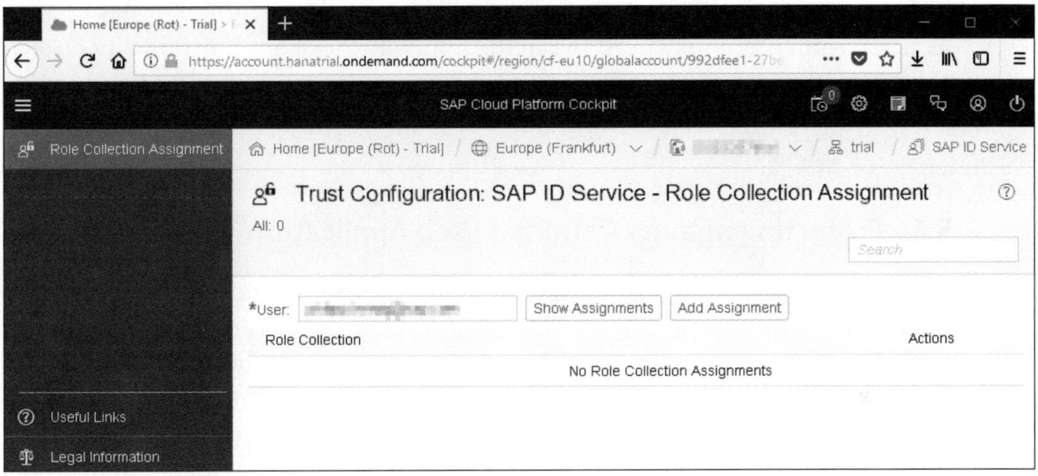

Figure 5.13 Selecting User Role Assignments

Then, click **Add Assignment** and choose the **Business Partner Manager** role collection from the menu to assign it to your user (Figure 5.14).

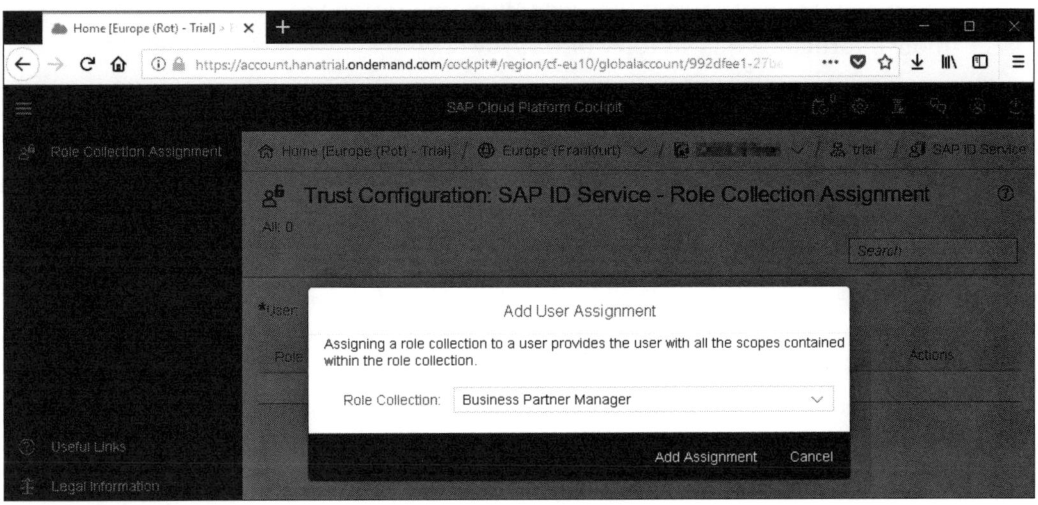

Figure 5.14 Assigning Role Collection "Business Partner Manager" to a User

Based on this role collection assignment, we can now use the application as before using our authenticated and authorized user while other users will no longer have access.

As noted earlier, you may need to call the AppRouter's logout functionality once to invalidate any existing sessions and retrieve a new JWT with the updated scope information.

5.4 Protecting against Common Web Application Threats

Besides protecting our application with authentication and authorization, the AppRouter, as well as the SAP S/4HANA Cloud SDK, provides additional capabilities to protect your application against standard attack vectors in web or cloud applications. We'll touch on some of these potential attacks in this final section. Note that enabling the features we describe do not mean your application is secure. Additional attack vectors are possible and require mitigation when building your application. For example, typical vulnerabilities such as SQL, Lightweight Directory Access Protocol (LDAP), or other path injections; cross-site scripting attacks; or the use of vulnerable third-party dependencies in your application code must be checked by different tools or methods. These additional aspects are beyond the scope of this book. We recommend that you consult the Open Web Application Security Project (OWASP) for more information on this topic (*https://owasp.org*).

5.4.1 Cross-Site Request Forgery

In simple terms, cross-site request forgery (CSRF) or, more specifically, *session riding* is an attack where an attacker convinces a user to follow a link that does something that the user did not intend to do (for example, deleting all records from a database if the user is the application's administrator). As a prerequisite to this attack, the user must be logged into the application, which can easily happen when session timeouts are unreasonably long, when login information has been stored by the user inside the browser for convenience, or login information is stored by the application for a long period of time in persistent cookies.

To prevent this attack, the client- and server-side code must share a secret unknown to an attacker. This secret is called the *CSRF token*.

Fortunately, in the Cloud Foundry environment of SAP Cloud Platform, the AppRouter enables CSRF protection for any HTTP method except `GET` and `HEAD` on routes that require authentication, that is, where the `authenticationType` attribute has not been set to `none`. If a route is CSRF-protected but the client-side application does not send a valid CSRF token as part of the `x-csrf-token` header, the AppRouter will reject the request with a 403 HTTP error code. To retrieve a valid CSRF token, the client-side code must first send a request with the HTTP header key-value `x-csrf-token: fetch`.

If you need to change this default behavior, you may use the `authenticationType` or `csrfProtection` attributes on routes in your xs-app.json, as shown in Listing 5.11.

```
"routes": [{
  "source": "^/api/(.*)",
  ...
  "csrfProtection": false,
  "authenticationType": "none"
}
```

Listing 5.11 Changing CSRF Protection in the AppRouter

Additionally, every microservice created using archetypes of the S/4HANA Cloud SDK also contain a CSRF protection filter defined in the web.xml file, as shown in Listing 5.12.

```
<filter>
  <filter-name>RestCsrfPreventionFilter</filter-name>
  <filter-class>
      org.apache.catalina.filters.RestCsrfPreventionFilter
  </filter-class>
</filter>
<filter-mapping>
  <filter-name>RestCsrfPreventionFilter</filter-name>
  <url-pattern>/*</url-pattern>
</filter-mapping>
```

Listing 5.12 CSRF Protection in Java Services

If you are using the AppRouter and have protected your backend microservice as described in this chapter, you can safely remove this protection. However, if you're exposing your service directly without the AppRouter (e.g., in the Neo environment), you should keep this protection in place to protect your application from being vulnerable to this attack.

5.4.2 Clickjacking

Clickjacking refers to an attack vector where the attacker embeds the vulnerable application, for example, using an HTML iframe, and overrides the visible intended actions with unintended actions. For instance, the user may intentionally click the playback button in a video application but instead unintentionally triggers a purchase in some retail application.

To prevent this attack, recent browsers can be instructed to block remote content embedded with iframes using the `X-FRAME-OPTIONS` HTTP header.

If you're using the AppRouter, the default setting of `X-FRAME-OPTIONS` is `SAMEORIGIN`, that is, the browser allows iframes only if the framed content originates from the same domain as the embedding application. You can either turn off this behavior by setting the AppRouter's environment variable `SEND_XFRAMEOPTIONS` to `false`, or you can override the value by specifying the `httpHeaders` environment variable (for example, setting it to `DENY` to completely forbid the use of iframes).

In backend microservices generated using the SAP S/4HANA Cloud SDK, the lines from web.xml, shown in Listing 5.13, introduce the same behavior.

```
<filter>
  <filter-name>HttpSecurityHeadersFilter</filter-name>
  <filter-class>
    com.sap.cloud.sdk.cloudplatform.security.servlet ↩
        .HttpSecurityHeadersFilter
  </filter-class>
</filter>
<filter-mapping>
  <filter-name>HttpSecurityHeadersFilter</filter-name>
  <url-pattern>/*</url-pattern>
</filter-mapping>
```

Listing 5.13 HTTP Security Headers in Java Services

You can remove these lines if your microservices are not directly accessible, for example, using the AppRouter. However, when your service is directly accessible, for example, when exposing Java-based services directly in the Neo environment of SAP Cloud Platform, you should keep this filtering setting in place.

In addition, you may use the Content Security Policy (CSP) header, which is currently recommended by the W3C (*https://www.w3.org/TR/CSP2/*) and supported by all modern browsers. We won't discuss this header further in this book, but recommend that you look into it yourself and use the standard HTTP header settings introduced in this chapter, since such policies are specific to each application.

5.4.3 Securing Session Cookies

In all SAP Cloud Platform environments, session IDs stored in cookies are used on the client to continuously identify a user across several stateless server interactions without requiring re-logins. Thus, these cookies are a primary target for attackers because they grant access to applications using the identities of compromised users. Therefore, sessions and their cookies must be protected in productive environments.

Fortunately, in the Cloud Foundry environment of SAP Cloud Platform, the AppRouter uses secure attributes by default when instructing browsers to store session cookies by specifying the `httpOnly` and `secure` options in the `Set-Cookie` response header, as shown in Figure 5.15. This process happens in the redirection phase (Step ❺ in Figure 5.2).

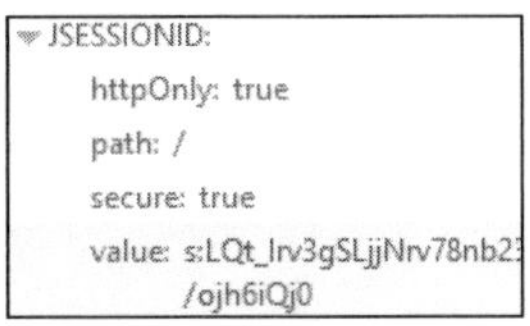

Figure 5.15 Example Set-Cookie Instruction Returned from AppRouter after Successful Login

The `secure` option instructs the browser to only send the session cookie over encrypted connections (that is, HTTPS). The `httpOnly` options instructs the browser that the cookie can be only accessed on real HTTP requests, for example, any JavaScript access is forbidden.

For testing purposes without encrypted connections, you might need to turn off this option by setting the AppRouter's environment variable `SECURE_SESSION_COOKIE` to `false`.

If you are using the Neo environment on the SAP Cloud Platform, no default security option exists. Thus, we recommend that you add the code shown in Listing 5.14 to your application's web.xml file.

```
<session-config>
  <cookie-config>
    <secure>true</secure>
```

```
    <http-only>true</http-only>
  </cookie-config>
</session-config>
```

Listing 5.14 Securing Session Cookies on SAP Cloud Platform Neo

5.4.4 Secure HTTP Headers

Finally, the backend microservices generated with the SAP S/4HANA Cloud SDK include `HttpSecurityHeadersFilter` in web.xml, which sets default headers for security. Besides the `X-FRAME-OPTIONS` headers we mentioned earlier in Section 5.4.2, `HttpSecurityHeadersFilter` also enforces the `Strict-Transport-Security` header, which instructs the browser to only allow cloud application access via the HTTPS protocol. In other words, no unencrypted HTTP traffic without TLS is allowed.

5.5 Summary

This concludes our chapter on how to protect a microservice-based application on SAP Cloud Platform. Based on these lessons, we'll turn, in the next chapter, to how to safely integrate our example application with SAP S/4HANA.

Chapter 6
Integrating with SAP S/4HANA

This chapter focuses on integrating cloud applications with SAP S/4HANA systems; that is, establishing analytical and transactional access to business data in SAP S/4HANA. First of all, this chapter explains the distinction between technical users and business users and then introduces the concept of principal propagation. Then, we'll dive into setting up the integration to both SAP S/4HANA Cloud and SAP S/4HANA. In the context of SAP S/4HANA Cloud, we'll present the concept of communication arrangements as well as discuss identity and access management. For SAP S/4HANA, we'll introduce the Cloud Connector. Both integration scenarios are demonstrated through our Business Partner Address Manager application.

So far in this part of the book, we've built our first cloud application (the Business Partner Address Manager app), based on the SAP S/4HANA Cloud SDK, and we've made the app run securely on the Cloud Foundry Environment on the SAP Cloud Platform.

In this chapter, we'll walk through the steps for connecting the application to an SAP S/4HANA system, whether on-premise or in the cloud. In the process, we'll extend our Business Partner Address Manager application further, using the same input values as we entered in the previous chapters. To help make integration concepts more concrete, we'll provide specific values wherever user input is needed. You are, however, free to use values of your choice. If you do so, be sure to follow a consistent approach.

6.1 Introduction

SAP S/4HANA and SAP Cloud Platform are a great example of how two systems can integrate with each other much like the pieces of a jigsaw puzzle. As standalone systems, both are pertinent and powerful in their own right: SAP S/4HANA for running highly intelligent, robust, and mature business processes, SAP Cloud Platform for providing a platform to build, deploy, run, and operate cloud-native applications that conform to the twelve-factor application principles outlined in Chapter 3.

In this chapter, we'll look at this integration in detail, in the context of both SAP S/4HANA Cloud and SAP S/4HANA on-premise.

We'll start with the various authentication and authorization entities that users and applications use when connecting to SAP S/4HANA systems. In addition, we'll explore the concept of principal propagation, which lets authentication and authorization information traverse between connected systems. Then, we'll turn our attention to the destination API of SAP Cloud Platform, which defines the physical connection to an external entity such as an SAP S/4HANA system. We'll then provide a hands-on explanation of configuring this connection further, on the semantic level and the logical level, first with SAP S/4HANA cloud, then with SAP S/4HANA on-premise. We'll take a deep dive into the overall integration architecture and the various entities that come into play along with their connections. At each step, we'll spend ample time looking at the configuration steps you'll need to take to create a seamless and secure connection. Where necessary, we'll take short detours to explain important theoretical concepts about the topic at hand.

6.2 Technical Users, Business Users, and Principal Propagation

After exploring the need to integrate our cloud application with SAP S/4HANA, we'll discuss the distinction between technical users and business users, since this distinction will affect authentication. We'll present principal propagation as the concept behind achieving integration with SAP S/4HANA by leveraging business users.

6.2.1 Technical Users and Business Users

To integrate your cloud application with SAP S/4HANA, you'll have to authenticate, that is, the caller has to prove its identity, to prevent unauthorized access to data and APIs inside SAP S/4HANA. The process of authentication includes identifying your user name. Once the user name has been identified by the mechanisms discussed throughout this chapter, SAP S/4HANA can conduct authorization checks with respect to the user's profile. As a result, every API inside SAP S/4HANA will be invoked in the context of a given user name. This user name must exist and be unlocked at the time of invocation.

In general, we can distinguish between *technical* and *business users*, which we'll explore next.

Business User

A business user commonly represents an existing, physical person working with the user interface (for example, an SAP Fiori application in SAP S/4HANA). Consequently, every call to SAP S/4HANA must be executed in the context of this business user. With respect to logging, we can trace back every recorded action to the relevant person.

Example: Integration via Business User

Let's assume that your cloud application allows you to manage business partners, and your application has several end users, each responsible for a different region. One user manages business partners in EMEA, the second one in APJ, and so forth. You'll need to grant fine-grained access to business partner data for each user, on the level of business roles. Moreover, your application will consist of a user interface and will execute requests to SAP S/4HANA in real time. Furthermore, to comply with data privacy regulations, you'll need a detailed trace of the data accessed by each user. This scenario is perfect for using business users to integrate the application to SAP S/4HANA.

Technical User

In contrast to a business user, a technical user may represent a technical system or external system and invokes certain APIs directly. Usually a user interface is not involved. With respect to logging the actions of technical users, we can identify the external system that invokes a particular API, but we won't have the granularity of individual user logging.

Example: Integration via Technical User

Let's assume that you need to integrate an external system with SAP S/4HANA Cloud to replicate business data in a regular manner. The data replication can happen overnight as the data consistency between the external system and SAP S/4HANA Cloud is not high priority. Therefore, the replication can be triggered by a batch job in the external system and invoke the relevant API in SAP S/4HANA. Moreover, defining fine-grained authorizations for this kind of business data isn't necessary anyway because all business objects are replicated. Additionally, let's say you don't need to log which users copied which business object, but instead only need to know from which external system the data originated. These circumstances meet the requirements for a scenario using technical users.

6.2.2 Authenticating as Business User via Principal Propagation

Before we go further, let's briefly discuss what principal propagation means. *Principal* refers to the identity of a given user inside an application. Therefore, *propagating the principal* means forwarding an identity from one system to another. This propagation is based on a trust relationship between two systems.

Let's say system S_1 has verified the authenticity of the user and has confirmed that the user's identity is I, then system S_2 can also assume that this user is I because S_2 trusts S_1. Perhaps S_2 recognizes the same identity under a different name. For instance, if I is known as U_1 in system S_1 and as U_2 in system S_2 and, therefore, both U_1 and U_2 refer to the same identity I, then we need a user name mapping between S_1 and S_2. This mapping can be made explicit or implicit.

Explicit User Mapping

We can maintain explicit user mapping by assigning all involved user names from S_2 to the corresponding user names in S_1. This mapping table must be stored in at least one of the systems S_1 and S_2. In the process of principal propagation, the system performing the authenticating looks up the user in the mapping table by considering the user name from the calling system.

Example: Explicit User Mapping

Your cloud application calls into SAP S/4HANA and claims that the logged in user is named JOHN_DOE. Due to the configured trust relationship between SAP S/4HANA and your cloud application, the SAP S/4HANA system assumes this claim is correct and looks in the explicit user mapping table. Perhaps this user has the user name DOEJOHN in SAP S/4HANA. Because of the explicit user mapping, the authentication is successful, and DOEJOHN is logged in.

Implicit User Mapping

In contrast to explicit user mapping, for implicit user mapping, we won't maintain the mapping on the level of concrete user names. Instead, for both S_1 and S_2, we'll define which field of the relevant user master data should be considered during principal propagation. This kind of mapping assumes that all users in S_1 have a field F_1 in their master data and F_2 is a field on the user master data in S_2. Implicit user mapping relies on the assumption that the values of F_1 in S_1 and F_2 in S_2 match syntactically.

Example: Implicit User Mapping

Let's say you specified that the field **Login Name** in the identity management of your cloud application should be the leading field for principal propagation. Your cloud application calls into SAP S/4HANA and claims that the logged in user is JOHN_DOE. Because SAP S/4HANA trusts your application, the system looks for a user with name JOHN_DOE by considering the field **User Name** in its user master data. If such a user exists, the authentication is successful.

In this section, we explored the distinction between business and technical users, provided relevant example use cases, and introduced you to the concept of principal propagation. In Section 6.4 and Section 6.5, we'll apply this knowledge when executing the configuration steps to set up the integration between the cloud application and SAP S/4HANA.

In the next section, we'll introduce the destination service on Cloud Foundry, describing its purpose and configuration. This component plays an important role in the subsequent configuration steps.

6.3 Using and Configuring Destination Service on SAP Cloud Platform Cloud Foundry

Now, let's say we want to integrate our Business Partner Address Manager application with a real SAP S/4HANA system. Because our goal is to build pure multitenant applications, we require a mechanism that allows customers to maintain the connection configuration at runtime, that is, without any interaction with the provider of the application. For this functionality, SAP Cloud Platform provides a destination service, which allows us to maintain the details of an external connection, including authentication flows.

6.3.1 Purpose of the Destination Service

The destination service on Cloud Foundry is a platform service that stores details about destinations and allows you to configure them for runtime. The destination configuration is possible on the subaccount/tenant level (see also Chapter 3 and Chapter 7). For instance, you can create an HTTP destination that points to the SAP S/4HANA system with which you want to integrate your SAP Cloud Platform subscription. Using the SAP S/4HANA Cloud SDK, you'll develop your cloud application to use a certain destination identified by its unique name. By default, the SAP S/4HANA Cloud SDK looks for a destination named "ErpQueryEndpoint" (see Chapter 4, Section 4.2.2). If necessary, destinations with other names can also be consumed by explicitly specifying their name in the application code.

Consider the code example in Listing 6.1 of a call using the virtual data model (VDM), as seen in Chapter 4:

```
new DefaultBusinessPartnerService()
  .getAllBusinessPartner()
     ...
  .execute(new ErpConfigContext("MY_DESTINATION"));
```

Listing 6.1 Calling the Business Partner API with a Custom Destination Name

Instead of using the default name implicitly, as before, we'll pass an instance of `ErpConfigContext` containing the required destination name as argument to the `execute` method (see Chapter 4, Section 4.2.1). In the given example, the SAP S/4HANA Cloud SDK looks up the destination with name "MY_DESTINATION." Thus, you can use uniquely named destinations or access more than one destination from your application. At runtime, the SAP Cloud Platform leverages the destination service, which will read the relevant destination and enriches, for instance, the HTTP request accordingly. In particular, you won't need deal with credentials, the URL of the destination, or its protocol while developing the cloud application. The SAP S/4HANA Cloud SDK will take over these activities and use the destination service to resolve the destination configuration at runtime.

6.3.2 Create and Subscribe to Destination Service

Now let's create and subscribe to a destination service.

Creating Service Instances

Before you can use destination service, you'll have to create a service instance (subscription to the destination service) and bind your application. To create the service instance, use the Cloud Foundry command line interface to enter this command:

```
cf create-service destination lite my-destination
```

After executing this command, you'll get a new service instance within your Cloud Foundry space where a service instance named `my-destination` for the `destination` service is using service plan `lite`. Alternatively, you can create a service instance using the SAP Cloud Platform cockpit, where you can also review all other existing service instances.

Binding the Destination Service Instances

So far, this service instance only exists and is not bound to a specific application yet. To bind your cloud application to the destination service, you'll have to refer to the destination service from within your manifest.yml file.

```
services:
  - ...
  - my-destination
```

After redeploying your cloud application, the binding to the new service instance will be established. Alternatively, you can bind the service instance using the following commands:

```
cf bind-service address-manager my-destination
cf restage address-manager
```

Note that `address-manager` represents the application name. You can then proceed with configuring your destinations. Figure 6.1 shows an example configuration to SAP S/4HANA where the user name JOHNDOE authenticates as technical user using Basic authentication.

6.3.3 Conduct Destination Configuration

You can configure destinations in the SAP Cloud Platform cockpit of your subaccount (see Figure 6.1). Open the **Destinations** submenu under **Connectivity** in the left-hand menu.

Click **New Destination** and fill in the required information:

- **Name**: By default, the SAP S/4HANA Cloud SDK accesses a destination named "ErpQueryEndpoint." You can also use different names, which you must mention in your application code accordingly.
- **Type**: Specify a communication protocol, such as HTTP or RFC. In order to invoke OData APIs in the SAP S/4HANA system, we'll use HTTP.

- **Description** (optional): Provide a meaningful description that explains the purpose of this destination.
- **URL**: This URL points to the SAP S/4HANA system with which your cloud application should integrate. Enter the protocol, the host name, and the port following the pattern: *https://<host>:<port>*.
- **Proxy Type**: To integrate with SAP S/4HANA, choose **OnPremise**. To integrate with SAP S/4HANA Cloud, choose **Internet**.
- **Authentication**: Choose the appropriate authentication method. In the context of the SAP S/4HANA Cloud SDK, the following methods are supported:
  - **BasicAuthentication**: Supported for integration with both SAP S/4HANA and SAP S/4HANA Cloud.
  - **PrincipalPropagation**: Supported for integration with SAP S/4HANA.
  - **OAuth2SAMLBearerAssertion**: Supported for integration with SAP S/4HANA Cloud.
- Depending on the chosen authentication method, further destination fields may be mandatory. Please refer to the Section 6.4.3, Section 6.4.4, and Section 6.5.5 for details.
- **Additional Properties**: Maintain the parameter `sap-client` and the relevant value to decide to which SAP client you want to authenticate.

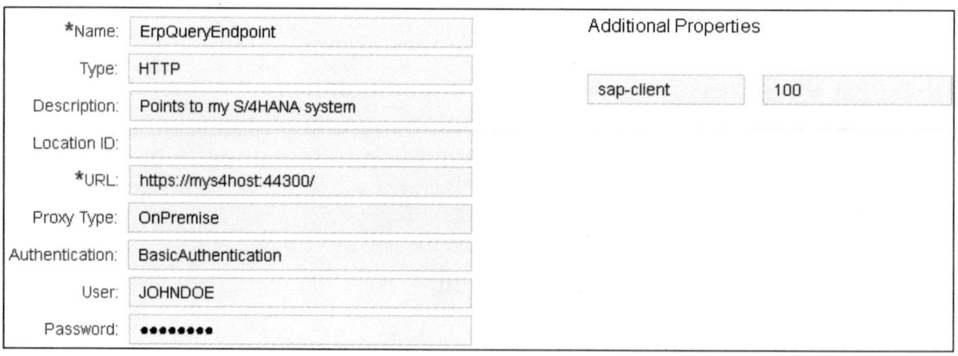

Figure 6.1 Example Destination Configuration

6.4 Integration with SAP S/4HANA Cloud

So far, in this chapter, we've discussed the following:

- The concepts of technical users, business users, and principal propagation
- Configuring a destination service on SAP Cloud Platform

We've now reached the heart of this chapter and are ready to understand how our Business Partner Address Manager application, developed securely in the previous chapters, can connect seamlessly to SAP S/4HANA Cloud. We'll assume that, as described in Chapter 5, you've created a binding of the application with the Cloud Foundry's Extended Services for User Account and Authentication (XSUAA). In addition, we assume you've also configured the use of destination service of Cloud Foundry, as described in the previous section, including its binding with the application.

As we've already seen earlier in this chapter, a connection to SAP S/4HANA Cloud may be established through Basic authentication. Another option is the SAML Bearer Assertion Flow for OAuth 2.0.

Between the two approaches, the latter is more relevant for practical use, for the simple reason that Basic authentication works only with a single, specific user. Thus, Basic authentication is more suitable to test scenarios or, in some cases, to test specific calls from specific clients, for example, an app calling another app. OAuth 2.0 SAML Bearer Assertion Flow, on the other hand, is more compelling for real-world users. For this reason, in this chapter, we'll first focus on the OAuth 2.0 mechanism. Later, we'll also cover Basic authentication, where we'll just work on top of our OAuth 2.0 configuration. Before we dive more deeply into OAuth 2.0 and Basic authentication, let's take a short detour and discuss the concepts behind authorization flow.

Specifications

Specifications for the various authentication frameworks mentioned in this chapter can be found at the following links:

- Basic Authentication: *https://tools.ietf.org/html/rfc2617*
- OAuth 2.0 Authorization Framework: *https://tools.ietf.org/html/rfc6749*
- OAuth 2.0 SAML Bearer Assertion Flow: *https://tools.ietf.org/html/rfc7522*

6.4.1 Security Assertion Markup Language

SAML is an XML-based security token format, used by applications and systems to share identity and security information with each other, across security domains. SAML is one of the important building blocks of what is popularly known as single sign-on (SSO) and, in our context, is used to exchange authentication information between systems.

6.4.2 OAuth 2.0 Authorization Framework

The OAuth 2.0 authorization framework enables an application to enjoy limited-scope access to another HTTP service, either for itself or on behalf of another request that may or may not have originated inside the app. If you've been an active user of the internet, you've likely already used OAuth 2.0 while accessing some websites.

Consider the following example where OAuth 2.0 concepts are used. Let's say you use Flickr to store your pictures, but now you want to use an online picture printing service to print out some pictures stored on Flickr. In this case, you can authorize the printing service to access your Flickr account on your behalf and select copies of pictures to print. In this scenario, not only can you authenticate the printing service to log in to Flickr, but you can also authorize it to only copy a select set of pictures and not, for example, delete or modify them. The benefit? You won't need a separate account in the printing service and can instead use your Flickr account seamlessly.

With a brief look at the concept of SAML and OAuth 2.0, let's now look at their implementation in the context of our cloud application.

For context, let's start with the big picture, in two parts—first, configuration and, then, runtime.

6.4.3 OAuth 2.0 SAML Bearer Assertion Flow Configuration

Figure 6.2 shows an overview of the main entities involved in the OAuth 2.0 SAML Bearer Assertion Flow from our cloud application to a service exposed by SAP S/4HANA Cloud.

Three entities are involved in this scenario:

- SAP Cloud Platform, where our Business Partner Address Manager application, will be deployed
- An Identity Provider (IdP), for example, SAP Cloud Platform Identity Authentication, formerly known as SAP Cloud Identity
- SAP S/4HANA Cloud

To establish the OAuth 2.0 SAML Bearer Assertion Flow, we'll need a three-way handshake between these entities, which involves the following relationships:

- A trust relationship between SAP S/4HANA Cloud and IdP.
- Entity metadata exchange between SAP Cloud Platform and the IdP.

- An SAP Cloud Platform signing certificate available in SAP S/4HANA Cloud, with an agreed application authorization scope between them. In particular, with respect to SAP Cloud Platform, you'll need XSUAA and destination service instances within the relevant subaccount.

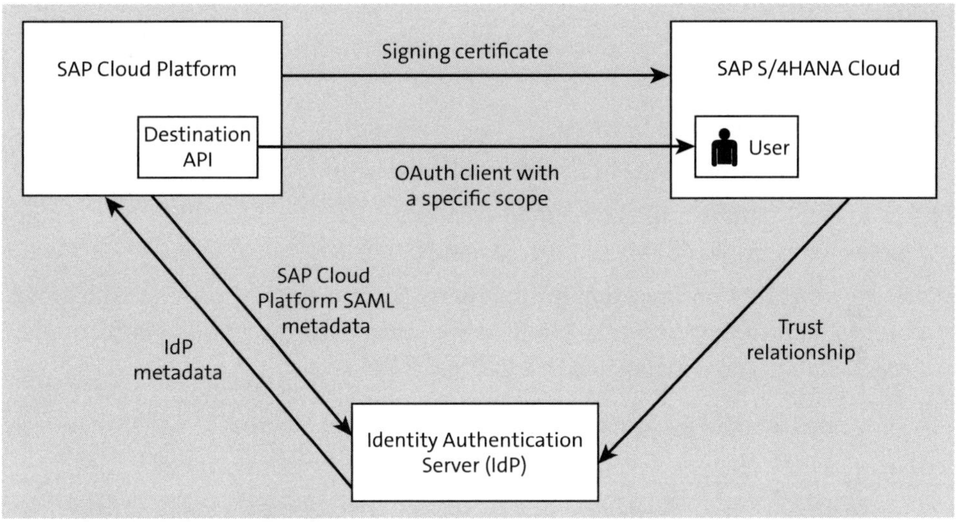

Figure 6.2 OAuth 2.0 SAML Bearer Assertion Flow: The Big Picture during Configuration

Let's now look at how to achieve this configuration. In our case, the SAP Cloud Platform Identity Authentication servers as the IdP.

Trust Relationship between SAP S/4HANA Cloud and IdP

You'll create this trust relationship when you set up user and authorization master data for the SAP S/4HANA Cloud system. While this process is outside the scope of this book, more information is available at *http://tiny.cc/scp-identity-auth*.

Metadata Exchange between SAP Cloud Platform and IdP

Let's look at the two sides of the configuration one at a time. First, focusing on the transfer of metadata from the SAP Cloud Platform to IdP, follow these steps:

1. Get the SAP Cloud Platform SAML metadata from the following URL:

   https://<your-tenant-id>.authentication.<your-region-host>.hana.ondemand.com/saml/metadata

Continuing with our example from Chapter 5, for our purposes, this URL will look like this: *https://p1942765239trial.authentication.eu10.hana.ondemand.com/saml/metadata*

Further Information

You can find further information on regions at *http://tiny.cc/scp-regions.*

2. Save the metadata.xml file on your local computer.
3. Login to SAP Cloud Platform Identity Authentication.
4. Go to **Applications** and choose **Add** to add a custom application. Then, enter a name, for example, "p1942765239trial," and click **Save**.
5. Go to **SAML 2.0 Configuration** for the newly created application. Click the **Browse** button next to the **Metadata File** field and upload the SAP Cloud Platform SAML metadata file you downloaded in Step 1. Click **Save**.

The end result should be similar to the screen shown in Figure 6.3.

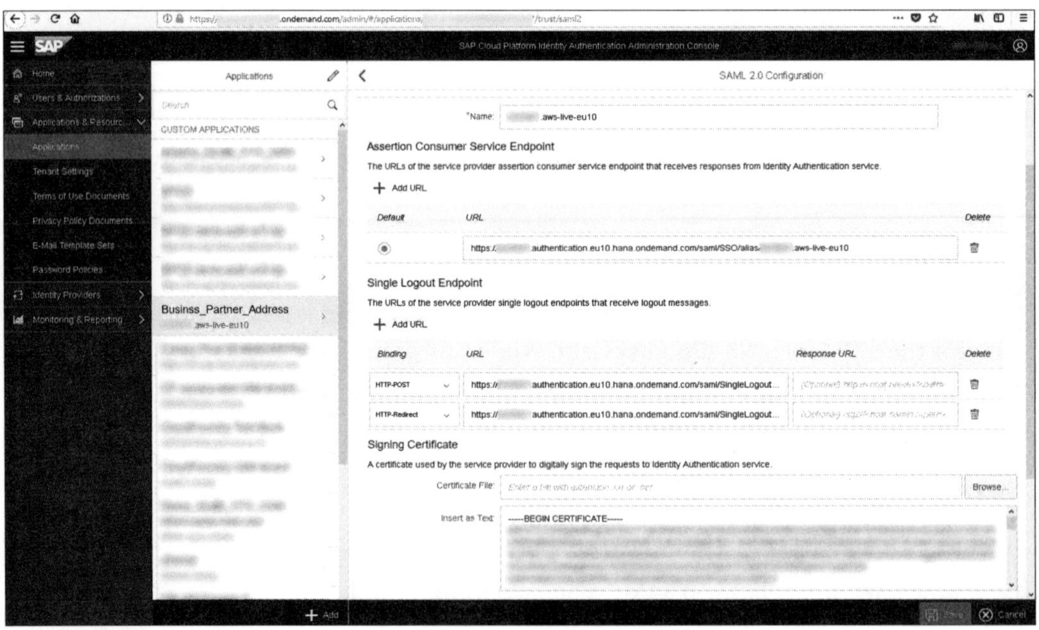

Figure 6.3 Configured Application in SAP Cloud Platform Identity Authentication

Second, to create the connection from Identity Authentication to the SAP Cloud Platform, follow these steps:

1. Log in to your SAP Cloud Platform Identity Authentication with administrator rights.
2. Navigate to **Application & Resources • Tenant Settings**, and then select **SAML 2.0 Configuration**. Next, click on **Download Metadata** to download the authentication server metadata file to your local computer, as shown in Figure 6.4.

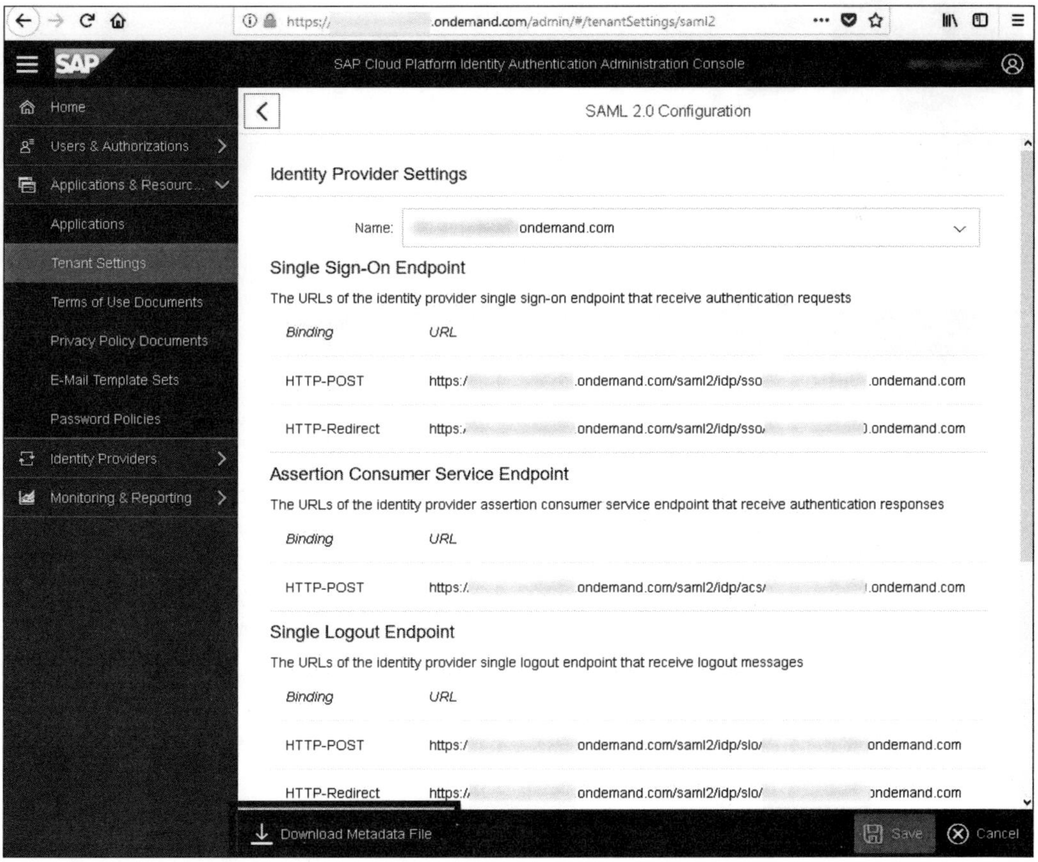

Figure 6.4 Download Metadata from SAP Cloud Platform Identity Authentication

3. Log in to your SAP Cloud Platform subaccount.
4. In the SAP Cloud Platform cockpit, navigate to **Security • Trust Configuration** on the left pane.

5. Click **New Trust Configuration**, as shown in Figure 6.5.

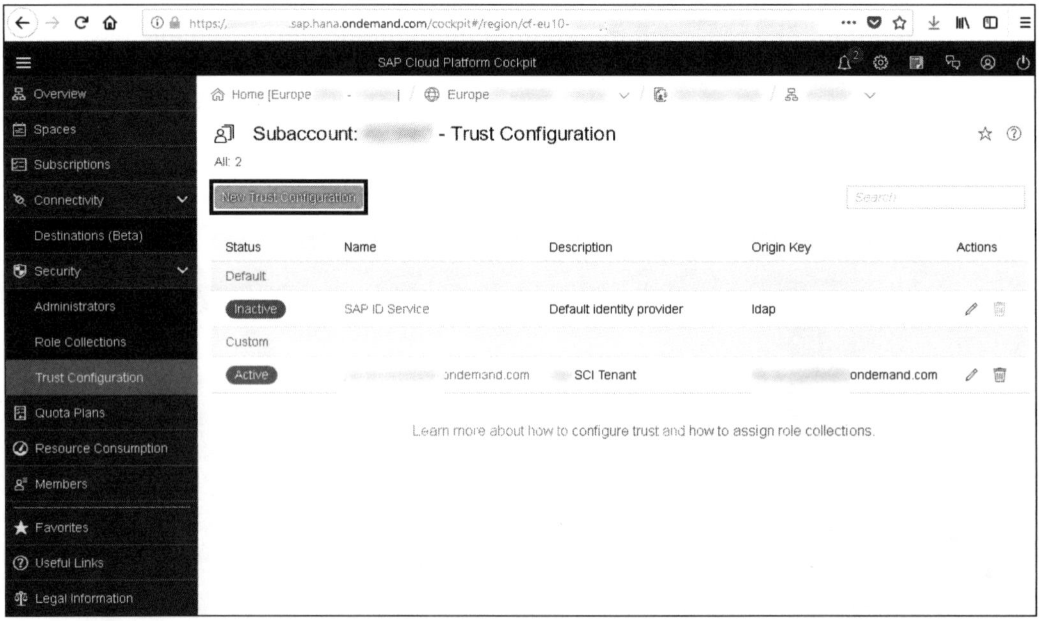

Figure 6.5 New Trust Configuration in the SAP Cloud Platform Cockpit

6. In the dialog box that opens, upload the Identity Authentication metadata you downloaded earlier, by clicking the **Upload** button next to **Metadata** field.
7. Click **Save**.

You've now completed the required configuration between SAP Cloud Platform and Identity Authentication.

Signing Certificate and OAuth Client with Scope Exchange between SAP Cloud Platform and SAP S/4HANA Cloud

In this step, we'll complete the following three activities:

- Setting up communication artifacts in SAP S/4HANA Cloud,
- Setting identity and access management in SAP S/4HANA Cloud
- Configuring destination parameters in SAP Cloud Platform

Before we dive into the more specific steps, let's be sure we understand the semantic meaning of these activities first. Without a long detour, let's take a brief look at the concepts of communication and identity and access management artifacts used by SAP S/4HANA Cloud to expose services for external use.

Communication Artifacts in SAP S/4HANA Cloud

Figure 6.6 shows an overview of the SAP S/4HANA Cloud artifacts that come into play in this process.

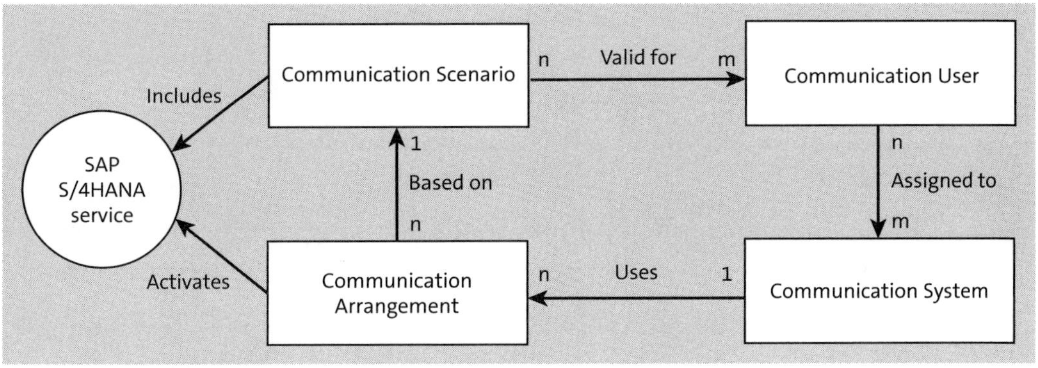

Figure 6.6 Overview of SAP S/4HANA Cloud Communication Artifacts

Let's look at these entities in a little more detail:

- **Communication arrangements**
  A communication arrangement acts as the primary integration point for an SAP S/4HANA Cloud system and allows you to configure inbound and outbound connections on a semantic level. A communication arrangement bundles a communication scenario and a communication system together and specifies necessary connection parameters such as authentication method and communication user information.
- **Communication systems**
  A communication system represents the SAP Cloud Platform subaccount through which you'll consume your cloud application. The communication system holds technical information such as hostname, IP address, user identity, certificates, etc.
- **Communication scenarios (also known as integration scenarios)**
  A communication scenario is the basis on which communication arrangements are configured. Delivered by SAP, communication scenarios bundle services exposed by SAP S/4HANA Cloud. As a user, you can also create your own custom communication scenarios.

- **Communication user (also known as technical user)**
  A communication user is assigned to communication system and is used by communication scenarios to log in to SAP S/4HANA Cloud system.

Identity and Access Management (IAM) Artifacts in SAP S/4HANA Cloud

Figure 6.7 shows the various IAM entities and their relationships with each other.

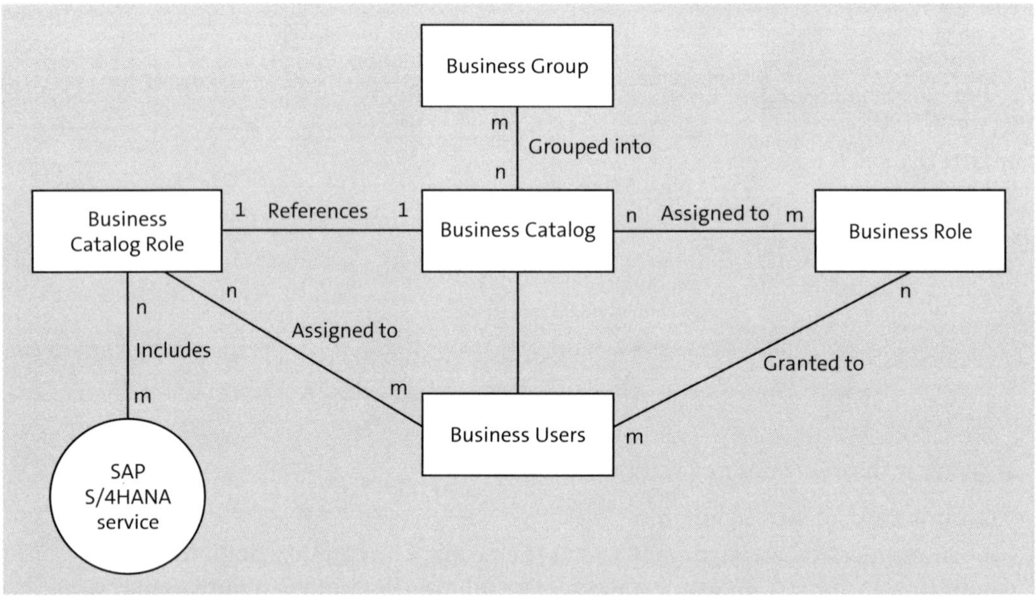

Figure 6.7 SAP S/4HANA Cloud Identity and Access Management Artifacts

Let's look at each entity briefly next:

- **Business user**
  As mentioned earlier in this chapter, a business user represents an existing, physical user, who would access an SAP S/4HANA Cloud service.
- **Business role**
  A business user is granted a business role, which models the end-user persona, for example, a business partner administrator.
- **Business catalog**
  Delivered by SAP, a business catalog is a collection of all applications and their relevant authorization restrictions that can be assigned to a business role. Technically business catalogs are collections of SAP Fiori tiles that a business user would access for day-to-day tasks. Business catalogs are grouped into business groups.

- **Business catalog role**
  Also delivered by SAP, a business catalog role is a ready-to-consume bundle of a given business catalog with its relevant authorizations required by end users to access applications in the business catalog.

Further Information

More information on communication management and identity and access management artifacts can be found at *http://tiny.cc/s4-ciam*.

In short, SAP S/4HANA Cloud's communication and identity and access management concept consists of powerful, robust, secure, and yet highly flexible set of entities that enable cloud application developers to access SAP S/4HANA services efficiently.

Now that we've had a brief look at the theoretical concepts, we're ready to perform the integration steps in the system.

Configuring Communication and Identity and Access Management in SAP S/4HANA Cloud

For this configuration, you'll have to switch back and forth between the SAP S/4HANA Cloud system and your SAP Cloud Platform Cloud Foundry cockpit.

Let's begin in SAP S/4HANA Cloud:

1. Log in to your SAP S/4HANA Cloud SAP Fiori launchpad as an administrator.
2. In the **Communication Management** section, click the **Communication Systems** tile.
3. On the **Communication Systems** screen, click **New** and then enter "BUSINESS_PARTNER_ADDRESS" as the **System ID** and **System Name**. Click **Create**.
4. Enter any value in the mandatory field **Host Name** (for example, "p1942765239trial.aws-live-eu10"). The actual value won't be used and thus you can choose freely. Click **Save**.
5. Click **Edit** and then the **+** icon to add a **User for Inbound Communication**.
6. On the **New Inbound Communication User** screen, click **New User** and make the following entries:
   - **User Name**: Enter "BUSINESS_PARTNER_ADDRESS."
   - **Description**: Enter a suitable description, such as "Business Partner Address."
   - **Password**: Enter a password and remember this password for a later step.
7. Click **Edit** and then the **+** icon to add a **User for Outbound Communication**.

8. On the **New Inbound User** screen, make the following entries:
   - **User Name**: Enter "BUSINESS_PARTNER_ADDRESS."
   - **Password**: Enter the password for this user, selected in a previous step.
9. Click **Create**, and then **OK**. **Save** the communication system.
10. Click on the user name and note the following information: the **Communication user ID** (with the pattern "CC...") and the user name specified earlier. Close the **Display Inbound Communication User** dialog box.

The end result should be similar to the screen shown in Figure 6.8.

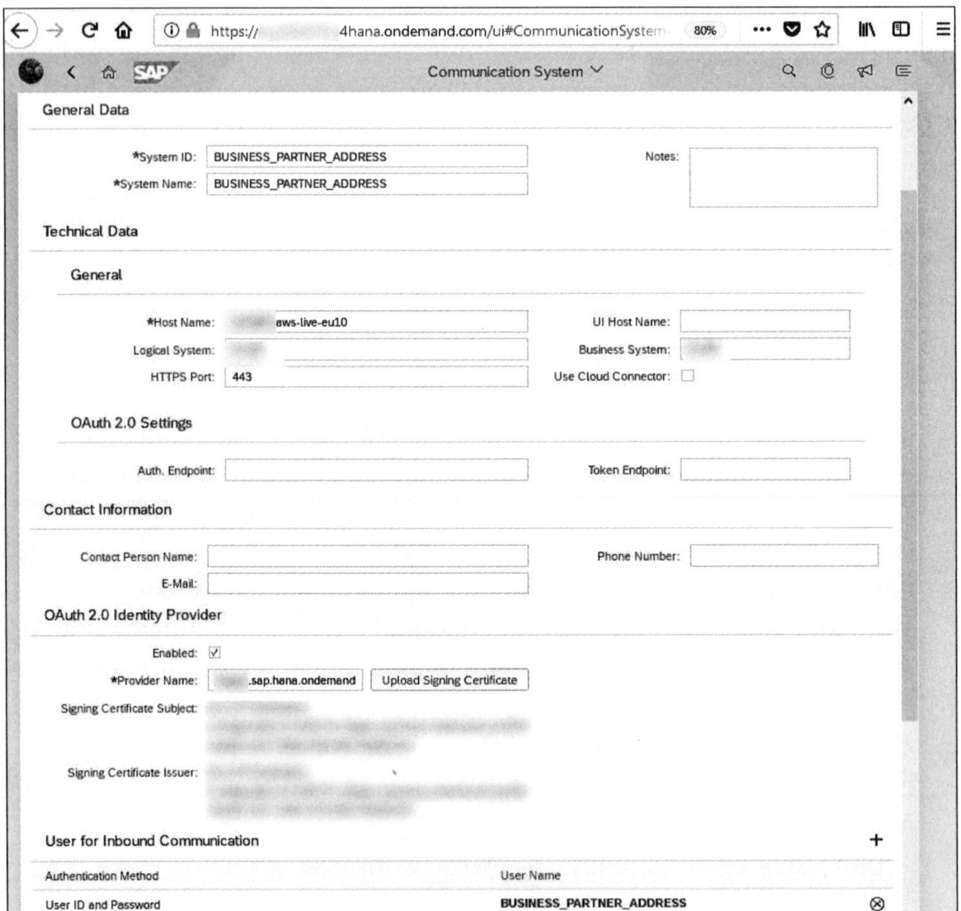

Figure 6.8 Communication System in SAP S/4HANA Cloud

Now, let's switch over to SAP Cloud Platform to perform the following steps:

1. Log in to your SAP Cloud Platform subaccount.
2. In the SAP Cloud Platform cockpit, navigate to **Destination**, as shown in Figure 6.10.
3. You should see the destination configuration you set up earlier in Section 6.3.
4. Click **Download Trust** to download your subaccount-specific key used to set up OAuth SAML bearer principal propagation to SAP S/4HANA system. You'll download this key to your local machine, as shown in Figure 6.9.

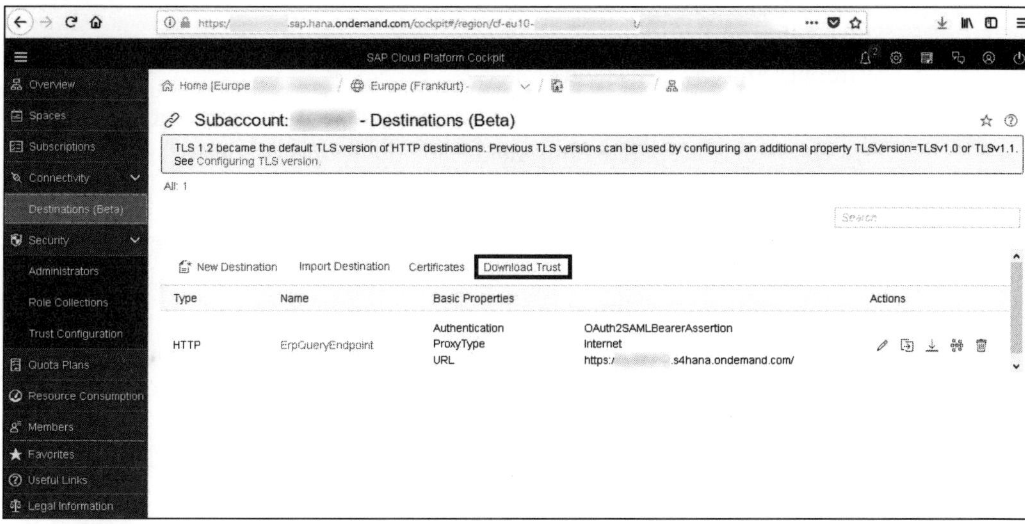

Figure 6.9 Download Trust Metadat from SAP Cloud Platform

5. Next, choose the destination you configured in Section 6.3, (for example, **Erp-QueryEndpoint**) and then click **Edit**.
6. Select **OAuth2SAMLBearerAssertion** from the **Authentication** dropdown list (if not already chosen). You should now see additional fields for input.
7. Enter the following values:
   - **Audience**: *https://<myNNNNNN>.s4hana.ondemand.com*
     - Replace *myNNNNNN* with the hostname of your SAP S/4HANA system. Make sure the URL does not end with a slash.

- **Client Key**: Enter "BUSINESS_PARTNER_ADDRESS," which is the communication user name that you specified earlier in this section.
- **Token Service URL**: Enter *https://<myNNNNNN>.s4hana.ondemand.com/sap/bc/sec/oauth2/token?sap-client=100*
  - Replace *myNNNNNN* with the host name of your SAP S/4HANA system.
  - Replace the sap-client number with your system-specific value.
- **Token Service User**: Enter "BUSINESS_PARTNER_ADDRESS," which again is your communication user name.
- **Token Service Password**: Enter the password of the communication user that you created earlier in this section.
- **System User**: Leave this field empty.
- **Additional Properties**: Click on **New Property** and enter information in the **Property Name** and **Property Value** fields. For the **Property Name** field, type these values, instead of choosing values from the dropdown menu.
  - `authnContextClassRef` = "urn:oasis:names:tc:SAML:2.0:ac:classes:X509"
  - `userIdSource` = "mail"
  - `nameIdFormat` = "urn:oasis:names:tc:SAML:1.1:nameid-format:emailAddress"
  - `scope` = "API_BUSINESS_PARTNER_0001"

Note

The scope parameter you specify in these steps is your application-specific OAuth scope, which will be checked against SAP S/4HANA Cloud, when you access the business partner service.

To find out your application-specific OAuth scope, refer to the service documentation at *http://api.sap.com*.

The end result should be similar to Figure 6.10.

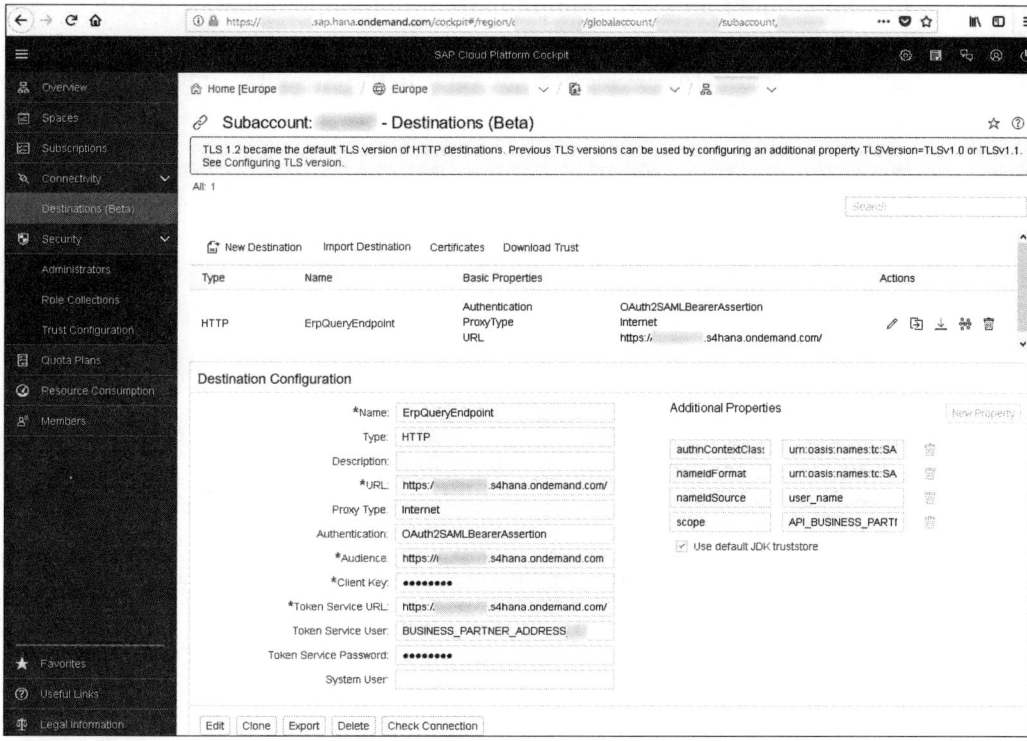

Figure 6.10 Configuring Destination Service of SAP Cloud Platform to connect to SAP S/4HANA Cloud

Now, let's switch back to SAP S/4HANA Cloud:

1. Log in to your SAP S/4HANA Cloud SAP Fiori launchpad as an administrator.
2. Under **COMMUNICATION MANAGEMENT** section, click the **COMMUNICATION SYSTEMS** tile. Then, choose the communication system you created earlier, **BUSINESS_PARTNER_ADDRESS**.
3. Edit the communication system.
4. Under **OAuth 2.0 Identity Provider**, select the **Enabled** checkbox.
5. Upload the certificate file representing the subaccount-specific signing certificate you downloaded during SAP Cloud Platform configuration earlier. You'll see that fields **Signing Certificate Subject** and **Signing Certificate Issuer** have been filled automatically. However, the mandatory field **Provider Name** is still empty.

6. In the **Provider Name** field, enter the ID of the owner of the signing certificate. This ID is available as the value of attribute "common name" (CN) of the signing certificate. To find this ID, look for the value in the attribute "common name" (CN) in field **Signing Certificate Subject**.

Example

If your **Signing Certificate Subject** is:

```
OU=CP Destination Configuration,
O=<your-organization>,
CN=<your-host-name>.hana.ondemand.com/<unique-id>,
```

then the **Provider Name** will be:

```
<your-host-name>.hana.ondemand.com/<unique-id>
```

7. Click **Save**.
8. Under **Communication Management**, click the **Communication Arrangements** tile.
9. On the **Communications Arrangements** screen, click **New** and then select the communication scenario SAP_COM_0008, which includes the OData service for business partners, exposed by SAP S/4HANA Cloud.

Information about Communication Scenarios

For information about communication scenarios for an SAP S/4HANA API, go to the respective API documentation at *http://api.sap.com*. For example, for the business partner API, the documentation is available at *http://tiny.cc/s4-api-hub-bp*, which also lists the communication scenario the API is a part of.

10. Enter "BUSINESS_PARTNER_ADDRESS" in the **Communication Arrangement** field and then click **Create**.
11. On the next screen, select the communication system you created during initial SAP S/4HANA Cloud configuration earlier ("BUSINESS_PARTNER_ADDRESS"). Notice that the relevant user for inbound and outbound communication has been chosen automatically.
12. Use the input help of the **User Name** field and select **OAuth 2.0** as the authentication method.
13. Deselect the **Service Status** checkbox in all subsections under **Outbound Services**.

14. Click **Save**.

The end result should be similar to the screen shown in Figure 6.11.

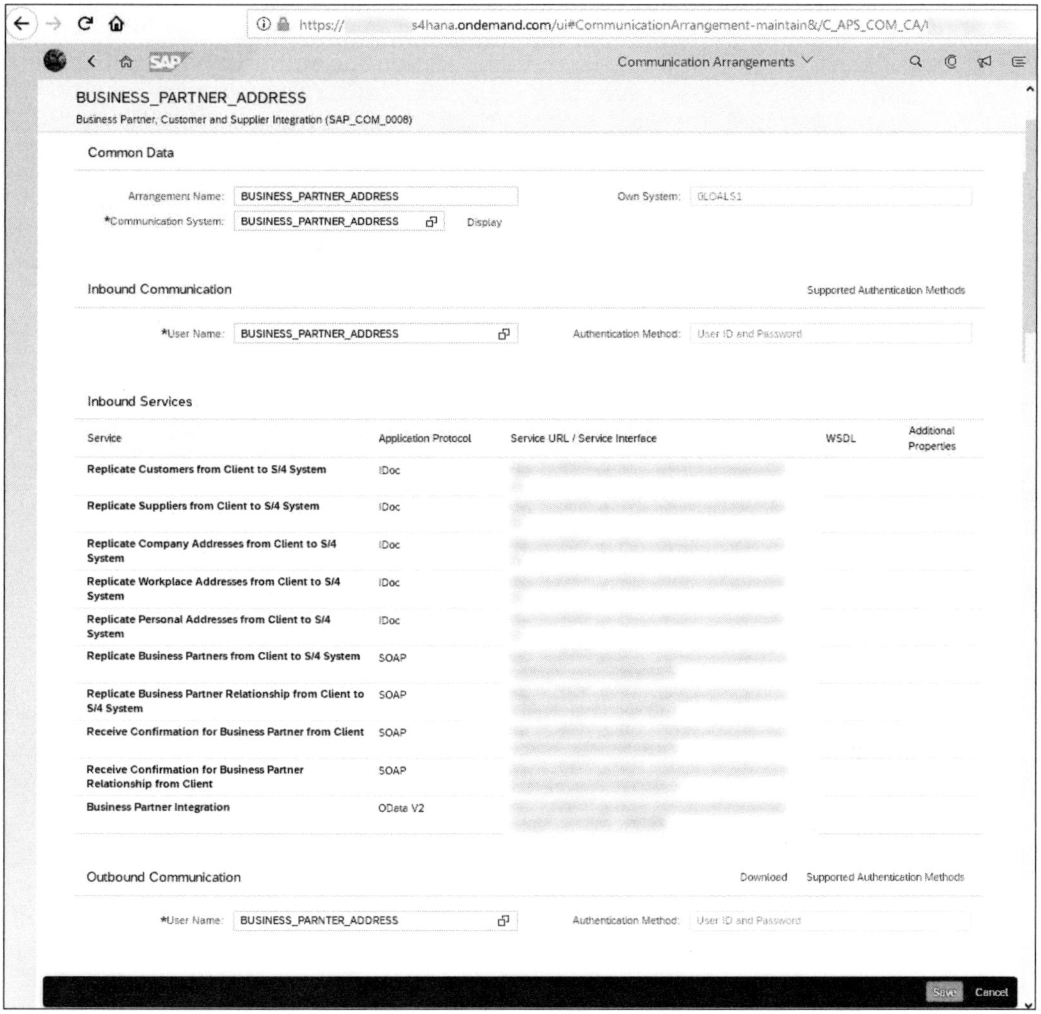

Figure 6.11 Communication Arrangement in SAP S/4HANA Cloud

At this point, you've configured a connection from our cloud-based Business Partner Address Manager application to SAP S/4HANA Cloud. Now, we're ready to run our application, but before we do, let's look at what happens under the hood when the application runs.

6.4.4 OAuth 2.0 SAML Bearer Assertion Flow—Runtime

Figure 6.12 shows the sequence of steps between when a user requests a business partner address from the application on SAP Cloud Platform and when the user gets results back. In this section, our discussion will be in the context of OAuth 2.0 SAML Bearer Assertion Flow as the chosen authentication and authorization mechanism.

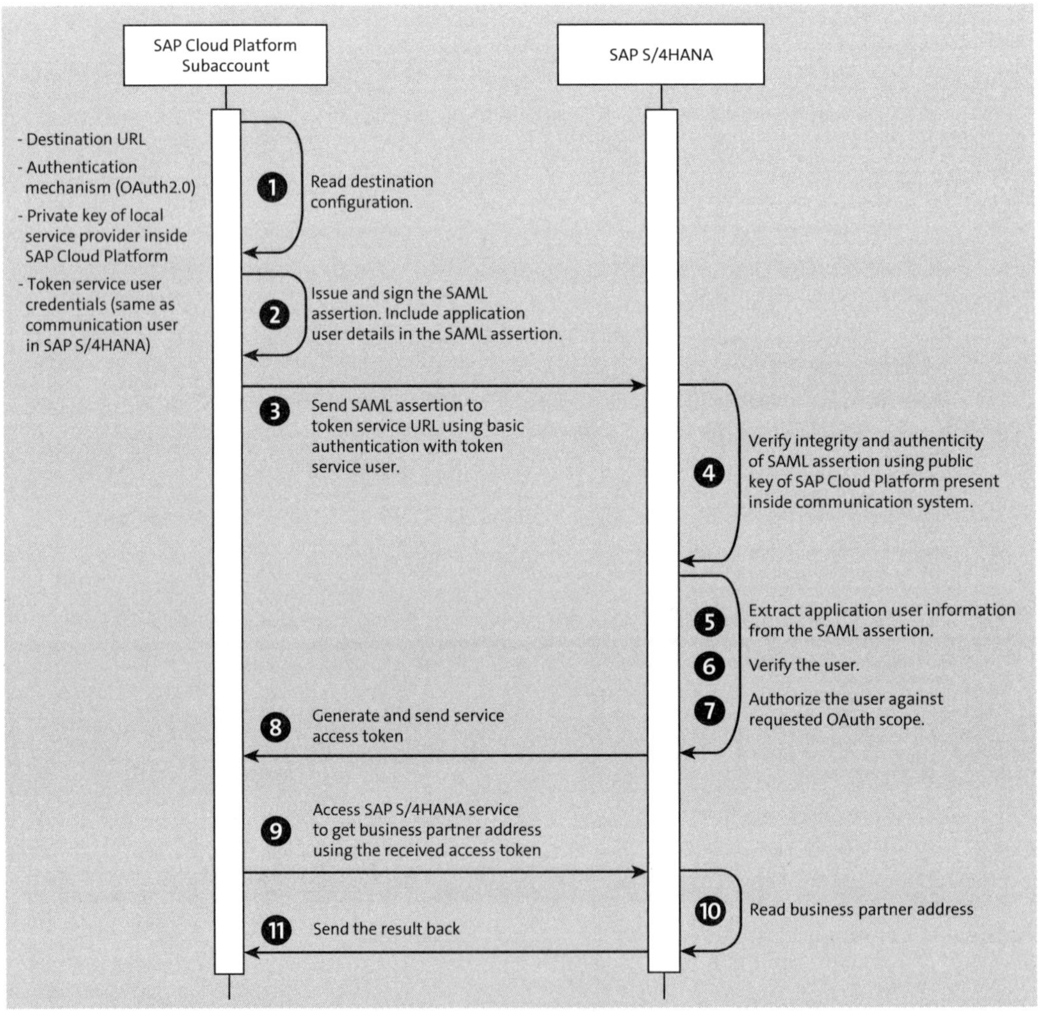

Figure 6.12 OAuth 2.0 SAML Bearer Assertion Flow: The Big Picture during Runtime

Let's look at these steps in detail:

1. As soon as the Business Partner Address Manager application receives a user request, the application accesses the destination and related configuration information on SAP Cloud Platform ❶. Specifically, the app reads the following information:
   - URL, the SAP S/4HANA Cloud endpoint
   - Authentication, in our case, "OAuth2SAMLBearerAssertion"
   - OAuth scope, which will be sent with the request
   - Private key of the local service provider inside SAP Cloud Platform with which to sign the SAML assertion.
   - Token service URL, user name, and password to access the SAP S/4HANA Cloud token service to get an access token.
2. Using this information, the SAP Cloud Platform issues an SAML assertion, which includes details about the application user. Then, the SAP Cloud Platform signs the SAML assertion with the private key. ❷
3. Then, the SAP Cloud Platform sends the SAML assertion to the SAP S/4HANA Cloud token service endpoint, using Basic authentication, with token service user name and password as login credentials. ❸
4. The SAP S/4HANA Cloud token service verifies the SAML assertion with the public key uploaded in the communication system. ❹
5. Upon successful verification, the SAP Cloud Platform extracts application user information from the SAML assertion ❺. Then, the SAP Cloud Platform looks for a matching business user inside SAP S/4HANA Cloud ❻ and checks whether this business user is authorized for the incoming OAuth scope ❼.

Note

The mechanism to check for a matching user depends upon the value in the `nameIdFormat` field, which you specified as an additional property in SAP Cloud Platform destination configuration.

- If `nameIdFormat = urn:oasis:names:tc:SAML:1.1:nameid-format:emailAddress`, which is how we've configured our example, then the user is matched using the `E-Mail` field.
- If `nameIdFormat = urn:oasis:names:tc:SAML:1.1:nameid-format:unspecified`, then the user is matched on fields other than `E-Mail`.

6. If the check is successful, the token service generates a temporary, session-specific access token and sends the token back to the calling application on SAP Cloud Platform. ❽
7. The application accesses SAP S/4HANA Cloud business partner service with this token, using "OAuthSAMLBearerAssertion" authentication mechanism. ❾
8. SAP S/4HANA Cloud service reads the requested business partner address. ❿
9. Finally, SAP S/4HANA sends the result back to the application. ⓫

All this happens under the hood, without the end user noticing.

Now that we understand the configuration and runtime mechanics of the OAuth 2.0 SAML Bearer Assertion Flow, let's turn our attention briefly to Basic authentication, which we'll discuss in the next subsection.

6.4.5 Basic Authentication

Using Basic authentication is different from using the OAuth 2.0 SAML Bearer Assertion Flow in the following ways:

- Setting up an OAuth client inside SAP S/4HANA Cloud is not required.
- In the SAP Cloud Platform **Destination Configuration**, **Authentication** is specified as "BasicAuthentication." The **Proxy Type** remains "Internet" to indicate that the connection is intended for SAP S/4HANA Cloud.
- In this approach, you'll only need to provide a login user name and password in the **User** and **Password** fields. This information may be for any user that has the authorization to run the requested service, in our case the business partner service, inside SAP S/4HANA Cloud.
- Maintaining additional parameters, as we did in OAuth, is no longer needed.
- In SAP S/4HANA Cloud, while creating the communication arrangement, when choosing the communication system, you'll select **User ID and Password** as authentication method for the relevant communication user.

At runtime, a call is made to SAP S/4HANA service using the user credentials provided in this list. Semantically, this process is equivalent to when a human being accesses the service using his or her login credentials.

Thus concludes our section on connecting our cloud application with SAP S/4HANA Cloud, using OAuth 2.0 SAML Bearer Assertion Flow or Basic authentication. In the next section, we'll look at how this connection may be achieved for SAP S/4HANA on-premise.

6.5 Integration with SAP S/4HANA On-Premise

In this section, we'll focus on the integration between the cloud application and SAP S/4HANA. After introducing the architecture and the relevant components, we'll describe an example flow and present the configuration steps to achieve the integration using a technical user or a business user.

6.5.1 Architecture and Involved Components

Figure 6.13 shows all relevant components.

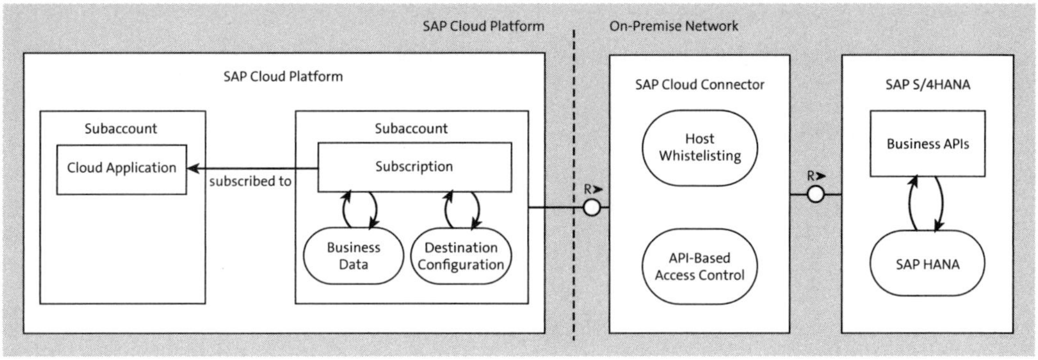

Figure 6.13 Architecture of Integration between SAP Cloud Platform and SAP S/4HANA over the Cloud Connector

Because our application runs on the SAP Cloud Platform, the Cloud Connector acts as reverse proxy between the SAP Cloud Platform and SAP S/4HANA. Both SAP S/4HANA and the Cloud Connector reside inside the on-premise network.

The cloud application will be consumed through a subaccount in SAP Cloud Platform. Either the application is deployed on the SAP Cloud Platform, or the relevant subaccount subscribes to the cloud application deployed in another subaccount. The cloud application may have its own database to store business data, depending on the use case. Furthermore, the destination configuration inside the subaccount is configured to point to the right SAP S/4HANA system.

Cloud Connector

Apart from the SAP Cloud Platform, the Cloud Connector is an independent technical component. The Cloud Connector is installed on a machine inside the on-premise network and connects to the SAP Cloud Platform subaccount to establish a secure and encrypted tunnel between the subaccount and the on-premise network, thus acting as a reverse proxy to the cloud application. Applications or subscriptions available in the connected subaccount can then send requests to the on-premise network, while the Cloud Connector receives the requests and checks whether the target host, port, and API are whitelisted. If so, the Cloud Connector forwards the request to the relevant target API of SAP S/4HANA.

Using whitelisting in the Cloud Connector, the administrator can grant fine-grained access to endpoints within the on-premise network. In other words, every request targeting an API not whitelisted will be rejected by default.

The Cloud Connector plays an important role in the process of principal propagation. Being in a trust relationship with the SAP S/4HANA system, the Cloud Connector issues the user identity from the cloud application to SAP S/4HANA.

SAP S/4HANA

The SAP S/4HANA system contains business data and provides business APIs to invoke business processes. The APIs are required if the cloud application are exposed by the SAP S/4HANA system. For instance, OData APIs must be activated in the SAP S/4HANA backend.

Apart from that, the SAP S/4HANA system will be configured to trust the Cloud Connector and, thus, will accept principal propagation as the authentication method.

6.5.2 Example Flow

Let's consider an example flow, as shown in Figure 6.14.

Let's assume that your cloud application invokes an OData API in the SAP S/4HANA system. This HTTP request will be created by the SAP S/4HANA Cloud SDK; will contain the target URL, the request header, and payload (if applicable); and will be sent to your SAP S/4HANA system.

On its way, the HTTP request will be considered, checked, and forwarded by the Cloud Connector. For SAP S/4HANA systems using whitelisted OData APIs, the request will be forwarded to SAP S/4HANA for further processing.

Authentication via Technical User

When leveraging technical users for authentication, the HTTP request generated on the SAP Cloud Platform will contain user credentials in the header. These credentials are retrieved from the configured destination within the subaccount.

The Cloud Connector forwards the HTTP request to the SAP S/4HANA system without inspecting the HTTP header. Thus, SAP S/4HANA receives the credentials in the header and initiates the authentication itself. If the authentication is successful, the OData API will be invoked in the context of the technical user.

Authentication via Business User

The sequence shown in Figure 6.14 depicts the example flow we described in this section. We assume that the business user has launched our Business Partner Address Manager application, which triggers the retrieval of business partner data from SAP S/4HANA.

The SAP Cloud Platform issues an SAML assertion, which contains user information, and sends the assertion to the Cloud Connector. The Cloud Connector verifies if whether the SAML assertion is trustworthy and, if so, extracts the user information.

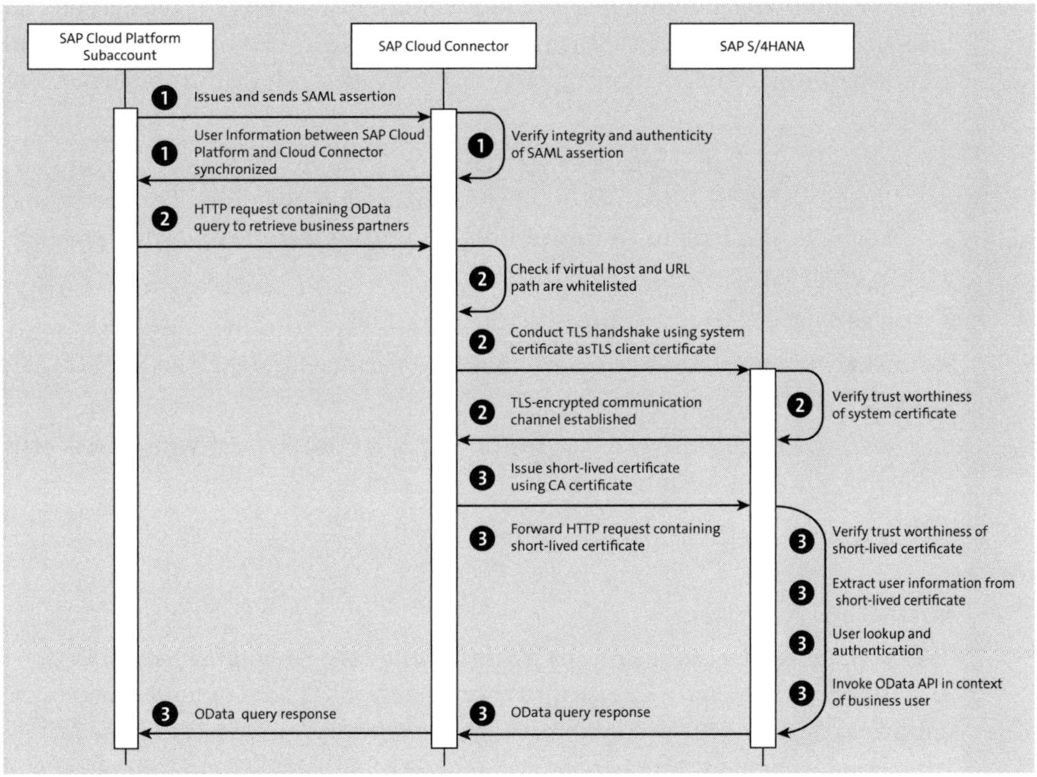

Figure 6.14 Example Flow of Communication between SAP Cloud Platform and SAP S/4HANA over the Cloud Connector

Subsequently, the HTTP request that contains the OData query will be sent to the Cloud Connector. After ensuring that the virtual host and the URL path of the request are whitelisted, the Cloud Connector will issue a certificate containing the user name from the cloud application as its subject. This certificate is also referred to as a short-lived certificate since it's only valid for a short time frame (by default, one hour). As the configuration of this integration included establishing a trust relationship between the Cloud Connector and SAP S/4HANA, SAP S/4HANA can verify this certificate. After extracting the user name from the short-lived certificate, SAP S/4HANA looks up the corresponding user name in the explicit mapping table. If a user name is found, and this user exists and is unlocked, the authentication will be successful. As a result, the OData API will be invoked in the name of the authenticated business user.

6.5.3 Integration Setup Independent from Authentication Method

In this section, we'll present the integration configuration steps you'll need conduct independently of the chosen authentication method. Later on, we'll introduce a separation between technical or business users and leverage this distinction in our configuration.

To integrate your cloud application with SAP S/4HANA, you'll have to configure several things, such as the destination of your application, the Cloud Connector, and your SAP S/4HANA system. In this section, we assume that the following prerequisites have been met:

- You've deployed your cloud application in your space on Cloud Foundry.
- You have administrative access to a machine residing inside the on-premise network.
- You have administrative access to the SAP S/4HANA system with which your cloud application will integrate.

Let's now turn to setting up the integration step by step.

Install Cloud Connector

The Cloud Connector can run on any machine within the on-premise network as long as it can access the public internet (to connect to your Cloud Foundry subaccount) and access the SAP S/4HANA system. For good performance, we recommend installing this component as close as possible to the SAP S/4HANA system. You can download the Cloud Connector at *https://tools.hana.ondemand.com/#cloud*.

On this web page, navigate to the **Cloud Connector** section and choose the right artifact depending on the operating system of your target machine.

We also recommend checking out the prerequisites page linked at that web page, which provides information about the technical prerequisites for the target machine. For example, the latest patch of Java Development Kit 7 or 8 must be installed. In the next step, launch the installer with administrator privileges and follow the installation steps guided by the wizard. Once the wizard is finished, the Cloud Connector will be installed, and you should be able to open a browser and visit the following URL: *https://localhost:8443/*.

6

Note

Change the port according to what you specified during the installation.

You should see a login prompt for the Cloud Connector, as shown in Figure 6.15, which proves that the Cloud Connector is running on the target machine.

Figure 6.15 Login Prompt for the Cloud Connector

Plenty more information is available at *http://help.sap.com* for topics beyond the scope of this book, such as securely setting up and operating the Cloud Connector. We also recommend you read the relevant help pages provided by SAP at *https://www.sap.com/developer/tutorials/hcp-cloud-connector-setup.html*.

Activate APIs in SAP S/4HANA

You'll need to ensure that the APIs inside SAP S/4HANA, which your cloud application needs to use, are exposed and, therefore, callable from an external system.

Let's assume that you want to consume OData APIs exposed by your SAP S/4HANA system. To activate OData APIs, use Transaction /IWFND/MAINT_SERVICE (Activate and Maintain Services). Check whether the relevant OData API is part of the list under **Service Catalog**. If so, you can utilize the SAP Gateway client to see if the API works by clicking **SAP Gateway Client**, as shown in Figure 6.16.

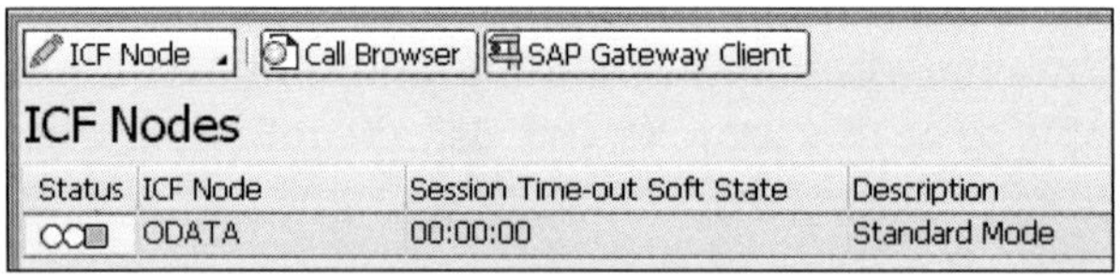

Figure 6.16 SAP Gateway Client Tool

Once the SAP Gateway Client has launched, click on **Execute**. If you receive an HTTP response on the right side of the screen, the API works as expected, as shown in Figure 6.17.

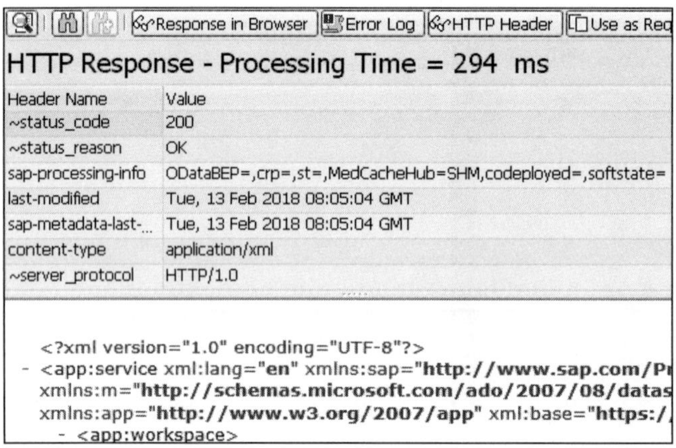

Figure 6.17 OData API Response after Invocation by SAP Gateway Client

If not, you'll have to activate the API before you can use it. Click on **Add Service**, choose the corresponding system alias, and click **Get Services**. SAP S/4HANA will fetch all installed APIs that have not been exposed. Select the required API and click on **Add Selected Services**. A popup window will open where you'll check and confirm the package assignment. After processing, you'll see a message that the metadata has been loaded successfully. The OData API is now activated.

So far, we've set up a configuration independent of any authentication method. In the following sections, we'll look at the configuration steps specific to each authentication method.

6.5.4 Integration Setup Leveraging Technical Users

In this section, we'll present the configuration steps to enable the integration with SAP S/4HANA leveraging technical users.

User and Role Management

The first step is to create a technical user. SAP S/4HANA distinguishes several user types, for instance:

- Dialog users: These are individual users, with specific and interactive access to system, typically representing a physical person.
- System users: These are used for internal system processes such as workflows or background processes.
- Communication users: These are used for system-to-system communication, such as function calls.

These user types differ in terms of their ability to conduct dialog processing, password expiry policy, etc. In the context of this section, we'll utilize a communication user since we do not need dialog processing for our purposes.

First, create a new user in Transaction SU01 (User Maintenance). Second, enter a chosen user name and then click **Create**. On the next screen, enter all mandatory fields, such as the surname. On the **Logon Data** tab, select **Communications Data** from the **User Type** dropdown list, as shown in Figure 6.18, specify a password and then save the user.

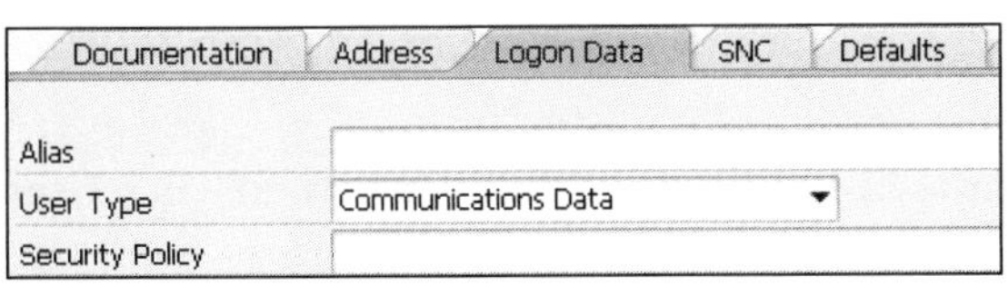

Figure 6.18 Specify User Type as Communications Data

Finally, you can leverage credentials to log on to SAP S/4HANA. However, the user still lacks the authorization to invoke the relevant OData API. Therefore, we'll need to use roles to assign privileges to our new user.

We can assign privileges to our user by creating a new role to be assigned to the newly created user. This role includes the OData API to grant the user the necessary authorization object (S_SERVICE). Follow these steps:

1. Open the transaction **Role Maintenance** (Transaction PFCG).
2. Enter the name of the new role and click on **Create Single Role**.
3. Provide a meaningful description for the role and click **Save**.
4. In the **Menu** tab, enter a new **Authorization Default**. In the popup window that opens, choose the following:
   - **Authorization Default**: TADIR Service
   - **Object Type**: IWSG
5. In the table shown in Figure 6.19, enter the name of your OData API surrounded by wildcards, such as "*API_BUSINESS_PARTNER*." Press F4 to open the input help and select the entry. Click **Return** and then **Copy**.

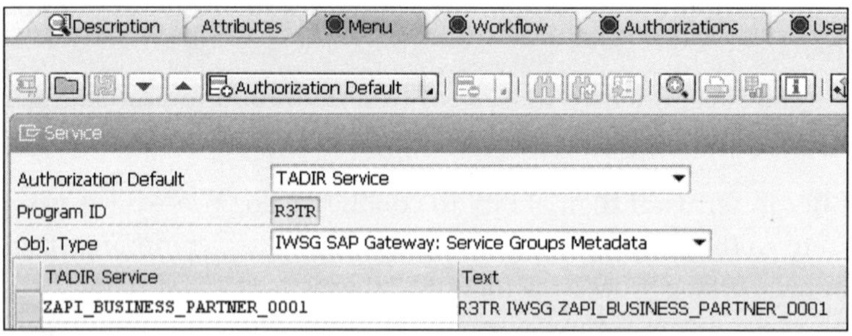

Figure 6.19 Enter OData API as Authorization Default

- In the **Authorizations** tab, click **Change Authorization Data**. On the next screen, you'll see the authorization object S_SERVICE (Figure 6.20) below the object class for **Cross-Application Authorization Objects**. In the menu bar, click the **Generate** button (checkered disc) to generate the corresponding profile. Return to Transaction PFCG.
- In the **User** tab, enter the user name of the newly created user. Then, click **User Comparison** to assign the generated profile to this user.
- Once all three tabs (**Menu**, **Authorizations**, and **User**) show a green indicator, the process is completed.

Your new user now has the required privileges to call the OData API.

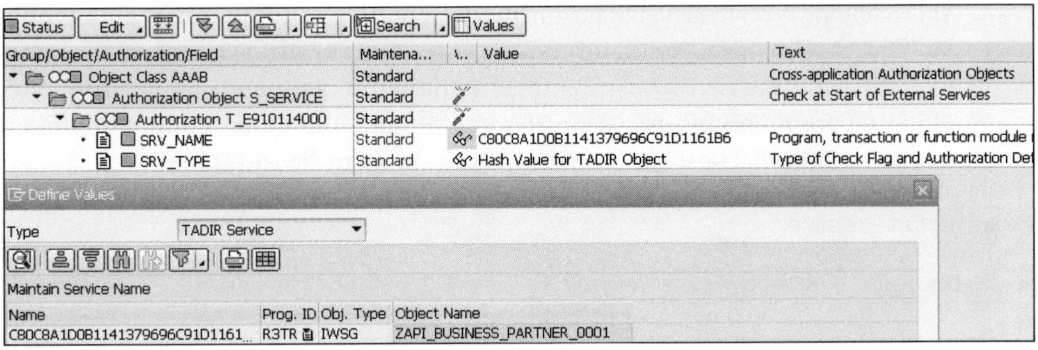

Figure 6.20 Authorization Object S_SERVICE Included in New Role.

Note that the OData API itself may conduct business-oriented authorization checks in addition to the initial check. If you encounter authorization problems, you can use Transaction SU53 (Display Authorization Data) to check which authorization objects, along with their values, are being checked at runtime. Based on this information, you may need to enhance your role.

Whitelist SAP S/4HANA System and APIs in Cloud Connector

The activated APIs in the SAP S/4HANA system are now callable from within the on-premise network; however, the APIs are not yet reachable from your cloud application. The Cloud Connector rejects all requests by default and only forwards requests targeted to explicitly whitelisted APIs.

We can whitelist requests in the Cloud Connector. Choose the corresponding subaccount and click on **Cloud To On-Premise** in the left menu pane, as shown in Figure 6.21. Navigate to the **Access Control** tab where you'll find the mapping between virtual and internal systems.

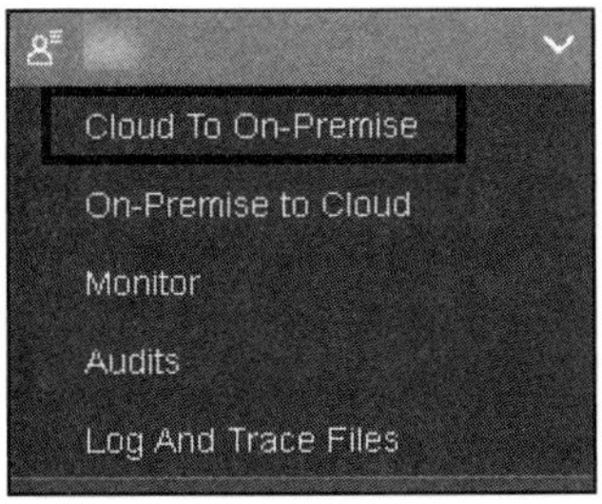

Figure 6.21 Choosing Cloud To On-Premise in Cloud Connector to Maintain System and for API Whitelisting

This mapping is on the level of host names and ports: A virtual host is mapped to an internal, physical host. The Cloud Connector extracts the virtual host from the HTTP request, that is, the virtual host is entered in the destination configuration in the SAP Cloud Platform cockpit. Based on the virtual host, the Cloud Connector checks whether an internal host has been mapped, as shown in Figure 6.22.

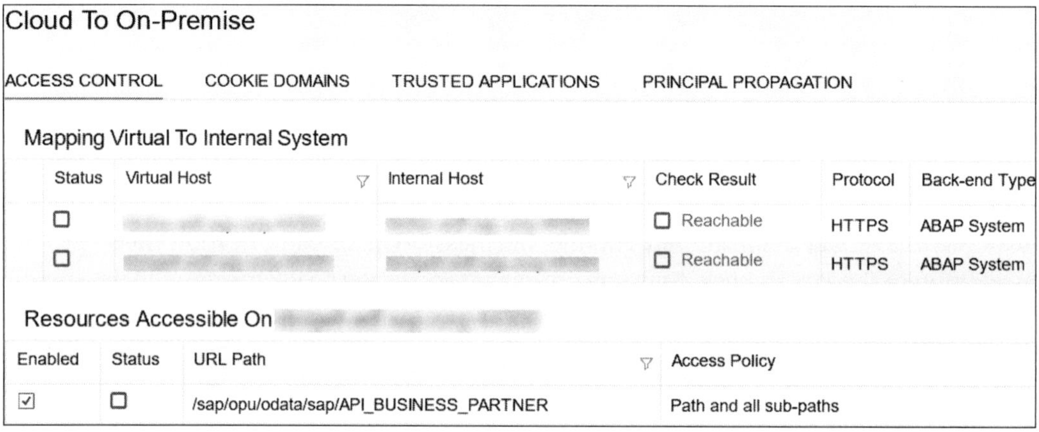

Figure 6.22 Example Access Control Maintained in Cloud Connector

We can add a new host mapping by clicking the + icon to open the **Add System Mapping** popup window. First, choose **ABAP System** as the backend type. In the next step, choose **HTTPS** as the communication protocol and then enter the internal host name and port. This information reflects the real host name and port for the SAP S/4HANA system. Then, maintain the virtual host, which you can specify according to your preferences. You can use the same values for both internal and virtual host. Finish the process by choosing **None** as the principal type, entering a representative description, and clicking **Finish**.

In addition to the host, we also need to whitelist URL paths on the relevant host. For example, we could whitelist all OData APIs in the SAP S/4HANA system by allowing access to the relative path */sap/opu/odata/* and all its subpaths. Depending on your security requirements, you can also whitelist exact paths only, as shown in Figure 6.23.

To whitelist a new URL path, click on the + icon to add a new accessible resource on the internal host.

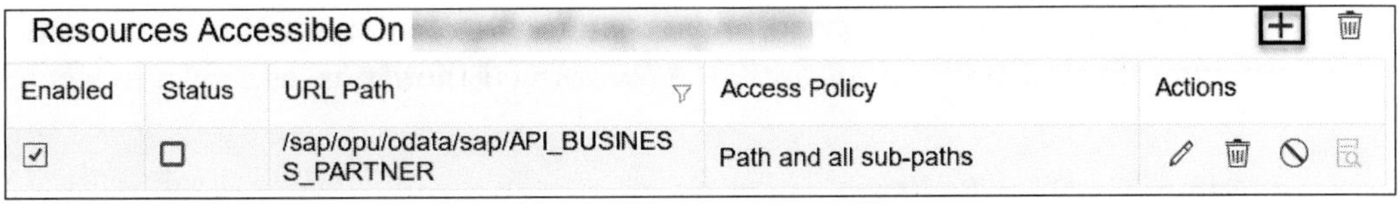

Figure 6.23 Choosing the + Icon to Add a New Accessible Resource

Enter the URL path of the target API in your SAP S/4HANA system, as shown in Figure 6.24. For instance, assuming your OData API is named `API_BUSINESS_PARTNER`, you would enter:

- **URL Path**: Enter "sap/opu/odata/sap/API_BUSINESS_PARTNER."
- **Enabled**: Select the checkbox.
- **Access Policy**: Select **Path and all subpaths**

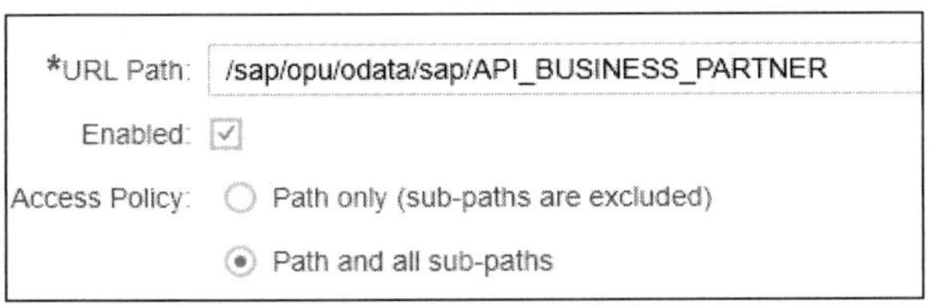

Figure 6.24 Whitelisting of OData API in the Cloud Connector

Click **Save** to save your settings.

The **Status** column of the two tables on this screen, as shown in Figure 6.25, indicates whether the given host and path are reachable from the Cloud Connector.

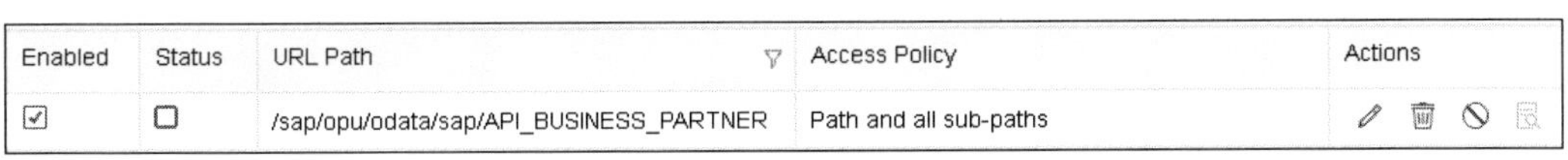

Figure 6.25 Maintained Whitelisting of OData API in the Cloud Connector with Green Status Indicating an Accessible API

Maintain Destination for Basic Authentication

By whitelisting the SAP S/4HANA system and the target API in the Cloud Connector, the system and the target API are callable from the SAP Cloud Platform over the Cloud Connector. Subsequently, we'll configure our destination in the SAP Cloud Platform to point to this API.

Open your Cloud Foundry subaccount and choose **Destinations** in the menu on the left. Click on **New Destination**. Enter the following information, as shown in Figure 6.26:

- **Name**: "ErpQueryEndpoint"
- **Type**: "HTTP"
- **URL**: The virtual host of your SAP S/4HANA system, following this pattern: *https://<host>:<port>/.*
- **ProxyType**: "OnPremise"
- **Authentication**: "BasicAuthentication"
- **User**: Enter the name of the technical user you defined in the beginning of this section.
- **Password**: Enter the password of the technical user you defined in the beginning of this section.
- **Additional Properties**: Enter a new property with key "sap-client" and the respective value (for example, "100") depending on which SAP client you want use to invoke the API.

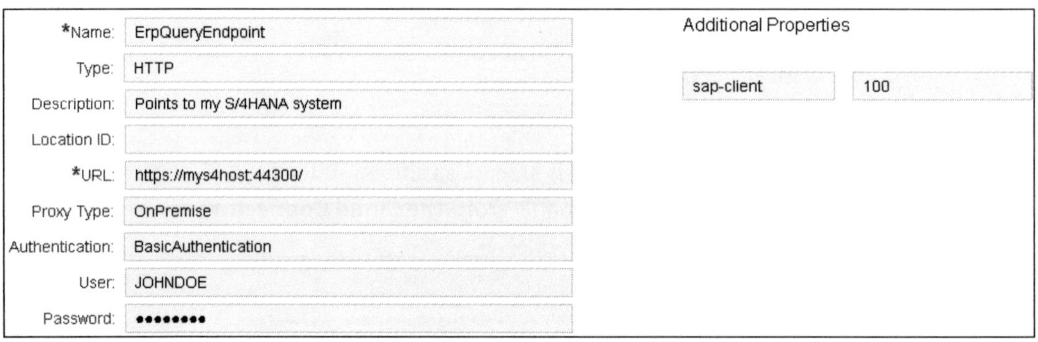

Figure 6.26 Destination Configuration Leveraging Basic Authentication via a Technical User

Click **Save**.

Launch Example Application Leveraging Technical User

In summary, we've conducted the following configuration steps so far:

- Cloud Connector has been installed and configured.
- OData API has been activated in SAP S/4HANA.

- A technical user has been created and its role assigned.
- The SAP S/4HANA system and OData API have been whitelisted in the Cloud Connector.
- The destination has been maintained.

Subsequently, we can launch our application (refer to Chapter 4 for a refresher). The business partner OData API will be invoked in the name of the technical user you created earlier in this section.

6.5.5 Integration Setup Leveraging Business Users

In this section, we'll present the configuration steps to enable the integration with SAP S/4HANA leveraging business users.

User and Role Management

The first step is to create a business user and assign a new role to the user.

Because business users represent persons interacting with user interfaces, we'll utilize dialog users in this section. The process of creating a business user is equivalent to creating a technical user (Section 6.5.4), except for the user type. For business users, choose **Dialog** as the user type.

Creating and assigning a new role to the new business user is equivalent to the steps we performed for the technical user in Section 6.5.4.

Whitelist SAP S/4HANA System and APIs in Cloud Connector

Whitelisting the SAP S/4HANA system and its APIs in the Cloud Connector also works the same way as for technical user, as described in Section 6.5.4.

The only difference is the principal type chosen in the system mapping. In this case, we'll choose **X.509 certificate** instead of **None**.

Maintain Destination for Principal Propagation

Open your Cloud Foundry subaccount and choose **Destinations** in the menu on the left. Click on **New Destination**. Enter the following information (Figure 6.27):

- **Name**: "ErpQueryEndpoint"
- **Type**: "HTTP"
- **URL**: The virtual host of your SAP S/4HANA system, following the pattern: *https://<host>:<port>/*

- **ProxyType**: "OnPremise"
- **Authentication**: "PrincipalPropagation"
- **Additional Properties**: Enter a new property with key `sap-client` and the respective value.

Figure 6.27 Destination Configuration Leveraging Principal Propagation via a Business User

Click **Save**.

Establish Trust Relationship between SAP S/4HANA and Cloud Connector

Now, let's establish a trust relationship between the SAP S/4HANA system and the Cloud Connector. This trust relationship is the basis for principal propagation. The Cloud Connector will provide a user identity to SAP S/4HANA, and since SAP S/4HANA trusts the Cloud Connector, the system will authenticate a user if a corresponding SAP S/4HANA user exists.

Generate and Sign Certificates

We assume that you have a process to issue and sign trusted certificates, that is, either you have established your own certification authority (CA), or you use an external certification authority. As an alternative, you can sign the generated certificates yourself.

In fact, we'll need two certificates to establish the secure connection between the Cloud Connector and SAP S/4HANA. First, a system certificate is used as a client certificate for the Transport Layer Security (TLS) handshake between the Cloud Connector and the SAP S/4HANA system. Second, a Certification Authority (CA) certificate is used by the Cloud Connector to issue short-lived certificates to establish a user's identity within the cloud application. You can use the same physical certificate for both purposes, or you can utilize different physical certificates. We recommend using the latest version of OpenSSL when generating keys and certificates. Depending on whether you require one or two certificates, you'll need to execute the following steps once or twice. First, generate a public and private key pair. At the time of this writing, utilizing an RSA key pair with a key length of at least 2,048 bits is recommended. Generate a public and private key pair with these commands:

```
openssl genrsa -out scc_private.pem 2048
openssl rsa -in scc_private.pem -pubout -out scc_public.pem
```

Second, create a certificate signing request with these commands:

```
openssl req -new -key scc_private.pem -out scc.csr
```

This signing request can be submitted to your own certification authority or an external certification authority. If you need to sign the certificate yourself, use the following command:

```
openssl x509 -req -days 365 -in scc.csr -signkey scc_private.pem -out scc.crt
```

Finally, let's add the private key and the corresponding signed certificate into a PKCS12 archive.

```
openssl pkcs12 -export -out scc.p12 -inkey scc_private.pem -in scc.crt -
chain -CAfile scc.crt
```

Upload Certificates to Cloud Connector

To upload certificates to the Cloud Connector, choose **Configuration** in the left-hand menu and select the **On Premise** tab. Upload the certificate both as a **System Certificate** and a **CA Certificate**. Verify that, for each uploaded certificate, the subject, issuer, and validity period are correct. See Figure 6.28 and Figure 6.29 for reference.

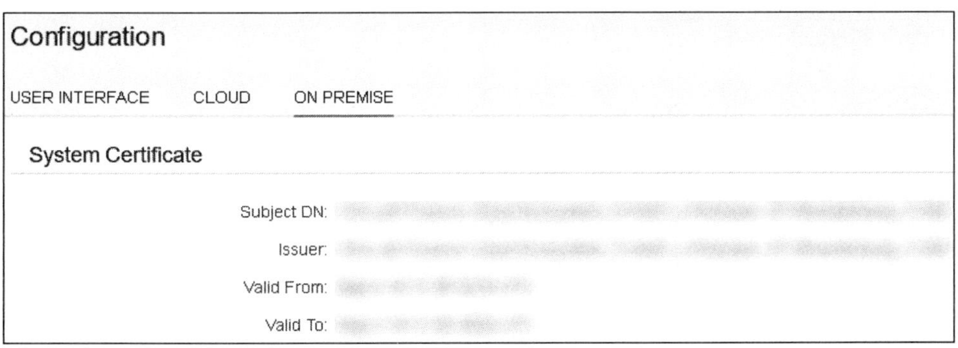

Figure 6.28 Uploaded System Certificate in the Cloud Connector

Figure 6.29 Uploaded CA Certificate in the Cloud Connector

Synchronize Trust between SAP Cloud Platform and Cloud Connector

Open the Cloud Connector, navigate to the settings for your Cloud Foundry subaccount, and click on **Cloud To On-Premise**. Select the **Principal Propagation** tab and then click the **Synchronize** button on the upper right-hand corner of the table.

Configure Subject Pattern in Cloud Connector

Open the Cloud Connector, choose **Configuration** in the left-hand menu, and select tab **On Premise**. Under **Principal Propagation**, specify the subject pattern as `CN=${name}`. This code tells the Cloud Connector to put the SAP Cloud Platform user name into the subject of a short-lived certificate.

Upload Certificate to SAP S/4HANA

Launch the Trust Manager (Transaction STRUST) in the SAP S/4HANA system and double-click the PSE (personal security environment) called **SSL Server Standard**. Switch to change mode using the corresponding button in the application tool bar. If the system certificate was signed by a certification authority, upload the certificate of this CA to this certificate list, as shown in Figure 6.30.

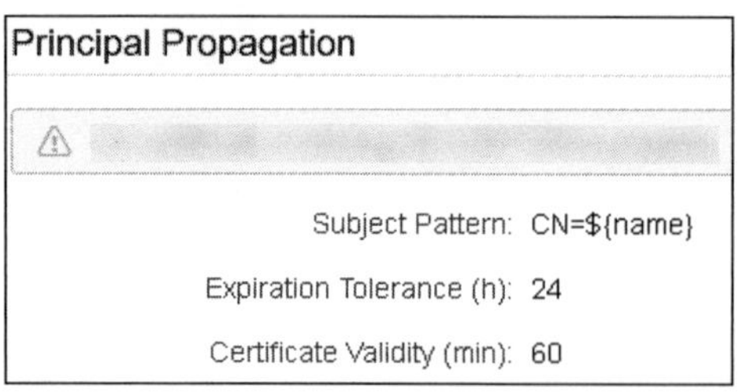

Figure 6.30 Specifying the Subject Pattern as CN=${name}

Example: System Certificate Signed by Certification Authority

The subject of the system certificate is given as `CN=SAPCloudConnector`, and its issuer is specified as `CN=MyCertificationAuthority`. Thus, upload the certificate with subject `CN=MyCertificationAuthority` into the certificate list.

If you signed the system certificate yourself, then you'll need to upload it to the certificate list, as shown in Figure 6.31.

Example: Self-Signed System Certificate

The subject and the issuer of the system certificate are equal when the system certificate is self-signed. Therefore, upload the system certificate itself into the certificate list.

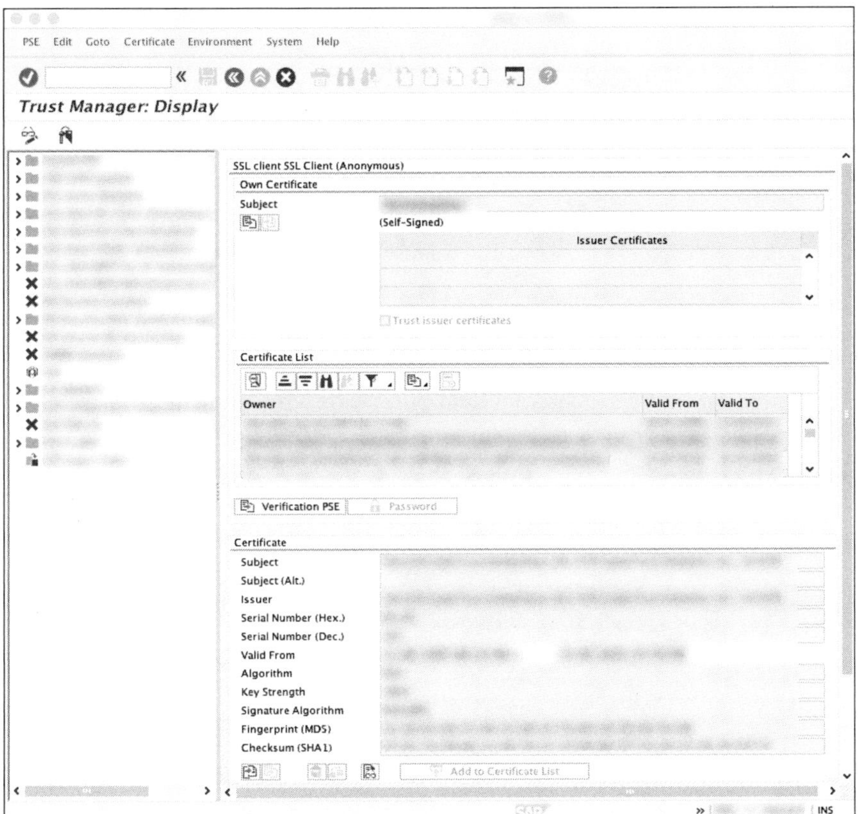

Figure 6.31 Certificate in the Certificate List of Transaction STRUST

As final step, click **Add to Certificate List** and then click **Save**.

Configure Internet Communication Manager in SAP S/4HANA

To make SAP S/4HANA trust the system certificate from Cloud Connector, we'll need to specify its subject and issuer in one profile in the Internet Communication Manager. Open the **Profile Editor** (Transaction RZ10) and choose the profile you want to edit. Click the **Extended Maintenance** button and switch to change mode.

Maintain the parameters as shown in Table 6.1.

Key	Value
icm/HTTPS/trust_client_with_issuer	The issuer of the system certificate
icm/HTTPS/trust_client_with_subject	The subject of the system certificate

Table 6.1 Profile Parameters in Internet Communication Management

Internet Communication Management Profile Parameters

If the subject of the system certificate is CN=SAPCloudConnector and its issuer is CN=MyCertificationAuthority, then maintain the parameters as in Table 6.2.

Key	Value
icm/HTTPS/trust_client_with_issuer	CN=MyCertificationAuthority
icm/HTTPS/trust_client_with_subject	CN=SAPCloudConnector

Table 6.2 Profile Parameters in Internet Communication Management

In contrast, if the subject and the issuer of the system certificate are both CN=SAPCloudConnector and are therefore equal (that is, the system certificate is self-signed), then maintain the parameters as shown in Table 6.3.

Key	Value
icm/HTTPS/trust_client_with_issuer	CN=SAPCloudConnector
icm/HTTPS/trust_client_with_subject	CN=SAPCloudConnector

Table 6.3 Profile Parameters in Internet Communication Management

Save the profile.

Open the **ICM monitor** (Transaction SMICM) and choose **Administration • ICM • Hard Shut Down • Global** from the menu.

Internet Communication Management will restart so that the maintained parameters are taken into account. Verify that the two parameters are consumed by choosing **Goto • Parameters • Display**. Choose the parameter keys and check their respective values.

Maintain Explicit User Mapping in SAP S/4HANA

As discussed in Section 6.2.2, we'll need to maintain an explicit mapping of the user's representation in SAP Cloud Platform and SAP S/4HANA. Thus, we'll maintain an explicit mapping between cloud and on-premise identities, as shown in Figure 6.32.

1. Open the view Transaction EXTID_DN (Assignment of External ID to Users). Add a new entry for every business user.
2. Specify the following details for every entry.
   - **External ID**: Enter "CN=<cloudIdentity>"
     (Example: `CN=JOHN_DOE`)
   - **User**: Enter the user name inside the SAP S/4HANA system.
   - **Active**: Select the checkbox.
3. **Save** all entries.

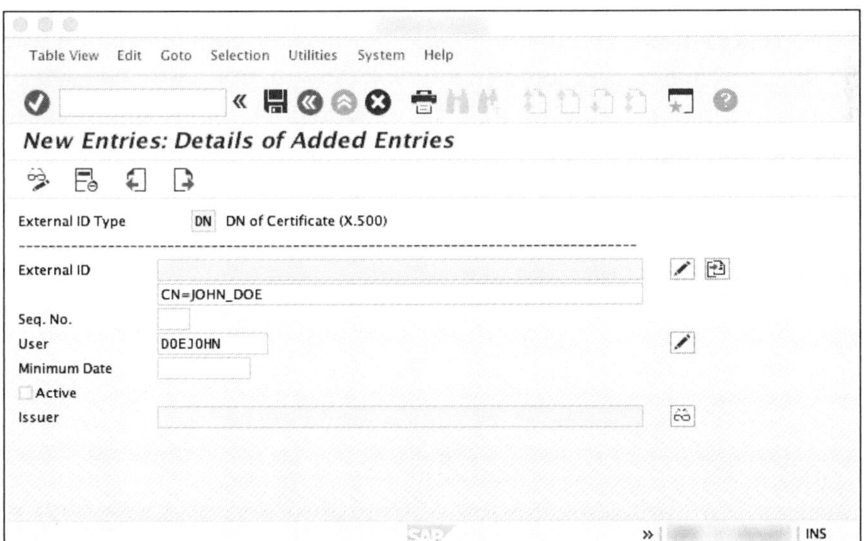

Figure 6.32 Explicit User Mapping between SAP Cloud User Name JOHN_DOE and SAP S/4HANA User Name DOEJOHN

Launch Example Application Leveraging Business Users

In summary, we've conducted the following configuration steps:

- Cloud Connector has been installed and configured.
- OData API has been activated in SAP S/4HANA.
- A business user has been created and its role assigned.
- The SAP S/4HANA system and OData API have been whitelisted in Cloud Connector.
- The destination has been maintained.
- A trust relationship between SAP S/4HANA and Cloud Connector has been established.

We can now launch our Business Partner Address Manager application. The business partner OData API will be invoked with the business user you created earlier this section.

6.6 Summary

In this chapter, we focused on integrating our example application with SAP S/4HANA to gain access to business data. After distinguishing between business users and technical users and introducing the idea of principal propagation, we presented the architecture, example flows, and the configuration steps for both integration with SAP S/4HANA Cloud and integration with SAP S/4HANA. In the next chapter, we'll introduce you the concepts behind multitenancy and multitenant implementations in the Cloud Foundry environment on the SAP Cloud Platform.

Chapter 7
Multitenancy

This chapter describes the architecture of multitenancy in the Cloud Foundry environment on the SAP Cloud Platform, from identity zones down to persistence level. We'll reflect on how multitenancy has already been applied via the SAP S/4HANA Cloud SDK in our example application (for example, for caching or to increase resilience). Then, we'll expand the scenario with an approval workflow requiring local persistence on the SAP Cloud Platform. Based on this example, we'll discuss some design trade-offs for application developers and demonstrate how to implement multitenancy on the database level.

In previous chapters, we explained the principles of and the rationale for building cloud-native side-by-side extensions for SAP S/4HANA in SAP Cloud Platform. In addition, with our Business Partner Address Manager application, we've shown you how to implement SAP S/4HANA integration, resilience, scalability, and security.

In this chapter, we'll take a deeper look at another important aspect that you'll need to consider when building cloud-native applications: multitenancy.

In Section 7.1, we'll explain the concept behind and the reasons for multitenancy in general. In Section 7.2, we'll outline the principles and theory behind implementing multitenant applications in the Cloud Foundry environment on the SAP Cloud Platform. In Section 7.3 and Section 7.4, we'll explain how these principles can be applied in practice. We'll use our Business Partner Address Manager application as a hands-on example and extend the app with tenant-aware persistence.

7.1 Motivations for Multitenancy

Treb Ryan, CEO of OpSource, once stated the following about multitenancy:

> *"Multi-Tenancy is a requirement for a SaaS vendor to be successful."*

What does this mean? Why is multitenancy so important? In the cloud, all costs for hosting and operating the software and its required technical resources rest with the application provider. Thus, reducing these costs is essential for running a cloud-based software-as-a-service (SaaS) business.

Multitenancy is defined as a software architecture in which the software is provided once on a server that serves multiple customers, referred to as *tenants*. Tenants share the same technical resources, but their data is separated, and identity and access management are strictly isolated.

Let's take a closer look at costs and how to reduce costs with the multitenant approach. The main cost drivers are operations and resources. Operational efforts include bug fixing, deploying new versions of an application, and monitoring applications. With only one instance of a software, the operations team must update it only once for all tenants to benefit from the update. Resource costs are caused by the different technical components used for storing and processing data like databases, message brokers, etc., as well as the cost of running the application during runtime. Usually, these components are offered at a fixed price. So, the more tenants are served by a single server, the cheaper the operations of the overall application will be. In addition, one large component is usually cheaper than multiple small instances.

7.2 Multitenancy on SAP Cloud Platform

Now let's explore how multitenancy principles are realized on the SAP Cloud Platform.

7.2.1 Tenant Onboarding and Offboarding

As outlined in Chapter 3, the SAP Cloud Platform subaccount represents the tenant at runtime in both SaaS and platform-as-a-service (PaaS) scenarios. In SaaS scenarios, subaccounts subscribe to applications to consume them. In PaaS scenarios, subaccounts consume services to develop their own applications. With the separation between global accounts and subaccounts, customers can manage multiple separate tenants, and the data for testing and productive usage, while still wrapping all tenants within their single global account.

Before a customer can use an application, the tenant must be onboarded, and the application must be notified to prepare tenant-specific persistence. The onboarding process is shown in Figure 7.1.

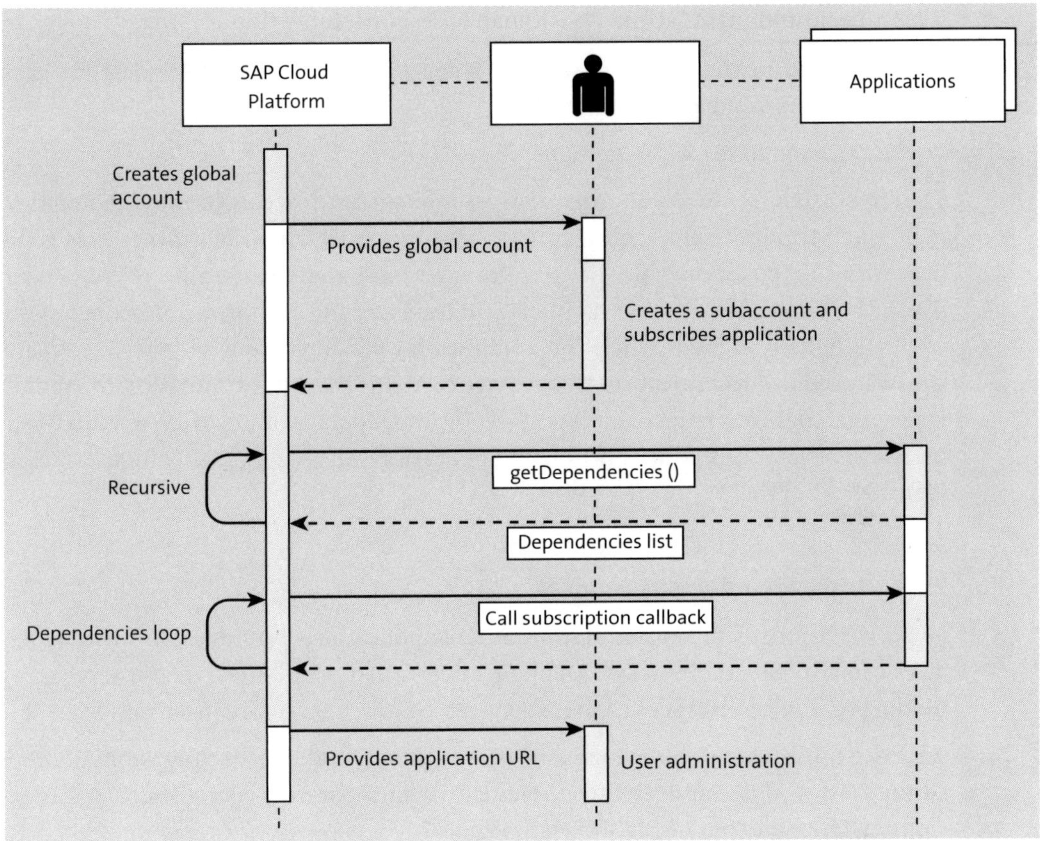

Figure 7.1 Tenant Onboarding Process

As a prerequisite, the customer needs a global account. Within this global account, the customer either uses an existing subaccount, if he wants to use the same tenant and share data between applications, or he'll create a new subaccount. From the subaccount, the customer can subscribe to the applications he is authorized for.

To notify the application about a new tenant, two callbacks are called recursively. First, the application is asked for the business services it depends on, for example, the business logging service. This request is repeated for all dependencies and their dependencies. Second, each component is notified that the tenant is subscribed to it. Consequently, tenant persistence has been created. Finally, the application URL is provided to the customer in the SAP Cloud Platform cockpit. Before the application can be accessed, the administrator will create business users and assign the relevant business roles to them.

7.2.2 Tenant Identification

As mentioned in the previous section, a specific application URL exists for each tenant. The URL follows the pattern:

<tenant>.<app-name>.<app-domain>

The application router (AppRouter) derives the tenant from this URL and redirects to the Cloud Foundry User Account and Authentication (UAA), which authenticates the user with the tenant-specific Identity Provider (IdP) and creates a JSON Web Token (JWT). This JWT contains the tenant, current user, and the authorization scopes of the user, all digitally signed. When the application calls dependent services internally, the JWT used to authenticate at that service contains the tenant, and thus, the tenant is propagated through the complete stack. For more details on security, refer to Chapter 5. Whenever required, a multitenant application can read a globally unique tenant identifier from the JWT.

7.2.3 Applications versus Services

So far, we've mostly talked about multitenant applications, but reusable business services can also be tenant-aware. An application usually combines several services by binding to service instances of these services, to which tenants can subscribe.

A service provides well-defined reuse business functionalities for programmatic consumption via APIs. Services can implement data separation along the two dimensions instance and tenant, as shown in Figure 7.2.

Service without Data Separation

The service is not tenant-aware and stores the data without tenant and service separation. Thus, the application binds against one service instance and connects to the service instance with a technical user.

Technical Service with Application Data Isolation

The service is not tenant-aware but realizes data isolation per service instance. Applications can realize tenant separation by creating several service instances to be managed by an application itself. As the tenant does not need to be identified, technical users with Basic authentication are sufficient.

Services that use containers to isolate data by service instance can leverage Cloud Foundry service broker APIs to create or delete a container when a service instance is created or deleted.

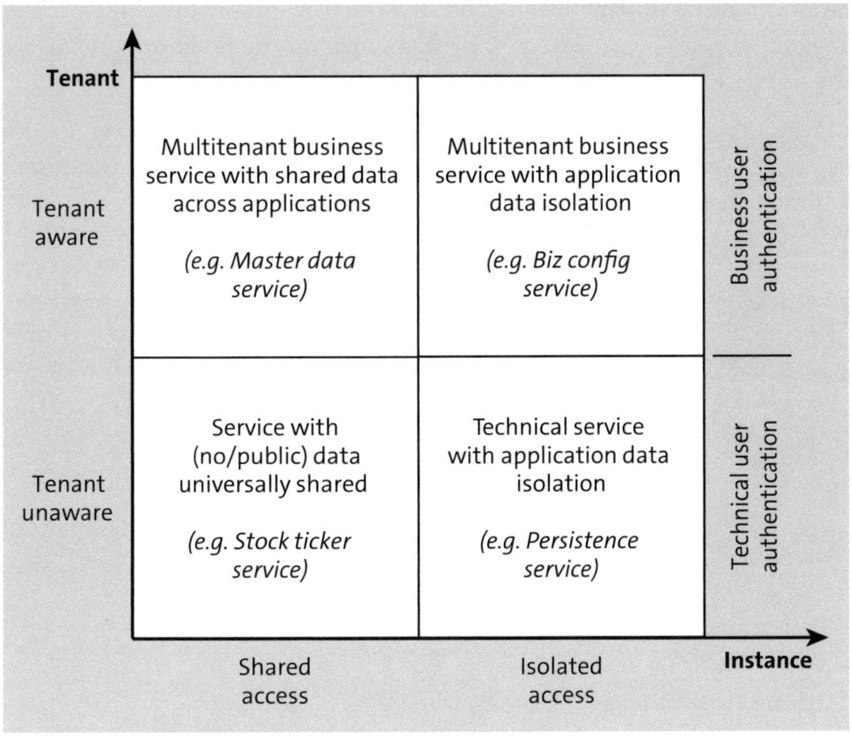

Figure 7.2 Dimensions of Multitenant Services

Tenant-Aware Service with Shared Data across Applications

The service is tenant-aware and is invoked with a business user. Thus, the service handles the tenant separation by itself, and the data of one tenant is shared across different applications.

Such a service is applicable for the tenant onboarding outlined for applications. This service will result in an onboarding callback wherein the service should instantiate its tenant-specific storage. In case of several onboarding calls due to consumption by multiple applications, only one container shall be created.

Tenant-Aware Services with Application Data Isolation

The service is tenant-aware and invoked with a business user. In addition, the data is separated by service instances. This option is usually the most complex. If needed, you can either have separate storage for each tenant and a discriminator column for keeping the service instance, or separate storage for each service instance with a discriminator column to distinguish tenants. For the first option, the regular tenant onboarding callback can be used to create the storage; for the latter option, the creation of the service instance could serve as a trigger.

If a consuming application needs to be identified in the persistence of a service, the service instance ID (which can be read from the JWT) should be used as the only identification of the consumer.

Figure 7.3 shows the consumption options we've discussed so far.

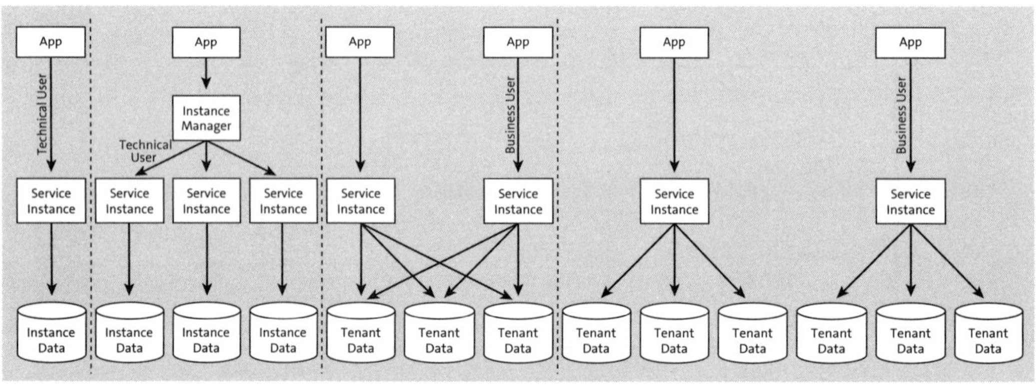

Figure 7.3 Options for Multitenant Service Consumption

7.2.4 Data Separation

As we've outlined, although tenants share resources, their data must be stored separate from each other so that one tenant is never able to access the data of another tenant.

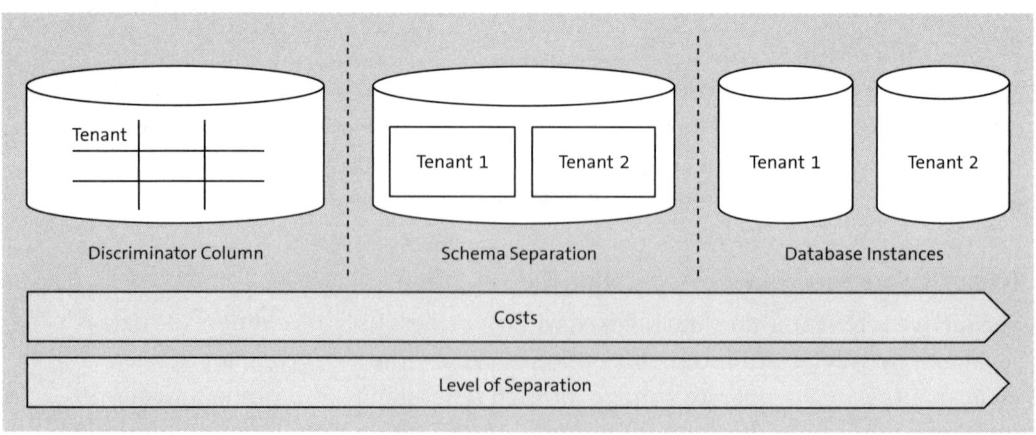

Figure 7.4 Options for Separating Tenant Data

Multiple options exist to separate the data, ranging from using a discriminator column to using distinct database instances that offer different levels of tenant isolation and costs, as shown in Figure 7.4. In the following sections, we'll take a closer look into data separation for databases.

Tenant Discriminator Column

All data is stored in the same schema of the same database, and tenant information is provided in a discriminator column. This option is the most cost-efficient, providing the lowest isolation. In this approach, tenant-specific extensions are more difficult to implement. Additionally, data backup and restore is usually only possible for all tenants at once. For applications that require data sharing among tenants, this option can be a suitable choice.

Schema Separation

In this approach, every tenant is assigned its own schema within the same database. If one database cannot serve all tenants, more databases are added. This option usually represents a good compromise between data isolation and cost efficiency. Customer extensions can be managed more easily by schemas. Furthermore, tenant-specific backup and restore can usually be achieved with less effort depending on the underlying database.

Database Instances

When relying on this approach, every tenant is assigned its own database instance. This option guarantees the highest level of data isolation. However, this option also results in higher costs, for example, for operating all of these instances. In particular, some database resources may be underutilized in this approach. Backup and restore usually require less effort as these activities can be done for each tenant separately. For customers with larger amounts of data, this option can be an appropriate choice.

Considering the criteria outlined in this section, schema separation is a good match for many projects. If some customers also require their own databases, projects can also mix schema separation with dedicated database instances, for example, by providing two licenses from which the customer can choose. If developers always separate by schema, whether the schema is deployed only once or multiple times into one database instance is a purely operational question.

For implementing schema separation in detail, please refer to Section 7.4.

7.3 Multitenancy Aspects in the Existing Application

In Chapter 3 and Chapter 4, we introduced our Business Partner Address Manager application. In this section and the next, we'll investigate how the multitenancy principles in the SAP Cloud Platform, which we've described in Section 7.2, can be applied to our application.

Let's assume that we have several customers who want to use our application to manage the addresses of their business partners. As explained in Section 7.1, we want provide the application as an SaaS solution and deploy a single instance in the provider account of the SAP Cloud Platform. To access the solution, customers can subscribe to the instance of the running application from their consumer accounts. In this set up, we need to make sure that the application properly separates the data, so that each customer can only see and modify the data of its own business partners. In other words, the application should be tenant-aware.

Depending on the complexity of the scenario, the integrated cloud platform services, as well as the SAP S/4HANA Cloud SDK components we're using, some multitenancy aspects were already covered by the SDK and the SAP Cloud Platform. For some aspects (such as the persistence service, discussed in Section 7.4), the SDK provides convenient components for implementing tenant awareness, such as a tenant accessor, which allows the system to easily retrieve the current tenant.

Figure 7.5 shows the high-level components in our Business Partner Address Manager application as well as the involved SAP Cloud Platform and SAP S/4HANA services relevant to this context. In the previous sections of this chapter, we discussed the structure of the example application in detail and the components required to run the application in SAP Cloud Platform.

Let's briefly recapitulate this architecture before we elaborate on the role of multitenancy in our example application:

- Customers of our example application can send HTTP queries to retrieve business partner master data and can create, edit, or delete business partner addresses. These requests are sent via a single point of entry into the application, namely, the AppRouter.
- The AppRouter, the Extended Services for User Account and Authentication (XSUAA) service, the configuration of identity zones, and Identity Provider (IdP) components are required to secure access to the application in the Cloud Foundry environment on the SAP Cloud Platform. This setup ensures tenant information is propagated to an application. For more details on these components, refer to

Chapter 5. For a step-by-step explanation of this setup, read the tutorial on SAP S/4HANA Cloud SDK online at *http://tiny.cc/sapsecurityblog*.

- `AddressServlet` and `BusinessPartnerServlet` represent services that receive requests from the AppRouter and are responsible for reading and writing data to SAP S/4HANA. Corresponding SAP S/4HANA requests are wrapped into commands to ensure resilience and to cache results (see also Chapter 4).
- The business partner service in SAP S/4HANA retrieves business partner data and to read, create, and modify addresses of business partners.

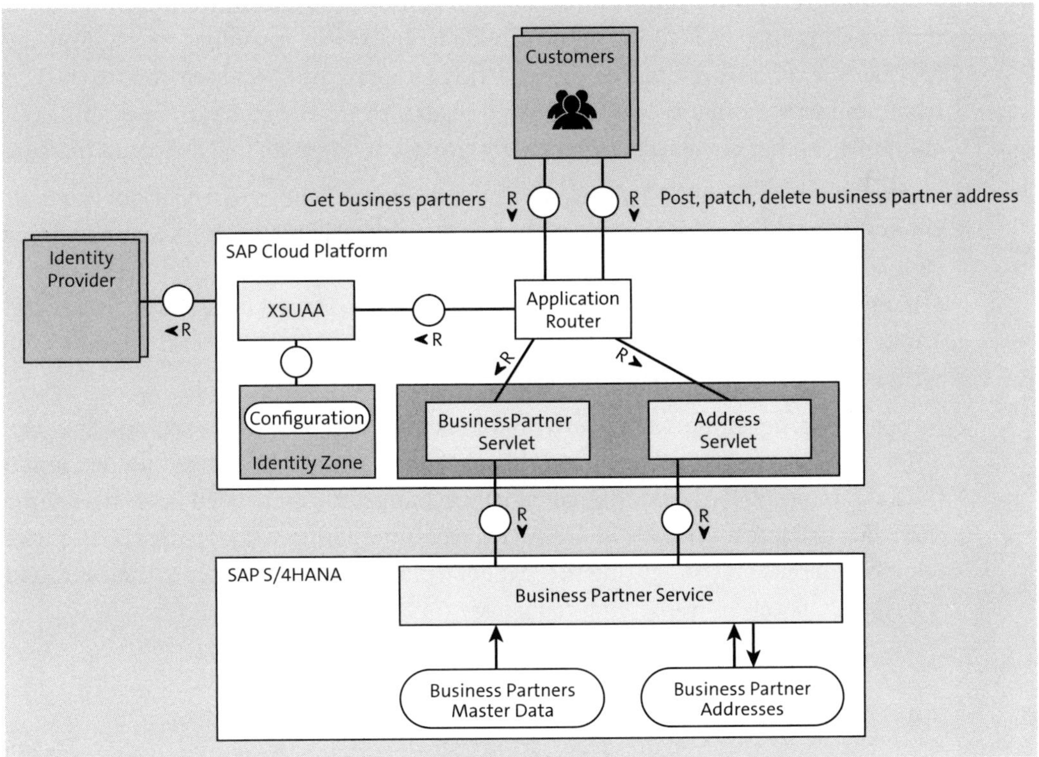

Figure 7.5 Building Blocks of the Business Partner Address Manager Application

As discussed in Chapter 6, we'll configure the destination service and the connectivity service of SAP Cloud Platform to establish the connection to SAP S/4HANA. When we develop an SaaS solution and when several customers subscribe to the application, each tenant will have its own destination configuration. Due to the multitenancy concept underlying the connectivity service, the requests are dispatched to the system configured for each tenant without any explicit handling by a developer.

In addition, separation in the SAP S/4HANA connectivity itself, other features in the current version of our example application require tenant separation: fault tolerance and caching.

The SAP S/4HANA Cloud SDK has extended the Hystrix framework with certain functionalities to better support multitenancy. These adaptations provide developers of side-by-side extensions for SAP S/4HANA with a powerful and proven toolset for resilience features. In our Business Partner Address Manager application, we'll wrap all the calls to SAP S/4HANA into `ErpCommand` or `CachingErpCommand` (see the implementation of `BusinessPartnerServlet` and `AddressServlet`), as described in Chapter 4, Section 4.6. This approach allows us to provide fallbacks and introduce a circuit breaker for calls to external systems like SAP S/4HANA. Due to the SDK extensions to the Hystrix framework, resilience logic is handled separately for each tenant. For example, circuit breakers that are usually triggered by command are triggered by tenant instead.

Furthermore, in Chapter 4, Section 4.6, we integrated the caching of query results when reading business partner data in our Business Partner Address Manager application. By default, the caching mechanism implemented in the SAP S/4HANA Cloud SDK ensures tenant and user separation, which is the desired behavior in most cases. Thus, in a usual provider-subscriber multitenant application, each tenant (subscriber) only has access to his own caches.

Nevertheless, developers can overwrite the default behavior of the caching and use a different level of isolation for cases where a dataset should be cached independent of the user or tenant. For example, currency exchange rates retrieved from an external service constitute a use case where such a custom caching strategy may be required. For more details on configuring the level of isolation, refer to the documentation for the class `CacheKey` in the GitHub repository for this book.

7.4 Adding Multitenant Persistence to the Application

In this section, we'll continue extending our Business Partner Address Manager application and take an in-depth look into how to set up tenant-aware persistence using SAP S/4HANA Cloud SDK components.

7.4.1 Introducing Addresses Workflow with Local Persistence

In the current version of our example application, users can create, update, and delete addresses of their business partners in SAP S/4HANA using `POST`, `PATCH`, and

DELETE HTTP methods on the */addresses* endpoint. The state diagram shown in Figure 7.6 describes the current possible state transitions for business partner addresses.

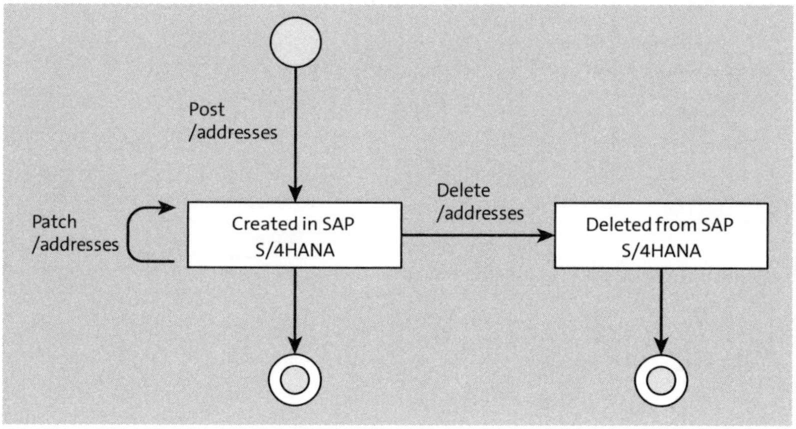

Figure 7.6 Business Partner Address Manager: State Diagram before Introducing Local Persistence

When building SAP S/4HANA side-by-side extensions on the SAP Cloud Platform, we have the flexibility to enrich data and business processes using various services of the SAP Cloud Platform.

As outlined in Chapter 3, we'll consider the following extension of the given workflow: Before a new address is written in SAP S/4HANA, it should be validated by a reviewer of the business partner master data. After the review, the new address can be approved or rejected. If approved, the address is automatically created in SAP S/4HANA. The new extended workflow is shown in Figure 7.7.

On the API level, we'll introduce the additional endpoint */addresses-local*. We'll provide this API to send a POST request to create a new address and to change the address status from "New" to "Rejected" or "Approved."

Of course, we'll also need to extend the existing application logic and the data model. We'll integrate a persistence service of SAP Cloud Platform for this purpose, and we'll handle new created business partner addresses and their current statuses ("New," "Approved," or "Rejected") in a separate local persistence service instance. Every time an address is approved, the creation of a corresponding record is triggered in SAP S/4HANA. Figure 7.8 shows a high-level block diagram for the extended version of our Business Partner Address Manager application, including the integration with the persistence service.

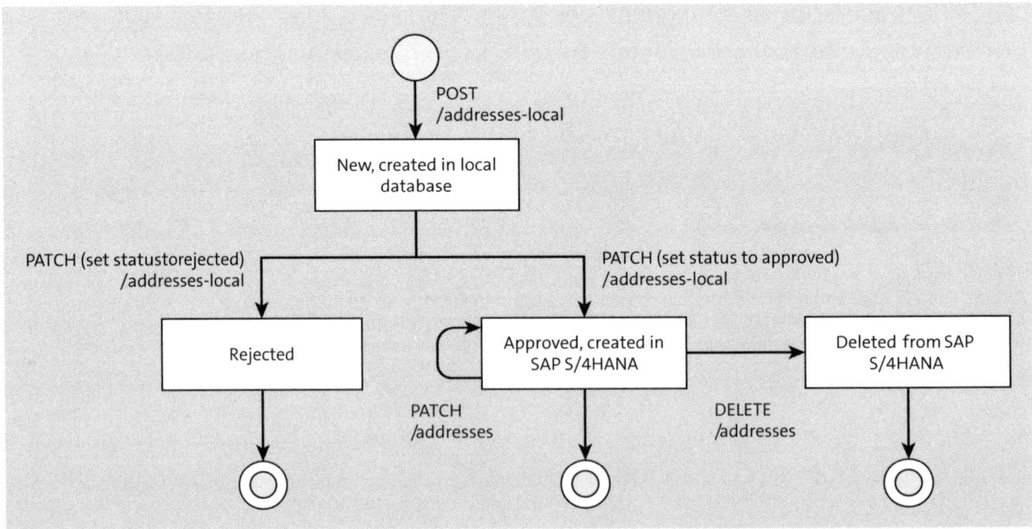

Figure 7.7 Business Partner Address Manager: State Diagram after Introducing Local Persistence

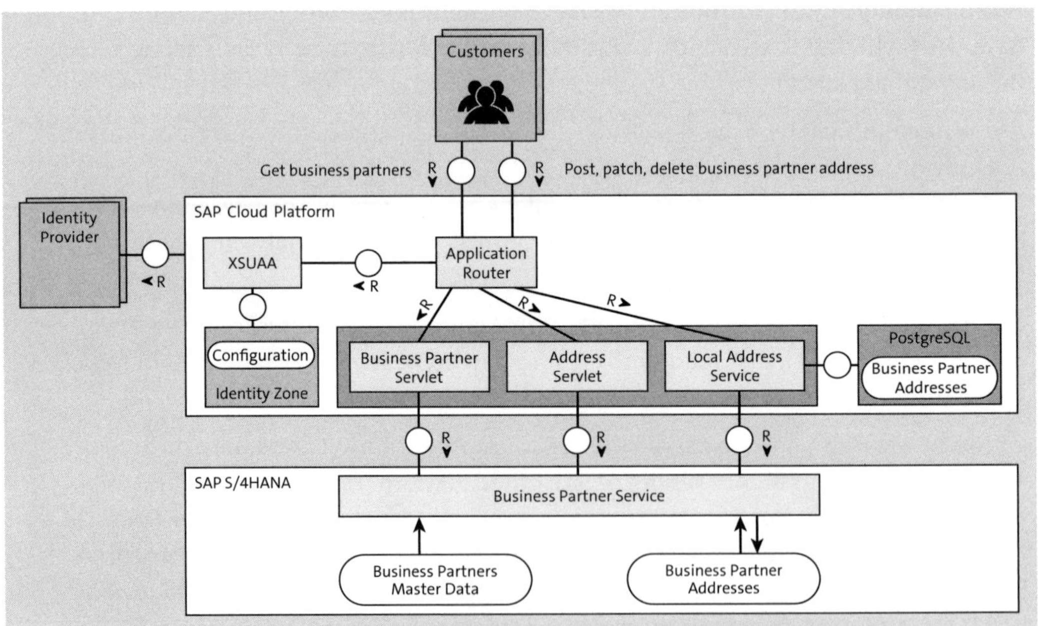

Figure 7.8 Business Partner Address Management: Additional Building Blocks

The following additional components are introduced:

- The `LocalAddressServlet`, which is a service that handles the creation of addresses and status updates in the local database. This servlet triggers the creation of an address in SAP S/4HANA, which will then need to be approved.
- An instance of a persistence service in SAP Cloud Platform, where all the local addresses are maintained. In our example implementation, we'll use PostgreSQL; however, you're required to use a concrete persistence service provider, when using the SAP S/4HANA Cloud SDK.

While extending the application with the persistence service, we'll need to ensure tenant separation at the data level. As described in Section 7.2.4, we can choose between three approaches for the tenant separation: column-discriminator, schema-based separation, or database instance separation. The SAP S/4HANA Cloud SDK supports any of these approaches, and we'll leave the final decision to the application developer.

Without loss of generality, we can adopt schema-based separation for our example application, because this approach strikes a good balance between level of separation and corresponding costs.

In the following sections, we'll explain step by step how to integrate tenant-aware persistence starting from the current state of our Business Partner Address Manager application. Note that the technology used in this section is not the only possible option for this setup. Multitenancy can also be implemented with different frameworks (for example, Spring Boot) and different persistence services (such as SAP HANA). When deciding among these options, you should consider various factors, from the volume of the data over the costs, to the preferences and skills of the development team and the architects. Let's look at the technology and concepts that we'll use to implement tenant-aware persistence in our example application.

- **Persistence framework**
  When writing your Java code, accessing and manipulating objects in a database, you can use plain SQL strings and connect your database instance with a Java SQL connection. Alternatively, you may include an existing Java Persistence API (JPA) implementation, like EclipseLink (*www.eclipse.org/eclipselink/*) or Hibernate (*hibernate.org*). Several benefits can be enjoyed using these frameworks instead of plain SQL strings. First, these frameworks allow you to focus on the high-level object model rather than on low-level SQL queries. Second, they provide a dialect-agnostic way of communicating with a database, making migrations between database providers easier. Last but not least, these frameworks are easily customizable

and help you avoid manual effort for implementing various scenarios. We can leverage this advantage to customize tenant-awareness in our example, where we've chosen Hibernate as our JPA implementation.

- **Development framework**
  Several frameworks are available for Java-based development of enterprise applications. These frameworks simplify and standardize typical operations such as data access, transactional business logic, communication between components, and communication with external systems. To focus on multitenancy, we won't deal with the specific properties of any framework in this section. Instead, we'll use servlets and application-managed persistence via Hibernate. We describe some concepts of industry standard Java frameworks, such as Java Platform, Enterprise Edition (Java EE) and Spring in Chapter 15. Also, for a step-by-step guide to implementing an example scenario with the Spring Boot framework, refer to the blog post at *http://tiny.cc/multi-tenant-persistence*.
- **Choosing a database**
  Another decision you'll have to make when developing a productive application is choosing a database provider. At the time of this writing, you can use SAP HANA or PostgreSQL services in the Cloud Foundry environment on the SAP Cloud Platform. You'll need to consider several factors when making a choice, such as the data volume, the type of queries, and the costs. Our example uses PostgreSQL, which is a legitimate choice for our Business Partner Address Manager application, considering the rather small amounts of data. Nevertheless, the SDK allows you to integrate SAP HANA persistence with multitenancy features as well. In fact, you can leverage SAP HANA Deployment Infrastructure (HDI) containers when working with SAP HANA in SAP Cloud Platform (see also *http://tiny.cc/hdi-containers*). More information can be found in our blog series at *http://tiny.cc/s4sdk-blogs* and in our example projects at *http://tiny.cc/s4sdk-examples*.
- **Data separation**
  We'll focus the schema separation approach. For more details on alternatives and their relative advantages and disadvantages, refer to Section 7.2.4.

Now, let's look at the most important aspects of implementing our scenario with the technologies and concepts we've mentioned so far. As shown in Figure 7.9, several components will be added to the initial implementation described in Chapter 4. For the full source code for this extended version of our application, refer to the code of the Business Partner Address Manager application in the GitHub repository for this book.

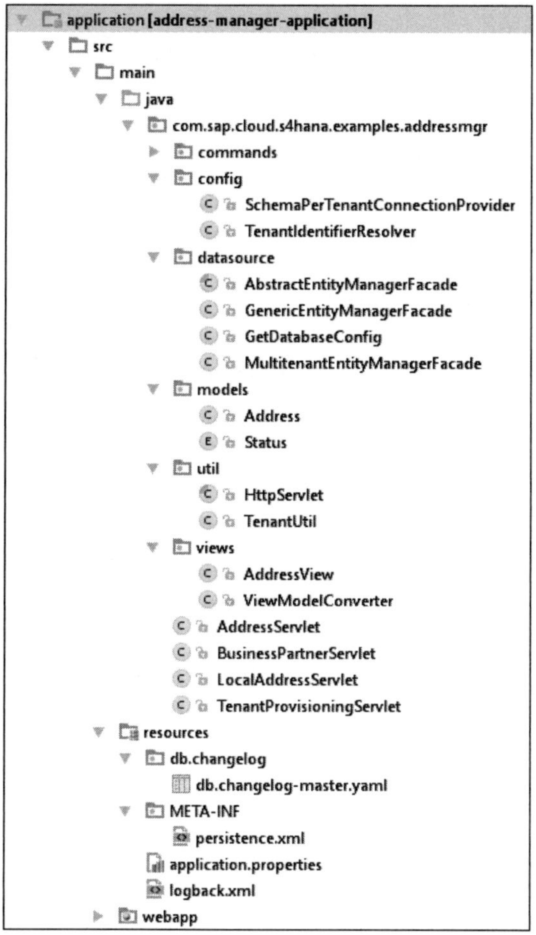

Figure 7.9 Project Structure after Implementing Multitenant Persistence

In the subsequent sections, we'll discuss the main dimensions of the components by covering the following topics step by step:

- Configuring a data source, located in package `datasource` (Section 7.4.2)
- Configuring tenant-awareness in Hibernate based on the class `MultitenantEntityManagerFacade`, the persistence.xml file, and the package `config` (Section 7.4.3)
- Application tenant onboarding and offboarding based on `TenantProvisioningServlet` and the Liquibase configuration residing in the file *db.changelog-master.yaml* (Section 7.4.4)

- Implementing the data model and accessing services in packages `models` and `views` as well as in `LocalAddressServlet` (Section 7.4.5)
- Configuring services and service bindings in the Cloud Foundry environment on the SAP Cloud Platform using the manifest.yml file (Section 7.4.6)

While outlining these aspects, we'll highlight the relevant components of the SAP S/4HANA Cloud SDK in each step.

7.4.2 Configure Data Source

Before we describe the configuration and implementation of the multitenancy logic, we first need to ensure that our application connects to the right data source. Therefore, in this section, we'll integrate application-managed persistence by creating an entity manager factory using the parameters of the database directly in our Java code.

The `AbstractEntityManagerFacade` class in the `datasource` package contains the generic configuration of the data source, such as the database user, password, and JDBC URL as well as generic Hibernate parameters, including the SQL dialect. Listing 7.1 outlines an example of how these parameters can be set for an `EntityManagerFactory`.

```
public class AbstractEntityManagerFacade {
  private EntityManagerFactory entityManagerFactory;

  protected AbstractEntityManagerFacade() {
    PostgresqlServiceInfo postgreInfo = GetDatabaseConfig ↩
        .retrieveDatabaseInfo("book-project-database", ↩
            PostgresqlServiceInfo.class);

    Map<String, String> properties = ↩
        buildProperties(postgreInfo);
    entityManagerFactory = ↩
        Persistence.createEntityManagerFactory( ↩
            "pu", properties);
  }

  protected Map<String, String> buildProperties( ↩
      PostgresqlServiceInfo postgreInfo) {
    Map<String, String> properties = new HashMap<>();
    properties.put("javax.persistence.jdbc.user", ↩
```

```
        postgreInfo.getUserName());
    properties.put("javax.persistence.jdbc.password", ↩
        postgreInfo.getPassword());
    properties.put("javax.persistence.jdbc.url", ↩
        postgreInfo.getJdbcUrl());
    properties.put("hibernate.dialect", ↩
        "org.hibernate.dialect.PostgreSQLDialect");
    properties.put("hibernate.show_sql", "true");
    return properties;
  }

  public EntityManager getEntityManager() {
    return entityManagerFactory.createEntityManager();
  }
}
```

Listing 7.1 AbstractEntityManagerFacade: Creating an Entity Manager

In Listing 7.1, we used `PostgresqlServiceInfo` to access the database parameters. Next, let's discuss how these parameters can be retrieved by an application running in the Cloud Foundry environment on the SAP Cloud Platform.

At runtime, all information related to bound backing services, such as persistence, is available via the `VCAP_SERVICES` environment variable For more information on environment variables in Cloud Foundry, refer to the documentation found at *http://tiny.cc/cf-env*. To retrieve the information for the PostgreSQL service, we'll parse the `VCAP_SERVICES` variable manually. Another option that simplifies the parsing is to use the Spring Cloud Foundry Connector. Listing 7.2 shows the dependency that you'll need to add to your pom.xml file in order to include this library.

```
<dependency>
  <groupId>org.springframework.cloud</groupId>
  <artifactId>spring-cloud-cloudfoundry-connector</artifactId>
  <version>2.0.1.RELEASE</version>
</dependency>
```

Listing 7.2 Dependency to Spring Cloud Foundry Connector

With this dependency in your project, you can parse your PostgreSQL service information as shown in Listing 7.3.

```
public class GetDatabaseConfig {
  public static <T extends ServiceInfo> ↩
      T retrieveDatabaseInfo( ↩
          String serviceId, Class<T> serviceInfoType) {
    return (T) new CloudFactory() ↩
        .getCloud().getServiceInfo(serviceId);
  }
}
```

Listing 7.3 GetDatabaseConfig.retrieveDatabaseInfo: Parsing VCAP_SERVICES Using Spring Cloud Foundry Connector

Having implemented these components, we'll use the `getEntityManager` method to obtain an entity manager, which automatically accesses the database parameters from the `VCAP_SERVICES` variable. In our example, we'll introduce two classes extending `AbstractEntityManagerFacade` as shown in Figure 7.10.

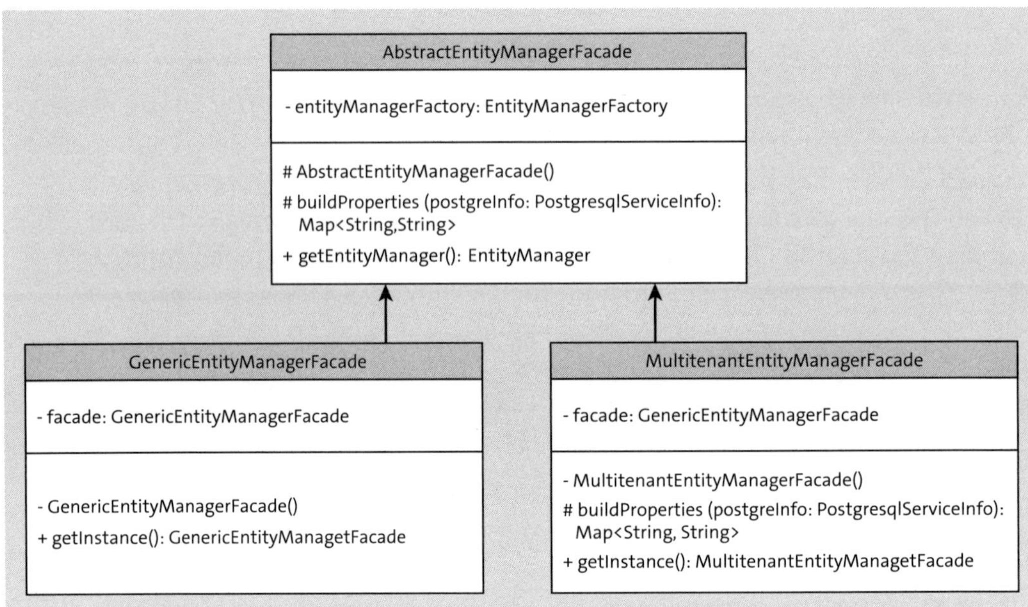

Figure 7.10 Entity Manager Facade Implementations

This step allows us to determine whether we need tenant-dependent or tenant-independent data source connections. We'll explain the implementation of `MultitenantEntityManagerFacade` in Section 7.4.3, covering the topic of customizing tenant-awareness. For now, in this class, we'll override the `buildProperties()` method, thereby extending the property map with additional Hibernate parameters to define the multitenant behavior. We'll use class `GenericEntityManagerFacade` in Section 7.4.4 for cases where tenant-independent connections need to be set up, such as for tenant onboarding.

Now that we've described how our data sources need to be configured for our example application, let's configure tenant-based data separation in a customized data source.

7.4.3 Configure Hibernate to Handle Tenant-Aware Queries

To customize the tenant-aware persistence, we'll combine SAP S/4HANA Cloud SDK components and Hibernate.

First, we'll add the dependency to Hibernate to the application pom.xml, as shown in Listing 7.4.

```
<dependency>
  <groupId>org.hibernate</groupId>
  <artifactId>hibernate-entitymanager</artifactId>
  <version>4.2.21.Final</version>
</dependency>
```

Listing 7.4 Hibernate Dependency

Next, we'll customize Hibernate using the persistence.xml file to activate application-managed persistence with `transaction-type` set to the value `RESOURCE_LOCAL`. We'll also specify Hibernate as the JPA provider, as shown in Listing 7.5. The file is located in the folder *src/main/resource/META-INF*.

```
<persistence xmlns:xsi= …>
  <persistence-unit name="pu" ↩
      transaction-type="RESOURCE_LOCAL">
   <provider>org.hibernate.ejb.HibernatePersistence</provider>
  </persistence-unit>
</persistence>
```

Listing 7.5 Configure Persistence Unit

The code `transaction-type="RESOURCE_LOCAL"` means that our application is responsible for creating and tracking the entity manager. Furthermore, the application needs to explicitly begin and commit each data access transaction. For more insight into transaction types, refer to the JPA concepts article at *http://tiny.cc/jpa-concepts*.

In Section 7.4.2, we configured the data source by implementing the buildProperties method of AbstractEntityManagerFacade. The class diagram shown in Figure 7.10 depicts the class MultitenantEntityManagerFacade that extends AbstractEntityManagerFacade and incorporates the additional customization of Hibernate's multitenancy functionality. Listing 7.6 sketches the implementation of this class.

```
public class MultitenantEntityManagerFacade ↩
    extends AbstractEntityManagerFacade {
  private static MultitenantEntityManagerFacade facade;

  @Override
  protected Map<String, String> buildProperties( ↩
      PostgresqlServiceInfo postgreInfo) {
    Map<String, String> properties = ↩
        super.buildProperties(postgreInfo);

    properties.put("hibernate.multiTenancy", "SCHEMA");
    properties.put("hibernate.tenant_identifier_resolver", ↩
        TenantIdentifierResolver.class.getCanonicalName());
    properties.put( ↩
        "hibernate.multi_tenant_connection_provider", ↩
            SchemaPerTenantConnectionProvider.class ↩
                .getCanonicalName());
    return properties;
  }

  public static MultitenantEntityManagerFacade getInstance() {
    if(facade==null) {
      facade = new MultitenantEntityManagerFacade();
    }
    return facade;
  }
}
```

Listing 7.6 Customizing Hibernate Multitenancy

Note that we'll override the method buildProperties and enable multitenancy by configuring some properties. The property hibernate.multiTenancy specifies that we'll use schema-based tenant separation. With the property hibernate.tenant_identifier_resolver, we'll set the class TenantIdentifierResolver, which resolves the current tenant identifier from requests that are sent to the application. Finally, the property hibernate.multi_tenant_connection_provider defines the class CurrentTenantIdentifierResolver, which sets up connections for the entity managers in Hibernate.

The last two classes constitute the key elements for implementing multitenant persistence in our application. For this reason, let's have a closer look at several implementation dimensions of these components.

The class TenantIdentifierResolver is responsible for resolving tenant identifiers at runtime by implementing CurrentTenantIdentifierResolver and its method resolveCurrentTenantIdentifier, which returns the tenant identifier. But how is the tenant identifier retrieved, and how can we access it in the application? In fact, the SAP S/4HANA Cloud SDK offers components to simplify access to tenant data and provide platform abstractions to hide internal platform details from application developers.

Listing 7.7 demonstrates how to implement access to tenant data using the SDK component TenantAccessor. You can find the full source code for the class TenantIdentifierResolver in the config package.

```
@Override
public String resolveCurrentTenantIdentifier() {
  try {
    return TenantAccessor.getCurrentTenant().getTenantId();
  } catch (TenantNotFoundException e) {
    logger.warn("Tenant not found", e);
    return DEFAULT_TENANT;
  }
}
```

Listing 7.7 TenantIdentifierResolver.resolveCurrentTenantIdentifier: Resolving the Tenant ID Using TenantAccessor

Under the hood, TenantAccessor uses a platform-specific implementation to retrieve the tenant information. For instance, in SAP Cloud Platform, Cloud Foundry, the tenant identifier is extracted from the zid field of the JSON Web Token, which is contained in the Authorization header of an HTTP request. The SAP S/4HANA Cloud SDK supports the Neo and Cloud Foundry environments on the SAP Cloud Platform, as shown in Figure 7.11.

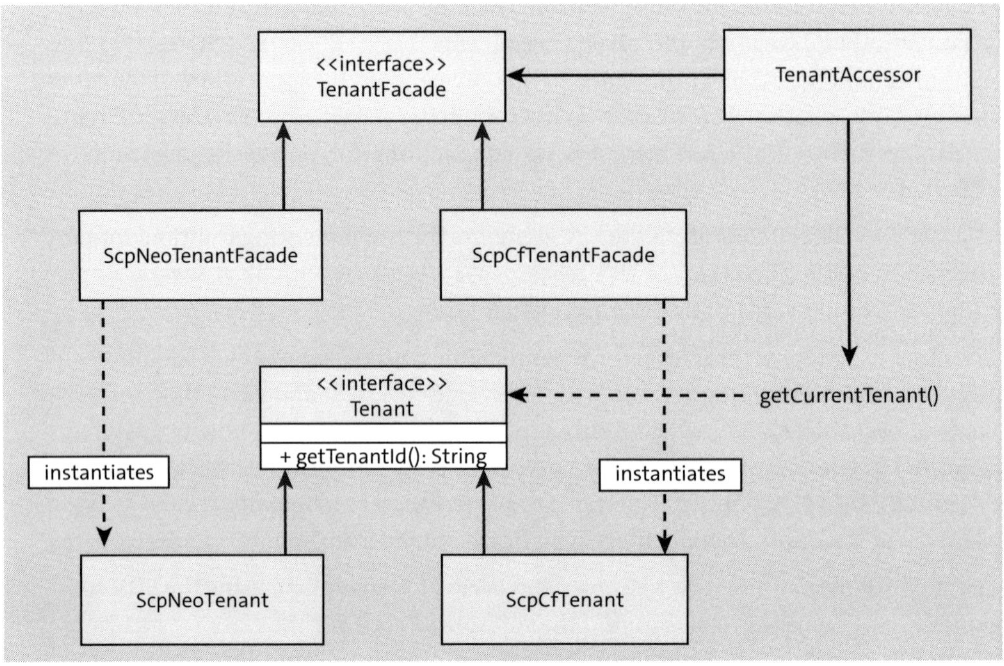

Figure 7.11 SAP Cloud Platform Abstractions in the TenantAccessor

Application developers can decide which implementation to use by specifying a corresponding platform dependency in the pom.xml file. This dependency includes platform-specific implementations of `TenantFacade` and `Tenant`. As the example application runs in the Cloud Foundry environment on the SAP Cloud Platform, we'll add the relevant dependency to our pom.xml file, as shown in Listing 7.8.

```
<dependency>
  <groupId>com.sap.cloud.s4hana.cloudplatform</groupId>
  <artifactId>scp-cf</artifactId>
</dependency>
```

Listing 7.8 Dependency to the Cloud Foundry Environment on the SAP Cloud Platform

More details on SDK's cloud platform abstractions are described in the blog post at *http://tiny.cc/platform-abstractions*. In summary, `TenantIdentifierResolver` retrieves the tenant identifier at runtime via the `TenantAccessor`.

Now, let's look at `hibernate.multi_tenant_connection_provider`. The class `SchemaPerTenantConnectionProvider` implements the `MultiTenantConnectionProvider` interface and is responsible for setting up a connection for each tenant. The method getConnection opens a connection to a dedicated schema for each given tenant identifier (Listing 7.9). As a result, the data for each tenant is separated by means of individual database schemata. The full version of the source code can be found in the class SchemaPerTenantConnectionProvider in the config package.

```
@Override
public Connection getConnection(String tenantId) ↩
    throws SQLException {
  Connection connection = this.getAnyConnection();
  try (PreparedStatement statement = ↩
      connection.prepareStatement(String.format( ↩
          "SET SCHEMA '%s'", ↩
              TenantUtil.createSchemaName(tenantId))))
  {
    statement.execute();
    connection.commit();
  } catch (SQLException e) {
    throw new HibernateException( ↩
        "Could not alter JDBC connection to schema [" + ↩
            TenantUtil.createSchemaName(tenantId) + "]", e);
  }
  return connection;
}
```

Listing 7.9 SchemaPerTenantConnectionProvider.getConnection: Setting Up Tenant-Specific Connections

7.4.4 Tenant Onboarding and Offboarding

In the previous section, we customized the tenant-aware processing of requests, meaning that each tenant is now redirected by Hibernate to its dedicated database schema. Another key aspect of the implementation is to ensure that the database schema and all related database objects exist for each new subscribed tenant. To ensure that an application running in the Cloud Foundry environment on the SAP Cloud Platform is notified of each tenant subscription, we'll create and register an API for tenant onboarding and offboarding. This API is called by SAP Cloud Platform each time an account subscribes to the application. The callback URL must be formed as follows: *<some-url-path>/<tenantId>*. Furthermore, you must implement a PUT request (to subscribe a new tenant) and a DELETE request (to unsubscribe a tenant). Keeping in mind that we are implementing schema-separated multitenancy, the onboarding and offboarding services in our Business Partner Address Manager application will create or drop database schemas for corresponding tenants.

Listing 7.10 shows an example implementation of the onboarding method provided by the class TenantProvisioningServlet in the addressmgr package. In this example, we'll use Liquibase (*www.liquibase.org*) along with the SchemaPerTenantProvisioner class, which is offered by the SAP S/4HANA Cloud SDK, to incorporate the subscription logic.

```
@Override
protected void doPut(HttpServletRequest request, ↩
    HttpServletResponse response) throws IOException
{
  String tenantId = retrieveTenantId(request);
  try {
    EntityManager entityManager = ↩
        GenericEntityManagerFacade.getInstance() ↩
        .getEntityManager();

    Connection connection = ↩
        ((SessionImpl)entityManager.unwrap(Session.class)) ↩
        .connection();

    SchemaPerTenantProvisioner schemaProvisioner = ↩
        new SchemaPerTenantProvisioner(connection, ↩
            LIQUIBASE_CONFIG, SCHEMA_PREFIX);
    schemaProvisioner.subscribeTenant(tenantId);

    connection.close();
    response.setStatus(HttpServletResponse.SC_NO_CONTENT);
  } catch (SQLException | LiquibaseException e) {
    logger.error("Subscription failed: {}.", tenantId, e);
    response.setStatus(HttpServletResponse.SC_BAD_REQUEST);
  }
}
```

Listing 7.10 TenantProvisioningServlet.doPut: Tenant Onboarding Using SchemaPerTenantProvisioner

At first, we'll retrieve JDBC connection from the Hibernate entity manager, and we'll need the connection to instantiate SchemaPerTenantProvisioner and to subscribe the tenant. Note that we can use the GenericEntityManagerFacade to create an entity manager in this case since we don't require a tenant-specific connection to onboard the tenant. Then, we'll instantiate the SchemaPerTenantProvisioner and call its method subscribeTenant with the tenant identifier provided as a path parameter in the initial HTTP request. The SDK components handle the required subscription steps behind the scenes: The subscribeTenant method creates a database schema for the tenant and performs the corresponding database migration using the provided Liquibase configuration file. Note that the Liquibase configuration file defines the database objects created in the new schema.

In our example scenario, we'll require a single table that stores business partner addresses; therefore, the structure of this file is simple and contains only a single table definition. We'll place the Liquibase configuration file in the folder *src/main/java/resources*. Note that, in some cases, the application's consumers may need to unsubscribe from the service and remove all related data. For those cases, we'll need to integrate support for tenant offboarding by implementing the doDelete method, as shown in Listing 7.11.

```
@Override
protected void doDelete(HttpServletRequest request, ↩
    HttpServletResponse response )
{
  String tenantId = retrieveTenantId(request);
  try {
    EntityManager entityManager = ↩
        GenericEntityManagerFacade.getInstance() ↩
        .getEntityManager();

    Connection connection = ↩
        ((SessionImpl)entityManager.unwrap(Session.class)) ↩
        .connection();

    SchemaPerTenantProvisioner schemaProvisioner = ↩
        new SchemaPerTenantProvisioner(connection, ↩
            LIQUIBASE_CONFIG, SCHEMA_PREFIX);
    schemaProvisioner.unsubscribeTenant(tenantId);

    connection.close();
    response.setStatus(HttpServletResponse.SC_NO_CONTENT);
  } catch (SQLException e) {
```

```
    logger.error("Unsubscription failed: {}.", tenantId, e);
    response.setStatus(HttpServletResponse.SC_BAD_REQUEST);
  }
}
```

Listing 7.11 TenantProvisioningServlet.doDelete: Tenant Offboarding Using SchemaPerTenantProvisioner

In Listing 7.11, we'll again leverage the `SchemaPerTenantProvisioner` to simplify the offboarding process. Like the onboarding step, we'll retrieve a JDBC connection and instantiate the `SchemaPerTenantProvisioner`. By calling the method `unsubscribeTenant`, we'll remove the schema corresponding to the given tenant identifier with all the included entities and their tables.

7.4.5 Implementing the Local Address Workflow

As shown in Figure 7.3, we'll introduce a new API to store, approve, and reject addresses in our example application using the `LocalAddressServlet` in the package `addressmgr`, which implements this API.

When the HTTP method `POST` is called on the API */addresses-local*, a local address is inserted into the PostgreSQL database in the schema that corresponds to the given tenant ID. The address is stored with the status "New." Because we're using application-managed persistence, the application will be responsible for opening and committing transactions. Listing 7.12 sketches how local addresses are persisted in the `LocalAddressServlet`.

```
EntityManager entityMgr = ↩
    MultitenantEntityManagerFacade.getInstance() ↩
    .getEntityManager();

EntityTransaction transaction = entityMgr.getTransaction();
transaction.begin();
entityMgr.persist(address);
transaction.commit();
```

Listing 7.12 LocalAddressServlet.doPost: Persisting a Local Address

Note that we'll use `MultitenantEntityManagerFacade`, introduced in Section 7.4.3, to create an entity manager. Thus, the correct database parameters will be set up for the connection, and `SchemaPerTenantConnectionProvider` will be employed for setting up tenant-specific connections. To approve or reject an address that exists in the local database, the user of the application calls the HTTP method PATCH on the API */addresses-local*. If the address is rejected, we'll update the status in the local database. In contrast, if the address is approved, we'll update the status and create a corresponding record in SAP S/4HANA. Listing 7.13 and Listing 7.14 show how to implement the approval and the rejection of addresses, respectively.

```
private void approveAddress(Address address, ↩
    EntityManager entityMgr)
{
  EntityTransaction transaction = entityMgr.getTransaction();
  transaction.begin();
  address.setStatus(Status.APPROVED);
  transaction.commit();

  BusinessPartnerAddress businessPartnerAddress = ↩
      convertAddress(address);
  new CreateAddressCommand(businessPartnerAddress).execute();
}
```

Listing 7.13 Set Status to "APPROVED" and Create Address in SAP S/4HANA

```
private void rejectAddress(Address address, ↩
    EntityManager entityMgr)
{
  EntityTransaction transaction = entityMgr.getTransaction();
  transaction.begin();
  address.setStatus(Status.REJECTED);
  transaction.commit();
}
```

Listing 7.14 Set Status to "REJECTED" in the Local Database

7.4.6 Configuring Service Bindings

At this point, we've implemented the application logic and customized the related data source and multitenancy configuration. However, before we can deploy and test our application, a few final steps are required. We'll create a new database instance and bind this instance to our application so that the parameters of the persistence service are written to the application environment variables, as discussed in Section 7.4.2.

The PostgreSQL service is available in SAP Cloud Platform Service Marketplace. Thus, you can instantiate the service in the SAP Cloud Platform cockpit or via command line by executing the command:

```
cf create-service postgresql v9.6-dev book-project-database
```

After the service has been instantiated, we'll bind the service instance to our Business Partner Address Manager application. To create the binding, we'll modify our existing manifest.yml file and add the required binding to the persistence service in the `services` section, as shown in Listing 7.15.

```
services:
  - myuaa
  - book-project-destinations
  - book-project-connectivity
  - book-project-database
  - log-service
```

Listing 7.15 Binding Services to the Business Partner Address Management

Once the application is bound to the service and deployed in SAP Cloud Platform, the new API */addresses-local* is available for the creation, approval, and rejection of business partner addresses in a tenant-separated manner in the database.

Thus concludes the steps required to extend and configure our Business Partner Address Manager application with tenant-aware persistence. For the full source code, please refer to the GitHub repository for this book.

7.5 Summary

Multitenancy is an essential aspect of cloud applications. In this chapter, we showed you how the concepts of multitenancy can be implemented in the Cloud Foundry environment on the SAP Cloud Platform. We discussed implementing various multitenancy dimensions, including SAP S/4HANA connectivity, resilience, and caching with the SAP S/4HANA Cloud SDK. Extending the initial workflow of our example application, we bound a persistence service and implemented schema-based tenant separation. In Chapter 15, we'll further developed this implementation by integrating Java enterprise frameworks such as Spring Boot and Java EE.

Chapter 8
REST APIs

Having focused purely on the servlet API specification so far, this chapter outlines the theory behind RESTful APIs and explains why you should use frameworks for building RESTful APIs. We'll explore the "API-first" approach using Swagger for decoupling view and data models to provide clean API contracts. Throughout this chapter, we'll provide examples for the REST framework as well as for OData service provisioning.

Before we explain how *Representational State Transfer* (REST) APIs are built, we'll explore why RESTful APIs have become so popular in recent years and why REST is currently the standard for writing web APIs. To understand the rise of REST, you must understand its historical development—or as Carl Sagan would say, "You have to know the past to understand the present."

Simple Object Access Protocol (SOAP) was the standard technology for building web APIs, before REST became popular. Initially developed by Microsoft in the late 1990s for the enterprise world, SOAP was recommended by the W3C in 2003. When we talk about SOAP, in general, we mean a combination of *Web Services Description Language* (WSDL) and schema definitions. This combination provides a rigorous contract for the exchange of structured information. Note that SOAP does not make any assumptions about the specific transport protocol, but HTTP or SMTP are the most prominent use cases.

While SOAP was being developed, the *Extensible Markup Language* (XML) was the favorite file format in town. Consequently, SOAP relies exclusively on XML as the file format for exchanging data (see *http://tiny.cc/xml-soap*). This format is an excellent choice for structuring data, but we won't go into too much detail on how a SOAP message is structured. The important point is that, for SOAP, you must follow a strict structure of envelope and body, as shown in Figure 8.1. The actual message is contained in the body; the WSDL defines its content, that is, the possible actions if the message is a request or the result data if the message is a response. Besides the content, error handling is also standardized by SOAP as seen by the fault block shown in Figure 8.1. In addition, features like security or attachments are included in the SOAP specification.

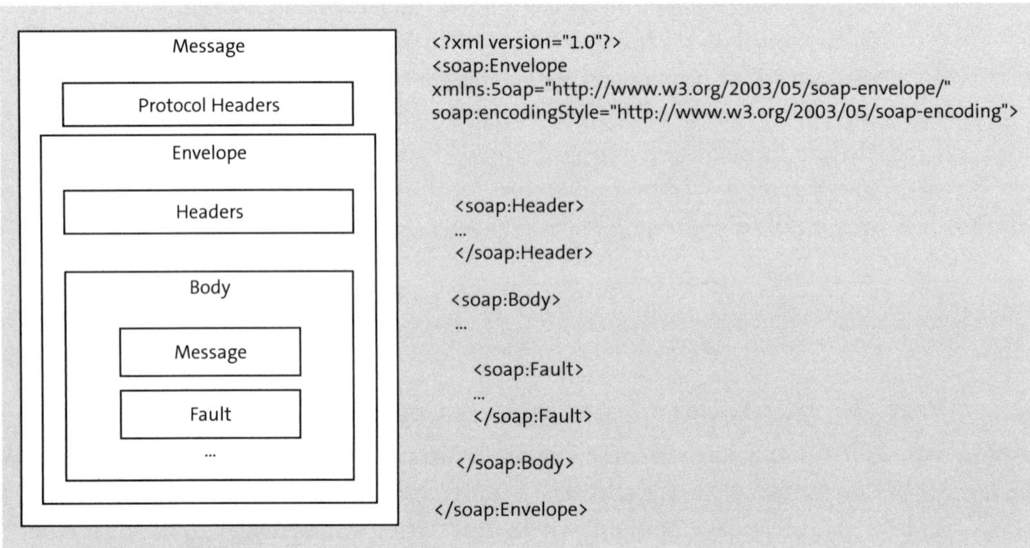

Figure 8.1 General Struture of a SOAP Message with the Schematic Message Structure and the Respective XML

Having elaborated on the development SOAP in detail, now we're ready to look at the future.

In today's highly connected and integrated world, APIs are crucial (*http://tiny.cc/history-apis*), and the question becomes "Should we build APIs using SOAP?" To answer this question, let's perform an experiment: Putting potential alternatives aside, let's assume we want to implement the API of our example application introduced in Chapter 4 using SOAP. The resulting SOAP API will illustrate the disadvantages of SOAP and naturally point us into the direction of RESTful services. First, let's quickly summarize, in Table 8.1, how the API was built using servlets in the previous chapters. Note that, for compactness, we'll shorten the relevant IDs to a single key parameter indicating the identifier.

Endpoint	Function
GET /api/business-partners	Retrieve all business partners
GET /api/business-partners?key=<key>	Retrieve a single business partner
POST /api/addresses	Create an address for a specific business partner
DELETE /api/addresses?key=<key>	Delete an address
PATCH /api/addresses?key=<key>	Update an address

Table 8.1 Implementation of Example API Using Servlets

This approach is not possible with SOAP, where you'll always post an XML message indicating what you want to do. In SOAP, the same API is shown in Table 8.2.

URL	Content SOAP Body
POST /api/business-partners	Empty
POST /api/business-partners	<businessPartnerId>BP id </businessPartnerId>
POST /api/addresses	<action>create</action> ...address data
POST /api/addresses	<action>delete</action> <addressId>address id</addressId>
POST /api/addresses	<action>update</action> <addressId>address id</addressId> ...address data

Table 8.2 Artificial SOAP Version of the API

Though we've skipped the header, the XML version information, and all redundant parts of the SOAP message for compactness, you should notice some overhead, in terms of message size and time-to-code, in creating these SOAP messages. The URL itself describes what we want to do. We can hide this information by using just a single URL and encoding the information in the SOAP message, as shown in Table 8.3.

URL	Content SOAP Body
POST /api/BPSoapApi	<businessPartner> <businessPartnerId>id</businessPartnerId> <!-- optional block --> <address> <action>{create,delete,update}</action> <addressId> address id</addressId> ...address data </address> </businessPartner>

Table 8.3 Realistic Version of Example API in SOAP Form

If we were using SOAP in the first place, this setup is the most likely form of the service we would build. We shift the complexity of creating two service endpoints (one for business partner data read actions and the other for manipulating addresses), because sending empty SOAP messages seems unnatural. These kinds of APIs, using plain old XML (POX), were called *the swamp of POX* by Leonard Richardson in his REST Maturity Model (*http://tiny.cc/maturity-model*). "Swamp" already indicates some negative associations, and, in the following, we'll discuss the problems related to this approach and then discuss the foundations of RESTful services.

Let's assume you are a new user of this API and you want to play around with the API using tools like Postman or SoapUI. In this case, you would have to look at the specifications, that is, the WSDL file, to build a proper payload. This process is tedious and error prone, especially if the payloads are long. So, a brief uniform interface comprising of HTTP keywords, with a URL to define the resources, is much more user friendly. Besides, a slim signature also has the advantage of decoupling functionality—each resource is related to a distinct URL. Such decoupling makes it easier for services to evolve with time, due to easier development and maintenance. Also, scaling becomes more efficient because computational power may be dynamically assigned, only activated when needed most.

Since SOAP results in adding more functionally within one service endpoint, the payloads tend to grow with time. This growth is not only a problem for humans who want to use the API but also for system performance in general because the server and client will have to parse potentially long XML files. Furthermore, more than just performance may be negatively impacted from XML parsing. Modern browsers make efficient use of caching, and the end user never knows whether a web application is fast due to intelligent caching or to powerful servers. However, the caching mechanisms of browsers only work with the GET method and do not apply to the POST method used in SOAP. The whole performance issue becomes even more relevant for applications running on mobile devices, with limited bandwidth, battery power, etc.

To summarize, we've identified a few potential shortcomings in SOAP services: slim uniform interfaces, decoupling functionality, scaling, performance, and caching. On the other hand, these topics are central to the concept of Representation State Transfer (REST), as proposed by Roy Fielding in his Ph.D. thesis at *http://tiny.cc/phd-fielding*.

Thus, we'll follow the REST approach to build our APIs and briefly present the theory behind REST in the next section. But first, let's look at the popular adoption of REST in the API world, which is an indicator of the quality and relevance of this approach.

Fielding's proposal was adopted the year he published his thesis (2000) by eBay, which rolled out a RESTful API together with its developer program, to encourage application development involving their marketplace. A few years later, other internet giants like Amazon (2002), Flickr (2004), Facebook, Twitter, and Google (2006) created APIs implemented in a RESTful manner. At this point, a critical mass was reached, and RESTful APIs started to dominate the landscape, which can be seen by comparing interest in SOAP versus interest in REST as measured by Google Trends (*http://tiny.cc/google-trend-api*). In particular, interest in REST started exceeding that of SOAP in 2008 (Figure 8.2). This development aligns with the onset of mobile devices and applications, where RESTful APIs could take full advantage of their strengths.

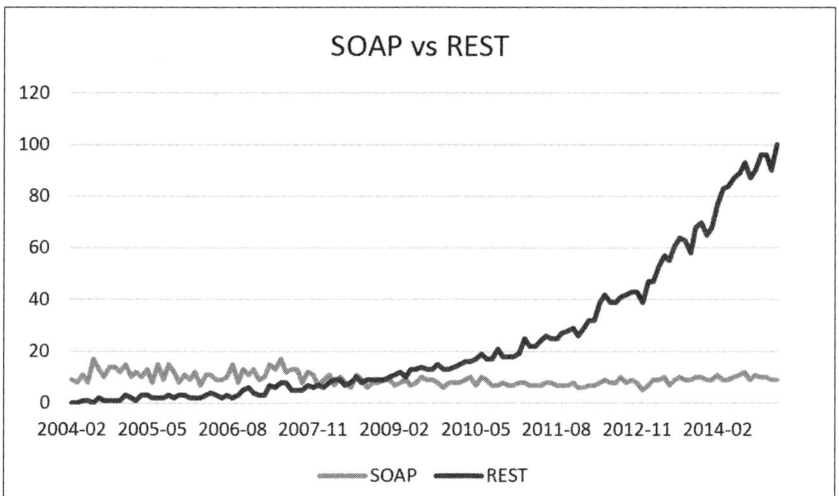

Figure 8.2 Interest in SOAP and REST as a Function of Time Measured by Google Trends (http://tiny.cc/google-trend-api)

Earlier in this section, we discussed the historical development of web APIs and explored what makes REST better compared to other approaches. Let's now focus on some concrete examples of REST, starting with the architectural constraints defined by Roy Fielding (*http://tiny.cc/phd-fielding*), as follows:

- **Client-server architecture**
  This constraint refers to separating the concerns of data storage and provisioning with that of requesting data, that is, the user interface.
- **Stateless system**
  This constraint requires that all application contexts or states are controlled by the client, and none of this information is held by the server. This constraint requires the client to repeatedly provide complete context to the server on each request. In most situations, the gain in reduced complexity, resilience, and scalability overcome the potentially inefficient request structure.
- **Cache**
  We addressed this constraint earlier in this section. Within HTTP requests, caching is supported. As a developer, your responsibility is to set the `Cache-Control` header correctly.
- **Uniform interface**
  We've already discussed how, in SOAP, each resource is represented by a URL and HTTP keywords, which represent the action performed on the data. We'll explain this constraint in more detail later in this chapter when we implement a concrete use case.
- **Code on demand**
  This constraint allows the client to run functions by the server via script files. With the popularity of JavaScript, this approach seems natural today but, in 2000, was revolutionary.

If these five constraints are fulfilled while implementing a service, an API is considered RESTful.

8.1 Designing RESTful APIs

In previous chapters, we explored why REST is a good choice for building web APIs. Now it's time to design the API for our Business Partner Address Manager application in a RESTful way. We'll follow SAP's API harmonizing initiative (*http://tiny.cc/sap-api-guidelines*), which is similar to other best practices on this topic (*http://jsonapi.org*).

For the actual process of defining an API, several tools are available, like Swagger, RAML, or API Blueprint, to help you define APIs. We decided to follow an *API-first* approach, in which we'll define the API using some descriptor file and then implement it. All definition tools share a common workflow:

1. Define the API in some definition or descriptor file.
2. Generate interfaces for the client stack (Java, Node.js, etc.).
3. Implement the interfaces.

We'll use Swagger as our definition tool, since it has currently the most momentum and flexibility. Swagger supports YAML and JSON as formats for the descriptor file, but we'll stick to YAML. Note that Swagger initially originated from the approach of annotating existing APIs to create documentation but fully supports the API-first approach we want to use in this chapter. As we go along, we'll describe certain best practices that API developers can use.

We'll start by defining the business partner endpoint, which provides all business partners. Let's look at the descriptor file in Listing 8.1.

```
swagger: "2.0"
info:
  description: "Managing addresses associated to business partners."
  version: "v1"
  title: "Address Manager API"
  contact:
    email: "frank.essenberger@sap.com"
basePath: "/api/v1/rest"
tags:
  - name: "businessPartnerService"
paths:
  /business-partners:
    get:
      operationId: "getBusinessPartners"
      description: "Get all business partners."
      tags:
      - "businessPartnerService"
      produces:
      - "application/json"
      responses:
        200:
```

```
          schema:
            $ref: "./schemas.yaml#/BusinessPartnersResponse"
500:
  description: "Server-side error"
```

Listing 8.1 First Part of Web Descriptor File Defining the API

The first info block provides basic information about the service like contact person, version, and title. Note that the `description` attribute is allowed almost everywhere, for example, in the `contact`, `tags`, etc., but we're not using it extensively so that our example files will be short. In real-world situations, descriptions help understanding the API and should be added accordingly.

The first thing we'd like to talk about is the `basePath` attribute. This attribute contains an API version number, which is important if we need to introduce breaking changes to the API in future. In such a case, the old API will remain available in parallel to the new version (for example, called v2) so that users can decide when to migrate their own codebase to the new version.

Best Practice I: Versioning

Include a version number in your API path, for example: */api/v1/rest*.

A second point we want to highlight in the description file is the path name for the resources. In naming, you should use plural nouns. In RESTful services, an action is defined by an HTTP method and not by a resource name. So, avoid path names like *getBusinessPartners*.

Best Practice II: Naming

Use plural nouns for your resource name, for example, */api/v1/rest/business-partners*. For more complex data models, you should avoid dashes, and we recommend using camel case to ensure the mapping of URL and JSON properties is aligned, for example, */api/v1/rest/businessPartners*.

At the end of the descriptor file, the response of the service is defined with HTTP status 200 if everything worked fine and 500 if a server-side error occurred. We haven't specified a response type in case of errors, which means an empty response. In principle, the service may also return 401 or 403 if users are not authenticated or lack permission. In our example, we'll skip defining these responses to keep our definition files shorter, but we'll discuss the usage of HTTP error codes later in this section.

First, we'll investigate the response type. The *$ref* tag links to the schema.yaml file where the response type is defined. This useful feature of Swagger helps structure the descriptor file. The schema.yaml contains the elements shown in Listing 8.2.

```
BusinessPartnersResponse:
  type: object
  properties:
    value:
      $ref: "#/BusinessPartners"
    error:
      $ref: "#/Errors"
BusinessPartners:
  type: array
  description: "List of Business partners"
  items:
    $ref: "#/BusinessPartner"
BusinessPartner:
  type: object
  description: "Business partner object"
  properties:
    id:
      type: string
Errors:
  type: array
  items:
    $ref: "#/Error"
Error:
    type: object
    description: "Error Object"
    properties:
      code:
        type: integer
      message:
        type: string
```

Listing 8.2 Schema Definition for Response Types of the Request

For later usage, we defined a single BusinessPartner object. For the moment, the object contains only a single attribute, id. We'll change this later, but for the moment, this simple definition is sufficient. This object is wrapped inside an array called BusinessPartners, which itself is returned in the BusinessPartnersResponse. We introduced this extra wrapper to be able to include a value attribute and an error attribute. The idea behind this wrapper to make it easier for the client to process a standard response.

Best Practice III: Response

Include a value attribute containing the data and an error attribute containing error information in your response object.

If an error appears during request processing, you can provide additional information on the error in this object. For example, for a bad request (code 400), offering guidance to the user on how to sanitize the request could be useful. The error object should contain at least a code attribute with an internal error code and a message. In principle, the message should be multilanguage depending on the accept-language header of the request.

The next feature we want to define is the search for a specific business partner. In the initial servlet, this functionality was created by passing a URL parameter. However, this method would not be RESTful, since we want to use the URL to identify the resource. So, in REST, we'll use the identifier directly in the URL path, for example, */business-partners/123*, to fetch the business partner with identifier "123." In the descriptor file, the new path would look like Listing 8.3.

```
/business-partners/{businessPartnerId}:
  parameters:
  - $ref: "./parameters.yaml#/businessPartnerId"
  get:
    operationId: "getBusinessPartnersById"
    description: "Get business partner by ID"
    tags:
    - "businessPartnerService"
    produces:
    - "application/json"
    responses:
      200:
```

```
        schema:
          $ref: "./schemas.yaml#/BusinessPartnerResponse"
404:
  description: "Not found"
500:
  description: "Server-side error"
```

Listing 8.3 Definition of Business Partner Lookup by ID

The content of the parameters.yaml file is shown in Listing 8.4.


```
businessPartnerId:
  name: businessPartnerId
  in: path
  description: "Id of business partner"
  required: true
  type: string
```

Listing 8.4 Definition of a Path Parameter

The new part is the definition of a parameter in the request. The parameter location (`in` attribute) is defined as `path`. Potential other values for this attribute are `query`, `header`, or `body`, indicating a parameter in the URL, header, or the request body, respectively. The rest of Listing 8.4 should be self-explanatory. Comparing the two services, we'll see a slight difference in the HTTP error codes. For the latter service, we included a 404 that was not present in the endpoint returning all business partners. For a list of objects, returning an empty list with error code 200 might be more intuitive if there are no business partners.

Best Practice IV: Resource Not Found

Use HTTP status code 404 if a single entity is not present. For a service that returns a list of items, use error code 200 and an empty list if no objects are present.

Now, we're finished defining the API related to the business partner itself. We'll proceed now with the address part, which has a one-to-many relationship with the business partner. The first method we'll define is the creation of a new address, which is done via a `POST` method, as shown in Listing 8.5.

```
/business-partners/{businessPartnerId}/addresses:
parameters:
- $ref: "./parameters.yaml#/businessPartnerId"
- name: address
  in: body
  required: true
  schema:
    $ref: "./schemas.yaml#/Address"
post:
  operationId: "createAddress"
  description: "Create address for business partner"
  tags:
  - "businessPartnerAddressService"
  produces:
  - "application/json"
  responses:
    201:
      schema:
        $ref: "./schemas.yaml#/AddressResponse"
    404:
      description: "Not found"
    500:
      description: "Server-side error"
```

Listing 8.5 Creation of Addresses for a Business Partner

We included an additional parameter in the body containing the data to be created. If the object is created, we'll return status code 201 along with the created object in the response.

Best Practice V: Creation

Use a POST request to create an object. On success, return status 201 and the created object in the payload. In addition, you should include the URL to the created object in the location header field.

We also added an additional tag to the API called businessPartnerAddressService because we wanted to keep a separation between business-partner and address logic in the later implementation. The tags used in this request will be considered when an interface is created. All paths with the same tag are included in one interface by the Swagger code generator. The delete and patch requests are the two missing requests we'll need to define next (Listing 8.6).

```
/business-partners/{businessPartnerId}/addresses/{addressId}:
    parameters:
    - $ref: "./parameters.yaml#/businessPartnerId"
    - $ref: "./parameters.yaml#/addressId"
    patch:
      operationId: "updateAddress"
      parameters:
      - $ref: "./parameters.yaml#/address"
      tags:
      - "businessPartnerAddressService"
      produces:
      - "application/json"
      responses:
        200:
          schema:
            $ref: "./schemas.yaml#/AddressResponse"
404:
  description: "Not found"
500:
  description: "Server-side error"
    delete:
      operationId: "delteAddress"
      tags:
      - "businessPartnerAddressService"
      produces:
      - "application/json"
      responses:
        200:
          schema:
            $ref: "./schemas.yaml#/AddressResponse"
404:
  description: "Not found"
500:
  description: "Server-side error"
```

Listing 8.6 Definition of Update and Delete Request for an Address

For updating or deleting existing addresses, we'll need to identify the object. Thus, we included the `addressId` parameter, which is analogous to the already existing `businessPartnerId`. Of course, an update request also needs the content of an address to update. For updating an object, we recommend using status code 200 and returning the changed object. If you only specify the house number when updating an object, then you would expect the other properties of the address object, like street, postal code, etc., to remain unchanged.

Best Practice VI: Update

Use a `PATCH` request to update objects. If certain properties of a resource are not specified by the update request, those properties must not be changed.

Since we're implementing a RESTful API based on HTTP, be aware that certain boundary conditions are imposed by the HTTP standard itself (*https://tools.ietf.org/html/rfc2616*). The `GET`, `DELETE`, and `PATCH` requests should be idempotent, meaning that multiple executions of the same request should have the same effect as a single execution. Note that the `GET` method is reserved for safe methods, that is, methods that do not change data and is therefore idempotent by construction. The return code and expiration headers are explicitly excluded from this rule. Thus, the first delete request on an object can return status 200 and the second one, status 404. If the status code wasn't excluded, you would need to include a delete flag on all your objects to distinguish a successfully deleted object from an object that never existed in the first place. This situation would quickly lead to an issue—servers would contain state information that violates one of the constraints for a RESTful API.

Best Practice VII: Safe and Idempotent

`GET`, `DELETE`, and `PATCH` requests must be idempotent, and `GET` requests must be safe.

At this point, we've configured the last service we need. However, before we proceed with the actual implementation of the services in the next section, we'd like to discuss a few more points. We've used a dummy business partner object for simplicity so far in our example, but let's now investigate a proper business partner object, as shown in Listing 8.7.

```
BusinessPartner:
  type: object
  description: "Business partner object"
```

```
  properties:
    id:
      type: string
    firstName:
      type: string
    lastName:
      type: string
    addresses:
      type: array
      items:
        $ref: "#/Link"
Link:
  type: object
  description: "Link to another object"
  properties:
    href:
      type: string
```

Listing 8.7 Business Partner Data Type

The first properties like `id`, `firstName`, and `lastName` are the basic properties of a business partner, and we already know their notation from previous objects. More interesting is the `addresses` property where we used a `link` property to indicate a path to an associated resource (e.g., */business-partners/123/addresses/456*). We didn't use a primitive type for the links although the object contains no additional information. Using a primitive type in this situation hinders extensibility. Let's assume we need to add meta information to the link. By having an object in place, instead of a primitive type, we can avoid a breaking change.

Best Practice IIX: Types

Wrap primitive types in objects before returning them.

Returning links in the response together with the standardized methods and response type metadata enables *Hypermedia as the Engine of Application State* (HATEOAS), a concept also proposed by Roy Fielding. HATEOAS means that the client explores potential actions by the provided response. In our example, we only provided some information, but you could extend this principle further to more complicated situations, for example, a scheduling API returning links to create new appointments in free time slots upon request. The benefits of this approach are the robustness of API changes and ease of use.

We'll conclude this definition section with a remark on HTTP status codes. In the software engineering community, you'll find a lot of discussion of what status code to use for which purpose. For some cases, the answer is clear; for others, this choice is unclear. To illustrate, let's assume an item is not present, for example, */business-partner/noExistingID*. We could return a 404 error code, which is correct with respect to the HTTP specification. However, the drawback of this code is that you would get the same code also if you have a typo in the URL, or the server is not available. So, in everyday development, returning 200 and an empty object instead of 404 may save time.

Or, another question, should you return 200 or 204 on a successful update? To avoid endless discussions on ambiguous status codes, you could, for example, follow the decision of the developers of the Facebook Graph API and always return 200 when a request is processed (for more details, refer to *https://developers.facebook.com/docs/graph-api*). All information on the status of the request is then given by the error object in the response with internal error codes. However, this extreme choice has implications on caching and on client expectations while processing requests. Therefore, we recommend a choice somewhere between "always 200" and "try to find the right one from more than 50 status codes" (*https://tools.ietf.org/html/rfc2616*).

For now, we'll stick to a handful of codes, and use the error object to provide extra information as we explained earlier in this section. This choice, as depicted in Best Practice IX below, has also been adopted by other big API developers like Google or Netflix (see *http://tiny.cc/error-codes* for more details).

Best Practice IX: Error Codes

Use only common HTTP error codes, such as the following:

- 200 – Everything Worked
- 201 – Item Created
- 400 – Bad Request (user input was not valid) and put additional information in the error attribute
- 401 – Not Authenticated
- 403 – Not Allowed
- 500 – Server-side Error

Error codes 401, 403, and 500 are common, and we've specified them in our API. However, you should only rarely code them by hand. In general, these error codes are set either by the web framework (401, 403) or by some exception mapper catching exceptions from server errors (500). We'll discuss this concept in the next sections.

Best Practice X: Error Codes

If possible, let your framework take care of authorization and server-side error handling.

8.2 Building RESTful APIs

So far in this chapter, we've defined our API using Swagger descriptor files, and we're ready to start the implementation now. We won't go over the implementation of all the methods in this chapter because the logic doesn't change from the previous servlet implementation we saw in Chapter 4. Instead, we'll focus on general concepts and only highlight some important differences from the servlet case.

Now, we can benefit from the code generation feature and create interfaces from the definition file. We'll use the Swagger code generation plugin for Maven (available at *http://tiny.cc/swagger-maven*), which provides a convenient way to generate code from the definition (Listing 8.8).

```
<plugin>
  <groupId>io.swagger</groupId>
  <artifactId>swagger-codegen-maven-plugin</artifactId>
  <version>2.2.3</version> <!-- use the latest version -->
  <executions>
    <execution>
      <goals>
        <goal>generate</goal>
      </goals>
      <configuration>
        <inputSpec>
          ${project.basedir} ↩
            /src/main/resources/api/api.yaml
        </inputSpec>
        <language>jaxrs-cxf</language>
```

```
          <configOptions>
            <sourceFolder>src/main/java</sourceFolder>
          </configOptions>
          <ignoreFileOverride>
            ${project.basedir}/src/main/resources/api/.ignore
          </ignoreFileOverride>
          <generateApiTests>false</generateApiTests>
          <output>
            ${project.build.directory}/generated-sources/api
          </output>
        </configuration>
      </execution>
    </executions>
</plugin>
```

Listing 8.8 Swagger Code Generation Plugin for Maven

Since the backend is written in Java, we'll use JAX-RS with Apache CXF (*http://cxf.apache.org*) as the language for the generated interface. JAX-RS defines the interface for building RESTful services in Java, and Apache CXF is the implementation. (We'll discuss other frameworks in Chapter 15.) If the frontend is written using TypeScript, we could execute the plugin twice and also create the interfaces for TypeScript. In this way, we can establish a clear contract between backend and frontend, which can be quite valuable for teams with distinct frontend and backend developers.

The setup shown in Listing 8.8 will follow the JAX-RS CXF standard and set the base path to root but requires you define the resource mapping in the web.xml file. Note that the .ignore file excludes the dummy implementation created by Swagger, which we won't use. Therefore, we'll include the parameter in Listing 8.9 in the `configOptions` of the plugin definition:

```
<additional-properties>
  useAnnotatedBasePath=true
</additional-properties>
```

Listing 8.9 Setup to Include the Base Path in the Resource Path

Note that, if you prefer servlet mapping in the web.xml file, set the option `generateNonSpring-Application=true`. Using the configuration depicted in Listing 8.9, the base path */api/vi/rest/* is used as a prefix to the resource path.

Remark on CXF

CXF versions before 3.0 cannot process multiple services with the same base path. As a workaround, you can include a custom `ResourceComparator` class. Refer to *http://tiny.cc/swagger-jaxrs-cxf* for more details on this class.

The result of the code generation process is a set of Java interfaces and classes, as shown in Figure 8.3. In the plugin definition, we defined the output directory to serve as the *target* folder of the application as this folder is not included in the GitHub repository for this book. The interfaces define the signature of the service and the classes of the relevant data model.

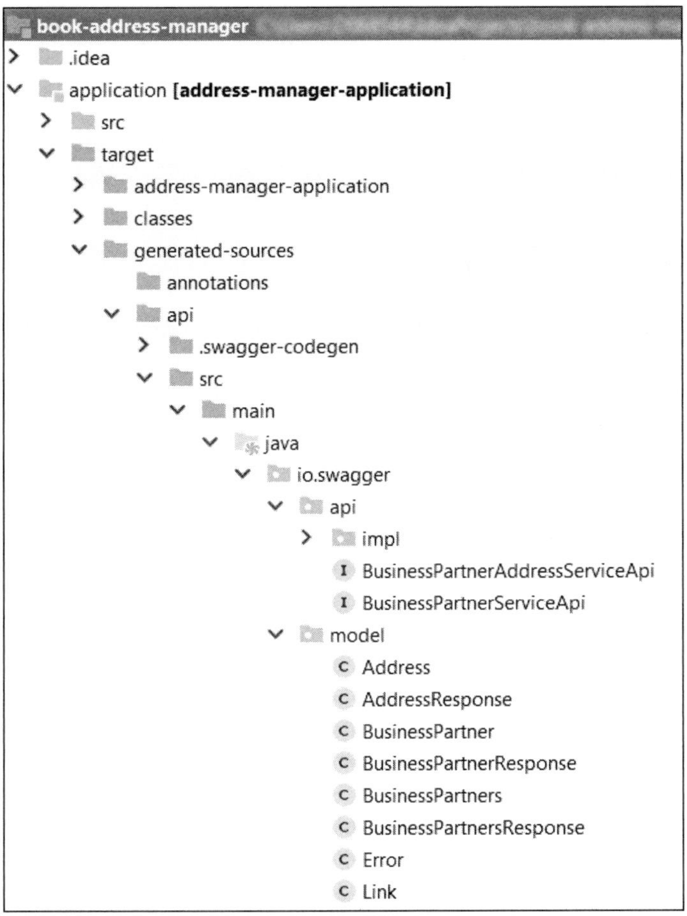

Figure 8.3 Interfaces and Classes Created from the Service Definition

As discussed earlier in the definition process, we introduced two tags, and consequently, we have two interfaces. As an example, let's quickly investigate the `BusinessPartnerServiceApi`.

In Figure 8.4, notice that the content of the interface represents the definition given in Listing 8.1 and Listing 8.3. We would like to emphasize that this bidirectional mapping also enables an *API-last* scenario in which you would add annotations starting with "@" to an existing service and create a descriptor file from these annotations. This approach makes sense if you already have an API ready, or you're creating a small private API, that is, for situations where the API-first approach would mean too much overhead. Either way, the annotations are processed on server startup, and the implementing class is invoked for an incoming request. The first step is a dummy implementation of the interface (Listing 8.10).

```
@Path("/api/v1/rest")
@Api(value = "/", description = "")
public interface BusinessPartnerServiceApi  {

    @GET
    @Path("/business-partners")
    @Produces({ "application/json" })
    @ApiOperation(value = "", tags={ "businessPartnerService",  })
    @ApiResponses(value = {
        @ApiResponse(code = 200, message = "", response = BusinessPartnersResponse.class),
        @ApiResponse(code = 500, message = "Server side error") })
    public BusinessPartnersResponse getBusinessPartners();

    @GET
    @Path("/business-partners/{businessPartnerId}")
    @Produces({ "application/json" })
    @ApiOperation(value = "", tags={ "businessPartnerService" })
    @ApiResponses(value = {
        @ApiResponse(code = 200, message = "", response = BusinessPartnerResponse.class),
        @ApiResponse(code = 404, message = "Not found"),
        @ApiResponse(code = 500, message = "Server side error") })
    public BusinessPartnerResponse getBusinessPartnersById(
            @PathParam("businessPartnerId") String businessPartnerId);
}
```

Figure 8.4 API Generated from Descriptor File

```
public class BusinessPartnerRestService ↩
    implements BusinessPartnerServiceApi {

  @Override
  public BusinessPartnersResponse getBusinessPartners() {
```

```
    return null;
  }

  @Override
  public BusinessPartnerResponse getBusinessPartnersById( ↩
    String businessPartnerId) {
    return null;
  }
}
```

Listing 8.10 Dummy Implementation of the Business Partner Interface Generated by Swagger

Once we have the dummy implementation, we can start the server. At this point, we recommend creating test cases to verify the server behaves correctly while implementing the logic. We'll go into more detail on testing in Chapter 9. The successful mapping between URL and handler method is indicated by log statements on server startup, as shown in Figure 8.5.

```
INFO:        Service URI: http://localhost:57711/4a6b731a-bde0-4756
 -a398-5e5b98d114f0/api/v1/rest
   -> Pojo com.sap.cloud.s4hana.examples.addressmgr.api
 .BusinessPartnerRestService
Jan 23, 2018 10:52:23 AM org.apache.openejb.server.cxf.rs
 .CxfRsHttpListener logEndpoints
INFO:                    GET http://localhost:57711/4a6b731a-bde0-4756
 -a398-5e5b98d114f0/api/v1/rest/business-partners
   ->        BusinessPartnersResponse getBusinessPartners()
Jan 23, 2018 10:52:23 AM org.apache.openejb.server.cxf.rs
 .CxfRsHttpListener logEndpoints
INFO:                    GET http://localhost:57711/4a6b731a-bde0-4756
 -a398-5e5b98d114f0/api/v1/rest/business-partners/{businessPartnerId
 } ->        BusinessPartnerResponse getBusinessPartnersById(String)
```

Figure 8.5 Mapping of URL and HTTP Methods to Java Methods

Notice that no exceptions are included in the method signature. This design decision was intentional by the Swagger team to enforce clean error handling. The processing of unchecked exceptions is based on an exception mapper. The best way to understand the concept of an exception mapper is by example. Let's implement the path for a specific business partner. Note that the `convert` method casts the SAP S/4HANA business partner type to the Swagger type (Listing 8.11).

```
@Override
public BusinessPartnerResponse getBusinessPartnersById( ↩
    String businessPartnerId )
{
  BusinessPartner businessPartner = ↩
      new GetSingleBusinessPartnerByIdCommand( ↩
          businessPartnerId).execute();

  if(businessPartner == null) {
    throw new NotFoundException();
  }

  BusinessPartnerResponse response = ↩
      new BusinessPartnerResponse();

  response.setValue(convert(businessPartner));
  return response;
}
```

Listing 8.11 Implementation of getBusinessPartnersById Method

The query logic is simply copied from our previous servlet implementation. However, now we'll throw an exception if the business partner can't be found, that is, `null`. In this case, the `ExceptionMapper` class comes into play. This class catches all exceptions and transforms them into HTTP responses. In the JAX-RS framework, functionality is extended using classes with a `@Provider` annotation implementing the corresponding interface. This interface may be an entity provider, context provider, or in our case, an exception mapper (Listing 8.12).

```
@Provider
public class ExceptionMapper ↩
    implements javax.ws.rs.ext.ExceptionMapper<Throwable>
{
  private final ErrorResponseBuilder responseBuilder = ↩
      ErrorResponseBuilder.newBuilder() ↩
          .withMapper(new NotFoundExceptionMapper());

  @Override
  public Response toResponse(Throwable throwable) {
    return JaxRsErrorResponseBuilder ↩
```

```
        .build(responseBuilder.build(throwable));
  }
}
```

Listing 8.12 Exception Mapper Handling NotFoundException

The toResponse method handles the translation from an exception to an HTTP response. Since we don't want to use the default handling, we included the NotFoundExceptionMapper from the SDK. The mappers are bundled in the SDK ErrorResponseBuilder containing the following features:

- Stack trace is logged on the server side with a reference identifier.
- The HTTP response containing this identifier is passed to the client, so that a reported error can be easily analyzed.
- ExceptionMapper-specific exceptions to a custom log level and HTTP response are included.
- Fallback to the default log level error takes place, with HTTP return status 500 by default, if no mapper handles the exception.

Using the exception mapper, handling exceptions in a consistent way in all your application modules becomes easy as does providing helpful responses for investigating log files. Furthermore, a hard encapsulation of the exception on the server is guaranteed because the exception mapper includes fallback handling for all unmapped exceptions. This useful quality is also a security benefit since no server information is extracted from the client side. We'll go into the exception mapper and logging in more detail in Chapter 13.

We'd like to close this section with one more interesting feature—the Swagger UI, as shown in Figure 8.6. This out of the box web client is created from the descriptor file. This client can serve as useful online documentation for the API and enables executing requests. The UI makes playing around with the API extremely easy because no extra tools are needed. You'll simply host the Swagger UI on the server from which you have access to the API descriptor files. For the simple address application, we included the UI within the .war file of the application. Note that the UI supports importing descriptor files from other services. This functionality makes enables you to reduce the UI for multiple services. However, providing the Swagger UI with each application has the advantage of not sharing internal details (how the model is exposed) between services, and you can set up UI-specific authorizations easily on the application level.

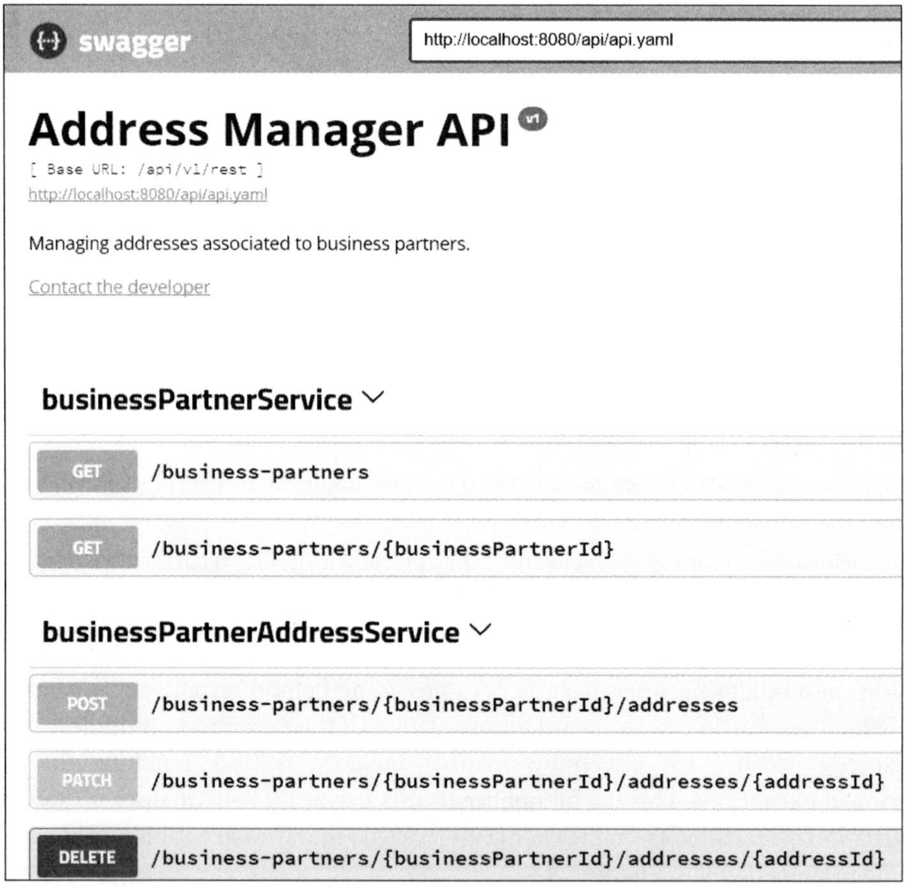

Figure 8.6 Swagger UI for the Business Partner Address Manager

8.3 Provisioning OData Services with the SAP Cloud Platform SDK for Service Development

We've seen how business partner data can be exposed as a RESTful API. Let's now look at exposing business partner information as an OData service for clients interested in consuming this data as an OData service.

Open Data Protocol (OData), as described at *www.odata.org*, is an open standard that defines a set of best practices for building and consuming RESTful APIs. An OData service complies to the OData standard and is the chosen protocol for SAP Fiori applications to communicate with SAP systems. OData is a common protocol of choice in the SAP space, both for user-facing apps as well as integration scenarios, since it allows you to define and easily access semantically rich services that are usually required for business processes and data.

SAP Gateway offers the tools and the APIs for building OData services on the SAP NetWeaver platform using ABAP as the programming language. The SAP Cloud Platform SDK for service development (SAP Cloud Platform SDK) provides Java and Node.js libraries and APIs for building applications that expose OData services on the SAP Cloud Platform. We introduced the SAP Cloud Platform SDK for service development in Chapter 3, Section 3.3, where we also explained its relationship to the SAP S/4HANA Cloud SDK.

In addition to the pure OData service provisioning capabilities, the SAP Cloud Platform SDK also provides simple APIs for the consumption of various data sources that could be useful for developers needing to connect data from different systems. An example data source could be an SAP S/4HANA system exposing an OData service. The SAP Cloud Platform SDK provides APIs that simplify the use of these OData services.

The following sections explain how to provision an OData service. As we walk through each step, we'll outline the capabilities and components being employed. We'll use Java as programming language and describe the provisioning of OData 4.0 the latest version of the specification with significant improvements over OData 2.0.

8.3.1 Introduction to Technical Components

The SAP Cloud Platform SDK allows you to implement business logic for provisioning OData services with simplified interfaces. These interfaces abstract the OData version dependency and help you focus only on the basic tasks necessary. You can implement the logic for some basic OData operations using the same code for provisioning an OData 2.0 and an OData 4.0 service (see Figure 8.7). We'll cover this process in detail once we discuss the runtime logic implementations in Section 8.3.4.

The SAP Cloud Platform SDK provides capabilities for enriching the implementations. By implementing the logic to fetch a collection of entity set resources, custom OData queries like `$count` and `$top` are available for the service, thereby enriching OData features on top of existing implementations. Nevertheless, you can also implement these features on your own, if you'd like to have an optimized implementation for your specific use case.

The SAP Cloud Platform SDK for service development enables you to build applications to deploy directly to the Cloud Foundry environment of the SAP Cloud Platform.

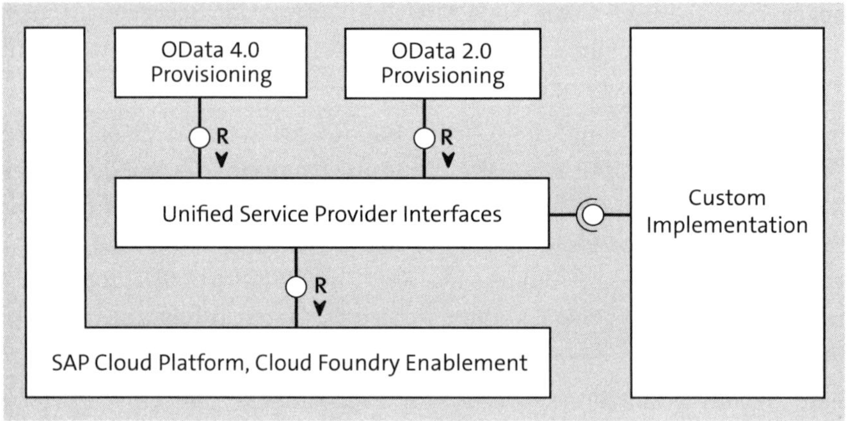

Figure 8.7 Technical Components of the SAP Cloud Platform

8.3.2 Setup and Installation

The SAP Cloud Platform SDK for service development is freely available at *https://search.maven.org/* under the SAP developer license. The prerequisites for the setup of the SAP Cloud Platform SDK are the same as the prerequisites mentioned in Chapter 4, Section 4.1.1. We recommend using its latest version as we continuously enhance its capabilities.

The project can be created using Maven archetypes. To generate the project from the Maven archetype, follow the process we described in Chapter 4, Section 4.1.2. In this chapter, we'll enhance our example application to add the functionality for OData provisioning. Therefore, the additional content shown in Figure 8.8 will be added to the web.xml file located in the *src/main/webapp/WEB_INF/* directory.

```
<servlet>
    <servlet-name>ODataServlet</servlet-name>
    <servlet-class>com.sap.cloud.sdk.service.prov.v4.rt.core.web.ODataServlet</servlet-class>
    <load-on-startup>1</load-on-startup>
</servlet>
<servlet-mapping>
    <servlet-name>ODataServlet</servlet-name>
    <url-pattern>/odata/v4/*</url-pattern>
</servlet-mapping>

<context-param>
    <param-name>package</param-name>
    <param-value>com.sap.cloud.s4hana.examples.odata.businesspartner</param-value>
</context-param>
```

Figure 8.8 Enabling OData Provisioning in the Deployment Descriptor

Package Name

Remember to specify the package name of the classes under the `context-param` tag as shown in Figure 8.8. The package name holds all the classes that will contain the implementations for the runtime logic that we'll implement. In the example, all the OData provisioning content is placed in the package `com.sap.cloud.s4hana.examples.odata.businesspartner`.

Add the dependencies shown in Figure 8.9 to the pom.xml file of the project to enable OData provisioning.


```
<dependency>
    <groupId>com.sap.cloud.servicesdk.prov</groupId>
    <artifactId>odatav4</artifactId>
</dependency>
```

Figure 8.9 Dependency for OData V4 Provisioning

8.3.3 Metadata

Every OData service must expose the metadata document at the URL *$metadata* relative to the service. A metadata document enables OData clients to discover how to operate with the OData service. The SAP Cloud Platform SDK allows you to place metadata documents as XML resource files within a project. A service with the same name as that of the metadata document is exposed when the project is deployed. More than one metadata document may be placed, and a service is exposed for each file with its respective name. The metadata XML files must be placed in the *edmx* folder in the project. Figure 8.10 shows how a service called `EPMSampleService` can be exposed.

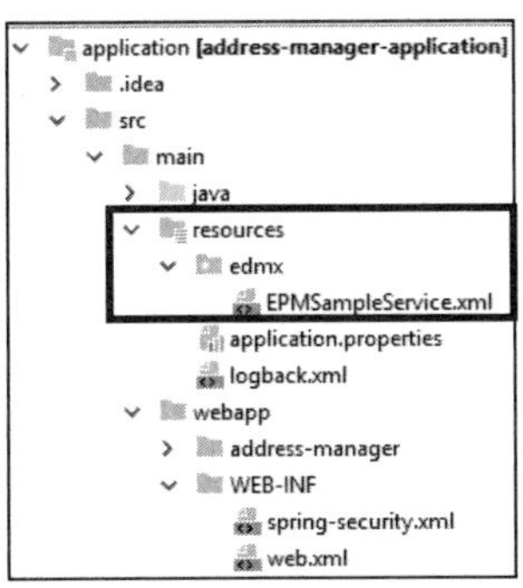

Figure 8.10 File Location for Service Metadata

For the metadata document of the OData service in this chapter, we'll use the snippet shown in Figure 8.11.

```
<?xml version="1.0" encoding="utf-8"?>
<edmx:Edmx Version="4.0" xmlns:edmx="http://docs.oasis-open.org/odata/ns/edmx">
    <edmx:DataServices>
        <Schema Namespace="EPMSample" xmlns="http://docs.oasis-open.org/odata/ns/edm">
            <EntityType Name="BusinessPartner">
                <Key>
                    <PropertyRef Name="id" />
                </Key>
                <Property Name="id" Type="Edm.String" Nullable="false" />
                <Property Name="firstName" Type="Edm.String" />
                <Property Name="lastName" Type="Edm.String" />
                <Property Name="email" Type="Edm.String" />
            </EntityType>
            <EntityContainer Name="EntityContainer">
                <EntitySet Name="BusinessPartners" EntityType="EPMSample.BusinessPartner" />
            </EntityContainer>
        </Schema>
    </edmx:DataServices>
</edmx:Edmx>
```

Figure 8.11 Metadata for Business Partner OData Service

At this point, our project could be built and deployed. However, the service runtime operations do not work yet. Nevertheless, the metadata document of the OData service would be available after deployment. We'll provide a basic implementation to make the service return data for certain operations.

8.3.4 Runtime Logic

Implementing the service runtime logic involves the following steps:

1. Define annotated methods for specific operations
2. Use the operation-specific interfaces of the parameters and return types
3. Implement the relevant business logic

We'll go through these steps for the operation that fetches all instances of entity set `BusinessPartners`, as we've defined in the previous section.

As a prerequisite, the classes where you'll implement the logic must be under the package specified when you created or configured the project.

Implementing a Query Operation

When the OData provisioning framework receives an OData call to fetch all business partners, it searches for the method you've specified to handle this. You'll indicate the method to use in this case by annotating it, as shown in Listing 8.13. The parameters to be used in the method are also indicated in this snippet.

```
@Query(serviceName="EPMSampleService", entity = "BusinessPartners")
public QueryResponse getAllPartners(QueryRequest partnerQuery) {
  /* processing logic */
}
```

Listing 8.13 Define Method to Handle Query Requests

The parameters to be used in each method depend on the respective operation. Table 8.4 outlines the parameters for each operation.

8

Operation	Return Type	Parameter	Annotation
Query	QueryResponse	QueryRequest	@Query
Read	ReadResponse	ReadRequest	@Read
Create	CreateResponse	CreateRequest	@Create
Update	UpdateResponse	UpdateRequest	@Update
Delete	DeleteResponse	DeleteRequest	@Delete
Function	OperationResponse	OperationRequest	@Function
Action	OperationResponse	OperationRequest	@Action

Table 8.4 Method Return Types and Parameters for OData Operations

We'll now continue with our implementation of the query operation and come back to this table when we implement other operations. After we define the annotated method to be used by the provisioning framework for handling the operation, you can implement the logic for getting the business data for the entity set specified in the annotation of the method (in this case, `BusinessPartners`). We won't look at any specific data sources in this example because the actual scenario will make all the difference, but let's look at how the data can then be returned as an OData response. The data could be returned as a collection of plain old Java objects (POJOs) or could be sent as a list of maps. The snippet shown in Listing 8.14 is an example where the data is fetched by the method `getPartnersFromDB` and is returned as an `ODataResponse`.

```
List<Partner> partnersList = getPartnersFromDB();
return QueryResponse ↩
    .setSuccess() ↩
```

```
    .setData(partnersList) ↩
    .response();
```

Listing 8.14 Defining the Response of an OData Query

If an error occurred while processing the logic to get business data, the framework will ensure that the OData client receives an error message. However, these messages may not be enough to resolve the issue. Thus, exceptions can be handled explicitly to provide meaningful error responses, as shown in Listing 8.15.

```
try {
  /* processing logic */
} catch (SomeException e) {
  ...
  QueryResponse.setError(ErrorReponse.getBuilder() ↩
      .setCause(e).setStatusCode(500).response());
}
```

Listing 8.15 Error Handling for Query Operation

Thus completes the steps necessary for implementing the query operation. You can look at the other methods of QueryRequest to see the different options available for handling query requests.

OData Provisioning Functionality

By implementing the query operation as we've described in this section, some operations like $top and $count would work without any additional implementation steps. The provisioning framework handles these additional calls based on your implementation. A $batch call that contains a query for business partners would also be able to return the responses.

If you want to implement $top in their optimized code, you would fetch the $top value specified by the OData client in the request with this code:

```
int topValue = partnerQuery.getTopOptionValue();
List<Partner> partnersList = getTopNPartners(topValue);
```

These code snippets enable you to work with business data represented as POJOs while the transformation to OData service operations is fulfilled by the OData provisioning framework.

Implementing a Create Operation

Let's look at a create operation looks according to the logic outlined in Listing 8.16.

```
@Create(serviceName ="EPMSampleService", ↩
    entity = "BusinessPartners")
public CreateResponse createPartner( ↩
    CreateRequest createRequest) {
  Partner partnerData = ↩
      createRequest.getDataAs(Partner.class);
  try {
    Partner createdPartner = insertPartner(partnerData);
    return CreateResponse.setSuccess() ↩
        .setData(createdPartner).response();
  } catch(SomeException e) {
    return CreateResponse.setError( ↩
        ErrorResponse.getBuilder().setMessage( ↩
            "Failed to add business partner.").setCause(e));
  }
}
```

Listing 8.16 Implementation of Create Operation

The data sent by the OData client for the create request can be obtained in the form of POJOs as shown in Listing 8.17 or also in the form of maps. The choice for a certain approach depends on the use case.

Implementing an Update Operation

When the OData client sends an update request, the URL of the request also contains the keys of the entity that the client wants to update. Accordingly, you'll need to obtain the keys for the update, which can be achieved as shown in Listing 8.17.

```
public UpdateResponse updatePartner( ↩
    UpdateRequest updateRequest) {
  String partnerID = ↩
      (String)updateRequest.getKeys().get("id");
  Partner updatedPartner = updatePartnerByID(partnerID);
}
```

Listing 8.17 Implementation of Update Operation

Implementing Functions and Actions

Unbounded OData function and action imports allow OData clients to perform operations that take parameters for execution from the URL. The response type of these operations could be any of the following:

- Empty
- One or more values of primitive type
- One or more complex type
- One or more instances of an entity set

Accordingly, the `OperationResponse` interface allows you to set this information into the response after processing the relevant parameters that can be obtained from the `OperationRequest` method parameter.

8.3.5 Building and Deploying

After the implementation is completed, the project can be built as usual with Maven. Open the command line prompt on the project root directory and execute the following command:

```
mvn clean package
```

This command builds the project and packages it for deployment. Afterwards, the application can be deployed to the Cloud Foundry environment using the same steps as described in Chapter 4 of this book.

The OData service will be available after the application is deployed in Cloud Foundry. To access the OData V4 service that we created, we'll simply append the segment */odata/v4/* to the URL obtained from the Cloud Foundry application list. Accordingly, the service should be available at:

https://hostname:port/odata/v4/EPMSampleService

8.4 Summary

In this chapter, you learned about the REST framework, how to build RESTful APIs, and how to provision an OData V4 service. With the evolution of core data services (CDS) as the central model for applications built in SAP, the SAP Cloud Platform SDK for service development will enable you to simply model business entities with CDS and get OData services for these models without the need to implement service provisioning logic. We'll further touch upon this topic in Chapter 22.

In the next chapter, we'll explore automated application testing.

Chapter 9
Automated Testing

With our example application running on the SAP Cloud Platform, we can now focus on the theory and practice of testing application code. In particular, we'll discuss how the SAP S/4HANA Cloud SDK makes testing of SAP S/4HANA side-by-side extensions easier, even without relying on an SAP S/4HANA system. Different types of tests such as unit and integration tests will be considered for our example application, covering topics like mocking, end-to-end testing, and testing complex applications. This chapter provides the basis for Chapters 10–13 where automated testing is an important aspect of quality assurance in the context of continuous delivery.

Testing should ensure that the application meets functional requirements and, to some extent, nonfunctional requirements, for example, security constraints or performance. Testing can be performed manually by developers during development all the time. Manual test scripts can be performed on a regular schedule either by team members or explicit testers. Explicit acceptance test schedules by external testers could be performed before a release. Except for manual testing, all of these other tests are more or less integration tests; the entire application will be tested, including eventual consumption of external resources such as a database or remote API calls.

For these repetitive, error-prone and tedious tasks, you could use code to test the application, automatically running tests during various stages of the application lifecycle. In this chapter, we'll focus on automated tests, offering hints and recommendations on how an application can be tested. Furthermore, we'll outline what capabilities the SAP S/4HANA Cloud SDK provides to facilitate automated tests.

Several reasons why you may want to use automated tests include the following:

- Ensuring functional correctness during builds can also be used as a measure of quality either during regularly scheduled builds or when a user submits code but before the submission is integrated into the main codebase (see also Chapter 12).

- Automated tests relieve you from performing extensive tests manually, especially for making sure that changes do not affect unrelated code. Writing tests is a one-time effort whereas manual tests need to be performed on each change.
- You'll have more confidence when refactoring code. In applications where features are added constantly, it will be necessary to refactor the code from time to time. A test suite where much of the application code is tested will make developers more confident that refactored code does not break anything.
- You'll avoid regressions when a new version of the application is developed or when bugs are fixed. If reported bugs are approached with a test-first mindset, having fixed bugs creep up again later on can be avoided.

For these reasons, we strongly encourage you create automated tests along with the implementation of application features. Tests should not be an afterthought, a topic we'll return to in Chapter 12, which outlines in detail how to implement continuous delivery. Whether you run a test-first approach or a more lax convention should be up to team culture. We recommend making tests part of the code review process and discourage delivering critical code without tests.

9.1 Concepts of Testing

In general, two fundamentally different types of automated tests exist:

- *Unit tests* test the smallest possible units of an application. Unit tests are not constrained by the design of your application but by the smallest unit allowed by your runtime that is technically testable. In the case of Java, the smallest unit is a class. Ideally, a unit test should test only one class and only that class and nothing else. Most classes have dependencies on other classes, and we'll see how to deal with dependencies throughout this chapter.
- *Integration tests* test larger chunks of your application even across module boundaries. Integration tests come in flavors of increasing dependency on resources outside the realm of the application code itself. Typically, integration tests will at least require being run within a container such as the Java Platform, Enterprise Edition (Java EE) for which the application is written to run. Even deeper coupling is required for integration tests, which need to make calls outside the application boundary such as requests to a database or requests to a remote API (for example, an OData call to an SAP S/4HANA system). Finally, end-to-end integration tests can be triggered from the user interface and route through the application, eventually hitting backend systems like a database or an SAP S/4HANA system.

For the remainder of this chapter, we'll dive more deeply into the concepts, advantages, and disadvantages of both approaches.

9.1.1 Unit Tests

As mentioned earlier, unit tests strive to test atomic parts of the application. Tests are written in a way that the call path through parts of the application affects as few units as possible. Ideally, the call path should affect only one class that is part of the application. However, most classes will have dependencies to classes either inside or outside your application. We'll discuss mitigation techniques to isolate theses dependencies later in this chapter. If we thoroughly isolate dependencies during testing by using these techniques, we'll be able to run the tests solely by firing up a Java virtual machine (JVM) together with only the language library and maybe the direct dependencies of the class under test, as well as the test framework dependencies. This selection ensures that we'll only test the functionality of the class under test, along with its controlled behavior and its dependencies.

Let's discuss advantages and disadvantages of this approach.

On one hand, the advantages are:

- **Isolated failure mode**
  If a test fails, the reason almost always lies in the class being tested or, in some cases, in the test code itself. The fact that the test can run without a container (such as a servlet container) makes isolating the cause easy.
- **Short turnaround times**
  As only few classes are loaded, tests generally run quickly. Accordingly, for a given time budget, more tests can be run in comparison to integration tests.

On the other hand, some disadvantages include:

- **No indication of contract violations**
  As the test does not call dependencies of the class under test, changes of the behavior of these dependencies will go unnoticed. This disadvantage can be partly mitigated by allowing dependencies in the tested class being called. However, the dependency can't itself depend on the used container and can't have outbound communication—directly or indirectly. For example, the class under test might use a class from the SAP S/4HANA Cloud SDK, which performs an outbound call to an SAP S/4HANA system. In this case, the dependency must be isolated, as discussed below in this section, to avoid outbound calls in unit tests.

- **Testing requirement during design**
  You'll need to design applications for testability, which can introduce additional complexity solely for the purpose of testing. The challenge of designing testable applications will be discussed in the next section.

The applications considered here will mostly have dependencies outside the application. To test your code in an isolated fashion, two main ingredients must be combined:

- **Mocking the dependencies**
  For dependencies of a class, *mock instances* can be used instead of real dependencies. These mock instances exhibit a prescribed behavior for a particular test, thus enabling a controlled environment for the testing where the class under test can be fed both valid and invalid data from the mocked instance. The expected behavior of the test class can be validated. Section 9.2 discusses how to use mocking in automated tests. With this technique, you'll need to ask how the tested class should make use of these mocked instances, which leads us to the next point.
- **Design for testability**
  You should use *dependency injection*, which results in the instances on which a class depends, wherever possible, to not be created within that class but instead be provided from outside of the class. The dependencies are either provided at creation time (constructor injection) as setters or by the container (servlet container or Java EE container). We'll shed more light on this topic in Section 9.2.

Unit tests follow a *white-box* approach, making use of knowledge about the inner workings of the tested objects. As a result, unit tests must evolve together with the code.

When setting up automated tests, you'll have to ask how you'll measure the quality of your tests. A good heuristic is to measure the parts of the application code that run during a test. Two metrics can be derived from this information: First, the (raw) *code coverage* denotes which parts of the application code is run *at all*. Second, the *path coverage* denotes which *code paths* out of the possible code paths are run. Let's consider the example in Listing 9.1.

```
public String testedMethod(int input, boolean prefixed) {
  StringBuilder output = null;
  if (prefixed) {
    output = new StringBuilder("Prefix: ");
  }
```

```
    if (input < 0) {
      return output.append("Negative").toString();
    } else {
      return (output != null ? output : "") + "Positive";
    }
}
```

Listing 9.1 Code Example for Code Coverage versus Path Coverage

Testing this with the input (-1, true) and (1, false) will achieve 100% code coverage but only 50% path coverage because two possible code paths are not included in this test run. In this case, despite 100% code coverage, a bug could slip by unnoticed because we only had 50% path coverage, which we could rectify, in this example, with the input (-1, false). However, striving for complete (or even a high proportion) of path coverage is not always economically viable due to a possibly exponential explosion of possible paths. Code coverage is a meaningful measure, and you should strive for high coverage in critical areas of the code. However, code coverage should be used with caution as an absolute metric. Setting hard targets for the code coverage to achieve can lead to optimization specifically towards that goal in your team, often with undesirable effects: Easy-to-test parts of the code could be tested when testing is not necessary (such as for pure Java Beans); critical code with lot of corner case handling might go untested because these tests are hard to write; or testing might only involve the happy path, which is of little value.

A final word on the effort required to write tests: In our experience, every line of code being tested requires an additional line of test code on average. The dominating factor is the number of decision points your application has, like conditionals or exceptions. You'll need a separate test for each decision point and that makes for a roughly equivalent codebase. As a result, effort for writing tests should be planned for. However, you'll be rewarded by higher-quality software, less time spent on bugs, and less time spent on evolving your application.

9.1.2 Integration Tests

Integration tests are set up to test parts or the entire application for a particular functionality. During integration tests, code flow doesn't only go through the application code. Dependencies in your application code will be called together with their transitive dependencies. In turn, even outbound calls such as database calls or calls to remote systems will be carried out. Because a container will likely be required, integration tests typically start or emulate the container your application is using. Various open source projects are available that facilitate running the most common containers during test runs. We'll discuss these projects in Section 9.3 in more detail.

Integration tests often follow a *black-box* approach. The input channels the application is designed for are used (such as HTTP requests). No further assumptions are made during testing regarding the inner workings of the application. Finally, the output is checked against expected output.

The advantages of integration tests are:

- Integration tests check whether the assumptions that code makes on its dependencies hold true, including assumptions about the container the code is running in. However, for this container, one caveat is that the container being tested may not be the same as the container on the deployed application as this container would be controlled by the cloud provider in many cases.

The disadvantages are:

- Often, only the happy path can be checked. In integration tests, only the regular input channels are used. Thus, you may be able to check how the application handles well-formed, malformed, or unexpected inputs. Still, error conditions that do not rely on inputs, like missing resources or failing outbound calls, are hard to trigger reliably during a test.
- The reason of failing tests can be hard to find. The error condition must be reproduced in an environment a developer has (debug) access to. With so many moving parts in an application, an error can occur on a build machine but not come up when running the same test on a developer machine. In such cases, good tracing in the application is helpful. Furthermore, the error might be triggered in one part of the application, but the root cause lies in another part of the application where the link is not obvious. The author of this chapter has hunted down more than one `NullPointerException` in some library where, due to several redirections, tracing down where in the code the `null` reference was set was hard. Even if your code is the culprit, the error may never appear in any stack trace. Missing or faulty entries in configuration files are also notorious for this problem. These bugs may be triggered spuriously especially during nightly builds and may be hard to hunt down.
- Integration tests can break due to no fault of the application code or an incompatible change of dependencies. Tests that rely on resources outside the application, such as file access, database calls, or remote HTTP calls, are especially prone to this problem. Take for instance network access, which may work well on a developer

machine but fail on your team's integration build server either spuriously or due to a different network setup. Experience shows that tests break more often due to these reasons than faults introduced through new code. Therefore, we recommend using integration tests sparsely and mainly to check assumptions about dependencies.

A middle ground between unit tests and integration tests exists which you can make successful use of. If possible, you can break away dependencies such as database access or remote HTTP calls outside the runtime. One example is mocking a database with a small in-memory database that can be fired up within the runtime during the test and that is wired to the framework used, such as a Java Persistence API (JPA) provider. Or, you could use a small, low-profile web server fired up during test runs to serve remote calls.

So far, we've discussed integration tests, which call the HTTP endpoint provided by your application provides. If the application also serves a user interface (UI), such as a rich web application, end-to-end integration tests may be useful. These tests start the UI and simulate user inputs, making sure that the application provides user feedback as expected. In Section 9.4, we'll discuss some frameworks that facilitate this kind of test. However, note that such end-to-end tests are even more brittle. Some UI frameworks like SAP UI5 offer good integration with test frameworks that can mock back-end calls and should be favored over full integration tests where possible.

9.2 Building Unit Tests

In this section, we'll describe the bits and pieces that you'll need to tie together to write meaningful tests. We'll focus on frameworks and libraries that facilitate writing code and running tests. Furthermore, we'll consider how to design your code for easier testability. Finally, we'll walk through an example that explains how all the bits fit together.

9.2.1 JUnit

In principle, writing unit tests is as simple as writing some code that instantiates the objects being tested, calls some methods on them, and checks either the return values or the desired side effects the method calls have. To facilitate running the tests and focusing only on the test code, test frameworks are used. For Java, the de facto, standard framework is JUnit (*https://junit.org*). JUnit manages the lifecycle of test classes during a test run and enables you to provide code to set up tests before they run and clean up after the tests have been run. Additionally, the framework contains helpers for different levels of abstractions to validate the expected outcomes of the tests. Due to its popularity, JUnit is integrated with almost all tooling covering integrated development environments (IDE) like Eclipse and build tools such as Maven (*http://tiny.cc/surefire*). Of particular importance is the fact that these tests can be run as part of automated builds and as such be part of the output qualification. In a Maven Java build, all classes placed under *src/test/java* in the project folder, which have names either starting or ending with `Test`, will be considered test classes and being run in the test phase.

9.2.2 Mocking

As explained in Section 9.1, it is essential for unit tests that dependencies are mocked away in a controlled fashion. In other words, dependencies must be replaced with instances whose behavior is under acute control of the test code and that provide reproducible input to the classes under test. The simplest way to achieve this is to either, for classes, develop subclasses for dependencies or, for interfaces, provide alternative implementations. This process can be quite tedious especially if you need to check the way in which the mocked instances are accessed, for example, which methods are called with which parameter values. Various open source libraries are available to facilitate this task, such as EasyMock (*http://easymock.org/*) or Mockito (*http://site.mockito.org/*). As the test helpers provided by the SAP S/4HANA Cloud SDK are based on Mockito, we'll focus on this library.

A mocking library offers mainly two things:

- An easy way to create a mock instance to replace the original one. The mock instance is of the target type and can as such serve as a replacement for the original. Additionally, this instance can be passed on to more helper methods which enable you to control the outputs of the methods called on the mock instance when called with a specific input. The helpers are commonly organized to return fluent interfaces (*http://tiny.cc/fluent-interface*) to facilitate comprehensive and easy-to-read code.
- A way to test which methods with which arguments have been called during the test run to enable you to check whether the instance has been used in the desired way. This test should only be used if really necessary, for example, in cases where reentrant calls are not desirable or input arguments to mocked instances need to be transformed in a complicated way that depends on the parameters input into

the test. If we don't capture all the relevant methods and arguments being tested, we might encounter tests breaking "for no good reason."

The design rules described we'll describe next in Section 9.2.3 stem mainly from the need to abstract away dependencies for testing.

9.2.3 Design Rules

A couple of rules you should adhere to can make code testable more easily. As a side effect, these rules generally make code easier to read and also can extend code. As mentioned earlier in Section 9.1.1, a crucial element is dependency injection. With dependency injection, any instances a class depends on are provided from outside of the class. As a result, instances can be swapped out easily. This may lead to very tedious code, with some exceptions:

- Classes from the language library can generally be used without further consideration. Only classes that, when used, lead to calls outside the runtime should be injected, like an HTTP client library or JDBC classes.
- Classes inside your application that can be tested safely together. Again, everything that leads directly or indirectly to calls leaving the runtime boundaries or that may rely directly or indirectly on a running container must be injected as well.

Dependency injection should be achieved in the order listed below as the complexity involved increases with each step:

1. Injection via the constructor, ideally into a final field, allows for a clearly defined lifecycle for the dependency (set once at the creation of the instance). Putting the dependency into a final field eases reasoning about code and enhances thread safety.
2. Injection via setter methods allows for a more flexible lifecycle of dependencies. However, injection can impede reasoning about code, giving rise to subtle bugs when dependencies are not set as expected by the downstream code or not set at all.
3. Injection via the container. Many containers and frameworks offer container-managed lifecycle of objects where the dependency is a field marked with an annotation. The concrete implementation is then defined through configuration provided to the framework. Accordingly, the default implementation can be overridden during tests. Choose this method if the lifecycle of the class containing the dependency is not under your control but instead controlled by the container or a framework

used within the container. The most basic way to achieve this is via JNDI injection. This method can be used with any container and can be mocked easily.

One should remember to handle the patterns consistently. If one class needs a dependency injected by container means, this dependency should be injected that way everywhere, which also results in more readable and maintainable code. To use dependency injection, static classes (classes having only static methods) should be avoided, at least if these classes have dependencies to outside libraries or perform outbound calls. These classes cannot be mocked easily. If a class has upstream dependencies of this kind, consider wrapping those dependencies into their own class and to refer only to this class in the application code. In this way, the upstream dependency can be mocked. For example, the Java language library contains some notorious examples of static classes such as `java.net.Authenticator`. If you need access to these, wrap them into interfaces or classes owned by the application.

Mocking frameworks must be able to replace the objects they mock, which can be facilitated by the application code. Ideally, all classes to be mocked should be abstracted as interfaces as these can be mocked in the most flexible way. If using dependency injection through a container, using interfaces is mandatory in most cases anyways. Nonfinal classes can also be mocked via inheritance and mocking frameworks make use of this. Final classes (or methods) are harder to mock although Mockito 2.x supports them as well. We recommend using interfaces wherever possible. Sometimes, to facilitate testing, you may need to introduce code within the application that is only needed for testing that class. An example case is if you provide a class that is instantiated by a container and has its dependencies injected using annotations. For testing, you might want to have a constructor using which you can inject these dependencies. In these cases, you should make the required code package-private and put the test code into the same package. Such code also should be clearly marked.

Classes that are intertwined with other classes in a circular dependency relationship make mocking particularly hard and should be avoided to improve code clarity. Even worse, circular dependencies can make for nasty bugs when involved in reentrant call stacks. Dependency injection via a constructor is an elegant way to avoid circular dependencies: If constructor dependency injection is not possible, a circular dependency is the likely culprit.

The application should be structured in a way that the tasks of some higher abstraction are made by a group of classes that belong together. These may be grouped into a separate package but don't have to be. Let's assume that your application has some emailing functionality, which likely breaks down to classes providing the formatting of the email body and classes for mailing of the body to recipients. The latter may depend on the former, and instantiating these classes is fine. But to use classes outside this realm, such as helper classes also used elsewhere, the new operator should be used cautiously, and those dependencies should be injected by one of the methods described earlier in this section.

These recommendations generally lead to code that is easier to maintain and extend. However, do not follow these recommendations blindly. For example, introducing interfaces everywhere may obscure the code, which is why we mentioned some exemptions earlier. In principle, if dependencies do not rely on a running container, or if they call resources outside of the test run, you can decide whether or not to mock them.

To summarize, the most important design recommendations for testability are the following:

- Use dependency injection mechanisms instead of the new operator.
- Do not use classes with static methods; these cannot be mocked easily.
- Use interfaces where mocking is required; final classes and application code for testing should be package-private.
- Avoid circular dependencies between classes.
- Structure the application to have sets of classes for some larger tasks that may be tested together; avoid the new operator outside this set.

9.2.4 Putting It All Together

Let's bring together what we've discussed so far in this chapter through an example that tests the GetAllBusinessPartnerCommand described in Chapter 4 (see Listing 9.2).

```
public class GetAllBusinessPartnersCommand
    extends CachingErpCommand<List<BusinessPartner>> {
  private final BusinessPartnerService service;

  public GetAllBusinessPartnersCommand(
      final BusinessPartnerService service) {
      ...
    this.service = service;
  }
}
```

Listing 9.2 Constructor Dependency Injection in GetAllBusinessPartnerCommand

Note how this class uses a constructor dependency injection to create an instance of the `BusinessPartnerService` provided by the SAP S/4HANA Cloud SDK (Listing 9.3).

```
@RunWith(MockitoJUnitRunner.Silent.class)
public class GetAllBusinessPartnersCommandTest {
  private MockUtil mockUtil;

  @Mock(answer = Answers.RETURNS_DEEP_STUBS)
  private BusinessPartnerService service;

  @Mock
  private BusinessPartner alice;

  @Before
  public void before() {
    mockUtil = new MockUtil();
    mockUtil.mockDefaults();
    mockUtil.mockDestination("ErpQueryEndpoint", ↩
        URI.create(""));
    // Invalidate cache ahead of each test
    new GetAllBusinessPartnersCommand(null) ↩
        .getCache().invalidateAll();
  }

  @Test
  public void testGetAll() throws ODataException {
    when(service
      .getAllBusinessPartner()
      .select(any(BusinessPartnerSelectable.class))
      .filter( ↩
          BusinessPartner.BUSINESS_PARTNER_CATEGORY.eq("1"))
      .orderBy(BusinessPartner.LAST_NAME, Order.ASC)
      .execute()
    ).thenReturn(Arrays.asList(alice));

    final List<BusinessPartner> result = ↩
        new GetAllBusinessPartnersCommand(service).execute();

    assertEquals(1, result.size());
```

```
    assertEquals(alice, result.get(0));
  }
}
```

Listing 9.3 Test Class for GetAllBusinessPartnersCommand

The annotation `@RunWith(MockitoJUnitRunner.Silent.class)` instructs JUnit to run the test with a test runner offered by Mockito. The annotation guarantees that tests won't fail due to strict checks on the generated stubs from Mockito.

The `MockUtil` instance is a mocking utility class provided by the SAP S/4HANA Cloud SDK. The `MockUtil` class helps create the mock instances required to simulate instances provided either by the platform or the container, such as the destination service or JNDI lookups.

9

Next, two mocked instances are provided by Mockito for the `BusinessPartnerService` and the `BusinessPartner` class. For the `BusinessPartnerService`, Mockito is instructed to create mocks for transitive method calls on that class. Using a library such as Mockito provides a great deal of boilerplate to work with to create mock instances from scratch, either by implementing the respective interface or inheriting from the class to be mocked. If you only need an instance without further requiring special behavior, that is all you need to do. We'll see in a moment how the behavior of the mock instances can be refined when required.

The code block starting with `@Before` will be called in preparation of each test run. JUnit will run each method annotated with `@Test` on a freshly created instance of the test class and ensure for each run that all methods annotated with `@Before` are run before the test method is called. Within this particular `@Before` method, a new `MockUtil` instance is created and instructed to create defaults for services that would be normally provided by the cloud platform or container. Then, the JUnit is instructed to mock the default destination that would normally contain the properties to connect against an SAP S/4HANA system. These mocks serve as replacements when `GetAllBusinessPartnersCommand` is instantiated. Finally, the (static) cache of the command is cleared. Thus, each test run starts with an invalidated cache as the cache is statically shared among all test runs.

Finally, a test method will be defined. Note that one test class may carry multiple test methods. This functionality can be used to group similar tests logically together. In most cases, a one-to-one relationship exists between test classes and classes under test. The first statement of the test method creates the `BusinessPartnerService` mock instance. The central Mockito class provides a static method `when`, which takes a function call on a mocked instance as a parameter. This parameter tells the library which function calls on the mocks to expect when the mock instance is finally used within the application code under test. Any eventual parameters passed into the methods will be recorded. The `when` method returns an object that can be created with expected return values for a method call. This return value will only be returned upon calling the method chain if all input parameters of the call chain meet those parameters given at the time the `when` method was called. Thus, the expected input to these methods can be matched to the expected output of these methods. The `when` method may be called multiple times with the same mock method, but with different parameters which are then associated to different return values in turn.

In our example, we'll simulate the method call chain as it occurs in our `GetAllBusinessPartnerCommand` class. Then, we'll create the mock to return the `BusinessPartner` mock we just wrapped in a new list. This example illustrates why unit tests are called white-box testing: Knowledge about the inner workings of a class is used for testing. Testing is thus intimately intertwined with development and must be considered during development.

The next step is actually calling code on the class being tested. In our example, a new `GetAllBusinessPartnersCommand` instance is created, which is then passed the `BusinessPartnerService` mock. Then, the `execute` method is called on that method. Finally, expectations about the class are checked. JUnit provides a few helper methods for this process, most prominently the various static `assert*` methods. These check expectations and throw appropriate exceptions that can be recognized by downstream tools such as JUnit runners in IDEs or reporting tools in build runs. In this case, the result returned by the `GetAllBusinessPartnerCommand` instance is checked to return the values provided by the created `BusinessPartnerService`.

More elaborate tests could check whether caching works as intended. As you can check the number of invocations on a mock (see Mockito documentation), you could verify that the service is only called once for multiple invocations of `execute` in the `GetAllBusinessPartnersCommand`.

9.3 Building Integration Tests

As stated earlier in Section 9.1.2, integration tests are black-box tests. The test code makes no or only few assumptions about the code being tested. Furthermore, the code is run within a suitable substitute for the container the code is to be deployed in, such as a servlet container. The test then triggers actions from outside the application and checks assumptions about the expected behavior of the application upon these actions. For middleware written using the SAP S/4HANA Cloud SDK, the application exposes one or more HTTP endpoints. Therefore, integration tests need to combine the following aspects:

- Providing the container into which the application is deployed
- Packaging and deploying the application code under test and its dependencies into the container
- Providing connectivity to systems or resources outside the application, such as an SAP S/4HANA system
- Calling an endpoint of the application and checking the returned data for expected values.
- Ideally, running tests within a well-known test framework like JUnit

Luckily, all of these requirements can be fulfilled with open source libraries and the SAP S/4HANA Cloud SDK. For the first two items, Arquillian (*http://arquillian.org*) provides suitable containers for our use case as well as the packaging machinery required. The `MockUtil` class provided by the SAP S/4HANA Cloud SDK can deal with connectivity to an SAP S/4HANA backend. The RestAssured library (*http://tiny.cc/rest-assured*) provides the functionality to call an endpoint in a container run by Arquillian and to test expectations on the responses when calling the endpoint. Arquillian enables you to run the integration tests as JUnit test. This capability makes testing accessible within any IDE providing JUnit supports and can be part of a build run capable of running JUnit tests, such as Maven.

These elements can be put together for a simple test for `BusinessPartnerServlet`, as shown in Listing 9.4.

```
@RunWith(Arquillian.class)
public class BusinessPartnerServletTest {
  public static final String BUPA_ID = "1000000";

  @Deployment
  public static WebArchive createDeployment() {
    return ShrinkWrap
      .create(WebArchive.class)
      .addClasses(BusinessPartnerServlet.class);
  }
```

```
private final MockUtil mockUtil = new MockUtil();

@ArquillianResource
private URL baseUrl;

@Before
public void before() {
  mockUtil.mockDefaults();
  mockUtil.mockErpDestination();
  RestAssured.baseURI = baseUrl.toExternalForm();
}

@Test
public void testGetAll() {
  when()
  .get("/api/business-partners")
  .then().statusCode(200)
    .contentType(ContentType.JSON)
    .body("$", hasSize(greaterThan(1)))
    .body("[0].BusinessPartner", not(isEmptyOrNullString()));
}
```

Listing 9.4 Simple Integration Test for BusinessPartnerServlet

As in the previous section, the first instruction lets JUnit run with a class provided by Arquillian, thereby ensuring that Arquillian will be able to properly start up the container. Next, a static method with the `@Deployment` annotation is required and returns an archive that contains the servlet class being tested to enable the container to start this class for an appropriate endpoint. Arquillian has various helper classes to facilitate the creation of the archive containing the required resources. Thus, we'll only need to include the servlet being tested, which already has its path annotated. A web.xml is therefore not required.

Then, we'll define the `MockUtil` instance we need for providing the SAP S/4HANA destination. As we do not have the cloud environment present when the test is run, the data contained in a destination must be injected during the test run. Next, to be able to call the URL under which the servlet can be reached, we need the URL for the container fired up by Arquillian. A property typed as `java.net.URL` annotated with `@ArquillianResource` will enable this capability.

As with the unit test, we'll need to do some programmatic setup for each test being run, again via a method annotated with `@Before`. This step initializes the `MockUtil` instance and then instructs it to provide the default destination to SAP S/4HANA. For this step, information about which system to contact is required, but various methods are available to achieve this (for more details, refer to the JavaDoc for `MockUtil.mockErpDestination()`. One possibility is to put the necessary content into *src/test/resources/systems.yml*, as shown in Listing 9.5.

```
---
erp:
  default: "ERP_SYSTEM"
  systems:
    - alias: "ERP_SYSTEM"
      uri: "https://<mys4hanasystem>"
      proxy: "http://<myproxyhost>"
```


Listing 9.5 Contents of systems.yml

You'll also need to provide credentials for connecting to the backend system. Either put the credentials into a credentials.json file into the same folder as systems.yml or pass the information as system property `test.credentials` formatted as `json` (without line breaks) to the process (Listing 9.6).

```
{"credentials":
  [{"alias":"ERP_SYSTEM",
    "username":"<...>",
    "password":"<...>"}]}
```

Listing 9.6 Contents of credentials.json or System Property test.credentials

The latter method is recommended because it prevents accidentally committing credentials into a code repository. The `before` method finally sets the base URL for the RestAssured library to the value previously set by Arquillian, thus enabling RestAssured to call relative URLs.

Finally, we have the test method `testGetAll`. RestAssured enables calling an endpoint and checking assumptions on the returned data in one fell swoop. The `when` method enables various types of HTTP requests, in this case, an HTTP `GET` request. The returned object allows you to check the response, again as fluent interface. First, the proper HTTP status code (200) is ensured. Then, the correct content type is checked. Finally, the body is tested against two assertions. The first selects the entire `json` object and ensures that the result is an array containing at least two members. The second selects the first array element and ensures that the property `BusinessPartner` is not empty. Note that the test is run against real SAP S/4HANA systems. For robust tests, the assertions should not be too specific, as the system is not under control of the test environment. As an example, you shouldn't expect a specific business partner instance, as business data may change in the remote systems. In case the targeted backend contains a large amount of data, requests also should also only fetch a few entries.

Integration tests will soon require a considerable amount of code for setting up and tearing down the tests. This code is likely reusable, and we recommend using mechanisms such as setting up JUnit rules (*https://github.com/junit-team/junit4/wiki/Rules*) to enjoy flexible composability.

9.4 Testing Complex Applications

Your application may have a user interface on top, most likely designed as a browser-based, Ajax-driven application. This interface can be tested in an end-to-end test where parts of the user interface are executed automatically. Technically, you'll use a suitable framework to trigger user behavior on a browser or browser stub. The test then "clicks" through the user interface and tests expected behavior, that is, the expected changes in the user interface. This framework will trigger most parts of the entire application starting from the frontend code all the way down to eventual backend services like an SAP S/4HANA system. As a result, end-to-end tests ensure that all parts of your application work together as intended.

As you can imagine, end-to-end testing involves a lot of moving parts that need to work flawlessly together at test time. You could argue that this requirement holds true for productive environments as well, with some caveats: Often, tests cannot be run against productive systems for data privacy reasons. Therefore, separate systems are required for tests. Development systems are unsuitable because they may not run a well-defined version of the software. Thus, you're left using quality systems, if available, but want to avoid setting up systems solely dedicated to automated end-to-end tests. You may encounter some of the following issues:

- Content in backend systems may change in an unexpected manner, making robust tests difficult to write.
- Test execution time tends to be long as outbound calls are being made. Depending on the size of your test suite, times may extend minutes. This constraint can

become prohibitive when executing end-to-end tests as part of the submit process into the main codebase.

- Connectivity can be an issue. Often, tests are part of a build pipeline, and backend systems may not be reachable from the machine where the tests are running. Also, locked test users are a notorious problem.
- Frontend tests can be plagued by subtle timing problems, especially for Ajax-driven applications. This problem can be exacerbated by the fact that the response times of systems can vary greatly, making tests fail spuriously.
- Even if the test catches a bug, the bug may be hard to hunt down. The cause of a failing test may even lie in code not directly touched by the specific call, for example, due to improper initialization code during application startup.

Although end-to-end tests have their merits, you should follow a pyramid approach for testing. As the base, the majority of test code should be tested in unit tests. These tests offer the most controlled test environment and can be easily fired up everywhere. Mocking is a powerful tool you should make extensive use of. On the next level are integration tests. These should be divided up into tests to check external assumptions, such as the semantics of remote systems being called, and tests that fire up the container used but mock external calls. This division isolates assumptions about the backend service from assumptions about application dependencies and makes finding bugs easier when tests fair. Finally, some strategic end-to-end tests can ensure that all the parts run smoothly together.

The implementation of UI-driven, end-to-end testing is beyond the scope of this book. However, multiple tools are available, like Selenium (*www.seleniumhq.org*) or nightwatch-cucumber (*http://tiny.cc/nightwatch-cucumber*). Interested readers can find a guide on writing tests compatible with the continuous delivery pipeline described in Chapter 10 and Chapter 11 at *http://tiny.cc/automated-testing*.

9.5 Summary

In this chapter we outlined how to test an application built with the SAP S/4HANA Cloud SDK. We started by introducing you to the fundamental principles of testing. We covered topics like unit tests and integration tests and discussed how code should be designed to ensure testability. Furthermore, we provided examples for testing our example application of this book.

Now that we've covered the basics of testing, in the following chapters, you'll learn about delivering and operating applications and how automated tests ensure quality during continuous delivery.

PART III

Delivering and Operating Side-by-Side Extensions

Chapter 10
DevOps and Continuous Delivery

This chapter introduces the concepts behind DevOps and two of its practices: continuous delivery and monitoring. First, we'll present companies that owe their success to mastering DevOps. Second, we'll present the theory behind DevOps and then outline how continuous delivery and monitoring practices can help you create high-quality software delivered in a quick and reliable manner. To illustrate the concepts through practical examples, the SAP S/4HANA Cloud SDK pipeline and a working model of a DevOps team will be presented. Interested readers will find a wide variety of references to related work in this field.

The ultimate goal of software development is to create value for end users. In this chapter, we'll introduce principles and practices of DevOps and continuous delivery. Together, these principles enable organizations to quickly deliver high-quality software that strives to maximize value for consumers. By increasing IT performance, DevOps in the end also contributes to improved business outcomes, as measured by productivity, profitability, and market share (N. Forsgren et al., *State of DevOps Report*). From a financial perspective, DevOps shortens the cycle time between idea and usable software because "Software delivers no revenue until it is in the hand of its end users" (J. Humble and D. Farley, *Continuous Delivery*).

10.1 The Importance of DevOps

Many successful companies, such as Netflix, Amazon, and Google, owe their success to the application of DevOps principles. Their stories show how DevOps can help establish and maintain high innovation speed, quick feedback loops within the value chain, and an organizational culture that encourages experimentation and fast learning. In fact, many companies we'll discuss have already managed to completely transform their IT foundations multiple times at critical points. Without these transformations, most of these players would probably be out of business and replaced by a competitor.

A study, based on 3,200 participants, showed that companies ranked as IT high performers strongly differ from IT low performers when looking at the frequency of software change deployments. Organizations from the group of high performers manage to deploy several thousand software changes daily in a reliable manner. On average, high performers deploy their code 46 times more often, have 440 times quicker lead times to production, 96 times quicker mean time to recovery from downtimes, and a 5 times lower change failure rate than low performers. Low performers are characterized by code deployments in monthly cycles or sometimes even less often (N. Forsgren et al., *State of DevOps Report*).

10.2 Introducing the Principles of DevOps

In this chapter, we'll introduce the theory behind DevOps, the convergence of various earlier philosophies and management movements, such as the lean principles, the Agile Manifesto, the Agile Infrastructure and Velocity movement, the Continuous Delivery movement, and Toyota Kata (G. Kim et al., *DevOps Handbook*).

On a high level, the authors define DevOps through three core principles:

- The principle of flow, which focuses on the quick delivery of software from development to customers
- The principle of feedback, which helps quickly sense problems in the value chain, leading to the continuous improvement of process and product quality
- The principle of continuous learning and experimentation, which establishes a culture that motivates experimentation, risk-taking, and learning from failures

10.2.1 The Principle of Flow

The concept of DevOps aims for a quick and reliable flow of work from ideas to end-user consumption. This section discusses exemplary practices so teams can optimize their work towards this goal.

Many organizations separate their teams by functions, such as development, testing, deployment, or operations, which leads to a matrix organization style. In such environments, many hand-offs take place before a feature is delivered to the customer. Information and context is lost on the way, delays are introduced if a team in the value chain is overloaded, and teams can easily start optimizing against local goals. While this style is great from the perspective of maximizing resource utilization, this structure can be an impediment to responsive, agile organizations that strive to optimize their global goal of quick time-to-value.

To make the global value creation process explicit, and the work in it measurable, DevOps teams typically use visual work boards, for example, a Kanban board. Based on the transparency regarding current work flowing through the value chain, stations with very high or low loads can be identified and optimized. For high loads, for example, applying reasonable limits for parallel work in progress might make sense to reduce the negative impact on efficiency caused by frequent work context switches.

By distributing the value creation process on numerous specialized functional units, the amount of work in process at a given point of time is high. This high volume inevitably leads to long cycle times from ideation to the delivery of a feature, with all associated negative effects, such as late error discovery and high repair costs. Instead, organizations should establish a *single piece flow* strategy, where a piece of work is propagated through the whole value creation chain by teams with end-to-end responsibility before new work is started. Figure 10.1 compares the timing difference between ideating (I), building (B), testing (T), and delivering (D) a software feature through large batches against a single piece flow. In a batch workflow, the first feature is finished rather late in the process, while with single piece flow, the deployment step is reached more quickly.

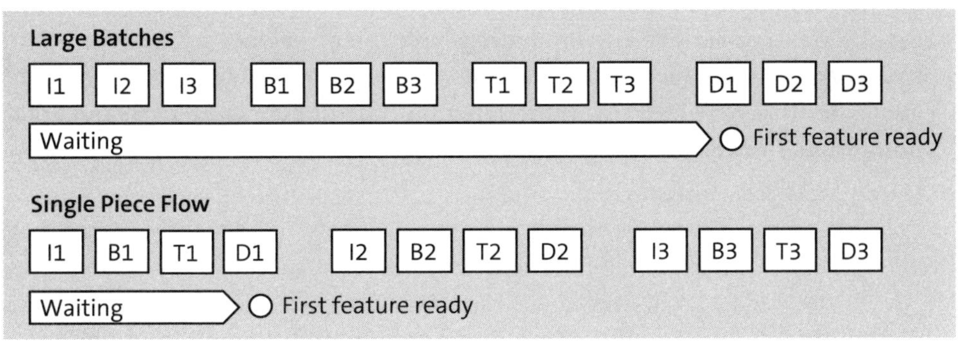

Figure 10.1 Time to Feature Readiness with Large Batch Methodology versus Single Piece Flow (Based on Stefan Luyten, 2014)

Once the flow of work is orchestrated in a single piece manner and without unnecessary hand-offs, the DevOps teams can focus on identifying and optimizing bottlenecks in the software value chain. In the following list, we highlight some frequent bottlenecks and ways to address them. Some of these problems have been already discussed in Chapter 4, Chapter 8, and Chapter 9 of this book:

- **Creation and maintenance of software environments**
  Manually managed software environments are hard to maintain and scale. Due to manual intervention, systems often diverge in their configuration, making it hard to guarantee the application behaves the same on all nodes. Modern cloud platform offerings provide a solution with on-demand, available, predefined execution environments. Typically, APIs are offered for automatable configuration management, thus making environments easy to set up and maintain.
- **Testing**
  Manual testing of software can be error-prone and highly repetitive. In consequence, it isn't feasible to achieve a high quality and at the same time a quick flow of work where even small changes are confidently and frequently deployed to production. Comprehensive and fully automated test suites offer a mechanism for efficient testing and quick flow of work towards production. Typical automated test suites comprise unit tests, integration tests, system tests, and acceptance tests.
- **Code deployment**
  Manual deployments are highly repetitive, time consuming, and not repeatable by definition. When these deployments fail, you may never know whether the failure was caused by an error in the deployed application or by the human conducting the deployment. Especially when deployments are complex, human execution may become error-prone. By automating deployment, engineers can avoid repetitive work and save the time they would otherwise spend following deployment guidelines that may lead them through a number of manual steps, hoping that nothing goes wrong.
- **Overly tight architectures**
  The architecture of a software product can make it hard to frequently update individual parts of it. Such issues may occur on both technical and organizational levels. On a technical level, overgrown, monolithic applications may require major deployments for even small changes. On an organizational level, responsibility for even one small application can be distributed among multiple teams, which can quickly lead to slow and bureaucratic change processes. Therefore, the technical and the organizational setup in which software is developed should be designed in such a way that allows the seamless updating of individual parts.

The last aspect of optimizing flow in DevOps is the avoidance of waste. Waste is defined as every type of work that could also omitted without negatively affecting the result. A popular type of waste is the implementation of unneeded features (M. Fowler, *Yagni*). In fact, a study at Microsoft found out that only one-third of new features resulted in their intended outcomes (R. Kohavi et al., *Online Experimentation at Microsoft*). Further types of waste comprise the time lost while waiting for others, between switching tasks, hand-off overheads, avoidable defects, and repetitive manual work.

10.2.2 The Principle of Feedback

The concept of DevOps aims for short and efficient feedback cycles in the whole value creation process of building software. This section discusses exemplary practices for DevOps teams to optimize their work model towards this goal.

While the principles of flow help to quickly move work from idea to production, the principles of feedback concentrate on the establishment of quick and efficient ways to backpropagate learning into earlier stages of the value creation process. In this way, the value creation process becomes increasingly safer and more resilient.

Complex software systems are hard to understand. Even when an individual component is well understood, changing it might impact the overall system in an unexpected manner. Therefore, failure in complex software systems is inevitable. DevOps teams do everything to establish a safe system of work where errors are discovered early before they can cause any serious damage. For this, you must constantly assert the working conditions of the system. This assertion can occur on the code level, for example, in the form of enforced contracts, or during operations in form of checks that monitor the relevant telemetry of the application, such as response times and resource consumption. By sharing an end-to-end responsibility for the application, a DevOps team can start equipping their products with qualities that make it easy to operate and troubleshoot.

Of course, quick feedback propagation is also important on the level between the customer and the development team. Even a perfectly implemented feature can fail to satisfy the actual needs of the end customer.

Short feedback cycles prevent problems from propagating through the value stream, where they can become exponentially more expensive to fix the further they propagate. With quick feedback, the DevOps team can become aware of a problem at a point when they still have full contextual awareness, allowing them to focus their work without major context switches. In the end, this focus helps to keep error-related costs low.

10.2.3 The Principle of Continuous Learning and Experimentation

This section discusses organizational practices that support the DevOps principle of establishing a healthy culture of continuous learning and experimentation within the organization.

IT is a rapidly evolving and transforming business. The best way of doing something today might soon be outdated and require new practices tomorrow. Therefore, your organization must establish a culture that enables individuals to challenge the status quo by trying new things and learning from mistakes. In this way, your organization can establish a continuously upward spiral of learning and adapting to new conditions.

Organizations should not only conduct daily work but also reserve time for experiments that allow optimizations of daily work. Failures, whether from daily work or in experiments, should undergo blame-free post-mortems. By identifying the root causes of failures and avoiding workarounds, the team ensures that *technical debt* does not accumulate. Technical debt is "a concept in programming that reflects the extra development work that arises when code that is easy to implement in the short run is used instead of applying the best overall solution" (*http://tiny.cc/technical-debt*). Like financial debt, technical debt is not always a bad thing. However, as technical debt accumulates, teams will find it increasingly harder to evolve and maintain a piece of software. In the long term, limiting technical debt helps reduce waste and unplanned work. Furthermore, the team culture and the codebase can stay in a healthy state, which allows to conduct agile experiments and decisions about the future instead of being continuously burdened by bad decisions from the past.

To effectively leverage the value of new lessons learned, DevOps teams aim to elevate local knowledge gains on a global level where value can be unfolded to a broader audience. This propagation of knowledge can occur via knowledge sharing sessions, wiki pages, or codified practices, such as libraries or new automated code checks.

Finally, the right leadership style is a crucial prerequisite for DevOps success. Organizations need to establish a healthy and generative organization culture, defined by openness for new ideas, active sharing of information, shared responsibilities, and constructive learning from failures. Instead of identifying granular goals and trying to make too many decisions, leaders should identify high-level goals. Together with their team, an iterative process can break high-level goals down to more concrete short-term goals. Towards these goals, leaders observe and coach their teams by asking the right questions, such as:

- What was your last step, and what happened?
- What did you learn?
- What is your next target condition?

In the long term, this process facilitates personal growth and maximizes the learning effects for each team member (Kim et al., *The DevOps Handbook*).

10.3 Introducing Continuous Delivery

The DevOps movement defines principles and goals with a broad range of organizational, cultural, and technical implications. One of these implications is typically the adoption of continuous delivery practices, which had been evolving even before the DevOps movement.

In this book, we define continuous delivery as an approach in which teams produce, test, deliver, and deploy software in short cycles and in a reliable, fully automated manner. The standard tool for realizing continuous delivery is the implementation of a continuous delivery pipeline, which starts with code commits and ends with deployments into productive systems.

10.3.1 Introducing Continuous Delivery Pipelines

No "one size fits all" definition or technology for realizing continuous delivery pipelines can be discussed because their realization depends on technical and organizational conditions. Concrete implementations typically vary in the structure and goals of their stages, the degree of automation, parallelization, and the technology used for implementing the pipeline itself. In the following section, we'll mainly focus on the continuous delivery of three-tier web applications, the most common architecture style of current enterprise applications.

For a better understanding of the design and value of continuous delivery pipelines, we'll use the *SAP S/4HANA Cloud SDK pipeline* as an example. This pipeline is the product of codifying SAP's own best practices as part of building cloud-native SAP S/4HANA extension applications on the SAP Cloud Platform. The SAP S/4HANA Cloud SDK pipeline helps extension developers quickly get started with continuous delivery in their projects and is actively maintained by SAP as an open source project on GitHub. Given the high-level structure shown in Figure 10.2, let's introduce the capabilities and qualities of the SAP S/4HANA Cloud SDK pipeline.

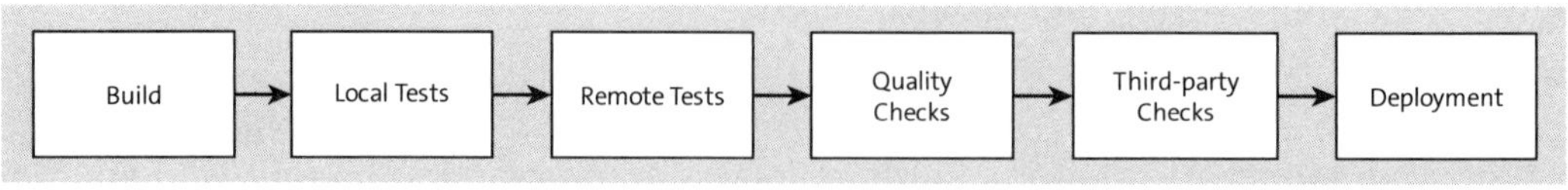

Figure 10.2 SAP S/4HANA Cloud SDK Pipeline Structure

The SAP S/4HANA Cloud SDK pipeline is triggered by any change of source files in the version control system (VCS) of the application. The pipeline is fully automated and starts with a *Build* stage that compiles and packages the application code with help of the relevant build tools. At this point, all dependencies are resolved, downloaded, and included into the build result. Once the resulting application artifact is packaged, this artifact is used throughout the whole remaining build process as is. Building application artifacts only once is a recommended continuous delivery practice. Compared to rebuilding an artifact multiple times, you'll save valuable time and ensure that all tests and checks are executed with exactly the same artifact (Y. Yehuda, *7 Best Practices for Continuous Delivery Success*).

After the application is packaged, the *Local Tests* stage is executed, which comprises frontend and backend unit tests as well as isolated backend integration tests that don't require a production-like environment, for example, by using a lightweight Java container and, if needed, a lightweight database (see Chapter 9). In addition, this stage also executes a set of static code checks that identify likely bad coding practices, such as omitting the original exception when logging an error. Finally, the *Node Security Platform* (NSP) is used to identify potentially vulnerable dependencies in the JavaScript parts of the application.

If all local tests have completed successfully, the application enters the *Remote Tests* stage. In this stage, the application is deployed into one or multiple production-like environments within SAP Cloud Platform. At this point, the application undergoes automated end-to-end tests that typically check that the intended usage scenarios work properly on the whole stack, typically also including relevant connected downstream services. In addition, this stage might be used to execute performance test scenarios.

SAP S/4HANA Cloud SDK-based projects automatically collect quality-related data during testing. Furthermore, the static code checks in the Local Tests stage also create result files of potential findings. In the *Quality Checks* stage, all quality-related logs are analyzed and checked for violations against SAP guidelines. We'll go into a detailed discussion of quality checks in the SAP S/4HANA Cloud SDK pipeline in Chapter 12.

The *Third-party Checks* stage subsumes further checks of optional external tools that try to identify security issues within the application. At the time of this writing, the pipeline supports *Checkmarx*, a tool for vulnerability scanning in application code (*https://www.checkmarx.com/*), and *WhiteSource*, a tool for dependency and legal compliance scanning in dependencies (*https://www.whitesourcesoftware.com/*).

Finally, if a change occurred on the productive branch, and if all previous stages went well, the *Deployment* stage of the pipeline deploys the validated artifact on a set of targets within SAP Cloud Platform. This process uses the blue-green deployment technique (Martin Fowler, *BlueGreenDeployment*), which ensures a seamless, zero-downtime switch from the old to the new version. On SAP Cloud Platform Cloud Foundry, this process additionally runs smoke tests on the new deployment before switching (Yehuda), thus adding a last layer of defense for detecting the unlikely errors not discovered before deploying to the actual production environment. If auditability is needed, the application artifact can further be deployed to a *nexus* artifact repository.

10.3.2 Enabling DevOps Principles via Continuous Delivery

The previous section used the SAP S/4HANA Cloud SDK pipeline as an example to introduce the function of continuous delivery pipelines. In this section, we'll discuss how continuous delivery pipelines contribute to the realization of DevOps principles.

Continuous delivery pipelines help organizations to massively streamline their flow of work by automating every step, from feature check-in to production deployment. For this part of the value chain, the single piece flow work style is implicitly realized by the pipeline, which also ensures that even small changes are handled and validated in exactly the same manner. For testing, the pipeline uses automatically deployed versions of the application, which run in production-like environments on SAP Cloud Platform. All of these features are achieved without introducing hand-offs or repetitive, error-prone tasks for human users. Thanks to the broad availability of cheap and scalable cloud computing resources, the continuous delivery infrastructure can easily be scaled to fit the volume of changes that need to be processed. Scaling and parallelization of the pipeline brings wait times down to a minimum. With a continuous delivery pipeline and automated testing, even big systems can be built and continuously improved in a reliable and fast-moving manner.

By automating builds and deployments, DevOps teams free up otherwise wasted time and capacity. With this time, they can gain the freedom to conduct experiments and to learn. Continuous delivery also supports continuous improvement in organizations, for example, by giving room for adapting new technologies or for refactoring parts of the product in a reliable way.

Moreover, the pipeline is a powerful tool for implementing and shortening feedback cycles. When a developer commits a change that causes an error in the overall system, he'll be informed quickly that something went wrong while building and testing the change. Furthermore, the team can take notice of the failed build via a continuous delivery dashboard. Usually, DevOps teams leverage a code review system that could be enhanced with the build results from the pipeline or even block the merging of the changes if the code does not meet quality expectations. Thus, a code reviewer can also take the build results into account. Accordingly, the developer as well as the whole team can quickly react while still having full contextual awareness and before the error propagates further through the value chain.

For decoupling the deployment from the release of a feature, developers can leverage the concept of *feature toggles*, which allow you to hide features from end users until explicitly activated. By activating features for selected user groups, these groups can be used for early testing in a production environment (see Chapter 11).

Sophisticated applications like SAP RealSpend typically have test suites that comprise thousands of tests. Thanks to scaling and parallel test execution, even in such cases, low cycle times (significantly below an hour) can be achieved. Because of the fail-early nature of the pipeline, you can typically get their feedback within a few minutes. Of course, you're still encouraged to execute local tests during development. However, the pipeline ensures that all changes are always tested with the full test suite.

With its quality checks, the pipeline, furthermore, ensures common quality standards. Static code checks help to identify flaws, such as information loss during error handling, which can make it hard to conduct proper root cause analysis of failures. Dynamic code checks help identify nonresilient invocations of downstream services, which can cause cascading errors that negatively impact multiple tenants of an application. Finally, enforcing sufficient code coverage in tests ensures that all parts of the system are properly tested. The checks in the pipeline ensure the compliance of functional and nonfunctional application requirements. Altogether, the pipeline enjoys the reliability needed for making automated deployment decisions. We'll introduce these quality requirements in more detail in Chapter 12.

Insights gained from failures can quickly be incorporated into new tests and checks can be executed as part of the pipeline. By this codification, local knowledge gained by investigating errors can be turned into global knowledge automatically be applied in all future runs of the pipeline. This feature helps avoid similar failures in the future and supports the DevOps goal of adding more safety to the system of work over time.

10.4 How to Monitor Applications

The use of a continuous delivery pipeline helps ensure a certain amount of compliance to functional and nonfunctional requirements during deployment. However, the pipeline cannot guarantee that the application and the environment in which it runs will forever stay in a well-functioning state.

Sudden changes in the load, unexpected malfunctions of downstream services, deeply hidden bugs, or even problems on the cloud platform level can emerge at any point in time and lead to bad end-user experiences.

Thus, convenient mechanisms must exist to detect malfunctioning system states early. Furthermore, these mechanisms need to support diagnosing and fixing these situations in a structured way. Preferably, these mechanisms should even be able to automatically send out alerts when the operational state diverges from the norm.

Typically, two mechanisms are available to establish operational transparency across the whole application stack:

- Logging of textual events that describe relevant events in the context of the application, such as an incoming HTTP request or users changing their stored settings.
- Collecting numeric metrics in time series that provide insights to specific countable information, such as CPU consumption or the number of failed login attempts.

Together, logging and metrics are subsumed as the gathering of *telemetry* data.

10.4.1 The Importance of Logging

The key components of log statements comprise their timestamp; their hierarchical source information (for example, the fully qualified class name); their level of severity; and the actual log message. Because logs can easily grow to many gigabytes in size, they are only stored for a predefined period, typically several weeks. In terms of severity level, we'll typically distinguish between the following types of messages:

- DEBUG
  Detailed technical information about interesting areas within the application code, such as an outgoing HTTP request with all its parameters. Some logging frameworks also offer the TRACE log level, which can be used for intensive application state logging at critical parts of the application. For performance reasons, DEBUG and TRACE log messages will typically not be recorded during the normal operation of the application. However, for troubleshooting, these logs will likely be turned on temporarily in relevant parts of the application.
- INFO
  General information that can provide a glimpse into how the application has been used over time. A configuration change event by a user will typically belong to this category, also information regarding business transactions.
- WARN
  An event in the application that represents a potentially dangerous situation, for example, a long-running HTTP request or malicious user input. In context of a metric-based alert, these messages will likely contribute valuable contextual information.
- ERROR
  Indicates an obvious error situation that should never occur, for example, a database connection issue or exception caused by a bug in the application code itself.
- FATAL
  A serious, unrecoverable error has occurred, and the application, or at least parts of it, cannot continue operations, for example, failed master data synchronization during application startup.

While the right number and severity of log statements can sometimes be hard to decide, generally, all security-related events should be logged. During troubleshooting situations, engineers will typically understand what data would have improved operational awareness. Thanks to continuous delivery, these engineers may quickly close any gaps with a new version of the application. In some cases, creating an audit log for access and changes to sensitive data, such as personal information or critical application settings, might be required.

In today's technological world, logging is well supported by software libraries and services on cloud platforms. SAP Cloud Platform, for example, provides specialized services for centralized log collection and analysis. A high-reliability audit logger is also offered to ensure full traceability of audit-relevant events and can easily be consumed via the APIs of the SAP S/4HANA Cloud SDK.

For further information on logging and error handling, refer to the OWASP Wiki (*Error Handling, Auditing and Logging*).

10.4.2 The Importance of Metrics

While logs can provide a detailed understanding of the operational state and its changes over time, they are not well suited for measuring and classifying the health of an application. A single failing request might, for example, not qualify as erroneous operational state. However, ten failing requests within a given timeframe may indicate an error state.

Netflix reported in 2014 that they collected and analyzed up to 1.2 billion time series at a given point in time with automated alerting when one of the metrics starts to show a suspicious pattern (B. Harrington and R. Rapoport, *Introducing Atlas*).

Application developers should be able to easily create and populate metrics with data. In this way, applications can build up a fine-mesh net of measurements to help identify problems that are just incubating, for example, a memory leak that may slowly lead to increasing memory consumption before an out-of-memory error finally forces the application into a nonfunctioning state.

Furthermore, metrics provide an objective, unambiguous reality for everyone in the organization. While problems in large organizations often lead to political tension, finger-pointing, and cover-ups, metrics allow the efficient formation and assessment of scientific hypotheses towards resolving issues. Finally, these metrics also help to leverage lessons on a global level.

Typical, basic application metrics comprise service response times, error rates, request rates, application availability, and the consumption of system resources, such as CPU, RAM, and disk, of both the application and its downstream services. Furthermore, measuring how long users need to complete a certain task and how often they fail on their way will often make sense.

In logging, blank spots should be filled in with metrics when needed, which requires proper support on the software side. Thanks to continuous delivery, new metrics can also quickly be brought into production.

10.4.3 Telemetry Consolidation

Log statements and metrics are worthless when scattered across many places, hard to extract, or only available to a special group of engineers. Accordingly, establishing a centralized infrastructure for collecting and processing this information is important. However, no "one size fits all" tool should be sought. Instead, using multiple, best-of-breed solutions that work well together will likely yield the best results in practice (M. Julian, *Practical Monitoring*). In logging, for example, we'll typically have different requirements in an audit logger than in a normal application event logger. The audit logger must be absolutely reliable, which requires a blocking implementation that writes to a persistent medium, of course, with trade-offs on performance. While we are willing to accept the associated costs of rare audit logs, the more frequently used event logs need to take performance into consideration. For event logs, we'll likely accept the risk of data loss in rare cases and go for a nonblocking, asynchronous logging mechanism.

Once data is centrally collected, we can easily set up services, such as visual metrics dashboards, automated anomaly detection, and proactive alerting. Furthermore, through a single central log file, we can simplify the tracing of activities in highly distributed and microservice-based systems.

To detect errors even earlier, telemetry gaps should be closed continuously. In many cases, software engineers will, for example, tend to concentrate on a telemetry metric relevant during development time. By also involving telemetry into operations activities, a feedback loop is established. These engineers will get a feeling for telemetry that also simplifies their work and start automatically writing more operations-friendly code in the future.

Overall, we strive for telemetry in the following categories:

- **Business level**
  Telemetry associated to the business features of the application, such as the number of active users or financial figures.
- **Application level**
  Technical telemetry of the application, such as service response times, database operation durations, or unexpected exceptions.

- **Infrastructure level**
  For platform-as-a-service (PaaS) offerings, these metrics will typically be provided by the platform and comprise statistics about basic resources, such as CPU, RAM, disk, or network.
- **Client software level**
  All user interactions that happen in the client software. Therefore, collecting information, such as errors, user interaction events, and metrics that measure user performance for specific tasks, makes sense.
- **Continuous delivery pipeline level**
  Telemetry in the context of the continuous delivery process and its environment comprises pipeline states, execution durations, or the health state of delivery-related systems. Finally, explicitly tracking the deployment of application updates also makes sense to provide valuable context for interpreting other telemetry.

As an additional feedback channel, visual dashboards can also broadcast onto public screens at offices. These displays could create transparency within the team of an application and transparency for people passing by. While the display is useful for discovering abnormal behavior in production systems, team members could also receive positive feedback if everything works flawlessly.

Often, applications emit development-related log information only. To facilitate the inclusion of operations-related logging, letting developers operate the application as well can make sense. Developers won't operate the application twenty-four hours a day, but that they should have access to the production environment like every operations engineer. Furthermore, developers are responsible, during normal working hours, for analyzing or fixing problems in production in the same way they are today responsible for writing their own automated tests instead of letting the testing be done by a dedicated quality assurance person.

So far, in this chapter, we introduced the theory and practice of DevOps and continuous delivery. Next, we'll introduce a team and its working model as a concrete example of how DevOps and continuous delivery can be brought to life in practice.

10.5 Case Study: Working Model of a DevOps Team

Inspired by the SAP RealSpend team, this section introduces the working model of an exemplary DevOps engineering team working on a continuously delivered, cloud-native application written in Java (backend) and JavaScript (frontend).

Our DevOps team is part of a large enterprise software company and builds an application to provides new, innovative features on top of existing capabilities. These capabilities are provided by well-established solutions with traditional update cycles spanning several months. The innovative cloud application runs on SAP Cloud Platform and integrates with the company's traditional systems in a loosely coupled, service-oriented manner via RESTful web services. In this way, the team can deliver changes quickly without depending on the slower release cycles of its downstream services.

Together with other teams, the DevOps team works with GitHub Enterprise, a central, company-wide source code repository. This decision establishes a high level of transparency in the whole organization because every developer can seamlessly inspect all implementation details of a software component of interest. By checking for an author, experts can easily be found and contacted. The contribution of changes or bugfixes is also simplified. Furthermore, the central repository can be used to understand how other teams solve specific problems or even to get a global understanding of dependencies and the reuse of software artifacts for the whole organization.

To facilitate efficient communication and information spread, the team uses Slack chat rooms and chat bots. In comparison to private emails or coffee break chats, chat rooms give every team member the chance to know what is going on or to reach out to the whole team in a nondistracting manner. Automated chat bots can establish teamwide contextual awareness and provide a history of technical events such as deployments or build failures.

To make value creation visible, the team identified and documented its value creation process. The process was structured into three main categories: product management, software development, and delivery, comprising twenty-one stages overall. The process started from new customer requirements or ideas and ended with the productive deployment of a change. Even though not all work was explicitly tracked end to end all the time, the team selectively measured the flow of work to identify and improve bottlenecks. Daily development work was tracked in Jira.

The development of new features happened in feature branches of the code repository. At all times, the team tried to minimize branch lifetimes to a minimum by regularly merging back into the main branch. This process maintained high team productivity by reducing the level of rework that would result from merging long-living, strongly diverging feature branches. To allow for merging to the main codeline often, new code was hidden behind feature toggles to separate deployment and release (see Chapter 11).

Every engineer who writes new code was also responsible for writing suitable corresponding automated tests, which reduced the rate of change failures for current and future changes.

Once a change was ready to be merged into the mainline, the engineer would create a *GitHub pull request* and nominates at least one colleague to conduct a review of the changes. Instead of following rigid, bureaucratic processes, the change author decides himself who the right expert for this task is. Typically, the list of reviewers comprises colleagues who worked on the same code earlier or those who act in a more senior or architecture-related role.

Experts who conduct a manual review discuss potential findings with the author. This fosters learning from each other and establishes an organic channel for communicating changes within the code base. In addition, this mechanism allows new colleagues to be onboard easily to the culture and art of writing the code in the project, which helps tremendously with getting new colleagues up to speed. If an engineer feels that an uninvolved colleague should be aware of a particular change or its related discussion, he can invite that colleague at any point in time to the process.

In addition to the manual review process, a new pull request, or any changes to an existing pull request, automatically triggers a run in an isolated instance of the S/4HANA Cloud SDK pipeline, which automatically validates the new version. Finally, the results of the pipeline execution are automatically published via Slack and as part of the Pull Request overview in GitHub Enterprise.

If all automated tests and manual reviews have completed successfully, the changes are merged into the main code, which again triggers a run of the pipeline. However, this time, the run will also try to deploy the new application to production in the form of a blue-green deployment. After the new version has been successfully smoke tested, the system will automatically flip the switch so that users will start using the just deployed version. One of the first users (typically, the product owner) reviews the change in production with real data and either approves the change or suggests follow-up activities. If approved, the change developer can now move his work item to "done" and start working on a new task.

The team uses platform-provided mechanisms for logging, monitoring, and alerting. Log files are centrally collected and can be analyzed by *Kibana*—a tool for log file transformation an analysis. The SAP Cloud Platform provides basic metrics for metrics like CPU usage, memory consumption, or database connection pool utilization. On the application level, the team built a set of additional metrics into the code, which captured information such as the number of business transactions, frequency of error events, or duration of downstream service invocations. For monitoring the continuous delivery server on the internal infrastructure, the team adopted *Nagios*, a tool for keeping the build environment in a healthy state. Alerting is used for critical metrics, and alerts are sent to the whole team.

Our DevOps team placed a big screen in the office workspace, as shown in Figure 10.3. The screen used an economical and energy-saving *Raspberry Pi* (*https://www.raspberrypi.org/*) to switch between multiple visual dashboards of the continuous delivery pipeline and metrics. In this way, everyone was always aware of ongoing deliveries, potential errors, and statistics about the delivery and operation of applications.

Figure 10.3 Continous Delivery Dashboard Display

The team regularly conducted knowledge exchange and learning sessions on multiple layers of the organization. Higher-level events mainly aimed to create awareness around overall activities and important achievements. Communities of practices were used to exchange information between colleagues of multiple teams who shared common interests and work focuses. Finally, team-level events were used to foster general knowledge sharing. Code reviewers were encouraged to discuss recurring quality problems in the code, which might be the result of a lack of effective communication or other factors such as skill gaps. To address these issues, findings are presented in a blame-free manner and discussed with regards to how a specific problem could be solved in a better way. Where possible, the team also tries to automate the discovery of code practice violations, for example, the improper use of logging.

10.6 Summary

In this chapter, we introduced DevOps with its three core principles: flow, feedback, and continuous learning and experimentation. In our experience, we recommend organizations aim for short cycle times from concept to customer value; create effective feedback cycles for noticing problems early; and encourage a culture that motivates experimentation, risk-taking, and learning from failures. Next, we introduced continuous delivery and monitoring practices to achieve the many goals of DevOps. Finally, we learned more about how DevOps principles can be realized by looking at the culture and working model of an example DevOps team.

In Chapter 11, we'll present how to implement the SAP S/4HANA Cloud SDK pipeline to continuously deliver our Business Partner Address Manager application. Furthermore, we'll dive more deeply into best practices for quality assurance as well as application monitoring, in Chapter 12 and Chapter 13.

Chapter 11
Implementing Continuous Delivery

This chapter introduces the continuous delivery artifacts provided as part of the SAP S/4HANA Cloud SDK in the form of open source components on GitHub and Docker Hub. In this chapter, we'll show you how to set up and configure a fully-fledged pipeline in less than five minutes and how to continuously ship an application to the SAP Cloud Platform with zero downtime. In addition, we'll discuss using feature toggling to decouple the deployment and release of new software features based on tools provided by the SDK.

With the theoretical foundations of continuous delivery established in Chapter 10, let's now step into implementing continuous delivery with the SAP S/4HANA Cloud SDK in detail.

11.1 The SAP S/4HANA Cloud SDK CX-Server

Using the *SAP S/4HANA Cloud SDK pipeline* (*CD pipeline*), you may automatically build, test, and deploy your application to the cloud. In a nutshell, the pipeline consists of two main parts. First is the continuous delivery pipeline itself, which from our experience, is a best practice-based sequence of build and quality jobs for SAP S/4HANA extensions on SAP Cloud Platform. Second is a completely codified infrastructure that aims at a simple setup of the entire system in an automated manner. This thorough automation reflects the ideas behind DevOps and continuous delivery we introduced in Chapter 10. We'll discuss both the pipeline itself and the infrastructure throughout this chapter in depth.

Definition: Microservice, Application, Repository

In this chapter, the terms "microservice" and "application" are used interchangeably. So far, we've concentrated on the notion of microservices for components that can be deployed and operated separately in this book because this is the leading architectural style in SAP Cloud Platform. An application is the aggregation of multiple microservices to perform a common business operation. The CD pipeline introduced in this chapter assumes, for the sake of standardization, a certain directory structure within the source code repository, depending on whether you're building a monolithic application or a single microservice. Consequently, if building a monolith, a single CD pipeline is used only, whereas in the case of microservices, one CD pipeline would exist per microservice. In contrast, having multiple microservices in one source code repository is not supported.

Before we dive into the specifics of implementation, let's introduce the basic design principles of the CD pipeline and discuss how these principles relate to the concepts behind DevOps and continuous delivery:

- **Embrace "pipeline as code"**
  The CD pipeline is defined as code in a domain-specific language (DSL), rather than in a graphical user interface. As a result, boundaries between development and operations are removed because the pipeline coexists with the application's source code in one repository, thus, applying the one root principle of DevOps. This would ensure a single-source-of-truth.
- **Strict isolation between pipeline runs**
  The CD pipeline builds your application from scratch every time. Otherwise, errors in one pipeline run may affect subsequent runs unintentionally.
- **Parallelized where possible**
  By running builds distributed on several servers, parallelizing the build can provide significant benefits in terms of combined build duration. The CD pipeline strives to parallelize as many parts of the build as possible.
- **Simple**
  The CD pipeline makes certain assumptions about how your project is organized and which tools are used. Although they are based on our experience, these assumptions may allow for a streamlined start, resulting in fewer errors, an easier setup, and a more standardized quality process.

In addition, the CD pipeline is available as open source software on GitHub, and Docker images are available on Docker Hub. If you're curious about the CD pipeline, you can obtain the source code from the GitHub repository for this book at *https://github.com/SAP/cloud-s4-sdk-pipeline*.

Based on the lessons from Chapter 3 through Chapter 9, Figure 11.1 presents a high-level overview of the workflow for building applications using the SAP S/4HANA Cloud SDK and testing them via the CD pipeline. Let's untangle what happens step-by-step.

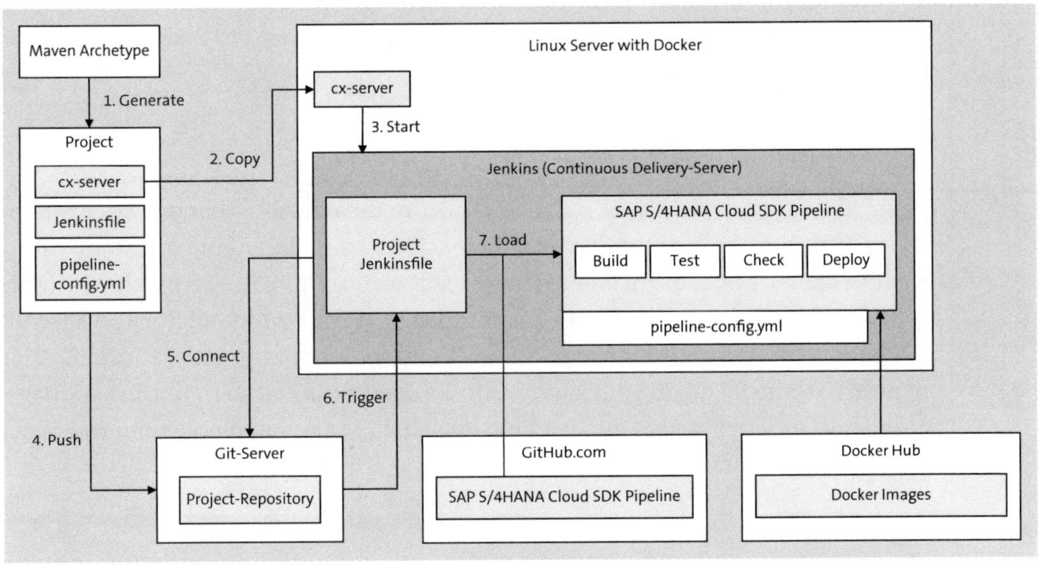

Figure 11.1 Schematic Overview of the SAP S/4HANA Cloud SDK Pipeline Workflow

First, the project is bootstrapped using one of the Maven archetypes introduced in Chapter 4. This process creates a local project folder that contains a *cx-server* directory, a *Jenkinsfile*, and a pipeline_config.yml file, amongst others. The *cx-server* directory contains a script called *cx-server* and a configuration file called *server.cfg*. These files start and manage the Jenkins build server. The *Jenkinsfile* describes how Jenkins builds the application. In our case, Jenkins will merely download the most recent CD pipeline from GitHub. This redirection allows for updates of the CD pipeline without requiring manual steps on your end. The pipeline_config.yml contains the configuration of the CD pipeline. This configuration comprises three main sections:

- `general` describes project-level settings. Most importantly, if your productive branch in the Git repository is not `master`, you can configure your branch in this section. We'll explain this concept later in more detail.
- `steps` includes the settings for the individual build steps. A build step is the smallest entity in the CD pipeline, which translates to invoking a tool to do a task like compile the source code.

- `stages` contain settings for build stages. A build stage consists of one or more build steps. For example, in this section, you can configure the credentials used to deploy to SAP Cloud Platform.

Jenkins

Jenkins is a open source build server providing a rich ecosystem of plugins that integrate many build tools and online services. More information on the Jenkins project can be found at *https://jenkins.io/*.

Second, the *cx-server* directory must be copied to the machine that will later run the Jenkins instance. As a prerequisite, this machine must be a Linux system with a recent version of Docker installed. Docker will be used to run the Jenkins instance itself as well as all tools used by the pipeline, such as the command line tools for the SAP Cloud Platform or the Apache Maven build tool. Consequently, those tools do not need to be installed on your server, but the pipeline pulls the right Docker images automatically from Docker Hub. For help on installing Docker, please refer to *https://docs.docker.com/install/*.

Docker

Docker is an open source container engine. Containers are a concept used in operating systems to isolate applications from each other. Docker as an implementation of those concepts makes heavy use of Linux kernel features such as *control groups* and *namespaces*. We use Docker to distribute our software artifacts independently from the Linux distribution. The images contain all required runtime components, such as the Java Runtime Environment (JRE). More information on Docker can be found at *https://www.docker.com/*.

Third, the Jenkins server can be started using the *cx-server* script. We'll explain this step in more detail in Section 11.2.

Fourth, the local project directory can be pushed to a version control system (VCS) such as Git. The Git server can be provided by software-as-a-service (SaaS) providers or as on-premise solutions such as GitHub (*https://github.com*), GitLab (*https://about.gitlab.com*), BitBucket (*https://bitbucket.org*), or Gogs (*https://gogs.io*).

Fifth, the build job for your new project needs to be configured in the Jenkins server. This step is necessary for Jenkins to know about your project and to know how to get the source code. We'll explain this step in detail in Section 11.2.

Sixth, the repository on the Git server must be configured with a trigger. Triggers are, in some systems, also called hooks. This small command is executed every time you push to your repository and informs the CD pipeline about this change in the version control system and subsequently initiates a new build.

Finally, your project is built. As a prerequisite to the build, the actual code of the pipeline is automatically downloaded from GitHub.com, and required tools such as Maven or npm are downloaded as Docker images from Docker Hub. Once downloaded, these images are available on the server locally. When a new version of the image is published, the changes between those images are downloaded automatically. Afterwards, the pipeline runs through all build stages and steps, which are shown in more detail in Figure 11.2, which also provides a nice overview of build stages running in sequence and in parallel.

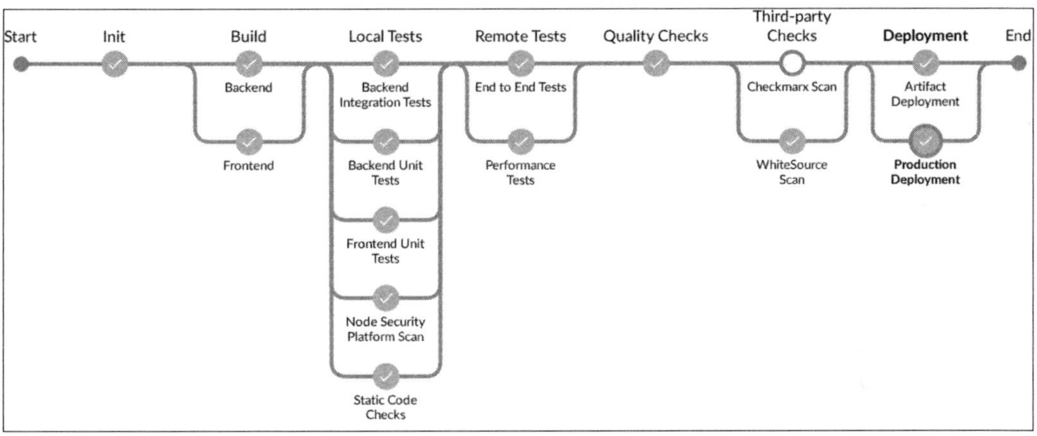

Figure 11.2 Example Instance of the Continuous Delivery Pipeline

The CD pipeline starts with the initial stage to prepare the build by checking out the source code of your application and preparing the build environment.

Second, the application is built. For backend code written in Java, in other words, the application is compiled, and the Java archive file (`jar`, `war`, or `ear`) is assembled. For frontend code written in JavaScript, the dependencies are downloaded, and the code might be minified.

Third, local tests are executed, comprising of unit tests for both the frontend and the backend, additional integration tests for the backend, *Node Security Platform* (NSP)

checks to search for known vulnerabilities in the JavaScript part of the application, and finally static code checks (see Chapter 12) to identify bad code practices.

Fourth, a remote test stage is executed that includes end-to-end as well as performance tests. The application is deployed into a development subaccount of SAP Cloud Platform, which should be as close to production as possible (according to the dev/prod parity principle). This step is important because, despite good unit and integration tests, some errors might only be spotted when the application is running in a productive environment.

Fifth, comprehensive quality checks specific to SAP S/4HANA qualities are performed. For example, the minimum acceptable code coverage will be checked or calls to the downstream services will be made resilient. We'll introduce these checks in more detail in Chapter 12.

Sixth, the third-party checks comprises of scans from third-party tools such as Checkmarx and WhiteSource. Again, we'll explain those qualities in more detail in Chapter 12.

Finally, the application is deployed, comprising of a productive, zero-downtime deployment to the SAP Cloud Platform, if you committed to the productive branch of your project (`master` by default). As a result, feature branches created during development will not be deployed to the SAP Cloud Platform. When merging branches to `master`, you must be aware that a deployment will be triggered. Additionally, the build artifact is uploaded to a Nexus repository, if configured.

This concludes our conceptual overview of the SAP S/4HANA Cloud SDK pipeline. In the next section, we'll show you how to set up a continuous delivery pipeline and infrastructure for your own projects.

11.2 Setting Up and Configuring a Continuous Delivery Server

In this section, we'll illustrate the necessary steps to set up your first CD pipeline with the help of the *cx-server* script. As a prerequisite, we must set up the environment first. We assume you already have access to a server or a virtual machine with a Linux operating system. As described in Section 11.1, the CD pipeline makes extensive use of Docker, so you'll need to install the latest version of the Docker on the server. After installation, add the user that will be used to run the *cx-server* script to the user group `docker` (*http://tiny.cc/docker-install*). That's all for the environment setup, and you're ready to set up your first CD pipeline now.

11.2.1 Installing Jenkins

Copy the *cx-server* directory to the server where you would like to set up your Jenkins server, for example, using `scp`. In addition, ensure that the *cx-server* script is executable by the user on the server.

> **Line Endings on Windows**
>
> If you are copying the *cx-server* from a Microsoft Windows machine, Windows line endings in the files can make the code unusable on a Linux server. Convert the line endings of *cx-server* script and configuration file *server.cfg* to the Linux format by using `dos2unix` or similar tools.

The *cx-server* script helps you with the lifecycle management of your continuous delivery server. The commands supported by the script include the following:

- `start`
  Use this command whenever you'd like to start your Jenkins server. This command will start an old container, if already existing, or will create a new Docker container from the image downloaded from Docker Hub.
- `stop`
  This command initiates a soft shutdown of Jenkins, waiting for all the executing build stages to complete. The remaining stages of the pipeline are executed once the Jenkins server is restarted. Please note, you'll need the Jenkins administrator privilege to execute this command.
- `remove`
  To upgrade your Jenkins Docker image to any newly available version, you'll need to stop the Jenkins container first and then use the `remove` command. This command will delete the old Jenkins container, without affecting your configuration and workspace. Afterwards, you can execute the `cx-server start` command to start Jenkins, which will automatically pull the latest Docker image from Docker Hub.
- `update`
  A check for updates for the *cx-server* script itself is initiated every time you launch the *cx-server* script. If an update is available, you can apply the automatically downloaded update using the `update` command. This command, however, *does not* update Jenkins. To update Jenkins, use the `remove` and `start` commands as explained earlier in this list.

Let's continue by starting our Jenkins instance. You'll need to run `cx-server start` from the *cx-server* directory. This command will pull a Docker image with a freshly installed Jenkins and start the container (Figure 11.3). The state of this Jenkins is stored in a persistent Docker volume named `jenkins_home_volume`. This volume contains all the critical data comprising the Jenkins configuration, plugins, and your Jenkins workspace. By default, the Docker volume is a directory on the host machine with which the Docker container can directly interact. Thus, restricting access control on the host that owns the *cx-server* is highly recommended.

```
   docker pull s4sdk/jenkins-master:latest
latest: Pulling from s4sdk/jenkins-master
723254a2c089: Pull complete
abe15a44e12f: Pull complete
409a28e3cc3d: Pull complete
503166935590: Pull complete
043a12c29ea4: Pull complete
303620452447: Pull complete
c61f95baa024: Pull complete
3f2018472a1f: Pull complete
a25f8a69c882: Pull complete
a5bb015454bf: Pull complete
7461eb8c83ac: Pull complete
67263fcabe87: Pull complete
697e4fd968c8: Pull complete
a2642707ca92: Pull complete
13ae5742459d: Pull complete
7efa2fa7e5b8: Pull complete
c6b2f10f9d8c: Pull complete
3ea47c16f3e0: Pull complete
714d2fded9d0: Pull complete
f3ee945a6cc3: Pull complete
04ad6f1f3d8f: Pull complete
731d78f836b6: Pull complete
722ad3833cff: Pull complete
2e0b268f3262: Pull complete
98a856d01c3f: Pull complete
649d98286fa1: Pull complete
28b62b2bf91d: Pull complete
eb05e47850df: Pull complete
Digest: sha256:f0c7c0b4325077f9c558873fd7b6ab4914cdd8b6ff888c268248a61a0edebc55
Status: Downloaded newer image for s4sdk/jenkins-master:latest
   docker run -u 1000:115 --name s4sdk-jenkins-master -d -p 80:8080 -v /var/run/
b68a5c584646140ba2f2d6967e863a17912b1c85ef7504754555f72909704059
Waiting for the S/4HANA Cloud SDK Cx server to start......... success.
```

Figure 11.3 Installing Jenkins with the cx-server Script

After the Docker images have been downloaded, the Jenkins server is ready for use and contains all the plugins required to execute the pipeline. To check whether your Jenkins instance has started successfully, open the server's hostname or IP address with the specified HTTP port in a browser (for example, *http://localhost*), and you should see the Jenkins welcome page as shown in Figure 11.4.

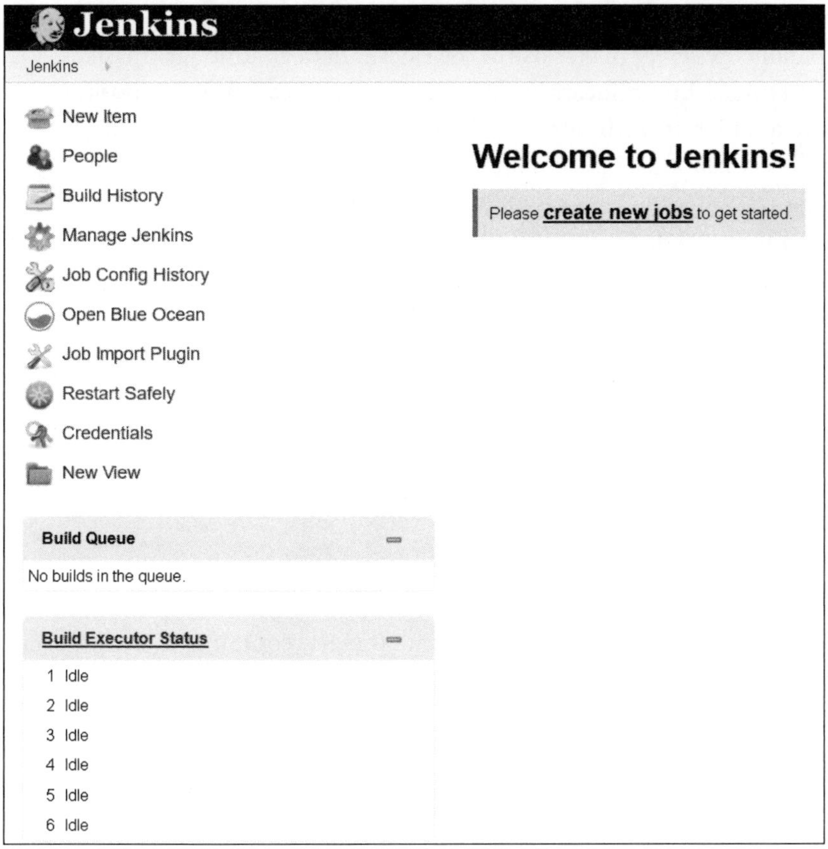

Figure 11.4 Jenkins Welcome Page

In some cases, you might need to change certain settings to accommodate your corporate IT infrastructure (for example, providing proxy settings). The *cx-server* provides the following options as part of the server.cfg file:

- `docker_registry` specifies the Docker registry to be used for pulling Docker images. For example, you can specify a local registry with this option. When no value is specified, the Docker engine will use Docker Hub as a default registry.
- `docker_image` controls the Docker image to be used for instantiating your *cx-server*. When no value is specified, the *cx-server* will pull the latest version of the `s4sdk/jenkins-master` image.
- `http_port` declares the port on which the Jenkins server can be reached. By default, port 80 is used.

- `jenkins_home` specifies a directory on the host to be used as the Jenkins home directory. By default, *cx-server* makes use of the Docker data volume `jenkins_home_volume` as the Jenkins home location. Alternatively, you can use an absolute path pointing to a folder on your host machine, for example, `jenkins_home="/var/jenkins_home"`.
- `x_java_opts` might be used to provide custom Java options to be passed to the Java virtual machine (VM) that runs Jenkins. For example, you can adapt the maximum heap size of the Java VM with `x_java_opts="-Xmx1024m"`. If you have any proxy settings relevant to the Jenkins process, you'll need to configure them as a `x_java_opts` as well.
- `http_proxy`, `https_proxy`, or `no_proxy` specifies the proxy settings for the Docker container. For example:

  ```
  http_proxy="http://proxy:8080"
  https_proxy="http://proxy:8080"
  no_proxy="localhost,.corp"
  ```

  If you change any of these values, make sure you always run `cx-server remove` before starting the Jenkins server again so that the new container is created taking these custom values into account.

Jenkins Home

The user inside the Jenkins container has a fixed `uid=1000`. Note that the user mapping between the host system and the Docker container is only based on the IDs, not on actual user names. If you choose to store your Jenkins home directory in a local folder, please ensure that the user with `uid=1000` can read and write within the folder you wish to set as the home directory. To avoid permission-related issues, we recommend using named Docker volumes.

After we've successfully started our first Jenkins instance, we'll need to provide some configuration information so that we can automatically build and deploy our project, which we'll explain next.

11.2.2 Credentials Management

As a first configuration step, we'll need to provide credentials for the various systems with which our CD pipeline interacts. This information includes, for example, credentials for the version control system (VCS), the protected SAP Cloud Platform application as introduced in Chapter 5, or an SAP S/4HANA test system we're utilizing for integration tests as discussed in Chapter 9. All these credentials must be stored in a secure way, and sharing them via the VCS is *strictly not recommended.* Instead, we'll use the credential management feature of Jenkins. To create credentials, navigate to Jenkins' **Credentials** menu item on the left-hand side of Jenkin's home screen. Add a user name and a password for the intended system, as shown in Figure 11.5. The **ID** you provide while entering the credentials will be used by the CD pipeline upon execution. We'll see how this field is used in the following subsection.

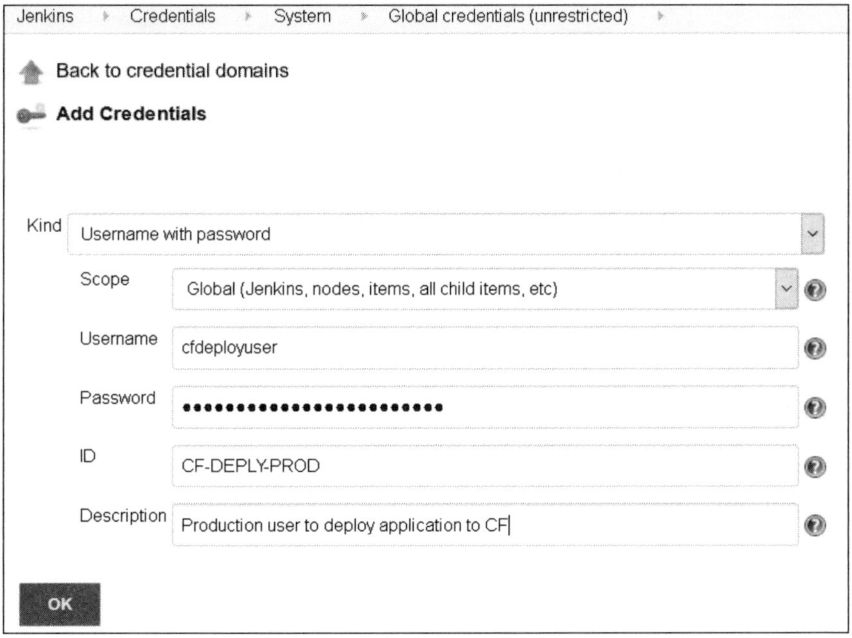

Figure 11.5 Credentials Management in the Jenkins Server

11.2.3 Setting Up Source Code Management

The Jenkins we installed so far does not yet know where our VCS is located (in this example, we'll assume GitHub for simplicity). Therefore, we'll need to set up a communication channel between our Jenkins server and the Git server. To create this link, navigate to the **Configure System** section under the **Manage Jenkins** menu, as shown in Figure 11.6. In the **GitHub** section, provide the API endpoint of the version control server and enter an appropriate name before saving the changes.

Figure 11.6 Configuring a Public GitHub Server in Jenkins

If you're using GitHub enterprise version, you can configure the Git server details under the **GitHub Enterprise Servers** section (Figure 11.7).

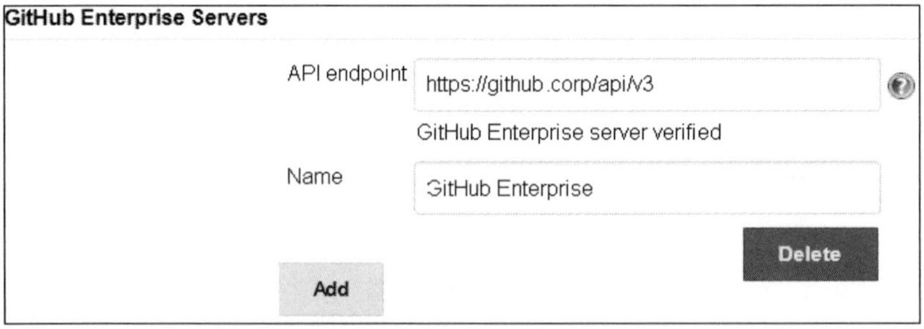

Figure 11.7 Configuring Enterprise GitHub Servers in Jenkins

11.2.4 Configuring Webhook to Jenkins

In the previous subsection, we configured Jenkins to communicate with our VCS. On the other side, we'll establish a channel from our VCS to Jenkins, if supported. This channel enables us to trigger the CD pipeline automatically whenever new code changes are pushed by the team.

For example, when using GitHub, we can configure what's called a *webhook*. An owner of the GitHub repository can create a webhook by navigating to the **Hooks &**

services menu under the **Settings** tab. Click on **Add services** and search for the Jenkins service. Provide the URL of your Jenkins server in the **Jenkins hook url** field. Furthermore, activate event notifications by checking the **Active** checkbox, as shown in Figure 11.8. After adding the service, GitHub will automatically inform our Jenkins instance when events occur, such as *push* or *pull requests*.

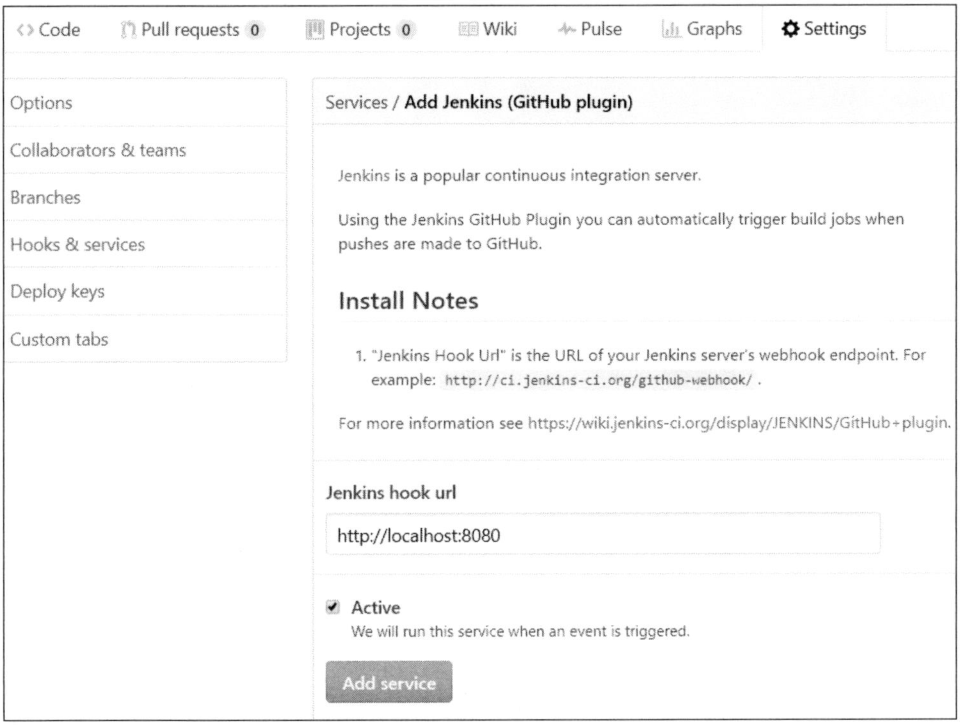

Figure 11.8 Webhook to Jenkins Server from GitHub

11.2.5 Multibranch Pipelines

We're just one step away from executing our first pipeline. The only thing left to do is to create a new item in Jenkins to start a dedicated build job. Click on **New Item** in the left-hand side menu on the Jenkins welcome screen. The build job should be able to build every branch of your repository. Thus, you'll need to create a multibranch pipeline and provide your VCS details in the window under **Branch Sources**, as shown in Figure 11.9. Use the credentials that you created in Section 11.2.2.

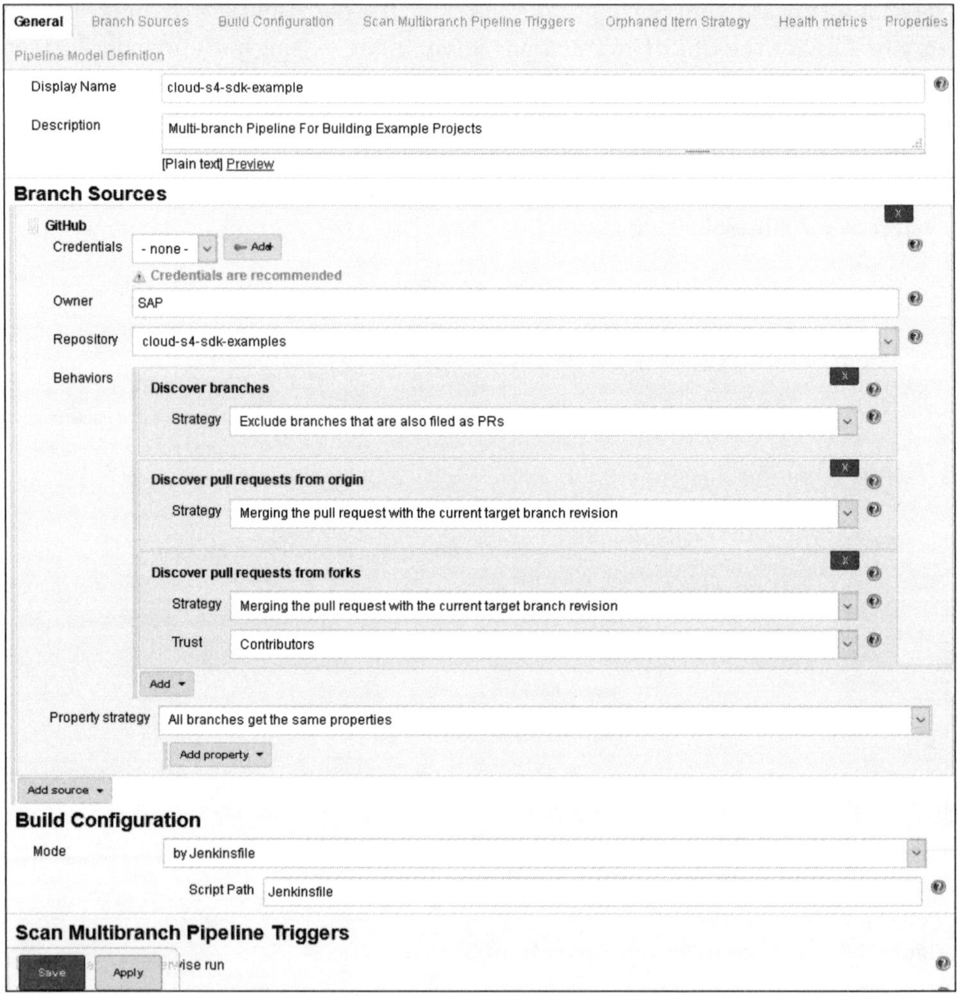

Figure 11.9 Configuring a Multibranch Pipeline in Jenkins

You've now successfully configured Jenkins for your application or microservice. To run the pipeline for the first time, just push some changes into the version control system or start the build job manually in Jenkins.

11.2.6 Securing Jenkins

The Jenkins server that we configured has still unrestricted access, that is, anybody who knows the URL can perform any operation including administrative ones. We *highly recommend* you configure an access restriction to your continuous delivery server so that only authorized people can view or edit the configuration. To access the security section, click on the **Management** menu and navigate to **Configure Global Security**. Jenkins supports multiple authorization profiles such as authentication using Lightweight Directory Access Protocol (LDAP), using Unix user groups, or via a user database in Jenkins. Select the profile best suited to your use case. If you need finely granular access, then matrix-based authorization might be helpful. We recommend consulting *http://tiny.cc/secure-jenkins* for more information on how to secure Jenkins.

In this section, you learned how to set up your own CD pipeline using the SAP S/4HANA Cloud SDK. Although we can run the pipeline, we're not ready to deploy our app into real SAP Cloud Platform systems. We haven't yet configured the target systems where the application should be deployed. Therefore, let's consider how to set up application deployment next.

11.3 Zero-Downtime Shipments to the Cloud

Earlier, we introduced several reasons why continuous delivery might be more beneficial than traditional enterprise IT delivery models. However, a major challenge is how to avoid perceived service downtimes from the end user's perspective, particularly if we deploy into production frequently. Continuous delivery with zero downtime is a delivery method where new features or fixes are delivered to a productive system in a transparent way so that the end user does not notice that the system has been updated. Technically, SAP Cloud Platform provides mechanisms to achieve zero-downtime deliveries, which are also supported by the CD pipeline.

11.3.1 Blue-Green Deployment

Blue-green deployment is a method to update a currently running cloud application with zero downtime. If done correctly, the end users of the application will not even notice that the application has been updated. Before we explain how this method works in detail, let's define the following terminology:

- **Load balancer**
  This component sits between the end user and the deployed backend services. The load balancer forwards incoming requests transparently to the backend services balancing the load between them.

- **Blue and green environments**
  Blue-green deployment involves two identically deployed environments. The environment that contains the currently running application in its old version is called the *blue* environment, and the environment where the new version of the application will be deployed is called the *green* environment.

Figure 11.10 presents the steps for blue-green deployment in more detail.

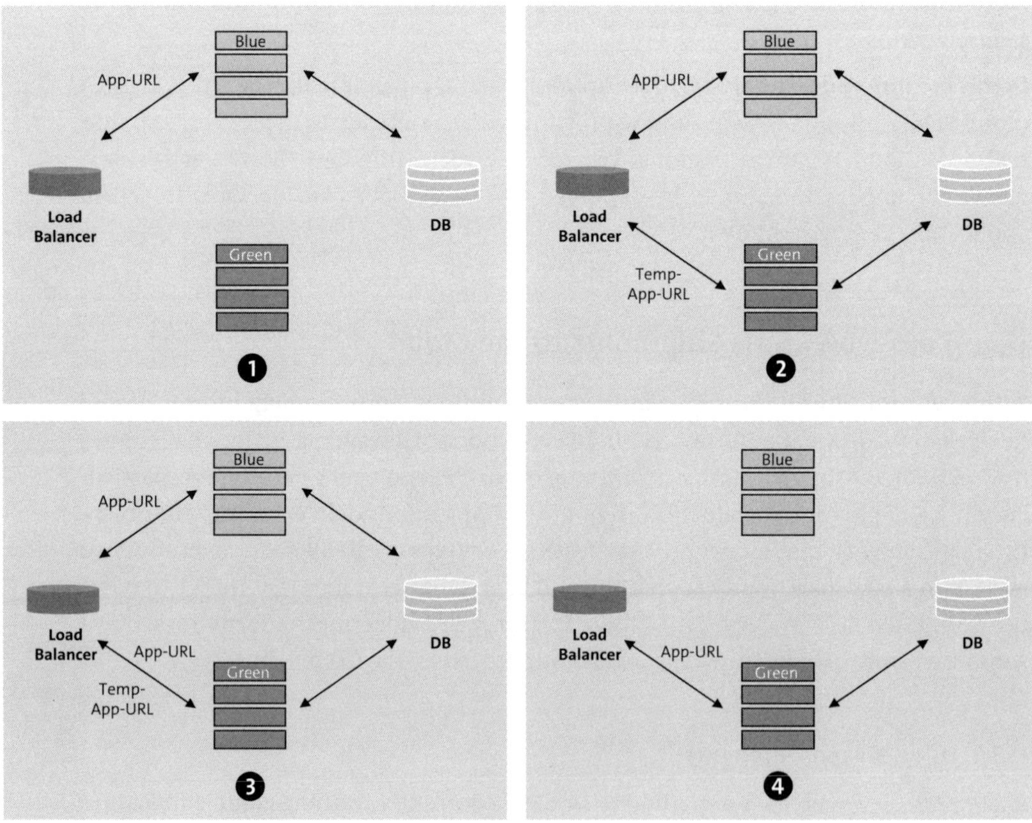

Figure 11.10 Steps Involved in a Blue-Green Deployment

❶ shows the initial scenario: a productive application running in the blue environment. The load balancer forwards all traffic to the application deployed in the blue environment. Therefore, any change to the green environment will not impact the availability of the application in the blue environment.

Now, the new version of the application is pushed to the green environment. Once the application is pushed to the remote server, a new application instance is created with a temporary link from the load balancer to the green environment (❷). Even though the production traffic is routed to the blue environment, you can access the green environment with the temporary link. In addition, you can execute a set of smoke tests against the application using the temporary link to confirm that the new version is behaving as expected.

In the next step, the original application route is mapped to the green environment. That is, the load balancer will now distribute the traffic to both the blue and the green environments as shown in ❸. Please note that, in Cloud Foundry, you'll typically find HTTP session stickiness, that is, end users who received a session from the blue environment continue to be forwarded to the blue environment, and only new users might be forwarded to the green environment. The temporary link to the green environment will continue to exist at this stage.

Next, the load balancer is instructed to stop forwarding traffic to the blue environment, for example, by unmapping the route to the blue environment. The temporary link to the green environment will be deleted as well. Once the whole procedure has been executed, the application in the green environment serves the production traffic. The blue environment will become free for future deployments. ❹ shows the postdeployment state.

Rollback in Blue-Green Deployment

Despite rigorous tests and careful validations, sometimes the application does not behave as expected. In such cases, the blue-green deployment method allows you to easily switch back to the old environment by remapping the routes back to the earlier version of the application.

11.3.2 Zero-Downtime Deployment to SAP Cloud Platform, Cloud Foundry

When you use the CD pipeline, zero-downtime deployment to the Cloud Foundry can be easily configured in the pipeline configuration file. All you need to do is to provide configuration details in the pipeline_config.yml file (Listing 11.1). To review the list of all configurable properties, refer to the configuration guide available at *http://tiny.cc/pipeline-config*.

```
general:
  productiveBranch: 'master'
steps:
  deployToCfWithCli:
    dockerImage: 's4sdk/docker-cf-cli'
    smokeTestStatusCode: '200'
    org: 'sap'
    appName: 'book-address-manager'
    manifest: 'manifest.yml'
    credentialsId: 'CF-DEPLOY'
    apiEndpoint: '<Cloud Foundry API endpoint>'
stages:
  productionDeployment:
    appUrls:
      - url: '<Application URL>'
        credentialId: 'e2e-test-user-cf'
    cfTargets:
      - space: 'Prod'
```

Listing 11.1 Example Pipeline Configuration for Deploying the Application to SAP Cloud Platform, Cloud Foundry Environment

As explained earlier in Section 11.1, the configuration file consists of three configuration sections. To deploy to Cloud Foundry, we need to configure them.

First, the `general` configuration section contains the name of the productive branch, which is "master" in our example. In a multibranch pipeline, the production deployment will be performed only for the branch configured as the `productiveBranch`. For all other branches, the deployment stage is skipped.

Second, the `steps` configuration section contains the `deployToCfWithCli` configuration, which is reused in multiple stages, such as performance tests, end-to-end tests, production deployment, and smoke tests. In our case, this section includes the name of the Docker image containing the Cloud Foundry command line interface tools, the application name that needs to be deployed, the name of the manifest file to be used, the API endpoint to our Cloud Foundry instance, and a credential ID to log in to the Cloud Foundry account.

Finally, the `stages`-level configuration `productionDeployment` consists of values related to the deployment stage only. For example, the `space` is where the application is to be deployed and the configuration for any smoke tests that should be executed. We'll learn more about smoke tests in Chapter 12.

With this example configuration in place, all the steps required to perform the application deployment to Cloud Foundry are taken care of by the CD pipeline.

11.3.3 Zero-Downtime Deployment to the Neo Environment on the SAP Cloud Platform

Like in the Cloud Foundry environment, the Neo environment on the SAP Cloud Platform offers a mechanism for zero-downtime updates, called *rolling-update*. The steps performed as part of the deployment are comparable to the blue-green deployment of Cloud Foundry.

Listing 11.2 provides a sample configuration for our pipeline_config.yml that enables the deployment of an application into the Neo environment. The deployment configuration is quite similar to the one used for Cloud Foundry deployment. In the `general` configuration section, we'll configure our productive branch. We'll make use of a Docker image that contains the Neo command line interface (CLI) tools to perform deployment. This information is configured within the `steps` configuration section. Under the `stages` configuration section, we'll configure the `host` value that contains the Neo host URL, and the `account` value will contain the subaccount value for the Neo environment. The `application` attribute will contain the name of our application. Furthermore, we'll also need to provide authentication details to the Neo environment. For this step, we'll make use of the credentials that we created in Section 11.2.2 and assign the ID to the `credentialsId`.

With this configuration in place, all the steps required to deploy an application to the Neo environment are taken care of by the CD pipeline.

```
general:
  productiveBranch: 'master'
steps:
  deployToNeoWithCli:
    dockerImage: 's4sdk/docker-neo-cli'
stages:
  productionDeployment:
    neoTargets:
     - host: '<URL to Neo Environment>'
       account: <Sub account name>
       application: ' book-address-manager'
       credentialsId: 'NEO-DEPLOY'
```

Listing 11.2 Example Pipeline Configuration for Deploying Our Application to SAP Cloud Platform, Neo Environment

Challenges in Zero-Downtime Deployment

Zero-downtime deployments ensure transparent upgrades of the application to newer versions. However, depending on your persistence strategy, changing versions can be tricky because they also require a change to the underlying database structures such as tables or schemas. As we aim to deploy applications as frequently as possible, performing such database changes manually may lead to downtimes and is highly error-prone.

Therefore, we'll also have to make the evolutionary design of the database schema part of the source code inside version control and automatically migrate changes to the database as part of the continuous delivery methodology. For this purpose, we can use automatic data migration tools such as Flyway (*https://flywaydb.org/*) or Liquibase (*https://www.liquibase.org/*). Liquibase has first-class support in the SAP S/4HANA Cloud SDK by providing additional convenience classes for SAP Cloud Platform. Because this topic has many facets beyond the scope of this book, we recommend interested readers refer to a comprehensive article at *http://tiny.cc/evodb.*

Even though continuous delivery aims at providing frequent deployments of the application to the production environment, not every feature deployed is ready for consumption by the end user. In such cases, you'll need a mechanism to differentiate the deployment of a feature into production from the release of a feature to our end users. Let's take a deeper look into this challenge and also the solution provided by the SAP S/4HANA Cloud SDK in conjunction with the CD pipeline.

11.4 Feature Toggles: Decoupling Deployment and Release

In the age of cloud computing, we can potentially deploy every change of our application into production. This ability goes along nicely with agile development practices, which aims to provide improvements on software in small and regular intervals. As we've seen in the previous section, these updates can happen without interfering with the user workflows via zero-downtime deployments.

Multiple ways exist for how a software development team can organize those changes. For example, many teams work with long-lived branches on the source code repository. Each feature is a branch in development, and those changes can be merged once the feature is ready. However, one potential problem with this approach is that long-lived branches can lead to costly and error-prone merges, which can only be prevented if developers update their feature branches regularly (which they generally don't do in order to focus on to finishing their feature only). Thus, a feature branch can become continuously unintegrated and needs to be merged with extraordinary effort in one shot. Furthermore, whether a feature is ready to be merged or ready from a customer's perspective is not always easy to determine because the feature might not have been tested with productive data loads yet or the customer or the product owner has not yet approved the changes.

Another approach is to work with short-lived feature branches, that is, we'll try to merge into master as early and often as possible, typically no longer than two or three business days. However, in this case, we'll need a mechanism that prevents us from releasing unfinished work into production. For this mechanism, we can leverage a pattern called *feature toggles*, which can deactivate unfinished features and then roll them out gradually to more users, which increases our confidence that the feature does what we want. In fact, the major innovation of feature toggles is that they allow us to decouple the activity of deployment from the activity of releasing, which otherwise would be inherently connected with each other. This pattern is discussed extensively in the developer community, which includes a canonical definition (*http://tiny.cc/feature-toggles*).

Toggles are categorized by the purpose they serve, as we'll discuss next.

11.4.1 Operation Toggles

Operation-specific toggles can be used to change an application's behavior based on the technical environment it is running on. For example, our application could adapt to a specific SAP Cloud Platform variant, such as the Neo environment or the Cloud Foundry environment.

11.4.2 Experiment Toggles

Experimental toggles can be used to roll out new features for a small subset of users to see how they react to the feature in comparison to users who have not been introduced to this feature. If the feature proves to be useful, it could be added to the backlog and be implemented as a full feature. Other experiments include checking whether the feature operates on real data because significant amounts of data might be only available in the production environment. These kinds of toggles are related to release toggles because they enable new features for some users only, but experimental toggles are used in a much earlier stage and should be enabled for a small group of selected users only.

11.4.3 Permission Toggles

With permission toggles, features might be enabled for users based on a certain group assignment. For example, we could differentiate users based on the price tier of our application and designate high-profile features only for gold-level subscriptions. We could also enable administrative features for users that are part of a dedicated group of administrators.

11.4.4 Release Toggles

Release toggles allow us to separate deployment from release. By "release," we mean that a feature can be used by our end users. New features can be disabled during the development phase, in particular, when they are not ready for production yet. Nevertheless, we can make them available to a small set of test users, for example the product owner, at any time as the functionality is continuously deployed into production through our CD pipeline. Once the feature is stable, the toggle can be removed. We'll focus on release toggles for the remainder of this chapter.

The SAP S/4HANA Cloud SDK offers a way to implement feature toggles using the well-known open source framework *Togglz*.

The different kinds of toggles we described in the previous subsection each require different strategies for activating toggles for certain users. The Togglz project provides a variety of strategies documented online at *http://tiny.cc/togglz-strategies*. In addition, the SAP S/4HANA Cloud SDK provides useful adaptations to Togglz so that it seamlessly works with concepts from SAP Cloud Platform. For example, the SDK provides out of the box support to toggle features by SAP Cloud Platform tenants, users, or combinations thereof.

11.4.5 Decoupling Deployment and Release

When you start implementing a new toggle-protected feature, you'll create a toggle for it that is disabled by default. You can enable a toggle for a selected group of users such as the development team, testers, the product owner, and hand-picked stakeholders in the organization. As a result, the group of early testers can quickly get a sense of this feature and determine whether the feature is worth further investment. Moreover, early testers will use the feature in the real systems with their real data rather than on a development snapshot with some generated test data.

As an example, let's use our Business Partner Address Manager application. Imagine we are implementing the feature that business partner addresses can be updated, but this feature is not quite production ready yet.

To implement the feature toggle, first add the togglz dependency provided by the SAP S/4HANA Cloud SDK to your application's POM file at *application/pom.xml*.

```
<dependency>
  <groupId>com.sap.cloud.s4hana.frameworks</groupId>
  <artifactId>togglz</artifactId>
</dependency>
```

Next, you can create an enumeration that extends the interface Feature. You'll need to implement isEnabled() and assertThatEnabled() from the interface, like in the example in Listing 11.3. This enumeration will be used in the source code to check whether the feature is activated or not at runtime.


```
public enum ReleaseFeature implements Feature {

  @Label("Update the address of a business partner")
  UPDATE_ADDRESS;

  @Override
  public boolean isEnabled() {
    return FeatureContext.getFeatureManager().isActive(this);
  }

  @Override
  public void assertThatEnabled() {
    if (!isEnabled()) {
      throw new FeatureNotEnabledException(this.name());
    }
  }
}
```

Listing 11.3 Example Implementation of a New Feature Toggle

Finally, you can protect the execution of any new feature by querying isEnabled(). For example, in the class AddressServlet, we may only execute the update command of addresses to SAP S/4HANA, if our new feature is enabled as shown in Listing 11.4.

```
if (ReleaseFeature.UPDATE_ADDRESS.isEnabled()) {
  new UpdateAddressCommand(address).execute();
}
```

Listing 11.4 Invoking the isEnabled() Method for Each Feature to Hide the Implementation until Finished

To use feature toggles within our unit and integration tests, you can use the JUnit rule provided by Togglz. We won't go into detail in this book since the comprehensive documentation for Togglz should be sufficient (*http://tiny.cc/togglz-testing*).

For managing your toggles at runtime, you can use the web-based administration console shown in Figure 11.11. The setup is described also in the official Togglz documentation (*http://tiny.cc/togglz-console*). You can enable or disable the toggles manually or define activation strategies to do this automatically.

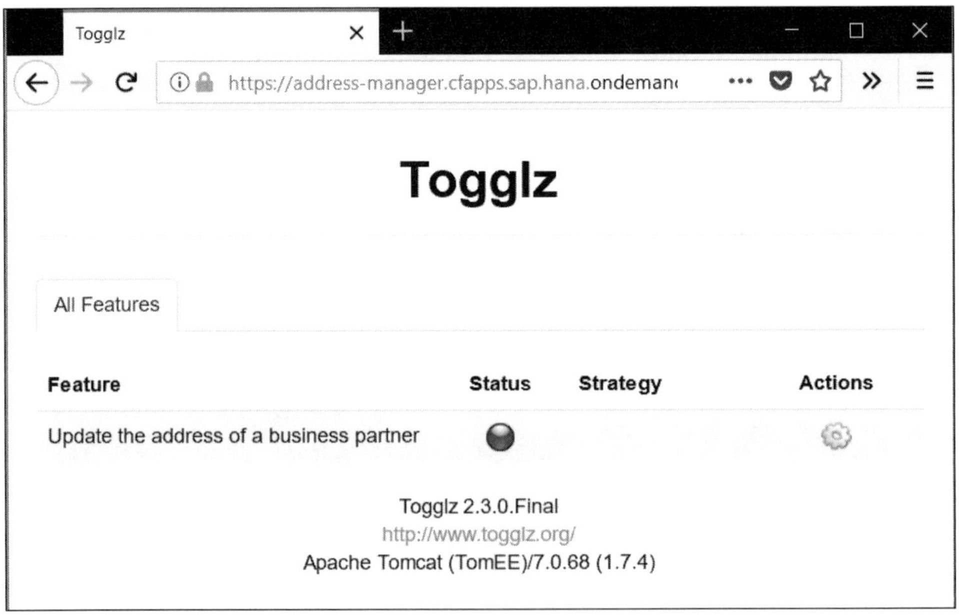

Figure 11.11 Admin Console Showing Our Feature Toggle

Once a feature is mature, the toggle should be removed as release toggles are meant to be temporary. You'll need to be aware of the added complexity to your codebase that comes from each additional toggle.

11.5 Summary

In this chapter, we learned about the SAP S/4HANA Cloud SDK pipeline and discussed how it helps implement DevOps principles and continuous delivery practices as well as how to set it up. Furthermore, we learned about zero-downtime deployments and how to separate the deployment of new functionality from its release using feature toggles.

In the next chapter, we'll take a closer look on the quality checks performed automatically by the CD pipeline in its various stages and steps.

Chapter 12
Quality Assurance

In this chapter, we'll discuss all design-time aspects that relate to software quality as provided by the SAP S/4HANA Cloud SDK. In particular, we'll introduce the static code checks, cloud quality checks, performance tests, etc., that are executed against the application's code and describe how you can continuously assess production code against these qualities while following the continuous delivery principles introduced in previous chapters. In addition, the chapter will explore advanced topics on how to provide and scale automated test suites for integration and end-to-end frontend tests.

High software quality is important to reach the goal of creating value for customers. Bad software quality decreases customer satisfaction. If an application does not behave as expected, or an outage occurs because of a defect in the software, the customer might consider another product in the future or may not renew their contract in the cloud. Furthermore, we learned in Chapter 10 that, following the DevOps theory and the continuous delivery principles, software needs to be checked continuously, ideally, in a fully automated way. In this chapter, we'll provide an overview of the software qualities that are important in the context of SAP S/4HANA extensions and how the SAP S/4HANA Cloud SDK helps to measure these qualities in an automated way.

12.1 What Is Software Quality and How to Achieve It?

The term "quality" is hard to define. One common definition is "fitness for use" (J. Juran and A. Godfrey, *Quality Handbook*). This definition takes the customer perspective into the focus. You should design products in a way that fits the needs of the people who will actually use them.

For software, this definition also means that you'll have to understand how the customer will use your application and what requirements derive from those uses.

Software needs to fulfill functional requirements and be free of bugs. Furthermore, software must also address nonfunctional requirements, such as performance, reliability, or resilience.

Software quality can be divided into internal and external characteristics (A. McConnell, *Code Complete*). External characteristics are perceived by users, such as correctness, robustness, reliability, or usability. Internal characteristics are perceived by developers, such as maintainability, flexibility, readability, or testability. Although in the end only the external characteristics matter, internal characteristics can affect external ones. For example, testable code may make it easier to write tests and, therefore, supports the correctness of the application.

In software projects, you should first identify and define the relevant characteristics for your project and plan how to measure and monitor them. In this way, you can constantly improve the quality of your application and identify flaws in the application as early as possible.

Different approaches exist to ensuring software quality and can be categorized as static and dynamic checks. The main difference is that static checks analyze the source code of the software whereas dynamic checks execute the software and test the behavior of the application.

Static checks mainly help improve the internal characteristics of software quality but can also support external characteristics. Some tools measure the complexity of the code or check that programming rules regarding the style are applied to improve the maintainability of projects. These tools may also identify common security-related bad practices and other factors that influence the functionality of the software.

Dynamic checks mainly help improve external characteristics. A common approach is to write software tests that compare the actual behavior with the expected behavior. You can write these tests on different levels, testing just a single component, or the whole application from the user's perspective. We already explained the concepts of testing in Chapter 9. With these checks, we can monitor the functionality of our software. Metrics exist to monitor the quality of these dynamic checks. Code coverage, for example, measures the amount of the source code that is covered by automated tests.

Furthermore, dynamic checks can also help to improve usability or reliability. Performance tests, for example, can simulate user interactions and test whether the application still responds within the expected time frame. These tests can also determine whether an application or system may crash because of high workloads.

Throughout this chapter, we'll show you the numerous static and dynamic checks built into the SAP S/4HANA Cloud SDK pipeline we introduced in Chapter 11. We'll also introduce additional dynamic checks to monitor the usage of SAP S4/HANA Cloud SDK-specific features to satisfy the quality characteristics of resilience and portability. We'll call these checks SAP Cloud quality checks.

12.2 Static Code Checks

To ensure internal qualities, most often, teams use some form of code review mechanisms such as pull requests within GitHub, which is suitable for small teams and small projects. However, as complexity grows, aligning with more team members regarding the rule sets based on which pull requests should be approved becomes difficult. In addition, manual review involves additional human effort that may be neglected when a certain deadline is approaching. Thus, automated analytical tools can play a key role because of their speed and the face that rule sets can be configured and shared. Your application can then able to benefit from the automated evaluation triggered by every single code change. Therefore, automated analytical tools can be used as a supplement to manual reviews.

FindBugs (*http://findbugs.sourceforge.net/*) and PMD (*https://pmd.github.io/*) are two static code analyzers used by the CD pipeline. For the most part, the warnings they covered are unique and don't overlap, so executing both might be worthwhile. Unnecessary return statements, for example, are only detected by PMD. The existence of an unclosed I/O stream, on the other hand, is only verified by FindBugs (N. Rutar et al., *A Comparison of Bug Finding Tools for Java*).

12.2.1 FindBugs

FindBugs is an open source, cross-platform application for Java programs scanning the bytecode. Integrated with Maven, FindBugs can also be executed as part of your continuous delivery pipeline.

FindBugs as Part of the Pipeline

The CD pipeline executes FindBugs in the *Static Code Checks* stage. To pass this step, your application must be without any major bugs, and the number of minor bugs must be under ten. Figure 12.1 shows the FindBugs trend graph, which can be found on the right side of the dashboard, if you go to a specific branch of your project running on Jenkins.

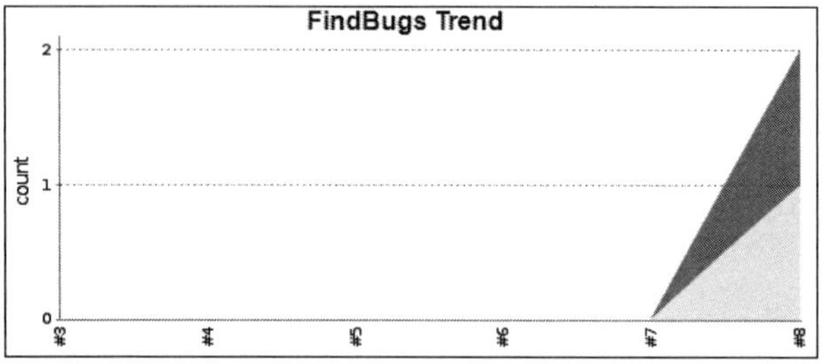

Figure 12.1 The FindBugs Trend Graph Showing the Number of Major (Red) and Minor (Yellow) Warnings in Recent Builds

The logs regarding major bugs may look like the console output shown in Listing 12.1.

```
[FINDBUGS] Plug-in Result: Failed -
<a href="findbugsResult">1 warnings</a> of
<a href="findbugsResult/HIGH">priority High</a> exceed the
threshold of 0 by 1
```

Listing 12.1 Logs of a Failed Pipeline Due to FindBugs Warnings

For more detail about any problems reported by FindBugs, no matter how major or minor, simply click the trend graph, and you'll be redirected to the details page as shown in Figure 12.2. If you click on the source file name shown on this page, you can then see the root cause of the warnings.

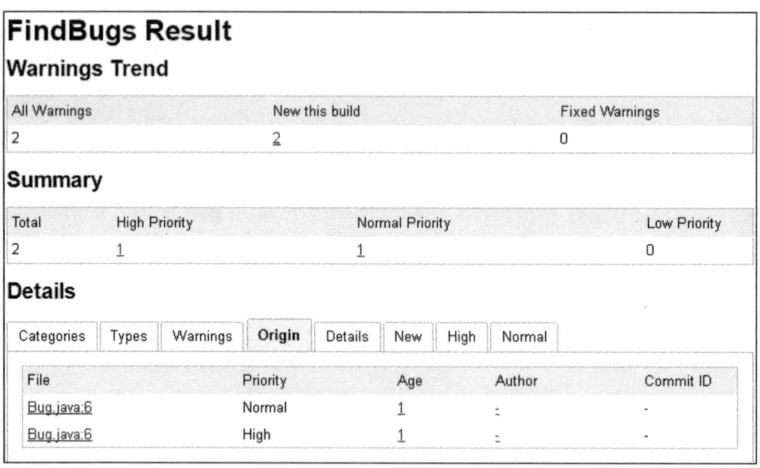

Figure 12.2 FindBugs Details Page Showing List of Warnings with Classnames Involved and Rules Violated

Suppress FindBugs Warnings

If a new warning is found, you should always try to fix it. All warning have a description of which rule was violated. However, in certain cases, the warning might be a false positive, but FindBugs has a convenient way to ignore designated warnings. Simply add an annotation `@SuppressFBWarnings` either at the class or method level. Please note, this approach is *not recommended* to "fix" FindBugs warnings and should be used as exception only.

FindBugs as a Maven Plugin

To reproduce the findings locally before committing to remote repositories, you can execute FindBugs as a Maven goal. FindBugs generates a findbugs.xml as the output file under your *target* folder. The property `findbugs.includeFilterFile` customizes which classes are omitted from analysis, as shown in the following:

```
$ mvn clean install findbugs:findbugs \
> -Dfindbugs.includeFilterFile=includeFilterPlaceholder
```


Since you'll need to replace the placeholder in the command with the path to your local include filter, check out the `cloud-s4-sdk-pipeline-lib` repository (Pipeline Library for the SAP S/4HANA Cloud SDK, n.d.). The preconfigured include filter can be found under the path *resources/s4hana_findbugs_include_filter.xml.*

12.2.2 PMD

PMD is another open source static code analysis tool for Java applications. One of the major differences between PMD and FindBugs is that PMD is executed against the source code.

PMD as Part of the CD Pipeline

The CD pipeline also executes PMD checks. If you encounter some PMD warnings, check the dashboard for any job on your Jenkins server, which contains the PMD trend graph of the latest builds, as shown in Figure 12.3.

By clicking the PMD trend graph, you can navigate to the detailed report as shown in Figure 12.4, which includes problematic classes, warning levels, and underlying reasons. The problematic lines of the code are highlighted with hints if you click on the specific class files, as shown in Figure 12.5.

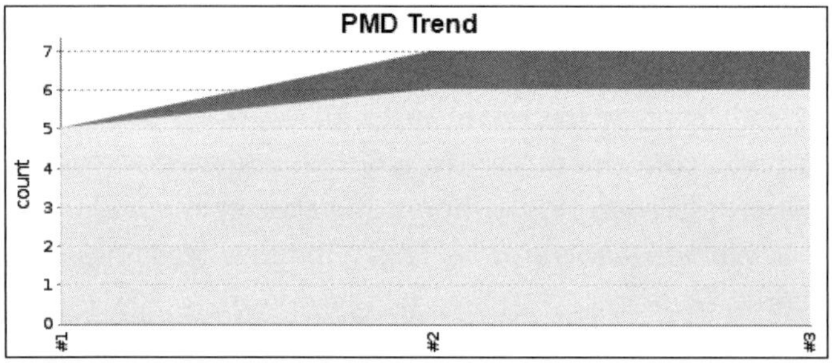

Figure 12.3 PMD Trend Graph Showing the Number of Warnings with Different Priorities in Most Recent Builds

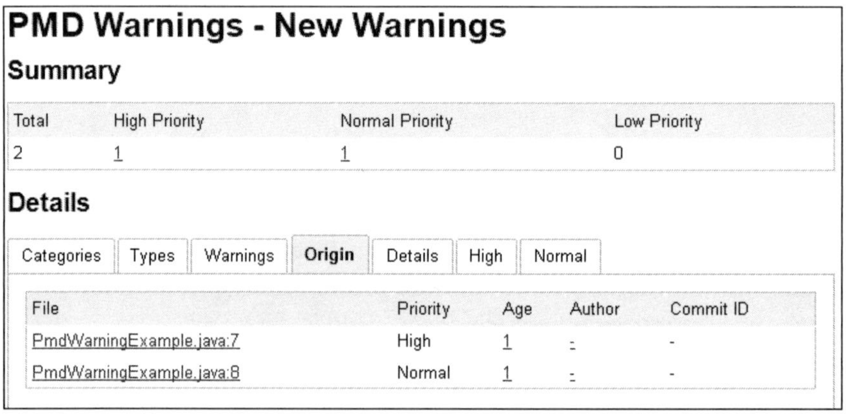

Figure 12.4 PMD Details Page Showing More Statistics

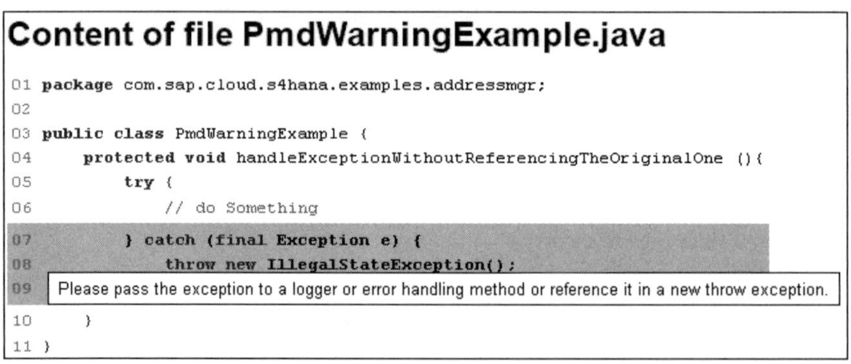

Figure 12.5 PMD Source Code Report Showing the Root Cause of Every PMD Warning

PMD as Maven Plugin

The Maven PMD plugin can also be leveraged to verify whether your local changes violate PMD rules. Use this Maven command to generate a report and an output file based on the configuration:

```
$ mvn clean install pmd:pmd
```

In addition to the standard PMD rulesets, the CD pipeline performs SAP-specific static code analyses using a custom PMD plugin together with custom PMD rulesets, which are integrated and shipped with the SAP S/4HANA Cloud SDK. To execute these checks manually, run the following command:

```
$ mvn com.sap.cloud.s4hana.quality:pmd-plugin:RELEASE:pmd -Dpmd.rulesets=
rulesets/s4hana-qualities.xml
```

In the following sections, we want to quickly introduce the additional SAP-specific PMD rules that are shipped as part of the SAP S/4HANA Cloud SDK. If these rules are violated, the plugin will mark the corresponding code as either a warning or error.

HandleExceptionsRule

One example of a specific SAP S/4HANA Cloud SDK rule is the `HandleExceptionsRule` enforcing proper error handling. To enable the application to be analyzed post-mortem, exceptions must be logged in the `catch` block, and the exception itself must be referenced as an argument. Listing 12.2 presents an example where the exception is not referenced in the log, thus resulting in a PMD warning.

```
try {
  // do something
} catch (final Exception e) {
  handleException();
}
```

Listing 12.2 Bad Code Example without Referencing the Exception in the Log

OnlyUseCloudLoggerFactoryRule

`CloudLoggerFactory` is implemented as part of the SAP S/4HANA Cloud SDK to help log all important results in a way that can be easily and consistently consumed by the SAP Cloud Platform. The code block shows how to correctly initialize a logger using the `CloudLoggerFactory`:

```
private static final Logger logger = CloudLoggerFactory.getLogger(Foo.class);
```

If we use a different logger factory, PMD would issue a warning.

ReferenceExceptionRule

When logging inside a catch block, the original exception has to be referenced for postmortem analyzability. Listing 12.3 shows how the exception is passed to the logger as a parameter.

```
try {
  // do something
} catch (final Exception e) {
  logger.warn("Some exception happened", e);
}
```

Listing 12.3 Reference Exception to Logger When Logging in a Catch Block

If we create a log entry without referencing the exception as parameter, PMD would issue a warning.

UseSdkPlatformAbstractionsRule

To allow an application to smoothly transfer between the Neo and Cloud Foundry environments, we should leverage the platform abstractions provided by the SAP S/4HANA Cloud SDK. The complete list of platform abstractions can be found at *tiny.cc/sdk-abstractions*.

12.2.3 Node Security Platform

Research shows that, in any application code, injection vulnerabilities are both present and not adequately addressed (C.-A. Staicu et al., *Understanding and Automatically Preventing Injection Attacks on Node.js*). An attacker may take advantage of APIs provided by Node.js to inject arbitrary code. For example, exec may introduce command injection, if the attacker can influence the string passed to exec, because exec spawns a shell command and executes the string in the shell. Similarly, eval enables code injection, because the string passed to eval is interpreted as JavaScript code.

The CD pipeline helps to keep a Node.js application secure by using the Node Security Platform (NSP) (*https://nodesecurity.io/*), which is an open source tool that checks known vulnerabilities in your project.

12.2.4 CheckMarx

CheckMarx CxSAST (*https://wiki.jenkins.io/display/JENKINS/Checkmarx+CxSAST+Plugin*) is another source code analysis tool for identifying security vulnerabilities, compliance issues, and business problems. CheckMarx, a remote service on the fly, saves your system resources from scanning and analyzing source code as well as generating reports. The CD pipeline also provides the extension to perform CheckMarx scans, and the configuration handbook can be found at *tiny.cc/pipeline-config*. However, a license is required.

12.2.5 WhiteSource

Today, approximately 2 million open source projects can be leveraged as dependencies in your project (*https://www.blackducksoftware.com/technology/knowledge-base*), and the percentage of vulnerable open source applications is increasing to reach approximately 80% (G. Bitz and H. Plate, *Open-Source Security Management and Vulnerability Impact Assessment*). Hackers may look for newly published vulnerabilities and try them on your application.

WhiteSource (*https://www.whitesourcesoftware.com*) is an open source security management tool that detects whether any issues have been reported for the open source components you're using in your application and whether new patches or versions are available. With WhiteSource, you can choose open source components that fit best and update them in a timely fashion. The CD pipeline executes WhiteSource automatically, if you configure it. You can find out more details regarding the configuration at *http://tiny.cc/pipeline-config*. Please note, the free policy is applicable to open source projects only; commercial projects may have to buy a corresponding license.

12.3 Automated Testing

Testing is a valuable approach to ensure that functional requirements, and to some extent nonfunctional requirements, such as performance, are met. These dynamic checks execute parts of the application and compare actual behavior with expected behavior. In Chapter 9, we learned how to implement tests for side-by-side extensions in order to validate the functional requirements. In this section, we'll learn how these tests are used in the CD pipeline. Furthermore, we'll also learn how to create and run performance tests in the CD pipeline.

12.3.1 Backend Unit Tests and Integration Tests

As described in Chapter 9, unit tests and integration tests in the context of the SAP S/4HANA Cloud SDK subsume tests that either test the smallest pieces of the application or spawn a small local web server to test the HTTP backend interface. Both can be run locally using Maven. In the CD pipeline, they are grouped as **Local Tests**. Both types of tests are run by the CD pipeline automatically. The stages are called **Backend Unit Tests** and **Backend Integration Tests**.

We also learned that integration tests can be used to validate assumptions about the communication with dependent systems, such as an SAP S/4HANA system. Destination configurations, such URLs or credentials, are provided by special configuration files in the *integration-tests* module. The file systems.yml defines the alias of the systems, the URLs, and additional properties, such as proxies. The file credentials.yml contains the credentials used to connect to these systems. However, we cannot commit the file containing the credentials to our version control system. Instead, the CD pipeline makes use of the credentials API provided by Jenkins. We already used this API in Chapter 11 to set up the zero-downtime deployment to SAP Cloud Platform. Now, we'll have to create additional credentials in Jenkins to execute the integration tests as well. Afterwards, we'll define, in the configuration file pipeline_config.yml, which credentials should be used for which systems. Listing 12.4 shows an example of this configuration.

```
stages:
  integrationTests:
    credentials:
      - alias: 'ERP_SYSTEM'
        credentialId: 'MY-CREDENTIAL_ID'
```

Listing 12.4 Configure Which Credentials to Use for Which System in the Integration Tests Stage

As described in Chapter 11, the configuration file contains a section called `stages`, which configures stage-specific behavior. Thus, in the section `integrationTests` representing the integration tests stage, we may create a subsection called `credentials`. For every system in the systems.yml, we'll create one entry in this section. The value for alias corresponds to the alias in the systems.yml. The value for `credentialId` corresponds to the Jenkins credentials that should be used for this system.

Afterwards, the CD pipeline executes these tests and displays the tests' results, as shown in Figure 12.6. The CD pipeline shows which tests passed and which failed. If a test fails, the result of the whole build is marked as "FAILURE."

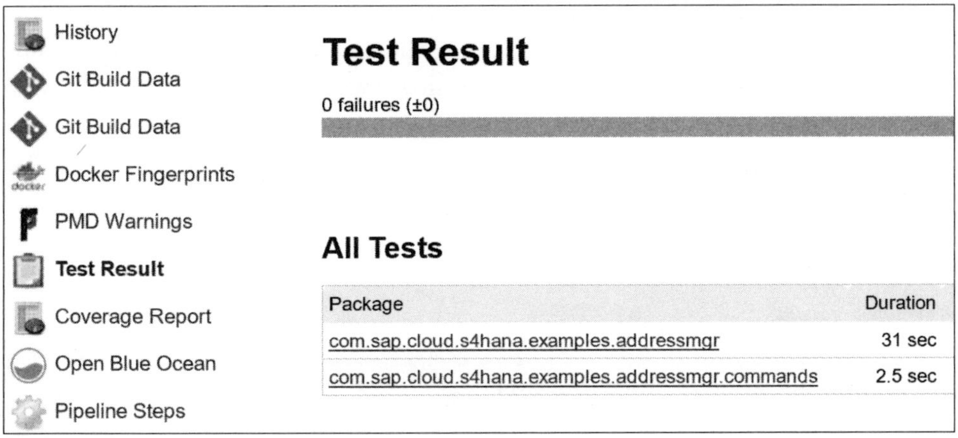

Figure 12.6 Jenkins Showing Last Test Results

12.3.2 Code Coverage

Code coverage is a commonly used measure indicating the degree to which the application's source code is covered by tests. Writings tests for the majority of the application is crucial since code without tests may contain undetected defects. In addition, without adequate code coverage, the refactoring of an existing project is not safe and may result in significant mistakes. However, please be aware that also the quality of the tests is important, as already discussed in Chapter 9.

The **Quality Checks** stage of the CD pipeline collects test statistics generated from the **Backend Unit Tests** and **Backend Integration Tests** stages, aggregates them, and demonstrates code coverage trends over time as a line chart, as shown in Figure 12.7.

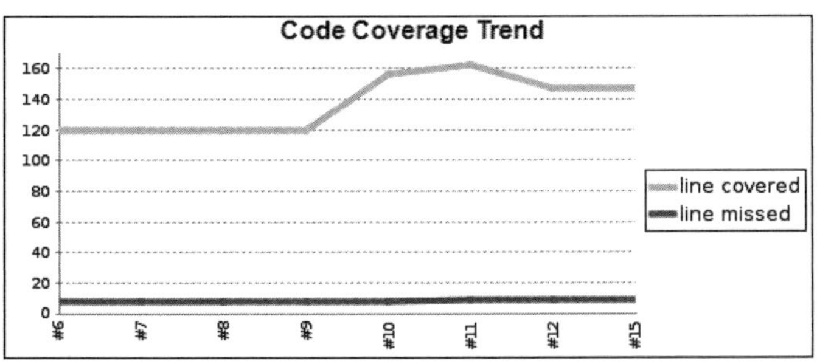

Figure 12.7 Code Coverage Trend Graph Showing the Number of Lines of Code Covered or Missed by Tests

For each individual Jenkins build, coverage statistics with different scopes such as overall coverage, package coverage, and source file coverage can be found via the link **Coverage Report**. Figure 12.8 is an example of an overall coverage summary, where for all classes and each individual package coverage statistics are listed.

Overall Coverage Summary

name	instruction	branch	complexity	line	method	class
all classes	94% M: 28 C: 466	75% M: 2 C: 6	89% M: 4 C: 31	94% M: 9 C: 147	94% M: 2 C: 29	100% M: 0 C: 8

Coverage Breakdown by Package

name	instruction	branch	complexity	line
com.sap.cloud.s4hana.examples.addressmgr	M: 13 C: 169 93%	M: 2 C: 4 67%	M: 2 C: 10 83%	M: 4 C: 53 93%
com.sap.cloud.s4hana.examples.addressmgr.commands	M: 11 C: 279 96%	M: 0 C: 0 100%	M: 1 C: 18 95%	M: 3 C: 89 97%
com.sap.cloud.s4hana.examples.addressmgr.util	M: 4 C: 18 82%	M: 0 C: 2 100%	M: 1 C: 3 75%	M: 2 C: 5 71%

Figure 12.8 Overall Coverage Summary Page with Code Coverage Statistics for Different Categories at the Package Level

As shown in Figure 12.9, if we open the source file coverage report, our source code will be marked with different background colors indicating which lines are covered (green/lighter shading) or not covered (red/darker shading) by our automated tests.

```
        logger.warn("Invalid request to delete - at least one mandatory
        response.setStatus(HttpServletResponse.SC_BAD_REQUEST);
        response.getWriter().write(
            "Bad request: please provide query parameters " +
                "businessPartnerId and addressId");
        return;
    }

    logger.info("Received delete request to delete address {},{}", bus
    new DeleteAddressCommand(businessPartnerId, addressId).execute();
```

Figure 12.9 Lines of Code Not Covered by Tests

We can also exclude certain classes from the code coverage report by adding properties in the pipeline_config.yml as shown in Listing 12.5.

```
s4SdkQualityChecks:
  jacocoExcludes:
    - 'com/yourCompany/generated/DataModel.class'
```

Listing 12.5 Adding Properties in pipeline_config.yml

The list of exception classes should be expressed in the Ant style pattern (*https://ant.apache.org/manual/dirtasks.html*). This option should only be used for generated code that we don't need to test. However, we recommend using this functionality cautiously because you should always consider adding more tests instead of using exclusions.

To demonstrate how the CD pipeline behaves if the code coverage is below a certain threshold, let's simply ignore the `AddressServletTest` of the address manager example application. As a result, the console output shown in Listing 12.6 illustrates a situation when the build fails due to a low code coverage.

```
[JaCoCo plugin] Health thresholds: JacocoHealthReportThresholds [minClass=
0, maxClass=0, minMethod=0, maxMethod=0, minLine=65, maxLine=70, minBranch=
0, maxBranch=0, minInstrction=0, maxInstraction=0, minComplexity=
0, maxComplexity=0]
[JaCoCo plugin] Apply Min/Max thresholds result: FAILURE
```

Listing 12.6 Console Showing the Health Status Threshold

So far, the CD pipeline checks the line coverage only.

- When line coverage ≥ 70%, the build status is "SUCCESS."
- When line coverage < 65%, the build status is "FAILURE."
- When line coverage is between 65% (inclusive) and 70% (exclusive), the build status is marked as "UNSTABLE."

Therefore, to fix the Jenkins build, we'll have to implement additional tests to achieve at least 70% line coverage using unit or integration tests. Please note that the thresholds mentioned in this subsection are not configurable.

12.3.3 End-to-End Tests

In Chapter 9, we learned that end-to-end tests can ensure that all parts of our application from the user interface to dependent systems in the backend work together in the intended way. Usually, these tests are executed against a running version of the application in an environment similar to the production deployment. For side-by-side extensions built on SAP Cloud Platform, the application is deployed into a test subaccount. Afterwards, the test framework starts a browser and navigates through the application's user interface.

Many test frameworks execute these kinds of tests, for example, nightwatch-cucumber (*http://tiny.cc/nw-cucumber*). The CD pipeline makes no assumption about any specific end-to-end testing frameworks. Instead, it just uses the script functionality of the node package manager (*npm*) as an interface to trigger the execution. We may create a package.json in the root folder of our project sources and define a block called `scripts` as shown in Listing 12.7. In this example, the script starts the test framework nightwatch.

```
...
  scripts": {
    "ci-e2e": "cd e2e-tests && nightwatch --skiptags=ignore"
  },
...
```

Listing 12.7 Example package.json for Running End-to-End Tests with Nightwatch

The pipeline expects that a script called `ci-e2e` exists, which starts the execution of the end-to-end tests using your preferred testing framework. The following *npm* command will start the tests:

```
npm run ci-e2e -- --launchUrl=https://url-to-my-app.com
```

The URL to the deployed application is injected over the parameter called `launchUrl`. If you also need credentials to log in to a secured application, these credentials are injected as environment variables. You can read the variables called `e2e_username` and `e2e_password` and pass the values to the application. Furthermore, the CD pipeline expects to store test results in the cucumber format in the folder *s4hana_pipeline/reports/e2e*. An example configuration for nightwatch-cucumber is shown in Listing 12.8. This configuration stores the launch URL and the credentials injected as parameters or environment variables in the nightwatch configuration. Furthermore, this code configures the test result output as required by the pipeline.

```
const argv = require("yargs").argv;
require('nightwatch-cucumber')({
  cucumberArgs: [
    ...
    '--format',
    'json:../s4hana_pipeline/reports/e2e/cucumber.json',
    ...
  ]
```

```
})
const options = {
  output_folder: '../s4hana_pipeline/reports/e2e',
  ...
  test_settings: {
    default: {
      launch_url : argv.launchUrl,
      ...
      globals: {
        user: "${e2e_username}",
        pass: "${e2e_password}"
      }
    }
  }
}
module.exports = options;
```

Listing 12.8 Example Configuration of Nightwatch

Now that we've completed configuring the framework, we can implement the tests. Details on how to implement end-to-end tests is beyond the scope of this chapter, but you can read the official nightwatch-cucumber documentation at *http://tiny.cc/nw-cucumber*. Furthermore, some examples of implementing tests with nightwatch can be found at *http://tiny.cc/s4sdk-testing*.

After implementing end-to-end tests, we'll have to configure the CD pipeline so that it first deploys the application and then runs the end-to-end tests with the right credentials against the right application. An example configuration is shown in Listing 12.9. As for the productive deployment in Chapter 11, we'll define, in `cfTargets`, where to deploy the application. Within the section `appUrls`, we'll define a list of URLs and the corresponding credentials to be injected into the test script defined in Listing 12.4.

```
stages:
  endToEndTests:
    appUrls:
      - url: 'https://url-to-my-app.com'
        credentialId: e2e-test-user
    cfTargets:
      - org: 'MyOrg'
        space: 'Test'
```

```
appName: 'exampleapp'
manifest: 'manifest-test.yml'
credentialsId: 'deploy-test'
```

Listing 12.9 Example Configuration for End-to-End Tests Stage

Afterwards, the CD pipeline will run the end-to-end tests and if one of the tests fails, it will fail as well.

We can also use end-to-end tests after the final production deployment. As we learned in Chapter 11, smoke tests after the final deployment check that the application has successfully deployed to production. To run just a subset of these tests, the name of the npm script is called `ci-smoke`. We'll have to register such a script in the package.json. Furthermore, we'll also have to add the section `appUrls` to the configuration of the production deployment in the pipeline_config.yml.

12.3.4 Performance Tests

To provide a responsive user experience, we should consider the following aspects. First, the response time a user experiences after sending a request to our application should not exceed a certain threshold (for example, one second). Second, given the existing infrastructure, our application should be able to serve a certain number of users concurrently. Therefore, performance tests should be executed to identify potential bottlenecks in the system.

Performance tests are simulated test cases that analyze statistics regarding response time as well as scalability and stability. To obtain precise reports, the simulation parameters must reflect the anticipated workload in production regarding the number of active users or the amount of data our system has to process

Making performance tests a part of the CD pipeline can be beneficial because then we can constantly check how changes in the code influence the performance of our application. The CD pipeline supports two different technologies, Apache JMeter and Gatling, which we'll discuss next.

Apache JMeter and Gatling

Apache JMeter (*http://jmeter.apache.org/*) is an open source performance test tool written in Java. This cross-platform tool is highly extensible, configurable, and user-friendly.

Especially if you are new to performance tests or do not want to write performance tests in a programming language, you can choose the GUI mode, where new test plans can be prepared manually and the test script recorder can generate ready-to-use test plans based on chosen templates (B. Erinle, *Performance Testing with JMeter*).

Gatling (*https://gatling.io/*) is another powerful open source load and performance testing tool for web applications. Gatling can simulate at least 1,000 to 2,000 users simultaneously without any problems from our experience, while with Apache JMeter a bottleneck occurs if approximately 400 to 500 users are active at the same time. This difference stems from the different underlying connection strategies. Gatling reuses connections for virtual, sequential users, while Apache JMeter does not (F. Toledo, *Gatling vs. JMeter*). On the other hand, Gatling-related Maven dependencies must be added to the code for writing test plans and generating corresponding reports. In addition, since Gatling test plans are written in the Scala programming language, the Scala Maven plugin has to be configured. For more details, please follow the demo in the next section.

Both JMeter and Gatling can be used in the Performance Tests stage of the CD pipeline. Next, we'll continue using Gatling to visualize the use of performance tests.

Execute Gatling Locally

In this section, we'll demonstrate how to execute Gatling locally with Maven. In our Business Partner Address Manager application, we'll now create a new Maven project for performance tests called `performance-tests`. This individual project should not be referenced as a submodule in the main pom.xml. Our pom.xml of the `performance-tests` project should look similar to Listing 12.10.

```
<dependencies>
    <dependency>
      <groupId>io.gatling.highcharts</groupId>
      <artifactId>gatling-charts-highcharts</artifactId>
      <version>${gatling.version}</version>
      <scope>test</scope>
    </dependency>
    <dependency>
        <groupId>io.gatling</groupId>
        <artifactId>gatling-app</artifactId>
        <version>${gatling.version}</version>
        <scope>test</scope>
```

```
    </dependency>
</dependencies>
...
<build>
    <plugins>
      <plugin>
        <groupId>net.alchim31.maven</groupId>
        <artifactId>scala-maven-plugin</artifactId>
        <version>${scala-maven-plugin.version}</version>
      </plugin>
      <plugin>
        <groupId>io.gatling</groupId>
        <artifactId>gatling-maven-plugin</artifactId>
        <version>${gatling-plugin.version}</version>
      </plugin>
    </plugins>
</build>
```

Listing 12.10 Gatling Dependencies and Plugins Configured in pom.xml

Then, we'll have to add a basic test, as shown in Listing 12.11, that measures performance when multiple users access our Business Partner Address Manager application at the same time. The corresponding test in Scala programming language is shown in Listing 12.11.

```
class RecordedSimulation extends Simulation {
  val httpProtocol = http.baseURL("https://yourUrl.com") ↩
    .inferHtmlResources(WhiteList(), BlackList())
  val headers = ...
  val headers = ...
  val scn = scenario("scenario").exec(http("home").get("/") ↩
        .headers(headers).check(status.not(404), status.not(500)))
  setUp(scn.inject(atOnceUsers(10)).protocols(httpProtocol))
}
```

Listing 12.11 A Gatling Test Plan Written in Scala Injecting 10 Users at Once

Now, we can run Gatling tests via the following command inside the *performance-tests* directory of the Maven project:

```
mvn clean gatling:execute
```

Gatling as Part of the CD Pipeline

To activate Gatling tests in the CD pipeline, we'll have to enable them using a feature toggle via the pipeline-config.yml file, as shown in Listing 12.12.

```
#Steps Specific Configuration
steps:
  checkGatling:
    enabled: True
```

Listing 12.12 Configure Gatling Performance Tests

Furthermore, we'll have to add the deployment configuration to the stage configuration named `performanceTests`. The syntax is the same as for deploying end-to-end tests and for productive deployment.

We can check out the initial test results from the Jenkins log and the Gatling dashboard of your Jenkins server, as shown in Figure 12.10. You can inspect response time statistics in bar charts, successful request rates in pie charts, and the number of requests/responses per second.

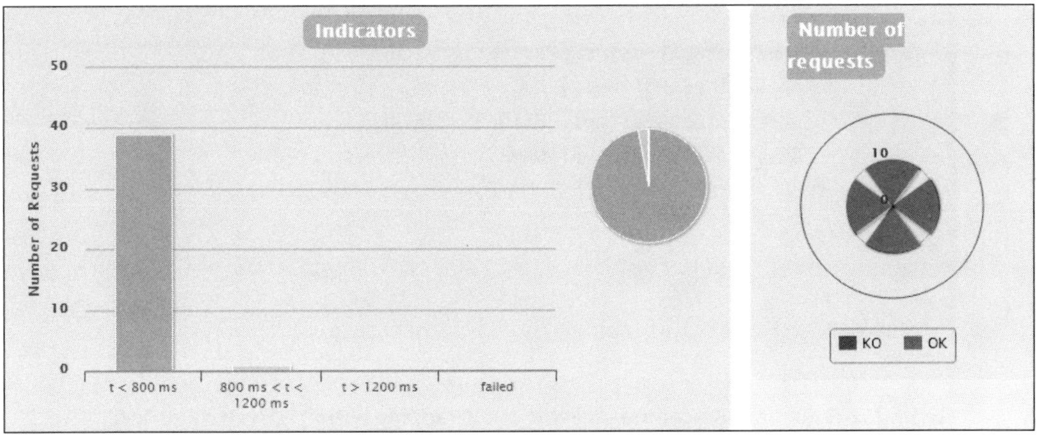

Figure 12.10 Example Gatling Dashboard with Response Time Distribution and Request Success Rates

12.4 SAP Cloud Quality Checks

To build your extension application on the SAP Cloud Platform with high quality, communication to third-party services must be taken into consideration. First, as discussed in Chapter 4, the SAP S/4HANA Cloud SDK builds upon libraries such as Hystrix to help your multitenancy application achieve resilience on an application level. The CD pipeline helps identify any nonresilient calls so that they can be corrected and isolated before being deployed into production. Second, unstable APIs may affect your productive application unintentionally at runtime when API contracts change without prior notice. The CD pipeline helps identify unstable APIs, that is, APIs from SAP that are not released as part of the public SAP API Business Hub.

12.4.1 Hystrix Checks

In this section, we'll demonstrate how the CD pipeline ensures that all remote procedure calls are sufficiently wrapped into Hystrix commands to keep your application resilient.

For instance, we may add a new servlet class containing the method shown in Listing 12.13 to our Business Partner Address Manager application. We'll reuse the same code block example as discussed in Chapter 4 before we introduced Hystrix.

```
protected void doGet(final HttpServletRequest request,
...
    result = new DefaultBusinessPartnerService()
        .getAllBusinessPartner()
        .select(BusinessPartner.BUSINESS_PARTNER,
            BusinessPartner.LAST_NAME,
            BusinessPartner.FIRST_NAME)
        ...
        .execute();
...
  response.getWriter().write(new Gson().toJson(result));
}
```

Listing 12.13 Remote Procedure Call without Wrapping within a Hystrix Context

As explained earlier in this section, the CD pipeline collects information about calls to third-party systems while executing tests and evaluating the results in the *Quality Checks* stage. Consequently, the pipeline will recognize that we forgot to use Hystrix and fails with the following error message:

```
ERROR: Your project accesses downstream system in a non-resilient manner:
  - HTTP access to 'https://xxx/business-partners' outside of Hystrix context
```

12.4.2 Stable ERP API Checks

In this section, we'll demonstrate how the CD pipeline behaves when we call a nonpublic API. For illustration purposes, let's assume that we are about to create a new class to call the private, nonreleased OData service *FCO_PI_COST_CENTER_PRIVATE* (Listing 12.14).

```
@Override
protected List<YourDataModel> run() throws Exception
{
    ODataQueryBuilder
        .withEntity("/sap/FCO_PI_COST_CENTER_PRIVATE",
                    "Collection")
        .execute();
}
```

Listing 12.14 Calling a Nonpublic API of SAP S/4HANA

Consequently, the CD pipeline will fail to pass the Quality Checks stage as shown:

```
ERROR: Your project uses non-official OData services: [FCO_PI_COST_CENTER_PRIVATE]
```

However, this mechanism applies to SAP S/4HANA systems only. If your application requires calls to other systems such as SAP SuccessFactors, you can introduce a whitelist of non-ERP destinations to the CD pipeline to turn off the check. To create this whitelist, you'll have to introduce the following property into the pipeline_config.yml:

```
s4SdkQualityChecks:
  nonErpDestinations:
    - yourDestination
```

To understand which APIs are safe to access, we recommend checking out the SAP API Business Hub at *https://api.sap.com* or using the virtual data model classes for Java as discussed in Chapter 4.

12.5 Scaling Quality Assurance with Distributed Builds

Checking all the qualities described in this chapter may become expensive; integration or performance tests may especially demand significant computing resources. Furthermore, deployments of applications to the SAP Cloud Platform and the end-to-end tests afterwards may consume a considerable amount of time. In this section, we'll show you how to scale the pipeline whenever we need to handle more workload.

12.5.1 Scaling the Build Pipeline

In Chapter 10, we learned that fast feedback is important in DevOps. The speed of the build pipeline has a direct impact on the productivity of teams. Especially in working modes using pull requests, developers usually commit their code to a version control system (VCS) and then wait until the pipeline has executed all quality checks. If these checks are slow, developers may not receive timely feedback and lose focus. As a consequence, changes won't be merged into the main code often, merge conflicts will occur more frequently, and the overall flow will start to break down.

To speed up the pipeline, many stages within the CD pipeline are already parallelized. For example, integration tests run in parallel to each other. Deployments for multiple targets and the execution of end-to-end tests for each target can be executed in parallel. However, to enable running multiple tests at the same time, the underlying infrastructure should scale.

Vertically scaling up a single server, that is, adding more processing units, might help to a certain extent. Fortunately, Jenkins also supports horizontal scaling, that is, adding more dedicated servers (agents) and distributing the workload across these agents accordingly. You can find additional documentation for this concept at *http://tiny.cc/jenkins-distribute*.

Our installation of Jenkins runs a *master node*, which by default runs everything. However, we can also add additional *agents*. Agents can take over certain tasks, for example, parts of the build pipeline, and run them on a separate server. Thus, we can use the Jenkins instance to run many projects or handle larger workloads.

The CD pipeline supports parallelization and distributed builds. In the next section, we'll learn how to set up the infrastructure for that and how to configure the CD pipeline correspondingly.

12.5.2 Distributed Builds with the CX-Server

In this section, we'll show how to prepare a new host to run an agent. We'll show how to connect an agent to the Jenkins master node and how to run a certain pipeline stage on this particular agent. Technically, for distributed builds, the Jenkins master node connects over *ssh* to another host and executes a Java command to start an agent over this channel. However, this flow is usually hidden from users.

Requirements

To add an agent to the Jenkins master node, we must fulfill the following requirements, which are similar to the requirements for the Jenkins master node:

- Access to a new server running on Linux
- Docker installed on this server
- The ability for the Jenkins master node to connect to the new server over *ssh*

We explained the first two requirements already in Chapter 11. Please also examine the documentation of your local infrastructure provider for further details on getting a new Linux server. We also learned that, in order to execute Docker images, the user needs to be in the group `docker`. In the following text, we'll call this user the "Docker user."

To fulfill the third requirement, we'll connect to the server running the Jenkins master first. Jenkins runs in the container called `s4sdk-jenkins-master`. To tap into this container, we'll execute the following command:


```
docker exec -it s4sdk-jenkins-master bash
```

Second, we'll generate a new public key and copy the content of the public key from the file *id_rsa.pub*:

```
mkdir ~/.ssh && chmod 700 ~/.ssh && ssh-keygen -t rsa
cat ~/.ssh/id_rsa.pub
```

Finally, we'll log into the new server using the Docker user and add the output of the previous command to the file *~/.ssh/authorized_keys*.

To test that everything works, we'll go back into the `s4sdk-jenkins-master` container on the master host and try to connect to our new server using *ssh*:

```
ssh <docker-user>@<host/ip>
```

If asked, we can also add the server's fingerprint to the list of known hosts. As a result, we can now log into the agent without a password.

Adding Agents to the CD Pipeline

Having set up the agent, we'll also have to add the agent to the CD pipeline.

From Jenkins home screen, go to **Manage Jenkins** on the left and select **Manage Nodes**. Click on **New Node** on the left to create a new agent, as shown in Figure 12.11. A new agent should be a **Permanent Agent**. Enter a name that can be used later to assign a particular stage to the agent and confirm by clicking **OK**.

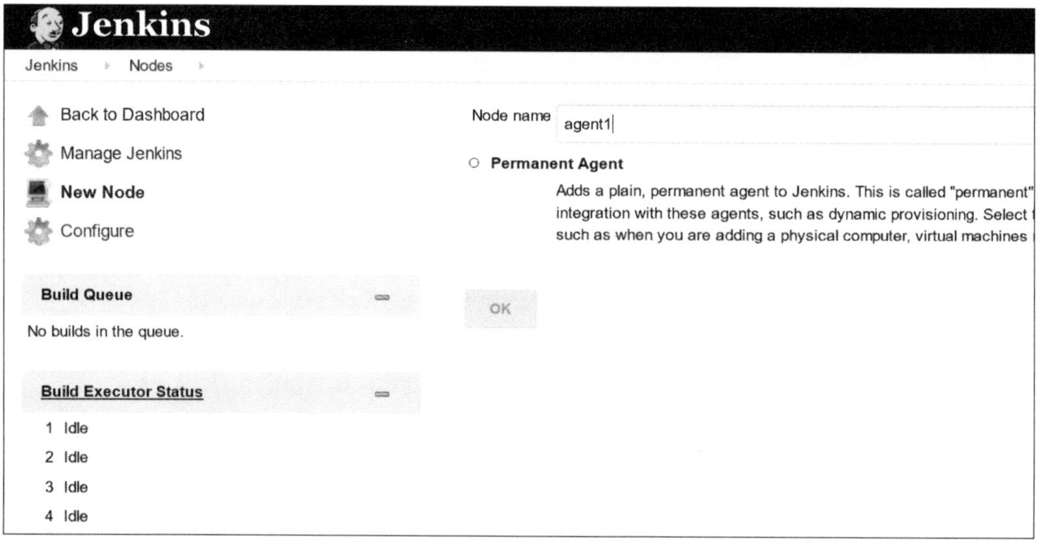

Figure 12.11 New Agents Created as Permanent Agent with a Node Name

Second, we'll have to configure the agent. Figure 12.12 shows an example configuration for a new agent. The agent is launched on the new host inside a Docker container. Therefore, we don't have to install any dependency the pipeline requires. A small script added to the Jenkins master Docker container will start the agent for us. To execute this script, we'll select **Launch agent via execution of command on the master** as the launch method and use the following template as the launch command:

```
./var/jenkins_home/launch-s4sdk-agent.sh <user> <host> [image]
```

Replace the placeholders `user`, `host`, and `image` with the corresponding values. The parameter `host` refers to address of our newly created agent. The parameter `user` references the Docker user on the agent. Optionally, you can also provide your own Docker image, if you require infrastructure-dependent configurations, such as the installation of certificates. The script will use these parameters to connect to the new server and spawn a new Jenkins agent inside a Docker image.

As for the Jenkins master, the agents also store temporary data such as sources, logs, or build artifacts in a local directory. Of course, agents require file access permissions to modify this folder. In the Docker container used for the agents, a folder already exists with the correct access permissions. As shown in Figure 12.12, we just have to configure the folder named */var/jenkins_home* as the **Remote root directory**.

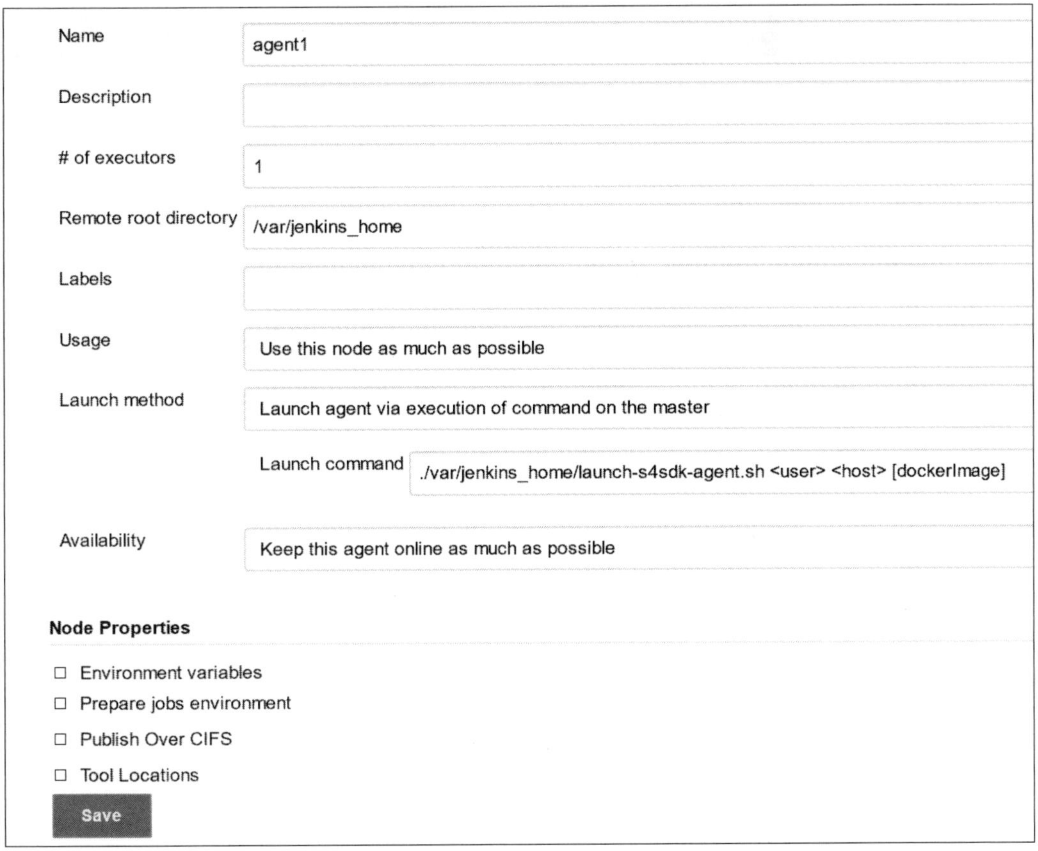

Figure 12.12 Configuring a New Agent from Jenkins

Assigning Pipeline Stages to Agents

Jenkins always tries to build the project on the same agent from the last build. However, in certain use cases, selecting servers might make sense, for example, to use a server with more CPUs only for certain tasks, such as expensive integration tests. To declare that an agent is only assigned by the master if explicitly specified, we'll change the configuration, as shown in Figure 12.12, to **Only build jobs with label expressions matching this node**.

In addition, the following configuration must be made in the pipeline_config.yml to run integration tests only on the agent we just created.

```
stages:
    integrationTests:
        node: 'agent1'
```

To validate that the build is executed in the correct agent, watch the **Build Executor Status** on the left side of the main Jenkins dashboard.

12.6 Summary

In this chapter, we introduced several characteristics of software quality, such as functionality, reliability, or maintainability. We presented how software quality can be ensured in general and how some tools, such as static code checks and performance tests, are integrated into the CD pipeline. Furthermore, we also introduced additional cloud quality checks designed specifically for extensions built with the SAP S/4HANA Cloud SDK. We demonstrated how these checks ensure your application is resilient and only relies on stable SAP S/4HANA APIs. Finally, we learned that the speed of the build pipeline is important for the productivity of teams. We demonstrated how parallelization and scaling with distributed builds can decrease build times even for complex automated quality assurance processes.

Chapter 13
Cloud Operations

This chapter complements the design-time parts of the previous chapter by presenting runtime quality aspects as provided by the SAP S/4HANA Cloud SDK and the SAP Cloud Platform. We'll touch on how to log and trace end-to-end across SAP Cloud Platform by using logging methods provided by the SDK based on the logging infrastructure. In addition, the chapter introduces how to conduct performance and health monitoring to ensure a smooth operational experience. Finally, we'll share best practices, mitigation strategies, and scaling considerations in conjunction with DevOps principles.

In Chapter 10, we learned that the principle of feedback is a core aspect of DevOps theory. Errors should be discovered early before they can cause any serious damage. This knowledge should be propagated back to earlier stages and solved there. However, even if you've created a great build pipeline and checked design-time aspects, the application may still break in the production enviroment. Thus, during operations of cloud software, we must gather telemetry data to detect malfunctional system states early. Furthermore, telemetry data may help you gain the knowledge to identify root causes and to set up mechanisms to solve and prevent these issues in the future. Under telemetry data, we include logging as well as metrics that provide insights into runtime aspects of applications. In this chapter, we'll show you how to gather telemetry data on the SAP Cloud Platform with the help of the SAP S/4HANA Cloud SDK and other tools. We also show you how to use telemetry to scale your application.

13.1 Logging and Tracing

The first type of telemetry data that we'll cover is logging. In Chapter 10, we introduced logging as the concept of storing textual information about relevant events in the context of executing applications.

We can distinguish between two types of events relevant for logging. This chapter covers events that help you understand an application internally and identify root causes of malfunctions. Typical examples are incoming requests, status codes, and exceptions in the application. In this section, we'll explain how to create and analyze these logs. The other type of event is for audit-relevant events. Typical examples include access to and changes of sensitive data or changes to critical application settings. These events are not covered by this chapter.

Although both types of event seem to be quite similar, their requirements, in terms of how the logging infrastructure handles these events, is quite different. A logger logging application internals must be fast because logging these events should not decrease application performance. In the best case, the logs are written asynchronously. The logger does not have to be reliable. Missing a few log entries is not a serious problem. Furthermore, these logs are only valuable while investigating recent problems and can be deleted after some time. For audit logs, however, the requirements are different. For legal reasons, these logs have to be retained longer. Furthermore, the logger must be reliable and safe. Thus, fulfilling these requirements with different tools makes sense.

In this section, we'll learn how to use the logging service in the SAP Cloud Platform, together with the SAP S/4HANA Cloud SDK, to produce and analyze logs. Both environments of the SAP Cloud Platform—Neo and Cloud Foundry—offer the ability to record and show logs directly for each service. However, because Cloud Foundry encourages a microservice architecture, it uses the open source tool *Elastic Stack* (*https://www.elastic.co*) as the central log aggregator. The tool collects logs from multiple services and enables analyzing these logs in one place using *Kibana*, the log analyzer of Elastic Stack. Therefore, we'll focus on producing and analyzing logs in the Cloud Foundry environment in this chapter.

Logging with a central logging service consists of two steps. First, the application or each individual microservice provides log messages with a certain structure. Second, a central log service collects the logs and makes them available in Kibana.

We'll use our Business Partner Address Manager application to illustrate these steps. In Chapter 4, we implemented the Java-based microservice of the application in such a way that it logs events like exceptions using the `CloudLoggerFactory` as shown in the following:

```
private static final Logger logger = CloudLoggerFactory ↩
    .getLogger(BusinessPartnerServlet.class);
```

Classical logs are often represented as plain text files. A stack trace, for example, is often distributed over multiple lines in the log file. However, to know which lines belong together or to build metrics based on the log, a best practice is to create structured log outputs. SAP offers dependencies, as shown in Listing 13.1, that may be added to your microservice to produce logs in the required JSON structure. We'll add these dependencies to *application/pom.xml*.

```
<!-- Cf logging -->
<dependency>
    <groupId>com.sap.hcp.cf.logging</groupId>
    <artifactId>cf-java-logging-support-logback</artifactId>
    <version>2.0.10</version>
</dependency>

<dependency>
    <groupId>ch.qos.logback</groupId>
    <artifactId>logback-classic</artifactId>
    <version>1.1.11</version>
</dependency>
```

Listing 13.1 SAP-Provided Logger Implementation Based on Logback

The logger implementation is based on logback (*https://logback.qos.ch/*), which provides additional configuration possibilities. We'll configure logback to use an encoder to produce log outputs in the required format. To use the SAP-specific encoder, we'll create the file *application/src/main/resources/logback.xml* with the content shown in Listing 13.2.

```
<configuration debug="false" scan="false">
  <appender name="STDOUT-JSON" ↩
      class="ch.qos.logback.core.ConsoleAppender">
    <encoder ↩
        class="com.sap.hcp.cf.logback.encoder.JsonEncoder"/>
  </appender>
  <root level="${LOG_ROOT_LEVEL:-WARN}">
    <appender-ref ref="STDOUT-JSON" />
  </root>
</configuration>
```

Listing 13.2 Formatter Configuration for SAP-Specific Log Encoding

Afterwards, the microservice produces log outputs in the required format, and we'll use the new output to deploy the microservice to the SAP Cloud Platform. The second step is to configure and use a logging service that collects all logs centrally, which can be achieved by a service available in SAP Cloud Platform. As done already multiple times in this book (see Chapter 5 and Chapter 6), we first must create an instance of this service in our SAP Cloud Platform space and then bind the service to our microservice.

In Chapter 11, we configured a pipeline that deploys our microservice into a public space on SAP Cloud Platform (e.g., *http://hanatrial.ondemand.com*). In this space, we'll create a new instance of the logging service, which can be done in two ways: Either we'll use the `cf create-service` command or the SAP Cloud Platform cockpit. In this chapter, we'll focus on the second approach.

To create a new logging service instance, open the SAP Cloud Platform cockpit and navigate to **Services • Service Marketplace** of our subaccount's space where the application is already deployed. We'll select the **application-logs** service from the available services, as shown in Figure 13.1, and enter an instance name (for example, "log-service") in the creation dialog, as shown in Figure 13.2.

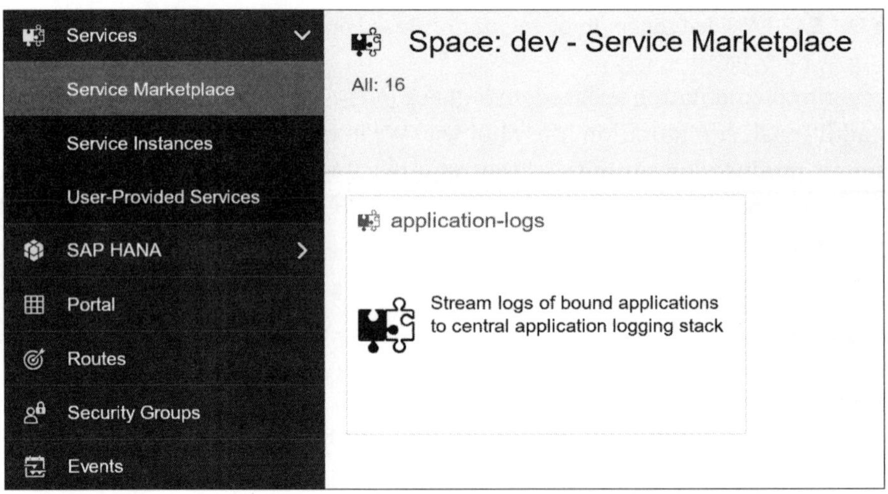

Figure 13.1 Choosing the Logging Services in SAP Cloud Platform

As shown in Figure 13.2, we can also choose the application to which the service should be bound. Binding a service means that configuration parameters, such as URLs and credentials, are made available in the environment variables of the application. However, as described in Chapter 10, a best practice is to store configuration as code in your repository. Therefore, we recommend always configuring bindings over the manifest.yml file of your application. The file manifest.yml is the deployment descriptor, as we discussed in Chapter 4.

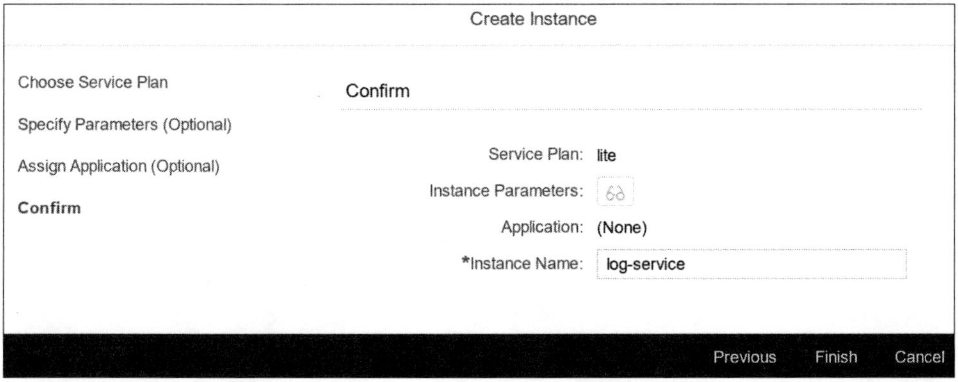

Figure 13.2 Creating a New Service Instance of the Logging Service

To bind our Business Partner Address Manager application backend microservice to the logging service, we'll add the lines shown in Listing 13.3 to the application definition in manifest.yml.

```
services:
  ...
  - log-service
```

Listing 13.3 Adding the Log Service Instance to the Deployment Descriptor

After committing the changes to our version control system (VCS), the pipeline deploys the application and triggers the service bindings. To view the logs, open, for example, *https://logs.cf.eu10.hana.ondemand.com* and enter your credentials. For the domain, you may use the same base domain to which the application has been deployed.

Afterwards, open the Kibana user interface, which has some predefined dashboards but you can even create your own. An example dashboard is shown in Figure 13.3, which consists of two basic elements: lists showing different events, such as requests to the application, and metrics aggregating and visualizing sets of events in diagrams such as pie charts. We can customize both types of dashboard elements. For event lists, we can define a filter query. For aggregations, we can define inputs, dimensions, and aggregation functions. In our example dashboard, we added a pie chart showing the distribution of log levels. Furthermore, a list of logs shows the log events for our Business Partner Address Manager application. For each log entry, we can analyze the error message and the potential stack trace.

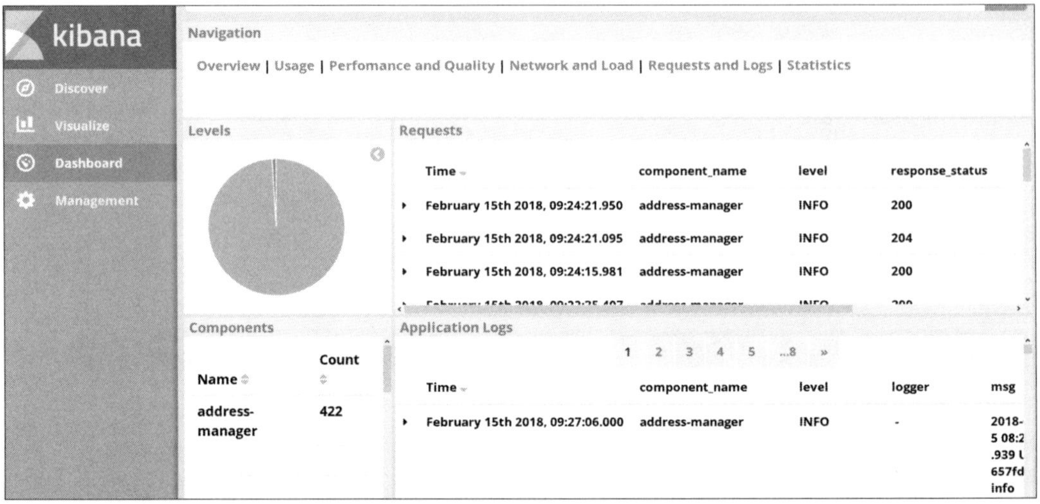

Figure 13.3 Customized Kibana Dashboard Showing Requests, Logs, and the Amount of Logged Errors

If users are affected by an error, you should inform them about what went wrong. Showing the user an error message indicating want went wrong and how the problem effects the user's workflow is invaluable. We recommend even providing a reference ID that users can provide in a bug report. The reference number should also be written into the log file. With the reference number, you can correlate the bug report and detailed error descriptions including all aspects you might need to investigate further.

13.2 Application Health Monitoring

Application metrics are the second type of telemetry data. In Chapter 10, we learned how metrics can help you measure and classify the health state of an application. A good health state means that the application and all its dependencies are available and behave in the expected way. Furthermore, the performance of the application should be within an acceptable range.

In this section, we'll first learn a manual approach to expose and monitor these metrics. Then, we'll introduce the tool *Dynatrace*, which automatically extracts and monitors some metrics. Dynatrace detects anomalies in these metrics, alerts administrators if problems arise, and tries to analyze root causes.

13.2.1 Health Status Endpoint

Let's consider a manual approach first. We'll instruct the application to collect certain metrics and execute some health checks. Application developers know best which components and dependencies are relevant and how they communicate with each other. Thus, a developer can use this information to provide an HTTP endpoint, which executes several checks and reports a health status. This approach uses what's called the *health endpoint*.

For example, Listing 13.4 shows a simple health endpoint that returns the status code 200 if the application is able to talk to the downstream SAP S/4HANA system. This code tries to get all business partners from an ERP system. The `GetAllBusinessPartnersCommand` will throw an exception if an issue arises in the communication with the ERP system. We'll report error code 500 as an indicator of poor health. Please note that this is just an example, and a real implementation can be improved by decreasing the amount of requested data, adding validations on the result of the command, or adding information about the failing dependency to the response.


```
@WebServlet("/api/health")
public class HealthServlet extends HttpServlet
{
  private static final long serialVersionUID = 1L;
  private final BusinessPartnerService service = new ↩
      DefaultBusinessPartnerService();

  @Override
  protected void doGet(HttpServletRequest req, ↩
        HttpServletResponse resp) ↩
        throws ServletException, IOException {
    try {
     new GetAllBusinessPartnersCommand(service).execute();
    }
    catch (Exception ex) {
      resp.setStatus( ↩
```

```
                HttpServletResponse.SC_INTERNAL_SERVER_ERROR);
            return;
        }
        resp.setStatus(HttpServletResponse.SC_OK);
    }
}
```

Listing 13.4 Simple Health Endpoint Checking the Connectivity to an SAP S/4HANA System

Likewise, we can also check other systems. To test database connections, for example, we can query a dummy database table that does not impact the performance of the database. Usually, other dependent systems offer similar APIs to check availability during runtime.

Finally, we can use standard tools, such as *Pingdom*, or write a script to visit our endpoint at certain time intervals. We can set up alerts to inform us if the health endpoint reports a bad status.

13.2.2 Application Monitoring with Dynatrace

So far, we've learned how to manually instruct an application to execute checks against dependent systems of the application. We could also extend the application to collect additional metrics, such as the response times for requests. In our health endpoint, we'll define time constraints based on which metrics determine whether the application is healthy.

However, collecting all these metrics can be cumbersome and further violates the principle of the separation of concerns. Building too many monitoring capabilities into the application makes the application more complex and distracts focus from its business value. A tool that collects the relevant metrics automatically without having to change the application code would be better.

In this section, we'll use Dynatrace as an example to do just that. Dynatrace collects metrics and determines the application's health. Dynatrace installs an agent into the container on Cloud Foundry and then tries to monitor different levels of the microservice, such as the container environment or the Java process. Thus, Dynatrace collects general metrics about the container, such as memory or CPU consumption, but it can also trace the execution of Java programs or monitor incoming and outgoing requests. Other tools can be used, and you should decide which tools fit your needs and your personal experience best.

Dynatrace License

Dynatrace is a full stack, automated monitoring tool by Dynatrace, LLC. To use Dynatrace, you'll need a license. In some license packages for SAP Cloud Platform, such as the multicloud starter pack, the developer edition of Dynatrace is already included (*http://tiny.cc/starter-packs*).

Setting Up Dynatrace

Dynatrace is one tool already integrated with the SAP Cloud Platform via the Java or Node.js community or SAP buildpacks. Therefore, we only need to configure the agent to connect to the server where we collect all metrics. On Cloud Foundry, we'll set up a user-provided service that is represented by configuration properties, such as credentials or URLs. In the SAP Cloud Platform cockpit, create a new instance in the **User-Provided Services** view under **Services**. Give the instance a name and enter the connection details as described in the Dynatrace documentation (*http://tiny.cc/cf-monitoring*). As standard services available in the marketplace on SAP Cloud Platform, user-provided services can be bound to applications, which makes the configuration available to the application via environment variables.

Afterwards, the Dynatrace agent uses the configuration injected over the user-provided service to connect to the Dynatrace server. Metrics in the application will be collected and then displayed in the Dynatrace dashboard. In the following subsections, we'll show you some examples of how to use Dynatrace to monitor and analyze these metrics.

Automatic Problem Detection and Analysis by Metrics Monitoring

Problems during the execution of applications can be characterized as unexpected behaviors or as behaviors that deviate from past behavior starting at a specific point in time. To detect problems automatically, a monitoring tool tracks behavior over time, builds a model that represents the usual behavior, and sends an alert if behavior deviates from this model.

However, metrics can also help identify root causes. Thus, in a complex scenario with multiple microservices and dependent downstream systems, a monitoring tool would collect metrics for all the individual services and try to correlate these metrics with each other. By also tracing the communication flow between microservices, the tool can build a communication model and judge whether an issue in one microservice is based on an issue in another microservice.

Let's illustrate this approach using Dynatrace as an example. As stated earlier in this section, a key element is to detect all the individual microservices and derive a communication model between the microservices. Dynatrace records requests between the components and models the communication flow, as shown in Figure 13.4. For all requests and API endpoints, Dynatrace collects metrics about the response times and response code types. With these metrics, Dynatrace can build a model that describes the usual behavior and detect, for example, performance degradation.

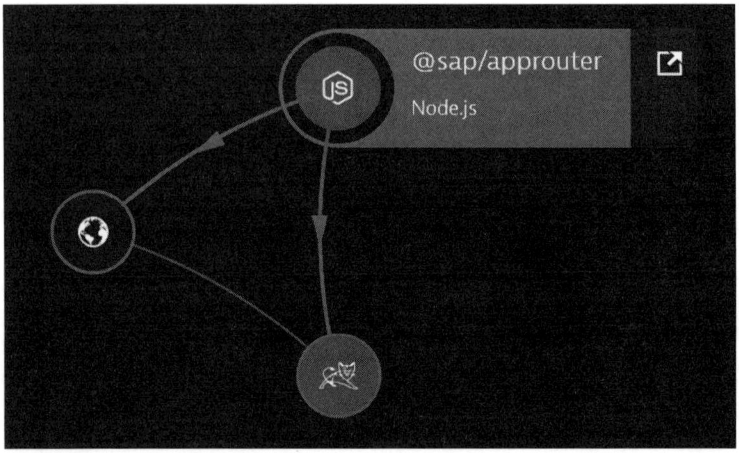

Figure 13.4 Example Communcation Flow Model in Dynatrace Using the AppRouter and the Business Partner Adress Manager Application

Let's conduct an experiment to demonstrate this functionality for our Business Partner Address Manager application. Our setup contains the application router (AppRouter) introduced in Chapter 5, which is the central entry point to our application and is responsible for authentication. The AppRouter dispatches all incoming user requests as a reverse proxy to the Business Partner Address Manager microservice, as shown in Figure 13.4.

Let's assume that we conducted some local testing in our microservice and disabled the caching mechanism of the `GetAllBusinessPartnersCommand` command. Unfortunately, we pushed our results into version control without reenabling the caching again, and the code reviewer didn't notice the change either. Furthermore, performance tests have not been implemented yet. Otherwise, these tests might have detected the degradation in application performance. Thus, the change is deployed into production. Let's assume further, that the network connection to the SAP S/4HANA system is slow.

After a few minutes, we get an alert from Dynatrace indicating that there is a performance degradation, as shown in Figure 13.5. The performance is below the autodetected baseline of the AppRouter. Notice that Dynatrace detected the performance degradation in the Business Partner Address Manager microservice as the potential root cause.

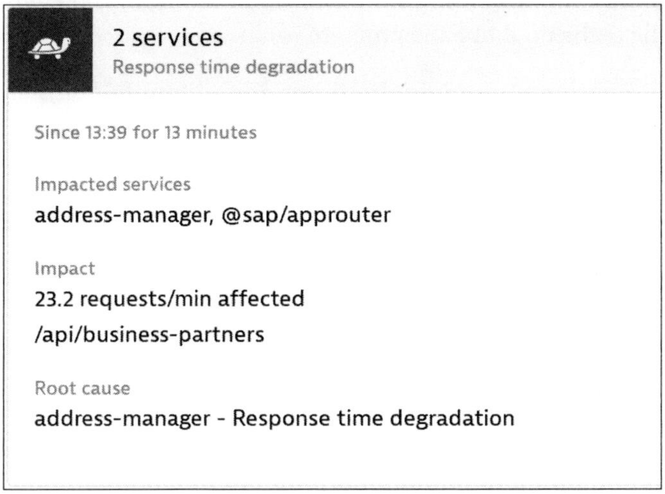

Figure 13.5 Dynatrace Showing an Performance Issue in the Endpoint /api/business-partners

Let's analyze this problem further. In Dynatrace, we can inspect the response time degradation, as shown in Figure 13.6. Dynatrace indicates that the issue is caused by a downstream component. Notice that, together with the performance of the AppRouter, the performance of calls to the business partner endpoint in our Business Partner Address Manager application has decreased.

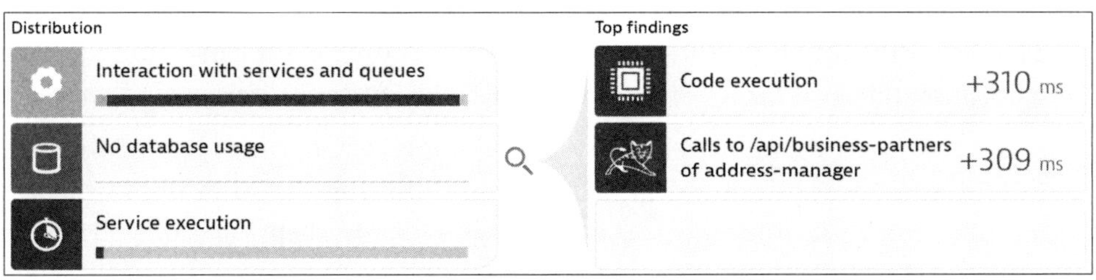

Figure 13.6 Analyzing Performance Degradation in the AppRouter and the Address Manager Microservice

Thus, we'll need to analyze the time hotspots in this endpoint. We can open the same analysis tool for our Business Partner Address Manager application as before. You'll see that a considerable amount of time spent is for calls to the SAP S/4HANA system. By clicking on this finding, another screen will open showing statistics on these calls, as shown in Figure 13.7. Notice that 100% of the calls to the business partner endpoint trigger a call to the SAP S/4HANA system, which is an increase of 100%—a good indication that an issue with the cache might be the problem.

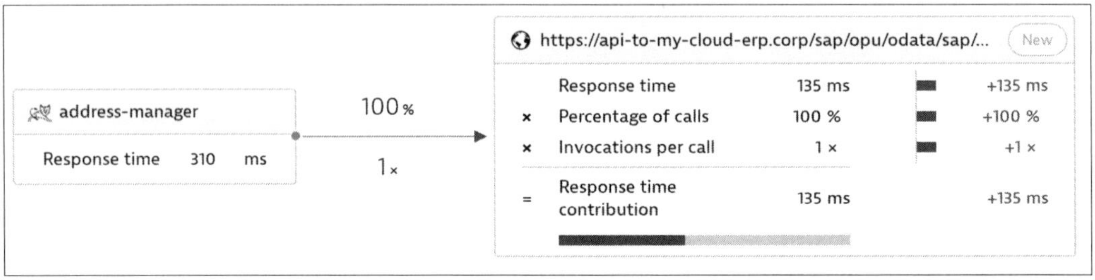

Figure 13.7 Statistic on Calls to the SAP S/4HANA System

Using these tools, we can get automatic alerts whenever performance degradations. Furthermore, monitoring tools such as Dynatrace can help you find and solve root causes quickly.

Adding Additional Metrics with JMX

Not all metrics are collected automatically by Dynatrace. Let's say we want to create our own application-specific metrics. A standard you can leverage for custom metrics is Java Management Extensions (JMX). JMX is a standard specification to manage applications and expose metrics in the Java world. To implement a JMX metric, simply create an interface and a plain old Java object (POJO) with several getters. You'll need to follow certain naming conventions for the interface and the class. Finally, you'll register the implementation in a JMX server. More details can be found in the Java documentation at *https://docs.oracle.com/javase/tutorial/jmx/index.html*.

The SAP S/4HANA Cloud SDK already offers some JMX features out of the box. The `CloudLogger` we introduced in Chapter 4 and Chapter 12, for example, records exceptions in the `ExceptionMonitor` bean. Whenever an exception is logged via the `CloudLogger`, the `ExceptionMonitor` records this exception. Furthermore, the `ExceptionMonitor` can be registered in the JMX server. Thus, we can retrieve the collected metrics via JMX at runtime. The `ExceptionMonitor` exposes several metrics such as the metric `TotalNumberOfExceptionsLast01h`. This metric indicates the number of exceptions logged during the last hour. The SAP S/4HANA Cloud SDK also exposes other JMX metrics. The class `CacheMonitor` monitors the size of the caches and statistics about their access. The class `ErpEndpointMonitor` collects statistics about the communication with the SAP S/4HANA systems.

Dynatrace only displays some standard metrics by default. All other JMX metrics have to be manually added via the **Monitored technologies** section of the Dynatrace settings. You'll have to upload a JSON file declaring which JMX metric to use as a source and declaring how to aggregate the metrics as a chart. The documentation for structuring the JSON file can be found at *https://github.com/dynatrace-innovation-lab/JMX-Extensions*. Listing 13.5 shows an exemplary source definition in JSON that uses the metrics from the `ExceptionMonitor`.

```
"source": {
  "domain":"com.sap.cloud.sdk.cloudplatform.monitoring",
  "keyProperties": {
    "name": "ExceptionMonitor"
  },
  "attribute": "TotalNumberOfExceptionsLast01h"
}
```

Listing 13.5 Adding the ExceptionMonitor from the SAP S/4HANA Cloud SDK to Dynatrace's JMX Plugin Definition

Now, you can click on the process serving your application in Dynatrace and select **Further Details**. You'll find a tab representing the chart we just configured, as shown in Figure 13.8.

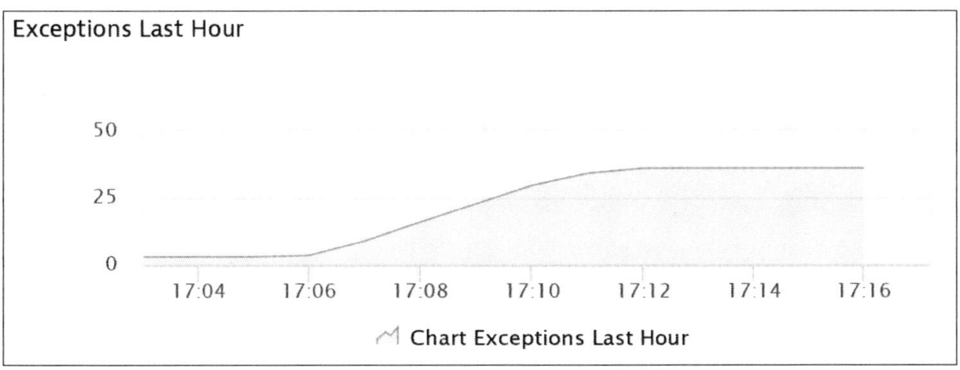

Figure 13.8 Dynatrace Showing JMX Metric of the ExceptionMonitor

13.3 Capacity Planning and Scaling of Cloud Infrastructures

Whenever you're starting with a new application or a new microservice, an important question is to determine the amount of resources the application requires. This question has two dimensions. First, how many resources will the application/microservice need to serve all requests while still offering an acceptable user experience? Second, what will be the resulting operational costs, and how will they influence the price of the application? In this section, we'll introduce some ways to calculate capacity requirements and show you how to collect the metrics required for adjusting scaling parameters in SAP Cloud Platform.

Two primary ways for capacity planning exist (M. Julian, *Practical Monitoring*). The first is to work backwards starting with a business requirement. This method focuses only on business requirements. If a business requires that a certain amount of data is transferred, we can calculate the size of the different components to handle this amount of data. The second approach is to forecast based on usage. This method requires that some system utilization data was already measured in a monitoring system. Based on these measurements, for example, we can take the last month and compute a forecast for the next few months. Based on this information, we can adjust the scaling parameters for our SAP Cloud Platform instances.

The Cloud Foundry environment on the SAP Cloud Platform provides vertical and horizontal scaling. Vertical scaling refers to an increase in computing resources (for example, disk, memory, CPU) within a single compute instance. Horizontal scaling refers to an increase in the number of computing instances.

As outlined earlier in this chapter, we recommend you persist all configuration values together with the code in the version control system. The scaling parameters can be set in the manifest.yml. Listing 13.6 shows an example. You can specify the memory space, the disk quota, and the number of instances.

```
applications:
  - name: address-manager
    memory: 768M
    disk_quota: 1024M
    instances: 2
```

Listing 13.6 Example manifest.yml to Configure Scaling

Note that you can always use the `cf scale` command to change the scaling parameters introduced in this code. Furthermore, SAP Cloud Platform, Cloud Foundry environment also offers a service called the *Application Autoscaler*, which you can use for advanced scaling. Based on certain rules, the Application Autoscaler service scales your application dynamically during runtime. More information on this mechanism is provided at *http://tiny.cc/autoscaler*.

For scaling, your account must have the corresponding resources available. If not, consider buying additional resources. You can use the pricing information for SAP Cloud Platform at *https://cloudplatform.sap.com/pricing.html*.

13.4 Summary

In this chapter, we learned how operations ensure a smooth user experience. We showed how logging, collecting, and analyzing metrics with a central tool can help developers react to issues early and to identify root causes quickly. We demonstrated how to use the SAP S/4HANA Cloud SDK and the tools available from SAP Cloud Platform to set up these approaches. Finally, we showed how you can use this knowledge to create your own scaling strategies.

PART IV

Advanced Concepts

Chapter 14
Building a Custom SAP Fiori User Interface

The focus of previous chapters has been on the backend—a web-based user interface (UI) was deployed as frontend, but not explored in more detail. This chapter briefly introduces concepts of building a web UI with SAPUI5. Besides developing the frontend, we'll also consider how to provision the frontend in the context of continuous delivery.

We first saw the frontend of our Business Partner Address Manager application in Chapter 4, where we simply copied the provided web application without exploring it in detail. In this chapter, we'll look at the sample user interface and its implementation. Even though building user interfaces is not at the heart of this book, we want to provide an overview and some initial pointers as starting points for your UI development.

The user interface of our Business Partner Address Manager web application loosely follows SAP Fiori design guidelines. SAP Fiori is SAP's design language for business web apps (*http://tiny.cc/fiori*) and is used in SAPUI5, SAP's JavaScript application framework. Of course, you can choose whatever frontend technology you prefer to connect to the frontend-agnostic backend.

In Section 14.1, we'll explain the architecture and implementation of this SAPUI5-based SAP Fiori frontend. Although we'll use an example SAPUI5 application, the main concepts of the remaining sections are technology independent. The overall considerations for provisioning the frontend as part of the overall deployment are discussed in Section 14.2. When operating the frontend in the continuous delivery mode as appropriate for our cloud-native application, we'll need to consider additional topics such as cache-busting and componentization. We'll also explain other necessary steps to ensure a consistent user experience in Section 14.3. We'll close with a look at current trends within the frontend development space in Section 14.4.

14.1 Explanation of the Frontend Application

In this section, we'll describe how to design the user interface for our Business Partner Address Manager application. We'll discuss the frontend architecture and how the web app can be implemented using SAPUI5. SAPUI5 is a web application framework from SAP (*http://tiny.cc/ui5*), which is based on the Model-View-Controller (MVC) architectural pattern. SAPUI5 provides UI elements that comply to SAP Fiori design principles and interaction patterns, which provide a consistent and holistic user experience for enterprise web applications. A web page that follows the layout and interaction guidelines of SAP Fiori can be implemented with SAPUI5.

14.1.1 Overview of the Architecture

For our application, we opted for the popular split-screen layout, also known as master-detail (*http://tiny.cc/fiori-split-screen*). This basic page layout is used by SAP Fiori and optimized for browsing a list of items quickly. The split-screen layout proposes a master list area on the left of the screen. The right area of the screen in a split-screen layout displays the details of the entity selected from the master list on the left. Thus, the layout is well suited for our requirements: users can manage the addresses of business partners by navigating from one business partner to the next and then exploring and modifying the details of the selected business partner as needed.

In the following section, we'll describe the frontend that was implemented based on this specification. We won't provide step-by-step instructions but rather explain the high-level mechanics of the source code. The starting point for our implementation is a template app provided by SAPUI5 (*http://tiny.cc/ui5-templates*). In particular, we'll use SAPUI5s master-detail template, which already implements the basics of a split-screen layout (*http://tiny.cc/ui5-master-detail*). We'll then adapt this example template to our business partner use case. This process mostly means adapting the presentation of business partner properties, connecting to our backend, introducing the table of addresses, implementing interactions with the addresses, and furthermore stripping down the template by removing functionalities not required by our application. You've seen the result previously in Chapter 4.

The application follows the MVC pattern, as SAPUI5 does in general. MVC is a general architecture pattern for user interface development. As the name suggests, the frontend is divided into three areas of responsibilities:

- The *model* expresses the domain of the application and manages the data, including its associated logic, independent of its representation in the user interface. In our example, this deals with the entities of business partners and addresses.
- The *view* describes the visual representation of the application and visually reflects the current state of the model. The view reacts to changes in the model via data bindings. In our case, the view consists of the master and detail pages, along with their contents, as well as some dialog boxes to interact with the user.
- The *controller* reacts to user input, such as mouse or keyboard events. The controller modifies the model or view and sends requests to the backend. In our case, the controller initially requests a list of business partners, updates the detail information based on user navigation, and handles user interactions like creating and deleting addresses.

Let's now look at how the sample source code provided in this book implements the functionality of our basic application. We'll proceed along the lines of MVC, considering each area in turn, starting with the model.

14.1.2 Model and View of the Sample App

The code for the model is quite minimal because we mostly used the implicitly defined JSON model of the backend API. The structure of the JSON objects used by the backend for business partners and addresses directly defines the JavaScript objects used by the frontend. The model hosts a list of business partners as well as the details of the currently selected business partner, which can be accessed by the view.

The view code uses the markup from the template, which has been adapted to our Business Partner Address Manager application. SAPUI5 offers different options to specify a view. In this case, we used the definition via XML views. Several *.view.xml files define the layout and components of the frontend, each handling one part of the frontend. The views are composed of SAPUI5 controls nested to achieve the desired layout. Figure 14.1 outlines which parts of the frontend are handled by which view and controller. Each fully-fledged view has a separate controller, which we'll discuss in Section 14.3. The overall page is represented by the App view, which simply consists of the split-screen SAPUI5 app layout.

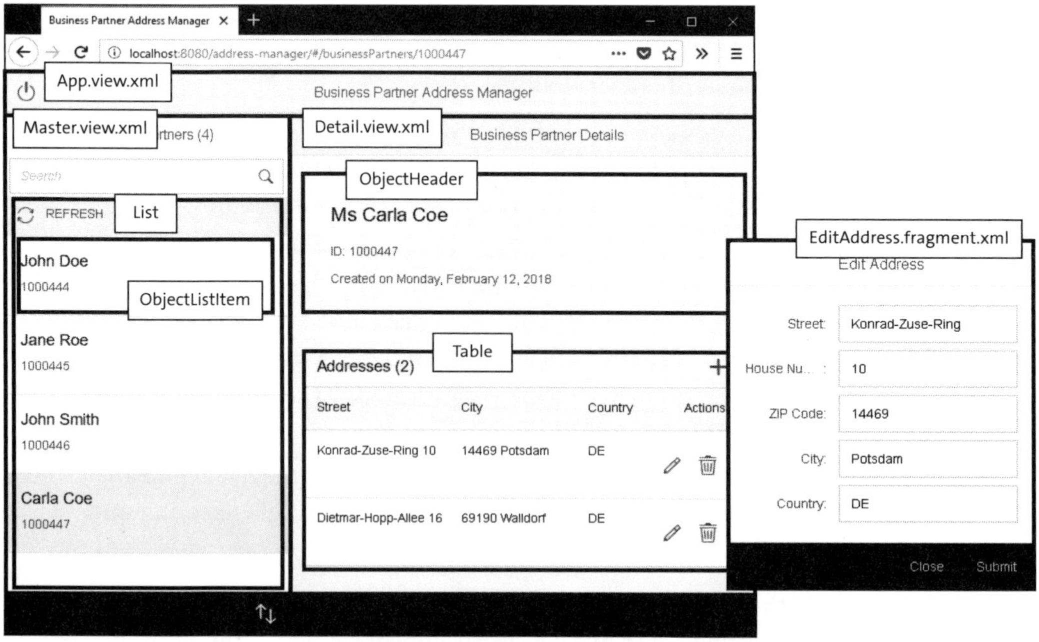

Figure 14.1 Overview of the Structure of the Views and Controls

Listing 14.1 displays the XML definition of this view to demonstrate how such an XML file looks like in principle: The root XML element defines the view and its properties. This root element contains a nested SAPUI5 element of type SplitContainer, which represents the split-screen layout.

```
<mvc:View
    controllerName="sap.ui.demo.addressmgr.controller.App"
    xmlns:mvc="sap.ui.core.mvc"
    displayBlock="true"
    busy="{appView>/busy}"
    xmlns="sap.m">
  <App>
    <Page>
      <SplitContainer id="idAppControl" />
    </Page>
  </App>
</mvc:View>
```

Listing 14.1 XML View Definition of the Overall App in App.view.xml (without Header)

The parts that make up the two areas of the `SplitContainer` according to the master-detail pattern are defined by the `Master` view and the `Detail` view. The routing configuration of the application defined in manifest.json at the root of the frontend project specifies when to display which view. Routing refers to the concept of mapping the high-level state of the application to a URL, and vice versa. From the routing, the SAPUI5 app deduces what to display. The detail part of the screen will display the `Detail` view for the business partner specified in the URL, if according to the route a concrete business partner has been selected for display.

The master page essentially consists of a SAPUI5 `List` control, decorated with a header and a sort bar. The excerpt shown in Listing 14.2 determines how the list should be defined within the `Master` view and how the data binding between view and model should be specified. The items of the list are bound to the root of the main model as defined in the curly brackets of the `items` attribute.

```
<List id="list"
    items="{/}"
    ...
    selectionChange="onSelectionChange">
  <items>
    <ObjectListItem
        title="{FirstName} {LastName}"
      <attributes>
        <ObjectAttribute text="{BusinessPartner}" />
      </attributes>
      ...
    </ObjectListItem>
  </items>
</List>
```

Listing 14.2 Excerpt of Master.view.xml Defining the List

The `List` control contains the `items` aggregation, which is used in Listing 14.2 to define an `ObjectListItem` control as a template for the individual objects in the list. In our case, the list contains business partners with the corresponding properties. We bound the title of the list item to the name of the business partner and displayed the `BusinessPartner` property that contains the identifier as an additional attribute. Furthermore, note that the function assigned to the `selectionChange` attribute of the `List` refers to a method of the controller that acts as the event handler for the corresponding event.

Similarly, the `Detail` view defines the detail page as a combination of an `ObjectHeader` control to display the detailed properties of the selected business partner and a `Table` to display the addresses. Events triggered by interactions with the buttons in the table are bound to their corresponding event handlers in the `Detail` controller. Additionally, we defined an `EditAddress` fragment for the address dialog, where the user can change or create an address. Fragments are lightweight UI parts that don't have dedicated controllers and can be used within views.

14.1.3 Controller of the Sample App

The controller code is conceptually split into two parts: first, the set of actual controllers for the view elements that handle the logic and events and, second, a service that encapsulates all calls to our backend API. As the service *businessPartner.js* is used by all controllers, let's look at this code first.

The service provides methods that act as JavaScript counterparts to each of the operations that the backend provides: reading business partners and creating, deleting, and updating addresses. Listing 14.3 contains the definition of the service method for deleting an address with a specific `businessPartnerId` and `addressId`. As with most of the methods of the service, the `delete` method transforms the parameters to the input for the asynchronous request to the backend. The `deleteAddress` method executes and returns a jQuery Ajax (Asynchronous JavaScript and XML) request using the HTTP method `DELETE`. The request is sent to a URL constructed by the `getAddressUrl` method. The other service methods work similarly—where necessary, the method adds a JSON representation of the address in the body. Each service method returns the promise created by the Ajax call to the caller, who can attach callbacks to be called when the request completes.

```
deleteAddress: function (businessPartnerId, addressId) {
  return jQuery.ajax({
    url: this.getAddressUrl(businessPartnerId, addressId),
    method: "DELETE"
  });
}
```

Listing 14.3 Excerpt of Service businessPartner.js for Deleting an Address

Cross-Site Request Forgery Handling

The service also generically handles cross-site request forgery (CSRF) tokens for modifying operations. These tokens are expected by the backend to protect against cross-site request forgery attacks. The service fetches a CSRF token once on startup and attaches a filter to all Ajax calls, which adds a header with the CSRF token to each `POST`, `PATCH`, and `DELETE` request.

Each of the views described in this section is backed by a controller of the same name that handles the logic. Most controllers make use of the service to interact with the backend to load data or modify addresses in reaction to user interaction. Controllers also contain event handlers that interact with the model or view in some other way, for example, by opening a dialog.

The top-level `App` controller loads the list of business partners from the backend service. The resulting JSON object is directly used as part of the model component. The application router uses the URL to represent and change the currently selected business partner, if any. The controller for the `Master` view reacts to the matched route. If the route matches a pattern, the `Master` controller modifies the internal state accordingly, for example, by setting the state of a list item as selected if a specific business partner is selected.

The controller for the `Detail` view reacts accordingly. The controller initiates navigation that is also visible in the route of the URL when the user selects a business partner from the list. This level of redirection via the route fosters proper decoupling and enables bookmarking and sharing of the URL. At any place in the application, for example, when looking at a particular business partner, a user can save the URL and revisit the same URL later to arrive at the same place. The `Master` controller also deals with the search and sort behavior of the list via corresponding event handlers. Note that both searching and sorting operate on the local model initialized by the `App` controller and do not trigger additional remote requests to the backend.

Similar to the `Master` controller, the `Detail` controller reacts to changes in the route and loads the details of the selected business partner using the business partner service. Furthermore, this controller handles all address modifications. The simplest interaction is the deletion of an address. Listing 14.4 shows the code of the event handler that is called when the user clicks on the **Delete** button next to an address. In line 3, we'll retrieve our main model. In line 4, we'll identify the source of the event and store the model binding path of the address as the variable `sPath`. We'll use this path to retrieve the IDs of business partners and addresses from the model in lines 8 and 9, which we then pass on to the business partner service for the address deletion operation. We'll invoke the deleteAddress method from Listing 14.3 and attach a callback that will always be called after the request to the backend completes. In this case, we'll only reload the business partner details from the backend, but this part would also be the proper place for error handling (not shown for the sake of brevity).

```
onDeleteAddress: function (oEvent) {
  var that = this;
  var oModel = this.getMainModel();
  var sPath = oEvent.getSource()
      .getBindingContext(this.mainModelName).getPath();

  businessPartnerService.deleteAddress(
      oModel.getProperty(sPath + "/BusinessPartner"),
      oModel.getProperty(sPath + "/AddressID"))
    .always(function () {
      that._reloadDetailsModel();
    });
}
```

Listing 14.4 Excerpt of Detail.controller.js That Handles the Deletion of Addresses

The user interactions for the remaining modifying operations are slightly more involved. When the user clicks the button to add or change an address, the controller opens the edit dialog by instantiating the EditAddress fragment, setting the model to the business partner in question, if any, and opening the dialog. Any events within the dialog are still handled by the controller of the Detail view. If the user confirms the dialog after entering the desired values for the address properties, the Detail controller handles the event by calling the appropriate service method. The values entered by users are automatically synchronized to the model via data binding.

On a high level, we've described the complete functionality implemented in the SAPUI5 app representing the frontend of our Business Partner Address Manager application. We didn't cover a few details, for example, the detail page that is shown if no business partner is selected, error handling, or internationalization, but the description in this section should give you a good starting point to dive more deeply, if desired. In the next section, we'll discuss the different options for provisioning the frontend as part of our overall application.

14.2 Provisioning the Frontend as a Microservice

The Cloud Foundry environment of the SAP Cloud Platform provides a great deal of flexibility with regards to the structuring of our overall application in separate microservices. This feature, in turn, offers different options for provisioning the application. In this section, we'll discuss the most commonly used alternatives for deploying an application that consists of a frontend and a backend. We'll also explain how to implement these alternatives on Cloud Foundry. The basis is, as usual, our Business Partner Address Manager application, which consists of two separate parts: the frontend implemented in SAPUI5 and the Java backend as developed in Part II. In addition, we already have an instance of the AppRouter in place as the central entry point to our application as required for security purposes, which we introduced in Chapter 5.

14.2.1 Overview of Alternative Approaches

On a high level, we'll distinguish between two categories of provisioning the frontend: either bundled as part of the Java application or as a Cloud Foundry app separate from the Java app. The bundled approach is less complex, but decoupling the frontend from the backend has advantages as well, first and foremost, increased flexibility. As shown in Figure 14.2, the latter method of separating frontend and backend comes in two flavors, depending on where exactly the frontend is hosted: We can either use the existing AppRouter to also host the static content of the frontend or create a separate app to serve this static content. Note that all three approaches use an AppRouter because the AppRouter provides the security setup of our application and the routes between Cloud Foundry apps. In the AppRouter hosting approach, the AppRouter additionally contains the frontend static content. Thus, we'll require two separate Cloud Foundry apps in total for either the bundled or the AppRouter hosting approach, and three apps for the dedicated apps approach, if we consider, for example, a microservice such as our Business Partner Address Manager app, which consists of one Java application and hosts a single frontend. The number of apps is only meant to give an overview and does not imply that fewer apps are always better.

In any case, the configuration of the AppRouter as well as the deployment differs depending on the chosen approach. So far, we've used the bundled approach as explained during Part II and Part III of the book. In the following sections, we'll explain the setup for the other two approaches, which both feature a separate frontend, and discuss the trade-offs between the two variants in the separated frontend category. But first, let's discuss the high-level advantages and disadvantages of bundling the frontend with the backend in contrast to separating them.

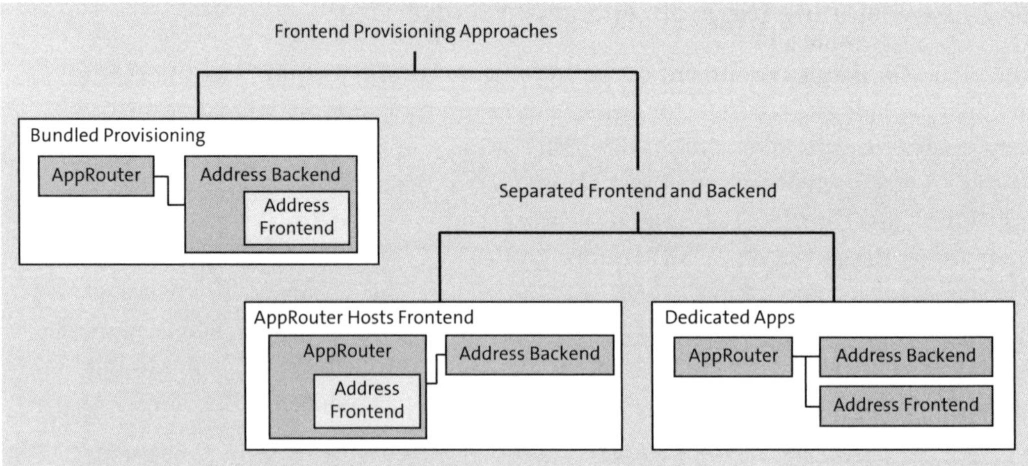

Figure 14.2 Categorization of Approaches to Provisioning the Frontend at the Example of the Address Manager Application

In the *bundled provisioning* approach, shown in Figure 14.3, the frontend content and the backend services of an application are combined into one application, in our case, a Java application. The Java Web Application Archive (.war file) not only contains the Java classes of the app, but also the content of the *webapp* folder. We'll use the capabilities of the Java application server to serve static content from those archives. In the previous parts of the book, we've seen that this approach works well and is simple to handle when the frontend and backend evolve together. Both during initial development and continuous delivery, we didn't need to pay any particular attention to the frontend, as it always existed as part of the same build and deployment artifact.

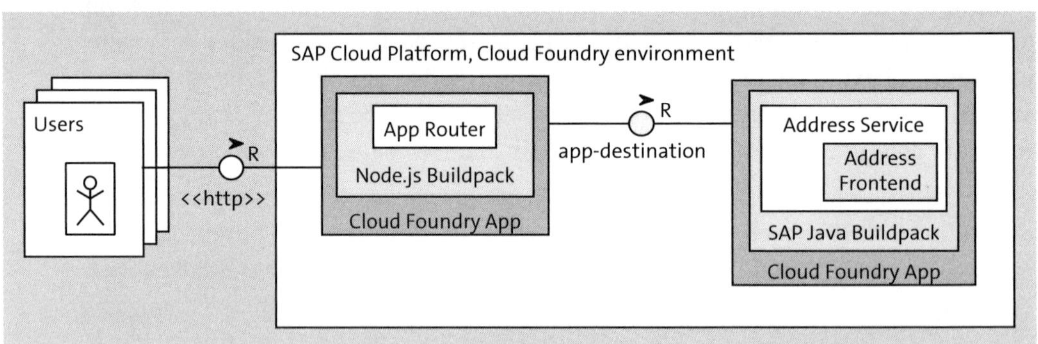

Figure 14.3 Landscape with Bundled Provisioning of the Frontend

Because frontend and backend are part of the same lifecycle and evolve together, we won't need to apply any special considerations on the source code level to keep the versions of backend and frontend in sync. Since we're dealing with a single artifact only, what version of the backend the frontend is accessing is always clear. No additional synchronization or versioning of the backend API is necessary. If we change the API of the backend, we can adapt the frontend in the same commit. The commit will run through the same continuous delivery pipeline as one build. The deployed versions of backend and frontend will always match, as they are built and deployed as one single artifact.

Thus, the infrastructure both during design and at runtime is as simple as possible, possibly reducing the operating costs of our application. During design, we have a single repository that hosts both frontend and backend code and a single pipeline that builds, tests, and deploys the commits. At runtime, the application is deployed in one Cloud Foundry app using the Java buildpack. The AppRouter only deals with authentication and routes all requests to the Java application, including the requests for the static content of the user interface such as HTML, CSS, JavaScript, or image files.

As with any monolithic approach, bundling leads to a higher risk of tight coupling between frontend and backend. The simplicity of the bundled approach comes at the expense of reduced flexibility. Any change in the frontend requires you rebuild, test, and redeploy the whole application. The application can only be scaled up by increasing the number of Java instances, which typically require more resources and thus are costlier than a simple web server.

Any approach that separates frontend and backend offers flexibility in many dimensions that cannot be changed in the bundled approach flexibly or independently. Generally, with these approaches, the frontend is not hosted together with the Java application; instead, a separate Cloud Foundry application hosts the static content that makes up the frontend. Depending on the exact setup, this separate application may also serve other purposes, for example, as the AppRouter. Due to this separation, we'll also need a component that routes requests between the frontend and the backend.

The immediate benefit of the separation approach is the independence of the frontend and the backend. Especially if different groups of developers are responsible for the frontend and the backend, putting the two together in all stages of the development lifecycle, as with the bundled approach, may be counterproductive. With separation in place, developers can make modifications to the productive frontend without impacting the backend at all, and vice versa, as long as the change doesn't depend on changes in other components. In that case, some kind of synchronization, versioning, or graceful fallback is required, which increases the complexity of this approach. Many changes will, however, only impact one component and can be built, tested, and deployed independently of other components.

Frontend developers use different tools than Java developers, which can be reflected in a separate pipeline for the frontend with specific build tools. Specialized server runtimes exist for hosting static content. Instead of serving all static content via a Java application server, we can use Cloud Foundry buildpacks that are more appropriate for static content. For example, the Staticfile buildpack of Cloud Foundry is well suited for efficiently serving static files (*http://tiny.cc/cf-static*). In addition to using an optimized environment for the various needs of frontend and backend developers, having separate applications also allows us to scale those resources independently, depending on the demands on each. Although the added complexity makes operating the application slightly more difficult, we benefit in terms of stability (see Chapter 4, Section 4.6) in other dimensions: If we have a separate application for the frontend, the web application can still at least serve the static content if the Java application is not available. Also, the separation follows the stability pattern of bulkheads by isolating different parts of the application from each other. With a separate frontend, stability issues in the frontend will not immediately impact the backend application, and vice versa, which allows us to focus our attention when issues arise.

Finally, the separated approach does not need to be limited to one backend (or frontend). The separation lays the basis for further splitting the backend into several separate microservices, all held together by the AppRouter.

Hopefully, the preceding discussion has equipped you with the information you need to decide which provisioning approach works best for you. Luckily, you can easily switch from the bundled approach to the separated approach, so you're not forced to stay with one approach as your project evolves. To help you implement your decision, we've explained the bundled approach up to now. In the following two sections, we'll explain the two variants of the separated approach and explain how to implement them as well.

14.2.2 Frontend Resources as Part of the AppRouter

The two variants of the separated frontend provisioning discussed in this chapter differ in how the frontend is being hosted. For the first variant, discussed, in this subsection and shown in Figure 14.4, we'll use the existing AppRouter to serve the static content of the frontend in addition to using the AppRouter to deal with security and deal with the routing between Cloud Foundry apps. The AppRouter provided by SAP out of the box supports serving static content that is deployed as part of the AppRouter.

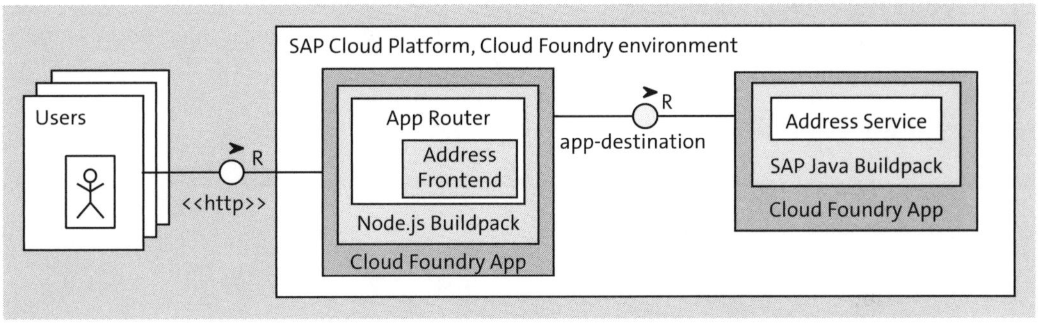

Figure 14.4 Landscape with Frontend Provisioned as Part of the Approuter

Hosting the frontend as part of the AppRouter represents a trade-off in the complexity of the infrastructure. Because the AppRouter is a mandatory component of our application anyway, we can forgo creating yet another application and still benefit from the separation of the frontend and the backend. As each application requires management, including continuous delivery, reusing the AppRouter reduces complexity. On the other hand, we thus mix two components of our application that don't necessarily need to be coupled; the AppRouter and the frontend.

However, hosting the frontend resources as part of the AppRouter has another distinct advantage: Frontend resources are secured out of the box because these resources are only available as part of the AppRouter, which requires authentication by default. In summary, reusing the AppRouter for the frontend may be a good choice for your project to keep the landscape of your application as simple as possible (while separating frontend and backend) and to secure the static resources of your application.

To host your frontend as part of the AppRouter we created in Chapter 5, you'll need to apply the following changes, starting from the previous state of a bundled application:

1. Move the entire frontend folder *address-manager*, located in *application/src/main/webapp*, to a new folder called *static-content*. That folder shall be located in the same folder as your AppRouter. In other words, the folder *static-content* must

be in the folder that also contains the package.json and xs-app.json files of your AppRouter.

2. Adapt the route for the frontend path in the xs-app.json file to the configuration shown in Listing 14.5, replacing the previous `target` and `destination` properties with a single property called `localDir` whose value specifies the name of the folder that contains the resources of the frontend. Note that we won't apply any target mapping, so the folder *static-content* must contain another folder, *address-manager*, whose resources are then served via this route.

```
"routes": [
  ...
  {
    "source": "^/address-manager/(.*)",
    "localDir": "static-content"
  }
]
```

Listing 14.5 Excerpt of xs-app.json with the Route for the Frontend as Part of the Approuter

3. Rebuild and redeploy the Java application, which now no longer contains the frontend resources.
4. Redeploy the AppRouter using `cf push`.

Now, you can access the application as before via the AppRouter. The `localDir` property specifies the folder within the working directory of the AppRouter from which static content on `GET` requests is served. With this configuration, we are explicitly mapping each path that begins with */address-manager/* to the static content folder. We'll instruct the AppRouter to search for the whole path of the requests within the folder of static content (since we did not specify a different target mapping). Of course, the AppRouter allows us also to configure other route mappings.

From now on, whenever we change anything in the frontend, we only need to redeploy the AppRouter. Most likely, you'll want to create a separate continuous delivery pipeline on your Jenkins server hosting the AppRouter and the frontend. However, this process is beyond the scope of this book.

While hosting the frontend as part of the AppRouter is an accepted approach, sometimes, we want to separate the lifecycle of the security-relevant AppRouter from the often-changing frontend. Thus, we may consider the second variant of the separate provisioning of the frontend, as discussed in the following subsection.

14.2.3 Dedicated Microservices

As briefly mentioned, AppRouter and the frontend are, in principle, two separate components of our overall application, each with a dedicated purpose. The AppRouter deals with security and routing, and the frontend contains the user interface for our web app. Thus, depending on your requirements and organizational setup, you may consider having the development team drive the separation one step further by splitting the frontend into an entirely separate Cloud Foundry application only dedicated to serving the static content. In this setup scenario, the AppRouter routes the requests to both frontend and backend, as shown in Figure 14.5. As a result, the separate microservice variant can be even more finely granular and specialized to work with the different components that make up the runtime of our application. This feature further increases flexibility and allows specific optimizations, although with additional complexity.

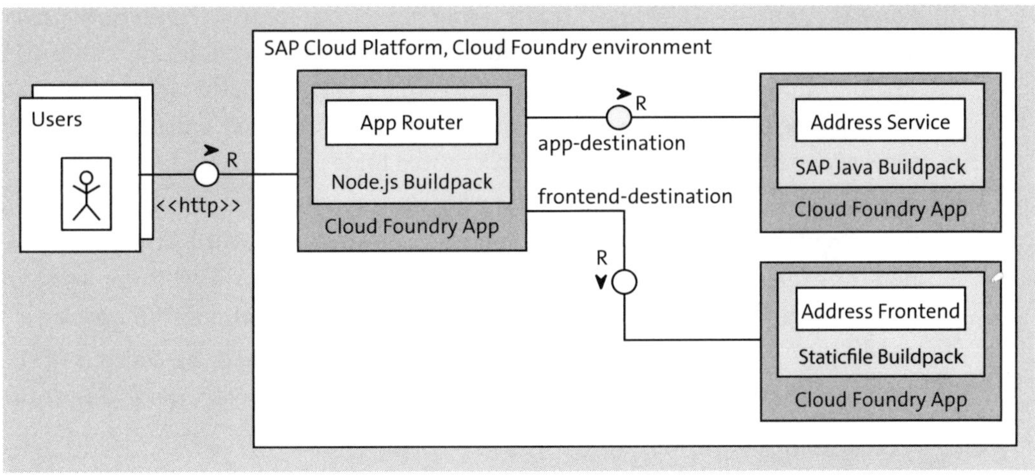

Figure 14.5 Landscape with Dedicated Microservices for the Java Application, Frontend, and Approuter

Cloud Foundry offers a dedicated Staticfile buildpack for serving static content, based on the lightweight nginx web server from *http://nginx.org*. In most cases, this buildpack exhibits better performance for the particular use case of serving static content when compared to using the multipurpose Node.js-based AppRouter to serve static content, as done in the AppRouter-hosted approach. This performance difference is especially true as content files grow. Hosting the frontend behind the AppRouter in a dedicated microservice makes deploying new versions with zero downtime via blue-green deployment much easier. As the lifecycle of AppRouter and frontend is decoupled, the route to the frontend in the AppRouter can be adapted once a new version of the frontend has been deployed in a separate instance of the frontend microservice.

One drawback of using a dedicated application for the frontend is the fact that the frontend resources are no longer access-protected by default. If the static content itself requires authentication, not only access to the backend, you'll need to implement this access protection separately. Often, this security feature will not be required, however, because the sensitive information should only be delivered by the backend, which we need to protect in any case, as described in Chapter 5.

The following steps describe the actions necessary to move the web application out to a dedicated Cloud Foundry app and configure the AppRouter accordingly. First, we'll create our dedicated frontend application as follows:

1. Move the content of the folder *address-manager*, so far located in *application/src/main/webapp*, to a new location for the source code of the frontend application. In the following steps, we'll use the name *webapp* to reference this folder that now contains the frontend. Note that the content of the frontend must be located in the *webapp* folder directly, not within a nested folder address-manager.
2. Within the new folder *webapp*, create a manifest.yml file with the content shown in Listing 14.6. Adapt the route by replacing `<unique-route>` with a unique identifier, for example, your user name on the SAP Cloud Platform. This deployment descriptor configures the frontend application to use the Staticfile buildpack.
3. Execute `cf push` within the folder *webapp*, which will upload the content of the folder and launch a web server that serves the static content of the folder at the root path of the configured route.

```
---
applications:
- name: address-manager-frontend
  routes:
    - route: address-manager-frontend-<unique-route>↩
.cfapps.eu10.hana.ondemand.com
  memory: 64M
  buildpack: staticfile_buildpack
```

Listing 14.6 Content of the manifest.yml file for the Frontend Application

Afterwards, rebuild and redeploy the Java application as before, now without the frontend. You can access the frontend resources at the specified route; however, for a working application we'll need to access it via the AppRouter, which will then route calls to the backend differently than the requests for frontend resources. We'll need to configure the AppRouter as follows:

1. Adapt the route for the frontend path in the xs-app.json file to the configuration shown in Listing 14.7.

```
"routes": [
  ...
  {
    "source": "^/address-manager/(.*)",
    "target": "/$1",
    "destination": "frontend-destination"
  }
]
```

Listing 14.7 Excerpt of xs-app.json with the Route to the Dedicated Frontend

2. Add `frontend-destination` as an additional entry next to `app-destination` to the JSON object of the destinations environment variable of the AppRouter, as defined in the manifest.yml of the AppRouter: `{"name":"frontend-destination", "url": "https://address-manager-frontend-<unique-route>.cfapps.eu10.hana.ondemand.com"}`. Replace <unique-route> as before.
3. Redeploy the AppRouter using `cf push`.

These steps configure the AppRouter so that any request to a URL whose path begins with */address-manager* is forwarded to the URL defined for the destination *frontend-destination*. Only the remaining path behind the initial part is used to access the target, as specified in the target mapping.

At this point, we've separated the different components of our application to a large extent and can update the frontend, the backend, and the AppRouter independently. Each component should be deployed by its own continuous delivery pipeline, which is, however, beyond the scope of this book. In the next section, we'll discuss the specific steps to keep in mind when continuously updating the files being served to users' browsers. These steps apply to all the approaches to provisioning the frontend, whether bundled or separated.

14.3 Considering Continuous Delivery of the Frontend

Based on the explanations in this book so far, we're in a good position to implement continuous delivery of our application, choosing any of the approaches to provisioning the frontend. When continuously deploying new versions of a web application, we'll need to consider browser caching. While embracing the performance advantage caching provides, we need to ensure our users get access to the changes we're making to our application, as opposed to accessing an older cached version of the application, which would happen if we don't consider this issue explicitly. This section briefly discusses concepts dealing with caching and performance.

To understand the impact of caching and how to deal with caching, we'll first look at the behavior of browsers when accessing a resource. When a web browser accesses a resource such as an HTML, JavaScript, or CSS file at a specific path for the first time, the browser retrieves the content from the web server. If the response headers contain instructions to cache the content of the resource for a specific time, the browser will locally store a copy of the resource. For each future request, the browser will serve the locally cached copy unless it has expired. In general, this behavior is desirable because it greatly improves the response time of our web application. However, we still want the ability to update our application at any time to leverage the benefits of continuous delivery. Often, these updates will also contain updated frontend resources. For users to access these new resources instead of their cached copy, we need a way to signal to the browser that it should retrieve the resources from the server instead of the cache.

The term *cache-busting* refers to techniques that allow exactly this instruction. In essence, most cache-busting techniques version the URL to the resource. Whenever a resource changes, we'll need to change its version, and this version needs to be referenced by the URL. As the browser did not cache anything for this new URL, the browser will retrieve the new version of the resource from the server. For this to work, the entry point to the application must not be cached.

For example, let's assume we have a JavaScript resource at the path */script.js*, which is referenced from our entry point, the index.html file. To implement cache-busting, we'll add the version of the JavaScript resource to its path, for example, */script.v1.js*. Our index.html is a slim HTML page that won't be cached and references all resources by their versioned path, such as the following:

```
<script src="/script.v1.js" />
```

We want all our resources to be cached except for the index.html to improve repeated loading times of our application. Whenever we update a resource, we'll increase its version and its path, for example, to */script.v2.js*. We'll then need to update the *index.html* file to reference the new version. The next time the browser requests our web application, the new index.html content will be retrieved because this file is not cached. Then, the browser will look for the script.v2.js file. This file cannot already be in the browser cache because we updated the filename, thus *busting the cache*. Thus, the browser will retrieve the new version of this resource.

In most cases, we don't want to update the version in the path manually, but instead rely on an automated build script. Most frontend task runners or bundling tools such as Grunt (*gruntjs.com*) or Webpack (*webpack.js.org*) provide extensions to automate this task as part of the build process. Instead of a manual version number, these tools will often use a hash of the file content as a cache-buster.

With cache-busting and proper cache control generally in place, we can further improve how we deliver our application to end users, if needed. For example, we could engage a *Content Delivery Network* (CDN) to serve the static content of our application from a distributed network of proxy servers. Especially with larger files, serving resources from servers that are geographically close to a user's location becomes important. Instead of hosting the content ourselves on different servers, we can use the services of a CDN for this purpose.

14.4 Outlook on Current Trends in Frontend Development

In the previous sections of this chapter, we investigated how to develop, deploy, and deliver a modern frontend application. In this section, we'll briefly consider micro-frontends and related trends in the area of frontend development. For reasons of space and focus, we can only mention these trends in this chapter. Still, we feel you should be aware of these frontend trends as far as they concern cloud-native development. We'll provide several references for these trends as starting points for further investigation.

We've discussed the concept of microservices primarily in the context of backend applications. Many web applications split the backend into separate microservices, which are then combined by a single frontend application. As a result, we'll already enjoy benefits to the backend development such as loose coupling, scalability, and flexibility, discussed earlier in the book. Nevertheless, these processes stop short as far as the frontend is concerned, which is still essentially a monolith. More recently, the term *micro-frontend* extends the idea of microservices to the frontend (*http://tiny.cc/thoughtworks16*). Several companies are currently leveraging this approach to build their frontends (*http://tiny.cc/soederlund17*).

In contrast to a monolithic frontend, a micro-frontend (*http://micro-frontends.org*) consists of smaller modules that are independent from each other but held together by a thin integration part that composes the full web application from the separate micro-frontends, while ensuring proper isolation. Each micro-frontend is responsible for a particular feature of the web application and can be implemented in a different framework, reside in their own source code repositories, and have their own lifecycles. A corresponding deployment process is required to bundle and deploy all micro-frontends as well as the integration component. In essence, micro-frontends enable companies to build truly self-contained teams, where each development team is responsible for their part of the overall experience, from backend microservice to micro-frontend.

Several ways to implement micro-frontends are available. On an abstract level, an approach to micro-frontends must solve the challenges that arise from composing modules written in different frameworks into a common web page. One approach coincides with another current trend in frontend development: *componentization* or *web components* (T. Savage, *Componentizing the Web*). Componentization refers to the approach to split a web application into several isolated parts that can be developed separately. A web component is a reusable and encapsulated component that acts similarly to standard HTML elements and fosters componentization. A web component encapsulates structure described by HTML, behavior written in JavaScript, and styling specified by CSS. Building separate parts of the frontend as individual web components not only enables reusability, but more importantly adds isolation and simplifies integration into a larger application, thereby reducing the overall complexity of building web applications.

Web components are in the process of being standardized under the umbrella term *web components* (*http://tiny.cc/web-components*), which includes a set of specifications that together enable building custom web components. Despite still being in the process of standardization, modern browsers already support many of these underlying concepts, while others can be enhanced with polyfills (workarounds that implement functionality otherwise not supported by the respective browser). Thus, web components are a useful tool to effectively develop the frontends of modern, complex web applications today as well as directly benefit from building componentized frontends like micro-frontends.

14.5 Summary

This brief outlook into current trends in frontend development concludes our discussion on developing modern, web-based frontends. In this chapter, we showed you how to develop your first web frontend using SAPUI5 and then discussed different options for provisioning the frontend. For the remainder of this book, we'll turn our focus back to the backend. In the next chapter, for instance, we'll consider how to integrate our side-by-side extension with state-of-the-art Java frameworks.

Chapter 15
Integrating with Java Frameworks

Standing on the shoulders of giants is an important principle for software development. Industry-standard Java frameworks such as Java Platform, Enterprise Edition (Java EE) or Spring Boot can significantly simplify development of enterprise software. In this chapter, we'll consider how to integrate the SAP S/4HANA Cloud SDK in projects based on these technologies.

This chapter explains how to use the SAP S/4HANA Cloud SDK with industry-standard Java frameworks such as Java EE or Spring Boot. We'll walkthrough the straightforward integration of the SDK using our Business Partner Address Manager Application as an example for these two frameworks. Developers experienced with these frameworks can use the SDK in whatever setting is most familiar.

The first section looks at the integration with Java EE. Section 15.2 then does the same for Spring Boot. Both sections assume basic knowledge of the respective framework. You can read these section independently of each other, so some instructions and explanations will appear similar in both sections.

Each of the sections is structured similarly. First, we'll present SAP S/4HANA Cloud SDK archetypes for creating new applications with regards to the target Java framework. Second, we'll consider what to do when an existing project needs to be adapted and explain how to include the essential modules, along with the recommended dependency management. Third, the next subsection for each framework will show convenient dependency injection using the Virtual Data Model (VDM) while going into details about framework-specific features. Fourth, we'll demonstrate how to define web services with each respective framework. We'll conclude the section for each framework with an explanation on how to build a multitenant persistence layer on top of the original application, drawing on our discussions from Chapter 7.

15.1 Integrating with Java Platform, Enterprise Edition

Application performance, transactional integrity, and information security are core topics in an enterprise software environment. Therefore, today's developers rely on server-side technology to compose distributed and portable applications. These applications are centrally managed and are bound to services, leveraging transactional communication with other enterprise software. With Java EE, large-scale business logic can be developed with greater speed and using fewer resources based on an industry specification adopted by many application servers. By introducing Java EE and its wide set of API-powered tools with a simplified programming model, we can reduce software complexity and repetitive code on the application side, which leads to fewer dependencies and lower development costs.

For web services, most application-related settings can be managed in dedicated XML deployment descriptors. By using Java EE, the developer can also declare configuration data as annotations directly inside Java source files. The annotations conveniently work best with Plain Old Java Objects (POJOs), enhancing the general code style. In this way, the specification of web services and their transactions are described directly next to their corresponding implementations, while simplifying the overall product setup and packaging. A Java EE enabled server hosting such an application will automatically look up annotated classes and configure the software component at deployment and runtime accordingly. By continuously shifting configuration from XML descriptors to annotations, you can maintain a single language scope without changing files, thus leading to significantly improved implementation productivity.

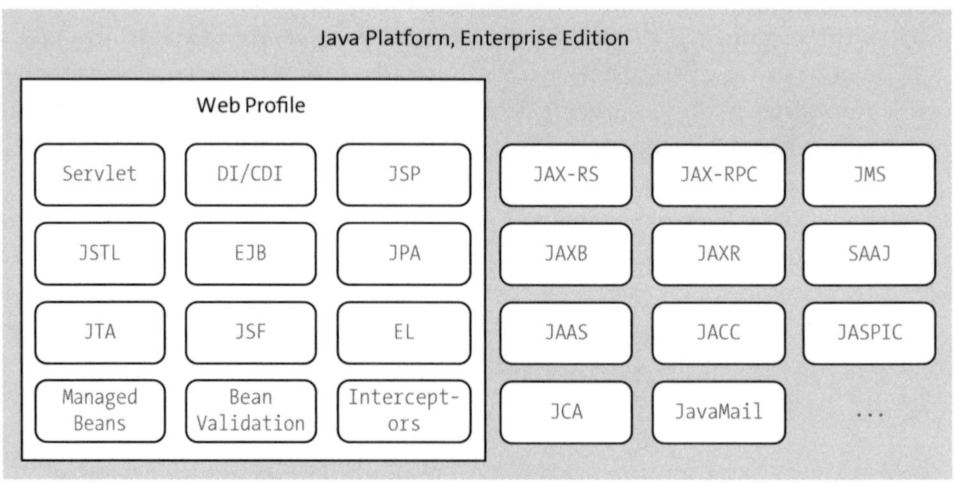

Figure 15.1 Profiles of Java EE and Their Components

The Java EE platform provides different sets of supported technologies based on the active profile. Two common configurations are the "Web Profile" for lightweight web applications based on the Servlet engine and the "Full Profile," for any full-scope enterprise application. Figure 15.1 shows the components included in the Web Profile and the Full Profile. The Java API for RESTful Web Services (JAX-RS) is also often used in web applications, although it is not part of the Web Profile.

15.1.1 SAP S/4HANA Cloud SDK Maven Archetypes for Java EE Projects

The SAP S/4HANA Cloud SDK provides Maven archetypes to help you kickstart a Java application with an already prepared setup including Java EE features.

Depending on your choice of SAP Cloud Platform environment, different archetypes with Java EE support are available:

- `scp-neo-javaee7` for Java EE 7 Web Profile with JAX-RS support on SAP Cloud Platform Neo, and
- `scp-cf-tomee` for Java EE 6 Web Profile with JAX-RS support on SAP Cloud Platform Cloud Foundry.

These Java EE versions are current on their respective SAP Cloud Platform environments at the time of this writing. For both target deployment platforms, the archetypes provide a multimodule Maven project with a simple "Hello World!" servlet, which we introduced in Chapter 4. In the following, we'll keep our focus on the Cloud Foundry environment. Thanks to the underlying Java EE platform and the SAP Cloud Platform abstractions of the SAP S/4HANA Cloud SDK, you can use the code shown in this section in both environments. See the blog post at *http://tiny.cc/scp-neo-start* for an introduction to the Neo archetype.

Java web applications for Cloud Foundry with Java EE version 6 can conveniently be created by the *scp-cf-tomee* archetype, as we've seen in Chapter 4. In the following section, we'll build on the information from Chapter 4 on how to generate and run projects locally, as well as how to deploy projects to Cloud Foundry. With the *scp-cf-tomee* archetype, both the local deployment as well as the runtime in Cloud Foundry use an Apache TomEE application server (*http://tiny.cc/apache-tomee*). TomEE provides the Java EE Web Profile stack on top of an Apache Tomcat server. Thus, out of the box, we can include Java EE features in our application, which is built on top of the TomEE archetype. The next section explains how to include the SAP S/4HANA Cloud SDK into an existing Java EE project that had not been created using one of the archetypes.

15.1.2 Including the SAP S/4HANA Cloud SDK in Existing Maven Projects

The libraries of the SAP S/4HANA Cloud SDK are publicly available on Maven Central and can be incorporated into any Java web application that uses the Java Servlet API. To ensure compatibility, the existing software project must be part of a Maven module and must be compiled—at the time of this writing—with Java version 1.8 or later. The application should support the Servlet 3.0 (or newer) API to have all features activated automatically during application startup. In this way, the components of the SAP S/4HANA Cloud SDK will be configured by Java annotations on startup.

Dependency Management Configuration

Instead of managing the dependency versions of each artifact separately, we recommend including the bill of materials (BOM) of the SAP S/4HANA Cloud SDK to the dependency management section of the project's pom.xml. This approach simplifies managing the modules of the SAP S/4HANA Cloud SDK that are involved and ensures a common setup for dependencies and their respective versions.

Add an entry to the `dependencyManagement` tag of the *application* POM, as shown in Listing 15.1. For a multimodule Maven setup, you should consider adding the code to the parent module so that inconsistencies in the dependency setup can be avoided.

```
<dependencyManagement>
  <dependencies>
    <!-- Keep any existing dependency imports -->
    <!-- SAP S/4HANA Cloud SDK dependency import -->
    <dependency>
      <groupId>com.sap.cloud.s4hana</groupId>
      <artifactId>sdk-bom</artifactId>
      <version>2.0.0</version>
      <type>pom</type>
      <scope>import</scope>
    </dependency>
  </dependencies>
</dependencyManagement>
```

Listing 15.1 SAP S/4HANA Cloud SDK Dependency Management in Maven

Now, any dependency of the SAP S/4HANA Cloud SDK can be easily included in the relevant Maven module. Version 2.0.0 is the latest release at the time of this writing, but use the latest available version when you start your project with the SAP S/4HANA Cloud, which can be found on the release notes page of the SAP S/4HANA Cloud SDK at *http://tiny.cc/s4-sdk-rel-notes*.

As dependency management is not technically required, you can still use the modules of the SDK without it, but you'll need to manage and specify the versions of each SDK module manually when including the module as a dependency. In the following sections, we'll assume that you're using the BOM.

Dependencies for SAP S/4HANA Integration

Listing 15.2 shows the standard set of dependencies that you must include in an application project to start using the central features of the SAP S/4HANA Cloud SDK. These dependencies are SAP Cloud Platform abstractions and the SAP S/4HANA integration. The former is a required dependency that must be present in one of two variants, either for Cloud Foundry or Neo, when using the SAP S/4HANA Cloud SDK. Listing 15.2 shows the variant for Cloud Foundry. Since the dependency import has been added previously, a version declaration for the artifacts of the SAP S/4HANA Cloud SDK can be omitted.


```
<dependencies>
  <!-- Keep any existing dependencies -->
  <!-- SAP S/4HANA Cloud SDK dependencies for CloudFoundry -->
  <dependency>
    <groupId>com.sap.cloud.s4hana.cloudplatform</groupId>
    <artifactId>scp-cf</artifactId>
  </dependency>
  <dependency>
    <groupId>com.sap.cloud.s4hana</groupId>
    <artifactId>s4hana-all</artifactId>
  </dependency>
</dependencies>
```

Listing 15.2 SAP S/4HANA Cloud SDK Dependencies for SAP Cloud Platform Cloud Foundry

> **Using the SAP S/4HANA Cloud SDK on Neo**
>
> If you're using the SAP S/4HANA Cloud SDK in a project on the Neo environment of SAP Cloud Platform, simply exchange the artifact `scp-cf` with `scp-neo`.

Dependencies for Unit and Integration Tests

For testing an application, the SAP S/4HANA Cloud SDK provides a test utility for testing ERP-related functions and easy mocking of SAP Cloud Platform entities as described in Chapter 9. The recommended method is to have dedicated modules for unit tests and integration tests. Each module can have the dependencies shown in Listing 15.3 attached to their respective POM. The `testutil` artifact provides mocking capabilities and is required for writing tests, as described in Chapter 9. The second dependency is used by the quality checks of the continuous delivery pipeline, as described in Chapter 12.

```
<dependencies>
  <!-- Keep any existing dependencies -->
  <!-- SAP S/4HANA Cloud SDK Testing dependencies -->
  <dependency>
    <groupId>com.sap.cloud.s4hana</groupId>
    <artifactId>testutil</artifactId>
    <scope>test</scope>
  </dependency>
  <dependency>
    <groupId>com.sap.cloud.s4hana.quality</groupId>
    <artifactId>listeners-all</artifactId>
    <scope>test</scope>
  </dependency>
</dependencies>
```

Listing 15.3 Test Utilities as Dependency in Unit and Integration Test Modules

Java Enterprise Edition Configuration

In addition to the Maven dependencies, we'll also need to configure the Java EE setup on SAP Cloud Platform Cloud Foundry where we want to deploy our application. The Java EE platform release schedule is behind the public JDK and JRE releases. While Java versions are regularly updated, most enterprise applications still run on older Java platforms because of cautious migration and elaborate certification processes on the enterprise platform side. For SAP Cloud Platform, the recommended target runtime at the time of this writing is Apache TomEE version 1.7.4 with a Java EE 6 Web Profile-certified software stack, based on a vanilla Apache Tomcat Java application server. Although part of the "Plus" profile of TomEE, JAX-RS has been activated by default on the SAP Cloud Platform and can be used without further setup steps. The SAP Java buildpack provides platform-related dependencies for security, logging, and service interaction on the platform.

The default manifest.yml file for SAP Cloud Platform Cloud Foundry-based applications shown in Listing 15.4 describes the required deployment parameters.

```
---
applications:
- name: [...]
  memory: 768M
  path: application/target/ [...] -application.war
  buildpack: sap_java_buildpack
  env:
    TARGET_RUNTIME: tomee
    JBP_CONFIG_SAPJVM_MEMORY_SIZES: 'metaspace:96m..'
  services:
    - mypostgres
```

Listing 15.4 Simplified manifest.yml Deployment Descriptor for SAP Cloud Platform Cloud Foundry

The buildpack and target runtime are specified manually. Without this configuration, the deployed container server may not satisfy all required application dependencies. A reserved memory of at least 768 MB is recommended in addition to the reserved metaspace size for the SAP JVM.

With these dependencies and configuration steps in place, or after creating a new project with an archetype, we can start using the SAP S/4HANA Cloud SDK in our Java EE project.

15.1.3 Using Dependency Injection with the VDM

An important feature of the Java EE platform is dependency injection, described in Java Specification Requests (JSR) 299 and 330. Dependency injection refers to the automatic insertion of object references to a software component or a resource by a runtime container. Instead of explicitly instantiating a resource dependency, such as a data source or a service, we'll declare that we depend on such a resource and expect it to be provided by the runtime container. Usually, we'll declare this dependency by adding annotations to classes, methods, and fields that signal to the runtime container to look up and inject the reference. Using dependency injection can greatly improve code quality and readability in the application sources by hiding the instantiation, lifecycle, and actual lookup of injected resources. Furthermore, dependency injection decouples the implementation of a client from the implementation of its dependencies.

The virtual data model of the SAP S/4HANA Cloud SDK supports dependency injection for services out of the box. Our Business Partner Address Manager app can be adapted to take advantage of dependency injection by adding a nonfinal field to the servlet classes that reference the VDM service, as shown in Listing 15.5. We'll choose the servlet to leverage the dependency injection because servlet classes are automatically being scanned for injectable fields.

```
@WebServlet("/api/business-partners")
public class BusinessPartnerServlet extends HttpServlet
{
    @javax.inject.Inject
    private BusinessPartnerService service;
    ...
}
```

Listing 15.5 Application Servlet Injecting a Component

By annotating the nonfinal, noninstantiated field `service` with `@Inject` in class `BusinessPartnerServlet`, we're requesting the Servlet container perform a dependency injection at runtime. Therefore, we can access the field and call the VDM with a statement such as `service.getAllBusinessPartner()`, without an apparent instantiation of the service. We don't need to expect a `NullPointerException` during runtime, which would be a clear sign of a failed dependency injection.

The Java EE-enabled platform will resolve the annotated field and, when no instantiation is given, will scan the current application class path for compatible classes that implement the type provided. A best practice is to only use interfaces in the application logic and provide the implementing classes as part of the class path. In our case, this implementation is provided by the SAP S/4HANA Cloud SDK, so we only need to declare the field with the interface and annotation we've done in this section.

15.1.4 Services Implemented with JAX-RS

The backend of an enterprise application can be exposed using different protocols. While web services classically have been implemented by using SOAP (XML), modern applications often rely on the JSON format provided by REST endpoints. Java API for RESTful Web Services (JAX-RS, defined in JSR 311) is a modern standard for developing and deploying RESTful web services using Java EE technologies. The standard provides an API that allows the formal declaration of web services by declaring Java annotations to application logic according to the REST (Representational State Transfer) architectural pattern. Popular open source implementations of JAX-RS are Jersey and Apache CXF.

While the former can easily be patched to existing Tomcat instances, the latter comes already packaged with current releases of TomEE. As a result, the API of Apache CXF is incorporated by the SAP Java buildpack on the SAP Cloud Platform. Developed by Apache, this web service framework provides additional frontend programming APIs like the Java API for XML Web Services (JAX-WS). One key aspect of Apache CXF is its emphasis on the variety of supported protocols besides RESTful HTTP, for example, SOAP based on WSDL and XML. In the following subsections, we'll consider how to implement the REST API of our Business Partner Address Manager application with JAX-RS based on Apache CXF. The SAP S/4HANA Cloud SDK additionally provides additional security handlers for Apache CXF, which we won't cover in the following subsections, but we recommend referring to the Javadoc of the SDK instead.

Implementing a Web Service

We can easily transform our Business Partner Address Manager application from servlets to a JAX-RS-powered web services. For the class `BusinessPartnerServlet`, the required change would look like the following simplified comparison. Listing 15.6 recaps the servlet, as developed in Chapter 4, simplified to focus on the excerpts relevant to the comparison with a JAX-RS-based implementation. The predefined servlet method `doGet` is registered for one path and its code needs to handle two different requests, depending on the optionally supplied request parameter `id`, for retrieving the specific business partner that we need to parse explicitly. The HTTP response content type is declared at runtime. and serialization of the response is handled manually as well.

```
@WebServlet("/api/business-partners")
public class BusinessPartnerServlet extends HttpServlet
{
  @Override
  protected void doGet( final HttpServletRequest request,
      final HttpServletResponse response )
```

```
        throws ServletException, IOException
  {
    final String id = request.getParameter("id");
    if(id == null) {
      // ...
    } else {
      // ...
    }
    response.setContentType("application/json");
    response.getWriter().write(...);
  }
}
```

Listing 15.6 Simplified Excerpt of the BusinessPartnerServlet Using Plain Servlet API

Using JAX-RS, we'll replace the `BusinessPartnerServlet` with the more convenient POJO class `BusinessPartnerRestService` from Listing 15.7. The new class is annotated with a dedicated service root path `@Path` for incoming requests and contains two separate methods, each responsible for handling one particular kind of request. The class is using speaking names for its public methods. The annotation `@GET` on a method signals to the backend JAX-RS environment that this Java method handles requests made with the HTTP `GET` method that match the path and further annotations of the Java method. The first method `getAll` matches the root path, while the second method `getById` handles requests to a particular subpath. JAX-RS enables the RESTful Web service to handle the optional `id` parameter as part of the request path like */api/business-partners/1* instead of as a query parameter. With the `@PathParam` annotation, we'll ask the container to inject the ID from the path conveniently into the corresponding method parameter. Instead of declaring response content types manually at runtime, the service endpoints are annotated in a clean and well-arranged way, at the method signature level. The deserialization of method parameters and serialization of method results are handled automatically by the JSON provider that is registered in JAX-RS. Different providers can be used for various content and media types. Compared with the servlet-based approach, JAX-RS allows us to declare our API in an explicit and clean way and handles a lot of the glue code otherwise necessary to handle request and response.

```
@Path("/api/business-partners")
public class BusinessPartnerRestService
{
```

```
  @Inject
  private BusinessPartnerService service;

  @GET
  @Produces(MediaType.APPLICATION_JSON)
  public List<BusinessPartner> getAll() {
    return new GetAllBusinessPartnersCommand(
        service).execute();
  }

  @GET
  @Produces(MediaType.APPLICATION_JSON)
  @Path("{id}")
  public BusinessPartner getById(
      @PathParam("id") String id) {
    return new GetSingleBusinessPartnerByIdCommand(service,
        id).execute();
  }
}
```

Listing 15.7 Retrieving Business Partners Implemented Using JAX-RS

This service class uses String-type arguments in the exposed methods, which will be mapped to the corresponding HTTP request path parameters. While this process is common for simple input variables for RESTful Web services, other service methods may require a different approach to handle complex input data. For example, to enable entity creation via an HTTP `POST` request, a method can expect an instance of a POJO class as an argument. In this case, the underlying framework will automatically deserialize parameters from the HTTP body of the request to create the instance and hand it over to the service method implementation. Besides deserialization during request mapping, the framework conveniently manages the serialization of the service response as well. A prerequisite for this data processing is a suitable JSON provider.

Including the Maven Dependencies

To enable the RESTful web services with an activated JSON provider in our Business Partner Address Manager application, the additional changes in Listing 15.8 are required in the pom.xml of the *application* module.

```
<dependencies>
  <!-- JAX-RS API -->
  <dependency>
    <groupId>org.apache.openejb</groupId>
    <artifactId>openejb-cxf-rs</artifactId>
    <version>4.7.5</version>
    <scope>provided</scope>
  </dependency>
  <dependency>
    <groupId>com.fasterxml.jackson.jaxrs</groupId>
    <artifactId>jackson-jaxrs-json-provider</artifactId>
    <version>2.9.4</version>
  </dependency>
  <!-- JAX-RS tools provided by SAP S/4HANA Cloud SDK -->
  <dependency>
    <groupId>com.sap.cloud.s4hana.frameworks</groupId>
    <artifactId>jaxrs</artifactId>
  </dependency>
</dependencies>
```

Listing 15.8 Application Dependencies for Provided JAX-RS API

The SAP S/4HANA Cloud SDK provides further tools to leverage application development for web services. For example, by including the `jaxrs` dependency, an elaborate exception mapper is registered into the servlet engine. This exception mapper takes care of handling runtime errors, automatically catches exceptions internally thrown by a web service, and maps these exceptions to prepared responses. The exception mapper processes error messages and stack traces, logs them to the underlying logging adapter, and exposes a prepared and comprehensible message with a dedicated error reference ID to the frontend. The user can report the application anomaly by using this unique error reference ID.

Configuring the JAX-RS Application

In specific circumstances, we may need to configure the JAX-RS application further. A Java EE application—being deployed locally or remotely on a TomEE or OpenEJB server—can customize the automatic scanning for Java EE components and classes, such as Enterprise Java Beans (EJB) or CDI beans, by providing exclusions and inclusions. Jar files are skipped from scanning when listed in a *WEB-INF/exclusions.list*, as prefixes or as full names, while packages and classes can be whitelisted in a *WEB-INF/scan.xml*, as shown in Listing 15.9, to include required application- as well as framework-specific packages.

```
<scan>
  <packages>
    <package>com.sap.cloud.s4hana.examples.addressmgr↩
</package>
    <package>com.sap.cloud.sdk</package>
    <package>com.fasterxml.jackson</package>
  </packages>
</scan>
```

Listing 15.9 Whitelisting Components in scan.xml

If we want a common root path for all RESTful web services of an application, we can declare an additional application configuration class. This class extends the JAX-RS `Application` class, as shown in Listing 15.10. We could also define components and supply web service metadata at this point, if required.

```
@ApplicationPath("/api")
public class MyApplication
    extends javax.ws.rs.core.Application {
}
```

Listing 15.10 Customizable JAX-RS Application Configuration

15.1.5 Multitenant Persistence

The EJB framework enables the lifecycle configuration of Java Beans and their components. The goal of Java EE is to reduce information redundancy and distribute commonly used resources to multiple service endpoints. However, for this process, you'll need to manage Java Beans with regards to their request dependencies. Components can be declared as stateful or stateless. A *stateful component* will be instantiated at least once for every request. Its value can be changed or processed only with regards to the invoking service request. Once the request is completed and the object is finalized by the container, the stateful component will be removed as well. On the other hand, a *stateless component* will be constructed once for the application. Its instance will only be removed once the Java application itself is terminated and no further references to the component are active in the container. Until then, the stateless component can be read and processed sequentially by any number of internal request handlers. Any reference to such a component instance is created by the field annotation @EJB.

With EJB technology, you can separate critical components from single applications, making it possible to share resources container-wide over several local and remote services. One popular example for using EJB components is accessing a context-aware, container-controlled EntityManager. Thus, you'll be able to switch from the application-managed persistence that we discussed in Chapter 7 to container-managed transactions, while resolving persistence properties for one application locally to a container-scoped setup, removing the necessity of explicit JNDI lookups. EJB also leverages JPA for persistence, but in contrast to Chapter 7, in this context, the container manages transaction handling.

To change transaction management of our example application, some steps are required, which we'll explain in the following subsections.

Setting Up Dependencies

Let's add the required configuration and dependencies to the application module pom.xml file, as shown in Listing 15.11.

```
<project>
  <!-- Required for DataSource Cloud Foundry Binding -->
  <repositories>
    <repository>
      <id>Spring Repo</id>
      <name>Spring Repo</name>
      <url>http://repo.spring.io/release/</url>
    </repository>
  </repositories>
  <dependencies>
    <!-- Persistence and Cloud Foundry Binding -->
    <dependency>
      <groupId>org.cloudfoundry</groupId>
      <artifactId>tomee-resource-configuration</artifactId>
      <version>1.4.0.RELEASE</version>
    </dependency>
    <dependency>
      <groupId>org.springframework.cloud</groupId>
      <artifactId>spring-cloud-cloudfoundry-connector↩
```

```
</artifactId>
      <version>2.0.1.RELEASE</version>
    </dependency>
    <dependency>
      <groupId>org.hibernate</groupId>
      <artifactId>hibernate-entitymanager</artifactId>
      <version>4.2.21.Final</version>
    </dependency>
    <dependency>
      <groupId>com.sap.cloud.s4hana.frameworks</groupId>
      <artifactId>liquibase</artifactId>
    </dependency>
  </dependencies>
</project>
```

Listing 15.11 Application POM file Additions for EntityManager Support

The new dependencies include implementations for `EntityManager` from Hibernate and the platform-related configurations and connectors for Cloud Foundry.

Configuring the Data Source and Hibernate

Now, we'll introduce a *WEB-INF/resources.xml* with a new `Resource` delegated from the Cloud Foundry platform, as shown in Listing 15.12. The name of the resource ID represents the bound database service instance name.

```
<resources>
  <Resource id="jdbc/mypostgres" type="javax.sql.DataSource"
      properties-provider="org.cloudfoundry.reconfiguration.↩
tomee.DelegatingPropertiesProvider"/>
</resources>
```

Listing 15.12 JNDI-featured DataSource in resource.xml

The persistence.xml file must be updated as shown in Listing 15.13. Instead of a persistence unit with transaction type "`local resource`," a "`JTA`"-powered persistence unit is being declared.

```
 <?xml version="1.0" encoding="UTF-8" standalone="no"?>
<persistence xmlns="http://java.sun.com/xml/ns/persistence"
  xmlns:xsi="http://www.w3.org/2001/XMLSchema-instance"
```

```
  version="1.0"
  xsi:schemaLocation="http://java.sun.com/xml/ns/persistence ↩
http://java.sun.com/xml/ns/persistence/persistence_1_0.xsd">
  <persistence-unit name="MyAppUnit" transaction-type="JTA">
    <provider>org.hibernate.ejb.HibernatePersistence↩
</provider>
    <jta-data-source>jdbc/mypostgres</jta-data-source>
    <properties>
      <property name="hibernate.dialect"
        value="org.hibernate.dialect.PostgreSQLDialect"/>
      <property name="hibernate.show_sql" value="true"/>
      <property name="hibernate.multiTenancy" value="SCHEMA"/>
      <property name="hibernate.tenant_identifier_resolver"
        value="com.sap.cloud.s4hana.examples.addressmgr.↩
config.TenantIdentifierResolver"/>
      <property
        name="hibernate.multi_tenant_connection_provider"
        value="com.sap.cloud.s4hana.examples.addressmgr.↩
config.SchemaPerTenantConnectionProvider"/>
    </properties>
  </persistence-unit>
</persistence>
```

Listing 15.13 JTA DataSource Descriptor in persistence.xml

While accessing the `mypostgres`-named JDBC resource, the classes `TenantIdentifier-Resolver` and `SchemaPerTenantConnectionProvider` can be reused.

Implementing the Local Address Workflow

A new EJB class is required, `LocalAddressBean`. This class will be given an injected instance of `EntityManager`, as shown in Listing 15.14.

```
@Stateless
public class LocalAddressBean {
  @PersistenceContext
  private EntityManager entityManager;

  public List<Address> getAllAddresses() {
    return entityManager.createNamedQuery("Address.findAll",
```

```
            Address.class).getResultList();
    }

    public void storeNewAddress(final Address address) {
      entityManager.persist(address);
    }

    public void updateExistingAddress(final Address address) {
      entityManager.merge(address);
    }
}
```

Listing 15.14 EJB with PersistenceContext for Managing Local Addresses

Note that transaction must not be managed manually (such as committing or rolling back if a problem arises). This limitation is due to the underlying database transaction being managed by the container instead of by the application as done before. Until a transaction is invoked internally, the entity is considered *managed* to the persistence layer, as shown in Figure 15.2, enabling you to change fields that will be kept up to date with the underlying database transaction. As soon as the persistence context is closed, for example, after request finalization, the remaining transaction is closed, and the entities become *detached*. Changes to the fields of detached entities will not be persisted.

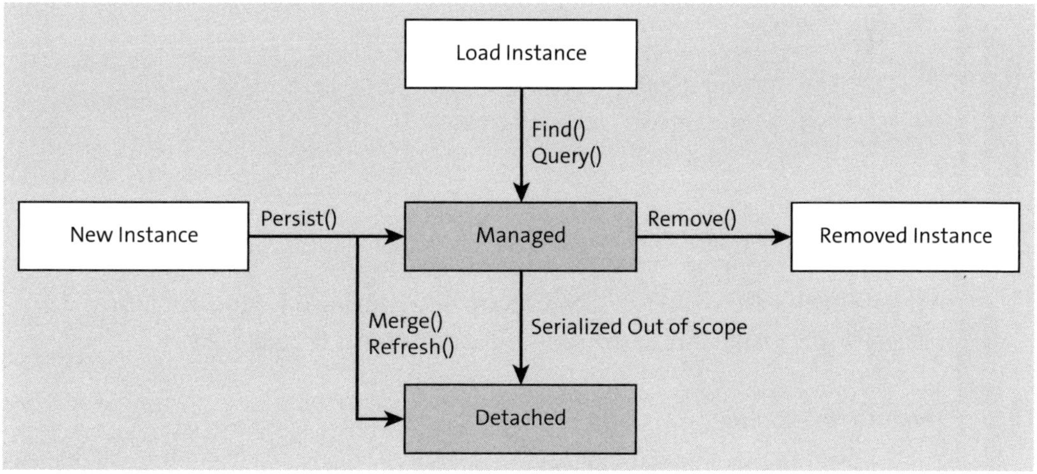

Figure 15.2 State of EJB Components in the Persistence Layer

The advantage of using this approach becomes apparent when changing the LocalAddressServlet class to a LocalAddressRestService class, including the newly created, injectable LocalAddressBean component, as shown in Listing 15.15.

```
@Path("/addresses-local")
public class LocalAddressRestService {
  @EJB
  private LocalAddressBean localAddressBean;

  @GET
  @Produces(MediaType.APPLICATION_JSON)
  public List<Address> doGet() {
    return localAddressBean.getAllAddresses();
  }

  @POST
  @Consumes(MediaType.APPLICATION_JSON)
  @Produces(MediaType.APPLICATION_JSON)
  public List<Address> doStore(final Address address) {
    localAddressBean.storeNewAddress(address);
    return localAddressBean.getAllAddresses();
  }

  @PATCH
  @Consumes(MediaType.APPLICATION_JSON)
  @Produces(MediaType.APPLICATION_JSON)
  public List<Address> doUpdate(final Address address) {
    localAddressBean.updateExistingAddress(address);
    return localAddressBean.getAllAddresses();
  }
}
```

Listing 15.15 LocalAddressRestService with Injected EJB

While switching from servlets to JAX-RS and introducing injections for EJBs and EntityManager, the readability of the service class improves dramatically.

Tenant Provisioning

The TenantProvisioningServlet class can be transformed as well. But instead of creating a new EntityManager, the data source will be read from the underlying persistence context.

To retrieve an instance of `java.sql.Connection` at runtime, the following statements were required:

```
final EntityManager entityManager = GenericEntityManagerFacade
    .getInstance().getEntityManager();
final Connection connection = ((SessionImpl)
    entityManager.unwrap(Session.class)).connection();
```

However, you can take advantage dependency injection again with the following statements:

```
@Resource(name="jdbc/mypostgres")
private DataSource dataSource;
```

The reference to the connection can be resolved by accessing the data source instance:

```
final Connection connection = dataSource.getConnection();
```

15.2 Integrating with Spring Boot

Spring is a popular open source Java framework for creating enterprise applications. Its main feature is its inversion of control container, which enables decoupling of code from the other services and modules it depends on. Spring also provides many modules that can be optionally included in your project to handle various use cases. One such module that we'll use extensively in this section is Spring Boot. This module provides a preconfigured and ready-to-run Spring environment that can run on its own without the need for separate middleware. Another module that we'll use in subsection Section 15.2.5 is Spring Data, which enables database access with a minimal amount of code and configuration.

This section assumes some basic knowledge about the Spring Framework and Spring Boot. For more information about these topics, refer to the **Guides** section of the Spring website, specifically *http://tiny.cc/spring-boot*. Another excellent resource for getting familiar with the Spring framework can be found at *http://tiny.cc/spring-framework*.

Note that the examples shown in this section and in the GitHub repository illustrate just one of many ways to implement Spring Boot applications with the SAP S/4HANA Cloud SDK. Newer versions of Spring may introduce features that change and/or simplify how applications should be developed, for example, new annotations.

15.2.1 Maven Archetype for Spring Boot Projects

For getting started quickly with both the SAP S/4HANA Cloud SDK and Spring Boot, the SDK offers a Maven archetype. At the time of this writing, this archetype uses Spring Boot version 1.5.9, which in turn uses Spring version 4.3.13. Spring Boots is also configured for deployment to the Cloud Foundry environment of SAP Cloud Platform as a Java main program. Generating a project with the Spring Boot archetype is almost the same as in Chapter 4, Section 4.1.2. Run the command shown in Listing 15.16 as a single line, without the ↩ symbols.

```
mvn archetype:generate ↩
    "-DarchetypeGroupId=com.sap.cloud.s4hana.archetypes" ↩
    "-DarchetypeArtifactId=scp-cf-spring" ↩
    "-DarchetypeVersion=RELEASE"
```

Listing 15.16 Generate Project Using Archetype

Also, for this archetype, Maven will ask for several parameters of the project to be generated. See Chapter 4 for an explanation and suggested values for our Business Partner Address Manager application. Similar to the other archetypes, the generated project contains a multimodule Maven project initially with three Java modules (*application, unit-tests, and integration-tests*) in separate subfolders. However, several differences exist with this archetype:

- The pom.xml file in the top-level folder of the project contains additional dependency management for Spring Boot and related libraries.
- The manifest.yml file is configured with the `main` target runtime. Therefore, Cloud Foundry will run the application as a Java main program.
- The *integration-tests* project is configured via its pom.xml to use the testing functionality offered by the Spring Framework instead of Arquillian.
- The sample integration tests themselves are also re-written to leverage the Spring Framework's testing capabilities.
- The *application* project is configured to package the application code as a JAR file instead of a WAR file.
- The sample "Hello World!" servlet is rewritten as a Spring controller.
- A bootstrapping class called *Application.java* is added to configure and initialize Spring Boot. Section 15.2.3 will go into more detail about configuring applications for Spring Boot.

Building the generated project is the same as other archetypes. Run the following command from the top-level project folder:

```
mvn clean package
```

To start the Spring Boot application, you can either run the `Application` class directly within your IDE, or you can use the following Maven command from the *application* project subfolder:

```
mvn spring-boot:run
```

This command instructs Maven to execute the Spring Boot plugin and start the application. Once the server has started, you'll see a line in the log output ending with a sentence similar to:

```
Started Application in 4.297 seconds (JVM running for 7.828).
```

By default, as before, the server is accessible at the URL *http://localhost:8080/* on your local machine. If you enter this URL in your browser, you'll see the standard static welcome page provided by the SAP S/4HANA Cloud SDK.

15.2.2 Including the SAP S/4HANA Cloud SDK in Existing Maven-Based Spring Projects

Throughout the book, we've been using Maven archetypes offered by the SAP S/4HANA Cloud SDK to generate projects with all of their dependencies preconfigured. If, however, you have an existing Maven project with Spring Boot and would like to start using the SDK, then this subsection will explain what modules to add to your pom.xml file.

Dependency Management Configuration

The first thing we strongly recommend is to add the bill of materials (BOM) of the SAP S/4HANA Cloud SDK to the dependency management section of your pom.xml. In principle, this approach is similar to the approach for a Java EE-based project, but a few specifics must be kept in mind, as shown in Listing 15.17, which contains version and dependency information for all of the modules of the SAP S/4HANA Cloud SDK. Although you could technically use parts of the SDK without the `sdk-bom` module, your pom.xml file would be more difficult to maintain because you would have to add version information for each SDK module you add.

```
<dependencyManagement>
  <dependencies>
    <!- Keep any existing dependency imports -->
    <dependency>
        <groupId>org.json</groupId>
        <artifactId>json</artifactId>
        <version>20170516</version>
    </dependency>
    <dependency>
      <groupId>org.mockito</groupId>
      <artifactId>mockito-core</artifactId>
      <version>2.10.0</version>
    </dependency>
    <dependency>
      <groupId>org.springframework.boot</groupId>
      <artifactId>spring-boot-dependencies</artifactId>
      <version>1.5.9.RELEASE</version>
      <type>pom</type>
      <scope>import</scope>
    </dependency>
    <dependency>
      <groupId>com.sap.cloud.s4hana</groupId>
      <artifactId>sdk-bom</artifactId>
      <version>2.0.0</version>
      <type>pom</type>
      <scope>import</scope>
    </dependency>
  </dependencies>
</dependencyManagement>
```

Listing 15.17 SAP S/4HANA Cloud SDK Dependency Management with Spring Boot

This code is similar to the main pom.xml in the Spring Boot archetype. Notice the explicit inclusion of Mockito v2.10.0 and org.json version 20170516.

Dependency Management

When using Spring Boot version 1.5.x and the SDK, Mockito v2.10.0 and org.json version 20170516 must be added and placed before the Spring Boot dependencies because both Spring Boot and the SAP S/4HANA Cloud SDK include Mockito and org.json as dependencies, but different major versions of them. The SDK depends on version 2.10 of Mockito and version 20170516 of org.json, while Spring Boot 1.5.x uses version 1.10.19 of Mockito and version 20140107 of org.json. We want the newer versions of Mockito and org.json to be used in the end so that unit and integration tests using the SDK testing features will compile and run properly. Alternatively, you can order the SDK and Spring Boot dependencies in such a way that the SDK is before Spring Boot. Then, the Mockito and org.json libraries bundled within the SDK can override the older libraries included in Spring Boot.

Dependencies for SAP S/4HANA Integration

After including the bill of materials POM module, you'll then need to include a cloud platform module, followed by modules of the SAP S/4HANA Cloud SDK features you want to use. If you're just running your Spring Boot application locally, we suggest using the Cloud Foundry module *scp-cf* as the default platform module.

The example shown in Listing 15.18 uses the *s4hana-all* module, which is a convenience POM module that includes everything related to integration with SAP S/4HANA from the SAP S/4HANA Cloud SDK. You can also use specific submodules of the SDK instead if you only need a subset of the SDK's functionality.


```
<dependencies>
  <!- Any number of dependencies -->
  <dependency>
    <groupId>com.sap.cloud.s4hana.cloudplatform</groupId>
    <artifactId>scp-cf</artifactId>
  </dependency>
  <dependency>
    <groupId>com.sap.cloud.s4hana</groupId>
    <artifactId>s4hana-all</artifactId>
  </dependency>
  <!- Other dependencies -->
<dependencies>
```

Listing 15.18 SAP S/4HANA Cloud SDK Dependencies in Sub-Projects

Spring Configuration

The SAP S/4HANA Cloud SDK has many servlet components and injectable classes. To fully integrate the SDK into Spring projects and use these components, some additional configuration is needed so that Spring discovers the SDK components. In a typical Spring Boot project, and especially with the SDK's Spring Boot Maven archetype, an embedded application server is used. Furthermore, usually a bootstrapping class annotated with `@SpringBootApplication` exists, In this bootstrapping class, we need to use both the `@ComponentScan` and the `@ServletComponentScan` annotations and add the package base path `com.sap.cloud.sdk` to both annotation values. As an example, consider the SDK's Spring Boot Maven archetype. Listing 15.19 shows how the bootstrapping class would look like when generated following the steps in Section 15.2.1. Note the highlighted parts of the annotations, which instruct Spring Boot to scan packages of the SAP S/4HANA Cloud with this base path for components so that they can be used in the Spring Boot application.

```
@SpringBootApplication
@ComponentScan({
  "com.sap.cloud.sdk", "com.sap.cloud.s4hana.examples"})
@ServletComponentScan({
  "com.sap.cloud.sdk", "com.sap.cloud.s4hana.examples"})
public class Application {
  public static void main(final String[] args) {
    SpringApplication.run(Application.class, args);
  }
}
```

Listing 15.19 Spring Boot Application Class with SDK Servlet Components and Injectable Classes

If you're using just the Spring Framework and not Spring Boot, then you only need to ensure that your Spring configuration is also scanning the class path `com.sap.cloud.sdk` for components. Listing 15.20 and Listing 15.21 show an example for annotation- and XML-based configurations, respectively.

```
@Configuration
@ComponentScan(basePackages = "com.sap.cloud.sdk …")
public class YourSpringConfiguration  {
  // your implementation
}
```

Listing 15.20 Class-Based Spring Configuration

```
<?xml version="1.0" encoding="UTF-8"?>
<beans xmlns=http://www.springframework.org/schema/beans …>
```

```
  <!-- some of your configuration -->
  <context:component-scan base-package="com.sap.cloud.sdk ..."/>
  <!-- rest of your configuration -->
</beans>
```

Listing 15.21 XML-Based Spring Configuration

15.2.3 Using Dependency Injection with the VDM

With the configuration in place, we're ready to use the dependency injection capabilities of Spring with the virtual data model of the SAP S/4HANA Cloud SDK, similar to the usage in a Java EE project described in Section 15.1.3. The Spring Framework, since version 3, supports JSR 330 annotations, so you can inject the VDM services as you would any other Spring bean. The example shown in Listing 15.22 illustrates how VDM services can be injected into a Spring Boot controller.

```
@RestController
public class BusinessPartnerController {
  private final BusinessPartnerService service;

  @Autowired
  public BusinessPartnerController(
      BusinessPartnerService service) {
    this.service = service;
  }

  /* Rest of controller implementation, omitted for clarity */
}
```

Listing 15.22 Injecting VDM Services in Spring Components

One reason for dependency injection in VDM services is the ability to mock these services in unit tests. In Spring Boot, we can use the `@MockBean` annotation to automatically inject mocked instances of VDM services into the controllers that we want to unit test. Listing 15.23 contains an example of unit testing the controller.

```
@RunWith(SpringRunner.class)
@WebMvcTest(BusinessPartnerController.class)
public class BusinessPartnerControllerTest {
  private static final MockUtil mockUtil = new MockUtil();
```

```
  @Autowired
  private MockMvc mockMvc;

  @MockBean( answer = Answers.RETURNS_DEEP_STUBS )
  private static BusinessPartnerService
    mockBusinessPartnerService;

  @BeforeClass
  public static void beforeClass() {
    mockUtil.mockDefaults();
    mockUtil.mockErpDestination();
  }

  @Before
  public void beforeEachTest() throws ODataException {
    when(mockBusinessPartnerService
        .getAllBusinessPartner()
        .execute(any(ErpConfigContext.class)))
        .thenReturn(new LinkedList<BusinessPartner>());
  }

  @Test
  public void testGetBusinessPartners() throws Exception {
    mockMvc.perform(MockMvcRequestBuilders
        .get("/api/business-partners"))
        .andExpect(status().isOk());
  }
}
```

Listing 15.23 Unit Testing with Mocked VDM Services

The important thing to note when mocking VDM services is that you have to enable deep stubbing. In our example, we did enable deep stubbing by setting the `answer` parameter in the `@MockBean` annotation. Without this setting, all of the fluent APIs would return null values, causing exceptions to be thrown in the unit tests. We want to mock the VDM service behavior, but at the same time, we want to return the mocked VDM service object whenever the fluent APIs are called.

15.2.4 Services Implemented as Spring Controllers

Once the necessary configurations (Section 15.2.2 and Section 15.2.3) are in place, writing Spring controllers with the SAP S/4HANA Cloud SDK is quite straightforward. For readers familiar with Spring, some additional considerations about SDK features when writing controllers include the following:

- VDM entities can be used directly as input parameters with the `@RequestBody` annotation in controller methods. The VDM entities support deserialization from JSON using Jackson (Spring default) and Gson. In your controller method's `@RequestMapping` annotation, make sure to set the `consumes` parameter to "`application/json`".
- Also, VDM entities can be directly returned with `ResponseEntity`. Again, VDM entities support serialization to JSON using Jackson and Gson. In your controller method's `@RequestMapping` annotation, make sure you set the `produces` parameter to "`application/json`".

Using VDM Entities in Requests and Responses

When using VDM entities directly, note that fields are (de)serialized to/from JSON using the property names from their matching OData entities and complex types. Thus you'll need to use upper camel case, except for associated entities (navigation properties) retrieved with the fetch methods. These associated entities usually have names prefixed with "to_". In more complex web applications, using dedicated Java objects to transfer data to and from the backend may be more suitable than reusing the VDM entities, because dedicated Java objects allow you to tailor the contract to the needs of specific consumers.

15

Listing 15.24 is an example of a Spring controller based on our Business Partner Address Management application from Chapter 4. This example also uses the `CreateAddressCommand` class, which is nearly identical to the command classes described in Chapter 4. However, the service is passed to instead of instantiated within the command classes, since the example is using dependency injection. Note how we leveraged VDM entity classes when dealing with the request and response body, based on the out of the box serialization capabilities of the VDM.

```
@RestController
@RequestMapping(
    value = "/api/addresses",
    produces = "application/json")
```

```
public class AddressController {

  private final BusinessPartnerService service;
  @Autowired
  public AddressController(BusinessPartnerService service) {
    this.service = service;
  }

  @RequestMapping(
      method = RequestMethod.POST,
      consumes = "application/json")
  protected ResponseEntity<BusinessPartnerAddress>
    createAddress(
        @RequestBody final BusinessPartnerAddress address) {

    final BusinessPartnerAddress addressCreated =
        new CreateAddressCommand(service, address).execute();

    return ResponseEntity
        .status(HttpStatus.CREATED)
        .body(addressCreated);
  }
  // Rest of controller operations
}
```

Listing 15.24 Example Spring Controller Using SDK Features

15.2.5 Multitenant Persistence

In Chapter 7, we described how to add multitenant persistence in a generic way without using frameworks such as Java EE or Spring. The basic principles and functionality offered by the SAP S/4HANA Cloud SDK can also be used in a Spring-based implementation. In this section, we'll summarize how to create such an implementation using Spring Boot and running on SAP Cloud Platform Cloud Foundry. We'll start with the Spring Boot Maven archetype (Section 15.2.1) and add multitenant persistence on top of it. In our examples, we'll use PostgreSQL for the database and Hibernate for the implementation of the Java Persistence API.

For the full source code of this Spring-based implementation, refer to the GitHub repository for this book. You'll also find a detailed step-by-step guide on implementing multitenant persistence using Spring on our SDK online resource (*http://tiny.cc/s4-sdk-mt-spring*).

Configuring the Data Source

For simple scenarios deploying to SAP Cloud Platform Cloud Foundry and using only one database service, Spring automatically sets up the data source. All you'll have to do is extend the `Application` bootstrapping class to extend `JpaBaseConfiguration` and provide a default implementation of the abstract methods.

Configuring Hibernate

By default, persistence libraries such as Hibernate are configured for simple single-tenant database access. We'll therefore need to perform some configuration steps to enable multitenant persistence. With Spring, you can achieve this configuration using Java classes. In our example, we'll need to implement three classes:

- A class annotated with `@Configuration`, which is the main Hibernate configuration class. In this class, we'll configure the JPA entity manager, set the parameters to enable multitenant persistence, and set the package(s) to scan for our classes that represent database tables (JPA entities). In our example project on GitHub, we named this class `HibernateConfig`.
- A class annotated with `@Component`, which implements the `MultiTenantConnectionProvider` interface used by the `HibernateConfig` class. This class provides tenant-specific connections to the database. In our GitHub example, we named this class `SchemaPerTenantConnectionProvider`. The `getConnection` method obtains a connection from the data source and sets the schema to the tenant-specific one. The `releaseConnection` finally sets the schema to the default tenant's schema and closes the connection.
- A class annotated with `@Component`, which implements the `CurrentTenantIdentifierResolver` interface also used by the `HibernateConfig` class. Its purpose is to obtain the identifier of the current tenant. This is where we use the `TenantAccessor` class from the SAP S/4HANA Cloud SDK to get the current tenant identifier.

Tenant Onboarding and Offboarding

When developing multitenant applications on the SAP Cloud Platform in the Cloud Foundry environment, you'll need to create services for tenant onboarding and offboarding. Once registered the SAP Cloud Platform automatically calls these services when users subscribe to an application. The onboarding service needs to handle the creation of the tenant database schema, while the offboarding service will perform the relevant cleanup actions of the tenant database schema (such as archiving or deletion of the schema).

The SAP Cloud Platform expects services in the following format:

- Onboarding service
  - URL: *some-url-path/tenantId*
  - HTTP method: `PUT`
  - Normal HTTP return code: 204 (no content)
- Offboarding service
  - URL: *some-url-path/tenantId*
  - HTTP method: `DELETE`
  - Normal HTTP return code: 204 (no content)

Now, we can follow the usual Spring conventions and implement a controller for the two services. Our GitHub example has an interface named `TenantProvisioningService` and an implementation named `DefaultTenantProvisioningService`, which is a Spring service. This service is invoked by a wrapping Spring controller, which is named `TenantProvisioningController`. The service uses Liquibase for easy creation of the tenant database schema.

Implementing the Local Address Workflow

The next step is to introduce the Java classes that represent the data, that is, the JPA entities, the database access logic, and the business logic using both.

With Spring Data, the only database access logic you need to write are interface stubs annotated with `@Repository`. Spring Data fills in the implementations, which provide basic operations to find, create, and delete JPA entities, which translates into database queries. Spring Data also takes care of the JPA entity manager and database transactions. In our GitHub example, we have repositories that extend the `CrudRepository` interface, which is a generic interface that requires two type parameters: one for the type of the JPA entity and the other one for the type of the primary key field.

```
@Repository
public interface AddressRepository
    extends CrudRepository<Address, Long> {}
```

Listing 15.25 Spring Data Repository Example

The JPA entities are almost the same as explained in other examples in the book and the SDK's online resources. However, some annotations such as `@NamedQueries` and

@NamedQuery aren't needed because the Spring Data repositories already provide queries for the entities.

Finally, you can include the Spring Data repositories into your own business logic services and controllers using the @Autowired annotation and access tenant-specific data with only a few lines of code. Simply call the methods provided by the Spring Data repositories and use the JPA entities.

Binding to Persistence Services

With the SAP Cloud Platform Cloud Foundry and Spring Cloud, configuring the database service requires only the following steps:

1. Create the database service in the SAP Cloud Platform. You can create a database service from the SAP Service Marketplace section of the SAP Cloud Platform cockpit or using the Cloud Foundry command line tool.
2. In the application, create a class representing a Spring configuration profile that uses Spring Cloud to scan for the Cloud Foundry database service. For simple scenarios like our GitHub example, create the profile as shown in Listing 15.26.

   ```
   @Configuration
   @Profile("cloud")
   @ServiceScan
   public class CloudConfig {}
   ```

   Listing 15.26 Spring Profile for Cloud Service Scanning

   For a more detailed explanation using more complex cases, please consult the Cloud Foundry documentation at *http://tiny.cc/spring-cf*.
3. Add a few lines to your manifest.yml to activate the Spring profile and bind the database instance to your application. For example see Listing 15.27.

   ```
   ---
   applications:
   - name: persistence
     memory: 768M
     host: persistence
     path: application/target/persistence-application.jar
     buildpack: sap_java_buildpack
     env:
       TARGET_RUNTIME: main
       JBP_CONFIG_SAPJVM_MEMORY_SIZES: 'metaspace:96m..'
   ```

```
    SPRING_PROFILES_ACTIVE: cloud
  services:
    - mydb
```

Listing 15.27 Cloud Foundry manifest.yml Example

15.3 Summary

In this chapter we've shown you how to combine the SAP S/4HANA Cloud SDK with popular Java frameworks such as Java EE and Spring Boot to develop side-by-side extensions with less effort. The next chapter will explain how to handle business events coming from SAP S/4HANA Cloud systems within side-by-side extensions.

Chapter 16
Event-Based Integration

In this chapter we'll show you how to build Java applications that consume business events from an SAP S/4HANA Cloud system. Event-based integration is an additional building block for side-by-side architectures, suitable in many cases where events should trigger a process. This chapter explains the foundation of event-based integration, the event mechanisms found in SAP S/4HANA Cloud, and ways to integrate event-driven aspects into side-by-side extensions.

Different approaches exist for how systems communicate with each other. In Part II, we mostly considered direct communication via API calls. In some scenarios, direct communication could lead to tight coupling and unwanted dependencies at runtime. Thus, communicating via messages or events can be desirable in some contexts. We also introduced Hystrix commands in previous chapters, which in addition to improving resilience can also serve to achieve asynchronous and reactive programming by wrapping API calls accordingly. However, we haven't yet considered the theory and concepts behind message-based interaction or described how to achieve event-based integration between SAP S/4HANA Cloud and applications on the SAP Cloud Platform.

Event-based integration, the topic of this chapter, thus expands the set of approaches available to us for designing a modern application architecture. We'll first explain the theory of reactive systems and how it relates to events and messages in Section 16.1. Section 16.2 relates the theory to the concepts of event-based integration as available with the SAP Enterprise Messaging service on SAP Cloud Platform. In Section 16.3, we'll describe the eventing capabilities in SAP S/4HANA Cloud and describe how to configure the system to send events from SAP S/4HANA Cloud to SAP Cloud Platform. Section 16.4 then describes the required configuration of the SAP Enterprise Messaging service on SAP Cloud Platform before we take a short look on how to integrate events into a Java application on SAP Cloud Platform.

16.1 Theory of Reactive Systems

By definition, side-by-side extensions run in highly distributed and heterogenic environments because they interact with SAP S/4HANA systems and possibly other dependencies that run in different environments. This situation results in new challenges for the development of your extensions.

As such, an extension is a system of distributed components. Our Business Partner Address Manager app will be appealing to users if it reacts immediately to user requests. To keep the extension responsive, we must cater to all situations, especially situations when any component might fail. Therefore, we need all components to be responsive when they run into errors and when they run under high loads.

We've seen some ways to achieve responsiveness under failure (resilience) and responsiveness in high or changing load situations (elasticity) in a traditional architecture built on RESTful web services in the previous chapters, especially Chapter 4. A relatively new approach to resilience and elasticity builds components as *reactive systems* (*www.reactivemanifesto.org*). Since the introduction of the term, reactive systems have gained a lot of traction. While they require a different approach to the architecture of distributed systems, reactive systems offer distinct benefits to make systems responsive.

The key element of reactive systems is the asynchronous message-driven communication between systems, as shown in Figure 16.1. Regardless of their location, reactive systems communicate in the same way with each other—via messaging, which allows loose coupling, efficient resource usage, and isolation between systems. Via messaging, reactive systems notify supervisor components about failures without blocking the process so that another component can take over the role of a failed system.

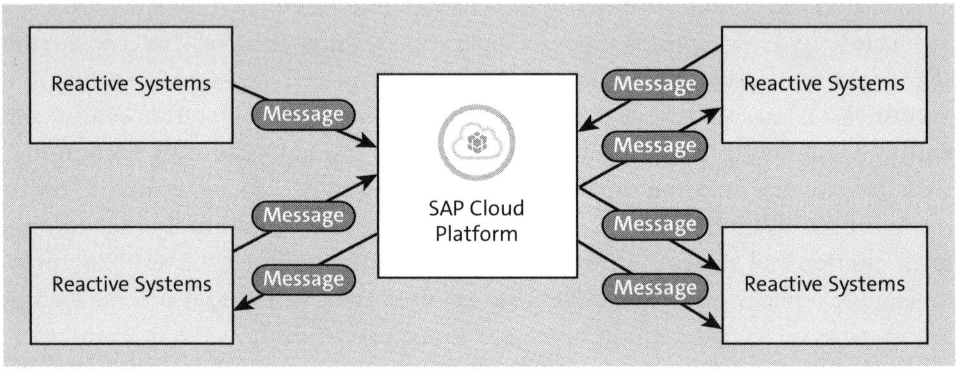

Figure 16.1 Messaging between Reactive Systems

Messages

Messages are distinct pieces of information that are sent, preferably asynchronously, to a clear and single destination and are used to communicate across a network.

Business-relevant applications implemented as extensions on the SAP Cloud Platform process business-related objects and data that are part of core business applications in the connected SAP S/4HANA environment. Traditional applications mainly use remotely accessible APIs to extract data—synchronous calls to an explicit endpoint on the right SAP S/4HANA system. As we never know from outside when changes occur, we would need to poll for those changes regularly on the connected suite system, if our application needs to stay up-to-date and react to changes.

To avoid too many calls being made to APIs, the system that owns the business data, in which the core business application runs, should actively inform potentially interested consuming applications on the SAP Cloud Platform when changes happen and exactly what happened. Knowing that a change happened, the consumer application can use the relevant API to fetch the new or changed business data. To achieve this connection, we can use the reactive programming approach shown in Figure 16.2.

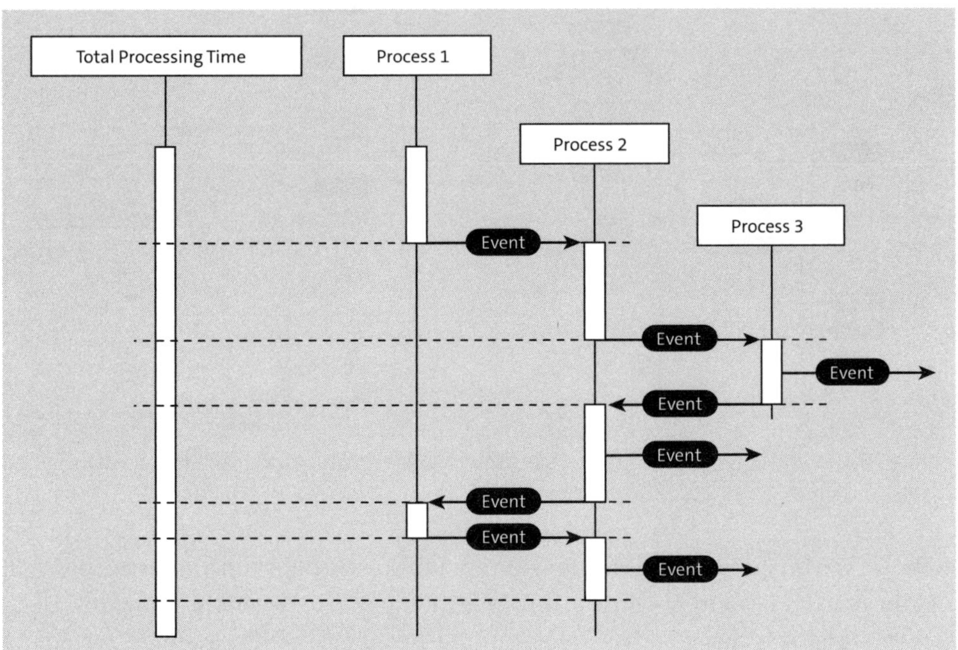

Figure 16.2 Reactive Programming Approach

Reactive programs work asynchronously when triggered by data flows (events) and remain inactive if no relevant change happens. Reactive programs are not controlling processes and are not waiting or blocking other processes. So, inside a reactive system, events are "controlling" the behavior of business processes.

Events

Events are facts for others to observe about situations (the result of an action, a certain constellation of parameters, etc.) that occur in business systems or applications, mostly happening outside of the system of receivers. Events can be relevant to a group of components as a trigger for subsequent actions in the system of receivers. Senders of events are not aware of event receivers.

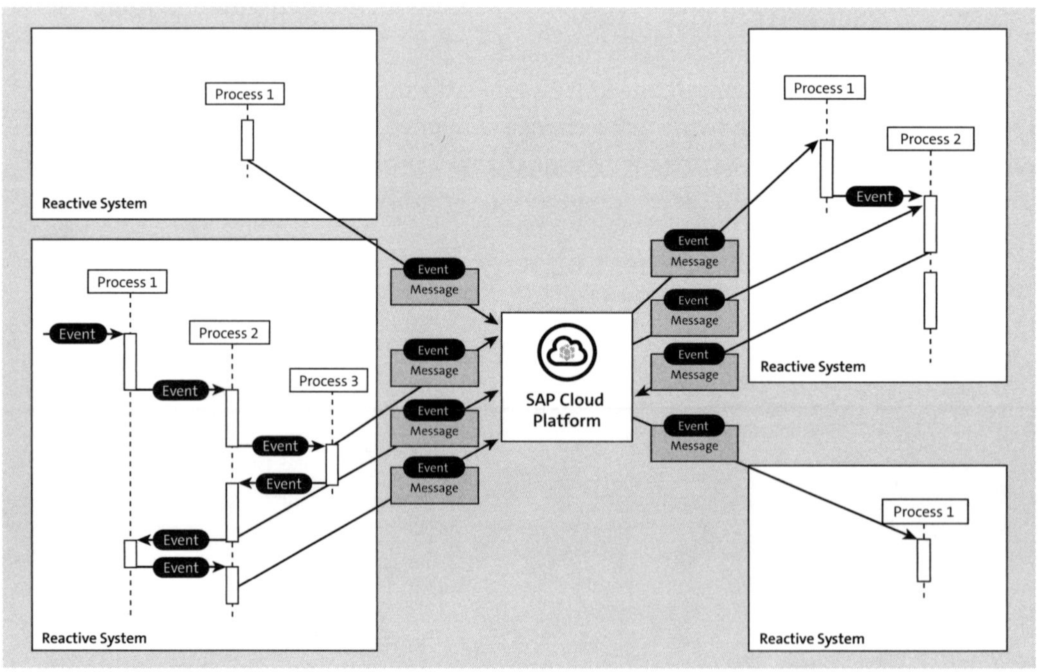

Figure 16.3 Event-Driven Systems across Networks: Messaging under the Hood with Events inside Messages

Now, we can finalize our target extension application through both approaches. We'll use the reactive systems architecture for the interaction between the individual components and use the reactive programming paradigm within a single system to implement the business logic. To transmit events raised inside the business logic of one specific system to other systems, messages are used as vehicles, as shown in Figure 16.3. How to leverage messaging to transport events will be described in the following sections.

When we expose events via messaging (raised, for example, in SAP S/4HANA Cloud), observable significant facts within business processes (being internal so far) are sent to the SAP Cloud Platform. In this manner, we can also expose the underlying core business process to be enhanced through applications built on SAP Cloud Platform, if they in turn react to external events. Thus, our extension can participate in core business processes and can add or change logic without affecting the original core business process or being limited by physical location.

16.2 Concepts of Event-Based Integration

The theory presented in the previous section makes a compelling case for reactive systems and communication via messaging. In this section, we'll explore in practice the capabilities of SAP Cloud Platform and SAP S/4HANA in this direction.

The SAP Enterprise Messaging service facilitates messaging capabilities in a robust, efficient, scalable broker architecture. The service includes out of the box integration with SAP's applications, such as SAP S/4HANA Cloud, to propagate events and enable reactive business processes across enterprise landscapes.

To achieve this integration, we'll need two major parts: a generic integration with the event-driven architecture in SAP S/4HANA Cloud and the SAP Enterprise Messaging service offered on SAP Cloud Platform. Both components communicate seamlessly with each other via standard state-of-the-art message and connection protocols.

With the first version of the SAP Enterprise Messaging service, SAP S/4HANA Cloud and the SAP Cloud Platform can act both as event sources to the SAP Enterprise Messaging service. Applications built on the SAP Cloud Platform can act as consumers. The SAP Enterprise Messaging service offers a design time interface for configuration and development tasks. At runtime, the service uses a message broker to deliver messages to consumer applications. Figure 16.4 shows a high-level overview of the service.

Event sources, such as an SAP S/4HANA Cloud system, expose their event metadata to the SAP Enterprise Messaging service. Apart from SAP S/4HANA Cloud, other SAP applications, for example, SAP SuccessFactors, SAP Hybris, and others, might expose events in the future.

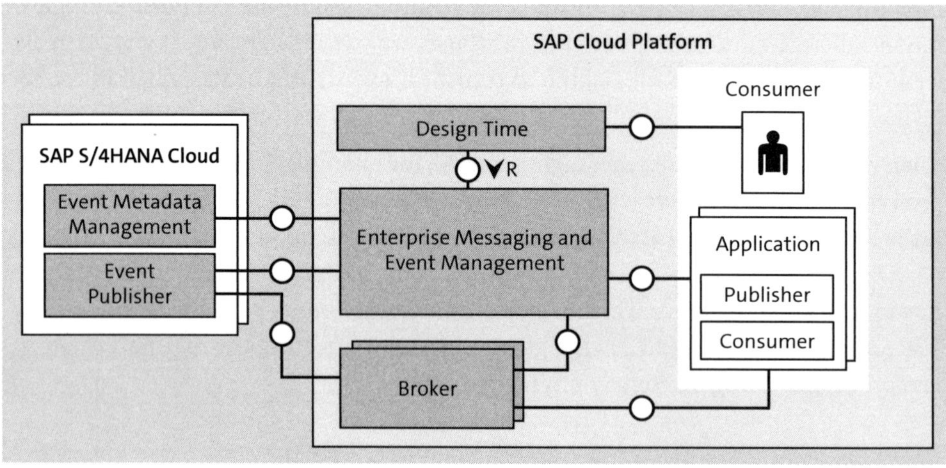

Figure 16.4 High-Level Component View of the SAP Enterprise Messaging Service

As senders of events are not aware of event receivers and cannot adapt their events to receivers, events look and feel the same to all receivers. A receiver—for example, your extension application—doesn't care about the technological context (for example, the type of the system or the technical transport layer) of the event source.

Instead, the receiver recognizes the semantics and the relevance of a specific event by looking at the metadata of an event. Therefore, using a unified and well-defined hierarchy for event types, as well as for the payload of events, can be beneficial. The event enablement provided within SAP S/4HANA Cloud systems is a thin layer that, on one hand, exposes metadata for events of the relevant system in a remote accessible way (via an OData service). On the other hand, connections to the SAP Enterprise Messaging service are managed and events published at runtime.

Event types are identified through *topics*, which describe what an event is about.

Topics

Topics identify event types. Topics organize event messages on the messaging infrastructure and are used for dispatching messages at runtime.

Each event is assigned to exactly one topic. Topics form a logical tree to organize messages, like a folder hierarchy in a file system. Topics are technically represented as strings, consisting of multiple segments, separated by a defined delimiter, like file paths.

Usually, the topic syntax depends on the transport protocol used and so must change each time the protocol is changed. Thus, consumer applications must adopt different ways to describe topics. To allow business applications to be stably configured, the SAP Enterprise Messaging service and event enablement in SAP S/4HANA Cloud use a unified topic syntax for transmitting events.

The messaging infrastructure used by the SAP Enterprise Messaging service uses topics to route and dispatch messages/events to the appropriate host of the message broker.

In SAP S/4HANA Cloud, event topics are composed as follows:

```
<channel topic space>/<service topic space>/<specific topic>
```

The individual parts are defined as follows:

- `<channel topic space>` identifies the source system of an event type, for example, `S4/SYS` would represent an SAP S/4HANA Cloud system with the system ID "SYS."
- `<service topic space>` identifies the provider implementation inside an event source system. For example, a provider for business events in SAP S/4HANA could use the value "BO" to represent business objects events. A provider for technical events inside SAP S/4HANA Cloud could choose the value "TECH."
- `<specific topic>` identifies the event type. In SAP S/4HANA Cloud, the event type mostly contains the object type the event belongs to. For example, the object "SalesOrder" can raise the "Created" event type, which would be expressed as "SalesOrder/Created" in the last part of the topic.

Here are two examples:

```
S4/SYS/BO/BusinessPartner/Created
S4/SYS/BO/SalesOrder/Released
```

You can bind your extension application as a consuming application on the SAP Cloud Platform to the instance of the SAP Enterprise Messaging service in your account. Through the design time interface of the SAP Enterprise Messaging service, you can explore events metadata catalogs from all event sources which have been connected to your consumer account. All events exposed by one source system through a specific channel are consolidated into one catalog.

Channels

Channel is a single connection for events between an SAP S/4HANA Cloud system and a service instance of the SAP Enterprise Messaging service on a SAP Cloud Platform account. Event types can be bound to channels.

To consume an event, your extension application must know the topic corresponding to the event. Through an event catalog, you can search for topics that correspond to certain event types.

Once we know the event we'd like to consume and we've found the corresponding topic in the catalog of the connected source system, we should understand how the consumption is realized. Note also that consumption has the same requirements as for topic syntax definition: The consumer will not deal with the technological context of the source system. Usually, the consumption depends on the underlying messaging infrastructure—which broker we are using—so it must change when the message broker is exchanged.

Message Brokers

A *message broker* is a component used for decoupling application components by using an asynchronous message-based communication approach. A broker enables an *n:m* communication between different parties in high-load scenarios and in highly distributed environments.

Therefore, the SAP Enterprise Messaging service offers a unified consumption API for subscription and for publishing messages/events. The SAP Enterprise Messaging service abstracts from a specific broker infrastructure, so your extension coding remains stable even if different brokers are used in the future.

16.3 Events in SAP S/4HANA Cloud

Now that we've established the basic concepts behind event-based integration, let's now look into the two components, the SAP Enterprise Messaging Service and SAP S/4HANA Cloud, in detail. In this section, we'll start with the SAP S/4HANA Cloud system as the first enabled event source of the SAP Enterprise Messaging Service apart from the SAP Cloud Platform to understand how event provisioning and delivery are implemented. A few configuration steps require information that we'll get from the SAP Cloud Platform configuration steps we explained in Section 16.4. In this section, we'll follow the flow of events from source to target as we describe the configuration to make the steps easier to understand.

16.3.1 Events Raised by SAP S/4HANA Cloud Applications

Business objects are the basis for event enablement. Business objects are well defined in the context of the SAP Business Suite and in SAP S/4HANA Cloud. A business object is a piece of business functionality that can be instantiated on its own. While business objects are used almost constantly, their types are only rarely considered explicitly. Within business applications, the types of the business objects are derived and known from the context in which they appear, but they are generally not explicit. An SAP Fiori app for managing business partners knows that it is dealing with business partner objects and does not need to inspect the type of business objects being handled. The actual business object type is relevant only at the fringes of the applications, generally when the application is interacting with some framework on a generic level or when you configure or extend the system.

A common type system shared by these frameworks is a prerequisite for generic interaction between them. Therefore, a new entity, the *SAP Object Type*, has been introduced. An SAP Object Type is a generalization of business object types. The repository for SAP Object Types holds information such as the SAP Object Category (business or technical), a description, the business object type, and additional data for administrative purposes.

SAP Object Types

An SAP Object Type is a well-defined, named abstract concept in SAP software representing a data model and a behavioral model of a concrete business or technical entity.

An SAP Object Type can define business events with a clear semantics for certain situations. An event can be raised when a certain action is executed on the business object or when the business object enters a certain state.

As soon as events are raised by business objects, a core API in SAP S/4HANA Cloud propagates these events to event processing frameworks. Thus, events are already built into the applications within SAP S/4HANA Cloud. Public events can be propagated to applications outside their origin systems.

Once a public event is raised, the event is handed over from business workflow to the business event handling framework. This framework maps from the internal technical representation of the event to its external human-readable representation and composes the specific payload. Now, the event can be emitted to the outside world.

16.3.2 Event Enablement

In our example, let's say we want to supply an extension we are building on the SAP Cloud Platform with information about significant occurrences—events—in an SAP S/4HANA Cloud system.

Two entities, the application on the SAP Cloud Platform and the SAP S/4HANA Cloud system, must be connected to each other in a standardized way to ensure all non-functional qualities and in a reliable way to allow events to arrive at your application at the time they occur. These requirements can be fulfilled by enterprise event enablement. Figure 16.5 shows the flow of an event. SAP Event Enablement communicates directly with the relevant instance of the SAP Enterprise Messaging service on the SAP Cloud Platform via a WebSocket connection. This connection remains open to ensure that events can be transmitted immediately without delay. An SAP ABAP core mechanism ensures that the connection is kept alive and reestablished whenever required, for example, after a network problem, expired credentials, or any other reason is resolved.

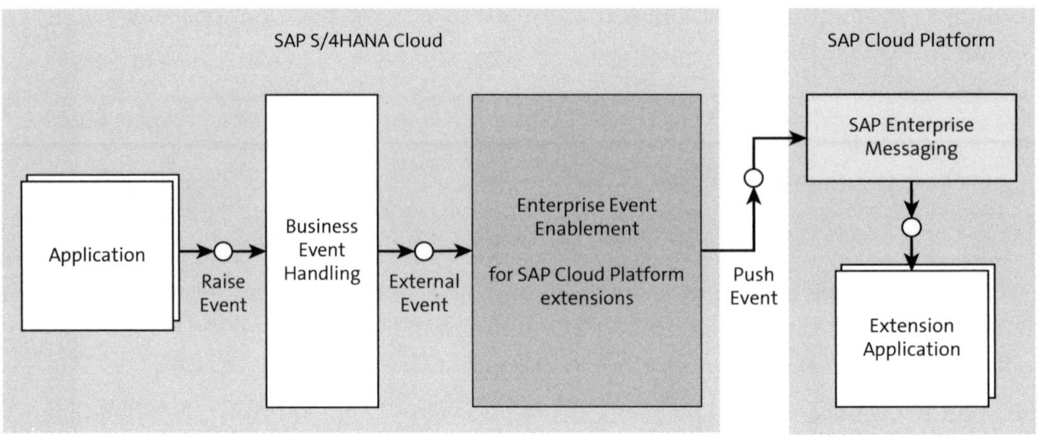

Figure 16.5 Propagation of an Event Raised in SAP S/4HANA Cloud

As pointed out in the previous section, messaging will be used as the transport mechanism for events. Therefore, SAP Event Enablement uses MQTT as the protocol for messaging. Events are transported as payloads of MQTT messages.

MQTT

MQTT (MQ Telemetry Transport) is a standardized protocol. MQTT was originally intended for machine-to-machine communication, as used in the Internet of Things (IoT). The protocol allows you to implement thin clients and to use small packet sizes to connect systems in distributed scenarios via publish/subscribe. For more information, refer to *http://mqtt.org*.

SAP Event Enablement places the event into the payload of an MQTT `PUBLISH` message and sends this message via the WebSocket connection to the SAP Cloud Platform.

An SAP S/4HANA Cloud system can be connected to different instances of the SAP Enterprise Messaging service. To manage these connections, the notion of a channel has been introduced. A channel is specified through the following attributes:

- **Channel name**
  Identifier of the channel.
- **Indicator for activation**
  Indicates whether the channel is active. An event can be sent via this channel if the channel is active.
- **Channel destination**
  Name of the destination that is targeting the messaging endpoint of the SAP Enterprise Messaging service.
- **Channel protocol**
  The message protocol used for the channel. Currently, only MQTT v3.1.1 is supported.
- **Channel outbound stream topic space**
  The first segment added to all topics of events send via this channel. With a channel topic space, topics on the receiver side are guaranteed to be unique.

Consider event types with different channel topic spaces as follows:

```
S4/SYS1/BO/SalesOrder/Created
S4/SYS2/BO/SalesOrder/Created
```

In these examples, the topic space indicates that one event type originates from different systems.

Additionally, parameters can be defined for a channel:

- `MQTT_QOS`
  Quality of service indicates the requirement towards the reliability of delivery. Two qualities defined by MQTT can be used:
  - 0 – At most once delivery—This quality of service does not guarantee the delivery of events. Use this option for event types that indicate changes that are not business or time critical.
  - 1 – At least once delivery—This quality of service guarantees the delivery of events. An event will be delivered at least once to the consumer. Use this option if events must not be lost.
- `OAUTH_20_CONFIGURATION`
  The OAuth2.0 configuration stores the client id, client secret, authorization endpoint, and the token endpoint. The SAP S4/HANA Cloud system requests an access token based on the client credentials flow, each time a new connection is established. All properties stored in the configuration are required for the logon via OAuth2.0 at the specific instance of the SAP Enterprise Messaging service.

Via the channel, we can also control the distribution of events across different service instances by binding event types to single channels.

Now, we can assign a specific event type of an SAP S/4HANA Cloud system to a certain channel to send events to a specific instance of the SAP Enterprise Messaging service, where the messages can be consumed by applications on SAP Cloud Platform.

Let's look at three examples of event-to-channel bindings.

If we have two event providers, "BO1" and "BO2," we can configure channel bindings as follows:

- **Example 1:**
  Channel: "Instance1"
  Bound event types:

  ```
  /BO1/SalesOrder/Created
  /BO2/SalesOrder/Created
  /BO1/BusinessPartner/Created
  ```

  Specific event types from different providers are bound to the channel.
- **Example 2:**
  Channel: "Instance2"
  Bound event types:

```
/BO1/SalesOrder/*
/BO2/SalesOrder/*
/BO1/BusinessPartner/Created
```

All sales order events are bound to the channel and a specific business partner event type.

- **Example 3:**
  Channel: "Instance3"
  Bound Event types:

  ```
  /BO1/*
  /BO2/*
  ```

  All events are bound to the channel.

16.3.3 Configuration

In SAP S/4HANA Cloud, we can use the communication management apps introduced in Chapter 6 and the applications for the event handling management to configure all parameters and settings for the event delivery. First, we'll create a communication system to represent the instance of the SAP Enterprise Messaging service that we want to connect. Second, we'll create a communication arrangement for the event handling communication scenario and the communication system. Finally, we'll configure the binding of events to channels.

16

To start, we'll need to log on to the launchpad of the relevant SAP S/4HANA Cloud system as an administrator. As first explained in Chapter 6, Section 6.4.1, we'll use the Communication Systems app to create a communication system with the sample system ID "BUSINESSEVENTS". We need to supply the following settings for the communication system, which are specific to the event handling case. Figure 16.6 shows those settings with some example values. You'll get these values from the service key of your SAP Enterprise Messaging service instance, as explained in Section 16.4:

- **Host name**
  For our business event scenario, this host is the endpoint of the SAP Enterprise Messaging service for the transmission of events at runtime.
- **Auth. Endpoint**
  This authorization endpoint in the SAP Cloud Platform will be used for authorization via OAuth 2.0.

- **Token Endpoint**
  This endpoint in the SAP Cloud Platform provides OAuth 2.0 tokens to the applications running on SAP S/4HANA Cloud systems.

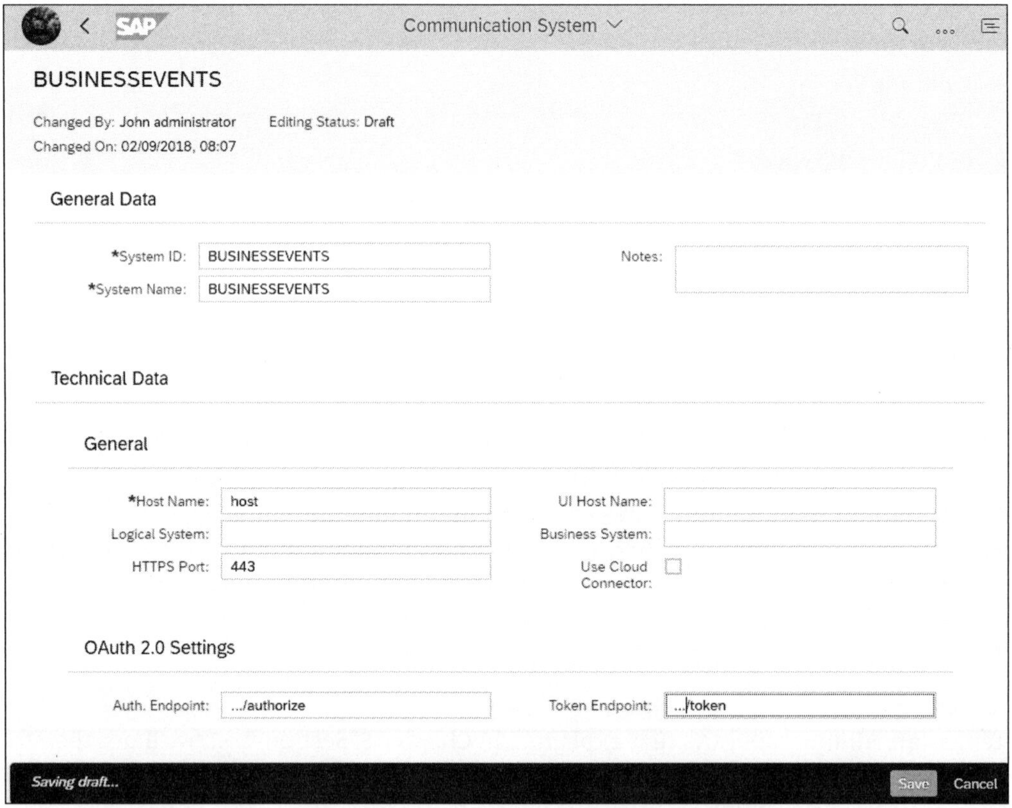

Figure 16.6 Event Management-Specific Settings in Communication System

As part of the communication system, we must create an inbound user. This user will be used by the SAP Enterprise Messaging service on SAP Cloud Platform to retrieve the catalog of event metadata from SAP S/4HANA Cloud systems.

For publishing business events at runtime, we'll also require a user for outbound communications. This user will be used by the SAP S/4HANA Cloud system to log on to the SAP Cloud Platform and to establish the WebSocket connection with the SAP Enterprise Messaging service. To specify the user, we'll use the option to add a new outbound user in the **User for Outbound Communication** section.

The process is slightly different than the one for creating an inbound user. In the popup box shown in Figure 16.7, we'll select **OAuth 2.0** as the **Authentication Method**. The fields **OAuth 2.0 Client ID** and **Client Secret** appear, which are provided by the SAP Enterprise Messaging service instance as part of the service key. Further details on these fields will be provided in the next section.

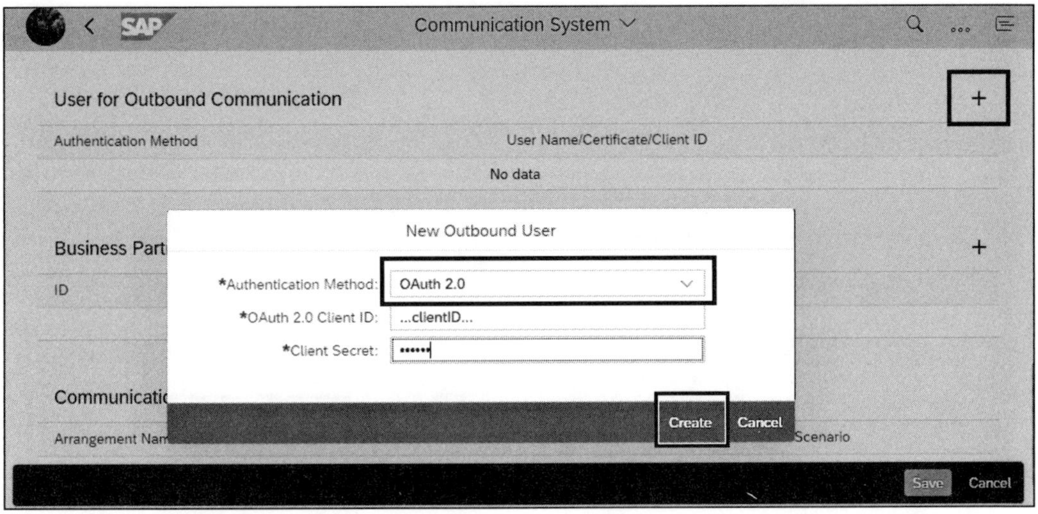

Figure 16.7 Creating a New Outbound User with Authentication via OAuth 2.0

16

Now, we can finish setting up the connectivity by creating the communication arrangement. Again, we'll proceed as first described in Chapter 6 and use the Communication Arrangements app to create a communication arrangement for the communication scenario SAP_COM_0092 (Enterprise Eventing Integration). This specific scenario supports the transmission of business events between SAP S/4HANA Cloud systems and the SAP Cloud Platform.

We'll assign the communication system that we created earlier, including the inbound communication user, to the new arrangement.

We'll need to provide the following details (shown in Figure 16.8), which are specific to the business event scenario and are necessary for internal processing:

- **Channel and Description**
  Assign a speaking name that identifies this connection in the next step where we'll bind event types to a channel. One channel corresponds to exactly one communication arrangement.

- **Topic Space**
  Assign a name for the first segment of topics for events emitted through this specific communication arrangement.

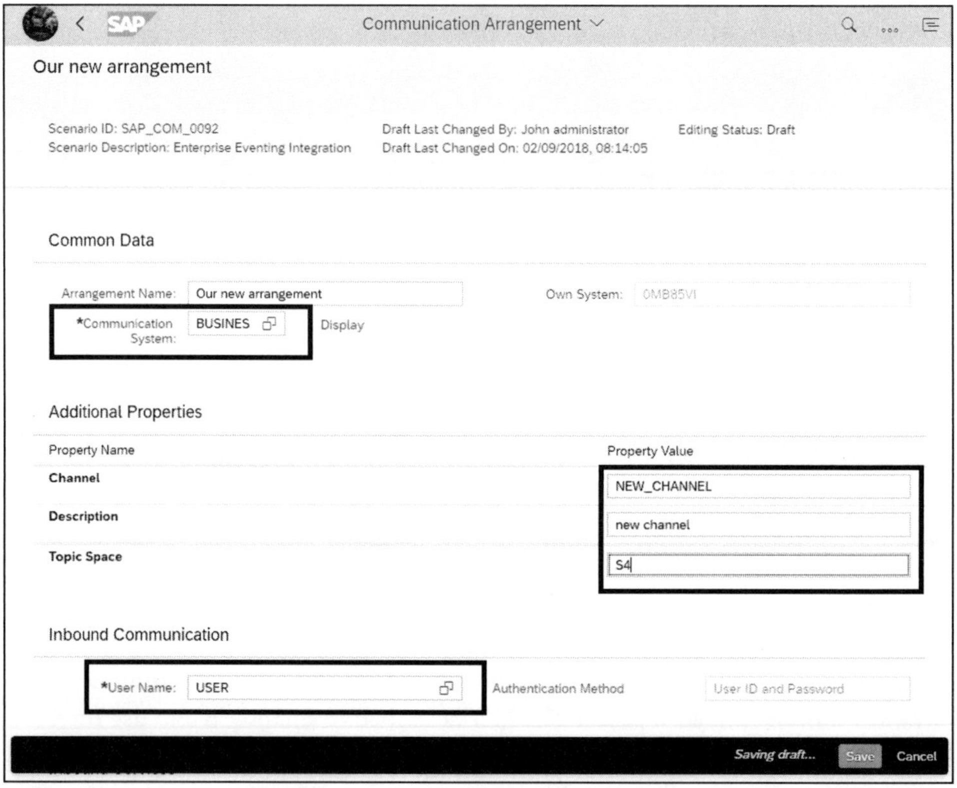

Figure 16.8 Event Management-Specific Settings in the Communication Arrangement

Once we save the new communication arrangement and it becomes active, the corresponding channel (as defined in the parameter **Channel**) will be created in the background. Let's further configure this channel entity.

To ensure that only the required events arrive in our subaccount on the SAP Cloud Platform, we'll need to maintain the *event-channel-binding* within our SAP S/4HANA Cloud system as the final configuration step. This configuration dispatches events of specified event types to the right channels in an SAP S/4HANA Cloud system.

Open the Manage Your Solution application on the SAP S/4HANA Cloud launchpad. In the application, search for a configuration item called "Event Handling" and select the entry from the search result. From the two configuration steps offered, choose the action **Configure** for the step **Maintain Event Topics**. On the next screen, you'll find that the channel we created earlier is now part of the new communication arrangement in the list of available channels.

After selecting the channel, a detail screen will appear in which you'll determine the topics—corresponding to the required event types—that will be transmitted via the new channel. To add new entries, you'll need to select the **New Entries** option and open the value lookup help for the **Topic Filter** table, as shown in Figure 16.9. Now, select entries by double-clicking individual lines in the resulting value list. Topics ending with "/*" indicate that all events defined for the entity specified in the previous segments are selected.

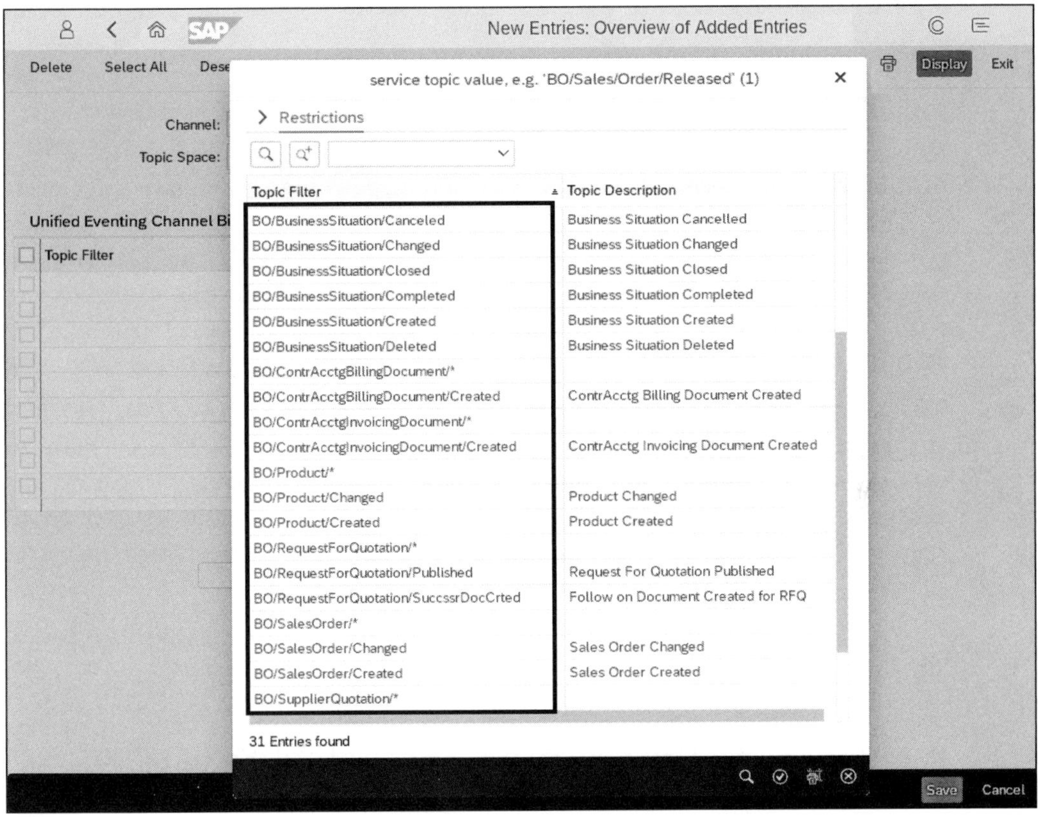

Figure 16.9 Maintaining Event Topics within the Manage Your Solution App

Our table of bindings could look like Figure 16.10, if we're only interested in a few event types.

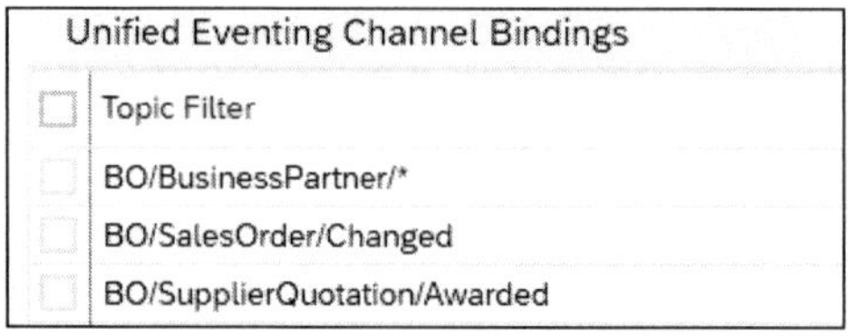

Figure 16.10 Event Binding in the Manage Your Solution App

Or, as shown in Figure 16.11, we could dispatch all event types to the new channel.

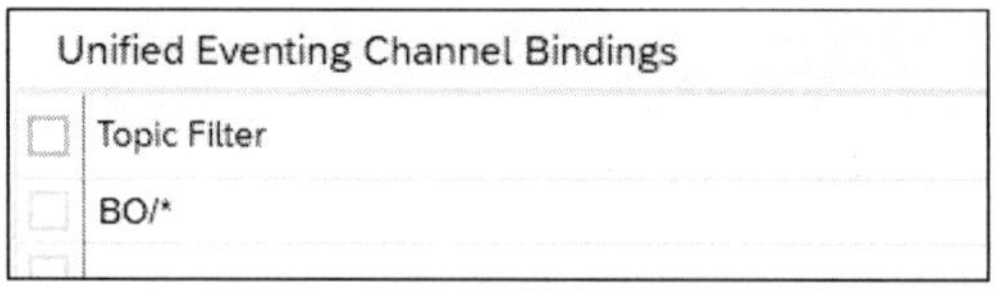

Figure 16.11 Second Event Binding Example

At this point, the necessary connectivity and dispatching configuration for event enablement in the SAP S/4HANA Cloud system is completed. The system will now send events to the SAP Enterprise Messaging service on the SAP Cloud Platform. The events raised by the SAP S/4HANA Cloud system contain the (set of) key(s) that enables the receiver to identify the affected business object. In the terminology of Martin Fowler, this follows the pattern of *event notification* (*http://tiny.cc/fowler17*).

This minimal payload has been chosen because events sent by SAP S/4HANA Cloud are meant as triggers for further processes. Also, the system sends those events automatically and without the immediate action of a named user. Thus, for security reasons, one must carefully select what the event shall transport in its payload. By keeping the event messages reasonably small, we make event-based integration scalable. The consumer of an event can, for example, use the information to query the SAP S/4HANA Cloud system using the methods we've presented in previous chapters, especially in Chapter 4.

16.4 Services for Handling Events on SAP Cloud Platform

In this section, we'll explain the steps you'll perform to consume events from SAP S/4HANA Cloud systems in our side-by-side extension on SAP Cloud Platform.

As described in Section 16.2, we need the SAP Enterprise Messaging service to consume events. Therefore, the first onboarding step is to create an SAP Enterprise Messaging service instance in your subaccount in the Cloud Foundry environment of

SAP Cloud Platform. With your service instance, the Cloud Foundry environment then takes care of providing a message host, a virtual broker exclusively used by your subaccount.

In the next step, we'll bind the SAP Enterprise Messaging service instance to one or multiple applications. You can either use the cockpit of the Cloud Foundry environment or the Cloud Foundry command line interface as seen in previous chapters.

Since we want to consume events from an SAP S/4HANA Cloud system, we'll need to create a service key for the new SAP Enterprise Messaging service instance. The service key contains the credentials such as the OAuth 2.0 client ID and secret, as well as the endpoints (host, authorization, and token endpoint) required for defining the communication system in the SAP S/4HANA Cloud system (see Section 16.3).

At runtime, before a connection is established with the SAP Enterprise Messaging service, the SAP S/4HANA Cloud system will use these credentials for authentication. Events are then sent by SAP S/4HANA Cloud to the SAP Enterprise Messaging service, which then forwards the messages (containing the events) to the message host of your subaccount based on a routing rule. Applications bound to the relevant messaging host can then consume the messages.

We can use the administration UI of the SAP Enterprise Messaging service to maintain queues and bind those queues to topics.

Queues

A queue is a component used to store messages for an asynchronous communication between systems. Senders and receivers do not interact with each other directly. A sender can transmit a message to a queue from which receiver(s) can retrieve messages later.

As discussed in previous chapters, topics are important for events as we can identify event types from their topics. A sending application (SAP S/4HANA Cloud system in our case) usually sends a message to a specifically named queue. With topic-to-queue bindings, applications can publish messages to a topic, which in turn are retained by a queue. In our case, messages can only be sent to a topic. A topic-to-queue binding ensures that the message is retained until consumed by the receiving application.

Besides the pure runtime perspective of the message/event exchange, SAP Enterprise Messaging service provides capabilities to explore and manage events from the clients. The administration UI of the SAP Enterprise Messaging service offers capabilities to explore event definitions raised by the clients.

The actual lookup of the event definitions is performed based on SAP Cloud Platform destinations, which you can maintain in your subaccount through the SAP Cloud Platform cockpit.

For administration purposes, you can create *event channel groups* to contain related events from different event sources. Therefore, you can select the relevant event source system from the list of your destinations and the channels you are interested in from these sources. The SAP S/4HANA Cloud system uses the channel entity to dispatch events.

For example, for an extension application processing sales orders, we would create an event channel group called "SalesEvents from system 1 and 2." To make our extension react on all sales order activities in the company, we could select all configured destinations that expose sales order events and assign the relevant channels to this group. Inside the event channel group, we can explore the topics corresponding to the different sales order event types.

16.5 Extending the Sample Application with Events

Now, let's enhance our extension with the necessary coding for consuming events. Messaging client libraries are available for Java and JavaScript. In this section, we'll look at the Java client library and explain how you can consume events in your Java source code.

Before the application can be deployed in the Cloud Foundry environment, we'll have to adapt the deployment descriptor for the project.

In the manifest.yml file, we'll define `SAP_XBEM_BINDINGS` with the structure seen in Listing 16.1 as an environment variable. The property value `service` directly points to our SAP Enterprise Messaging service instance. In this way, we bind inputs/outputs of our messaging client in the Java application to the actual messaging broker instance. The property value `address` points to the topic your extension is interested in that has been bound to a queue in the administration UI of the SAP Enterprise Messaging service, as described in the previous section.

If we decided to process different events or to use a different message broker in our extension in the future, we would only change the topic value in the environment variable `SAP_XBEM_BINDINGS` to a different value. The coding of the application would remain the same.

```
# Manifest
...
  env:
    SAP_XBEM_BINDINGS: >
      {
        "inputs": {
          "S4Events": {
            "service": "broker",
            "address": "topic:S4/BO/SalesOrder"
          }
        },
        ...
      }
```

Listing 16.1 Environment Variable for Event Consumption in manifest.yml

The following coding snippets demonstrate how the library can be used to implement the most important steps for consumption.

In Listing 16.2, we'll create an initial connection to the binding displayed in the listing earlier. To get a `MessagingService` instance of the Messaging Client Java API via the service connector, we'll use tools provided by the Spring Cloud framework (*http://tiny.cc/spring-cloud*). Spring Cloud helps implement common patterns in Cloud Foundry-based applications, such as configuration management. For our purposes, Spring Cloud provides us easy access to the artifacts specified in the configuration via environment variables.

With the `MessagingService` instance, we can establish the binding of our Java application to the configuration with name `S4Events` specified in the environment variable inside the deployment descriptor. This binding results in a new instance of a `MessagingEndpoint`.

```
final Cloud cloud = new CloudFactory().getCloud();
final MessagingService messagingService =
            cloud.getSingletonServiceConnector(
                    MessagingService.class, null);
final MessagingEndpoint messagingEndpoint =
            messagingService.bind("S4Events").build();
```

Listing 16.2 Establish Connection of Your Code to the Binding

Listing 16.3 shows how you can subscribe to our binding and receive events available from the bound topic when the call is made. In this example, we'll use features introduced by Java 8 such as stream processing to process the available messages in bulk. We'll define a sequence of functions to apply on each received message to convert its content to a string and to log the message text.

```
Stream<Message<byte[]>> stream = messagingEndpoint.subscribe();
stream.map(Message::getContent)
      .map(String::new)
      .forEach(msg -> logger.info("Received message " + msg);
```

Listing 16.3 Consume Events

For reasons of brevity and focus, we won't cover how to integrate event handling into the larger context of an application, possibly in a reactive manner. The code snippet in Listing 16.3 should give you an idea of how to use the Java client library to handle messages. For more details on the SAP Enterprise Messaging service and the available API, please refer to the documentation at *http://tiny.cc/sap-messaging*.

16.6 Summary

Hopefully, this chapter provided you with a good understanding of what event-based integration is all about. Events are a complementary approach to using APIs that make applications more scalable in a hybrid and fast-evolving environment. The SAP Enterprise Messaging service, in combination with the eventing capabilities of SAP S/4HANA Cloud, enables event-based integration in our side-by-side extensions. In the next chapter, we'll continue to explore current innovation topics with a look into machine learning and blockchain. Then, we'll walk through an example of reactive programming with the SAP S/4HANA Cloud SDK.

Chapter 17
Extending SAP S/4HANA with Machine Learning and Blockchain Technologies

The SAP Cloud Platform and the SAP S/4HANA Cloud SDK make using and integrating innovative technologies in SAP S/4HANA extensions easy. In this chapter, we'll show examples involving machine learning and blockchain use cases, which offer a glimpse into the portfolio of cutting-edge technologies available on the SAP Cloud Platform.

Innovation and experimentation has never been foreign to SAP ERP developers: The open architecture of the system lends itself exceptionally well to customization and experimentation. On the other hand, experimentation on the core of an enterprise is a challenging and slow process. This contradiction can be solved by applying innovations in big, widely spaced leaps—usually during a system migration to a new version.

Applying innovations in big rare upgrades has proven too slow and risky, and this problem is exactly where SAP S/4HANA extensions provide a solution: Experimentation and productization can happen in many separate, parallel spaces on the SAP Cloud Platform while the core stays unaffected by experimentation. Matched with many rich APIs, SAP S/4HANA Cloud thus provides a great environment for experimentation, implementation, and the productization of ideas—the stepping stones of innovation. SAP Leonardo adds cutting-edge technology ready for experimentation and productive use to this environment. Thus, side-by-side extensions contribute to the drive behind making the ERP intelligent. Extensions can further expand on the intelligent capabilities already delivered by SAP S/4HANA, especially for differentiating requirements of customers and partners beyond the standard functionality.

In Section 17.1, we'll first discuss how the SAP S/4HANA Cloud SDK integrates into SAP's innovation strategy and how it conceptually is well-suited for use in applications integrating innovative services on the SAP Cloud Platform. Then, in Section 17.2, we'll use our Business Partner Address Manager app to show how machine learning services can be integrated in a side-by-side extension app. In Section 17.3, we'll do the same for blockchain services.

17.1 SAP Leonardo and the Innovation Commitment of the SAP S/4HANA Cloud SDK

SAP Leonardo is the digital innovation system that enables companies to rapidly innovate and scale that innovation to redefine their business for the digital world (*http://tiny.cc/sap-leonardo*). SAP Leonardo brings machine learning, the Internet of Things (IoT), blockchain, analytics, and big data together on SAP Cloud Platform using design thinking services.

With SAP Leonardo, SAP delivers innovation capabilities and services as industry accelerators to integrate with core business applications so that customers can seamlessly bridge between operating and innovating. In this chapter, we'll focus on the newest additions: machine learning and blockchain. We'll show you how cutting-edge technology is easily within reach and how to make our SAP S/4HANA development projects intelligent and establish new levels of trust.

Destined for fostering innovation, the SAP S/4HANA Cloud SDK makes integrating the cutting-edge SAP Leonardo technologies easy and affordable, both from a risk perspective as well as a cost perspective. Enabling early adoption was and is the goal of the SDK, even for early stage technologies such as machine learning and, even more so, blockchain. The integration strategies we explain in this chapter will be valid and applicable for other new technologies and services.

Many features of the SAP S/4HANA Cloud SDK make it especially well suited for acting as glue code, the code required to integrate different parts of a software system. Glue code makes an indirect contribution towards meeting functional requirements by enabling you to create code quickly. What sounds bland is in fact one of the hottest areas of innovation in the software domain, and the SDK bears witness to that. The SAP S/4HANA Cloud SDK makes the integration of innovative services with SAP S/4HANA systems easy, while guaranteeing high standards for nonfunctional requirements like security and efficiency.

17.2 Extending a Sample Application with Machine Learning

Machine learning has many potential applications in the field of master data management for our Business Partner Address Manager application: Data cleaning, duplicate mapping, fraud screening, and the clustering of potential new business partners into categories are just a few. For this chapter, we'll start with a simple example: translation. We chose this task mostly due to logistics: We can start without requiring a body of data for training or inference. The goal is to talk about the technological integration—and translation will work splendidly for that.

Machine Learning in a Nutshell

With machine learning, machines are not told an algorithm but instead learn a solution by being provided with good and bad examples or by discovering structures in the input data automatically. SAP Leonardo Machine Learning provides services usable out of the box, one of which is translation. Advanced development resources also allow you to deploy your own custom models (called the *bring-your-own-model approach*).

Many resources are available for you to go beyond the examples in this chapter:

- SAP Leonardo Machine Learning Foundation: *http://tiny.cc/sap-leonardo-ml*
- openSAP data science class, with a focus on classical methods: *http://tiny.cc/opensap-ds*
- openSAP enterprise machine learning in a nutshell, with a focus on deep learning: *http://tiny.cc/opensap-ml*

17

Let's imagine our product owner and the user experience (UX) designer asked us to integrate a translation feature in our app for any text element displaying business partner master data. He argues that this is exactly the kind of feature that will help bring down the wall separating personal communication and computer user interface interaction: A new level of context will be created where foreign names can be easily translated and, also, made more easily pronouncable for a foreign speaker, especially if we expanded the app to also handle organizations with foreign company names, in addition to persons.

SAP Leonardo Machine Learning offers a translation service as part of the functional services listed on the SAP API Business Hub at *http://api.sap.com*, as shown in Figure 17.1. The entry on the SAP API Business Hub provides documentation, an option to try the service on the spot, and a possibility to even generate example code.

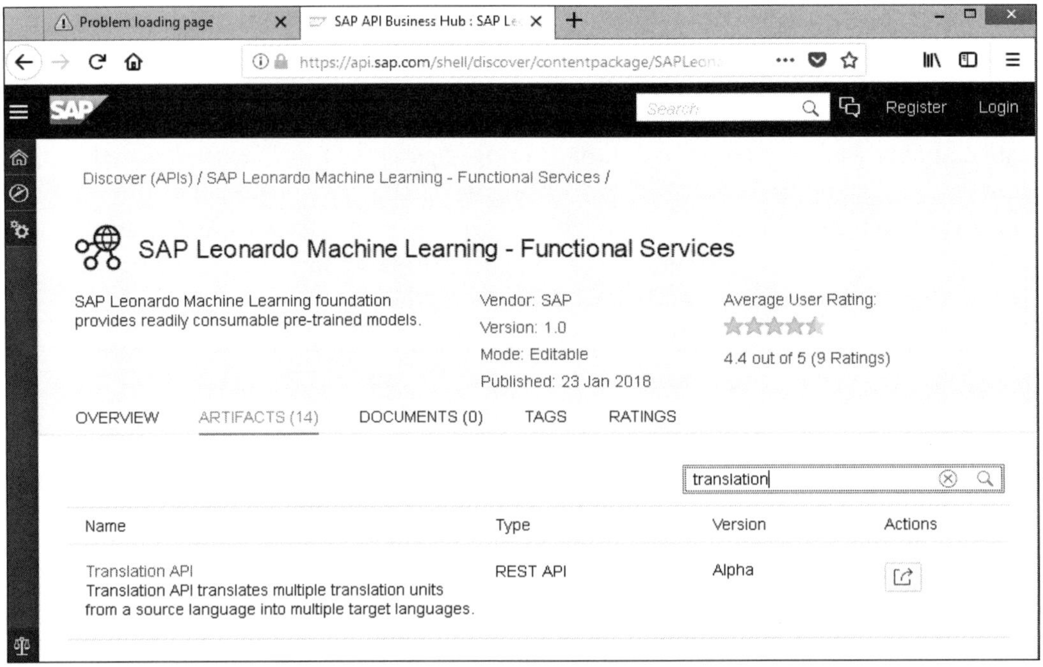

Figure 17.1 The Translation API on SAP API Business Hub

Now, let's imagine we're asked to quickly integrate the functionality so that our colleagues can start testing it with users. The code generation seems an easy enough way to get started—but which code do we generate? Javascript for the frontend or Java for coding in the backend? We recommend integration in the backend for the following reasons:

- **Security considerations**
  The authentication for the translation service requires passing an API key along with the service request. Implementing authentication in the frontend would expose the key to the users of the service as part of our browser-side code.
- **Interface stability and consistency**
  Changes of the backend service can be accomodated by defining our own interface and hiding changes in the backend service from the frontend code. Furthermore, the frontend stays more nimble by consistently communicating only with our own backend via our interface definitions.
- **Performance and cost optimization opportunities**
  Machine learning services can take a while to execute and are frequently priced on

a per-use basis. Therefore, caching might be considered. Caching on the client side might be far less efficient because we cannot exploit similarities between requests of the possibly thousands of our users.

This nonexhaustive list of reasons justify the common pattern of backend integration for microservices, which we'll use for our translation feature.

To understand how to call the translation service, let's study the documentation in the SAP API Business Hub by clicking on the **POST** endpoint of the translation service. From the documentation shown in Figure 17.2, we learn that the service requires us to provide the source language of the texts we want translated. We can imagine that the UX designer will not be pleased if we expect users to specify the source language. Instead, the source language should be detected automatically. So let's browse again to find the language detection API right next to the translation API in the catalog of **SAP Leonardo Machine Learning - Functional Services**. To fulfill our requirement, we'll have to call those two services (source language detection and translation) in sequence.

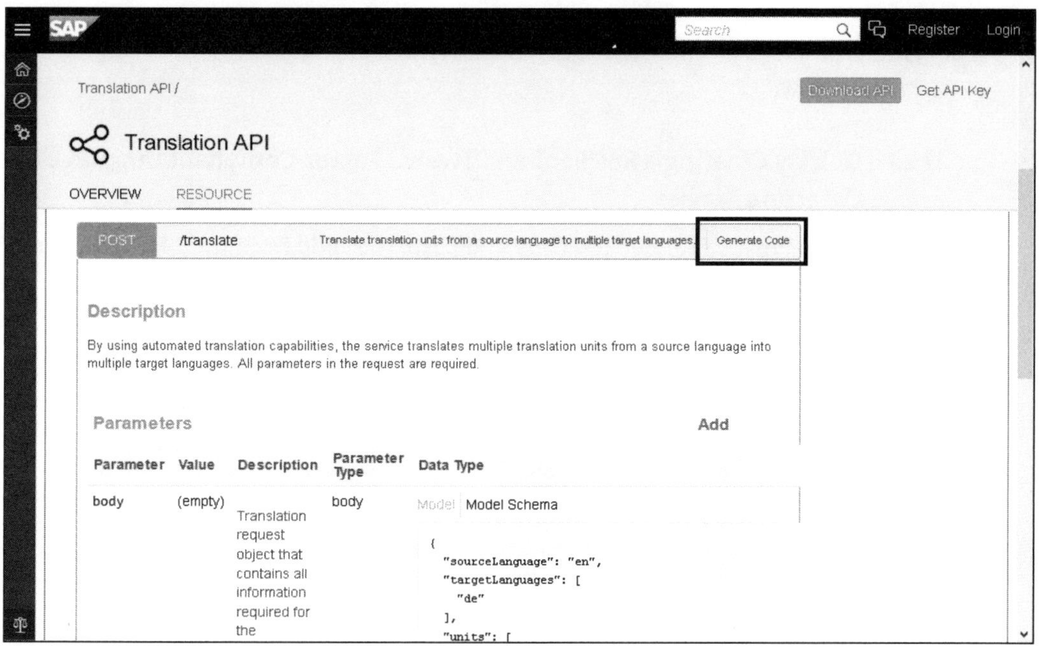

Figure 17.2 SAP API Business Hub Documentation of Interfaces, Code Generation, and API Keys for Evaluation

Calling two services sequentially, passing the results from one to the next, is a quite common pattern for microservices. Therefore, this example is a good opportunity to introduce how the SAP S/4HANA Cloud SDK handles such a situation. Before we work on the more complex task of calling two services, let's start with a simple scenario and make just the language detection service available via a dedicated servlet.

Alpha Services

The following example uses services that are still in the early testing phase and marked as *alpha* versions on the SAP API Business Hub. The intent of our example is to demonstrate how, in principle, an integration of such services would proceed with the SAP S/4HANA Cloud SDK. No guarantee is given that these services can be used in the future in the manner described in this book.

At the time of this writing, alpha services cannot be consumed via a Cloud Foundry service binding. Instead, we'll call the URL from the sandbox API provided by the SAP API Business Hub. This approach is viable for integrating many other services available on the network. Be aware, however, that calling the productive service works slightly differently and requires Cloud Foundry service binding. Section 17.3 integrates SAP Cloud Platform Blockchain via a service binding.

17.2.1 Quickly Creating a Resilient and Twelve-Factor-Compliant Language Detection Servlet

We *could* just create a servlet and copy and paste the code from the SAP API Business Hub's **Generate Code** feature into the servlet's `doGet` method. You can find the code generation feature on the right side of the header of each operation on the SAP API Business Hub, as highlighted in Figure 17.2. But the generated code contains infrastructure code that we would get out of the box with the SAP S/4HANA Cloud SDK. Moreover, we want the functionality to be reusable in other servlets or contexts, and make it resilient. So, instead of using the generated code directly, let's apply what we learned in Chapter 4, Section 4.6, and implement a Hystrix command for the service call. This choice should become second nature as using Hystrix commands improves the stability of your microservice architecture. The servlet can be quite straightforward: As shown in Listing 17.1, the servlet responds to requests on path */api/langdetect* and retrieves one parameter from the request. A Hystrix command instance will be created that implements access to the machine learning service. The service access is facilitated with a `MlService` utility class. Executing the command yields a result object with the language code of the detected language, which we'll serialize to JSON and send as an answer to the requestor.

```
protected void doGet( … ) throws … {
  final PrintWriter responseWriter = response.getWriter();
  final String input = request.getParameter("input");
  if (StringUtils.isBlank(input)) { … }
  final MlService mlService = new MlService();
  try {
    final MlLanguageDetectionResult output =
        new MlLanguageDetectionCommand(
            mlService, input).execute();
      response.setContentType("application/json");
      responseWriter.write(new Gson().toJson(output));
  } catch (Exception e) { … }
}
```

Listing 17.1 Simple Language Detection Servlet to Delegate the Work to a Reusable Hystrix Command

Depending on the framework you're employing in your project, you might deal with service injection differently. In our example, we opted for the in-line creation of the required `MlService` and then pass it via the constructor of the command for transparency's sake. The `MlService` class encapsultates the functionality for accessing the machine learning destination configuration, making it reusable by other commands accessing similar remote services.

Next, let's look at the command in Listing 17.2 to see how little had to be changed.

```
public class MlLanguageDetectionCommand
    extends Command<MlLanguageDetectionResult> {
  public MlLanguageDetectionCommand(
        MlService mlService, String input) {
    super(HystrixCommandGroupKey.Factory.asKey(
        "LeonardoMlFoundation-langdetect"), 10000);
    this.input = input;
    this.mlService = mlService;
  }
```

```
  @Override
  protected MlLanguageDetectionResult run()
      throws Exception  { … }
}
```

Listing 17.2 Simple Language Detection Command Boiler Plate

Note that the command is not extending the ErpCommand that we used before, but uses a simple Hystrix command from the SDK. This is because no ERP call needs to be executed in the command, and so the additional functionality of the ErpCommand is not required. The ErpCommand implements best practices for calls to an ERP that are not required for calls to a machine learning service.

We'll put the command into a new command-specific isolation group, following a straightforward isolation strategy. (Refer to Chapter 4, Section 4.6, for more information and other options, such as the fine-grained control of thread pools.) We selected ten seconds for the timeout since the machine learning services available for testing on the SAP API Hub are nonproduction services and will at times respond more slowly. We'll then move on to the run method, which implements the actual call to the machine learning service based on the generated code from the SAP API Business Hub, as shown in Listing 17.3.

```
DataOutputStream dataOut = null;
BufferedReader in = null;
try {
  String url = mlService.getLeonardoMlSandboxUrlOrThrow()
      + "/languagedetection/language";
  URL urlObj = new URL(url);
  HttpURLConnection connection =
      (HttpURLConnection) urlObj.openConnection();
  connection.setRequestMethod("POST");
  connection.setRequestProperty("Content-Type",
      "application/json");
  connection.setRequestProperty("Accept",
      "application/json;charset=UTF-8");
  connection.setRequestProperty("APIKey",
      mlService.getMlApiKeyOrThrow());
  connection.setDoInput(true);
  connection.setDoOutput(true);
  dataOut = new DataOutputStream(
    connection.getOutputStream());
```

```
  dataOut.writeBytes(
      new Gson().toJson(Collections.singletonMap(
          "message", input)));
  dataOut.flush();
  … // response handling, result: StringBuilder 'response'

  final MlLanguageDetectionResult mlLanguageDetectionResult =
  new Gson().fromJson(
      response.toString(), MlLanguageDetectionResult.class);
  return mlLanguageDetectionResult;
} finally { … }
```

Listing 17.3 Simple Language Detection Command Run Method with Differences to Generated Code Highlighted

In Listing 17.3, notice how the generated code has been quickly adapted to reach a higher level of reliability and configurability. Its basic structure is unchanged: The service is accessed via the standard Java `URLConnection`, the authentication, and the content configuration set up via the request property abstraction of the `URLConnection`, using URL and API key here provided via a service that retrieves this information from application configuration. As a result, HTTP headers are set on request. Then, we'll handle the input and output to the service via the respective streams offered by the `URLConnection`. The reading of the response via the input stream provided by the `URLConnection` gives the response as one string, similar to the generated code. Error handling for the response HTTP status code is not shown in this book for the sake of brevity. The response is then parsed directly into a plain old Java object (POJO) with the help of the Gson library (*http://tiny.cc/gson*). The POJO is then returned as result of the command. We've added the following features to the barebones generated code:

- The configurable service URL and API key are provided in a way that is conforming to the twelve-factor specification (*http://12factor.net*). Thus, the application can be deployed in different environments (for example, test, staging, and production) without recompiling code.
- JSON processing is handled with a Gson library so as to ensure proper escaping and error handling.
- Results are parsed into a simple POJO so as to be easily consumed by users of the command.

To understand this better, let's have a look at the classes MlService and MlLanguageDetectionResult.

Listing 17.4 shows that MlService retrieves the API key from a destination. We'll use the destination configuration as introduced in Chapter 4 and Chapter 6 to store the API key as an additional property on the destination. We're free to define our own properties as needed for our destinations, but we need to avoid redefining already-used property names like proxy. A simple method would be to use a prefix; in our example, the prefix "ml" is used. The URI of the service is simply configured as the destination URL.

```
public class MlService { ...
  public static final String ML_API_KEY = "mlApiKey"; ...
  public String getMlApiKeyOrThrow() {
    Map<String, String> destinationProperties =
        getMlDestination().getPropertiesByName();
    if(destinationProperties.containsKey(ML_API_KEY)) {
      return destinationProperties.get(ML_API_KEY);
    }
    throw new IllegalStateException(...);
  } ... // similar for the sandbox url, but using
      // getMlDestination().getUri() instead of properties
}
```

Listing 17.4 MlService Providing Access to Configurable API Key

In Listing 17.5, the MlLanguageDetectionResult class is shown as being indeed a POJO—an object not linked with any library or framework. This class is therefore ideally suited for use in the public interface of the command. POJOs avoid leaking internal implementation details to the users of an interface.

```
public class MlLanguageDetectionResult {
  private Double confidence;
  private String langCode;
  private String langStr;
  // getters and setters required but not shown here
}
```

Listing 17.5 MlLanguageDetectionResult POJO, for Gson JSON Parsing

When executing this code locally, doing integration tests, or deploying the application on the SAP Cloud Platform, we'll need to make sure that the required destination configuration is present—either as environment variables, as a mocked configuration, or as a configuration of the destination service. See Chapter 4 and Chapter 6 for an introduction to configuring destinations and Chapter 9 for mocking configurations for unit testing.

SAP's recommendation at the time of this writing is to use SAP Leonardo Machine Learning services on Cloud Foundry for production. This scenario would require a different authentication method, as explained in Section 17.3. Nevertheless, the method shown is required to sample the sandbox services and to integrate a great variety of non-Cloud Foundry machine learning services or other services, which can be valuable for going beyond the scenario presented earlier.

Now that we've set up our first service and run a trial of the architecture, in the next subsection, we'll tackle the complete challenge.

17.2.2 Improving the Integration and Chaining Services for a Complete Machine Learning Solution

To complete the backend service, we're still missing the real deal: the translation service integration. Let's step right into it with the command. In this section, we'll look at an even more refined version, where the generated code has been heavily refactored to leverage more features of the SAP S/4HANA Cloud SDK. The interesting part starts in the translate method, so let's focus on that in Listing 17.6.


```
private List<String> translate(
    String sourceLang, String targetLang, List<String> texts)
    throws Exception {
  final String requestJson =
      createRequestJson(sourceLang, targetLang, texts);
  final String responsePayload =
      executeRequest(requestJson);
  Map<String, String> inputToTranslations =
      parseResponse(responsePayload);
  // … removed validation, reformatting, and error handling …
  return translationsInCorrectOrder;
}
```

Listing 17.6 Translate Method of the Class MlTranslationCommand

The logic is divided into three steps, resulting in a structure that is both cleaner and easier to test: request content preparation, request execution and response parsing.

We'll prepare the content to be sent to the server in JSON format, set up and execute the request, perform a first error handling run, and then transfer the results to parsing. The parsing of the response is handled without Gson in this command, to provide an example of this, too. Please refer to the online resources to see it. With manual parsing, you can adapt to dynamic structures and provide fine-grained logs and error handling.

Let's dive more deeply into the executeRequest method in Listing 17.7. Keep in mind that some constant values have been inlined for readability.

```
private String executeRequest(String requestJson)
    throws Exception {
  HttpPost request =
      new HttpPost(new URI("/translation/translate"));
  request.setHeader("Content-Type", "application/json");
  request.setHeader("Accept",
      "application/json;charset=UTF-8");
  request.setHeader("APIKey", mlService.getMlApiKeyOrThrow());
  HttpEntity body = new StringEntity(requestJson,
      ContentType.APPLICATION_JSON);
  request.setEntity(body);
  // Use cached http client for reuse of resources
  final HttpResponse response = HttpClientAccessor
      .getHttpClient(mlService.getMlDestination())
      .execute(request);
  // retrieve entity content (requested json with Accept
  // header, so should be text) and close request
  final String responsePayload =
      HttpEntityUtil.getResponsePayload(response);
  final StatusLine statusLine = response.getStatusLine();
  switch (statusLine.getStatusCode()) {
    case HttpStatus.SC_OK:
      break;
    case HttpStatus.SC_REQUEST_TOO_LONG:
    case HttpStatus.SC_BAD_REQUEST:
      // this exception doesn't trigger resilience
      throw new HystrixBadRequestException(
          "Malformed request: " + statusLine.getStatusCode());
    default:
```

```
        throw new ShouldNotHappenException(
            "Service seems unavailable: Received response: "
                + statusLine);
    }
    return responsePayload;
}
```

Listing 17.7 ExecuteRequest Method Demonstrating Use of the Reusable HTTP Client in the SAP S/4HANA Cloud SDK and Hystrix-Compatible Handling of User Error

The executeRequest method demonstrates how to improve configurability and performance by employing SAP S/4HANA Cloud SDK tools. First, the request is set up, and only the path to the service is specified. The service URI prefix is provided via a destination configuration later. The setup is completed with headers, which are quite similar to the language detection example, and the provisioning of the request content body. Then, we'll retrieve the HTTP client from the SDK cache, providing the destination information so as to cache different clients depending on the configuration and server. The SDK handles the retrieval of the destination from the SAP Cloud Platform service and makes use of one of the most reliable and powerful HTTP client implementations available, the Apache HTTP client library. Caching the HTTP client is important for connection reuse—one of the main pitfalls of naïve HTTP service consumption. Finally, the response payload is retrieved via an SDK utility method, which also takes care of verifying the content type and decompression. The code also features a proposal for improved error handling.

Let's now put these services together in the translation servlet, which offers at path */api/translate* the service our frontend developer is asking for. Our focus here is on the code linking the two services, which leverages *RxJava*, a Java implementation of the ReactiveX API, to set up an event-driven link between the two services, passing results as well as errors through the link. Using this method allows you to solve the C10k problem of serving thousands of clients concurrently from one machine without dying the death of a thousand threads and makes for more neat error handling.

C10k and the Asynchronous, Event-Driven Architecture Style

The C10k problem (*http://tiny.cc/c10k*) is the problem of handling 10,000 client connections simultaneously. The classic Java style of using a thread for each connection is cumbersome at best, because each thread requires memory and because timesharing between that many threads is inefficient. ReactiveX is an API based on asynchronous patterns, allowing handling thousands of clients with only one thread, if the framework is consistently adhered to.

```
String translate(String input, String targetLang) … {
  Observable<String> result =
      new MlLanguageDetectionCommand(mlService, input)
      .observe() // Commands support RxJava patterns
      // flatMap channels results to the given lambda
      .flatMap(ldResult -> {
        String sourceLang = ldResult.getLangCode();
        if (StringUtils.isBlank(sourceLang)) {
          return Observable.just("");// not determined
        }
        // after check and prep pass to next command
        return new MlTranslationCommand(
            mlService, sourceLang, targetLang,
            Collections.singletonList(input))
            .observe()
            .map(strings -> {
              if (strings.isEmpty()) {
                // error, no results, mask
                return "";
              }
              return strings.get(0);
            }); });
  return result.toBlocking().single();
}
```

Listing 17.8 Linking Two Services with RxJava and Error Handling

Listing 17.8 shows you how to pass the output of one command as an input to another command using RxJava. The results are also adapted and checked for possible error conditions on the fly. We'll instantiate the first command as usual but then call `observe` instead of `execute`. `observe` yields an `Observable`, the cornerstone of the RxJava API. Events and errors can be observed on an observable. In our example, the result of the `MlLanguageDetectionCommand` is an event to observe. Via the `flatMap` method of the `Observable`, an observer-lambda is installed as tranformation of the result, which retrieves the detected language code; verifies that detection was successful; and, if successful, creates the next command in the sequence, the translate command. Translation requires, as input, the source language, the input text, and the target language. After successful language detection, we'll have the source language readily available.

Thus, we can create and execute the translate command, again starting the process with the `observe` method of the command interface. Again, we'll apply a transformation with the `map` method of the observable. This transformation verifies that a translation is indeed returned from the service call, masking a missing translation as fallback. The `map` method is used instead of `flatMap` in this case because the transformation of the translate command does not result in an `Observable`. The benefit of using `flatMap` in the outer block is that observables nested in an observable are unwrapped.

At the end of Listing 17.8, we still convert to a blocking, thread-consuming synchronous execution model with `toBlocking`, but to see how to get rid of superfluous thread consumption, take a look at an example of an asynchronous `TranslateServlet` in the book's GitHub repository.

At this point, we've finished our integration of machine learning into the backend. We started by quickly integrating generated code for machine learning service consumption in our backend. Then, we gradually transformed this generated code into a reliable and powerful backend service orchestrating two machine learning services, each wrapped in an easily reusable Hystrix command. We won't consider the frontend integration of our new service, which is beyond the scope of this book. Instead, we'll focus our attention on blockchain integration as another scenario illustrating SAP Leonardo service integration into a backend application.

17.3 Extending Our Sample Application with Blockchain

Blockchain has shown great promise with hundreds of potential use cases over all domains of enterprise software. Although known as the technology enabling cryptocurrencies like Bitcoin, blockchain technology is not at all limited to this application. Blockchain is also part of the SAP Leonardo portfolio—a digital innovation system to help quick innovation at scale by combining different technologies and services. At the time of this writing, a beta offering of the blockchain service is available to gain experience. This service is not intended for productive use and should be used at your own risk, without expecting any commitment regarding general availability. In this section, we'll build a sample service that delivers blockchain functionality using the Hyperledger Fabric infrastructure on SAP Cloud Platform.

Blockchain in the Enterprise

Blockchain is a concept for recording and sharing data across a multiparty network. At its core, blockchain provides a tamper-proof, easily auditable database: Data is only added and never deleted. The mainstay of its security is that the data is replicated to all participants in a blockchain network—so nobody can change the data on his own if these changes violated preset rules, called *smart contracts* or *chaincode*. Digital signatures ensure authentication of authority. Nevertheless, access to this network can still be restricted, and public blockchain networks, such as Ethereum, differ from so-called permissioned chains to which a governing body grants access. Many enterprise scenarios call for such a setup, and Hyperledger Fabric is an open source implementation of a permissioned blockchain. SAP is a member of the Hyperledger project of the Linux Foundation.

Let's walk through a scenario: One member of our board just returned from an industry leadership summit with the idea of setting up a blacklist to vet (new) business partners. The goal is to warn other partners of possible fraudulent behavior by listing perpetrators on the blacklist. Our board member and his peers agreed that blockchain technology could finally make this long-term project bear fruit. So far, the idea seemed sound to everybody on a high level, but the implementation had been missing.

The participants in the summit, each from different companies, would like to jointly blacklist business partners that have shown fraudulent behavior. This sharing would expose these perpetrators to all the participants who could then react prudently in accord with their own policies. So far, the problem was that, when looking for a location for the central database, no agreement could be reached about which cloud provider to trust or which summit participant should run the database centrally. This year, the leaders at the summit had heard about blockchain and learned that it solved the problem of who to trust to host a network. So, our boss surprised them (and us) by proposing he could have a close-to-production proof-of-concept blacklist ready within three months—integrated with the in-house ERP test landscape!

17.3.1 SAP Cloud Platform Blockchain-Based on Hyperledger Fabric Technology

Happy to be entrusted with this task and horrorstruck with the timeline, we breathed a sigh of relief when we discovered that SAP offers a ready-to-use blockchain platform: SAP Cloud Platform Blockchain (beta). The blockchain offering is technology agnostic, supporting different blockchain implementations. We'll opt for the Hyperledger Fabric technology. Since we know how to create side-by-side extensions for

SAP S/4HANA Cloud and run them on the SAP Cloud Platform, let's look at how blockchain can be used for the task.

One hesitation around using blacklists is the worry that blacklist entries might be added without anyone taking responsibility. Thus, besides the actual entries, we'll want to store the person adding the entry to the chain. Another challenge was the different policies on interpreting blacklist entries across peers, so another goal is to show how many peers had added partners to the blacklist—each peer can add an entry for a partner. Counting the total number of partners that have blacklisted an entry gives participants a handle on the seriousness of the allegation.

Chaincode (aka Smart Contract)

Chaincode is the concept of deploying and running programmed logic directly on the nodes making up a blockchain network. The chaincode is installed by common decision of network participants. A chaincode governs its own area of the blockchain, ensuring that all data in that area was validated by it. A chaincode can also implement query functionality for simplifying interfaces. Since chaincodes must be installed and upgraded by a majority of participants to function, they represent a kind of contract agreed to by the participants, with adherence enforced by the blockchain network. Hyperledger Fabric requires the chaincode be implemented in the Go programming language. For more information, see the help on chaincode in SAP Cloud Platform Blockchain at *http://tiny.cc/sap-blockchain*.

We'll use chaincode to implement the blockchain logic, as opposed to just using the blockchain as a "dumb" database and interpreting the information on the client side. As a result, interpretations will be more cleanly aligned across peers. Let's look at the design for the chaincode interface:

- `add(objectType, entryValue, creator)`
  Adds an entry to the blacklist, allowing different types of entries to be more flexible.
- `count(objectType, entryValue)`
  Counts blacklist entries (from different creators) for the same `objectType` and value.
- `remove(objectType, entryValue, creator)`
  Removes an entry from the blacklist but will only remove the entry added by the given creator. Note that this adds an entry negating the previously added entry—on the blockchain nothing can be removed. So the old entry will continue to be visible on inspection, as will the negation added later, of course.

We've implemented this logic as go chaincode, which is available in the GitHub repository for this book. Now, we can deploy the chaincode on the SAP Cloud Platform Blockchain (beta) on the SAP Cloud Platform. But first we'll need to create a SAP Cloud Platform Blockchain service instance on our SAP Cloud Platform account and create a channel in that instance. A channel represents a space in which communication happens for all channel participants to see. We'll then create a matching channel service instance for the channel, which hosts the channel's dashboard and test environment. Multiple channels can be used to implement confidentiality by separating participants or for organizing communication among participants. In SAP Cloud Platform Blockchain, chaincode is deployed to a node and linked to a specific channel during deployment.

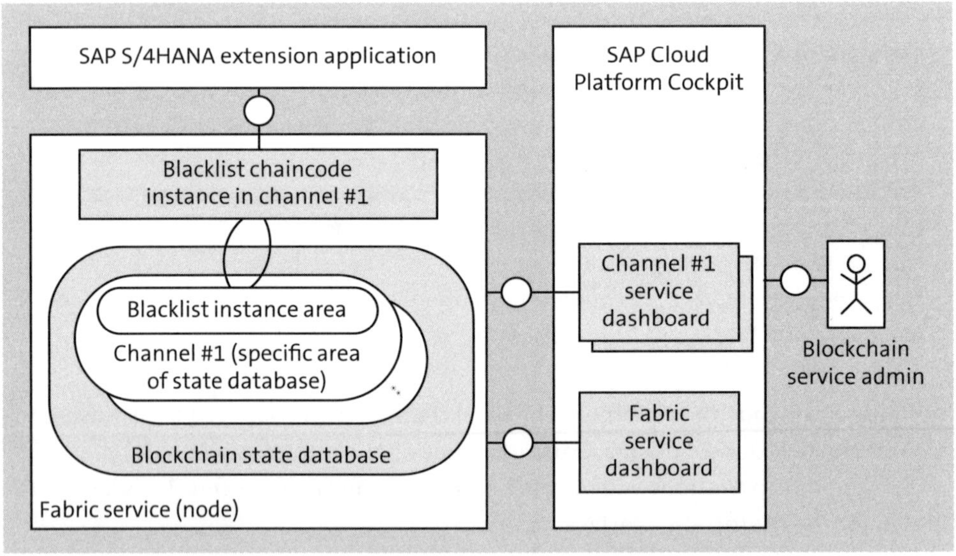

Figure 17.3 Structure of SAP Cloud Platform Blockchain Based on Hyperledger Fabric Technology

The relationship between the different entities is shown in Figure 17.3. A Hyperledger Fabric service supports many channels, and we'll have to associate a chaincode with a channel. Nothing can be stored outside of a channel. For the management of channels and nodes, the SAP Cloud Platform cockpit makes available several distinct dashboards. The SAP S/4HANA extension application we're building communicates with the blacklist chaincode, which has a reserved part of a channel available for exclusive use. All channels together make up the state database—the core of the blockchain.

17.3.2 Creating Required SAP Cloud Platform Blockchain Services and Deploying the Blacklist Chaincode Example

In this section, we'll set up the blockchain landscape and deploy the blacklist chaincode. You can find the main service in the service marketplace of SAP Cloud Platform, and the installation should be easy enough. Be aware that your SAP Cloud Platform account needs a quota to consume this service. Only with a quota will you see the service in your service marketplace, as shown in Figure 17.4. If you cannot find the service, your account might lack quota allocation for this service. The quota needs to be assigned to the subaccount that hosts your application.

Quota Requirement for SAP Cloud Platform Blockchain Service

At the time of this writing, we cannot yet publish a plan for general availability and for a potential trial offering of SAP Cloud Platform Blockchain. Please refer to the SAP Cloud Platform Blockchain documentation to determine the best way to get a service quota.

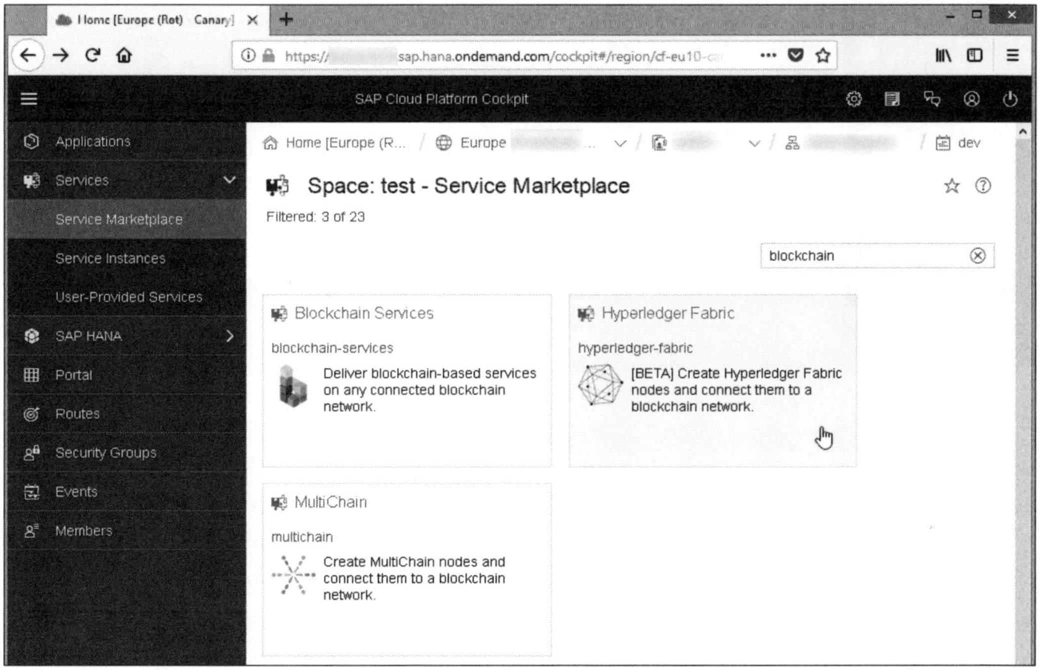

Figure 17.4 Blockchain Services Marketplace Preview (Example)

SAP follows best-of-breed strategies when it comes to blockchain technology selection—offering many options and do not preclude early—so every application can choose the blockchain technology that best fits its requirements. Therefore, you may find multiple blockchain service offerings on the SAP Cloud Platform.

After creating an instance of the fabric service, switch to its dashboard, shown in Figure 17.5, to create a channel. The channel needs to be reflected with its own service instance in Cloud Foundry, and the fabric service dashboard offers a button to create that channel service instance in our account (see Figure 17.6). This channel service instance has its own dashboard. Now, instead of the button for creating the channel service, a button on the fabric service dashboard provides access to the channel dashboard.

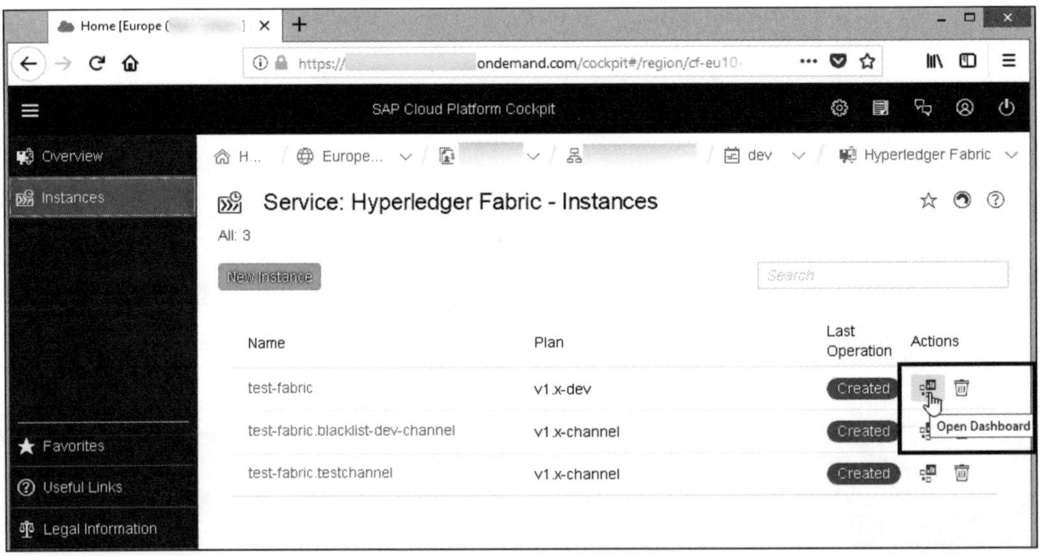

Figure 17.5 Creating a Hyperledger Fabric Service Instance and Opening Its Dashboard

If you recall the structure of the SAP Cloud Platform Blockchain based on Hyperledger Fabric technology we described in the previous subsection, remember that the channel dashboard is the spot to deploy our chaincode example. A chaincode needs to be associated with a channel. SAP Cloud Platform Blockchain supports a chaincode packaging format that helps with managing, testing, and using chaincodes, basically a ZIP file of source code with some metadata and an optional interface description. You can download the example chaincode from the GitHub repository for this book, where you'll also find documentation on how to create the packaged chaincode. Once you have the chaincode package available, simply locate the **Chaincode** screen in your channel dashboard to deploy the chaincode package.

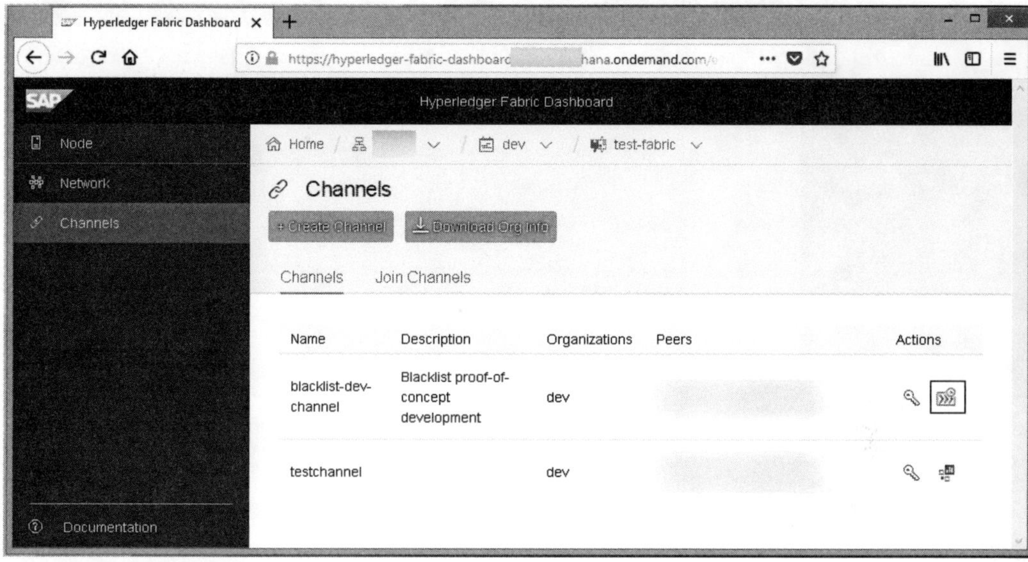

Figure 17.6 Hyperledger Fabric Service Dashboard: Creating Channels and the Required SAP Cloud Platform Blockchain Channel Service Directly

17.3.3 Cloud Foundry Service Authorization for SAP Cloud Platform Blockchain

After we've deployed the chaincode, all that's missing to enable calling it from our application on the SAP Cloud Platform is passing authorization checks. Note that, as a peer in the blockchain network, we'll need to run a node and assume the authority of a node owner, that is, take up our position in the governance of the network. The SAP Cloud Platform Blockchain services and their dashboards facilitate all of this.

Since the SAP Cloud Platform Blockchain services are provided on Cloud Foundry, authorization is handled via Cloud Foundry security. Cloud Foundry manages and provides authorization for access to the services, and we can instruct Cloud Foundry via the SAP Cloud Platform Cockpit to provide access to an application. This access is created by binding a service to an application (restricted to the same space) or by using the service key (which allows cross-space service usage). The important point is to bind the channel service and not the Hyperledger Fabric (node) service, as shown in Figure 17.7.

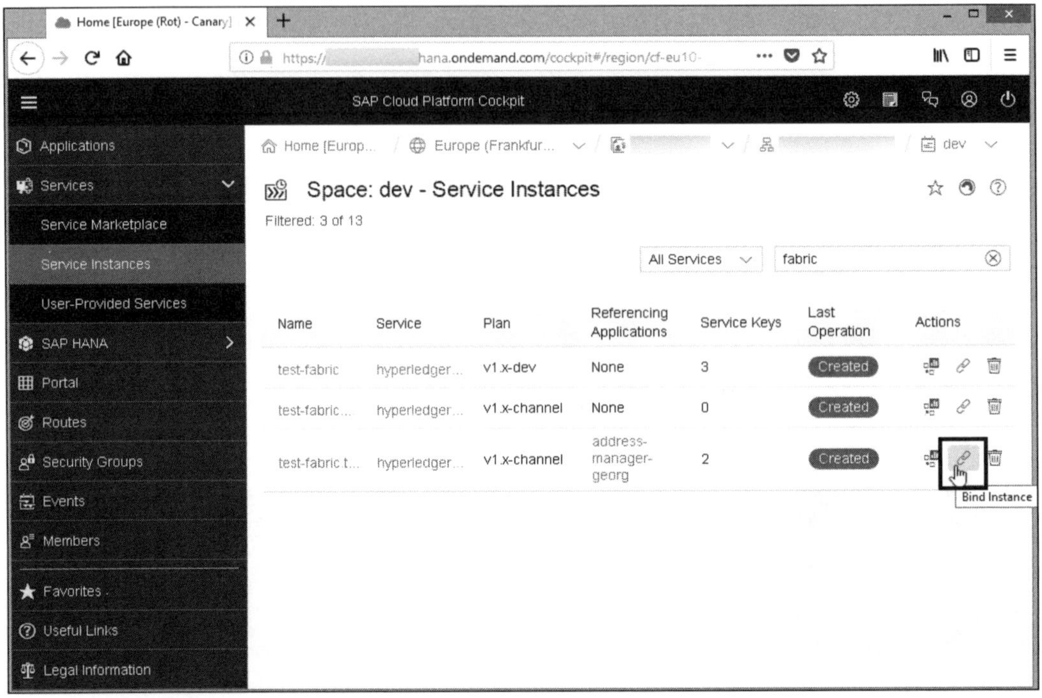

Figure 17.7 Binding a Service to an Application via the Service Instances Screen of a Space

After the service has been bound to the application, we'll see the updated VCAP_SERVICES variable in the **Environment Variables** screen of the application, which is handy for setting up a local test and debug environment.

The integration in our example application requires extracting the service information from the VCAP_SERVICES variable and acquiring an OAuth 2.0 bearer token from the provided authentication service. Although this interaction adheres to the OAuth standard, generally speaking, no overarching standard governs service access in Cloud Foundry. The lowest common denominator is using the VCAP_SERVICES structure for passing binding information to the application. Each service can choose its own information structure and authentication method. Therefore, authentication and parsing of VCAP_SERVICES is service-specific. An in-depth explanation of the source code to implement the authentication flow is out of scope for this book. However, we've provided the code for authentication in our sample application in the GitHub repository for the book. Take a look at the method createByGettingTokenViaCfServicesConfig of the class BlockchainService.

17.3.4 Interacting with the Deployed Chaincode

Next in line is actually using the landscape and the deployed chaincode in a side-by-side extension of our own making, which is what we'll do now. The actual interaction with the chaincode is almost anticlimactic after the complexity of the service setup, deployment, and authentication details—but let's keep in mind what we've accomplished: setting up a whole single-node blockchain network! For your next blockchain project, you can bypass the landscape creation steps by reusing the landscape that we'll set up in this section, thereby directly jumping to chaincode deployment.

The chaincode interaction basically requires making REST calls to the service URL provided in the service credentials, passing the ID of the deployed chaincode to identify chaincode and channel. The `BlockchainService` class implements generic calls to chaincode interfaces in the `invokeOrQuery` method, following the ideas laid out in the previous section on machine learning service invocation (see Listing 17.9). Since the service URL is provided by Cloud Foundry, we won't use the destination service.

```
public String invokeOrQuery(
    BlockchainInvocationType invocationType,
    String chaincodeId, String function, String... args)
    throws Exception {
  final HttpPost chaincodeEndpointRequest = new HttpPost(
      new URI(getServiceUrl()
          + "/chaincodes/" + chaincodeId
          + "/latest/" + invocationType.getPathParamValue()
      ).normalize());
  chaincodeEndpointRequest.setHeader(
      "Authorization", "Bearer " + getBearerToken())
  chaincodeEndpointRequest.setHeader("Accept",
      "application/json;charset=UTF-8");
  final JsonObject requestBody = new JsonObject();
  requestBody.addProperty("function", function);
  requestBody.add("arguments", new Gson().toJsonTree(args));
  requestBody.addProperty("async", false);
  final String json = new Gson().toJson(requestBody);
  chaincodeEndpointRequest.setEntity(
      new StringEntity(json, ContentType.APPLICATION_JSON));
  final HttpResponse response = HttpClientAccessor
      .getHttpClient().execute(chaincodeEndpointRequest);
  final StatusLine statusLine = response.getStatusLine();
```

```
  final String responsePayload =
    HttpEntityUtil.getResponsePayload(response);
   // Check for success with result status ...
  }
}
```

Listing 17.9 Invoking a Chaincode's Functions Generically

The generic `BlockchainService` is simply accessing a REST service, which makes a chaincode available via its identifier as path parameter and which expects function and arguments encoded in JSON in the request body. Blockchain-specific is the query type: Much slower than read requests, write requests are handled differently and must be specified as path parameters on the request URI. `BlockchainInvocationType` provides two request types:

- **Invoke**
  This request type permits the chaincode to alter the state database. Requests of this type are verified on every node connected to a channel, and all their parameters and actions are logged in the transaction log. This request type therefore executes much more slowly than query.
- **Query**
  The *query* request type doesn't allow changes to the state database by the executing chaincode, permitting a much faster execution strategy. A query request should always be used when a chaincode request will not lead to changes in the state database. Reading the blacklist status should clearly be implemented as a query request.

The result of the call is passed through to the caller. The method shown in this section is intended for use for specific services and commands, such as the `BlacklistService`, shown in Listing 17.10, which is exposing the chaincode functionality as straightforward Java methods for consumption in backend code. This code assumes that the ID of the chaincode to call is stored in the field `blacklistChaincodeId`, which in our case is initialized from an environment variable.

```
public class BlacklistService {
  // Initialization and reading chaincode id from environment
  public void addEmailToBlacklist(String emailAddress)
      throws Exception {
    blockchainService.invokeOrQuery(
        BlockchainQueryType.INVOKE,
```

```
        blacklistChaincodeId, "add", "email", emailAddress);
  }
}
```

Listing 17.10 Putting Chaincode ID Reading and Interface Function Calls in an Easily Consumable Service

With the service implemented in Listing 17.10, chaincode running on the blockchain is accessible via a simple function call in the backend code. Similarly, we could check the blacklist when creating a new business partner, assuming we expanded our sample application to include this functionality. Having come this far, we're pretty sure we'll finish the proof-of-concept for our boss before the deadline. The SAP S/4HANA Cloud SDK, SAP Cloud Platform Blockchain, and our `BlacklistService` utility class make creating integrated services as easy as writing any normal backend service.

17.4 Summary

This chapter has been a tour-de-force overview of how the SAP S/4HANA Cloud SDK and the SAP Cloud Platform facilitate innovation. The technologies already available on the platform today are bound to unleash great powers of innovation when put in the hands of developers. With what we learned in the chapter, this power is at our fingertips, ready for both today's cutting-edge technologies and for tomorrow's innovations.

In the next few chapters, we'll for a brief moment move away from side-by-side extensions and instead focus on in-app extensions, later tying them back to our Business Partner Address Manager application on SAP Cloud Platform.

PART V

In-App Extensibility

Chapter 18
In-App Extensibility in SAP S/4HANA

This chapter gives an overview of in-app extensibility of SAP S/4HANA systems to complement the side-by-side extensibility options presented so far. In this chapter, we'll introduce the overall concept behind and architecture of in-app extensibility and discuss some of the most compelling use cases for in-app extensibility.

The high demand to adapt enterprise business software originates from the nature of this software and its usage in customer landscapes. Cloud products especially aim for best practices in the business processes they facilitate. Adapting these best practices to cover the specific requirements of your own processes is highly desirable—especially in times of digitalization and quickly changing business processes. In SAP S/4HANA, self-service configuration tools allow you to adapt the business configuration. Some adaptations go beyond configuration but still need to be closely integrated with core business processes. These adaptations are best implemented in an integrated, in-app manner customized by key users, instead of as side-by-side extensions created by developers.

This integrated, in-app manner of extending core function is covered by the field of in-app extensibility, which we'll discuss conceptually in this chapter, before explaining the available tools in more detail in Chapter 19 and the integration of in-app extensions into applications on SAP Cloud Platform in Chapter 20.

For cloud products, normally project decisions and their realization are performed much more quickly than in on-premise systems and are focused more on lines of business (LOBs). Thus, extensibility designed for the cloud therefore addresses key users of LOBs as the main personas. Key users are assumed to have sound business knowledge but low technical skills; thus, they need a specific set of key user tools to fulfill the most important tasks of extensibility that impact the complete system with all users. With good key user tools in place, developers with high technical skills are only required in complex extension projects, for expert-oriented tasks like database design, integration, or coding.

The goal of extensibility for integrated scenarios is end-to-end-extensibility along business processes, realized by simple and robust extensibility mechanisms fulfilling cloud qualities. We'll discuss those expected cloud qualities in Section 18.1, before looking at the different in-app extensibility patterns and tools in Section 18.2. Section 18.3 discusses specific aspects of in-app extensibility to consider in integration scenarios.

As described in Chapter 2, we can enhance a software on a different platform specialized for side-by-side extensions or directly on the same stack where the extended software runs with in-app extensibility. In Section 18.4, we'll advise you about when to use in-app extensions. Throughout this chapter, we'll describe patterns and tools available in both SAP S/4HANA Cloud and SAP S/4HANA on-premise. In Section 18.5, we'll close the chapter with a look at the specifics of on-premise in-app extensibility.

18.1 Cloud Qualities of In-App Extensibility

In addition to the functional requirements expected of extensibility, companies using SAP S/4HANA require several cloud qualities to ensure that their extensions are future-proof and simple to maintain. The following qualities are the most important ones for extensibility, which we'll discuss in this section: reliable data interfaces, simplicity, and decoupling.

The first cloud quality, reliable data interfaces, means that data interfaces (like APIs or code exits) need to be semantically rich, on the one hand, and stable, on the other. Thus, only a stable subset of all SAP S/4HANA software artifacts can be enhanced, called or referenced by extensions. Depending on the kind of usage (internal or external), different contracts are defined to ensure stability. The basis of all contracts is that no cloud released artifacts (also called whitelisted artifacts) can be deleted or have its behavior changed. The same applies for its elements. For in-app extensibility, several types of objects are released. The most important ones are the following:

- Business contexts (i.e., business object nodes), which are part of applications that can be enhanced by custom fields or logic
- Code exits for custom ABAP code (so-called BAdIs; see Section 18.2.4 for more information about logic extensibility)
- Core data services (CDS) views, which are used for data declaration and data selection
- ABAP class-based APIs

- Data types used as interfaces of BAdIs and API classes or for type declarations within custom code

The second cloud quality is simplicity. In the cloud, extensibility tools must also be easily consumable. Technical objects (OData services, SAP Fiori UIs, custom code, view extensions and associations, database changes) are generated in the background without further interaction by the tool user. This process guarantees cloud-like stability and allows key users to create extensions without needing an understanding of the technical details.

For the third cloud quality, decoupling, in-app extensions must be loosely coupled from the SAP standard. Thus, the following rules are fulfilled:

- Regular SAP updates must not require adaptations to custom/partner code.
- Customer/partner extensions must never block an SAP software update.
- A clear logical separation must exist between custom/partner objects and SAP standard objects.
- Access to SAP objects must occur only via cloud-released APIs.
- No modifications are allowed, only enhancements following the guidelines described in this chapter.

In practice, decoupling is realized in a way that the SAP lifecycle of SAP is separate from the lifecycles of custom objects, but in all relevant runtime artifacts, both SAP and customer elements are combined in a stable and controlled way—allowing extensions to benefit from SAP HANA's capabilities.

Note

In SAP S/4HANA Cloud, only cloud-released software artifacts are visible and ready to be extended or consumed. These objects represent a public and stable model for key users or developers. All other objects are either hidden or only visible for information purposes. Besides the restriction to key user tools, this visibility is the major difference between SAP S/4HANA Cloud and SAP S/4HANA on-premise from the perspective of extensibility.

18.2 In-App Extensibility Patterns and Key User Tools

In-app extensibility can be structured along different extensibility patterns, which subsume the different in-app extensibility options described in the following:

- Content adaptation (forms, analytics, UI layout, terminology),
- Structural or data model extensibility (custom CDS views, field extensions, custom business objects)
- Business logic and process extensibility
- Integration extensibility (Section 18.3)

All of these extensibility patterns require implementation steps that impact technical artifacts across the complete SAP S/4HANA stack. As mentioned in Section 18.1 on cloud qualities, in SAP S/4HANA, key user tools generate these technical artifacts. Depending on the extensibility pattern, the following software artifacts are generated in the background, most of them hidden from the key user: ABAP dictionary appends, CDS extend statements, CDS views, data elements and domains, custom database tables, custom ABAP code, OData service extensions, custom OData services, user interface (UI) layout changes, and custom UIs.

In SAP S/4HANA, for the patterns mentioned earlier, a set of key user tools allow you to define the required extensions. All of these tools are integrated with each other, building a suite of tools supporting extensibility for extensibility patterns we've described. In the following sections, we'll introduce the main patterns. Chapter 19 describes the key user tools most relevant to side-by-side extensions and explains their use.

18.2.1 UI Adaptation

Adapting UIs to business and personal need is a strong desire of all software users. Business users want to personalize their UIs for their own usage (e.g., hiding or moving elements, adding fields, changing labels). Further, key users can perform these UI adaptations for the whole system and all its users.

As key users are expected to work in a UI-oriented environment (rather than using APIs or writing code), you can adapt SAP Fiori UIs directly within a running application via the UI runtime adaptation. This feature allows you to specify changes like adding fields, hiding elements, moving elements, and changing labels in a modification-free way as delta to the SAP standard. Runtime adaptation is available to all users with the key user role assigned.

Other UI technologies also support extensibility. Web GUIs (also known as SAP GUI or Web Dynpro) dynamically show extension fields in a specific tab. Web Dynpro UIs can be adapted by the floorplan manager (FPM).

18.2.2 Custom CDS Views

Defining and extending the data model of SAP S/4HANA is a major cornerstone of most extensibility projects, along with the retrieval and consumption of the data.

ABAP CDS entities and the ABAP virtual data model (VDM; not to be confused with the Java VDM of the SAP S/4HANA Cloud SDK) are important concepts to understand SAP S/4HANA's data model and the way it is exposed. These concepts form the basis for extending the data model, for custom analytics, and for consuming data in custom logic or side-by-side extensions.

Core data services are modeling entities that:

- are defined by a data definition language (DDL) that enhances the SQL;
- represent definitions of views (including joins, unions, expressions for calculations);
- allow defining relations between CDS entities by associations;
- can be enriched by annotations that define domain specific metadata (e.g., layout information for rendering SAP Fiori element-based UIs);
- contain an authorization concept with data control language (DCL); and
- are technically represented by ABAP dictionary views and SAP HANA database views.

Like ABAP dictionary structures, CDS entities and their metadata are extensible by available built-in extension options that you can use for defining sextensions manually (in the on-premise version of SAP S/4HANA) or via key user tools.

The SAP S/4HANA ABAP VDM leverages these characteristics of the CDS and represents the simplified and harmonized, business-oriented and semantically enriched data model of SAP S/4HANA. The VDM consists of several layers, the deepest of which is more data access-oriented, while other layers represent business objects, and expose data for consumption for a particular purpose (e.g., analytical queries).

Some CDS views of the VDM are released for cloud usage, and custom code can select data from these views. Also, the key user tool Custom CDS Views creates custom CDS views based on released SAP CDS views. The tool supports joining several CDS views, calculations, and aggregations. Custom CDS views can also be exposed as OData services.

18.2.3 Field Extensibility

Field extensibility allows you to add customer-specific fields in a 1:1 relation to an extensible part of an application, for example, to add custom attributes to a sales order item or customer address. The behavior of custom fields is identical to SAP standard fields. Normally, these custom fields are even persisted in the same database table.

For a simple and pragmatic application model for key users, applications are structured into business contexts. These business contexts correspond to extensible parts of applications (like sales order item).

A more formal structure model is described by business objects and business object nodes types, as known, for example, to developers using BAPIs. Business contexts refer to business object nodes, helping experienced users gain a deeper understanding of the application's structure.

Business contexts normally correspond to the CDS view that represents the business object node. Also, each business context is associated with one or several application database tables to be extended by the key user tool for field extensibility.

After an extension field has been defined, all necessary software artifacts are generated by the extensibility tool, as mentioned in the previous section. Prepared for this kind of extensibility, applications do consider and handle these extension fields, so we can use the generated fields directly in all other key user tools.

Directly from the UI adaption mode, a key user in SAP S/4HANA can add fields to an SAP Fiori app in a simple dialogue. The key user can edit or translate the field properties like data type, label, or code list values and texts.

18.2.4 Business Logic Extensibility and Process Extensibility

Beyond UI extensibility, which allows to adapt an application's appearance, and field/table extensibility, which allows you to enhance the data structure of applications, a further important extensibility capability is the enhancement of the behavior of applications and processes.

Prominent use cases include the following:

- Validation or checks
- Calculation or determination (e.g., for default values)
- Mapping standard and extension fields within applications and processes.

To make business processes more flexible, a process may offer custom checks (for example, for approval steps) or may offer the ability to remove process steps or define additional steps. Further use cases include the application of domain-specific topics like tax calculation or price determination.

Technically, SAP S/4HANA realizes business logic extensibility by application specific code exits, known as Business Add-Ins (BAdIs). BAdIs are predefined and stable interfaces, designed by SAP for specific extension purposes, that the application logic calls directly. Customers can implement the BAdI interfaces with ABAP classes to implement their business logic. Data transfer into the custom code happens via `IMPORTING` parameters, data transfer back to SAP business logic via `CHANGING` parameters. Some BAdIs also support a filter mechanism that allows several BAdI implementations to exist for one interface. At runtime, filter criteria specify the implementation to be called.

To be consumable in SAP S/4HANA Cloud, a BAdI must fulfill several requirements: It must be released for cloud usage, allow multiple implementations, and have simple and stable data types (instead of dynamic ones). Such a BAdI is called a *Cloud BAdI*. Implementations of a Cloud BAdIs can be developed in the SAP Fiori-based web editor for ABAP, which offers an appropriate user experience for key users. This editor allows an easy exploration of APIs, key user documentation, syntax checks, syntax highlighting, and code completion.

Unlike SAP S/4HANA on-premise, SAP S/4HANA Cloud does not only limit logic extensibility to released objects, but the ABAP language itself has a restricted set of instructions. No direct database operation (except selection from released CDS views) is allowed, no influence on task or transaction handling is possible, no dynamic programming or code generation is supported, and obsolete statements of the language have been removed. More details on this restricted version of ABAP are available at *http://tiny.cc/s4-restricted-abap*.

These restrictions allow ABAP to be used for logic extensibility even in SAP S/4HANA Cloud by ensuring robustness, security, and data consistency.

18.2.5 Custom Business Objects

Custom business objects (CBOs) refer to a self-contained type definition with a set of customer-specific fields that are not coupled to SAP business contexts. The fields are independent of a predefined business context and have their own dependencies, enabling associations between different custom business objects or parent-child relations.

In contrast to field extensibility, custom business objects lead to new customer-specific tables in the database. For each custom business object, generic and generated

APIs support create, read, update, delete (CRUD) operations: API ABAP classes, CDS views, OData services, and an SAP Fiori app.

Thus, entities for custom business objects can be created and modified through a UI within SAP S/4HANA or from other customer systems, for example, applications on SAP Cloud Platform. The key user tool for custom business objects also allows defining custom code lists that contain values for dropdown lists as well as for facts or dimensions in analytical scenarios. We can leverage CBOs to contain any custom specific data that we want to consider in extensions to application or process logic.

To allow adaptation of business logic, each custom business object has a set of code exits that can be implemented by means of business logic extensibility.

18.2.6 Further Tools

Further tools for key users around extensibility and adaptation are mentioned in this section only briefly because they are beyond of the scope of this book.

The SAP Fiori apps of the **KPI Design** group allow you to define new key performance indicators (KPIs) based on released SAP or custom CDS views (or OData services). The KPIs can be shown on new SAP Fiori tiles in the launchpad.

With the Custom Analytical Queries SAP Fiori app, customers can create their own analytical queries based on released analytical data sources (specific SAP or customer CDS views).

Also, you can create custom print forms with the Maintain Form Template SAP Fiori app. In this app, customers can create new form templates (e.g., copied from SAP templates) based on OData services and define the layout with Adobe Forms Designer.

All these tools support field extensibility and offer extension fields of the related objects for selection, as appropriate.

18.2.7 Lifecycle Aspects

As mentioned in Section 18.1, lifecycle events of extensions and of the core system by SAP must not interfere with each other. This separation is important, as extensions are expected to run after each SAP upgrade or patch without customer or partner effort.

To ensure stability, key user extensibility is only possible in the quality (Q) system and can be transported to the productive (P) system. The key user can transport extension objects from the quality to the productive system without interaction with the service provider. Further, this transfer must occur outside of the maintenance window of the service provider. For this purpose, the transport tool used by key users (the *ATO tool*) guarantees the completeness and integrity of transports and takes care that transports do not interfere with SAP lifecycle events.

18.3 Integration Aspects

Extensibility is an important feature in the domain of integration across systems. Extensibility enables a standardized cloud product, such as SAP S/4HANA Cloud, to play a role in a highly customer-specific system landscape. Integration, for example, brings together side-by-side extensions and the core SAP S/4HANA system with its potential in-app extensions.

The following patterns and requirements for integration extensibility are the most relevant in this context and discussed in the following subsections:

- Adding custom fields to SAP S/4HANA standard APIs
- Exposing SAP S/4HANA data via custom APIs
- Defining custom business logic for integration scenarios

18.3.1 Field Extensibility

In most cases, field extensions apply to all architecture layers (for example, database, business logic, UI) accordingly, but isolated extensions are possible as well, for example attributes that are calculated and not persisted in the database. For integration scenarios, external APIs need to reflect extensions with custom fields.

To enable the enhancement of APIs, in-app key user field extensibility can generate extensions into the appropriate APIs of the extended applications. Technically, SOAP services, OData services, IDocs, and even BAPIs are enabled for field extensibility, with BAPIs only exposed in on-premise systems. To allow the consumption of extension fields, the SAP S/4HANA Cloud SDK has its own measure to deal with field extensibility, which is described in Chapter 20.

18.3.2 Custom APIs

Another important pattern is the exposure of custom and standard data in custom APIs. This exposure is especially relevant because SAP cannot possibly foresee every possible externally required API with the desired granularity.

All externally available APIs are described and documented on the SAP API Business Hub, available at *https://api.sap.com*. If we need a combination of SAP and custom data, or if we need to join SAP data in a customer-specific way, creating your own custom APIs is possible. This process is either performed automatically on top of custom business objects or with the Custom CDS View app, which allows you to expose CDS views as OData services.

To make these OData services visible to the outside world (and thus to SAP Cloud Platform), an appropriate communication scenario and communication arrangement are required. The key user tools for this task are the Communication Arrangements and Custom Communication Scenarios SAP Fiori apps. In Chapter 20, we'll describe how the SAP S/4HANA Cloud SDK consumes these custom OData services in a side-by-side extension on the SAP Cloud Platform.

18.3.3 Business Logic

Custom business logic is not only relevant for application logic, but is also needed for integration within business processes. In custom business logic, we can perform local calculations, but we can also call external web services for each of the use cases described in the next section. Based on these capabilities, we can realize parts of the integration business logic as an in-app extension via BAdIs as described in the previous section.

A common pattern is to *validate* data as part of integration scenarios, for example, a stricter credit limit check before sending an order to the outside world. Validation includes simple value checks (for example, checking against code values of a dropdown list) or more sophisticated checks that consider several attributes or states, possibly even consider external resources.

A further typical use case is *mapping*, for example, the mapping of internal data representation to the representation expected by business-to-business (B2B) standards. We can realize mapping as in-app logic extensions for simple cases. Nevertheless, if for more complex requirements, middleware products like SAP Cloud Platform Integration are recommended. Using middleware, we can realize more complex extensibility patterns, like data transformation, splitting and combining of messages, message reduction, data enrichment or filtering, and distribution.

Key user field extensibility automatically takes care that appropriate mapping between APIs and application data occurs and that validation against customer-defined code values is done. As a consequence, the normal one-to-one exposure of custom fields in an API requires no business logic extension.

Another potential use case for custom business logic in integration scenarios is *triggering* a business process via a call to an external service. For example, we can issue a call to a REST endpoint of an application on SAP Cloud Platform and provide data available in the context of the BAdI. We'll describe an example of this in Chapter 19, Section 19.9.

18.4 When to Use What

As stated in this chapter and other chapters, the degree of freedom in key user extensibility is limited by the boundary conditions of the cloud qualities. This limitation is especially obvious when comparing the in-app extension options with developer tools on a platform-as-a-service (PaaS) product like SAP Cloud Platform. Nevertheless, strong use cases exist for in-app extensibility: It is the first choice when the focus is on context-aware extensions and tight integration, such as in the following scenarios:

- **Transactional integration**
  The extension should be part of a transaction within the SAP S/4HANA system and the integration into SAP S/4HANA system shall ensure transactional integrity and a low latency, for example, an additional check before creating a sales order or determining a currency exchange rate at the time of posting an accounting document.
- **Data integration**
  Custom data, either as new custom fields or custom business objects, should be deeply aligned with SAP core data to leverage the full power of SAP HANA for data retrieval and reporting, for example, to offer analytics with customer-defined dimensions.
- **Process integration**
  Creating custom APIs, as well as extending released SAP APIs, helps expose appropriate business data into business processes on top of SAP S/4HANA, for example, to an existing third-party application or a new side-by-side extension.

For extension scenarios where customer applications are self-contained, that is, only loosely coupled to SAP S/4HANA, side-by-side extensibility is a better choice. If the extension is about enhancing the reach beyond the typical users of an ERP system (for example, customer portals, mobile apps, consumer apps, or specialist apps) or about integrating with other cloud solutions, side-by-side extensions are the way to go.

Defining common rules about when to use in-app extensibility and when to use side-by-side extensibility is difficult. The choice will depend on the details of customer projects, the skills of the employees, the history of existing extensions, and the customer project roadmap. In the end, in many cases, a combination of both techniques will be the answer: functionalities that need proximity to the ABAP stack make sense as in-app extensions, while the other functionalities may be more suited as side-by-side extensions on SAP Cloud Platform that consume a public or custom API via the SAP S/4HANA Cloud SDK.

18.5 In-App Extensibility in SAP S/4HANA On-Premise Systems

In contrast to SAP S/4HANA Cloud, on-premise in-app extensibility is not restricted to key users. You can access the backend and use ABAP development tools (ADT) to enhance or even modify the software artifacts. This method is called *classic extensibility*.

In-app key user extensibility has been designed for the cloud but is also available in SAP S/4HANA on-premise systems. While in-app extensibility is limited in scope when compared to classic extensibility, some benefits for on-premise developers include the following:

- Following best practices in extensibility patterns and using released APIs optimizes the upgrade and patch process, since side effects of custom extensions are minimized.
- In-app extensibility enhances speed and efficiency of the development process.
- The simplicity of in-app extensibility tools does not require deep technical skills.

Adopting in-app extensibility with these benefits represents an important first step on the way to the cloud. In this case, extension implementations already fulfill most cloud qualities, making a later cloud migration much easier.

The features of in-app extensibility are quite similar in SAP S/4HANA Cloud and in SAP S/4HANA on-premise, but some differences need be considered on-premise, as follows:

- Transport of extension artifacts is performed via ABAP transport tools (CTS, correction and transport system) instead of using key user tools.
- On-premise systems do not support navigating from an application UI to the key-user extensibility tools supported.

- No predefined key user roles are available, instead custom user roles need to be built from predelivered role templates.
- Access to ABAP development tools allows the reuse of generated key user extension artifacts.
- No mandatory restrictions exist on cloud-released objects.

Many on-premise customer projects will involve a mixture of key user and classic extensions. One the one hand, this scenario stems from the limited scope of in-app extensibility; on the other hand, from customer history, which may involve older SAP ERP releases.

In cases that require freestyle ABAP development, we strongly recommend avoiding modifications and restricting the custom code to cloud-released objects. Following these rules will strongly decrease negative side effects and reduce the effort required when applying support packages or feature packages.

If customers are on a roadmap towards SAP S/4HANA Cloud, we recommend creating customer extensions using side-by-side extensibility and key user in-app extensibility. Only with these extensibility measures will migrating extensions into SAP S/4HANA Cloud be possible in the future.

18.6 Summary

With the conceptual overview given in this chapter, you should have a good understanding of the different options for in-app extensions and when to use them. We also explained how in-app extensions fulfill the expected cloud qualities and why they are useful also on-premise. In the next chapter, we'll look at the key user tools for in-app extensibility and explain how to create in-app extensions.

Chapter 19
Forms of In-App Extensibility

In this chapter, we'll explain how to use in-app extensibility as introduced conceptually in the previous chapter. We'll introduce key user tools for user interface (UI) and layout adaptations, custom business logic, custom core data services (CDS) views, and custom business objects. We'll also discuss in-app extensibility options that are particularly relevant to side-by-side extensions with specific reference to our Business Partner Address Manager application in the next chapter.

In the previous chapter, we learned about the basic concepts behind SAP S/4HANA's in-app extensibility. In this chapter, we'll show you how to use the tools for in-app extensibility step by step. We'll use key user tools to extend SAP standard objects with structural as well as logical enhancements. In Chapter 20, you'll then learn how to use in-app extensions from within your side-by-side application.

We'll start in Section 19.1 with an explanation of the necessary setup and authorization steps to use the key user tools for in-app extensibility. Section 19.2 introduces the Extensibility Cockpit as an important source of information for extension projects. The remaining sections each consider particular areas of in-app extensions.

19.1 Setup and Authorization to Use In-App Extensibility

In-app extensibility features are built into SAP S/4HANA. Thus, as outlined in previous chapters, key users can access all in-app extensibility features via web-based tools. Installing additional tools is not required.

To use in-app extensibility, your user requires special authorizations. In SAP S/4HANA Cloud, predefined roles are provided by SAP. In SAP S/4HANA Cloud, as an administrator, go to the Maintain Business Users app and assign the roles listed in Table 19.1 to the key users to enable the use of in-app extensibility.

Business Role	Business Role ID as Delivered by SAP
Extensibility	**SAP_BR_ADMINISTRATOR**
Configuration Expert (access to the Extensibility Cockpit)	**SAP_BR_BPC_EXPERT**
Analytics Specialist	**SAP_BR_ANALYTICS_SPECIALIST**
Software Collection Import	**SAP_CORE_BC_SL_IMP**
Software Collection Export	**SAP_CORE_BC_SL_EXP**

Table 19.1 Roles Required to Configure In-App Extensions

Required Business Catalog

In general, your user must be assigned to a business role that contains the respective business catalog mentioned in Table 19.2, like **Extensibility** (SAP_CORE_BC_EXT).

For our example, the roles listed in Table 19.2 also must be assigned to your user.

Business Role	Business Role ID as Delivered by SAP
Master Data Specialist - Business Partner Data	**SAP_BR_BUPA_MASTER_SPECIALIST**
Communication Management	**SAP_CORE_BC_COM**

Table 19.2 User Roles Required for Example

SAP S/4HANA On-Premise

Identity and access management is different in SAP S/4HANA Cloud and in SAP S/4HANA on-premise. For more information about maintaining business users and how to assign roles in SAP S/4HANA on-premise, please visit the relevant documentation: At *https://help.sap.com*, search for SAP S/4HANA and select **Product Assistance (English) • Enterprise Technology • SAP NetWeaver • General Functions for Key Users • App-Specific Implementation and Configuration Information** (*http://tiny.cc/s4-auth-op*).

Users that have the proper roles assigned will find the key user tools in the business catalogs **Extensibility, Transport Management**, and **Extensibility Explorer**, respectively, as shown in Figure 19.1. You can organize these tiles to your needs by opening the side bar and clicking the **Edit Home Page** button.

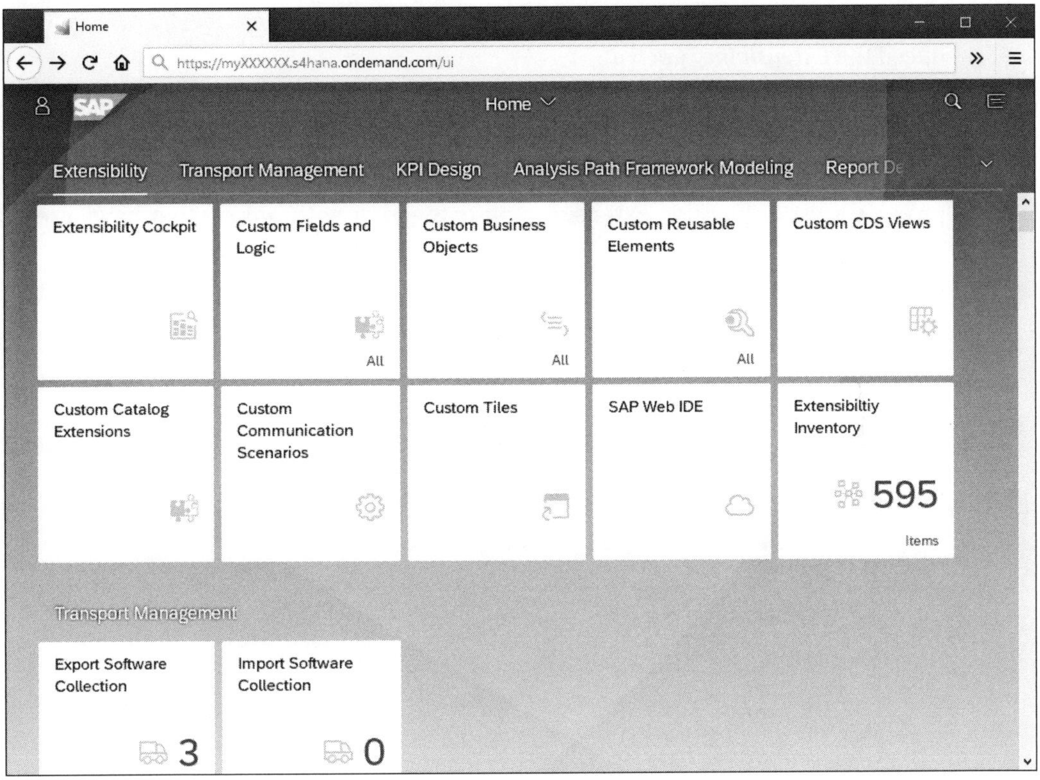

Figure 19.1 Extensibility Key User Tools of an SAP S/4HANA Cloud System

After assigning the relevant key user roles, you'll now have access to the key user tools for maintaining and configuring in-app extension objects. Also, you should have access to the business partner catalog and its respective applications.

In the following sections, we'll describe the various native SAP S/4HANA in-app extension options. In these sections, you'll learn how to find available extension points and how to extend an SAP standard object with custom-specific fields in our Business Partner Address Manager app. You'll add those fields to the UI and to the standard OData services. In addition, you'll create a custom business object to store arbitrary data and implement enhancement logic to illustrate SAP S/4HANA's in-app validation capabilities.

19.2 Extensibility Cockpit

Because key user tools operate directly on the object level but users searching for extensible objects might be searching on the business process level, SAP has introduced the *Extensibility Cockpit*.

With the Extensibility Cockpit, the user can navigate from a business level, like a solution scope or a business process, to the underlying technical objects (business context). Furthermore, the app also allows you to search directly on technical level to produce a list of possible extension points together with objects that have already been extended.

Besides the top-down navigation from the solution scope to a business context, a full-text search is available that also takes detailed descriptions into consideration and includes objects not attached to a scope item or a UI.

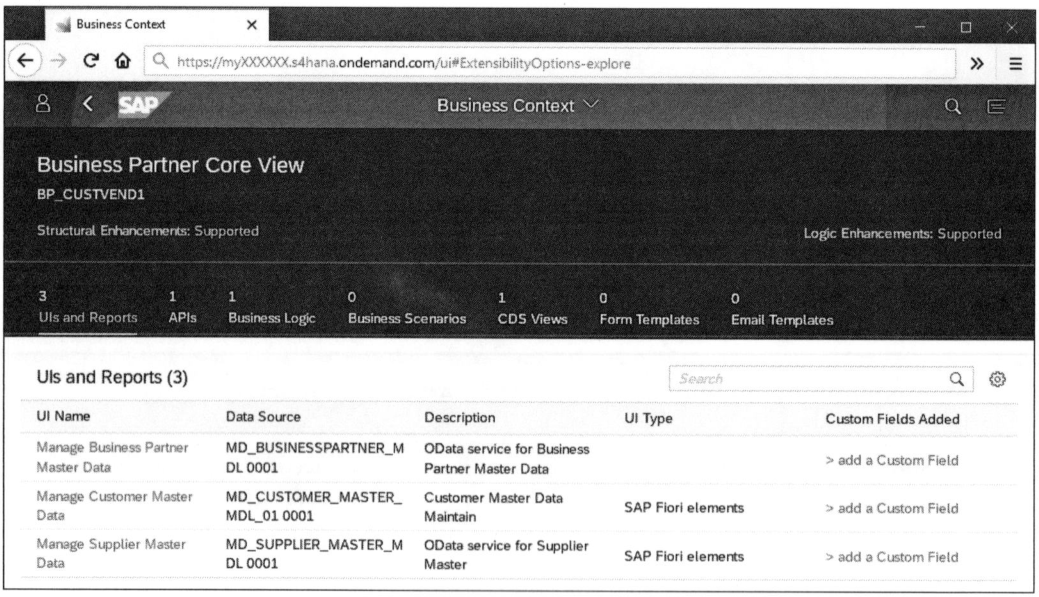

Figure 19.2 Extensibility Cockpit, Showing Available Extension Points of the Business Partner

Once you've found the correct business context, for example, the business partner, you'll see all extensible objects in this context, as shown in Figure 19.2. You can find details about extensible artifacts, such as user interfaces and reports, APIs, CDS views, or business logic, and also see already extended objects. From the detailed view, you can directly navigate into key user tools like Custom Fields or access further documentation by following links to the SAP API Hub.

19.3 Custom Fields

As described in Chapter 18, field extensibility refers to the ability to add customer-specific data to a standard business object like a sales order or the product master.

For our Business Partner Address Manager application, we'll add two custom fields to the `Business Partner Core View` business context, which we'll use to store information about the last address check for a business partner.

To create a new field, open the Custom Fields and Logic application from the catalog **Extensibility** and click the **+** icon to open the entry screen shown in Figure 19.3.

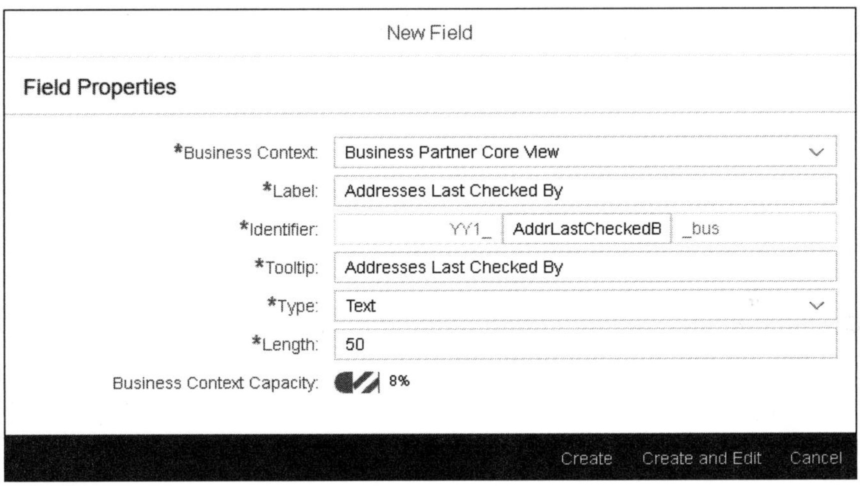

Figure 19.3 Entry Screen for Custom Fields

For **Business Context**, select **Business Partner Core View** and enter a label, for example, "Addresses Last Checked By." The identifier is automatically derived but can be adapted, for example, by entering "AddrLastCheckedBy." For our example, select **Text** from the **Type** dropdown list. Enter a **Length** of "50." Repeat these steps to create a second field with the label "Addresses Last Checked On," the identifier "AddrLast-CheckedOn," and the type **Date**.

As you can see, SAP S/HANA offers various types for custom fields. Table 19.3 provides an overview about available types and their meaning.

Type	Description
Amount with Currency	Numerical amount and currency selection.
Association to Business Object	An association allows you to link another SAP standard object or custom business objects (Section 19.5). The field provides value lookup help and forward navigation to the selected object.
Checkbox	Yes/no selection
Code List	Allows you to predefine a list of keys and values from which a user can choose. Code lists can be displayed as a dropdown list or using value lookup help (if many entries exist). After a field has been published, its published code values can no longer be deleted.
Date	Calendar year/month/day input.
Email Address	Email addresses.
Number	Numerical input with decimal places.
Quantity with unit	Numerical quantity and unit selection.
Text	Single line text with a specified length of up to 255 characters.
Time	Hour/minute input.
Web Address	Uniform resource identifier.

Table 19.3 List of Types Available for Custom Fields

The entry screen also shows the **Business Context Capacity** indicator. This indicator reflects how much available storage capacity of a business context this field will consume. The amount consumed by a field is determined by its type and length. Every business context has an independent, limited storage capacity available to ensure smooth operations. Thus, in some cases, you might switch to a custom business object for larger objects (Section 19.5).

After completing the fields on the entry screen, confirm by clicking **Create and Edit**. The detail screen will open where you can maintain further adjustments and enable the field for usage in various artifacts, like UIs, OData APIs, or email templates. Within the detail screen, select the **UIs and Reports** tab and enable the field for usage in **OData service for Business Partner** by clicking the **Enable Usage** button next to the field as shown in Figure 19.4. Now, the custom field is available in UIs that use this internal OData service.

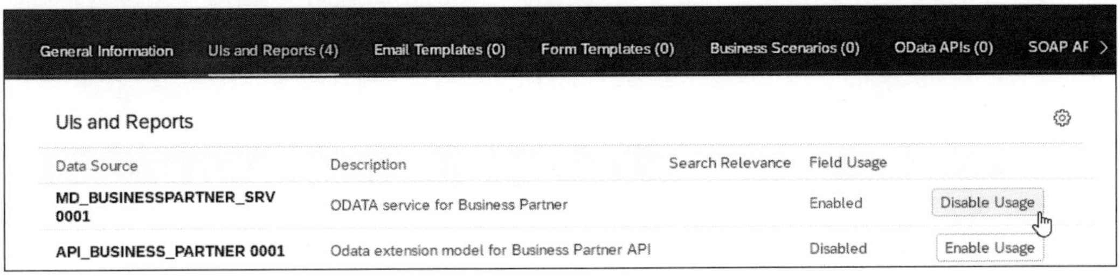

Figure 19.4 Detail Screen to Enable a Custom Field within a Specific UI or Report

To access and populate our custom fields from our side-by-side application later in Chapter 20, we'll now also add them to the standard OData service by enabling usage for the respective API data source (in our example, **API_BUSINESS_PARTNER**). After creating the two fields, navigate back to the overview screen, select both fields, and trigger the publishing process by clicking **publish**. The necessary database columns will be created, and all related artifacts will be extended with the new fields.

Navigating the SAP Fiori App

If the **Data Source** column is not shown, you can add it via the column options dialogue (click the gear icon). Also note that, in some cases, APIs might be listed on the tab **OData APIs**.

When now reading from the business partner API, the custom fields will be automatically appended to each entity in the response payload. They can be used for projection and filtering like any other property. Listing 19.1 shows a sample request and response when reading a single business partner via the OData service.

```
GET https://myXXXXXX-api.s4hana.ondemand.com/ /sap/opu/odata/sap/API_BUSINESS_
PARTNER/A_BusinessPartner('12910006')

{
  "d": {
```

```
    "BusinessPartner": "12910006",
    "PersonFullName": "Pascale Roy",
    ...
    "YY1_AddrLastCheckedBy_Bus": "Administrator",
    "YY1_AddrLastCheckedOn_Bus": "/Date(1473206400000)/"
  }
}
```

Listing 19.1 Sample Result Showing the Response of an OData Service with Two Custom Fields Included

In addition to standard APIs, custom fields can also be used within other CDS views. This capability allows you to use custom fields also within custom forms, custom reports, custom business logic, or custom email templates.

In this section, we learned how to add customer-specific fields to SAP standard objects and how they natively integrate into the ABAP virtual data model (VDM) within SAP S/4HANA. In the following sections, we'll add the fields to the standard SAP Fiori-based maintenance UIs as well as use these fields within validation logic.

19.4 UI and Layout Adaptations

As a key user, you can adapt the UI of standard applications to fit to the particular tasks and processes of your company—intuitively and without having to write code.

Adaptations made with the UI adaptation at runtime mechanism apply to the whole application and therefore also to all users of the app. In contrast, when an individual user personalizes an app, this customization applies only to this individual user.

As a prerequisite, your user requires access to the application to be adapted, as well as authorization for in-app extensibility (Section 19.1). Also, the fields must have been created and published as outlined in the previous section.

In our example, let's adapt the screen that displays and allows a user to modify the details of a business partner. To adapt the UI of an application, open the relevant app from the SAP Fiori launchpad, like the **Manage Business Partner Master Data** app under catalog **Business Partner Master** shown in Figure 19.5.

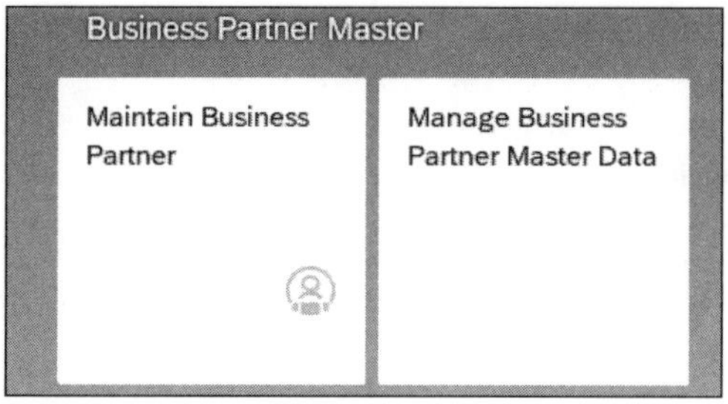

Figure 19.5 SAP S/4HANA SAP Fiori Launchpad with Both Maintenance Applications for Business Partners

Open one of the existing business partner entries to get to the detail screen that we want to adapt. On the detail screen, click the user profile icon on the top left of the screen to open the sidebar and click **Adapt UI** to switch to the UI adaption mode, as shown in Figure 19.6.

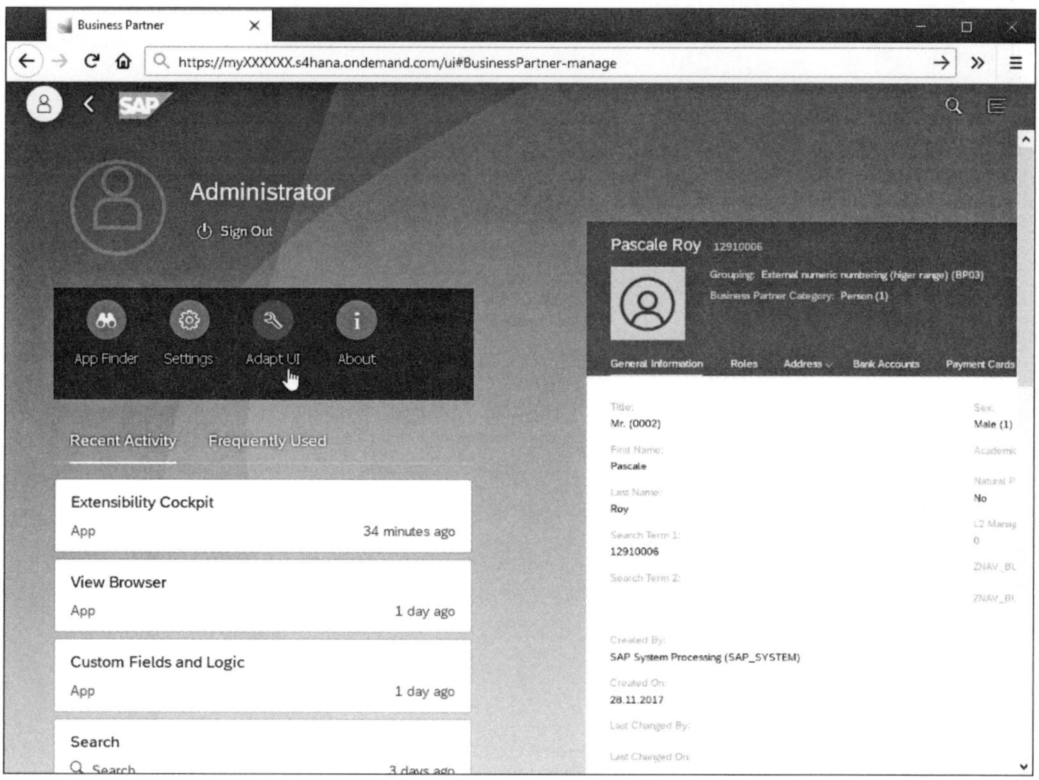

Figure 19.6 Sidebar Showing the Button to Activate the UI Adaption Mode

As shown in Figure 19.7, in UI adaption mode, the header of the app will change and show a new control that allows you to switch between the UI adaption and navigation mode. The first mode allows you to alter and rearrange elements on the screen, while the navigation mode allows you to navigate and switch from edit to view mode.

Sections that can be adapted light up as soon as you move your mouse over them. Right-click the field **Natural Person** and select **Add Field** from the dropdown menu to add the two custom fields below this field.

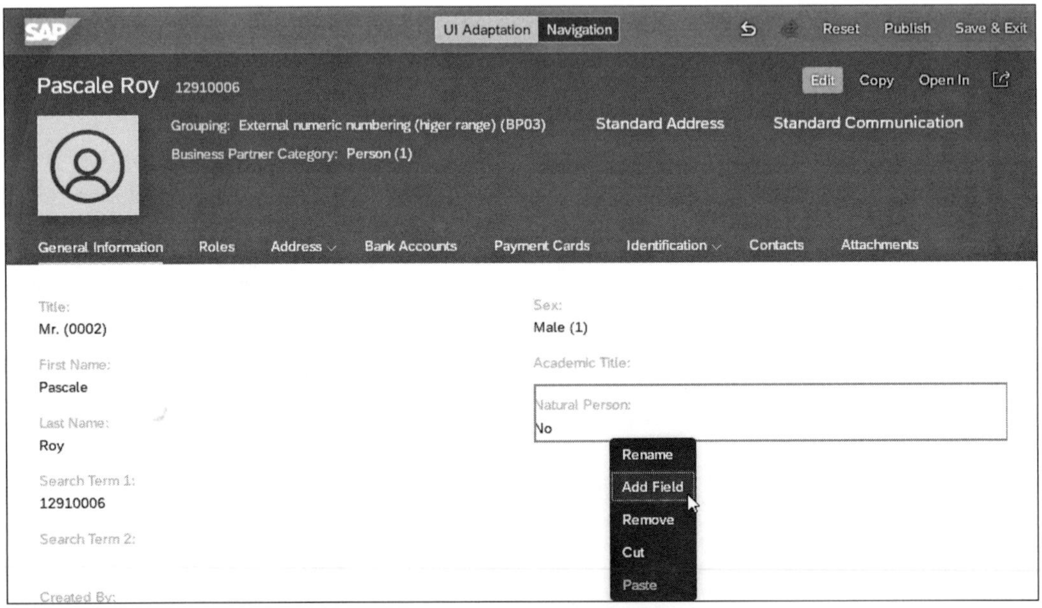

Figure 19.7 Business Partner Detail Screen in UI Adaption Mode

The selection screen lists all available fields under the context of the object `Business Partner`. Select both fields (**Addresses Last Checked By** and **Addresses Last Checked On**) created in Section 19.3 and confirm by clicking **OK**.

You can now switch to the entry screen by clicking the **Edit** button. The UI element for the custom field will also automatically show a corresponding value help, if the custom fields are of the type code list, date, or association. The final screen should now look similar to Figure 19.8.

Besides adding fields, you can also remove or rename standard fields, as well as create new sections or move sections within a screen.

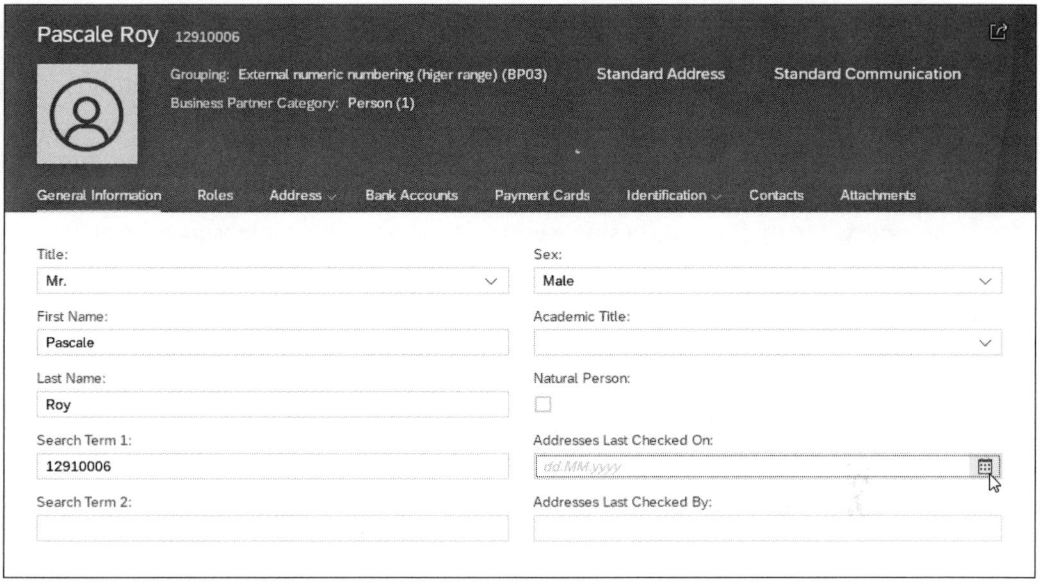

Figure 19.8 Two Custom Fields Added to the Business Partner Maintenance App, Shown in Edit Mode

A Note on Adaptations for Different UI Technologies

The UI adaption mode shown here only applies to applications using the *SAP Fiori* technology. Applications using *WebGUI for HTML* or *SAP WebDypro* technologies do not offer the same UI adaptation experience. Some still will show custom fields; however, these custom fields are typically bound to specific areas of the screen and cannot be moved around.

19.5 Custom Business Objects

As outlined in Chapter 18, custom business objects allow you to store arbitrary data in customer-specific tables.

A custom business object first of all consists of a root node with a set of fields that can be freely defined using the key user tools. Fields have a label, a technical identifier, and a type as listed in Table 19.3. Fields can also be marked as key fields. Furthermore, additional subnodes can be created, which themselves again contain a freely definable set of fields. Subnodes always represent a 1:*n* relationship towards the root node, for example, representing master/detail or header/line item structures. The automatically generated UI reflects this structure, which first allows users to maintain entries on root level. To this end, the UI shows a tabular list of the root entries of a custom business object on the entry screen. Filter, search, sorting, and grouping capabilities are automatically derived from the set of fields and provided in the UI. Second, when maintaining a single entry, the UI allows maintaining entries for each subnode.

For our example application, we'll use a custom business object to store the social media accounts of our business partners. Thus, we'll create a simple custom business object with one additional subnode. In the root node, we'll maintain a direct 1:1 association to a business partner, while the actual entries (the social media accounts) are stored in a 1:*n* relationship within a subnode. By using this approach with two separate nodes, the resulting UI will be more comfortable to use. In addition, this structure allows an association between the SAP standard object of a business partner and our custom business object by using a custom field. After defining the structure of the custom business object, we'll generate a maintenance UI for our business users.

To start, navigate to application **Custom Business Objects** in catalog **Extensibility** and then click **New**.

As shown in Figure 19.9, enter "Business Partner Social Media Account" (singular) into the **Name** field. The technical identifier is automatically derived out of the name but can be adapted. For example, enter "BpSocialMediaAccount" in the **Identifier** field to provide a more meaningful abbreviation. The plural name is suggested and can be adjusted if required. Confirm by clicking **Create**. You'll be redirected to the detail edit screen for our new custom business object.

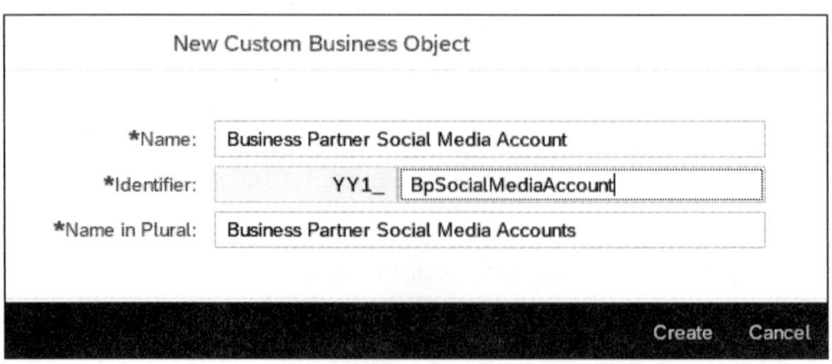

Figure 19.9 Entry Screen to Create a New Custom Business Object

The first tab allows you to maintain the basic data of the custom business object. Select the **Can be Associated** checkbox to allow associations from custom fields (Section 19.3), select the **UI Generation** checkbox to have the system generate a maintenance UI, and select the **Service Generation** checkbox, which will later allow you to access the data via an OData service.

To maintain a 1:*n* relationship between business partners and social media accounts, we'll create a subnode named `Social Media Account` (singular) by clicking **New** on the **Nodes** tab. Rename the root node to "Business Partner" to arrive at the state shown in Figure 19.10.

Figure 19.10 Root Node and Subnode of Our Custom Business Object

Switch to the **Fields** tab to access the field definition screen. Add the field shown in Table 19.4 to the root node (Business Partner).

Label	Identifier	Type	Key
Business partner	BusinessPartner	Text (length 10)	yes

Table 19.4 Fields Added to the Root Node

19

This field will be used as key field and hence provides a 1:1 relationship of entries within our custom business object and the standard object of a Business Partner. Also keep the standard field *Description*, which is generated automatically. Navigate to the subnode (Social Media Account) and add the fields listed in Table 19.5.

Label	Identifier	Type	Key
Service	Service	Text (Length 10)	no
Account	Account	Text (Length 60)	no

Table 19.5 Fields Added to the Subnode

Validation Logic and Actions in Custom Business Objects

Custom business objects also allow you to implement validation logic and actions in ABAP. Validation logic is automatically executed before or after an entry is saved and can be leveraged to implement validation, calculation, or even calls to external services. The result of such a check can be returned to the end user as a warning or error message. Actions behave similarly but need to be manually triggered via the UI. For details, refer to Section 19.8, which discusses custom business logic in the context of a standard object.

Start the generation of artifacts, like database tables and UI screens, by clicking the **Publish** button. After the generation process has finished, the log within the custom business object will show the following confirmation:

```
Success: Business object YY1_BPSOCIALMEDIAACCOUNT published
```

To access the automatically generated maintenance UI for our custom business object, we need to assign it to a business catalog and thereby assign corresponding permissions to users having access to this business catalog. To create the assignment, switch back to the **General Information** tab of our custom business object (Business Partner Social Media Accounts). Click the **Maintain Catalogs** link on the main screen of the custom business object to get to the Custom Catalog Extensions app.

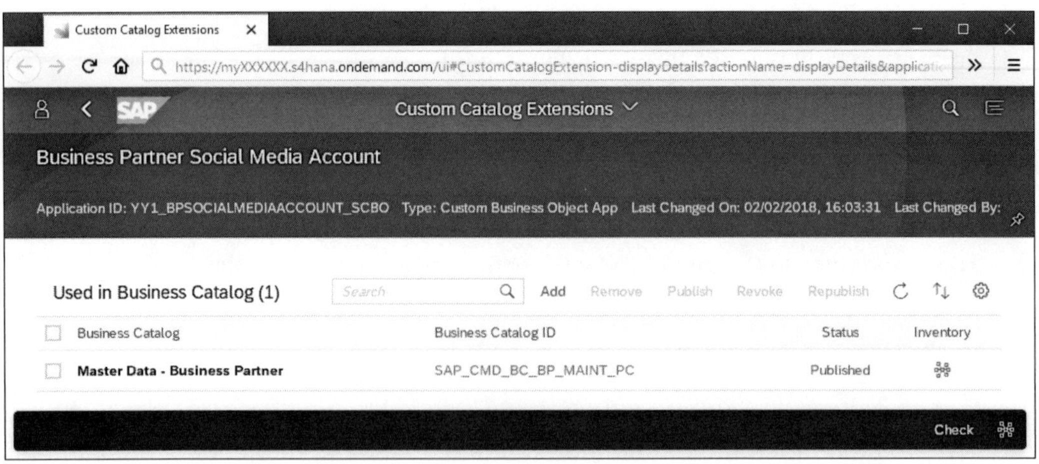

Figure 19.11 Catalog Assignments for a Custom Business Object

In this app, add the business catalog **Master Data - Business Partner** and publish the catalog extension by selecting the entry and clicking the **Publish** button. The result should look like what's shown in Figure 19.11. Because the maintenance app was added to a catalog already assigned to our user, we can now find the Business Partner Social Media Accounts app in the SAP Fiori launchpad under **Business Partner Master,** as shown in Figure 19.12.

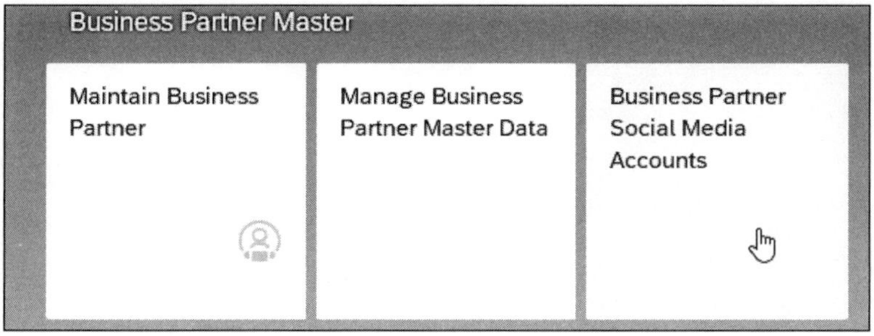

Figure 19.12 Maintenance App Added to the SAP Fiori Launchpad

Authorizations for Custom Business Objects

By assigning the UI application to a business catalog, all users that have access to this catalog will automatically be authorized to read, create, change, and delete entries in the custom business object.

Open the Business Partner Social Media Accounts app to create a first entry for one of our business partners with a UI, as shown in Figure 19.13. Note that you can also use the UI adaption mode to modify the generated maintenance application to your specific needs.

19

Custom UI Applications

The standard, automatically generated maintenance UI application often provides a sufficient and adequate user experience and functionality for basic data entry. For more sophisticated requirements, you can also replace the generated UI application with a custom developed UI application. Using the SAP WebIDE as the development environment, you can import the metadata of your custom business object and implement a freestyle UI application in a model-driven development approach. Afterwards, the application can be deployed back to the SAP S/4HANA system. For more information, please see the corresponding tutorial at *http://tiny.cc/s4-custom-ui.*

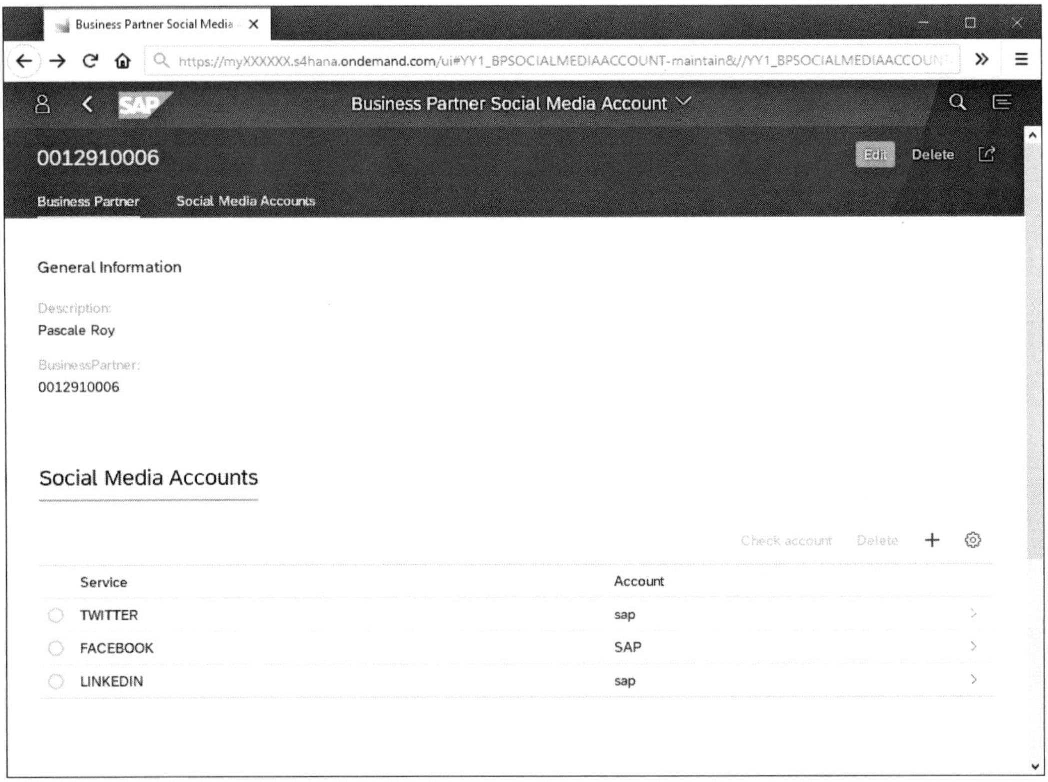

Figure 19.13 Autogenerated Maintenance UI of Our Custom Business Object

Custom Code Lists

Similar to custom business objects, you can also create reusable custom code lists. A code list contains a list of values and descriptions and is used, for example, to provide dropdown lists on UIs. In the Custom Business Object app, you can define a code list data type for your solution and use this data type when you create your custom business object. Code lists can be created and assigned directly to a field of a custom business object. Then, you could replace the type field with a custom code list to provide a predefined list of social media platforms rather than allowing the user to enter text freely.

In this section, we learned how to store arbitrary data within an SAP S/4HANA system. We generated a maintenance UI and assigned it to a business catalog so that our end users can maintain data. In the next section, we'll look at using custom CDS views to read data via custom queries.

19.6 Custom CDS Views

CDS views give access to SAP standard objects, as well as to custom fields or custom business objects. These views often serve as basis for further artifacts like custom reports, key performance indicators (KPIs) or as additional data source for external applications.

In this chapter, we'll create a new custom CDS view based on the standard view for business partners and the custom social media account business object we created in Section 19.5. The resulting view will return a list of all business partners including their assigned social media accounts. As a prerequisite, the steps outlined in the previous section must have been performed.

Start creating the custom CDS view by opening the **Custom CDS Views** application in catalog **Extensibility**. Click the **Create** button to get to the first entry screen. Enter a technical name (for example, "YY1_BP_SocialMedia") and define a descriptive label. To access a CDS view externally as an OData service, select the checkbox **OData API**. Add the standard view `I_BusinessPartner` as primary data source by clicking the **Add** button. Repeat the same steps to add the view `YY1_BPSOCIALMEDIAACCOUNT` as the associated data source, as shown in Figure 19.14. In relational database terminology, in these steps, we're defining a left outer join between the entries of the standard business partner object and the entries of our custom business object.

Click the edit association properties (paperclip) icon on the associated data source and maintain the association condition. Select the **BusinessPartner** field on the left-hand side, as well as the **BusinessPartner** field on the right-hand side, as shown in Figure 19.15. From the **Cardinality** dropdown list, select **Exactly one hit**. This option will try to join each entry of the standard view `I_BusinessPartner` with one entry in our custom business object. The join condition in this process is the identifier of a business partner. Finish the association editing by clicking **OK**.

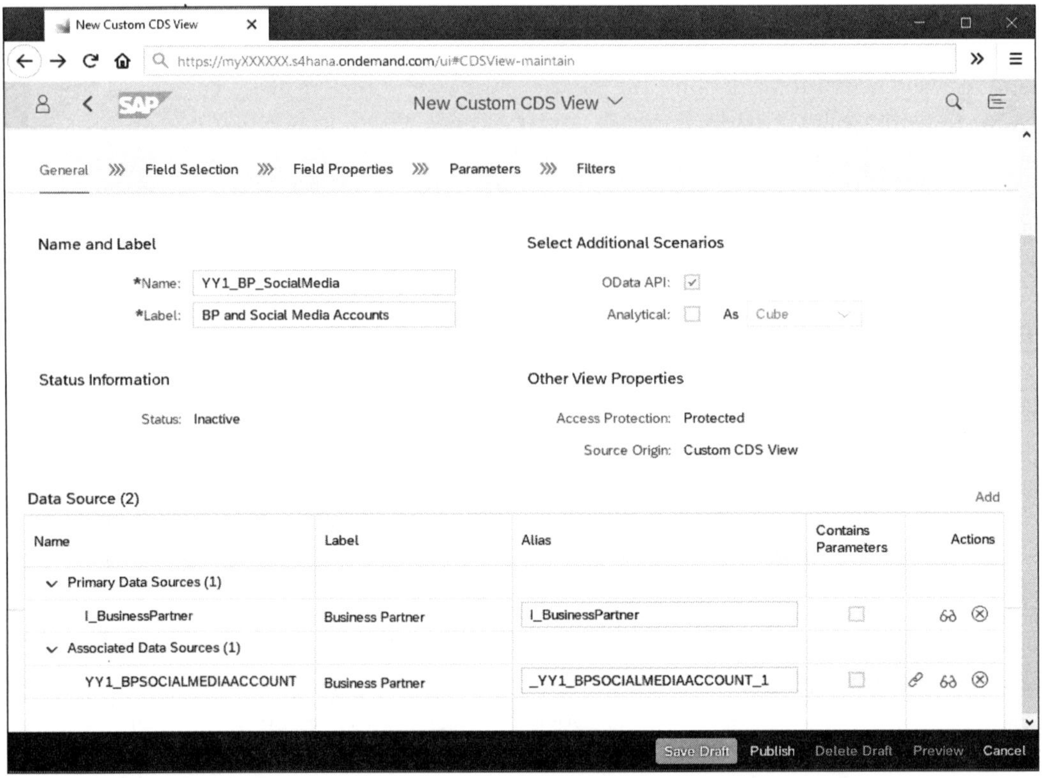

Figure 19.14 Custom CDS View Based on a Standard View and a Custom Business Object

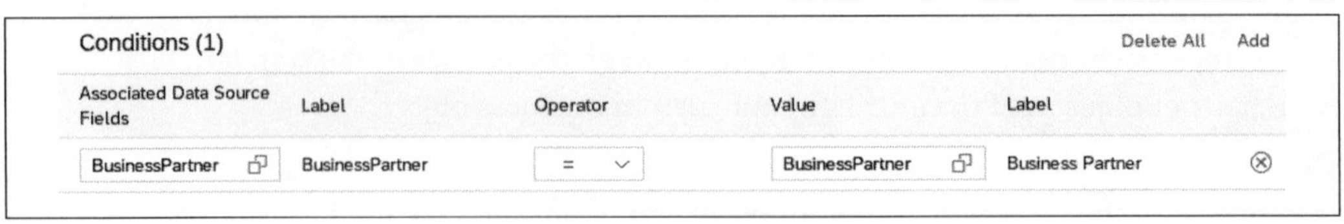

Figure 19.15 Association Condition between the Business Partner and Our Custom Business Object

Next, we'll define the fields of the data sources that will be part of our custom CDS view. Go to next tab, **Field Selection**, and select the **BusinessPartner**, **BusinessPartner-Category**, **FirstName**, and **LastName** fields from the node **I_BusinessPartner**. Out of the nested child node for social media accounts, select the **Account** and **Service** fields. Save the draft and click the **Preview** button to preview the results. If you've already defined social media accounts for one or more valid business partners, for example, using the generated maintenance UI, you should see a result similar to Figure 19.16. Note that the preview only shows a limited amount of data, so you might want to add a filter condition based on the test data you've used. Also, when maintaining test data, ensure you use the same identifier as for the business partner, including leading zeros.

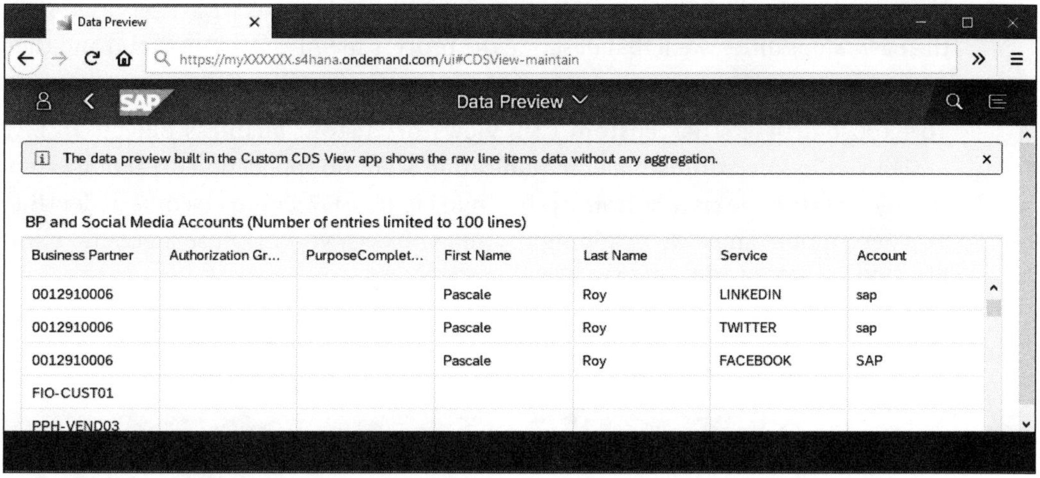

Figure 19.16 Data Preview of a Custom CDS View, Showing Standard Fields and Custom Fields

Besides selecting data from one or more views, custom CDS views also allow you to perform field calculations, aggregate data, or filter result sets based on freely definable conditions or parameters.

At this point, we've created a custom CDS view that can now be used in custom reports, within custom business logic, or from external systems via an OData service.

19.7 Exposing CDS Views and Custom Business Objects as OData Services

As outlined in the previous sections, custom CDS views and custom business objects can be exposed as OData services for consumption from external systems. In contrast to the standard APIs used in previous chapters and custom business objects, OData services based on custom CDS views only allow read/query operations. While limited, the custom CDS views can still be helpful for example when combining multiple data sources or when aggregations or fields are calculated. In this case, the processing occurs in the backend system, and only the result is transferred to the client, which often helps to reduce bandwidth and response times. OData services exposing custom business objects also support create, update, and delete operations and therefore allow full access to the data.

In this section, we'll expose our previously created artifacts as OData services. Since the basic steps differ, we'll first describe the process in SAP S/4HANA Cloud and then cover SAP S/4HANA on-premise.

To expose artifacts like custom CDS views or custom business objects in SAP S/4HANA Cloud, go to **Custom Communication Scenario** application in catalog **Extensibility** and click the **New** button, as shown in Figure 19.17. Enter a technical identifier and description. Since we're adding multiple objects, you may use a generic name like "YY1_CUSTOMOBJECTS_ADDRESSMANAG."

In the **Inbound Services** tab, click the **+** icon and add the custom business object we created in Section 19.5 as well as the custom CDS view we created in Section 19.6.

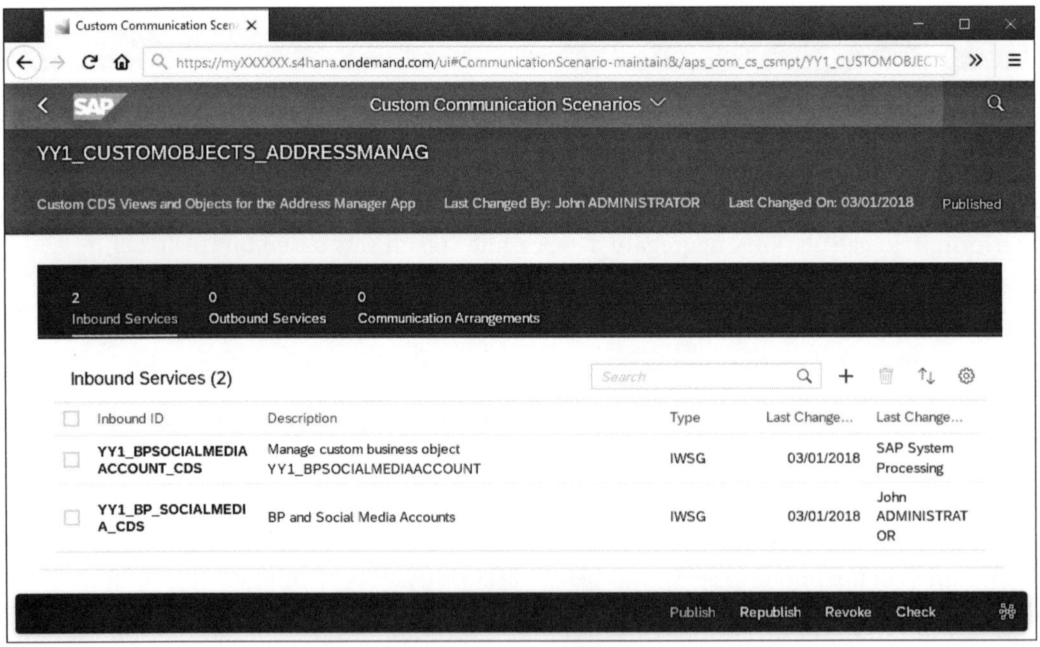

Figure 19.17 Custom Communication Scenario in SAP S/4HANA Cloud

With the custom communication scenario in place, you can now create a communication arrangement based on this scenario, as described in Chapter 6, Section 6.4 for SAP S/4HANA Cloud in general.

Activating OData APIs in SAP S/4HANA On-Premise Systems

To activate OData APIs in SAP S/4HANA on-premise, use the Transaction /IWFND/MAINT_SERVICE (Activate and Maintain Services). Click on **Add Service**, choose the corresponding system alias, and then click **Get Services**. SAP S/4HANA will fetch all installed APIs that have not been exposed. Select your custom CDS view and custom business object and then click on **Add Selected Services**. In the popup window, check the package assignment and confirm. After processing, you'll see a message stating that the metadata was loaded successfully. The OData API is now activated.

At this point, we've completed the configuration independently from the authentication method. Proceed with the configuration steps specific to the desired authentication method (technical or business user) as described in Chapter 6, Section 6.5.

19.8 Custom Business Logic

Business Add-Ins (BAdIs) is the standard code exit technology within SAP S/4HANA. BAdIs can be used to add custom business logic, like extended data validation or calculating results during predefined exit points within a business process.

In this section, we'll implement a standard BAdI available for validation in the context of the business partner. This BAdI will automatically be executed by the system whenever a business partner is changed. In this simple example, we'll check whether the field search term was maintained for business partners of type "persons" so that we'll prevent users from storing business partners without maintaining that field. Search terms greatly help to find a business partner in a more natural, faster way. For example, for people, a nickname or short name can be maintained. With this additional validation logic, we'll ask users to also provide a search term when creating a person.

To implement an enhancement object, go to the **Custom Fields and Logic** application and select the **Custom Logic** tab. Click the **+** icon to create a new enhancement implementation. For business context, select **Business Partner Core View**, and select **Validate BP BADI** in the **Definition Description** field. The listed definitions represent the different available exit points can be implemented within a business process. Enter a meaningful label to represent the purpose of your implementation. For our example, enter "BP_Custom_Validation_Logic" and click **Create**. The web-based ABAP editor will open, as shown in Figure 19.18. The web-based editor features syntax highlighting; static code checks; code completion, accessible via `Ctrl`+`Space`; and a pretty printer, accessible via `Shift`+`F1`, among other things.

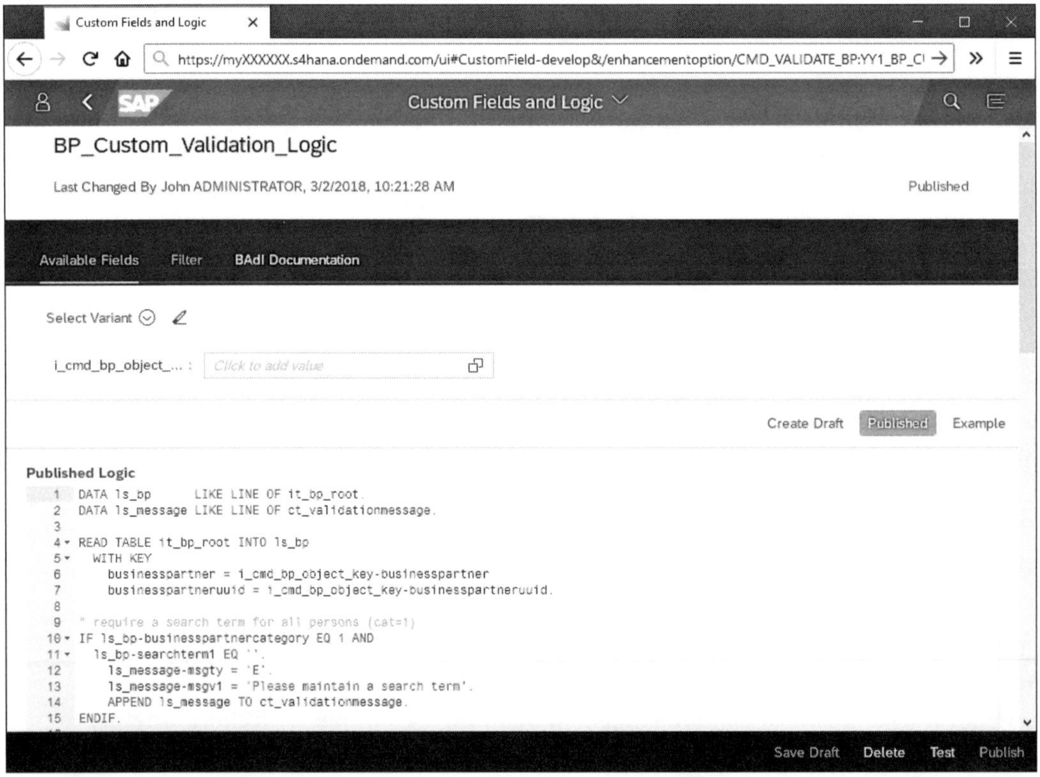

Figure 19.18 Web-Based ABAP Editor in Custom Fields and Logic

To implement our additional check, click **Create Draft** and add the lines shown in Listing 19.2 into the ABAP editor. We'll first load the user input into a local variable (`ls_bp`) for convenience. If the business partner belongs to the category "organization" (`category=1`) and the field "search term" is maintained with an empty value, we'll throw an error (`msgty=E`) that will prevent the user from saving the entry.

```
DATA ls_bp      LIKE LINE OF it_bp_root.
DATA ls_message LIKE LINE OF ct_validationmessage.
```

```
READ TABLE it_bp_root INTO ls_bp
  WITH KEY
    businesspartner = i_cmd_bp_object_key-businesspartner
    businesspartneruuid =
      i_cmd_bp_object_key-businesspartneruuid.
" require a search term for all persons (cat=1)
IF ls_bp-businesspartnercategory EQ 1 AND
      ls_bp-searchterm1 eq '' .
  ls_message-msgty = 'E'.
  ls_message-msgv1 = |Please maintain a search term|.
  APPEND ls_message TO ct_validationmessage.
ENDIF.
```

Listing 19.2 Custom Enhancement to Validate Entered Data in ABAP

To test the implemented enhancement point, you can use the built-in test functionality. First, maintain test input data in the upper section of the screen. Then, click the **Test** button to execute the enhancement implementation. The result (output parameters) is shown in the lower part of the screen.

ABAP for Key Users

To learn more about ABAP for Key Users, press F1 and click **What's this app**. The reference documentation lists allowed statements. In general, ABAP for Key Users is a subset of standard ABAP. To get started with the ABAP language in general, we recommend *Complete ABAP* by Kiran Bandari (SAP PRESS, 2017, *www.sap-press.com/3921*).

19

Click the **Publish** button to activate the enhancement implementation system-wide. To test the result within the standard maintenance application, navigate to the Manage Business Partner Master Data app and trigger a change of a business partner. If a change to the business partner violates the condition, the system will display an error message, as shown in Figure 19.19, and the user cannot save the entry without having a search term defined.

Reusable functions

Code blocks that need to be referenced from various places can also be moved into a separate library. Create a library in the Custom Reusable Elements application and add your methods as reusable elements.

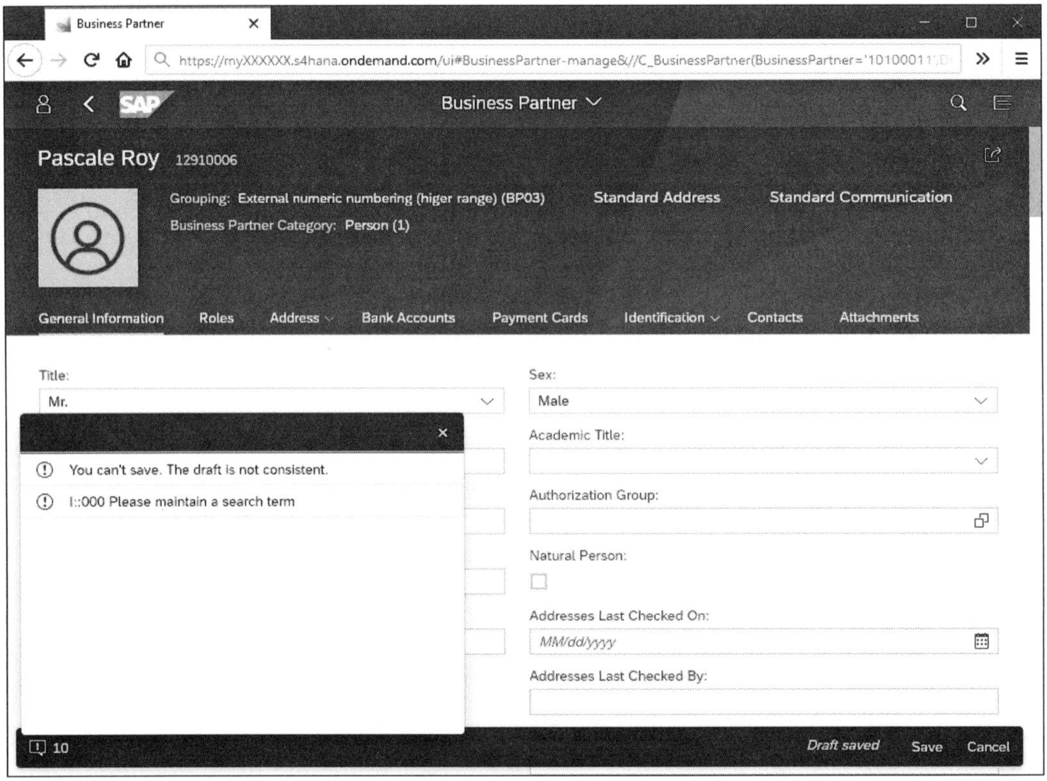

Figure 19.19 Error Message Passed to the User When Violating a Custom Validation Logic

At this point, we've now learned how to implement a predefined enhancement point with custom business logic using ABAP. For the sake of simplicity, our example was kept as short as possible. In general, custom business logic allows sophisticated implementations, like reading from the SAP S/4HANA VDM by using CDS views. Also, depending on the BAdI's parameter definition, we can change or enrich business data to control subsequent processing. We can even perform calls to external services, a typical requirement in integration scenarios, which we'll explain in the next section.

19.9 Custom Business Logic for Calling Web Services

In the previous section, we implemented a simple validation logic executed entirely within the SAP S/4HANA system. The enhancement points of custom business logic also allow calls to external web services. For example, you can trigger processes outside SAP S/4HANA or swap out calculation or validation logic to a side-by-side service running on the SAP Cloud Platform.

In this section, we'll use an external call to validate whether a social media account maintained in our custom business object exists or not. A user will be able to trigger the social media account check by clicking a button on the user interface. As a prerequisite, you'll need to have completed the steps outlined in Section 19.5.

For simplicity and brevity, we'll use standard HTTP response codes to check whether a Twitter account is valid. We'll issue an HTTP HEAD request to the public page of the target Twitter account. If the account exists, Twitter will respond with HTTP status code 200 (OK). Otherwise, HTTP status code 404 (not found) will be returned, as shown in the two request-response pairs in Listing 19.3.

```
> HEAD /sap HTTP/1.0        > HEAD /not-existent HTTP/1.0
> Host: twitter.com         > Host: twitter.com

< HTTP/1.0 200 OK           < HTTP/1.0 404 Not found
```

Listing 19.3 Explanatory HTTP Call to Check Twitter Accounts for Existence

We'll proceed in two steps: In the first subsection, we'll create the necessary configuration within the SAP S/4HANA system. In the second subsection, we'll implement the call to the external service.

19.9.1 Communication System and Arrangement

To separate configuration from implementation, we'll first create a communication system that represents the target system, Twitter, and a communication user that represents the user within the target system. In addition, we'll need a custom communication scenario representing the service endpoint within the target system and, as usual, a communication arrangement that combines all these entities.

Navigate to the Communication Systems app and create a new system named "TWITTER." Enter "twitter.com" without any path suffix as the **Hostname**. In the **User for Outbound Communication** section, click the **+** icon to add a new user. Since we're creating an unauthenticated call, chose **None** as the **Authentication Mode**. The result should look similar to Figure 19.20.

Go to the Custom Communication Scenarios application and create a new entry named "YY1_TWITTER." In the **Outbound Services** section, create a new entry named "YY1_CHECKACCOUNT_REST" with the URL path "/", as shown in Figure 19.21.

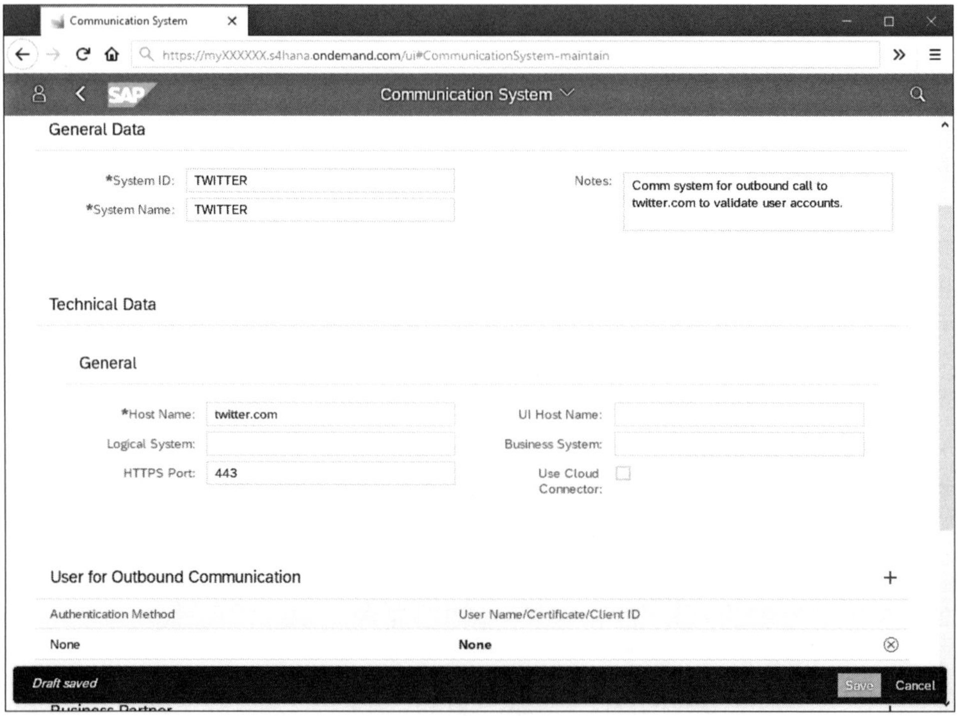

Figure 19.20 Communication System

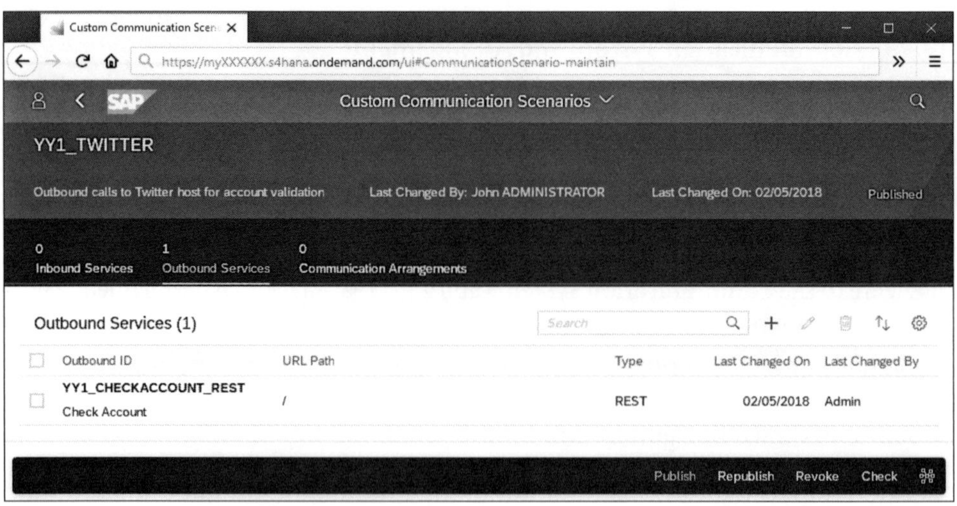

Figure 19.21 Custom Communication Scenario

Finally, go to the **Communication Arrangements** application and create a new entry by selecting the previously created custom communication scenario (**YY1_TWITTER**). For communication system, select your communication system (**TWITTER**) and select the **None** from the **Authentication Method** dropdown list under in the **Outbound Communication** section. You can trigger a connection check by clicking the **Check Connection** button, which should display a success message, as shown in Figure 19.22.

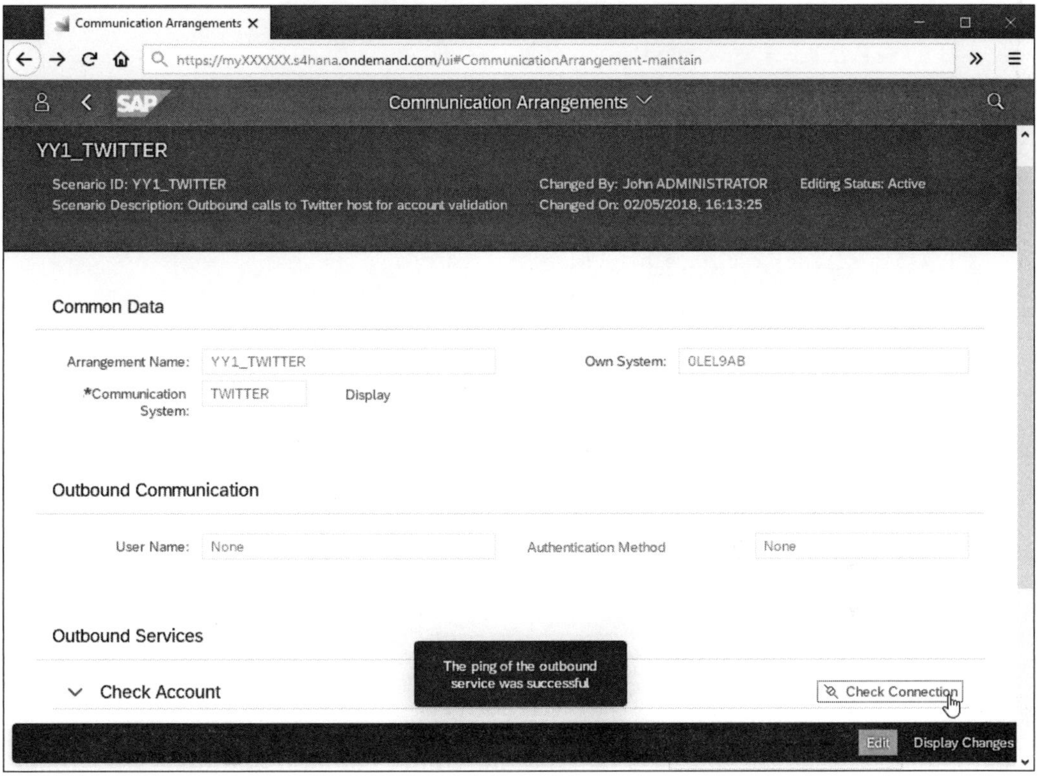

Figure 19.22 Communication Arrangement Triggering a Connection Check

At this point, we've configured all artifacts to issue an outbound HTTP call, which we'll implement in the next subsection, using the configuration we just created.

19.9.2 External Call Implementation

Open the Custom Business Objects application and navigate to the `YY1_BPSOCIALMEDIAACCOUNT` object we created in Section 19.5. Click the **Edit draft** button to switch to editing mode and navigate to the **Logic** section of the subnode `SocialMediaAccount`. Click the **new** button and create a new method named "Check Account."

After creating a new method, the custom business object needs to be published by clicking the **Publish** button before we can add our source code. Then, navigate into the newly created method (`Check Account`) by clicking its title. Click the **Create draft** link to start your implementation and then enter the ABAP code shown in Listing 19.4.

```
IF socialmediaaccount-service NE 'TWITTER'.
    message = VALUE #(
      severity = co_severity-warning
      text     = 'Only Twitter accounts can be validated.'
    ).
    RETURN.
ENDIF.

DATA(lo_client) = cl_ble_http_client=>create(
    communication_scenario = 'YY1_TWITTER'
    outbound_service       = 'YY1_CHECKACCOUNT_REST'
).

DATA(request) = cl_ble_http_request=>create(
)->set_method( 'HEAD'
)->set_resource_extension( socialmediaaccount-account ).

TRY.
    DATA(response) = lo_client->send( request ).
    message = VALUE #(
      severity = co_severity-success
      text     = 'Account @' && socialmediaaccount-account
                 && ' is valid.'
    ).
    CATCH cx_ble_http_exception INTO DATA(lx).
        message = VALUE #(
          severity = co_severity-error
          text     = 'Error account not found! Status code: '
                     && lx->status_code
        ).
ENDTRY.
```

Listing 19.4 ABAP Implementation of an Outbound HTTP Call

The implementation code in Listing 19.4 first checks the type of the service. Since our implementation only covers Twitter, all others will lead to a warning. Next, we'll instantiate an HTTP client based on the communication scenario and outbound service.

We'll build up the request by calling the `create` method of the HTTP client. Because we're only interested in the status code and not the actual body that would be sent in response, we'll use an HTTP `HEAD` request since a `GET` request is not relevant to this scenario. The `set_resource_extension` method will compile the path for the HTTP call.

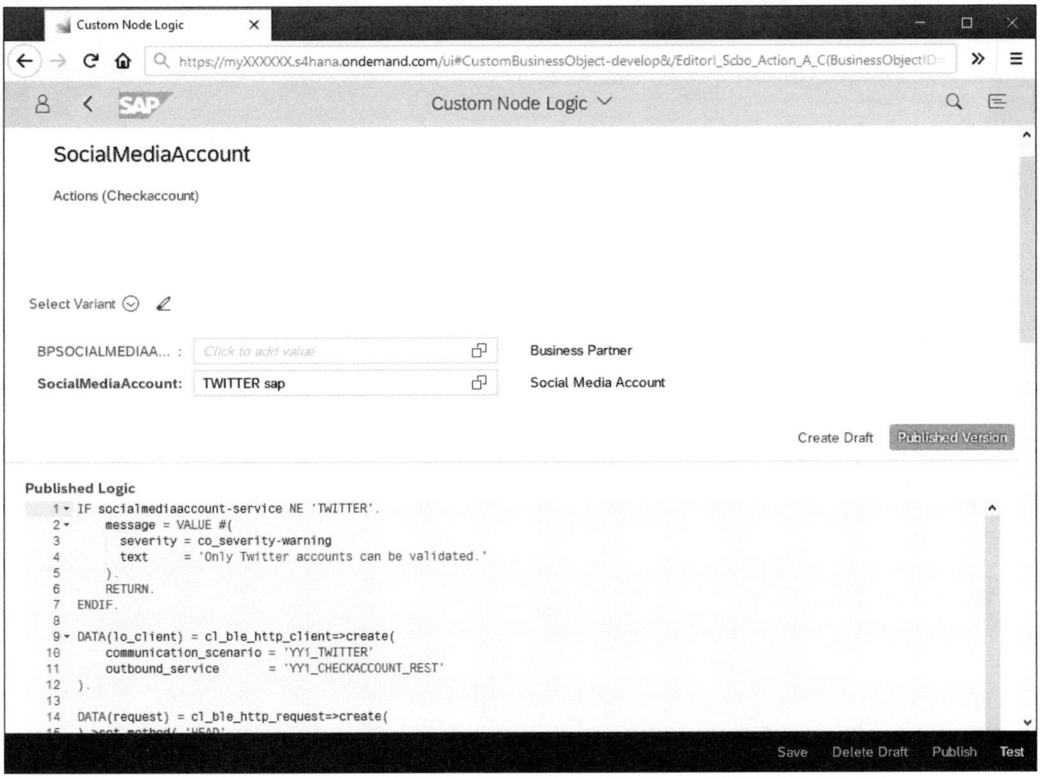

Figure 19.23 Implemented Method "Check Account" within Subnode "Social Media Account"

The full URL is then derived during runtime out of the communication system (host name), the communication scenario (path prefix), and the string passed to `set_resource_extension`. By calling the `send` method, we'll issue the actual HTTP request. If the server returns an HTTP status code starting with "2xx," the method call will be successful and return a valid response, which will result in a success message being sent to the user. Otherwise, the send method of the ABAP HTTP client will throw a cx_ble_http_exception exception, which we'll handle accordingly to raise an error to the frontend.

You can now test the implementation directly within the web-based editor, as shown in Figure 19.23, or you can navigate to the autogenerated maintenance application Business Partner Social Media Account. To call our validation method, open an entry; select a social media account with a service equal to "TWITTER"; and click the new button, **Check account**. A message on the screen will show the results, as shown in Figure 19.24.

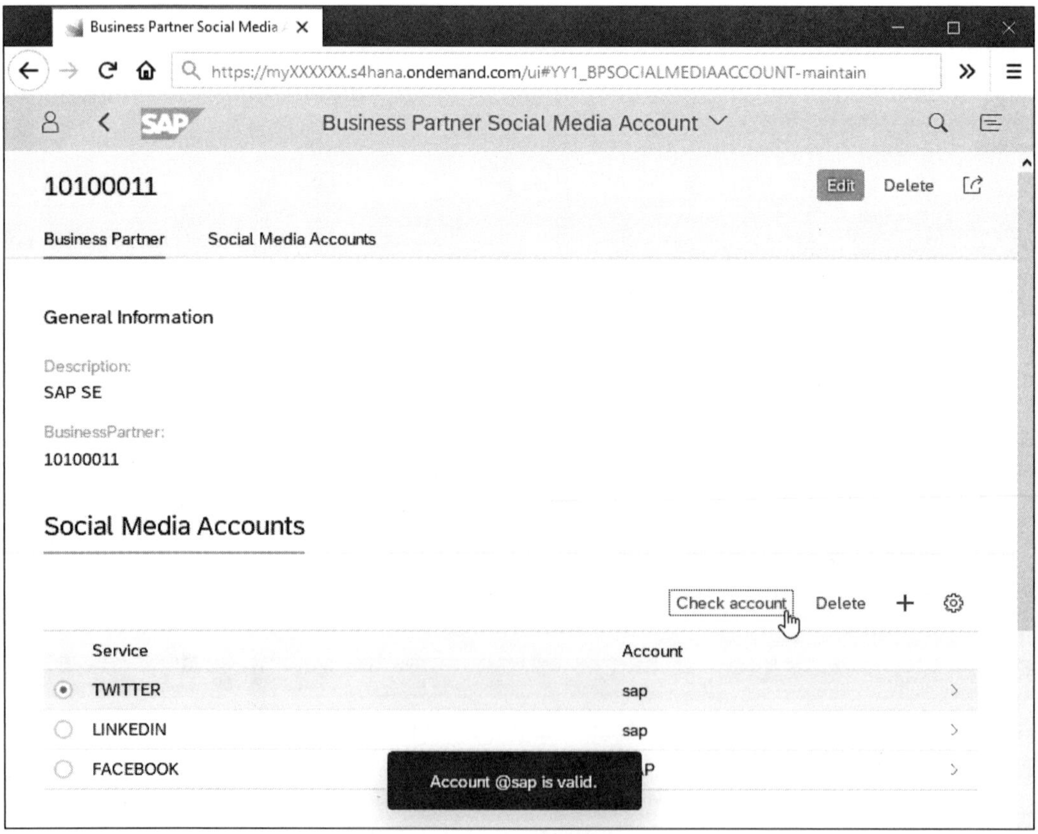

Figure 19.24 New Check Account Function and Results

In this section, we learned how to call an outbound HTTP service in the context of a custom business object. In general, we can also call external services in enhancement points of SAP standard objects, which allows for a tight integration of external services within standard processes.

Limitations of External Service Calls

Note that calls to external services implicitly create a dependency to the target system. Unavailability or overload situations on the target side will have a direct influence, as described in Chapter 4, Section 4.6. To avoid this dependency in productive cases, we highly recommend you avoid using outbound calls but instead reverse the direction of communication or decouple the communication by using an event-based approach (see Chapter 16). Otherwise, using a middleware system with high availability, introducing timeouts, and refining error handling can help to improve overall reliability.

19.10 Summary

We now have a good conceptual and practical overview of the in-app extensibility options in SAP S/4HANA. In the next chapter, we'll explore how we can leverage in-app extensions in our side-by-side Business Partner Address Manager application on SAP Cloud Platform to implement more advanced integration scenarios.

Chapter 20

Consuming In-App Extensions in a Side-by-Side Extension

The previous two chapters explained in-app extensibility from the point of view of an SAP S/4HANA system. In this chapter, we'll explain how to consume certain in-app extensions in a side-by-side extension such as our Business Partner Address Manager application. The SAP S/4HANA Cloud SDK provides corresponding features, which we'll discuss in detail.

This chapter joins two threads of the book: the side-by-side extension we've been building as a Java application on SAP Cloud Platform with the help of the SAP S/4HANA Cloud SDK during Parts II and IV, and the in-app extensions we created in SAP S/4HANA in Chapters 18 and 19. In this chapter, we'll explain how to consume certain in-app extensions in a side-by-side extension with the help of the SAP S/4HANA Cloud SDK. In this way, we'll extend our Business Partner Address Manager application with additional capabilities that in turn leverage in-app extensions.

Particularly relevant for consumption in an application on SAP Cloud Platform are in-app extensions that can be exposed in the form of OData services as part of a customer's SAP S/4HANA system. As we've described, first in Chapter 4, the SAP S/4HANA Cloud SDK provides a virtual data model (VDM) for easy consumption of OData services that are part of the standard public API of SAP S/4HANA. This chapter will discuss the capabilities of the VDM beyond this standard public API.

In particular, on one hand, in-app extensions that impact OData services are custom fields that become part of the properties of an OData entity. The first Section 20.1 explains the built-in capabilities of the virtual data model to handle such custom fields across their entire lifecycle. On the other hand, in-app extensions via custom business objects or custom core data services (CDS) views create entirely new custom OData services that are by definition not part of the standard API. Section 20.2 discusses the code generator that the SAP S/4HANA Cloud SDK provides to easily integrate such custom OData services into Java applications on the SAP Cloud Platform. Finally, Section 20.3 briefly touches on topics to consider when delivering side-by-side extensions that are based on in-app extensions.

20.1 Extending the Business Partner Address Manager Application with Custom Fields

We described how to create custom fields in SAP S/4HANA in Chapter 19, Section 19.3, where we created two custom fields for the business partner to store when and by whom addresses were last checked. In this section, we'll first describe a use case that uses both fields in our Business Partner Address Manager application, which we'll then implement in the backend. Thus, we'll explain the corresponding capabilities of SAP S/4HANA Cloud SDK's virtual data model and how to use them in our application. Then, we'll extend the API and frontend of our application. The last subsection discusses further topics to consider when building productive applications that work with custom fields.

20.1.1 Overview of Planned Use Case

So far, our Business Partner Address Manager application allows users to view and modify the addresses of business partners, potentially with an approval workflow. Let's imagine the following additional requirement: Users should be able to mark that they have checked and updated the addresses of a business partner as a whole. Other users, perhaps in other departments, should be able to see when and by whom a business partner's address was last checked to determine how confident the company can be that the addresses are up-to-date. Other departments outside the core user audience of our side-by-side app will not necessarily use our application directly but instead operate within SAP S/4HANA. For example, the distribution center could use the core functionality of SAP S/4HANA to ship deliveries to customers. Thus, they'll need status information about the last address check available within SAP S/4HANA. This use case is a good match for an in-app extension via custom fields because the data will be stored within SAP S/4HANA and can be displayed in the SAP S/4HANA SAP Fiori apps by using the methods we explained conceptually in Chapter 18 and practically in Chapter 19. At the same time, custom fields can be used consistently in side-by-side extensions as well.

The workflow within our Business Partner Address Manager side-by-side extension app will be as follows, with a user interface as shown in Figure 20.1:

1. When a business user with the appropriate authorization confirms that the address information of a business partner is accurate, he can click a button to mark the business partner's addresses as checked.
2. The application will store the information of the current user on SAP Cloud Platform and the current date in the custom fields of the business partner in SAP S/4HANA.
3. The details page for the business partner in our application will display the user information and the date of the last check to all users.

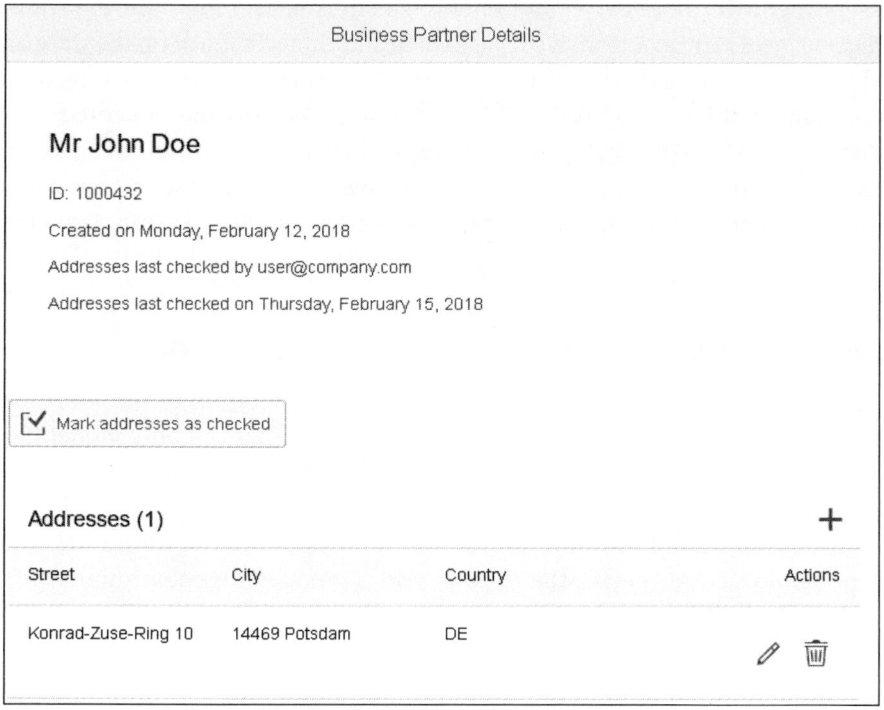

Figure 20.1 Sample Application with the Extension for Marking a Business Partner as Checked

What Data Will Be Stored Where?

The information will only be stored in and retrieved from the SAP S/4HANA system, using the two fields "Addresses Last Checked By" and "Addresses Last Checked On" we created in Chapter 19 on the business partner level. We'll mark this information on the business partner to signal that the complete set of addresses has been confirmed.

We'll store the name of the user as defined on SAP Cloud Platform, that is, his email address, and the current date when the user checked the address.

To implement these capabilities, we'll extend the backend with an additional operation that will set the two custom fields of a given business partner to the current user's name and current date. We'll also extend the information returned for a single business partner with those two custom fields. Finally, the user interface will show two additional fields and a button. We'll base these additional features on the state of the application, which we discussed in Chapter 4. To know the currently logged in user, the security features described in Chapter 5 must have been implemented. The other chapters, in which we further augmented our application, are not mandatory, so we can minimize assumptions. With the knowledge we've gained so far, however, integrating local persistence, as seen in Chapter 7, or providing the new functionality via an advanced REST API, as explained in Chapter 8, should not be difficult.

20.1.2 Using the SAP S/4HANA Cloud SDK to Consume Custom Fields

The VDM of the SAP S/4HANA Cloud SDK is a Java representation of the standard public API of SAP S/4HANA. The Java representation of entities can only model the standard properties of the OData services that are available in any SAP S/4HANA system with a certain release. Out of the box, the VDM cannot provide representations for custom fields because those representations will change from each SAP S/4HANA system to the next. Nevertheless, the VDM provides premier, type-safe support for custom fields via generic methods that provide read and write access to any custom field via the name of the custom field.

As we learned in Chapter 4, Section 4.2.3, the VDM models each property as a Java property representation, such as `BusinessPartner.LAST_NAME`. To handle custom fields easily and in a type-safe manner, we should first create such a property representation for our custom fields as well. Listing 20.1 shows the Java representation for the two custom fields used in our example use case. These definitions reside in a separate class `BusinessPartnerCustomFields` from which they can be referenced in commands that interact with SAP S/4HANA where needed. For each custom field, we'll create an instance of the subclass of `EntityField` that corresponds to the entity that has the custom field as a property. In our case, this entity is the business partner. We'll supply the identifier of the custom field in SAP S/4HANA to the constructor and the Java type of the field as generic type parameter. In our case, the field "Addresses Last Checked By" with identifier YY1_AddrLastCheckedBy_bus has type String to represent the email address as text and the field "Addresses Last Checked On" with identifier YY1_AddrLastCheckedOn_bus has type LocalDateTime to represent a date. In this way, we've encapsulated the technical information about the custom fields at one place. From now on, we can operate with these Java representations so as to easily interact with our custom fields in a type-safe manner.

```
public class BusinessPartnerCustomFields {
  public static final BusinessPartnerField<String>
      ADDRESSES_LAST_CHECKED_BY =
        new BusinessPartnerField<>(
          "YY1_AddrLastCheckedBy_bus");

  public static final BusinessPartnerField<LocalDateTime>
      ADDRESSES_LAST_CHECKED_ON =
        new BusinessPartnerField<>(
          "YY1_AddrLastCheckedOn_bus");
}
```

Listing 20.1 Property Representations for Custom Fields in Java

First, we'll use the property representations to retrieve the values of the custom fields when getting the detail information of a single business partner from SAP S/4HANA. Listing 20.2 highlights the required changes: We'll simply supply the property representations as two additional fields to the select method of the fluent helper for the get-by-key operation of the business partner service.


```
final BusinessPartner businessPartner = service
    .getBusinessPartnerByKey(id)
    .select(BusinessPartner.BUSINESS_PARTNER,
        BusinessPartner.LAST_NAME,
        ...,
        BusinessPartnerCustomFields.ADDRESSES_LAST_CHECKED_BY,
        BusinessPartnerCustomFields.ADDRESSES_LAST_CHECKED_ON,
        BusinessPartner.TO_BUSINESS_PARTNER_ADDRESS.select(
            ...
        ))
    .execute();
```

Listing 20.2 Excerpt of the Run Method Adapted to Retrieve Custom Fields in GetSingleBusinessPartnerByIdCommand

The business partner entity returned by the call to SAP S/4HANA will automatically contain the value for these two custom fields as Java objects. We can access the value, as shown in the code snippet in Listing 20.3, which will return the value of the given custom field as a LocalDateTime type object.

```
final LocalDateTime value = businessPartner.getCustomField(
    BusinessPartnerCustomFields.ADDRESSES_LAST_CHECKED_ON);
```

Listing 20.3 Accessing Custom Business Partner Field

In our case, however, we'll simply return the object to the frontend in JSON format as before. The VDM also takes care to serialize the custom fields, that is, converting them to the proper JSON format.

Next, we'll implement a Hystrix command to mark a business partner as checked. We'll update the business partner, setting the values of the two custom fields to the information provided when constructing the command. Assuming those values are stored in two fields of the MarkBusinessPartnerAsCheckedCommand, which are called checkedByUserName and checkedOnDate, the run method of the command contains the instructions shown in Listing 20.4. We'll first construct a business partner instance with the correct identifier. Then, we'll use this instance as a parameter to the update method to hold the updated information. Then, we'll set the values of the two custom fields on this instance. To this end, all entity types of the VDM, such as BusinessPartner, provide the setCustomField method. We'll supply the property representation and the value of the custom field, which will again encourage user interaction in a type-safe manner, as only values of the type specified by the property representation in Java will be accepted. For example, we cannot provide a String for the "Addresses Last Checked On" field. Finally, we'll send this entity, including the custom field values, to SAP S/4HANA using the, by now, well-known fluent helpers.

```
final BusinessPartner businessPartnerToUpdate =
    BusinessPartner.builder()
        .businessPartner(businessPartnerId)
        .build();
businessPartnerToUpdate.setCustomField(
    BusinessPartnerCustomFields.ADDRESSES_LAST_CHECKED_BY,
    checkedByUserName);
businessPartnerToUpdate.setCustomField(
    BusinessPartnerCustomFields.ADDRESSES_LAST_CHECKED_ON,
    checkedOnDate);
```

```
final ODataUpdateResult updateResult =
    new DefaultBusinessPartnerService()
        .updateBusinessPartner(businessPartnerToUpdate)
        .execute();
```

Listing 20.4 Instructions to Update a Business Partner with User Name and Date of the Last Address Check

At this point, we've handled custom fields on the level of the SAP S/4HANA integration. With the property representation of custom fields in Java and the method for handling custom fields on entity types, we have everything we need to deal with custom fields. In the next subsection, we'll integrate the just implemented command into our API and describe, on a high level, how to adapt the frontend.

20.1.3 Updating the API and UI of the Sample Application

Marking a business partner's addresses as checked is an operation on the business partner API. Since only a specific subset of fields of a single business partner is being modified, the appropriate HTTP method is PATCH, and we'll use the API endpoint */api/business-partners?id=<id>*. We can determine the current user and date within the backend logic; the API consumer does not need to enter this information. Instead, we'll define that the JSON body of this request should only contain the property AddressesChecked with the value true if the addresses have been marked as checked.

To implement this API, we'll add a doPatch method to our BusinessPartnerServlet, which we created in Chapter 4, Section 4.5.3. We'll extract the identifier of the business partner into a variable id and check whether the body of the request contains the expected content. As this should be straightforward to implement based on your knowledge so far, Listing 20.5 only shows the code to instantiate the command with the expected parameters and execute it. In the second line, we'll use SAP Cloud Platform abstractions of the SAP S/4HANA Cloud SDK, described in Chapter 3, to access information about the currently logged-in user. On any environment of SAP Cloud Platform, this simple line will give us the name of the user. Furthermore, we'll use the current date as the third parameter to the command.

```
new MarkBusinessPartnerAsCheckedCommand(id,
     UserAccessor.getCurrentUser().getName(),
     LocalDateTime.now();)
    .execute();
```

Listing 20.5 Instantiating and Executing the Command to Mark a Business Partner

Based on the enhanced capabilities of our backend API, we can adapt the user interface by applying the knowledge gained in Chapter 14. To keep focused on the capabilities of the SAP S/4HANA Cloud SDK for custom in-app extensions, we'll only describe the necessary changes on a high level. For more details, you can always refer to the provided complete source code available from the GitHub repository for this book.

We'll expand the `Detail` view with two additional object attribute elements that display the value of the custom fields returned by the API, along with corresponding formatters and internationalized texts. In addition, we'll add a button to the Detail view below the object header. When this button is pressed, the resulting event is handled by a new event handler method `onMarkAddressesChecked` in the `Detail` controller. To implement this event handler, we'll first extend the business partner service class with a method that calls our new API operation by sending a `PATCH` request via Ajax that contains the expected JSON-formatted body to the URL of the current business partner. In the Detail controller, we'll implement the event handler `onMarkAddressesChecked`, which is similar to the other functions that interact with the service by calling the service method, to which we'll supply the identifier of the currently selected business partner. After that request completes, we'll reload the model from the backend to display the new information.

20.1.4 Further Considerations

The implementation of the additional functionality in the previous section should be straightforward, as the functionality is based on the custom fields in SAP S/4HANA and leverages features from the VDM of the SAP S/4HANA Cloud SDK.

In more complex scenarios, you may need to deal with the custom fields in different places and operate a more advanced logic with them. The straightforward approach we took in Section 20.1.2 may be too simplistic because the custom fields are only available via the specific methods, not as Java properties. To work around this limitation, creating a new Java class that represents the extended entity, including custom fields as normal Java properties with getter and setter, may be beneficial. For example, you could extend the entity type Java class such as `BusinessPartner`. The extended class should provide a `get` and `set` method for each custom field that delegates to the custom field handler methods available from the extended type. This class can also host the property representation of the custom field. When you need to construct entities including custom fields, you can then use this new method.

If you also need to handle custom fields on entities returned by calls to the OData services via the fluent helpers, you may want to consider generating your own virtual data model for the extended OData service. In the next section, we'll discuss this use case while addressing OData services that are not available in the virtual data model at all.

20.2 Extending the Virtual Data Model for Custom OData Services

In some scenarios, custom fields will be too difficult to handle via the generic methods presented be in the previous section, or custom OData services based on custom business objects or CDS views in SAP S/4HANA will be a better approach. For these cases, extending the virtual data model could be beneficial. Essentially, we need to create the components of the VDM for such customized OData services, similar to the VDM that is delivered with the SAP S/4HANA Cloud SDK for the standard public API of SAP S/4HANA Cloud. To create these components, the SAP S/4HANA Cloud SDK also allows access to the generator that is used to generate the predelivered VDM.

In this section, we'll explore how to use this generator. First, we'll discuss scenarios where extending the virtual data model in a development project makes sense and describe the corresponding benefits. Afterwards, we'll explain how to use the generator.

20.2.1 When to Extend the Virtual Data Model

In Chapter 4, we described the benefits of the VDM, most importantly, its type safety and ease-of-access. In the previous section, we saw how custom fields can be handled with generic methods provided by the VDM, again with basic type safety. However, these custom fields need to be modeled manually to achieve the type safety and ease-of-access. In many cases, this manual approach is sufficient, for example, if only a few custom fields are handled at confined places in the source code. In those cases, the generic methods for handling custom fields provide quick access to those fields, and this approach can be quickly integrated into the development workflow, as no code generation is required. The VDM also provides methods that allow you to check whether a certain custom field is present, so that this manual approach can also be used if some SAP S/4HANA systems connected to the application lack those fields.

Scenarios with custom fields may go beyond the simple case outlined earlier. For example, we may want to handle entities in multiple layers of our application or deal extensively with the custom fields. In those circumstances, generic methods may get in our way as we write idiomatic code for our domain. Instead, we want the full benefits of the virtual data model but for custom fields. Using the VDM generator to create our own version of the VDM allows us to enable end-to-end support of custom fields just like any other property of the OData entities, without special handling. We also won't need to model the Java representation ourselves, which is particularly handy when the set of custom fields becomes more complex. For custom fields, the generated VDM supports the same operations as the original OData service, only with the custom fields also represented in Java as first-class properties.

Besides scenarios with custom fields, the VDM generator is naturally suited to deal with any other custom OData service, which may have been created in an SAP S/4HANA system for a custom business object (see Chapter 19, Section 19.5). A custom business object represents an entirely new entity type with several fields that can store arbitrary data. The predelivered VDM cannot support such a service out of the box because such a service is custom to the SAP S/4HANA system. Using the generator to generate a VDM for a custom OData service allows us to immediately create, read, update, and delete entities of the custom business object from our Java code with the known fluent API style of the VDM.

A custom CDS view (see Chapter 19, Section 19.6) is another potential origin of a custom OData service. In contrast to a custom business object, the OData service for a CDS view only supports read access, which will be reflected by the generated code. The VDM for a custom CDS view only supports reading operations.

In addition to the custom OData services of an SAP S/4HANA system, we can also use the generator for any other OData service that follows a similar structure. In particular, the OData service needs to comply to version 2 of the OData specification (*http://tiny.cc/odata-v2*). Generating a VDM for arbitrary OData services may require more manual work to specify the supported operations of each OData service.

Accessing Custom OData services without the VDM

Of course, in projects using the SAP S/4HANA Cloud SDK, you can call any OData service, including custom OData services in SAP S/4HANA, using the manual approach to building OData requests that we briefly discussed in Chapter 4, Section 4.2.3. Generating a VDM adds type safety and greatly simplifies the usage of our source code.

In all cases, the generator creates the same set of Java artifacts for the custom OData service that is also available for any standard OData service of SAP S/4HANA Cloud.

These components—service interface and default implementation, fluent helpers, property representations, and entity types—are described in more detail in Chapter 4, in Section 4.2.3.

20.2.2 How to Extend the Virtual Data Model

To run the generator, we'll need up to two artifacts for each OData service that together describe the OData service and are used as inputs to generate the VDM. First, we'll need to supply the metadata document of the OData service. Second, the generator can optionally consume a Swagger file that describes the available operations, that can be used to override defaults, and that provides documentation of the service.

You can download the metadata document from the custom OData service of your SAP S/4HANA system by appending */$metadata* to the URL of your custom OData service. For example, if you want to generate an updated VDM for the business partner API including custom fields, the URL will be like: *https://myXXXXXX-api.s4hana.ondemand.com/sap/opu/odata/sap/API_BUSINESS_PARTNER/$metadata*. For a custom OData service for a business object, the path may be similar to */sap/opu/odata/sap/YY1_BPSOCIALMEDIAACCOUNT/$metadata*, as displayed by the communication arrangement for the custom communication scenario. To access the metadata document, you'll need to supply the credentials of the technical user of the communication arrangement. Store the metadata document in XML format as a file with ending *.edmx* in a new folder *input*.

Authentication with a Technical User in a Browser

When opening the URLs mentioned earlier for the metadata of a service in an SAP S/4HANA Cloud system in a browser, you'll be redirected to the standard login screen of the system that does not accept the technical user. Append *?saml2=disabled* to the URL in order to get a prompt for the credentials of the technical user (communication user in SAP S/4HANA Cloud). Alternatively, use a REST client and supply the credentials via Basic authentication.

We first discussed Swagger in Chapter 8. The generator optionally consumes a Swagger file in JSON format and uses it to extract information about the OData service that is not apparent from the metadata document, as well as documentation. If you don't provide a Swagger file for a service, the generator will only consider the metadata and derive sensible default values for the information that would otherwise be provided via the Swagger file. Depending on the kind of OData service you're generating a VDM for, you can obtain the Swagger file in one of two ways:

- If dealing with a standard OData service and only extending a VDM with custom fields, we can download the JSON from the SAP API Business Hub (*http://tiny.cc/s4-api-hub*). Navigate to the OData API for which you want to extend the VDM and click on **Download API**, then choose **JSON**. If you are logged in, this process will download the Swagger file in JSON format.
- If dealing with a custom OData service, we can create the Swagger file on our own, based on templates provided by the generator. The following information is required:
  - The base path
  - The available paths, which essentially are the names of the entity types of the OData services
  - The available operations for each of these paths
  - Optionally, additional fields used for documentation that will be part of the generated Javadoc

  For an explanation of these properties, see Chapter 8 for more details on Swagger, and see the documetation of the generator to find out how to provide a Swagger file for custom OData services.

Store the file in the same *input* folder as the metadata document, with the same file name, except for the file extension *.json*. You can store metadata and, if wanted, a Swagger file for multiple services in the same folder and generate a VDM for all of them with one run of the generator. Optionally, you can also provide a file that defines the mapping of technical service names to Java class and package names. This file will be generated by the first run of the generator, if not present. You can use this generated file to understand the expected structure and modify the names of generated services and packages per service.

Once we have the expected input ready, we can run the generator in one of several ways: via the command line, using a Maven plugin, or from a Java program. We'll focus on the command line approach in this section. You can use the same options with the Maven plugin. Running the generator from a Java program provides the same functionality via a Java API. For more details on how to run the generator programmatically, see the Javadoc of the class `DataModelGenerator` in module `com.sap.cloud.s4hana.datamodel:odata-generator`.

The command line variant of the generator is available as a Java archive (JAR file). The module is called `com.sap.cloud.s4hana.datamodel:odata-generator-cli` and can be downloaded from Maven Central (*http://search.maven.org*). Search for this module (replace the colon with a space to quickly find the module) and download the JAR file. Rename the file to odata-generator-cli.jar and put the file into the parent folder of the *input* folder you created earlier.

Open a command line shell and navigate to the folder where you've placed the JAR file for the generator. This folder contains the input folder with the metadata and Swagger file(s). Simply type the following command to run the generator:

```
java -jar odata-generator-cli.jar
```

The generator looks for the input files, prints the information it will use to generate the VDM for the custom OData service, and then generates the Java source files for the VDM. By default, the generator will create a folder *target* that contains the output of the generation run. If you run the command with the flag `-h` appended, you'll see the list of options that allow you to control the behavior of the generator and which folders it operates on.

Whatever method and parameters we choose to generate the VDM for our custom OData services, the result is a set of Java source files in a certain package structure. You'll supply the package via the command line parameter `-p`. To quickly use the generated VDM, put the whole generated folder structure from the target folder, including all files, into the Java source code folder of your application. If your Java project has all of the usual dependencies to the SAP S/4HANA Cloud SDK, for example, when created using one of the archetypes, you'll only need to add Lombok as an additional dependency into *application/pom.xml*, as Lombok is used by the VDM entity classes (Listing 20.6).

20

```
<dependency>
  <groupId>org.projectlombok</groupId>
  <artifactId>lombok</artifactId>
</dependency>
```

Listing 20.6 Adding the Lombok Dependency

Depending on your IDE, you may also want to add Lombok as a plugin to your IDE as explained on the Project Lombok website (*http://projectlombok.org*). Afterwards, we can use our extension of the VDM in our code. We'll access the new service classes in the same manner as we access the predelivered VDM services. Thus, we'll benefit from simple and type-safe access to any OData service, not just the predelivered API. In the next section, we'll consider how to handle additional requirements around custom fields and custom OData services that may arise as you start delivering side-by-side extensions that partly rely on in-app extensions.

20.3 Delivering Side-by-Side Extensions That Rely on In-App Extensions

The generated source files of extensions to the VDM, as created in the previous section, are specific artifacts. In this section, we'll discuss how to integrate such generated code into the overall development lifecycle. We'll also consider how to deal with any type of custom OData service specific to some SAP S/4HANA systems, that is not part of the standard API.

In the previous section, we invoked the generator and manually copied the generated source files into our application project. While this process is sufficient for a one-off generation, running the generator more frequently, for example, because custom OData services change, can quickly become cumbersome. Instead, we can integrate the generation step into our Maven lifecycle to be run on each build of the application via the Maven plugin `odata-generator-maven-plugin`. More details on this process can be found in the documentation for the SAP S/4HANA Cloud SDK. In general, but particularly when following this approach, you should treat the created source files as a generated source and never change them by hand. Otherwise, you'll lose the ability to quickly regenerate the extended VDM, which is not only helpful if the custom OData service changes, but also allows you to benefit from improvements in newer versions of the VDM and the generator. You can simply rerun the generator when a new version of the SAP S/4HANA Cloud SDK brings new features to the VDM and leverage this new version also in your extended VDM. Even simpler, you can use the Maven plugin to always generate a fresh VDM on each build.

Furthermore, you may want to consider placing the generated VDM in a separate Maven module that acts as a library for your application. This approach increases encapsulation and makes using the same extended VDM in other projects easier. This separate Maven module needs to include the standard dependencies to the SAP S/4HANA Cloud SDK as discussed earlier.

In addition to the question of how to deal with the generated code, we need to consider how our applications should handle the fact that it no longer only relies on the standard public API of SAP S/4HANA. This question is independent of whether we access custom fields manually or use the generator. As custom fields and custom OData services in general are specific to one SAP S/4HANA system and need to be created in each SAP S/4HANA system, our application may be connected to an SAP S/4HANA system that may not (yet) have these custom OData services, for example, because they haven't yet been activated in the productive SAP S/4HANA system.

To comply with the patterns for resilient applications discussed in Chapter 4, we'll need to explicitly consider what happens when, for example, a custom field is not exposed by the OData service that we use. Of course, if this field is a mandatory requirement for our application, we cannot work around this problem, but we'll still need to handle this case gracefully, which is especially important for a multitenant application with different customers served by the same software-as-a-service (SaaS) solution. Feature toggles, as described in Chapter 11, may be a helpful way to gracefully degrade the functionality of an application.

The patterns to handle this situation are the same as handling any error but need to be discussed nonetheless. We should use resilient engineering to avoid repeating the same call over and over again if the call is doomed to fail, to supply helpful error messages, and to possibly proactively check in our code if the connected SAP S/4HANA system fulfills our expectations. Refer to Chapter 4, Section 4.6 to implement such resilience.

20.4 Summary

With these measures in place, we can safely develop side-by-side extensions that leverage the potential of in-app extensions, such as custom fields, custom business objects, and custom CDS views, providing even richer integration to SAP S/4HANA. As described in this chapter, the SAP S/4HANA Cloud SDK makes integrating in-app extensions into our side-by-side application on SAP Cloud Platform simple. In the next chapter, we'll again look at side-by-side extensions but now with a real-world, partner-built application using the SAP S/4HANA Cloud SDK.

PART VI
Partner Case Study and Outlook

Chapter 21

Partner Application Development Using the SAP S/4HANA Cloud SDK (Case Study)

This chapter introduces a partner scenario build with the SAP S/4HANA Cloud SDK. First, we'll describe the business scenario and give a short description of the project setup for the development of an industry solution as a partner. You'll then learn about the architecture and design of the cloud-native reinsurance application developed using SAP S/4HANA Cloud SDK and find out how SAP S/4HANA Cloud SDK was used to implement the architecture and the design of our application. In this chapter, you'll get firsthand insight on how a partner company used and benefitted from the S/4HANA Cloud SDK.

To bring together everything you've learned so far, we'd like to showcase an external partner project to illustrate application development using the SAP S/4HANA Cloud SDK. In this chapter, you'll see how SAP S/4HANA Cloud SDK can be applied to real-life business problems, the benefits it brings, and what lessons we can learn from this project.

21.1 Introduction

In this section, we'll provide a brief overview about our company msg and the business scenario we built on SAP Cloud Platform using the SAP S/4HANA Cloud SDK, including the cross-functional requirements for our scenario. We'll close the chapter with an introduction to our project setup.

21.1.1 About msg

msg is an independent group of companies with around 7,000 employees worldwide. The company's holistic service portfolio, composed of innovative consulting and intelligent, sustainable, and profitable IT solutions, has earned the company an excellent reputation as an specialist in a variety of industries, including automotive, banking, food, insurance, life science and healthcare, the public sector, telecommunications, travel and logistics, and utilities. Since the company was founded in 1980, msg continues to have this reputation today.

msg has enjoyed a close partnership with SAP since 1998, especially as part of their coinnovation efforts. The service portfolio covers every facet of the SAP partner program: from the distribution of SAP software and cloud solutions to consulting and implementation services for SAP products, not to mention the development of SAP industry solutions and add-on developments that perfectly complement the SAP portfolio. The SAP service portfolio is then rounded off by application management services for SAP applications, putting msg in an excellent position to offer SAP applications as end-to-end solutions from a single source—and do so worldwide.

21.1.2 Reinsurance Domain

Before we describe the business scenario in detail, we'll briefly explain the reinsurance domain to give you a basic understanding about the main processes our solution targets. Wherever necessary for a better understanding, we'll favor simplification of description over functional correctness.

Let's start with a scenario from our daily lives: We want to insure our house against the risk of storm damage. Thus, we'll apply for an insurance policy at an insurance company. The policy specifies the risk and coverage as well as the premium that we as policyholder must pay. If we make a claim, we'll get a disbursement from the insurance company to cover the loss. Our motivation for a policy is to mitigate the financial risk of costly damages like storms.

Now, let's switch the perspective from that of the policyholder to that of the insurance company, also called *primary insurer*: On a larger scale, the insurance company will have many policies that cover the risk of storm damage. We assume the policies accumulate at a specific geographical area. If a storm hits that area, the insurance company must disburse many claim cases. Consequently, the insurance company wants to mitigate the financial risk they face. The company achieves this by transferring the risk, or parts of it, to other insurance companies—the so-called *reinsurers*. The policy in this case is usually called *treaty* or *contract*. As the policyholder, the primary insurer has to pay a premium for the reinsurance and, in the case of a claim, gets money from the reinsurer. The cash flow is defined in the *cession*. The chain of transferring risk can continue between reinsurance companies via *retrocession* and a *retrocession treaty*. So roughly speaking, reinsurance is about insuring insurances. The overall process is shown in Figure 21.1.

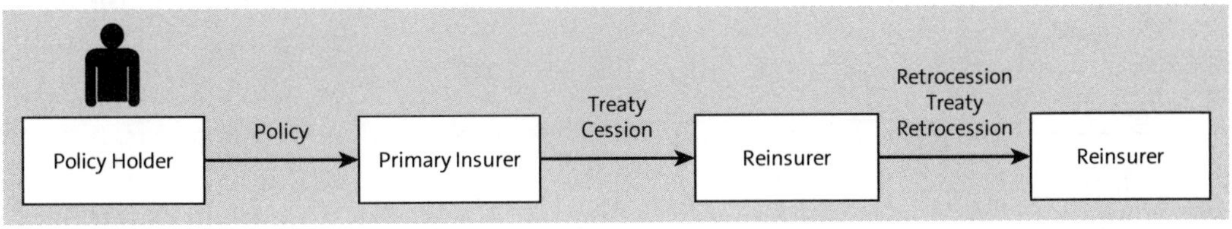

Figure 21.1 Reinsurance Process Flow

21.2 The Business Scenario

msg has a strong background in the insurance domain in general and specifically in the reinsurance domain. We developed and still evolve SAP Reinsurance Management as an SAP standard solution, which covers the complete process described in the previous section. However, in the age of digitalization and with the promises of the cloud, we asked ourselves if the solution is still the right fit, especially for small and medium-sized primary insurers interacting with reinsurers. We came to the conclusion that a software-as-a-service (SaaS) offering would be perfect for this customer segment. Consequently, we decided to design a new solution from the ground up, rethinking the business processes of the target group, which led to a cloud-native reinsurance solution offered as SaaS on the SAP Cloud Platform.

21.2.1 Functional Description

We developed the solution in an iterative and agile approach. The first use case we developed covers a basic scenario: The primary insurer wants to reinsure risks and handle the corresponding cash flow with its reinsurers. To implement this process, we needed information about insured risks, the involved reinsurance companies, and the premiums as well as the loss payments exchanged between policyholders and the primary insurer.

As shown in Figure 21.2, this scenario is handled by two user roles. One user role is the *reinsurance expert* who:

- Reinsures the insured risks
- Uploads the premium payments
- Uploads the losses

The other user role is the *senior reinsurance expert* who manages the reinsurance contracts or treaties concluded between the primary insurer and the reinsurer. To avoid confusion, from now on, we'll exclusively use the term "contract" in the rest of the chapter.

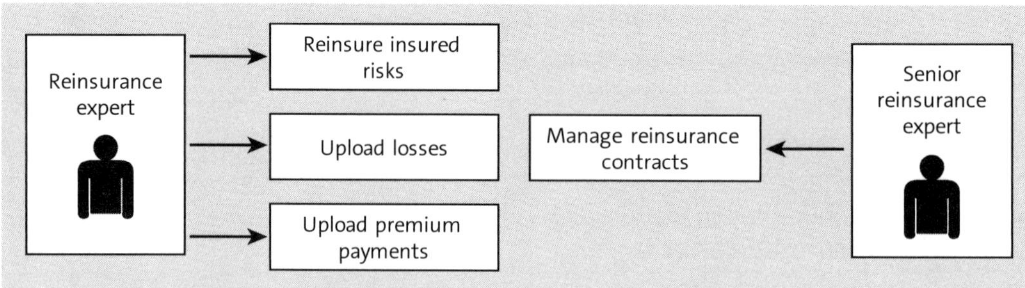

Figure 21.2 Use Case Diagram

From a process perspective, our solution provides interfaces for uploading risks, for example via Microsoft Excel files. The solution automatically processes these risks against reinsurance contracts. When the solution assigns a risk to a reinsurance contract, it reads the accounting information from the contract and uses this information for further processing. If the system detects an uncovered risk, automatic processing is no longer possible, and user interaction becomes necessary. The senior reinsurance expert must find a fitting reinsurance contract for the uncovered risk and assign it. If no contract exists, the senior reinsurance expert concludes a new contract with a reinsurer. He consequently creates the new contract in the system. After creating the new contract, the system processes and assigns the affected risks automatically. Then, the data foundation for processing the premium and claim cash flow is available.

When the primary insurer receives a premium payment, our solution offers interfaces for uploading data, for example, via Excel files. The system processes the premium based on the conditions of the reinsurance contract, namely, the distribution of the premium in accordance to the agreed terms and conditions. The analogue process is executed in case of a claim.

21.2.2 Essential Cross-Functional Attributes

To satisfy the expectations of our customers, our solution has to cover several cross-functional qualities:

- **Instant applicability**
  We want our customers to start working with our software from the moment they subscribe. Business configuration is done on the fly thus avoiding the typical implementation phase of classic software products.
- **Simplified, delightful, and role-based user experience**
  Although we want to *maximize automation*, user interaction is still necessary. We'll achieve this goal leveraging the SAP Fiori design guidelines.
- **Security**
  Access to the application must be secured, and customer data has to be isolated from each other while our application remains profitable from the economy of scale.

21.3 Project Setup

As mentioned in Section 21.2, we'll build a cloud-native SaaS solution. As a foundation, we decided for a specific project setup that supports this goal.

The overall methodology of the project is *SCRUM*, so our development teams work in an agile manner, which perfectly fits the ideas behind a cloud-native application with its fast evolution. Each development team has all the experts it needs, from application developers to test automation engineers to UX designers and product owners.

We decided to use *domain-driven design* (DDD) to translate our industry knowledge into the building blocks of our software. The microservice architecture reflects these building blocks. One strength of DDD in this context is its *ubiquitous language*, which means that terms are defined centrally and reused throughout the whole development process, from requirements to actual implementation. This ubiquitousness helps reduce overall complexity through unification and facilitates close collaboration between business experts and developers.

To complete the promises of a cloud-native application, namely, its ability to rapidly bring features and bug fixes into production, we committed to using *continuous deployment* (CD) from the beginning. This decision led to the following constraints in our project:

- To assure high quality in the software, we stuck to *test-driven development* (TDD). Every piece of functionality is preceded by a fitting automated test.
- To enable CD, we set up the required infrastructure for continuous integration and continuous delivery, including a central source code repository and a build pipeline.

The following sections will describe how the SAP S/4HANA Cloud SDK supported the realization of our solution and the achievement of our overall goal to develop a cloud-native SaaS product as a partner.

As a natural byproduct of the cloud-native development journey, we made some mistakes and learned from them, which we'll explore in Section 21.6.

21.4 Architectural Overview

The goal of this project was to build a cloud-native software-as-a-service (SaaS) offering on the Cloud Foundry environment on the SAP Cloud Platform. Some requirements for our application included the following:

- Scalability
- Reliability
- Resilience
- Enterprise-grade qualities like multitenancy

We achieved these goals by using a *microservice* architecture, leveraging the native capabilities of the Cloud Foundry environment on the SAP Cloud Platform. This architectural style allowed us to develop new features in an isolated way and deploy them to production independently, consequently reducing our time to market.

Advantages for Customers

As our application is offered as SaaS, we are in charge of its operation. As soon as a customer subscribes, he gets his own tenant including isolated data storage. The onboarding process also comes with the tenant preconfigured. Following this paradigm, the customer is ready to start right after subscribing, without any tedious implementation effort.

Aligned with the *principle of one*, we connect our solution to business functionality already available in SAP S/4HANA, such as SAP Business Partner and SAP Contract Accounts Receivable and Payable.

From an organizational perspective, each microservice is owned by exactly one development team that is responsible for the development as well as the maintenance of the service.

Freedom of Choice versus Governance

During our development, we learned that high-level governance makes sense when developing microservices. This governance model enables our development teams to "do the right thing," which means to develop and operate microservices in a *sustainable* manner, while keeping a high degree of freedom of choice for the teams.

21.4.1 Architecture and Design

Let's explore the macro- and micro-architecture of the application.

Macroarchitecture

Figure 21.3 gives you a basic overview of our reinsurance solution embedded in the Cloud Foundry environment on the SAP Cloud Platform. Multiple tenants can subscribe to the solution. The onboarding process allows a connection to their own SAP S/4HANA system either deployed in SAP S/4HANA on-premise or in SAP S/4HANA Cloud.

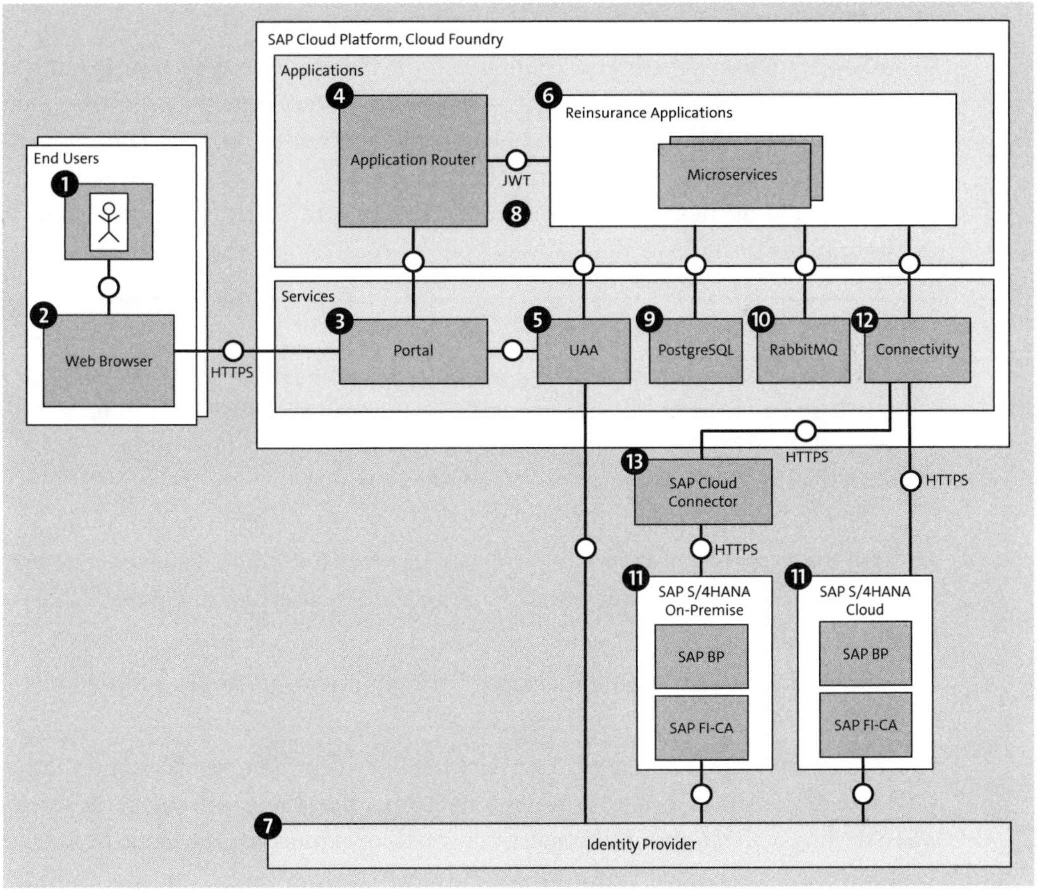

Figure 21.3 Macroarchitecture

As already mentioned in Section 21.3, we used domain-driven design to split our reinsurance solution in independent and business-driven bounded contexts. Every bounded context corresponds to at least one SAP Cloud Platform application implemented as a microservice. The microservices communicate via REST interfaces and events are served by message queues.

Walking through Figure 21.3, we'll start at the end user ❶. End users of multiple tenants access the user interfaces of our application via a web browser ❷ over HTTPS connection. To route end users to the right tenant, the necessary tenant information is part of the URL. The end user then starts the application from the SAP Fiori launchpad.

The SAP Fiori launchpad is served by the portal ❸ service, which provides the corresponding templates. The portal service is connected to an application router (AppRouter) ❹, which acts as a secured single sign-on (SSO) gateway, routing every request to the right microservice.

To authenticate users, the *user account and authentication service* (UAA) ❺ binds to every reinsurance application ❻ and the AppRouter. Every tenant has his own Identity Provider (IdP) ❼ in his SAP Cloud Platform subaccount. During tenant onboarding, the scopes defining the authorizations in the application are delivered by the application and pushed into the customer's subaccount. Customers can assign the scopes to his own roles.

User Authentication between Microservices

Because users are authenticated against the application router, a JSON Web Token (JWT) ❽ is forwarded with every request. Each service checks whether users have the right scope to access the resource. The JWT is also forwarded if one microservice calls directly another one, assuring a consistent user authentication.

We used the PostgreSQL ❾ service as a backing service for data persistence of each tenant. The persistence strategy is to store the data in a separated database schema per microservice.

The asynchronous exchange of messages between microservices is achieved by the RabbitMQ ❿ service.

To ensure secure and reliable connectivity between our microservices and the SAP S/4HANA ⓫ systems of our customers, we'll integrate the connectivity ⓬ service. When dealing with on-premise connections, customers must use the Cloud Connector

⓭ as a proxy between the SAP Cloud Platform and their SAP S/4HANA on-premise system.

Microarchitecture

Figure 21.4 depicts the microservice design in detail. All of our microservices are based on the SAP S/4HANA Cloud SDK's Spring archetype and use *Spring Boot*. Consequently, we used the SAP Java buildpack of SAP Cloud Platform.

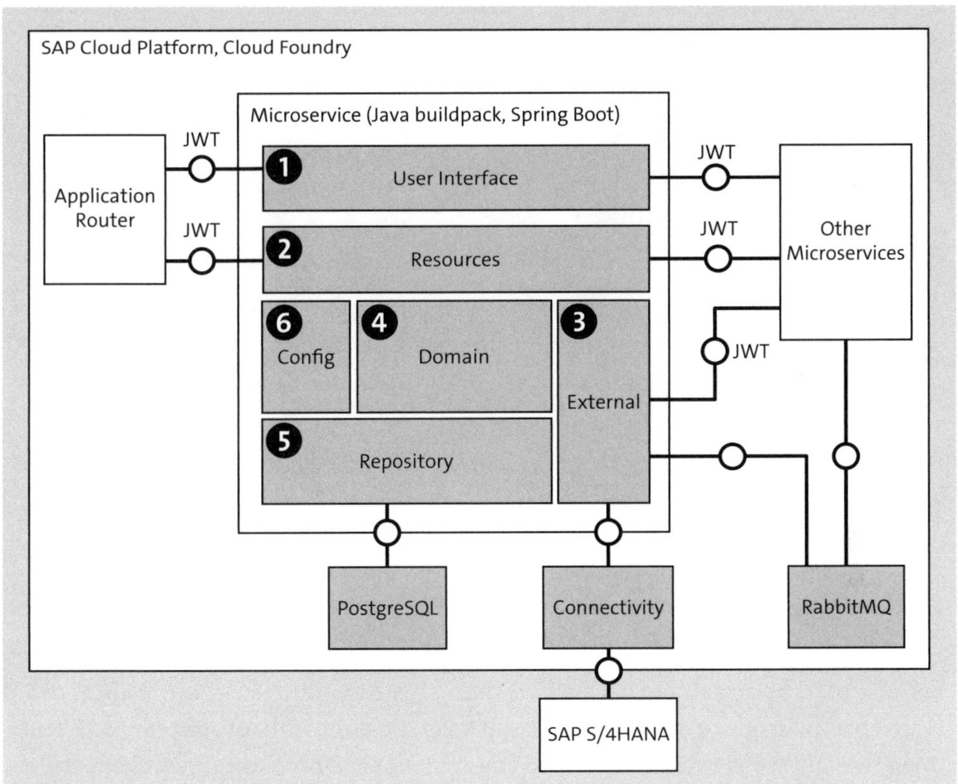

Figure 21.4 Microarchitecture

Every microservice contains its own SAPUI5 user interfaces in the user interfaces ❶ package. Sticking to the SAP Fiori design guidelines helps us to achieve a consistent user experience and enables us to integrate the different microservices on user interface level.

The resources ❷ package contains all the communication interfaces, provided by the microservice. Different technical interfaces can be provided for the same functionality, for example, OData or REST interfaces.

Every microservice can consume a number of external collaborators, called *downstream systems*, which consist of SAP S/4HANA systems as well as any other service or microservice. This communication is made explicit by placing the corresponding logic inside the external ❸ package.

Mocking Downstream Systems

Making the dependency to external collaborators explicit is an important aspect for handling dependencies, which is also handy when we look at automated testing as a pillar for continuous integration and continuous deployment. We'll rely on inversion of control to create our dependencies, which allows us to easily mock the downstream collaborators and, hence, simplify our automated tests.

The domain ❹ package contains our business logic and is the core of our reinsurance solution. Driven by domain-driven design, we'll develop *aggregates*, *entities*, *value objects*, and *domain services*, making use of the Spring ecosystem.

The repository ❺ package encapsulates the database connection for our entities. We used *Hibernate* as the Java persistence API to support schema-based multitenancy.

The config ❻ package contains all Spring Boot configurations for the microservice.

21.4.2 Design Decisions

During our development, we decided to use PostgreSQL as a relational database because of its low costs and because we didn't need the functional capabilities of SAP HANA for the scope of our scenario. We'll keep the possibility of adopting SAP HANA open though, as some future scenarios might favor it. One example would be the easier implementation of OData services that facilitate the usage of SAPUI5 analytical tables.

We also decided to package the UI part into our microservices because we wanted to avoid versioning problems. Our reasoning was that most microservice REST endpoints were to be consumed only by one user interface. Independent deployability was therefore not required right now and avoiding versioning conflicts by coupling those artifacts was more important.

21.5 Using SAP S/4HANA Cloud SDK in Partner Applications

The SAP S/4HANA Cloud SDK is the key element flowing through our development process and our application. In this section, we'll highlight the role of the SAP S/4HANA Cloud SDK in our application. We'll end the section with a short glance at our collaboration with SAP.

21.5.1 Using the SAP S/4HANA Cloud SDK in the Overall Application Architecture

As mentioned earlier, the SAP S/4HANA Cloud SDK accompanied our development at several spots. The following section represents some highlights of its usage.

Project Structure

We used the Spring archetype of the SAP S/4HANA Cloud SDK to create our microservices. The project structure ensures the seamless usage of the continuous integration server provided by the SAP S/4HANA Cloud SDK, as well as an easy deployment of the microservices to SAP Cloud Platform. We also use the provided pipeline configuration file to configure the desired pipeline steps needed for every microservice.

SAP S/4HANA Connectivity

One central need, in the context of a federated suite, is the application's communication with SAP S/4HANA, for example, to manage business partners in SAP Business Partner module. We used a set of capabilities provided by the SAP S/4HANA Cloud SDK to realize the connectivity, such as the following:

- **Virtual data model for OData**
  We used the virtual data model to consume whitelisted OData services of SAP S/4HANA published on the SAP API Business Hub. The provided service offers easy and type-safe access with full OData capabilities like sorting, filtering, deep insert, or expand.
- **Resilience with Hystrix**
  Downstream systems like SAP S/4HANA may not be available concerning system failure or network issues. To avoid downtimes in our application, the communication must be implemented in a resilient way. We use the `ErpCommand` of SAP S/4HANA Cloud SDK, which uses Hystrix to ensure resilience. Hystrix comes with

many interlocking mechanisms, for example timeouts, thread pools, or circuit breakers to protect our microservices from failure.

- **Destination and connectivity service**
  We used the Cloud Foundry destination and connectivity service to create and publish tenant-specific URLs to SAP S/4HANA systems. We implemented the service discovery feature of SAP S/4HANA Cloud SDK to easily consume the destination service in our microservices. In case of on-premise communication, we benefit from the fact that the Cloud Connector is automatically connected to the connectivity service. In addition, the destination service eases the setup of a secured communication via Basic authentication or user propagation to the SAP S/4HANA system.

Tenant-Aware Persistence

We used *Hibernate* with multitenancy to isolate tenant data in different database schemas. Hibernate uses a tenant resolver class, which we implemented using SAP S/4HANA Cloud SDK to determine the current tenant.

> **Why We Use Hibernate and Not EclipseLink**
>
> In the beginning, we used EclipseLink to implement multitenancy using discriminator column as the multitenant strategy. Later, we had a requirement that each tenant should have its data in different database schemas. Thus, EclipseLink did not work for us anymore, and we decided to use Hibernate, which operated immediately without any problems.

Mocking

Due to our test-driven development approach, the possibility to test and run our microservices efficiently in a local environment is an essential aspect. We use a set of SAP Cloud Platform abstractions provided by the SAP S/4HANA Cloud SDK to set up, configure, and mock the local environment. The provided mock utility makes mocking the context access to the platform, tenant, and user easy.

21.5.2 Collaboration and Working Model with SAP

We were given the great opportunity to closely collaborate with the SAP S/4HANA Cloud SDK development team already in the beta phase of the SDK. The collaboration was extremely fruitful for both sides. In regular sync meetings, we discussed our proceeding and addressed our questions as well as possible improvements for the SAP S/4HANA Cloud SDK. Extensive topics like tenant-aware database persistence or security implementations were discussed in dedicated workshops. Completed implementation tasks were accompanied by code reviews from the SAP S/4HAHA Cloud SDK development team, which helped improve our solution based on valuable feedback. Later, we additionally used open source channels like GitHub and Stack Overflow to intensify our collaboration.

21.6 Benefits and Lessons Learned

As an early adopter of the SAP S/4HANA Cloud SDK, we can clearly state that the provided technology, documentation, example projects, and best practices of the SDK sped up our development and increased the quality of our product. In this section, we'll describe our view on the benefits of SAP S/4HANA Cloud SDK as well as our lessons learned.

21.6.1 Overall Experience of Using SAP S/4HANA Cloud SDK

The SAP S/4HANA Cloud SDK gives a best-practice path for a lot of decisions. Its holistic approach to the software development lifecycle paves a way that is easy to pursue: starting from a predefined project structure right up to continuous deployment into production, accompanied by comprehensive blog posts that support decision-making. In short, the complete package delivered by the SAP S/4HANA Cloud SDK served as technological lighthouse for our development. The package guided us as we built a cloud-native application on SAP Cloud Platform.

21.6.2 Benefits of Using SAP S/4HANA Cloud SDK

Based on our experiences, let's look at some of the benefits we've found using SAP S/4HANA Cloud SDK for our application.

Continuous Integration and Deployment

At the start of our development, we invested a lot of effort to explore how to do things right. Finding the right strategy for continuous integration and setting up the corresponding infrastructure was especially tiresome. The SAP S/4HANA Cloud SDK provides a *dockerized* Jenkins server that made our self-managed continuous integration setup obsolete. In minutes, we had a completely preconfigured continuous integration infrastructure running, by using the cx-server script contained in the Maven archetypes of the SAP S/4HANA Cloud SDK.

Enabling Continuous Integration

Before you can build applications with Jenkins, Jenkins has to know the location of your source code. The source code should be stored in a version control software like Git. To allow for smooth integration with Jenkins, you should keep the available integration possibilities in mind when choosing a version control software for your project. When you decide for Git, you should take care that the selected implementation (like GitHub or Gogs) automatically supports your *Git workflow*. This combination of tools minimizes the manual effort to manage the integration of the source code repository with Jenkins.

The SAP S/4HANA Cloud SDK team keeps the continuous integration infrastructure up-to-date. The infrastructure is based on *Docker containers*, so updates are painless and fast. A typical update takes about two minutes without the need for manual interference.

The central Jenkins build pipeline is of equal importance. Our projects connect to the publicly available SAP S/4HANA Cloud SDK Jenkins build pipeline. As long as we decide to use the latest release of the pipeline, we can automatically benefit from the latest features and bug fixes.

We can autodeploy the built artifacts to Nexus repositories as well as directly to SAP Cloud Platform. Either way, we only need a minimal set of application specific-configuration to achieve this.

In conclusion, the functionality delivered with the SAP S/4HANA Cloud SDK has taken the burden of setting up the continuous integration and deployment environment from scratch off us and, consequently, has allowed us to focus on the development itself.

Automated Tests

The SAP S/4HANA Cloud SDK's archetype project structure contains folders for automated tests. Jenkins executes all automated tests in these folders during build time without any additional effort. The test results as well as code coverage reports are analyzed and displayed in Jenkins. The Jenkins plugin that measures and displays the code coverage of the Java code under test also brings preconfigured quality metric thresholds with it. As long as this threshold is not surpassed, the build breaks and prevents automatic deployment, which helps to increase software quality instantly and in a hassle-free way.

Static Code Checks

The SAP S/4HANA Cloud SDK's continuous integration pipeline runs a set of *static code checks*. After we connected our projects to the continuous integration pipeline for the first time, the checks discovered a list of previously unnoticed quality issues. We easily resolved the issues, and the quality improved. Offering default as well as SAP Cloud Platform-specific PMD and Findbugs checks, syntactical code correctness is covered without further manual effort.

> **Static Code Checks**
>
> Being experienced SAP ABAP developers, we were used to having our code permanently and actively scanned for syntactical issues by the *ABAP Test Cockpit*. These tools are not as tightly coupled to the development environment in Java and JavaScript, as they are in the SAP NetWeaver Application Server ABAP. The SAP S/4HANA Cloud SDK closes this gap and integrates essential quality checks into your application's continuous integration build pipeline. Serious or too many issues will cause your build process to halt, preventing continuous deployment to production until the reported quality issues are resolved.

SAP S/4HANA Connectivity

Our multitenant SaaS solution integrates with our customers' SAP S/4HANA systems. The SAP S/4HANA Cloud SDK allows us to connect to those systems, regardless of the deployment, whether SAP S/4HANA Cloud or SAP S/4HANA on-premise. The connectivity service and the destination service of SAP Cloud Platform are used behind the scenes. We only need a service binding in our microservices. The heavy lifting of configuration is handled by the SAP S/4HANA Cloud SDK. On the tenant side, only the destination properties need to be maintained in the customer's SAP Cloud Platform subaccount. At runtime, the underlying connectivity service dynamically picks up the current tenant's configuration and dispatches outgoing requests to the correct system.

Besides the infrastructural aspect of connecting our solution to an SAP S/4HANA system, the SAP S/4HANA Cloud SDK also simplifies the call of whitelisted APIs available in the SAP *API Business Hub*. For this task, the SAP S/4HANA Cloud SDK contains type-safe virtual data model representations of these APIs. As a consequence, the consumption of the APIs is convenient. No deep knowledge of the underlying technical protocol or implementation is necessary. We can easily leverage OData capabilities—if supported by the API. As a result; we can, for example, perform deep insert operations to create a cascade of data with one single API call. This feature helped us a lot when we create new business partners in SAP S/4HANA with a list of roles assigned to them. All this tasks can be achieved with a few lines of type-safe code.

21.6.3 Lessons Learned

A year of experience in the field of cloud-native, microservice-based application development resulted in many lessons learned. In this section, we want to highlight what we learned.

Microservices

A microservice-based architecture comes at the cost of integration efforts. Before we start to implement a new API, we create a specification with *Swagger*. This specification is the API contract for consumers as well as for the producer of this API and allows parallel and independent development of both parts. After getting used to this process, the upfront definition of APIs works very well, and the definition is quite stable. As development goes on, our APIs nevertheless evolve over time. To ensure the stability of our overall system, we introduced *consumer-driven contract tests*. Every microservice that consumes an API provided by another microservice of our application must create an automated test for this consumption. The test reflects the API call as exactly as possible and is added to the set of automated tests of the microservice providing the API. Consequently, every microservice has tests for all the consumers of its APIs, and our developers can confidently make changes to the source code. As soon as a change breaks one of the consumers, the automated test—and with it the build in Jenkins—fails. The developer can then react properly and either create a second version of the API or avoid the breaking change.

Microservice or Monolith First?

When you start a software development project, you typically lay out the cornerstones of your architecture based on the facts gathered so far. Microservices seem to be a natural choice as architecture for cloud-native applications. Based on our experience, starting with a *structured monolith* instead is perfectly reasonable: You would cut your application into logical units, as you would do in a microservice architecture. But instead of creating independent software projects, you would keep all the source code in one project and ensure module encapsulation by technical governance. You can later split up your structured monolith into several microservices and take care of the necessary communication overhead when you are sure that the benefits of a microservice architecture will pay off.

Test-Driven Development

Continuous deployment requires unrestricted trust in the quality of your application. We achieved this trust with high-quality automated tests and a nearly 100% code coverage. We decided to adopt *test-driven development (TDD)* right from the start. In theory, before we develop any new functionality, we write an automated test that exactly specifies the programming interface as well as the expected behavior. We learned that this approach has direct and positive impact on the software quality. On the other hand, we learned that TDD comes with some challenges. One challenge is testing the frontends. We're still learning how to build maintainable, meaningful, and sustainable unit tests for our SAPUI5 user interfaces. The automated tests have to find a balance in detail depth: Tests have to be high-level enough to decouple productive code implementation details from the test code. At the same time, the tests need to establish enough trust to allow courageous software development without fear of deployment to production.

21.7 Summary

The development of a cloud-native SaaS application is a huge challenge. Learning how to develop such an application is constant, ongoing work. Our experts have to translate their knowledge of building in SAP NetWeaver ABAP to the new application development ecosystem. The SAP S/4HANA Cloud SDK accompanies and guides us on this path. All in all, the SAP S/4HANA Cloud SDK, together with the close collaboration with the SAP development team, has helped us focus more on the development of our business logic rather than on dealing with tedious technology issues.

At the time of this writing, we've developed our cloud-native application. The next step will be operating the solution in the SAP Cloud Platform. As in development, we expect a lot of challenges and hard lessons in that area. However, we're confident that the foundation of our solution, the SAP S/4HANA Cloud SDK, is a reliable basis for the whole lifecycle of our software solution.

Chapter 22
Outlook

In this final chapter, we'll summarize the content we've covered in this book and provide an outlook of future innovations for building extensions with the SAP Cloud Platform.

In this book, we learned how to extend SAP S/4HANA Cloud or SAP S/4HANA on-premise. We introduced two main types of extensibility: in-app extensibility and side-by-side extensibility. Based on the rationales and the design principles underlying SAP S/4HANA, we introduced technologies, such as the SAP S/4HANA Cloud SDK and the SAP Cloud Platform SDK for service development, to develop comprehensive extensions to SAP S/4HANA, no matter whether you're implementing simple applications for your own business or developing fully-fledged solutions that could be sold to thousands of customers worldwide. Thus, we presented the entire development lifecycle of an application from building the application to continuous lifecycle management and operations in the cloud. We also saw how SAP partner msg leveraged the tools and methods presented throughout this book to develop a cloud-native application for a specific industry case.

SAP Application Development Partner Center

If you'd like to partner with SAP and build SAP S/4HANA extension applications, using the SAP S/4HANA Cloud SDK, visit the SAP Application Development Partner Center at *http://tiny.cc/partner-app-dev.*

While we thoroughly discussed the standard application development approaches, for example, with SAP Cloud Platform or the SAP S/4HANA Cloud SDK, we're aware that we probably did not answer every question that you may have and could not handle every topic that might be of interest in your particular application scenarios. For example, we introduced microservice-based architecture as a key pillar of cloud-native application development and centered our descriptions around microservice design principles. However, we didn't touch in detail on how to design microservices.

For these topics, we recommend you study the wealth of related literature such as Martin Fowler's blog posts on microservices (*https://martinfowler.com/articles/microservices.html*) and on bounded contexts (*https://martinfowler.com/bliki/BoundedContext.html*) or Eric Evans' excellent book, *Domain-driven Design: Tackling Complexity in the Heart of Software*.

Similar to such concepts that help when designing a cloud-native application, the SAP ecosystem also provides additional technologies that can be relevant to the day-to-day development work. Due to space restrictions, we also didn't cover SAP technologies such as the SAP Web IDE as a web-based IDE for SAP Fiori and full-stack development *http://tiny.cc/sap-webide* nor did we discuss multi target application (MTA) technology. MTA enables aspects such as combining multiple software artifacts that share the same lifecycle but may be inherently distributed or use different technologies at runtime (for example, multiple microservices or application components that must be deployed in lock-step). Furthermore, MTA allows for the creation of deployment assemblies that can be deployed by different persons into multiple target systems and environments. If you are interested in MTA, we recommend studying the various blogs that introduce MTA (*http://tiny.cc/mta-overview*) and the deployment models it enables (*http://tiny.cc/mta-deployment*).

If you have additional questions, feel free to visit our book page or our GitHub page for more details or check out the various community links provided in the preface of this book. We hope that you've enjoyed reading this book and that it serves as a useful resource for your future SAP projects.

Before we close, we want to provide a brief outlook to potential future innovations in the context of extending SAP S/4HANA.

22.1 Outlook

In this book, we described the various extensions mechanisms for SAP S/4HANA Cloud and SAP S/4HANA on-premise as they are available today using the SAP Cloud Platform. By introducing the various forms of extensibility and providing a clear how-to guide for both in-app and side-by-side extensibility, we believe that building application extensions for partners and developers is simple and can be used to develop great extensions.

Nevertheless, SAP doesn't stops here. In fact, numerous ideas exist to make the entire SAP platform even more powerful, integration between SAP solutions even easier, and application development even more efficient.

We'll outline some of our potential ideas in the following subsections.

22.1.1 Introducing Declarative Programming Approaches

In this book, we focused on application development without introducing too many dependencies to additional frameworks and programming methods. In other words, we described concepts in a mostly generic nature and that might be combined freely with other technologies and tools. Sometimes, this approach is also referred to as "freestyle" programming.

SAP Cloud Platform may complement the freestyle approach by introducing further declarative techniques and generic frameworks to significantly reduce the amount of code that needs to be written.

In particular, with SAP *Fiori elements*, SAP provides a powerful technology to apply a pattern-based application approach, for example, for master-detail user interfaces for master data (for example, products) or list views for line item-based data (for example, general ledger line items). In such cases, the required logic for the backend and the capabilities of the frontend are often quite similar and only primarily differ by metadata. In such cases, a purely freestyle programming approach is unnecessarily repetitive, cost-intensive, and error-prone.

As the basis, the *core data services* (*CDS*) could be used to define the persistence models as well as service interfaces of the application. Based on CDS models, physical persistence models in databases like SAP HANA as well as the OData entity data model can be automatically generated (Figure 22.1).

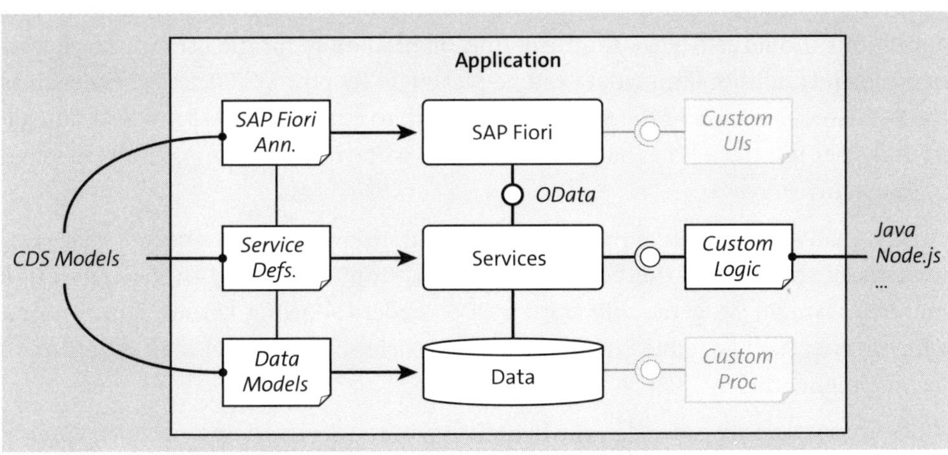

Figure 22.1 Core Data Services on SAP Cloud Platform

Given the declarative mapping between service interfaces and the underlying persistence, a generic service provider implementation can be provided which automatically handles the majority of create, read, update, delete (CRUD) requests from the client without writing any additional code. Furthermore, certain qualities such as multitenancy, internationalization, or extensibility can be supported in a harmonized manner to provide a consistent behavior across several similar applications.

In contrast to the handcrafted OData endpoints we introduced in Chapter 8, where the application developer is responsible for implementing the entire business logic for incoming OData queries or updates, such a model-driven methodology provides most of the capabilities (for example, standard queries) out of the box. Therefore, developers only need to focus on their custom logic by using model breakouts or custom handler mechanisms and let the runtime framework take care of the standard application functionality.

CDS has become prominent inside SAP S/4HANA (*http://tiny.cc/abap-cds*). Therefore, adding it to the SAP Cloud Platform would allow us to leverage known practices and skills and foster interoperability. While CDS has its roots in the SAP HANA database, we see that, for the SAP Cloud Platform, different databases beyond SAP HANA have to be supported in order to allow for multilingual persistence in microservice environments. Furthermore, the CDS methodology should be useable within different language runtimes such as Java or Javascript. In every supported language runtime, the CDS artifacts should be highly interoperable with the respective standard frameworks, for example, the Java Persistence API (JPA) for Java-based cloud applications (Chapter 15).

To deliver on the promise of an end-to-end, model-driven approach, the CDS service definitions should also allow for the definition of markup for the user interface. This markup and additional metadata can be picked up by powerful frameworks such as the SAP Fiori elements of the SAPUI5 framework to automatically provide a capability-rich user interface for typical user interface patterns such as master-detail views or line item list views.

Finally, many of the deployment- and configuration-related descriptors that were introduced throughout the book (for example, AppRouter, XSUAA, or application manifests) might be generable from a CDS model following certain conventions, which would further reduce development costs significantly and make application development efficient.

While we see and acknowledge the benefits of a model-driven approach for application development, also note that fully model-driven applications are always bound to the capabilities and expressivity of the model language itself (that is, its metamodel). Therefore, the declarative approaches of CDS allow for breakouts to introduce custom processing logic beyond the model's structure and standard behavior, which may range from simple data validation handlers to complex logic written in a freestyle manner. For the latter, in particular, we envision that the capabilities of the SAP S/4HANA Cloud SDK and related technologies can be seamlessly used in any of the breakouts. Consequently, we conclude that both the freestyle and model-driven approaches have to be highly interoperable so that developers can pick the best one for their requirements.

For example, a partner may start developing an industry-specific business-to-consumer application in a freestyle manner and then decide to use models for certain parts of the solution such as administration or master data user interfaces. In another example, a customer may start with a model-driven approach providing standard business-to-employee productivity applications but later may override certain limitations with an arbitrary, freestyle implementation.

As a result of this rationale, CDS on SAP Cloud Platform must be a nonintrusive, highly interoperable, and complementary technology that developers may easily include whenever they require a fast model-driven application programming method.

22.1.2 Seamless Integration

Loose coupling was already justified several times in this book as a main design principle and requirement. Loose coupling is achieved by clearly separating internal objects and implementation details, which may change in the future without prior notice, from the objects that have been made publically available and that offer a stable contract to any consuming client. With loose coupling, the agility and innovation speed of SAP S/4HANA, in particular on the cloud, is maintained while partners and customers may still extend the solution easily using either in-app or side-by-side extension capabilities.

22

The consequence of this loose coupling for side-by-side extensions is that there are at least two independent stacks that are inherently distributed and without investment are not integrated with each other by default, are required. Therefore, providing seamless integration is a key criterion to ensure the sustainable success of the platform strategy. Customers should perceive extensions as an integral part of the entire solution, which holds especially true on the user interface layer but touches every other lower layer. For example, customers using applications from the SAP Cloud Platform and SAP S/4HANA shouldn't notice when they're navigating between the solutions but instead should experience this in a transparent, seamless manner. Likewise, a user of an application on the SAP Cloud Platform should not perceive any performance degradation because of an additional latency premium for remotely communicating.

Figure 22.2 shows multiple integration aspects with SAP S/4HANA (left) as well as with the SAP Cloud Platform (right).

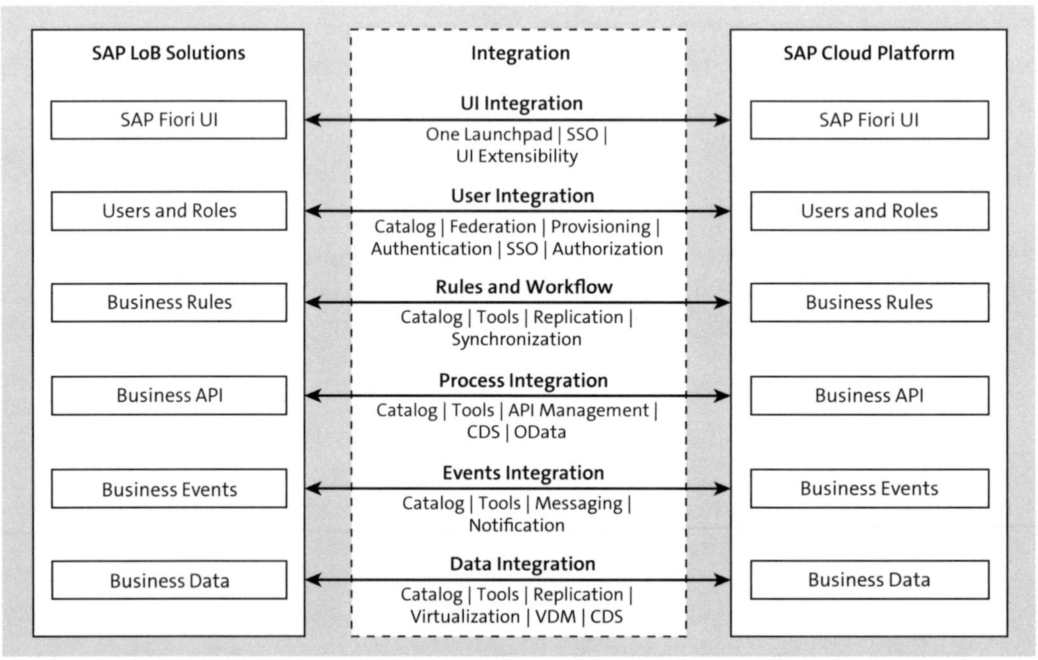

Figure 22.2 Integration Aspects of SAP S/4HANA and SAP Cloud Platform

Quite a few patterns for integration, latency tolerance, or identity and access management have been thoroughly introduced in this book (for example, Chapters 3–9 on side-by-side extensibility). However, this picture provides a frame to identify and derive future innovations on top of the existing possibilities that have been covered in this book.

In the following subsections, we'll discuss some additional aspects that outline our vision on how the platform can provide enhanced capabilities for developers and end users that blur the boundaries between SAP S/4HANA, SAP Cloud Platform, and other line of business (LOB) solutions even further.

22.1.3 UI Integration

In the various chapters of this book, we explained how to create and adapt SAP Fiori applications using either in-app or side-by-side extensibility. Furthermore, SAP Fiori applications can be easily composed and presented in SAP Fiori launchpads on your various stacks. For example, in Chapter 19, we mentioned that a custom SAP Fiori application can be added to the SAP S/4HANA Cloud launchpad. On the SAP Cloud Platform, you can aggregate and present multiple SAP Fiori applications in an SAP Fiori launchpad using the SAP Cloud Platform Portal. This feature is even possible for multitenant-enabled SAP Fiori launchpads (*http://tiny.cc/fiori-launchpad*).

However, a central place that spans applications from different platforms and LOB solutions is not available at the time of this writing. Users would like to access all applications relevant to daily work from a central place, independent whether they are predelivered apps in SAP S/4HANA Cloud, custom extensions by partners, or their own IT. Therefore, we envision a central SAP Fiori launchpad capable of exploring SAP Fiori applications from the various platforms, making them consumable and customizable in a single place.

As a prerequisite, this also requires that users and business roles carrying various business authorizations can be reused from a central place. Therefore, user and role federation is required, which we'll discuss next.

22.1.4 User and Role Federation

As discussed in Chapter 5 on application security, the SAP Cloud Platform allows you to define authorizations in a granular way for each microservice of an application. Later, these fine-grained authorizations can be composed into more coarse-grained roles and role collections that may span multiple microservices and applications based on the customer's preferences. At runtime, the central XSUAA service resolves the various authorizations based on the role collections that are assigned to the relevant users; therefore, users may use several microservices or applications completely transparently.

We envision a similar concept when thinking beyond the SAP Cloud Platform, in particular, when integrating with SAP S/4HANA but also other SAP solutions such as SAP

SuccessFactors, SAP Concur, etc. For these integrations, an integrated role concept is required that allows the federation of roles and users across platforms. A federated role may contain access to capabilities from SAP S/4HANA, SAP Cloud Platform, and other SAP solutions. For example, in the context of our Business Partner Address Manager application, the *viewer* role defined on the SAP Cloud Platform application might be composed with the business role in SAP S/4HANA that gives access to the business partner API.

Such a federated role can then be assigned to a federated user, that is, an abstract user that might be represented as different concrete users in the various target systems. As a result, an automatic switch between concrete users can be realized when communicating between the different systems and platforms. For example, the explicit mapping of user representations between SAP Cloud Platform and SAP S/4HANA, as introduced in Chapter 6, would be superfluous when a federated user concept would be consistently implemented.

22.1.5 Transparent Data Access or Business Data-as-a-Service

In this book, we have primarily looked at API-based and event-based integration to access and distribute business data of all kinds. Considering the integration patterns available on the cloud, these two approaches are also the most prevalent ones. The beauty of these approaches is that they provide a stable public contract despite the high innovation speed in the cloud. You'll be able to develop loosely coupled clients that can be shipped independently from the provider systems that they depend on.

However, in some heavily data-driven scenarios, for example, machine learning or analytical scenarios, you might need to directly integrate over data and lower-level access channels. While this data integration usually increases the coupling between provider and client, you'll reap certain benefits such as performance or minimal invasiveness in exchange. For example, accessing the data directly from the provider may speed up development on the client side, since the client won't have to wait until the provider ships a tailored API. Furthermore, the client may optimize its queries based on the nature and structure of the data instead of using generic APIs where the query performance is solely based on the provider implementation.

For this purpose, we envision a flexible infrastructure to reuse existing data from SAP S/4HANA also in SAP Cloud Platform. In this scenario, developers may define the qualities that are required by the application such as resilience, performance, or consistency and the infrastructure automatically provides and holds the data where most appropriate in the distributed system. For example, a developer may define that an analytical application has to respond within two seconds. At the beginning of the application usage, response times based on a remote access from SAP Cloud Platform to SAP S/4HANA might suffice. However, certain data is requested more often than other data, such as master data, which is required in almost every interaction with the system. This may trigger a transparent replication of the master data into SAP Cloud Platform so that this data is available faster in the future. Furthermore, when adoption of the application increases, response times may degrade because many users start to use the application at peak times and in parallel. To stay within performance constraints, the infrastructure (or an administrator) may decide to replicate even more data from SAP S/4HANA to the SAP Cloud Platform application to improve response times trading it off against data consistency for a certain time window.

Such a mechanism should be based on all the standards introduced by SAP S/4HANA, that is, the core data services, the virtual data model, and the structured query language. Access to the data is transparent at any given point in time, that is, any CDS or SQL query from an application on SAP Cloud Platform does not know at design-time whether it queries data from a local persistence or from a remote SAP S/4HANA database.

Furthermore, with data replication, business data along with business authorizations are replicated as modeled and defined in SAP S/4HANA. Otherwise, protected data from SAP S/4HANA might be accessed by unauthorized users on the SAP Cloud Platform.

22.1.6 Workflows and Business Rules

Workflows and business rules provide a convenient way to enhance and customize the logic and behavior of the system without requiring a fully-fledged programming language. Typically, business rules can be modeled to reflect simple *if-then* decision points or assignment statements where a business rule returns a value based on a certain state of the business. These decisions might be consumed by subsequent business rules or workflows.

Business rules are often modeled via graphical editors that provide the relevant conditions and consequences or provide decision tables. Today, various SAP solutions provide different tools and runtime implementations for business rules that must be integrated to define common business rules across lines of businesses and platforms.

Therefore, we envision a central repository to model and store business rules with a common user interface leveraging the virtual data model from SAP S/4HANA as well as the other public data models from LOB solutions such as SAP SuccessFactors. Despite being modeled in a central rule service, we see that rule execution has to happen decentralized in the relevant solutions to allow for high-performance rule evaluation as well as consistent decoupling. Thus, the envisioned business rule service may distribute the designed rules into the solutions where the data resides.

Business rules are also the basis to enabling comprehensive workflows across platforms and can achieve a coupling between independent workflows of the different SAP platforms. For synchronous workflows, the cross-platform APIs from the SAP API Business Hub can be used to evaluate the state whether a certain workflow needs to be triggered and can also be used to set the state of certain business objects whenever a workflow is completed. Likewise, asynchronous workflows can be triggered and completed using the event mechanisms introduced in this book. Events might be received from and sent to various SAP solutions such as SAP Leonardo Internet of Things (IoT), SAP Data Hub, or SAP S/4HANA.

With these ideas for future innovations, we close our book on extending SAP S/4HANA. The ideas, concepts, and technologies presented in this book should equip you with everything you need to craft future-ready, cloud-native applications that extend SAP S/4HANA with extraordinary quality and speed.

However, this book is not where the journey ends. Technology is always in flux and constantly evolving. Therefore, we invite you to continue studying many references and related resources we provided throughout the book.

Moreover, you may use any of the introduced feedback channels for future suggestions, ideas, or clarifying any open questions.

22.2 Summary

If you made it in sequence to this point, you probably worked through a lot of content and information. We hope that this book will be helpful for your future development projects in the context of SAP S/4HANA, no matter your role.

Appendix A
Bibliography

A.1 Books

Bandari, Kiran. *Complete ABAP*. (Boston, MA, SAP PRESS, 2017)

Erinle, Bayo. *Performance Testing with JMeter 3*. (Birmingham, United Kingdom, Packt Publishing, 2017)

Evans, E. *Domain-Driven Design: Tackling Complexity in the Heart of Software*. 1st edition. (Addison-Wesley Professional, 2003)

Humble, J., D. Farley. *Continuous Delivery: Reliable Software Releases through Build, Test, and Deployment Automation (Addison-Wesley Signature Series (Fowler))*. (Addison-Wesley Professional, 2010)

Julian, M. *Practical Monitoring: Effective Strategies for the Real World*. (O'Reilly Media, 2018)

Kim, G., P. Debois, J. Willis, J. Humble. *The DevOps Handbook: How to Create World-Class Agility, Reliability, and Security in Technology Organizations*. (IT Revolution Press, 2016)

Long, Josh, Kenny Bastani. *Cloud Native Java: Designing Resilient Systems with Spring Boot, Spring Cloud, and Cloud Foundry*. (O'Reilly Media, 2017)

Newman, Sam. Building Microservices: *Designing Fine-Grained Systems*. (O'Reilly Media, 2015)

Nygard, M. T. *Release It! Design and Deploy Production-Ready Software*. (Raleigh/Dallas, The Pragmatic Programmers, 2007)

Staicu, C.-A., M. Pradel, B. Livshits. *Understanding and Automatically Preventing Injection Attacks on Node.js*. (Darmstadt, 2016)

Stine, Matt. *Migrating to Cloud-Native Application Architectures*. (O'Reilly Media, 2015)

A.2 Journals and Reports

Forsgren, Nicole, Gene Kim, Jez Humble, Alanna Brown, Nigel Kersten. "State of DevOps Report." Puppet + DORA (2017).

Fox, Armando, Eric Brewer. "Harvest, Yield and Scalable Tolerant Systems." Proc. 7th Workshop Hot Topics in Operating Systems (HotOS 99), IEEE CS (1999): pg. 174–178

Juran, J., A. Godfrey. *Juran's Quality Handbook.* (New York, McGraw-Hill 1999)

Kohavi, Ronny, Thomas Crook, Roger Longbotham, Brian Frasca, Randy Henne, Juan Lavista Ferres, Tamir Melamed. "Online Experimentation at Microsoft." *Data Mining Case Studies*, 11. (2009)

Leland, W. E., Taqqu, M. S., Willinger, W., & Wilson, D. V. On the Self-Similar Nature of Ethernet Traffic (extended version). *IEEE/ACM Transactions on Networking*, 2(1) (1994): pp. 1–15.

Little, J. D. A Proof for the Queuing Formula: L= ? W. *Operations Research*, 9(3) (1961): pp. 383–387.

McConnell, S. *Code Complete: A Practical Handbook of Software Construction.* (Redmond, WA, Microsoft Press, 1993)

Rutar, N., C. Almazan, J. Foster. A Comparison of Bug Finding Tools for Java. *Software Reliability Engineering, 2004. ISSRE 2004. 15th International Symposium on.* (Saint-Malo, IEEE, 2004)

Stonebraker, Michael. "The Case for Shared Nothing." *A Quarterly Bulletin of the IEEE Computer Society Technical Committee on Database Engineering*, 9(1) (1986): pp. 4–9.

Taylor Savage. *Componentizing the Web. Queue* 13(8) (2015): pp. 60–79.

A.3 Websites and Blogs

"Richardson Maturity Model." RESTful API Tutorial, n.d.
https://restfulapi.net/richardson-maturity-model/ (*http://tiny.cc/maturity-model*)

Agarwal, Akhil. "What Is What? Your Quick Reference to Communication Management, and Identity & Access Management Artifacts in S/4HANA", September 15, 2017.
https://blogs.sap.com/2017/09/15/what-is-what-your-quick-reference-to-communication-management-and-identity-access-management-artifacts-in-s4hana/ (*http://tiny.cc/s4-ciam*)

Ajjugunti, Dileep Kumar Reddy. "Replicate ABAP CDS Views from SAP S/4HANA Cloud to SAP Cloud Platform", December 8, 2017.
https://blogs.sap.com/2017/12/08/replicate-abap-cds-views-from-sap-s4hana-cloud-to-sap-cloud-platform/ (*http://tiny.cc/data-replication*)

Bitz, Gunter, Henrik Plate. "Open-Source Security Management and Vulnerability Impact Assessment." RSAConference. 2016.
https://www.rsaconference.com/writable/presentations/file_upload/asd-f02-open-source-security-mgmt-and-vulnerability-impact-assessment.pdf

Bonér, Jonas, Dave Farley, Roland Kuhn, Martin Thompson. " The Reactive Manifesto. " September 2014.
www.reactivemanifesto.org.

Conway, Melvin E. "How Do Committees Invent?" F. D. Thompson Publications, Inc. April 1968. Retrieved from *http://www.melconway.com/Home/Committees_Paper.html* (*http://tiny.cc/conways-law*)

Duemont, Alexander. "Step 2 with SAP S/4HANA Cloud SDK: HelloWorld on SCP Neo. " May 21, 2017.
https://blogs.sap.com/2017/05/21/step-2-with-sap-s4hana-cloud-sdk-helloworld-on-scp-classic/ (*http://tiny.cc/scp-neo-start*)

Dusseault, L., J. Snell. "Request for Comments: 5789." Internet Engineering Task Force (IETF). March 2010.
https://tools.ietf.org/html/rfc5789

Fiedler, Thomas. "ABAP Custom Code Adaptation for SAP HANA – The Efficient Way", April 22, 2016.
https://blogs.sap.com/2016/04/22/abap-custom-code-adaption-for-sap-hana-the-efficient-way/ (*http://tiny.cc/s4h-abap*).

Fielding, Roy T. "Architectural Styles and the Design of Network-Based Software Architectures", 2000.
http://www.ics.uci.edu/~fielding/pubs/dissertation/top.htm (*http://tiny.cc/phd-fielding*)

Flower, Martin, James Lewis. "Microservices", March 25, 2014.
https://martinfowler.com/articles/microservices.html (*http://tiny.cc/microservices*)

Flower, Martin. "MonolithFirst", June 3, 2015.
https://martinfowler.com/bliki/MonolithFirst.html (*http://tiny.cc/monolith-first*)

Fowler, Martin, "*What Do You Mean by "Event-Driven"?*" February 7, 2017.
https://martinfowler.com/articles/201701-event-driven.html (*http://tiny.cc/fowler17*)

Fowler, Martin. "BlueGreenDeployment." January 3, 2010.
https://martinfowler.com/bliki/BlueGreenDeployment.html

Fowler, Martin. "FluentInterface", December 20, 2005.
https://martinfowler.com/bliki/FluentInterface.html

Fowler, Martin. "What Do You Mean by "Event-Driven"?", February 7, 2017.
https://martinfowler.com/articles/201701-event-driven.html (*http://tiny.cc/event-driven*)

Fowler, Martin. "Yagni." May 26, 2015.
https://martinfowler.com/bliki/Yagni.html

Geers, Michael. "Micro Frontends: Extending the Microservice Idea to Frontend Development." 2017.
http://micro-frontends.org

Hamm, Roland. "SAP S/4HANA System Conversion – At a Glance", November 2, 2016.
https://blogs.sap.com/2016/11/02/sap-s4hana-system-conversion-at-a-glance (*http://tiny.cc/s4h-conversion*).

Harrington, B., R. Rapoport. "Introducing Atlas: Netflix's Primary Telemetry Platform. " December 12, 2014.
https://medium.com/netflix-techblog/introducing-atlas-netflixs-primary-telemetry-platform-bd31f4d8ed9a

Heitkoetter, Henning. "Step 18 with SAP S/4HANA Cloud SDK: Your Multi-Tenant Application in SAP Fiori Launchpad on SAP Cloud Platform Cloud Foundry." October 9, 2017.
https://blogs.sap.com/2017/10/09/step-18-with-sap-s4hana-cloud-sdk-your-multi-tenant-application-in-sap-fiori-launchpad-on-sap-cloud-platform-cloud-foundry/ (*http://tiny.cc/fiori-launchpad*)

Herzig, Philipp. "Secure your Application on SAP Cloud Platform Cloud Foundry", July 18, 2017.
https://blogs.sap.com/2017/07/18/step-7-with-sap-s4hana-cloud-sdk-secure-your-application-on-sap-cloud-platform-cloudfoundry/ (*http://tiny.cc/sapsecurityblog*)

Hodgson, Peter. "Feature Toogle (aka Feature Flags)." October 9, 2017.
https://martinfowler.com/articles/feature-toggles.html (*http://tiny.cc/feature-toggles*)

Kopecz, Klaus. "Multi-Target Applications and Microservices – How Both Concepts Relate to Each Other." January 5, 2018.
https://blogs.sap.com/2018/01/05/multi-target-applications-and-microservices-how-both-concepts-relate-to-each-other/ (*http://tiny.cc/mta-deployment*)

Kopecz, Klaus. "Multi-Target Applications, Microservices and APIs." January 5, 2018. (*http://tiny.cc/mta-overview*)

Kruse, Ekaterina. "Deep Dive 6 with SAP S/4HANA Cloud SDK: Extend Your Cloud Foundry Application with Tenant-Aware Persistency." December 20, 2017. *https://blogs.sap.com/2017/12/20/deep-dive-6-with-sap-s4hana-cloud-sdk-extend-your-cloud-foundry-application-with-tenant-aware-persistency/* (*http://tiny.cc/multi-tenant-persistence*)

Kruse, Ekaterina. "SAP S/4HANA Cloud SDK Blogs." May 10, 2017. *https://blogs.sap.com/2017/05/10/first-steps-with-sap-s4hana-cloud-sdk/* (*http://tiny.cc/s4sdk-blogs*)

Kurzynski, Daniel " Step 13 with SAP S/4HANA Cloud SDK: Automated Testing ", September 19, 2017. *https://blogs.sap.com/2017/09/19/step-12-with-sap-s4hana-cloud-sdk-automated-testing* (*http://tiny.cc/automated-testing*)

Lane, Kin. "History of APIs", December 20, 2012. *https://apievangelist.com/2012/12/20/history-of-apis/* (*http://tiny.cc/history-apis*)

Liebherr, Ulrike. "SAP S/4HANA Extensibility Tutorial", January 20, 2017. *https://blogs.sap.com/2017/01/20/sap-s4hana-extensibility-tutorial/* (*http://tiny.cc/in-app-tutorial*)

Luyten, Stefan. "Single Piece Flow – Why Mass Production Isn't the Most Efficient Way of Doing 'Stuff.'" August 8, 2014. *https://medium.com/@stefanluyten/single-piece-flow-5d2c2bec845b*

Mulloy, Brian. "RESTful API Design: What about Errors?", December 5, 2011. *https://apigee.com/about/blog/technology/restful-api-design-what-about-errors* (*http://tiny.cc/error-codes*)

Sadalage, Pramod, Martin Fowler, "Evolutionary Database Design." May 2016. *https://www.martinfowler.com/articles/evodb.html* (*http://tiny.cc/evodb*)

Schneider, Thomas "S/4HANA Extensibility Concept Details: Restricted ABAP." March 18, 2016. *https://blogs.sap.com/2016/03/18/s4hana-extensibility-concept-details-restricted-abap* (*http://tiny.cc/s4-restricted-abap*)

Schneider, Thomas. "SAP S/4HANA Extensibility: Use Case Overview, September 12, 2016. *https://blogs.sap.com/2016/09/12/s4hana-extensibility-use-case-overview/* (*http://tiny.cc/in-app-overview*)

Sharma, Tushar. "ABAP Core Data Services – Introduction (ABAP CDS view)." September 9, 2017.
https://blogs.sap.com/2017/09/09/abap-core-data-services-introduction-abap-cds-view/ (*http://tiny.cc/abap-cds*)

Söderlund, Tom. "Micro Frontends. A microservice Approach to Front-end Web Development." 2017.
https://medium.com/@tomsoderlund/micro-frontends-a-microservice-approach-to-front-end-web-development-f325ebdadc16 (*http://tiny.cc/soederlund17*)

Tilkov, Stefan. "Don't Start with a Monolith", June 9, 2015.
https://martinfowler.com/articles/dont-start-monolith.html (*http://tiny.cc/dont-start-monolith*)

Toledo, F. "Gatling vs. JMeter." January 10, 2017.
https://dzone.com/articles/gatling-vs-jmeter

Wagner, Frank. "SAP S/4HANA Custom Code Migration Worklist", February 2, 2016.
https://blogs.sap.com/2016/02/02/sap-s4hana-custom-code-migration-worklist (*http://tiny.cc/s4hworklist*).

Wiggins, Adam. "*The Twelve-Factor App.*" 2017.
http://12factor.net

Wozniak, Sander. "Deep Dive 3 with S/4HANA Cloud SDK: Cloud Platform Abstractions. September 19, 2017.
https://blogs.sap.com/2017/09/19/deep-dive-3-cloud-platform-abstractions-in-the-sap-s4hana-cloud-sdk/ (*http://tiny.cc/platform-abstractions*)

Yalcin, Merve. "Tutorial to Create a Custom UI for SAP S/4HANA on SAP Cloud Platform." February 20, 2018.
https://www.sap.com/developer/tutorials/abap-custom-ui-tile.html (*http://tiny.cc/s4-custom-ui*)

Yehuda, Y. "7 Best Practices for Continuous Delivery Success." September 11, 2016.
https://devops.com/7-best-practices-continuous-delivery-success

Appendix B
The Authors

Dr. Philipp Herzig heads three two-pizza teams responsible for the SAP S/4HANA Cloud SDK and SAP RealSpend at the SAP Innovation Center in Potsdam. Over the years, he has worked as a software engineer, architect, and product owner at SAP. He holds a Ph.D. in Computer Science from Technische Universität Dresden.

Dr. Henning Heitkötter is the product owner of the SAP S/4HANA Cloud SDK at the SAP Innovation Center in Potsdam. He strives to make the SAP S/4HANA Cloud SDK a value-adding framework for SAP S/4HANA extensibility. At SAP, he has also been responsible for cloud-based applications such as SAP Financial Statement Insights. He completed his doctorate degree in business information systems at the University of Münster.

Dr. Sander Wozniak is the chief architect and lead engineer of the SAP S/4HANA Cloud SDK at SAP Innovation Center in Potsdam. He has worked as a software engineer and architect on various projects in the areas of finance and healthcare at SAP. He was the lead engineer of SAP RealSpend and was responsible for defining the architecture and implementing several of its core components and services. He earned his Ph.D. at Technische Universität Ilmenau.

Akhil Agarwal is a development architect at the SAP Innovation Center in Potsdam, specializing in SAP S/4HANA Cloud SDK integration with the SAP S/4HANA suite. His career at SAP spans more than sixteen years, during which he has worked on several large-scale, global projects in development and managerial roles. He has a background in electrical engineering and holds a master's degree in information technology from IIIT-Bangalore and an MBA in strategy and finance management from IIM-Kozhikode.

Dr. Johannes Wust is the head of several agile development teams with the SAP S/4HANA development organization, with a goal of enabling cloud-native extensions for SAP S/4HANA with SAP Cloud Platform. In the past, Johannes co-led the global development organization for financial solutions at SAP. Johannes received his Ph.D. from the Hasso Plattner Institute for Software Systems Engineering.

Richard Birenheide is an architect at SAP SE. He works for the Suite Architecture division which oversees the overall software architecture for SAP's Business Suite. He has more than 17 years of experience in full stack application architecture and development. Richards's role includes guiding application development in its transition into the cloud.

Marco Dahms is senior developer and acts as scrum master in the SAP S/4HANA Cloud SDK development team at the SAP Innovation Center located in Potsdam. He joined SAP in 2008 and worked in several custom development projects in the field of Treasury and Commodity Risk Management. Later, he contributed to and led the development of several SAP Fiori applications in the finance area and participated in bringing the SAP RealSpend solution to life. He holds a master's degree in computer science from the University of Hagen.

Alexander Dümont works as a Java developer at the SAP Innovation Center in Potsdam. He contributes to the SAP S/4HANA Cloud SDK by integrating and leveraging modern web frameworks and backend technologies. He is also driving cloud platform enablement to partners by providing library consumption support and publishing best practice implementations along with online tutorials.

While studying computer science in Berlin, he was employed as faculty system and virtualization administrator. At the university he worked as application developer for database and signal processing research projects.

Michael Emerson works in the Products & Innovation board office as a product strategist. Previously, he provided guidance to Line of Business Finance development organization. Before joining SAP, Michael worked at Société Générale Corporate Investment Banking in Paris. He studied mathematics and computer science at the University of Edinburgh, and obtained an MBA from the Sauder School of Business at the University of British Columbia.

Dr. Frank Essenberger works as an application developer at the SAP Innovation Center in Potsdam. Besides developing features for SAP RealSpend, he focuses on evaluating and introducing new technologies for existing and future products. Before joining SAP, he worked for maihiro, an SAP Gold Partner. He has a background in physics and holds a diploma from Freie Universität Berlin. He earned his Ph.D. at the Max Planck Institute of Microstructure Physics in Halle (Saale).

Jürgen Göbl is the lead IT consultant at msg system ag. He started his work at msg in 2006 and gathered extensive know-how in SAP standard development during the product development of SAP Reinsurance Management (FS-RI). Since 2017, he has focused on cloud-native development.

Benjamin Heilbrunn is the architect and lead engineer of the SAP S/4HANA Cloud SDK continuous delivery machinery. His goal is to enable SAP's ecosystem to reliably deliver high-quality applications at high velocity. In the past, Benjamin acted as lead engineer for integrating SAP RealSpend and SAP SuccessFactors. He has a strong background in enterprise software development, software architecture, and has worked on numerous cloud projects.

Ramachandra Kamath is a developer in SAP S/4HANA Cloud SDK team at the SAP Innovation Center in Potsdam. He has over six years of experience in software engineering field. In his current role, he is working on bringing CI/CD best practices to applications built using SAP S/4HANA Cloud SDK, by providing an out-of-the-box CI/CD infrastructure solution. He holds a master's degree from Technical University of Darmstadt in distributed software systems.

Ekaterina Kruse was born in Voronezh, Russian Federation. She possesses two degrees: specialist in applied mathematics from the National Research Nuclear University, Moscow and an M.Sc. in IT systems engineering from the Hasso Plattner Institute in Potsdam.

Being passionate about connecting business and technology, Ekaterina has been working with SAP since 2008 in solution consulting and software engineering roles. In 2015, she joined SAP S/4HANA Cloud SDK core development team in Potsdam.

Helmut Königseder is software architect at msg system ag. After joining msg in 2008, he became familiar with product development in the SAP NetWeaver Java and ABAP environments. The switch to cloud-native application development took place in the start of 2017, when he joined the department of technical guidance at msg. Since then, Helmut Königseder has built up expertise in product development on SAP Cloud Platform.

Georg Köster started his SAP career in the Finance LoB. He is now the blockchain topic owner and is coordinating machine learning solutions in the SAP Cloud Platform Innovation unit of the suite development organization, building SAPs market-leading ERP solution.

He has a background in software engineering, business, and design thinking, which he studied at the Hasso-Plattner-Institute in Potsdam and the design thinking schools in Potsdam and Stanford, amongst others.

Daniel Kurzynski works as a software developer at the SAP Innovation Center in Potsdam, and is responsible for the continuous delivery infrastructure and pipeline for apps built with SAP S/4HANA Cloud SDK. Prior to his current role, he worked on innovative cloud applications in the area of finance, integrating with SAP S/4HANA and SAP SuccessFactors. Before joining SAP, he completed his master's degree in IT systems engineering at the Hasso Plattner Institute in Potsdam.

Dr. Christian Lechner is software architect at msg system ag. He earned his Ph.D. in physics and then began working at msg in 2005, where he gathered extensive knowledge about SAP standard and custom development. As of January 2017 Christian has lead the technical guidance unit of msg, focusing on cloud-native development. He is an active member of the SAP Community and an SAP Mentor.

Arun Bhaskaran Nair is a development architect working at SAP in the technology unit, responsible for provisioning of OData services in SAP Cloud Platform. Before joining his current unit, Arun worked on building backend services for mobile applications in ABAP and also on integrating desktop applications with SAP systems.

Tatjana Pfeifer has worked for SAP since 2001. Currently, she is product owner and development expert in the area of the SAP Cloud Platform SDK for Service development and event enablement. Prior to that, she was product owner for SAP Gateway in SAP NetWeaver.

Jan Rumig is development architect for SAP Leonardo, in the Internet of Things area. He is one of the key drivers for the overall architecture of all applications within Internet of Things. In addition, he is an expert in multi-tenancy in the SAP Cloud Platform.

Mathias Rup is a product manager for SAP S/4HANA, focusing on evangelization and enablement of developer and partner extensions for SAP S/4HANA. Mathias has held various positions as a technology consultant and in different customer-facing roles and product management areas at SAP.

Junjie Tang is a software developer for the SAP S/4HANA Cloud SDK at the SAP Innovation Center in Potsdam. He specializes in the SAP S/4HANA Cloud SDK pipeline that helps build, test and deploy cloud extension applications to the SAP Cloud Platform automatically.

He holds a master's degree in advanced computer science from the University of Manchester.

Felix Wente joined SAP more than 20 years ago, after earning a degree in physics. Over the years, Felix has worked in the areas of middleware, integration, and extensibility, with the business scope of SAP Customer Relationship Management and SAP Business ByDesign. He now works in the central architecture department of SAP S/4HANA, in the area of extensibility, mainly focused on extensibility mechanisms of the ABAP stack.

Florian Wilhelm studied computer science at Hochschule Karlsruhe, where he received his Bachelor of Science degree in 2015. Since then, he has worked as a software developer with a strong focus on the Java platform, agile development, and DevOps practices. He joined SAP in 2017 and works at the SAP Innovation Center in Potsdam, as part of the cloud enablement unit, to bring a streamlined continuous delivery pipeline to SAP partners.

Carsten Ziegler has more than 20 years of experience driving the development of several SAP products and managing international teams.

At SAP he has worked in multiple areas including SAP Business ByDesign, SAP Strategic Enterprise Management, SAP Master Data Framework. He has also led the development of SAP Business Rules Framework plus (BRFplus) and SAP Decision Service Management from inception to mass adoption.

As a key contributor to SAP's business suite strategy, Carsten has guided many large-scale projects end-to-end. He also provides expert support to SAP customers, and sales, consulting, development, and solution management teams. He has been a chief architect for SAP's IoT platform. In his current position at SAP, he takes care of the architecture of side-by-side extensibility of SAP S/4HANA with SAP Cloud Platform and big data technologies.

Index

T

U

V

W

X

Y

Z